# 501

## MUST-VISIT WILD PLACES

# 501

## MUST-VISIT WILD PLACES

Bounty
Books

**Publisher:** Polly Manguel

**Project Editor:** Emma Hill

**Designer:** Ron Callow/Design 23

**Production Manager:** Neil Randles

*Chapters Written By:*
**Canada** – *Fid Backhouse and Joe Toussaint*
**USA** – *Fid Backhouse, Kieran Fogarty and Janet Zoro*
**Mexico** – *Kieran Fogarty*
**Central America** – *Kieran Fogarty*
**Caribbean** – *Jackum Brown and Janet Zoro*
**South America** – *Roland Matthews and Janet Zoro*
**Africa** – *Jackum Brown (Benin, Cape Verde, Cote d'Ivoire, Gabon, Gambia, Morocco, Tunisia, Senegal and Sierra Leone), Arthur Findlay (Djibouti, Ethiopia, Kenya, Malawi, Mozambique, Rwanda, Tanzania, Uganda and Zambia), Kieran Fogarty (Botswana, Lesotho, Namibia, South Africa and Swaziland), Joe Toussaint (Cameroon, Chad, Ghana, Mali, Mauritania and Niger), Janet Zoro (Egypt and Libya)*
**Europe** – *Fid Backhouse (Armenia, Latvia, Lithuania, Ukraine), Jackum Brown (Spain, Portugal and Italy), Arthur Findlay (Netherlands, British Isles and France), Kieran Fogarty (Denmark, Estonia, Finland, Iceland, Norway and Sweden), Roland Matthews (Austria, Czech Republic, Germany, Poland, Russian Federation, Slovakia and Switzerland), Joe Toussaint (Bulgaria, Hungary and Romania), Janet Zoro (Albania, Croatia, Greece, Serbia and Slovenia)*
**Eastern Mediterranean** – *Jackum Brown and Janet Zoro*
**Middle East** – *Jackum Brown*
**Central Asia** – *Kieran Fogarty and Joe Toussaint*
**South Asia** – *Jackum Brown and Janet Zoro*
**South East Asia** – *Arthur Findlay, Roland Matthews and Joe Toussaint*
**East Asia** – *Arthur Findlay and Kieran Fogarty*
**Oceania & Antarctic** – *Fid Backhouse and Roland Matthews*

First published in Great Britain in 2010 by Bounty Books,
a division of Octopus Publishing Group Limited,
Endeavour House, 189 Shaftesbury Avenue, London WC2H 8JY

A CIP catalogue record is available from the British Library

ISBN: 978-0-753720-14-1

Printed and bound in China

**Please note:** We now know that political situations arise very quickly and a city or country that was quite safe a short time ago can suddenly become a 'no-go' area. Please check with the relevant authorities before booking tickets and travelling if you think there could be a problem.

The seasons given in this book relate to the relevant hemisphere. Be sure to check that you visit at the correct time.

# Contents

# Introduction

The dictionary defines the word 'wild' as describing uninhabited and unspoilt regions, and also plants or animals that live independently of humankind. But this evocative word has as many nuances as there are people who use it. For some unapologetic city lovers, a wild place is anywhere more than 30 minutes away from a decent restaurant, warm bath and comfortable bed. At the opposite extreme others feel the 'wildness' of a remote island can be ruined by a distant glimpse of another person. In between are those who simply want to appreciate the breathtaking variety of Nature's bounteous natural wonders. *501 Must-Visit Wild Places* provides an overview of many different types of wild place around the world, with the aim of surprising and satisfying every reader . . . whatever their definition of 'wild'.

Despite today's booming travel industry and easier access to parts of the world our grandparents had barely heard of, it is practically impossible for any individual to see more than a fraction of Planet Earth in a lifetime. And for reasons of climate and politics, there will forever be wilderness areas that are hard to reach. Always check in advance whether a wild place could also be a dangerous one – particularly near borders where there are hostilities or countries where extremists target tourists to try and score crude political points. Take official advice about travel and safety arrangements.

Even when nearer home common sense should prevail when going off the beaten track. Leave information with family or friends about the latest adventure and where you expect to be on certain dates. Take a detailed map, torch, lightweight warm-and-waterproof clothing, water and even a whistle with which to attract attention. More elaborate survival packs may be bought from specialist shops or made up following advice on adventure-travel websites.

It almost seems unfair to single out any of the amazing places featured in this book, but a perfect example of the unexpected is Dasht-e Lut in Iran. One of the hottest places on earth, it is such a hostile environment that no flora or fauna live there. However, it can be seen from settlements in the surrounding hills and is a quite remarkable sight. For most, it is enough just to have seen it from afar. Other extraordinary places are endangered by the number of visitors they attract, putting rare plants, animals and sometimes the landscape itself in jeopardy. It goes without saying (but is still worth repeating) that visitors must behave responsibly to help conserve precious wilderness areas. Observe basic rules such as not lighting fires in tinder-dry forests or digging up plants imagining that just one won't matter. And if advised to stay on tracks do just that. In Jamaica's Cockpit Country, a fascinating region, exploring tempting virgin forest off-trail can lead to disaster. In many places what appears to be solid rock is actually a deceptively thin layer covering deep sinkholes beneath.

Of course, it's not necessary to travel to distant lands to experience the untamed natural world. Some places that appear familiar in daylight – say a local wood – can seem very different in the moonlight when night birds call and badgers, foxes, stoats and weasels go about their business. Nature is full of surprises. A beautiful but sparse hillside in the west of England, grazed by sheep, became an extraordinary wild place in the autumn of 2009 when thousands of poppies in every shade from red to cream appeared spontaneously, having lain dormant throughout living memory. Unusually warm and sunny weather and a local farmer turning over a field to aerate the soil prompted this unexpected reclamation of the land by wild flowers. In a few short weeks they were gone.

Not everyone wants to visit truly wild places, preferring instead to visit the national parks that preserve some of the world's landscapes, animals and plants before returning to civilization for a good night's rest. And some of us have a deep desire to see a specific place or animal during our lifetime. It might be mountain gorillas in Rwanda or Royal Bengal tigers in Nepal, lemurs in Madagascar or the hundreds of thousands of water birds that rest at Lake Ichkeul in Tunisia . . . perhaps simply the sun setting over the Pacific from a lonely palm-fringed beach in the company of a loved one or true friends. Whatever the dream, it may be possible to make it come true. Hatch a firm plan, start saving and go with an enquiring mind and open heart.

# AMERICAS & THE CARIBBEAN

# The Yukon

**HOW TO GET THERE:**
Fly into Erik Nielsen Whitehorse International Airport from various Canadian cities, including Vancouver and Calgary, or long haul from Europe in the summer months.
**WHEN TO GO:**
Late May to September
**DON'T MISS:**
Seeing Mount Logan, the second-highest mountain in North America after Mount McKinley in the neighbouring US state of Alaska. Mount Logan is in Yukon's spectacular Kluane National Park and Reserve.
**YOU SHOULD KNOW:**
The Klondike Gold Rush that began in the late 1890s was sparked by the discovery of a rich gold deposit in Rabbit Creek – which soon became Bonanza Creek in honour of the untold wealth it produced for the lucky ones among tens of thousands who stampeded to the then Yukon Territory from all over the world, seeking the life-changing wealth that could be found in the chill waters of the Klondike River and surrounding creeks. It was not in vain – nearly 400 tonnes of gold have been recovered from the Yukon since 1897.

*The Ogilvie Mountains in beautiful Yukon*

The Yukon in the far west is the smallest of Canada's three federal territories, and down from a desolate arctic coast in the north is one of the wildest – and loneliest – places on earth. Some 35,000 people occupy an area of 482,400 sq km (186,250 sq mi) and intrepid travellers should be prepared for an adventurous experience. It will start in Whitehorse, where most of the territory's population lives. This thriving city on the Alaska Highway is famed for its beautiful natural setting on the banks of the Yukon River.

However, Whitehorse is but a staging post for those visiting Yukon because they love wild places. The territory largely consists of the Yukon River's watershed, a fabulous landscape dotted with snow-capped mountains and long alpine lakes fed by glaciers, often surrounded by a sporadic growth of stunted trees. Elsewhere, dense pine forests surround crystal-clear meltwater lakes. The Yukon supports a fascinating diversity of animals and birds and the whole place comes alive with a brilliant display of wild flowers in summer. Vast areas are completely undeveloped, and much of the Yukon is strictly protected by National Park or other conservation status.

To the delight of visitors who want to get away from it all, the destructive hand of man has barely touched this pristine wilderness. That can make exploration difficult or even dangerous, but happily the locals are welcoming and many of them make a good living from helping visitors to enjoy individual access to this unique environment. Every settlement has its own airstrip and outfitter, while guides may be found for numerous rewarding activities ranging from simple backcountry trekking through angling, kayaking, skiing, snowboarding, dog sledding, ice climbing and snowmobiling to exceptional opportunities to observe the varied local wildlife.

# Tuktoyaktuk and the Pingos

A visit to the atmospheric Pingo National Landmark on the Arctic Ocean shore of Canada's Northwest Territories is an experience to treasure. The protected area contains just eight pingos – hydrolaccoliths to the scientifically minded – but these are representative of 1,350 in the surrounding coastal region, a quarter of the world's pingo inventory. These amazing domed ice hills in areas of permafrost have been formed over time by the slow build-up of ice during the long winters. The landmark extends to 16 sq km (6 sq mi) and in addition to large pingos rising from the watery landscape, it contains fine examples of impressive frozen features like massive ice blocks and wedge ice that forms intricate patterns of interlocking tundra polygons.

Before accessing the landmark's unique natural wonders, it is necessary to reach Tuktoyaktuk, located on Kugmallit Bay in the far north. This is an Inuvialuit settlement usually referred to simply as Tuk, and many of the local Inuit people still follow a traditional way of life – hunting, fishing, trapping, herding caribou, picking berries and gathering driftwood. But to that may be added thoroughly modern oil and gas industries plus transportation (mainly by tugs and barges). Tuktoyaktuk has around 900 inhabitants, and some of them cater for determined travellers who wish to explore the nearby Pingo National Landmark, just west of town.

This is best done by boat. The National Landmark has no facilities, although plans for a boardwalk and interpretive trail have been mooted. The sensible option is to secure the services of a local guide – there are several specializing in individual pingo tours – although experienced wilderness hikers might prefer to go in on foot. As ever, the unpredictable Arctic weather can at best spell a change of plans and at worse mean real danger.

*An aerial view of snow-covered Tuktoyaktuk*

**HOW TO GET THERE:**
Only by air from Inuvik (small planes) to Tuktoyaktuk/James Gruben Airport

**WHEN TO GO:**
Summer (June to August), although in May, September and October the temperature is only just below zero. Adventurous winter visitors can drive the famous Tuktoyaktuk Winter Road along the frozen Mackenzie River's delta channels, as featured in TV's *Ice Truckers*.

**DON'T MISS:**
Ibyuk Pingo in the National Landmark, at 49 m (160 ft) the largest pingo in Canada and the world's second-biggest example of this rare natural feature.

**YOU SHOULD KNOW:**
The Pingo National Landmark has unique recognition as Canada's only National Landmark – not as a result of being the country's finest landmark, impressive though the pingos may be, but rather because they were the first area to be awarded such status . . . after which the programme was abandoned.

*The majestic beauty of Pangnirtung Fjord on the Cumberland Peninsula*

# Cumberland Peninsula

Baffin Island in Nunavut is an outpost of Canada's northland and the demanding climate ensures that the population consists of no more than 10,000 hardy souls. This remote place is mostly above the Arctic Circle, so the sun sets in late November and does not rise again until mid January, while night doesn't fall at all during three-and-a-half summer months when eerie twilight is the darkest part of an endless day.

One unusual specialist leisure activity for which Baffin Island is well known is BASE-jumping, thanks to a profusion of high cliffs scattered around the island, but more traditional possibilities still seduce dedicated backcountry adventurers. One ideal destination is the east coast's Cumberland Peninsula, home to Auyuittuq National Park. The latter consists of classic Arctic wilderness, where granite mountains rub jagged shoulders with sweeping glaciers, rugged fjords and polar sea ice. The name means 'land that never melts' in the language of indigenous Inuits, although it remains to be seen whether global warming will eventually call for a rethink.

This opportunity to experience the majestic beauty of the Arctic is not for the unfit, faint-hearted or budget travellers. It's hard enough to reach the access points – Qikiqtarjuaq on Broughton Island or Pangnirtung – and registration is required at either park office. Would-be explorers must then attend an orientation session before proceeding to the park with a local guide by boat, snowmobile or dog sled, depending on the time of year. This is a harsh and dangerous land, and it is essential to go equipped for every eventuality – adjusting to the weather's rhythms and being prepared to sit out a sudden storm or high winds in a tent for days on end. But those prepared to meet the challenges posed by this extraordinary park will enjoy the experience of a lifetime.

**HOW TO GET THERE:**
The park can be reached only from Qikiqtarjuaq or Pangnirtung, which are served by scheduled or chartered light aircraft from the regional hub of Iqaluit.

**WHEN TO GO:**
March to May (overland access) or August and September (boat access). The park is inaccessible when the ice is breaking up or new-season ice has not yet formed, and winter conditions are treacherous.

**DON'T MISS:**
The rare but compelling opportunity to see polar bears in their natural habitat

**YOU SHOULD KNOW:**
It is almost certain that Baffin Island was the Helluland described in Icelandic sagas and artefacts indicating that the Vikings arrived on the island around AD 1000 have been found, along with mysterious evidence of even earlier European visitors.

# Gwaii Haanas National Park

This unspoiled archipelago, consisting of 138 of the southernmost Queen Charlotte Islands, is 130 km (80 mi) off the coast of British Columbia. It is well worth the considerable effort needed to reach this magical destination from the mainland. Gwaii Haanas – or to choose a specific destination Gwaii Haanas National Park Reserve and Haida Heritage Site – is home to Canada's indigenous Haida Nation. These indigenous people have maintained a pristine environment protected by sustainable management practices. With the advent of NMCAR (National Marine Conservation Area Reserve) status, the whole of Gwaii Haanas from mountain top to seabed will be protected forever.

The dramatic landscapes of Gwaii Haanas Park range from rugged mountains to deep fjords, alpine meadows to sub-alpine tundra, wetlands to rushing streams, dense forests to beguiling lakes. Within this unique environment distinct flora and fauna have evolved. The local animals – such as a subspecies of black bear larger than its mainland cousin – have been joined by imported species such as beaver, squirrel, racoon and Sitka black-tailed deer. There are great opportunities for wildlife-watching and in addition to four-footed inhabitants there is a thriving bird population. This includes extensive seabird colonies where nesting can be observed along the shorelines between May and September. Bald eagles are a common sight and many different species stop off as they migrate along the Pacific flyway.

Carefully managed tourism is important to the local economy and for those who like to escape from the madding tourist crowd Gwaii Haanas is a destination to die for – happily, with a little help from knowledgeable local guides, it shouldn't come to that – although many backcountry expeditions are not without a whiff of danger that heightens the senses and intensifies the experience.

**HOW TO GET THERE:**
By boat (BC Ferries out of Prince Rupert), sea kayak, chartered helicopter or floatplane only (from Moresby Island)

**WHEN TO GO:**
Summer (spring or autumn for spectacular displays of migrating birds)

**DON'T MISS:**
Ninstints (officially Sgang Gwaay Llanagaay, which translates as 'Red Cod Island Village') – a UNESCO World Heritage Site on Anthony Island at the southern end of Gwaii Haanas that is a former Haida village site complete with a large collection of totems in their original locations and ruined cedarwood houses.

**YOU SHOULD KNOW:**
The best way to experience the natural beauty of Gwaii Haanas and its unhurried pace of life is to book an inclusive package that offers transport to the islands, rustic homestead accommodation, home-cooked food and local guides. This is definitely not a place where nature lovers can turn up and expect to explore unaided.

*Mosquito Lake and Cumshewa Inlet form part of the dramatic and unspoilt landscape of Gwaii Haanas National Park.*

# Hotsprings Island

**HOW TO GET THERE:**
Kayak, boat or floatplane
**WHEN TO GO:**
May to September for *al fresco* hot
bathing
**DON'T MISS:**
The opportunity to see a pod of
orcas swimming past the island from
the relaxing vantage point of a
natural hot tub.
**YOU SHOULD KNOW:**
Camping is not permitted and there
are no facilities for overnight stays
on Hotsprings Island – a policy
policed by watchful guardians from
the Haida Nation.

Within Gwaii Haanas National Park Reserve is Hotsprings Island (also known as Gandla'kin), one of the jewels in the crown of the Queen Charlotte Islands. Located off the east coast of Moresby Island in Swanson Channel, the island's name suggests its principal attraction. There are numerous hot springs in British Columbia, many of which have been developed into popular tourist resorts. But other examples of this impressive natural phenomenon are found only in remote locations where a real effort is required from those who wish to experience the ultimate pleasure of relaxing in warm spa waters amid the spectacular scenery of an unspoilt wilderness.

Hotsprings Island definitely falls into the latter category, and simply getting there calls for a well-planned expedition. It can be independently reached by kayak, or alternatively it's possible to book a trip as part of a select group who will be decanted into kayaks from a mother ship, close to the island. These expeditions often take in more than Hotsprings Island during the day-long outing, offering a more general chance to explore the wondrous Gwaii Haanas Reserve. For those whose wallets are bigger than their muscles, hiring a floatplane from Moresby Camp might be the answer.

Whatever the means of transport, once on Hotsprings Island the first delight is exploring the fascinating shoreline and craggy interior. There are stunning scenic views out over Juan Perez Sound – a kayaker's paradise – and to the San Christoval Mountains back on the west coast of Moresby Island. After that, what could be more relaxing than dabbling in the island's dozen hot springs and seeps, followed by a plunge into one of the spring-fed hot pools carved into the volcanic rock – an experience sure to nourish both body and soul.

# Jedediah Island

The phrase 'small but beautifully formed' could have been coined to describe British Columbia's Jedediah, located between the larger islands of Lasqueti and Texada in the Straits of Georgia, off Vancouver Island. Jedediah Island is a tranquil haven that extends to 2.4 sq km (0.9 sq mi). It was privately owned – and occupied – by the Palmer family until 1994, when it became a Marine Provincial Park following an enthusiastic fundraising campaign. In the best Canadian tradition, there are no restrictions on camping, so the place becomes a favourite summer haunt for kayakers, recreational boaters and wilderness campers attracted by the pristine marine environment.

The island has five bays that offer safe harbour, with excellent camping areas around Long Bay and more isolated possibilities along the eastern shore. The coastline has bays, rocky coves, deep anchorages and sandy beaches. The unspoiled interior consists of rocky outcrops surrounded by forest containing a variety of tree species including arbutus and the ubiquitous Douglas fir, plus flat meadow areas that are ideal for pitching camp. Although a campfire ban is sometimes in operation for safety reasons, fires are generally allowed below the high-tide mark. There are a number of established hiking trails that connect the secluded bays, and visitors are asked to keep to these designed paths rather than striking off into the woods (beware – there are sometimes bears on the island!). No formal campsites exist and the only facilities provided on Jedediah Island are four pit toilets, located near the most popular anchorages. Anyone with the get-up-and-go to reach Jedediah will be aware of the 'Leave no Trace' camping ethic, and respect it for the benefit of those yet to visit this enchanting island. The park is open all year round.

**HOW TO GET THERE:**
By kayak or boat from Lasqueti Island (itself served by passenger-only ferry from French Creek near Parksville on Vancouver Island)

**WHEN TO GO:**
The island gets quite busy at the height of the summer kayak-touring season (July and August), so those who prefer solitude should consider the months either side. The climate is mild and April to September are the driest months.

**DON'T MISS:**
Remains of an aboriginal fish weir, one of four archaeological sites to be found on Jedediah Island.

**YOU SHOULD KNOW:**
The first in a mysterious and gruesome series of discoveries that saw at least eight severed human feet found along British Columbia's shoreline was made on Jedediah by a visitor in August 2007. The lonesome foot was wearing a sock and size 12 Adidas training shoe.

# Nootka Island

Waterborne adventure beckons for those willing to take to their boats and explore the fabulous waters that envelop Nootka Island off the wild west coast of Vancouver Island in British Columbia. The island is surrounded by Nootka Sound, Nuchatlitz Inlet, Esperanza Inlet, Tahsis Inlet and – last but by no means least – the mighty Pacific Ocean. There are a number of published kayak trails that offer inspiring vistas of breathtaking coastal scenery for those who prefer to remain afloat, but – however rewarding – that would mean ignoring the solid delights of Nootka Island itself.

The island covers an area of 534 sq km (206 sq mi). The main settlement is Yuquot (Friendly Cove), where modern-day British Columbia was born when the Royal Navy's Captain James Cook, who arrived in 1778, made the initial European contact with BC's First Nations people. The interior is a wilderness that cries out to be explored by the experienced hiker who loves solitude and magnificent scenery. Well-established trails along the island's awesome west coast and through the interior – that may be combined for a round trip – are not for the inexperienced.

Previous hikers have generally marked these routes but there are no man-made improvements, some of the terrain can be tricky and the risk of involuntary diversions in the wooded interior is ever present. Neither trail is excessively demanding, although the remoteness, unpredictable weather and lack of potential assistance in case of unexpected difficulties (take emergency medical supplies) makes exploring Nootka a true challenge. The circuit can be done in three days of hard tramping but a week is the ideal duration.

*Approaching Yuquot on
Nootka Island*

There are black bears on the island so it is wise to avoid foods with a distinct aroma and store provisions high in a tree overnight.

# Northern Rockies

In the top right-hand corner of British Columbia the Rocky Mountains offer amazing opportunities for lovers of wild places. Around 80 km (50 mi) to the southwest of Fort Nelson on the Alaska Highway is the Northern Rocky Mountains Provincial Park. Further along the road is Stone Mountain Provincial Park, while to the south is Kwadacha Wilderness Park. They offer a unique contiguous wilderness that encompasses much of BC's northeastern mountain landscape.

The largest is Northern Rocky Mountains Park. This expanse of valleys and ridges has a huge variety of water features – glaciers, lakes, large rivers, rushing mountain streams, waterfalls and white water. The smaller Stone Mountain Park encompasses some of Canada's finest scenery. For the truly dedicated backwoods explorer, the vast Kwadacha Wilderness does just what it says on the packet. It's accessed via a 150-km (93-mi) trail from the Alaska Highway at Trutch, or an alternative route from Sikanni Chief Canyon, and offers pristine wilderness untouched by the acquisitive hand of man. This one is for experienced trail hikers and horse riders only, although it is possible to be flown in.

The diverse habitat of the three parks supports over 70 species of bird, including eagles, hawks, grebe, duck, various warblers and even the occasional Lapland longspur. Many and varied animals include bears (black and grizzly), wolves, wolverines, weasels, mountain goat, marten, moose, elk and deer. In addition to incomparable wildlife-watching, these parks together offer every sort of natural outdoor recreational activity. Hiking is pre-eminent, with plenty of opportunities to explore or follow established trails for anything from half a day to a week or more. To that may be added hunting, fishing, horse riding, boating, primitive camping and guided adventure tourism. Best of all, everything takes places against the backdrop of breathtaking Rocky-Mountain scenery.

**HOW TO GET THERE:**
Initial access is from the Alaska Highway but planned trips to the interior can be by helicopter, light aircraft, boat, horse . . . or on a pair of good old hiking feet.

**WHEN TO GO:**
May to mid September

**DON'T MISS:**
Magnificent vistas across Stone Mountain Park from the Alaska Highway – take a spare memory card for the camera.

**YOU SHOULD KNOW:**
It is essential to go equipped for every eventuality, even in summer. The parks are remote and weather conditions can change abruptly.

*Northern Rocky Mountains Provincial Park – serene at sunset*

*The Tarn at Jumbo Pass in the magnificent Purcell Mountains*

# Purcell Wilderness

**HOW TO GET THERE:**
Drive to trailheads from Highway 31 at Meadow Creek (west side) or Highway 93/95 starting at Toby Creek (along gravelled roads used by heavy logging traffic).

**WHEN TO GO:**
May to September. Would-be hikers should note that many of the river crossings are difficult (or impossible) before the end of July, although a few have simple self-operated cable cars.

**DON'T MISS:**
Dewar Creek hot springs – too hot to bathe in, but an impressive sight as steaming water rich in minerals like sulphur, calcium and magnesium is expelled through a number of surface vents. The round trip (on foot or horseback only) should be made from the trail registry at the end of Dewar Creek Road. Allow four hours to hike there and back.

**YOU SHOULD KNOW:**
For those who don't like going it alone, there are a number of local guide-outfitters who offer hunting, fishing, wildlife viewing and hiking trips into the park, for one or more days.

It's a mouthful – namely the Purcell Wilderness Conservancy Provincial Park and Protected Area – but don't be put off by that. This is a magnificent 2,027-sq-km (783-sq-mi) mountainous landscape where no wheeled traffic whatsoever is permitted, and nor are the sort of helicopter drops well-heeled tourists sometimes use to reach remote wilderness destinations without doing the hard approach work. The park encompasses six large catchments that drain into the Columbia River and the original ecosystem is undamaged – remaining the only intact ecosystem in southeastern British Columbia. The park is located to the northeast of Nelson and northwest of Kimberley, not far from the US border with Washington, Idaho and Montana.

This is a truly wild place that offers determined explorers a choice of experiences to savour. Recreational opportunities include hunting, fishing, canoeing, horse riding, historic sites, climbing, wildlife observation and of course hiking. None of these is for the inexperienced, as the park contains no shelters, improved trails, public communications or supply points. Self-sufficient wilderness travellers will not be daunted, but indeed encouraged, by the opportunity to truly escape civilization. Even those who don't intend to venture into the park's rugged interior will find a day visit worthwhile, if only for splendid mountain scenery. Take plenty of food and drink plus warm clothing, as the weather can change rapidly and there are often violent thunderstorms in the summer months.

Overnight camping is permitted (beware of grizzly bears!) and there are established trails, notably the long Earl Grey Pass Trail (East and West) and the Fry Creek Trail. These should only be attempted with the help of proper equipment and trail maps. Other wildlife to look out for includes around 90 species of bird and animals such as elk, deer, wolverine, marten, beaver, coyote and wolves.

# Strathcona Provincial Park

*Fishermen on Buttle Lake in Strathcona Provincial Park*

Vancouver Island's largest provincial park was founded back in 1911, and now includes the UNESCO Biosphere Reserve at Clayoquot Sound, which encompasses three important watersheds in the western part of the park. Strathcona Provincial Park in the island's centre provides an unspoilt but relatively accessible tract of beautiful wild country. It can easily be reached from the surrounding communities of Gold River and Campbell River and – while there are no commercial tourist locations within the park – it does offer visitor facilities at Forbidden Plateau, Buttle Lake and Ralph River. These provide a choice of ideal bases with established campsites (mostly 'first come, first served') from which to sally forth into the surrounding wilderness, using a network of established trails.

Trekkers will find that this rugged wilderness offers a wonderful display of assorted wild flowers in the summer months, with mixed forest covering much of the park's valley areas and foothills. The most common trees are Western red cedar, Douglas fir, amabilis fir and Western hemlock. The intermediate slopes are home to creeping juniper, mountain hemlock and sub-alpine fir. Strathcona's rugged mountains remain snow-capped all year and higher elevations experience heavy snowfalls from November to March, with snow sometimes remaining on the ground, even at lower levels, until July.

The park is birdwatcher heaven, with unique Vancouver Island white-tailed ptarmigan to be found along with grouse, band-tailed pigeon, Steller's jay and many other species including chestnut-backed chickadee and red-breasted nuthatch. Many mammals common elsewhere in British Columbia are not found here, while some species are different from their mainland cousins. These include the Roosevelt elk, Vancouver Island marmot, Vancouver Island wolf and black-tailed deer. The most popular recreational activities are hiking, canoeing, climbing, cycling, fishing and snow sports. Horse riding is permitted only in the Kunlin area.

**HOW TO GET THERE:**
Car ferry from Vancouver or Horseshoe Bay to Nanaimo and drive north or, the shortest route, ferry from Powell River to the Comox Valley area and drive west. Alternatively fly-drive into Comox Valley or Campbell River, the principal access locations for the park.

**WHEN TO GO:**
This is an all-year destination but the park's campgrounds are only open from around the beginning of May to the end of September.

**DON'T MISS:**
Delta Falls in the southern section of the park – with an impressive drop of 440 m (1,440 ft) over three cascades, this is one of Canada's highest waterfalls.

**YOU SHOULD KNOW:**
Those interested in becoming proficient in backcountry exploration can take outdoor education courses in necessary wilderness skills at the Strathcona Park Lodge, cleverly combined with customized adventure holidays. This commercial facility is located close to the park along scenic Highway 28, the Gold River Highway.

# Wood Buffalo National Park

Straddling the border between Northwest Territories and Alberta, south of Great Slave Lake, is Wood Buffalo National Park. The name contains a clue to the park's *raison d'etre* that would hardly tax Sherlock Holmes or Hercule Poirot – it was established in the 1920s to protect wood bison, a subspecies of the American bison (widely called 'buffalo') that once roamed North America's grasslands in huge numbers. Duly protected, the park's population of 5,000 is now the largest herd of free-ranging bison to be found anywhere.

The park is Canada's biggest, encompassing a vast tract of wilderness that ranges from Caribou Mountains to the Peace-Athabasca Delta, the world's most extensive inland delta. The park's headquarters is in the town of Fort Smith on Slave River, with an outstation at Fort Chipewyan, a hamlet dating from 1788 that is one of the oldest European settlements in Alberta. The park protects a perfect example of Canada's Northern Boreal Plains and enjoys UNESCO World Heritage Site status for its biological diversity.

In addition to the eponymous wood buffalo, the park contains much wildlife. Notable among many bird species is the critically endangered whooping crane. Animals include bears, moose, wolf, lynx, beaver and snowshoe hare. There is also a large population of garter snakes that have communal dens within the park. In addition to wildlife-watching, there are plenty of other attractions for intrepid adventurers. Not for the inexperienced, backcountry trips on foot or by canoe (along proven routes or breaking new ground) come as close to wilderness paradise as it's possible to get. The possibilities for hiking, canoeing, boating, camping and fishing – with or without guides – are virtually limitless. It's even worth the effort of going to Wood Buffalo National Park simply to enjoy the stunning landscapes.

*Aspens turning a stunning shade of red in Wood Buffalo National Park.*

# Head-Smashed-In Buffalo Jump

If there's any lonely place in the world worth visiting for the name alone, it's surely this one. And Alberta's Head-Smashed-In Buffalo Jump tells it just as it is, or rather was. For this special natural feature provides an atmospheric reminder of the simple way of life followed by the indigenous people of Canada long before Europeans arrived – simple, perhaps, but certainly effective.

The location of this historic site is a point where prairie starts to give way to the foothills of the Rocky Mountains, close to the US border and not far from the town of Fort Macleod. The importance of this place in Native American history is underlined by its status as a UNESCO World Heritage Site and a fascinating museum of Blackfoot culture, consisting of an interpretive centre built naturalistically into a sandstone cliff. This presents archaeological evidence gathered from the area and explores the mythology, ecology, lifestyle and technology of the Blackfoot peoples. The centre also offers tepee camping and a number of special events take place throughout the year, including workshops on relevant aspects of native life such as moccasin-making and a Christmas festival that showcases the very best of First Nations' art and craft work.

But standing on the edge, the jump itself remains just as it has looked since time immemorial. This 10-m (33-ft) mini-cliff above a steep slope has been used to kill bison for at least five millennia. The buffalo were driven from a favoured grazing ground in the nearby Porcupine Hills, being channelled into narrowing lanes by many hundreds of artificial stone cairns before going off the 'jump' at full gallop. The resulting plunge broke legs and disabled these heavy beasts, allowing the hunters to finish them off at leisure and process the spoils at a nearby camp.

**HOW TO GET THERE:**
Drive for 18 km (11 mi) to the northwest of Fort Macleod on Highway 785.

**WHEN TO GO:**
Any time

**DON'T MISS:**
Fort Macleod's Fort Macleod – the town subsequently grew up around the North West Mounted Police barracks established in 1884 and now offers both the interesting NWMP Museum and a restored Main Street with original buildings dating back to 1874.

**YOU SHOULD KNOW:**
Don't be fooled into thinking that the correct name should be 'Broken-Leg Buffalo Jump'. According to legend, during one hunt a young Blackfoot decided to watch from below the jump, but was hit by falling buffalo and found dead beneath a pile of animals . . . with his head smashed in.

*The poignant Head-Smashed-In Buffalo Jump*

*The strikingly ice-blue Moraine Lake*

# Valley of the Ten Peaks

Alberta's Banff National Park in the Rocky Mountains is Canada's oldest and covers an extensive 6,640 sq km (2,564 sq mi). It consists of mountainous terrain with many ice fields and glaciers. Dense pine forests that crowd the many lakes counterpoint the park's wonderful alpine landscapes. There has been tension between conservationists and developers since the park was established back in 1885, but one undoubted highlight of the park's protected wilderness is the magical Valley of the Ten Peaks, which contains ice-blue Moraine Lake.

Moraine Lake is an easy drive up from Banff along the Trans-Canada Highway (Highway 1), although a more scenic route is the parallel Bow Valley Parkway. There's parking at the lake's northeastern end, from whence the short but rewarding interpretive Rockpile Trail may be taken. It will take less than an hour to get to the top of the eponymous heap of rocks and back, with gentle ascent of rock-slab steps required. The effort will be rewarded by sensational vistas from viewpoints that overlook the lake and some of the famous Ten Peaks. The latter range from Deltaform Mountain at 3,424 m (11,234 ft) down to Mount Perren's still-impressive 3,051 m (10,010 ft). Together with nearby peaks like Mount Temple, Eiffel Peak and Mount Babel, they combine to create some of the most spectacular scenery to be found anywhere in the Rockies.

For those who want to overdose, a number of trails start at Moraine Lake, from two-hour round trips (Consolation Lakes) to five-hour there-and-back tramps (Eiffel Lake or Sentinel Pass) with unbelievable views all the way. Ultra-experienced wilderness hikers can follow the Perren Route – a hard day's climb up to the Neil Colgan Hut in a breathtaking location on the Fay Glacier.

**HOW TO GET THERE:**
From the small settlement of Lake Louise beside the Trans-Canada Highway, follow Moraine Lake Road to the south.

**WHEN TO GO:**
May to September. Awesome scenery means the Valley of Ten Peaks attracts a large number of visitors in high season (July and August).

**DON'T MISS:**
Photographing the stunning reflection of snow-capped peaks in the blue waters of Moraine Lake.

**YOU SHOULD KNOW:**
The Valley of the Ten Peaks featured on Canadian $20 bills issued in 1969 and 1979, and the exact spot from which the scene was captured is on the Rockpile Trail – known, inevitably, as 'Twenty-Dollar View'.

# Writing-on-Stone Provincial Park

One of the most interesting places in Alberta contains both the works of nature and the impressive creations of Native Americans. The clue is in the name, for Writing-on-Stone Provincial Park contains the most concentrated collection of rock art to be found on the North American Great Plains. There are over 50 sites and literally thousands of pictographs (paintings) and petroglyphs (carvings), still held sacred by the Blackfoot people and other native tribes. The Canadian government has filed an application for UNESCO World Heritage Site status under the Blackfoot name *Áísínai'Pi*, meaning 'it is pictured'.

The park is a 17.8-sq-km (6.9-sq-mi) area of protected prairie, set against the glowering backdrop of Montana's volcanic Sweetgrass Hills to the south. It occupies part of the Milk River, where ancient grassland is broken by spectacular rocky outcrops. There are numerous coulees – low-lying areas with water in the bottom. This ideal habitat supports an impressive array of wildlife, which is high on the list of the park's sights. Animals include mule deer, pronghorn antelopes, bobcats, skunks, marmots, raccoons and northern pocket gophers. Among many bird species are prairie falcons, kestrels, cliff swallows and owls, along with pheasants and grey partridges. Reptiles include various frogs, spadefoot toads, tiger salamanders and assorted snakes.

But the park's unique attraction is the native rock art, dating back into the mists of time. Much was created by nomads passing through a sacred landscape consisting of the rocky hoodoos (stone spires) that adorn the park, and tells of the everyday lives and dramas of those who created them. From the mid 17th century the tales started to include the horses, guns and metal goods introduced by European incomers, whose influx would change and ultimately destroy the indigenous way of life in less than 150 years.

**HOW TO GET THERE:**
Drive in – the park is some 100 km (62 mi) southeast of Lethbridge and 45 km (28 mi) east of the Milk River settlement.

**WHEN TO GO:**
The park is open for camping at the official site (full facilities) all year round. High season is May to September.

**DON'T MISS:**
The fascinating North-West Mounted Police outpost, reconstructed exactly as was after a catastrophic fire destroyed the original shortly after World War I. It's part of the protected cultural site.

**YOU SHOULD KNOW:**
The most sensitive areas of the park have been named as a Provincial Historic Resource to protect the rock art from vandalism, graffiti and theft. Access to these areas is by official guided tour only. The Hoodoo Trail does provide access to freely available rock art but be warned – it gets very hot in summer.

*Spectacular rocky outcrops are dotted throughout the park.*

# Agawa Canyon

There's an easy way and a hard way for those seeking to experience the natural delights of Northern Ontario's Agawa Canyon Wilderness Park. The park lies in a shallow canyon created by the erosive action of the Agawa River, between the Boreal Forest and Great Lakes-St Lawrence Forest regions. This ensures that the flora of both is represented along the well-wooded canyon, with an abundance of flowering plants in spring and summer.

The area was opened up when rail tracks were laid through the canyon in 1911, and exploited in the early 1950s when the railway company cleared a picnic area. And travelling by the Algoma Central Railway's Agawa Canyon tour train is still the easy way to visit the wilderness park, departing from the depot in downtown Sault Ste Marie. The city's grimy industrial area soon gives way to variegated woodland, rivers crossed by impressive trestle bridges and occasional panoramic vistas. It's over three hours each way, with just two hours to explore the canyon in between, choosing between five short nature trails that criss-cross the park area connecting a number of waterfalls. The experience is still very rewarding for anyone who does not have the time – or inclination – to hike in. That adds up to plenty of people and tour trains are usually packed.

But after the train has gone, those who make the effort to walk into this rugged wilderness park will more or less have the place to themselves. Even going the hard way is best essayed with a little help from the railway company. Seasoned hikers could plan their own expedition, but many prefer to opt for assistance from Algoma Central, which operates various lodges along the line. These offer the ideal starting point for a hiking trip to Agawa Canyon.

*An aerial view of the railway line that runs through Agawa Canyon Wilderness Park*

# Algonquin Provincial Park

*Smoke Lake in Algonquin Provincial Park*

It may seem a curious suggestion, but the best place to start an exploration of Canada's oldest and most famous provincial park is in downtown Toronto. It is here that you will find the Art Gallery of Ontario, home to many of the works of Tom Thompson, Canada's greatest artist. Thompson spent every spring and summer hunting, fishing and canoeing in the park, and producing small studies of the landscape. He then returned to his studio in winter to develop these into larger oils on canvas which, almost unbelievably, were created using just four colours. Thompson's interpretations of Canada's wildernesses marked an epiphany in European settlers' attitudes to the country they had come to live in. The beauty of his work, as well as waking up a backward-looking art establishment, helped European Canadians to shake off their 'garrison mentality' and view the country around them no longer as 'Nature the Monster' but as a place of great beauty to be discovered and enjoyed.

It is possible to visit the museum in the morning, have a brunch of pancakes and maple syrup and be paddling a canoe on one of the park's many thousand pristine lakes in the afternoon. The park is vast and covers an area about one third the size of Wales. It has over 1,600 km (995 mi) of navigable waterways and innumerable hiking trails, which can be explored on skis, snowshoes or snowmobile in winter and on foot or on the water in summer. Its vast interior is characterized by maple-covered hills, fast-running streams, craggy ridges and spruce bogs. This environment supports a vast array of wildlife. Moose, black bear, beaver and wolves live alongside over 250 reported bird species and over 40 species of (non-poisonous) amphibians and reptiles. It is a place that the phrase 'Go explore' could have been written for.

**HOW TO GET THERE:**
Highway 60 runs through the south of the park; its northern section can be accessed from the trans-Canada Highway.

**WHEN TO GO:**
All year round

**DON'T MISS:**
Of all the sensory experiences available in the park, perhaps the most evocative of the Canadian wilderness is the howl of the wolf. Organized 'wolf howlings' take place in late summer when park staff encourage a wolf chorus by imitating their howls. Once the wolves get going on their own, they create a haunting melody that will live long in the memory.

**YOU SHOULD KNOW:**
Being within easy reach of Toronto and Ottawa, the park is very popular. Its sheer size means that it seldom seems crowded on the trails and waterways, but there is pressure on the campgrounds and chalets and advanced booking is recommended during the summer (July and August).

*Sunset over George Lake in Killarney Provincial Park*

# Killarney Provincial Park

If there is one thing Ontario has in abundance it is well managed provincial parks ripe for exploration on foot, snowshoe or by canoe. Killarney Provincial Park, located by the shores of Georgian Bay, itself an arm of Lake Huron, is perhaps the most spectacular in terms of scenery. Although it is small for a Canadian park at just under 500 sq km (193 sq mi), it offers a spectacular variety of landscapes. Tectonic compression has changed the area's sandstone into brilliant white quartzite, producing the year-round appearance of snow-capped hills. This contrasts beautifully with the deep-blue lakes and the rich green of pine ridges. Ideally, active exploration should be punctuated with rests at the best vantage points to view the effects that sudden changes of light have on this striking palette. It was this landscape that drew the great artist A Y Jackson to the area and he later successfully lobbied for the creation of the Provincial Park, enjoyed by so many today.

Another Group of Seven artist, Franklin Carmichael, gave the world the iconic image of the park with his painting *La Cloche, Silhouette*, after which the park's most challenging trail is named. The La Cloche Silhouette Trail takes around a week to complete and leads the hiker into a sumptuous wilderness of glacial lakes, hardwood forest, rugged mountain peaks and stunning views over Georgian Bay. There are numerous shorter trails for those with less time or ambition. Each season clothes the park in a new kind of beauty and it provides the perfect habitat for bears, beavers, bobcats, moose and otters and over 100 species of birds.

**HOW TO GET THERE:**
Join Highway 637, 40 km (25 mi) south of Sudbury.
**WHEN TO GO:**
All year round
**DON'T MISS:**
The view of Silver Peak from the shores of David Lake
**YOU SHOULD KNOW:**
A compass and good navigational skills are a must, particularly for those thinking of going off-trail. The topography of the park can play tricks with the senses as the trails wind their way up and down this rugged terrain.

# Point Pelee National Park

Point Pelee is a 20-sq-km (8-sq-mi) spit of land that juts out into Lake Erie, tapering gracefully to the point that marks the southernmost tip of mainland Canada. It sits on the same latitude as Northern California and has a climate that allows for the greatest biodiversity in Canada. Created by hunters in 1918 as an outdoor playground, soon the motorized transport that was liberating North Americans in their pursuit of pleasure started to strangle the park. Over the years the area became crammed with summer homes and campgrounds, and traffic jams often rivalled those of rush-hour in downtown Los Angeles.

Radical action was needed to restore the area to its former glory and, in 1972, a white knight duly arrived. Legislation was passed and all land was placed under the ownership of Parks Canada, traffic was greatly restricted and a transit service was introduced to ferry visitors deep into the park. Today, the area is home to a stunning array of wildlife. It marks the take-off point for a vast number of birds heading south and the assembly point for one of the greatest migrations on Earth. Each autumn, hundreds of thousands of monarch butterflies gather on the narrow peninsula, waiting for a kind wind to assist their passage over the Great Lake and eventually on down to Mexico.

Point Pelee contains an astonishing variety of terrain for an area of its size. Long sandy beaches invite a slow amble, while boardwalks take the visitor out deep into marshland. Canoeists can wend their way through reed beds and there are numerous trails suitable for navigation all year round. Large swathes of savannah grassland are framed by lush deciduous forest in a park that has something for everyone, whether they have two wings, four wings or none.

*Point Pelee boardwalk enables visitors to wander deep into the marshes.*

**HOW TO GET THERE:**
Follow the Parks Canada beaver signs from Highway 3 as you leave Leamington.

**WHEN TO GO:**
All year round – the shuttle service to the tip operates only from April to mid October.

**DON'T MISS:**
Standing at the very tip, virtually surrounded by the waters of Lake Erie, is probably the closest that a mere mortal can get to the feeling of walking on water.

**YOU SHOULD KNOW:**
While Point Pelee marks the most southerly point of mainland Canada, Pelee Island is its southernmost inhabited territory. Further out, the uninhabited Middle Island marks the most southerly point that flies the Maple Leaf flag.

# Pukaskwa National Park

Pukaskwa National Park is a place defined by its proximity to Lake Superior – the largest freshwater lake in the world. It is a body of water so vast that it can generate great storms capable of sinking large ships and hidden currents can have a dramatic effect even up stream, on the rivers that run into it. Its year-round average temperature is only a couple of degrees above freezing, perfect for alpine flora to blossom on its shores.

The park itself covers 1,878 sq km (725 sq mi) and is virtually all wilderness, with vehicular access available only to the administration office and the Hattie Cove campground. The landscape is boreal forest, typical of the Canadian Shield, where spruce and balsam mix with that most Canadian of trees – the Jack pine. Tip Top Mountain rises to a height of 630 m (2,067 ft) above sea level and marks the park's highest point, and a 60-km (37-mi) trail follows the shoreline of Lake Superior. A hop-on hop-off boat-hire service operates during the summer, allowing the hiker to experience this unique marine environment more intimately. The waters of Horseshoe Bay are shallow and calm enough to allow swimming in high summer and the shoreline is the perfect place to paddle a canoe.

Pukaskwa National Park includes land that is the domain of black bear, moose, beavers, wolves and the endangered woodland caribou. There is only one official campground (at Hattie Cove), but camping elsewhere in the park is allowed. It is important to be aware of the wildlife and secure all supplies above ground and adopt a policy of zero-trace camping by taking everything you brought in away with you.

*Halfway Lake in Pukaskwa National Park*

# Cape Spear National Historic Site

Marking as it does the easternmost point of continental North America, Cape Spear attracts a lot of attention. People roll up to its historic lighthouse, take a quick photo as evidence that they were there and then roll away again. However, the centre of the Historic Site is well worth an hour or two of anyone's time. It contains the oldest surviving lighthouse in Newfoundland – dating back to 1836 – complete with renovated lighthouse-keeper's quarters. It was also the site of much activity in World War II, when a series of tunnels and fortifications was constructed. Two gun emplacements remain as a reminder of more troubled times.

*The historic lighthouse on rugged Cape Spear*

Venturing away from the man-made structures on show, the Cape has much to commend it to those looking for a rugged, if sometimes very bracing hike. The area has bird life in abundance, including shearwaters which can usually only be seen some distance out to sea. In late spring huge icebergs drift slowly down the coast like ghostly facsimiles of the rugged cape landscape. The headland is dotted with secluded coves which, in summer, provide the best land-based whale-watching in North America. Orca, minke and finback whales all come to feed on herring and capelin in the waters off the cape. Harbour seals, otters and dolphins may also be observed from these natural vantage points.

Great waves crash against the shore and high winds pummel the headland almost all year round. The cape has a good system of hiking trails and it is essential to keep to them, no matter how benign the weather may seem. It is a place of great beauty for those who like nature at its most raw. Standing on the edge of a mighty continent, it is easy to feel humbled by the forces of nature that have shaped this craggy promontory.

**HOW TO GET THERE:**
Take Highway 11 (Cape Spear Drive) from St John's, Newfoundland.
**WHEN TO GO:**
The grounds are open all year round. The lighthouse is open from mid May to mid October.
**DON'T MISS:**
Watching the waves roll in from Blackhead. This is particularly impressive in late spring when the water is laden with ice.
**YOU SHOULD KNOW:**
Cape Spear is so called not for its shape, although it does look like a giant blunt arrowhead. Rather it is a corruption of the Portuguese *Cabo da Esperança* – literally, Cape of Hope.

# Cape St Mary's Ecological Reserve

Located at the very tip of Newfoundland's Avalon Peninsula, Cape St Mary's Ecological Reserve is about as wild a place as you could wish to find in North America. The wind roars so ferociously off the Atlantic Ocean that 100-year-old trees struggle to reach waist height. Waves crash against the rapidly eroding cliffs that mark the reserve's land boundary, while mist and fog shroud the peninsula most days.

*Ecotourists come to admire the gannets that perch precariously on the rock face.*

**HOW TO GET THERE:**
A two- or three-hour drive from St John's, Newfoundland, via Highway 90

**WHEN TO GO:**
Best between May and July.

**DON'T MISS:**
The performances put on by the gannets. They mate for life and have only one chick that spends the first weeks of its life perched perilously on the rock face, battered by wind and rain, held on by a harness-like nest of woven seaweed. Parent birds greet each other in both French and English styles (appropriately for Canada) – with a raised beak salute followed by alternating cheek beak taps.

**YOU SHOULD KNOW:**
The reserve has an interpretive centre which is the perfect place to start a visit to the area. Staff there will advise on current conditions and the best places to see the wildlife.

But when the wind abates and the fog clears one of the most beautiful seascapes on Earth is revealed. A lush green carpet of grass and moss covers the headlands and the land falls sharply away into the azure waters of the North Atlantic.

The reserve was established in 1983 and covers both the headland and the immediate waters around it. The main objective of the reserve was to create a low-pollution environment where birdlife could thrive. The result is a birdwatcher's paradise. Out to sea, the appropriately named Bird Rock is a limestone outcrop which has become separated from the mainland by years of erosion. Its detachment means that it is free from predators and pearly white gannets flourish to the point that every square inch of the island is occupied by them. Kittiwakes, gannets and murres all plunge into the fish-rich waters in their thousands, making the sea fizz with activity.

Great care should be taken while walking around the reserve, especially when conditions are misty or wet underfoot. As befits a wilderness, there are no signs warning you of the dangers. But, if you come well equipped and take extra care, the reserve offers many fantastic vantage points from which to witness the everyday trials and tribulations of vast colonies of majestic seabirds.

# Gulf of St Lawrence

In geographical science the term 'gulf' is used to describe a partly landlocked sea and although the Gulf of St Lawrence (Golfe du Saint-Laurent) seems to fit the bill, it is a misnomer. In reality the 'Gulf' is the estuary of a 'super-river' formed at the end of the last ice age. The colossal erosive powers of the river carved out a huge basin and, once the melt had finished, the sea levels rose and saltwater pushed the freshwater of the river back to leave what is now the world's largest estuary.

The Gulf of St Lawrence is massive, covering an area of around 234,000 sq km (90,350 sq mi). It is bounded by Nova Scotia to the south, Newfoundland to the east, Labrador to the north, New Brunswick to the west and is of immense strategic value as it links the Great Lakes to the sea via the St Lawrence River and Seaway. It contains many of the Maritimes' most beautiful and formidable islands, including Prince Edward and Bonaventure Islands as well as the Magdalen Archipelago. Cruise ships that ply their trade in the Gulf in summer can take weeks to complete their tours, yet only scratch the surface of discovery.

The Gulf has long been of vital importance and many First Nations bands chose to live on its edge to exploit its fish-rich waters. Ever since its discovery by Europeans in 1534 it has been a vital shipping route into Canada and the point at which the Gulf flows into the river is named the Jacques Cartier Strait, after its European discoverer. The lands around the Gulf are home to moose, caribou, bears and beavers, while its waters contain over 200 species of fish, which provide food for vast colonies of seals and huge pods of whales.

**HOW TO GET THERE:**
By air to St John's, Newfoundland, or by boat from Quebec City
**WHEN TO GO:**
The Gulf is usually ice free from May to November.
**DON'T MISS:**
Port Aux Basques – a beautiful old French fishing station right at the very tip of Newfoundland as it juts out into the Gulf.
**YOU SHOULD KNOW:**
Although ice adds to the stark winter beauty of the area, ice floes are a hazard to shipping during the spring melt. The Canadian Coastguard runs a fleet of 18 icebreakers to keep their eastern trade routes open.

*Limestone cliffs overlook the Gulf of St Lawrence.*

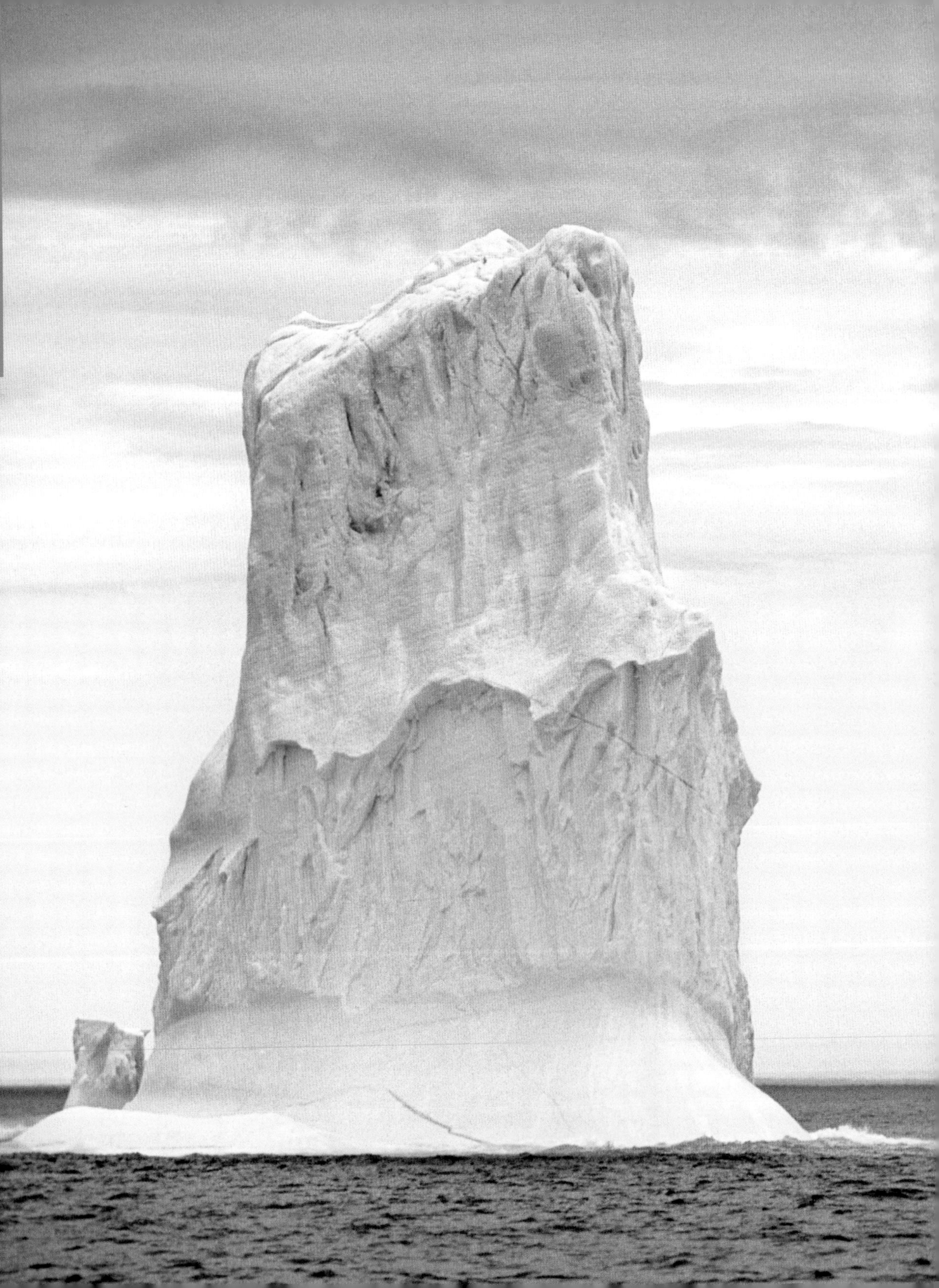

# Witless Bay Ecological Reserve

If you have any fear of birds and maybe have to hide behind the sofa when watching Hitchcock's *The Birds*, it is probably best to give the superbly named Witless Bay Ecological Reserve a wide berth. The reserve consists of four craggy islands – Green, Great, Gull and Pee Pee – each of which is a protected area and home to hundreds of thousands of birds. The only access to the waters of the bay is via escorted tours by locals, many of whom take time out from their regular work to show visitors this amazing landscape.

If you visit the area before the end of June, you are treated to the sight of icebergs moving across the bay like giant ice cubes, slowly melting as they drift south to warmer waters. July sees the icebergs depart, only to be replaced by even more spectacular giants of the sea. Large pods of humpback, minke and finback whales come to the area to feed on capelin, a tiny fish found in abundance at this time of year. The finback whale can measure up to 30 m (98 ft) long and a fluke (tail) thrashing display is an awesome sight.

Finally it is time to get up close and personal with the birds. As you approach the islands you gradually realize that what seemed like the colour of the rocks is actually the plumage of birds. The islands are completely covered by them, like bees swarming around a hive. Murres, puffins and kittiwakes all jostle for position on these prime pieces of avian real estate. Murres are particularly argumentative little creatures but, as they nest at such high density that they often rub wings with their neighbours, that is hardly surprising.

**HOW TO GET THERE:**
It's a 30-km (19-mi) drive south from St John's, Newfoundland, along Route 10.
**WHEN TO GO:**
Tours run from June to September.
**DON'T MISS:**
A small detour takes you to The Spout – a giant wave-propelled geyser which squirts water at a ferocious speed through a small aperture in the rocks. Many of the guides include this in a tour of the islands.
**YOU SHOULD KNOW:**
Landing on the islands is prohibited except for those engaged in research. Keeping the islands safe for the birds has been highly successful since the islands were protected in 1962 and the total bird population has increased several hundredfold.

*A whale-watching boat sails through icebergs in Witless Bay Ecological Reserve.*

# Magdalen Islands

**HOW TO GET THERE:**
By ferry from Souris on Prince Edward Island or by air from Montreal and Quebec City, landing on Havre aux Maisons Island.
**WHEN TO GO:**
All year round; the best weather is found from April to September.
**DON'T MISS:**
Swimming in one of the islands' many lagoons, which are ephemeral sea lakes caused when dunes connect. While the waters around the islands are generally chilly and rough, the waters of the lagoons are calm and can reach a positively balmy 21°C (70°F) in late summer (August).
**YOU SHOULD KNOW:**
The cliffs that line the islands are composed of extremely fragile sandstone and hikers should avoid walking within 3 m (10 ft) of the edge.

The Magdalen Islands (Îles de la Madeleine) form an archipelago located in the middle of the Gulf of St Lawrence, some 210 km (130 mi) from the Gaspé Peninsula. The islands, which are the visible peaks of a sub-marine ridge, run for over 60 km (37 mi) and comprise a dozen main islands along with innumerable rocky outcrops. Half of the islands are connected by long, slender sand dunes. The comparatively warm waters of the Gulf protect the island group from the harsh winters experienced on the Quebec mainland. The islanders are known as *les Madelinots* and are descendents of Acadians who escaped deportation to the south in 1755. Traditionally, agriculture and fisheries were the islands' mainstay, but farming has declined and only a small trawler fleet remains.

The islands' interiors are characterized by gently contoured verdant hills, while their shorelines are marked by fragile sandstone cliffs which have been eroded into spectacular arches, tunnels and caves by the combination of powerful winds and waves. The eroded stone from the cliffs impacts greatly on the islands' littoral zones and about one third of the islands' landmass is made up of dunes and sand bars. It is easy to find solitude along its many dune-lined strands, where only the roar of the sea and the squawks of seabirds can be heard. During the spring melt, seals can be observed hitching a ride on ice floes, while in summer the surrounding waters are ideal for windsurfing. When the wind drops, as it does every so often, the islands assume an appearance so benign that they might be from a lower latitude. But when it roars it provides a reminder that the elements govern the climate and topography of this remarkable archipelago.

*Cap Herrise Lighthouse, Magdalen Islands*

# Mingan Archipelago

*A hiker walks through rock stacks on Niapiskau Island.*

The Mingan Archipelago is a chain of around 30 islands and over 1,000 islets which runs for 150 km (93 mi) across Havre-Saint-Pierre on the north shore of the Gulf of Saint Lawrence. Comprised of limestone bedrock with granite outcrops, this ribbon of islands has, over millions of years, been sculpted by the awesome power of sea and wind into a remarkable landscape of natural monuments. Each of these huge rock stacks has weathered uniquely, some resembling giant monsters newly emerged from the sea, while others are reminiscent of the *inuksuit* (stone figures) left as markers by First Nations peoples.

Although the archipelago has the appearance of a fairly barren landscape, it is in fact part of a rich and diverse marine environment. The nutrient-laden waters of the Saint-Jean and Aguanish Rivers mix with the colder oxygen-rich waters of the Gulf to create ideal conditions for both flora and fauna. Grey, harbour and harp seals can be spotted sunning themselves on the rocks to raise their body temperature, in between fishing forays in the area's icy-cold waters. The abundance of fish and enormous shoals of plankton also attract dolphins and whales as well as Atlantic puffins, sea and eider ducks. On land, snowshoe hare, ermine and beaver flourish and the chief predators are red foxes and wolves.

The total landmass of the island chain may only be around 39 sq km (15 sq mi) but it boasts a dazzling array of landscapes. Peat bogs, coniferous forests, barrens and salt marshes as well as mile upon mile of shoreline all add up to a uniquely diverse ecosystem and the area is home to many rare and endangered wild flowers. There is also ample room for camping and hiking and, once the winter ice has melted, the surrounding waters are ripe for sea kayaking and diving.

**HOW TO GET THERE:**
It is a full day's drive along Highway 138 from Quebec – a bus also serves this route.
**WHEN TO GO:**
From May to September is best.
**DON'T MISS:**
Watching the sun rise or set behind the magnificent monoliths that line the islands.
**YOU SHOULD KNOW:**
Beavers, which are native to the area, favour lilies in their diet. The plant needs still water to grow, so the industrious beavers build dams so that the lilies flourish. The instinct to dam is so strong in the beaver, it has been demonstrated that even when played a tape recording of running water, the beaver will start building a barrier.

# Restigouche Estuary

The Restigouche (or Ristigouche) River marks the boundary between New Brunswick and Quebec and spills out into a large estuary at the western end of the Bay of Chaleur. At its most expansive the estuary is almost 8 km (5 mi) wide and only narrows some 25 km (16 mi) upstream at Campbellton. The estuary, although wide, is fairly shallow, allowing its waters to warm up quickly once the winter ice has melted. This encourages wildlife to flourish and the estuary is an important habitat for Atlantic salmon. Mussels and clams attract vast colonies of seabirds, including tens of thousands of black scoter which frequent the area in early spring.

The river's name is a corruption of the local First Nation word *Listuguj* – meaning five fingers. It is fed by fast-running streams that rise in the North Appalachians and which often teem with shoals of wild salmon. The shores of this bountiful river have for centuries been the home of the Mi'kmaq people who now live on reserved land at Pointe-à-la-Croix on the Quebec bank of the estuary. Although the surrounding land offers an opportunity for moderately challenging hiking, exploration of the area is best done on the water. A myriad of tributaries flow into the estuary and could not have been better designed for canoeing and rafting, but it is for fishing that the Restigouche is most renowned. The chance to catch and display a salmon as big as the fisherman has drawn people from around the world and the estuary was a favourite spot of former President Jimmy Carter. For all its bounty, the estuary is a delicate ecosystem and there have been numerous incidents when fish stocks have been all but exhausted by commercial fisheries. There is also still tension surrounding the First Nation people's ancestral fishing rights.

# Grand Manan Island

It may be only an hour-and-a-half ferry ride from Blacks Harbour, but Grand Manan Island has a remoteness that belies its proximity to the mainland. Home to a year-round human population of fewer than 3,000, it is also a significant stopping-off point for North American bird migration and attracts birdwatchers from around the globe. The island's name is probably a shortening of *Mananook* – meaning island place in the local First Nation's language. For centuries the Malecite-Passamaquoddy Indians would risk life and limb to canoe across the often-turbulent waters to hunt, fish and collect seaweed. Norse explorers found the island over 1,000 years ago, but it was only settled by Europeans in the late 18th century.

Nearly all of the settlements are dotted around the southeast coast, in comfortable little coves that provide some degree of shelter from the often ferocious wind and sea. Away from the coast Manan has a rugged interior which becomes ever more spectacular the further north and west one travels. A network of trails takes the hiker over a barren landscape of 200-million-year-old igneous rock before the land falls away into the sea via towering 120 m (394 ft) cliffs. Never crowded, the 34-km (21-mi) long island has a good system of roads which are often no more than winding country lanes and best explored by bicycle. Away from the land, the nutrient-rich waters of the Bay of Fundy attract whales and a host of seabirds, while the shallower waters closer to the shore are the perfect place to learn sea kayaking. Each season on Manan brings its own beauty. The island is covered by a carpet of wild flowers in spring, and summer and winters are tempered by the comparative warmth of the sea.

**HOW TO GET THERE:**
By ferry from Blacks Harbour
**WHEN TO GO:**
All year round. The weather is best from May to September.
**DON'T MISS:**
The Seven Days Work cliff formation at Whale Cove
**YOU SHOULD KNOW:**
Although the island was ceded to Britain by the Treaty of Utrecht in 1713, the USA disputed its ownership until 1817 when they swapped the island for three that are now part of Maine.

*Sunrise on the remote Grand Manan Island*

# Tobeatic Wilderness

**HOW TO GET THERE:**
A three-hour drive from Halifax, Nova Scotia
**WHEN TO GO:**
All year round
**DON'T MISS:**
The Shelburne River Canoe Route – a system of lakes connected by a river that flows from the centre of the area.
**YOU SHOULD KNOW:**
If travelling to the area in summer (June to August) it is vital to carry insect repellent and avoid using hairspray, perfume and the like, as the area is home to billions of insects waiting to take a bite out of you.

The Tobeatic Wilderness Area, affectionately known as 'the Toby', straddles five counties of Nova Scotia and is the largest protected wild region in the Maritimes. Its name comes from the local Mi'kmaq language and means 'site of the alders'. It is an area sculpted by major glaciers of previous ice ages and its barren and semi-barren landscape is dotted with moraine and eskers. Its remoteness provides an undisturbed habitat for the rare Nova Scotia moose as well as a healthy population of black bear. The abundant wetlands of the area are also the ideal home for a vast array of bird life. Founded as a game reserve in 1927, the area has now grown to cover 1,040 sq km (400 sq mi). In 1968 it was afforded Wildlife Management Area status, which has helped to limit the impact of logging in the park.

Nine major river systems have their headwaters in 'the Toby' and their journeys to the Fundy and Atlantic coasts are interrupted by seemingly countless lakes. A network of streams, rivers and lakes makes for interesting and diverse canoeing expeditions and solitude is almost guaranteed as the canoeist heads even a little way into this remarkable wilderness.

In autumn the colours of the mixed woodland are spectacular, but this soon gives way to a long cold winter. It is then that the wilderness assumes an eerie calm. Covered in a blanket of snow and with the lakes frozen over, the mammals of the area take their long hibernation. On such nights, when the moon is full, the 'Toby' exudes an almost electric radiance and the silence is broken only by the hoot of the barred owl. April sees the ice melt and, as the black bears awake from their slumbers, the Tobeatic Wilderness springs back into life again.

*A couple canoe down the Tusket River in the Tobeatic Wilderness.*

# Sable Island

Sable Island lies like a sleeping leviathan in the North Atlantic Ocean, detached from the coast of Nova Scotia by 160 km (100 mi) of often-turbulent water. It sits on the boundary between the warm Gulf Stream and the frigid Labrador Current, which often leads to the island being shrouded in thick fog. It is surrounded by barely submerged shifting sandbanks which, over the years, have first scuppered and then swallowed more than 300 ships. The treacherousness of its waters has earned it the tag 'Graveyard of the Atlantic'. Over the years it has been home to many stranded sailors, although today the only human inhabitants are scientists working for Canada's Environment Agency.

The island is long and narrow and is so battered by the elements that it is constantly changing shape. Since its discovery by Portuguese navigators, it has probably halved in size. Currently, it is around 40 km (25 mi) long and a mere 1.6 km (1 mi) wide at its broadest point. What it lacks in natural protection, the government of Canada has made up for in regulatory safeguards. Visitor numbers are strictly rationed and a code of practice must be adhered to. Indigenous wildlife includes harbour and grey seals that breed along the island's shoreline. However, there is one animal above all for which Sable Island is renown: a group of more than 250 displaced horses roam wild on the island, providing a curious sight in this harsh, treeless environment. While there are several interesting and conflicting stories about how these equine exiles happened to get to the island, it is probable that they were imported in the 18th century and then abandoned. Sable Island is a place like no other, starkly beautiful and wonderfully isolated, with a surreal charm all of its own.

*Wild horses canter across the beach on Sable Island.*

**HOW TO GET THERE:**
By small aeroplane (from Halifax, Nova Scotia) or by boat
**WHEN TO GO:**
From July to October
**DON'T MISS:**
For all its wild beauty the highlight of any trip to Sable has to be the horses. While there are numerous wild herds of horses in the world, few exist without some sort of interference by humans. The horses of Sable Island may not be indigenous, but they have adapted well to their environment and have no detrimental impact on the area's ecosystem.
**YOU SHOULD KNOW:**
In the early 20th century a plan was hatched to protect the island from erosion by planting tens of thousands of trees. Such was the ferocity of the wind, coupled with the paucity of the soil, that they all died – leaving just low-growth vegetation.

# Alexander Archipelago

The Alexander Islands are named after Tsar Alexander II, the former owner, but proudly fly the Stars and Stripes nowadays – the USA purchased Russia's Alaska territories for less than two cents an acre, the bargain of the 19th century. The 485-km (300-mi) long archipelago is off Alaska's southern coastline and is a chain of over one thousand islands (although *not* the home of the famous salad dressing, that honour belonging to the Thousand Islands in the St Lawrence River). Once part of the mainland, these islands – the tops of submerged mountains – are close to shore. The northern section of the Inside Passage from Washington's Puget Sound to the Alaska Panhandle winds through the archipelago, which protects seagoing vessels from sometimes-violent Pacific weather.

These islands offer massive doses of everything wilderness addicts crave – they have steep coastlines with dramatic fjords, while rugged interiors have dense evergreen and temperate rain forests. Much terrain is officially protected and the Alexanders are thinly populated, offering resourceful travellers with the necessary survival skills every opportunity to find and explore virgin terrain without seeing another human being (apart from any like-minded companions) from one day's end to the next. There are indigenous occupants – the Tlingit and Kaigani Haidas and Tsimshians who arrived from British Columbia in the 1800s – plus those concerned with the main commercial activities of logging, fishing and tourism.

In the latter context, guides are available for those who love wild places but prefer not to go it alone. The main islands are Admiralty, Baranof, Chichagof, Dall, Kupreanof, Prince of Wales, Revillagigedo and Wrangell. These all have scattered communities that provide an ideal starting point for backcountry expeditions. But a visit can prove very rewarding for those who simply want to see and appreciate this unspoilt archipelago.

*A humpback whale at sunset in Frederick Sound*

# Brooks Range

This impressive chain of mountains crosses Alaska from west to east, ending in Canada's Yukon. The Brooks Range is virtually uninhabited, having only a few tiny settlements such as Coldfoot and Deadhorse. Sole road access is from the Dalton Highway that runs through the Atigun Pass *en route* from Fairbanks to Prudhoe Bay's oilfields. The mountains include portions of the vast Arctic National Wildlife Refuge and encompass the Gates of the Arctic National Park. Together with the adjacent Noatak National Preserve, the latter is the USA's largest wilderness.

The Brooks Range marks the summer position of the Arctic front, ensuring that summers are relatively mild and providing a window of opportunity for visitors. It's possible to drive along the Dalton Highway and enjoy its rugged grandeur but, for those who want to see more, the answer is a trip organized by locals familiar with the spectacular but inhospitable terrain. Individual expeditions are possible, but even those experienced in self-sufficient wilderness travel should think twice before going it alone. The best way in is by floatplane and most adventurers wisely choose an expedition that includes hiking, kayaking or rafting with the help of experienced local guides.

The Brooks Range is the finest unspoilt mountain terrain in North America – a pristine wonderland of craggy granite, rivers and lakes teeming with wildlife. But it's that way for a reason. For the delights of the Brooks Range will never suffer the fate of so many natural wonders in the modern world – seeing a huge influx of the sort of visitors drawn to wild places whose presence ultimately devalues the very thing that attracted them in the first place. A visit to this magical place is simply too challenging for any but the most determined adventurers, able to dig deep into their wallets for the ultimate wilderness experience.

*An aerial view of Atigun Pass in the stunning Brooks Range*

**HOW TO GET THERE:**
Fly to a specific destination from Fairbanks or take the Dalton Highway and explore from there. Floatplane trips can be booked from Bettles.

**WHEN TO GO:**
Summer (June to August) is best.

**DON'T MISS:**
Wildlife watchers will be enchanted by the huge variety of fauna; be sure to witness the amazing caribou migrations through the mountains in spring and autumn.

**YOU SHOULD KNOW:**
Despite wilderness status and being almost entirely free from human disturbance, the Brooks Range is still home – at its western tip – to the world's largest zinc mine. The huge Red Dog opencast mine is responsible for around ten per cent of world zinc production and sits on land owned by the NANA Regional Corporation, created in 1972 to settle aboriginal land claims. The mine has operated since 1989 and hopes to continue extracting zinc, lead and silver until around 2030.

*Brown bear with yearlings on the McNeil River*

# McNeil River Game Sanctuary

The main attraction in the remote McNeil River State Game Sanctuary is the world's largest gathering of Alaska brown bears, which takes place annually where a series of cascades on the McNeil River provides an obstacle for migrating chum salmon. This makes them relatively easy prey for normally solitary bears, which duly congregate in large numbers to feast on Nature's bounty and fatten up for the harsh winter. A hundred or more turn up at the height of the salmon run in July to fight, play, feed and mate. A similar but smaller spectacle may been seen a little earlier at nearby Mikfik Creek, where up to 25 bears can be seen hunting red salmon in the ice-cold water.

The sanctuary extends to an unspoilt 462 sq km (178 sq mi) in southwestern Alaska. The nearest town is Dillingham, but the area has no roads and is untouched by modern development. The McNeil River originates high in the Aleutian Mountains and protected terrain surrounds the falls where the bears gather, close to the river's discharge point in lower Cook Inlet, 400 km (250 mi) from Anchorage as the light aircraft flies. A visit to this unique sanctuary to see the bears isn't a 'gimme'. In order to offer what the name suggests, access during the bear-watching season is strictly limited and permits – that should be applied for online to the Alaska Department of Fish and Game before March 1 each year – are issued by ballot.

Those who win a coveted four-day ticket to view form into small groups (consisting of no more than ten people plus a guide) that hike to prime bruin-watching spots to spend six or seven hours watching and photographing the congregation of bears, overnighting at an established campground and eating in a primitive cabin after a memorable wilderness experience.

**HOW TO GET THERE:**
The sanctuary is accessible by boat but most visitors fly in from Homer using one of several available air charters.

**WHEN TO GO:**
June 7 to August 26 is the period when permits are issued for bear-watching.

**DON'T MISS:**
The other wildlife to be seen in the refuge. Bears may be the main attraction, but those who don't make bear watch can still see (among others) moose, caribou, harbour seal, arctic ground squirrel, wolves and red fox – even the occasional lone bear – alongside numerous bird species including bald eagles and harlequin ducks.

**YOU SHOULD KNOW:**
No bears (or humans) have been injured since the restricted-access programme was introduced, but those lucky enough to take a bear-watching trip are reassured by the presence of an armed member of the sanctuary's staff.

# North Cascades National Park

The Cascade Range begins in British Columbia and extends through Washington and Oregon into Northern California. The Washington section is known as the North Cascades, and there the national park of the same name may be found. In fact, the North Cascades National Park is a complex extending to around 2,800 sq km (1,080 sq mi) that consists of four linked areas – north and south park units plus Ross Lake and Lake Chelan National Recreation Areas. As 93 per cent of the park has been designated as wilderness, for those willing and able to survive in the wild there are plenty of opportunities to enjoy awesome mountain hiking in complete solitude.

The two recreation areas are destinations of choice for anyone keen to experience the ambiance of these rugged mountains without mounting a major backcountry expedition. Ross Lake National Recreation Area, close to the Canadian border, is the most accessible. This corridor along the Skagit River bisects the park's north and south units and encompasses three reservoirs used to generate power for Seattle, including eponymous Ross Lake.

Recreational activities include hunting, fishing, kayaking, canoeing, hiking and climbing. There are trailheads connecting to an extensive network of established hiking routes, including those that continue into adjoining wilderness. The North Cascades Highway passes through the recreation area from east to west, providing access and allowing travellers to enjoy superb mountain scenery that has earned the nickname 'American Alps'. There are a number of campsites along the road. The Lake Chelan National Recreation Area is more remote, but equally impressive. It covers just 250 sq km (95 sq mi) at the north end of the lake. The Pacific Coast Trail passes through and in summer there is an off-road bus service that connects the trail and the town of Chelan at the south end.

**HOW TO GET THERE:**
Ross Lake is accessible from North Cascades Highway or the gravel Silver Skagit Road to the Hozomeen campground. There's no road access to Lake Chelan, but it's possible to hike in, use the floatplane or take a ferry up the lake from Chelan.
**WHEN TO GO:**
April to October
**DON'T MISS:**
The North Cascades Visitor Centre and Skagit Visitor Centre, both to be found in Newhalem, Washington.

**YOU SHOULD KNOW:**
The magnificent vista seen from Desert Peak Lookout is reached by a 10 km (6 mi) trail from Ross Lake. The lookout is staffed in wildfire season and was manned in 1956 by Beat Generation writer Jack Kerouac, who used the experience as inspiration for his novel *Desolation Angels*.

*Mount Shuksan, Washington*

# Trapper Creek Wilderness

**HOW TO GET THERE:**
There are no roads within the Trapper Creek drainage, but a number of primary and secondary unpaved forest roads skirt this wilderness area, which is just to the northwest of the town of Wind River.

**WHEN TO GO:**
May to September for the best weather

**DON'T MISS:**
The nearby Government Mineral Springs Recreation Area, where it's possible to imbibe – you guessed it – mineral water from the legendary Iron Mike Well.

**YOU SHOULD KNOW:**
The drive to Trapper Creek – just north of the Columbia River Gorge that divides Washington and Oregon – involves travelling the Columbia River Highway, built as a scenic route between 1913 and 1922. This has some spectacular sights, including Cascade Locks, the Bridge of the Gods and over 75 waterfalls.

The Gifford Pinchot National Forest in southern Washington stretches for 115 km (70 mi) along the western slopes of the Cascade Range, covering an impressive 5,300 sq km (2,050 sq mi). This vast area of wild country contains Mount St Helens National Volcanic Monument plus official wilderness areas such as Goat Rocks, Tatoosh, Mount Adams and Indian Heaven. One of the most interesting is the smallest – Trapper Creek drainage. This extends to a mere 240 sq km (93 sq mi) but is no less appealing for that. Trapper Creek Wilderness is a pristine area within the Wind River watershed and contains one of the largest blocks of original low-growth Douglas-fir forest in the state. To that may be added a rugged landscape full of rushing streams, waterfalls as tall as 30 m (100 ft) and huckleberry fields at higher elevations.

Anyone with limited time to explore the national forest would do well to focus on Trapper Creek, which offers accessible day hiking along established trails, although some are primitive and not for the inexperienced. For those capable of getting there (it requires physical effort and stamina), the outlook from the top of aptly named Observation Peak with its abandoned fire-watch post is awesome, encompassing Goat Rocks and Mounts Jefferson, Rainier, Adams and Hood. Catch it if you can! Soda Peaks Lake in the southwest corner of the drainage is another highlight that rewards a shortish hike.

Wildlife is varied and there is a good selection of birds – including barred and spotted owls, woodpeckers and goshawks – while commonly seen animals include Roosevelt elk, black-tailed deer and black bear. Rarer but still spotted occasionally are bobcat, cougar, pine marten and grizzly bear. For those with eyes to see beyond the striking scenery, it's a dimension that adds a special something to this beautiful wilderness.

# Willamette National Forest

After the Cascade Range duly cascades down into Oregon its western slopes are occupied by the 180-km (112-mi) length of Willamette National Forest, a protected area that offers a hugely varied landscape of mountains, canyons, rushing streams and extensively wooded slopes. There are almost limitless possibilities for open-air recreation and touring – a point underlined by the fact that there are 10,300 km (6,400 mi) of roads within Willamette Forest, including designated scenic routes such as Aufderheide Memorial Drive, Clackamas-Breitenbush Road, Diamond Drive, Quartzville Creek Road and the McKenzie Pass-Santiam Pass loop.

But for those who do not have the luxury of limitless time to explore this vast wild place a narrower focus is required. The forest contains a number of wilderness areas sure to appeal to adventurous explorers, but with no fewer than 1,550 sq km (600 sq mi) of uninhabited terrain to choose from further refinement is called for. One sure-fire winner is the Diamond Peak wilderness, surrounding the shield volcano of the same name. This lonely place straddles the crest and is located within two national forests – Willamette to the west and Deschutes to the east. The Pacific Crest National Scenic Trail passes through and some 200 km (125 mi) of established routes may be found within the wilderness, including the 16-km (10-mi) Diamond Peak Trail. A jewel-like ring of small lakes surrounds the peak's snow-capped summit.

The area features impressive stands of mixed trees such as mountain hemlock, western white pine and lodgepole. Abundant alpine flowers provide bright colour in season along the trails, on lakeshores and in meadows. Other than hiking, popular activities are camping, horseback riding, fishing and mountain climbing. Good base camps for the ascent of Diamond Peak may be found at Divide Lake, Marie Lake and Rockpile Lake.

*Proxy Falls in Willamette National Forest*

**HOW TO GET THERE:**
Access the forest from the Salem, Albany and Eugene areas of the Willamette Valley. The main highways are US Route 20 and Oregon State Routes 22, 58 and 126. The nearest town to Diamond Peak is Oakridge.

**WHEN TO GO:**
Avoid winter conditions (November to March), unless the main attraction is cross-country skiing or snowshoe trekking.

**DON'T MISS:**
Abundant wildlife. Large animals to be seen around Diamond Peak are black-tailed and mule deer, elk and black bear. Small animals include foxes, pine martens, snowshoe rabbits and marmots. There are numerous feathered residents such as Clark's nutcracker, Oregon jays, ravens and water ouzels

**YOU SHOULD KNOW:**
Day or overnight trekkers entering the Diamond Peak wilderness area between Memorial Day (the last Monday in May) and October 31 must obtain a permit. These are free and can be self-issued at approved trailheads.

# Kalmiopsis Wilderness

Tucked away at the heart of southwestern Oregon's Rogue River-Siskiyou National Forest is a hidden gem. The Kalmiopsis wilderness area is not small at around 730 sq km (282 sq mi), although that must be measured against the national forest's 7,300 sq km (2,820 sq mi). Even though it only occupies one tenth of the forest, Kalmiopsis is undoubtedly the star of the show. This unique wild place has extraordinary geology, with an amazing variety of rock formations supporting a huge diversity of plant life of great

*A ranger hiking by Western White Pine in Siskiyou National Forest*

botanical interest that has evolved to survive in harsh soil conditions caused by high concentrations of heavy metals such as magnesium, iron, chromium and nickel leaching from serpentinite and peridotite rocks.

The landscape of this rugged wilderness ranges from a lowly 150 m (500 ft) to a maximum elevation of 1,554 m (5,098 ft) at Pearsoll Peak. It is characterized by sharp ridges and plunging tree-clad canyons carrying rushing streams and white-water sections of the Illinois, Chetco and North Fork Rivers that attract rafters prepared to carry their craft in. There are also nearly 250 km (155 mi) of hiking trails in the area. These can be challenging, as many are steep and rocky, and were not made easier by the major Biscuit Fire of 2002 that devastated much of the forest following a lightning strike. The flora is regenerating but damage to the tree cover is still apparent, making trails even more hazardous in places. Many routes incorporate sections of old mining roads and can become confusing, so a trail map is essential. Popular day hikes are those to Babyfoot and Vulcan Lakes. But those seeking solitude can take any other trail into the wilderness and be virtually guaranteed there will be no sight or sound of other people.

**HOW TO GET THERE:**
There are more than a dozen trailheads, most accessible by regular car. Easiest access is from Highway 199 near Cave Junction in the Illinois Valley or Highway 101 at Gold Beach or Brookings.

**WHEN TO GO:**
June to September inclusive are the 'dry' months. Snow often blocks roads to the trailheads into spring and the Illinois River cannot be forded at Collier Bar until August.

**DON'T MISS:**
*Kalmiopsis leachiana*, the plant after which this wilderness area is named. Discovered in 1930 by Lilla Leach, this evergreen has fabulous purple flowers, is a relic of the pre-ice age and the oldest known member of the *Ericaceae* (heather) family.

**YOU SHOULD KNOW:**
Don't be tempted to leave marked trails to travel cross-country – the terrain is steep and treacherous with dense vegetation.

# Channel Islands National Park

Despite proximity to the urban sprawl of Los Angeles, the Channel Islands – close to California's southern coast – are largely unspoilt. Five of them form the Channel Islands National Park, a world apart from the bustling mainland. The islands offer a stunning display of wild flowers after the winter rains and have large seabird colonies, while surrounding waters support abundant marine life including whales, seals and sea lions.

Santa Cruz is the big one at around 245 sq km (95 sq mi) and preserves a fascinating microcosm of the Californian coastal environment as once it was. There are mountains, canyons, cliffs, tide pools, pristine beaches and sea caves – including one of the world's largest, the famous Painted Cave. There are numerous reminders of former occupants – both Chumash Indians and 19th-century incomers. Nearby Santa Rosa has cliffs, beaches and central peaks and – like its neighbours – supports a considerable diversity of flora and fauna, much of it unique to the islands.

The three islets of East, Middle and West Anacapa have towering cliffs, sea caves and the Arch Rock that serves as the park's symbol. In the summer on East Anacapa rangers dive in Landing Cove with video cameras, allowing visitors to glimpse the magical undersea world of the kelp forest . . . without getting wet. The smallest island is Santa Barbara, a 260-ha (640-ac) triangular rock with steep cliffs that is returning to its former self as the National Park Service reverses the effects of human interference like the introduction of rabbits and cats, which did huge damage to bird populations. Wild and windswept San Miguel is the outermost island, home to tens of thousands of pinnipeds (sea lions and seals by any other name) around Point Bennett, which may be viewed in season as part of a day-long hike guided by a ranger.

*Anacapa islands at sunset*

# Death Valley National Park

**HOW TO GET THERE:**
California Highway 190 crosses Death Valley National Park from west to east, where US Route 95 runs close to the park.
**WHEN TO GO:**
May to September should be avoided. December and January are the coolest months, with average daytime temperatures of around 18°C (65°F). Spring is the most popular season with visitors.
**DON'T MISS:**
Seeing Zabriskie Point – not the 1970 Michelangelo Antonioni movie, but the original, that extraordinary erosional landscape to be found in the Amargosa Range within Death Valley National Park.
**YOU SHOULD KNOW:**
A temperature of nearly 56.7°C (134°F) was recorded at aptly named Furnace Creek in 1913. That's fractionally below the all-time world high of 57.7°C (136°F) logged in Libya a decade later.

If ever a descriptive name was appropriate, it must surely be Death Valley. This is the lowest, driest and hottest location just about anywhere, and must have seemed a fearsome place to pioneers crossing the uncharted southwestern USA during the California gold rush of 1849. Despite adverse conditions, the valley has been home to the Timbisha tribe (formerly called Panamint Shoshone) for a millennium.

Situated within the Mojave Desert, Death Valley boasts the lowest elevation in North America at 85.5 m (280 ft) below sea level. Ironically, less than 125 km (78 mi) east is the highest point in the contiguous USA – Mount Whitney's soaring 4,421-m (14,505-ft) peak. The 7,800-sq-km (3,012-sq-mi) hotspot of Death Valley is in the Great Basin, enclosed by the Sylvania and Owlshead Mountains, Panamint and Amargosa Ranges. It mostly lies in California, with small areas invading Nevada. The valley forms the greater part of the national park that bears its name, which also includes surrounding mountains, Saline Valley and most of Panamint Valley. Park headquarters is at Furnace Creek along with a visitor centre, museum, gas station, campgrounds, the world's lowest golf course and a desert resort. The visitor centre offers fascinating talks on a variety of valley-related subjects between mid October and mid April. To the north, Scotty's Castle makes a great stopover. This Spanish-style mansion was completed in the 1930s and guided tours of the interior and a network of underground tunnels are available.

Death Valley is not the place for inexperienced people to try backcountry exploring, although hiking, camping, mountain-biking and birdwatching are popular activities. A network of dirt roads allows exploration off the beaten track in a 4x4 vehicle, although precautions like notifying someone of plans are sensible, as the chance of finding help in remote locations is small to negligible.

*Leaving footprints in sand dunes in Death Valley National Park.*

# Inyo Mountains Wilderness

This stark place encompasses a large portion of the Inyo Mountains, a short range to the east of California's Sierra Nevada that stretches for 130 km (81 mi) from the Westgard Pass at the southern end of the White Mountains. The Inyos separate arid Owens Valley from the equally parched Saline Valley in the Mojave Desert. The Inyo Mountains Wilderness covers 810 sq km (313 sq mi) and to the north is the Inyo National Forest, home of the world's oldest tree (Methuselah, a Great Basin bristlecone pine at a secret location that's been around for nearly 4,850 years).

There is usually a good reason why wild places have remained uncolonized, and in this case it's the sheer ruggedness of the terrain. That doesn't stop the park showing evidence of long-abandoned mining activity like old cabins, decaying aerial tramways and an old stamp mill. Four hiking routes are historic mining trails. These are the Burgess Mine Trail, pivotal Lonesome Miner Trail, French Spring Trail and one of the most accessible hikes, the Snowflake Mine Trail starting from the Snowflake Talc Mine and climbing the Beveridge Ridge before dropping down to the old mill site. The Beveridge Canyon Trail leads to the main mining area in an isolated location in the Mojave Desert. These are not smartly waymarked trails, so can be hard to follow and are sometimes seriously overgrown or even lost altogether to rock slides.

This is, therefore, a destination only for experienced survivalists – although cautious day hikes are feasible. Most trailheads can only be reached using a 4x4 off-roader and the wilderness is hazardous territory with dense vegetation, while steep slopes covered in loose rocks wait to trap the unwary at every turn. Be warned that no assistance is available and few people use the trails.

**HOW TO GET THERE:**
The easiest access is from Lone Pine, Inyo County (on US Route 395).
**WHEN TO GO:**
April to October
**DON'T MISS:**
For those with the determination to get there, the ruined Five-Stamp Mill above Beveridge Canyon, surrounded by the remains of miners' cabins, serves as an atmospheric reminder that even more determined individuals once wrested valuable minerals from this inhospitable landscape. From the mill a well-defined trail leads up to historic Frenchy's Cabin, which is reasonably intact.
**YOU SHOULD KNOW:**
Although vehicles are not permitted in the USA's wilderness areas, the official boundaries in Inyo are 9 m (30 ft) back from unpaved roads and 90 m (100 ft) back from paved roads. Camping is allowed with a 14-day limit on one site, after which the camp must be shifted by at least 40 km (25 mi).

*Inyo Mountains*

# Owens Peak Wilderness

The highest point in the southern Sierra Nevada is Owens Peak at 2,574 m (8,445 ft), which gives its name to the 300-sq-km (115-sq-mi) wilderness occupying the broken eastern face of the mountains beneath this saw-tooth landmark. The steep terrain has an assortment of canyons, many of them expansive, some containing springs surrounded by lush growth. This Californian wilderness is located where three ecosystems meet – those of the Mojave Desert, Great Basin and Sierra Nevada – resulting in an interesting assortment of vegetation that ranges from creosote bush scrub, cacti, classic yuccas, low-level oak and cottonwood trees to juniper-pinyon woods with pine and sagebrush at higher elevations.

Some hardened backpackers will just be passing through – the Pacific Crest Trail crosses the wilderness – but this is a great place for a day hike, although camping is permitted for those who like to explore more thoroughly. Other recreational activities include horse riding, mountain-biking, scenic viewing from the network of dirt roads and climbing. Some of the most challenging climbs in the southern Sierras are to be found here, with names like Lamoont Spires, Sawtooth Peak and Spanish Needles telling the tale. Those willing and able to reach the higher elevations are rewarded with sensational mountain vistas, notably from anywhere along the 35-km (22-mi) stretch of Pacific Crest Trail. But be warned that it gets very hot in summer and there's no guarantee that water will be found, especially higher up.

A 4x4 vehicle is desirable and in most cases essential – many approaches and wilderness dirt roads are impassable to anything with low ground clearance. Although no vehicles are allowed in the wilderness itself, parking is permitted beside established roads for those tempted to get out and stretch their legs. Unfortunately, despite the rule, this wilderness attracts drivers who attempt extreme off-road feats.

# Yosemite National Park

Central California's Yosemite National Park attracts three-and-a-half million visitors each year to the western slopes of the Sierra Nevada range, but it's still a wild place. The park covers 3,100 sq km (1,200 sq mi) and the vast majority of those eager tourists are interested only in Yosemite Valley, a tiny 18-sq-km (7-sq-mi) fraction of the whole. This is the main entry point to the park and contains a concentration of visitor facilities – but also natural wonders that make this a scenic sensation to savour. It contains the Merced River, fed and carried down the valley by a succession of eye-catching waterfalls, while high granite walls rise to stunning rock features that

include the El Capitan monolith, Cathedral Rocks, Cathedral Spires, Sentinel Rock and the Three Brothers.

Appreciating the enormity of these famous sights is mandatory, but for those who seek wide-open empty spaces there's plenty more to enjoy. Beyond the valley lies the 95 per cent of the park's area that has been designated as wilderness. This craggy landscape contains two major rivers, numerous streams and thousands of lakes and ponds. There are mountains, glaciers, meadows and forests within a vast expanse of unspoiled alpine scenery. The total area forms one of the largest undisturbed habitat blocks in the Sierra Nevada mountains, supporting a diversity of plants and animals within five distinct vegetation zones ranging from chaparral/oak woodland at lower levels up to alpine higher as the park's elevation rises from 600 m (1,970 ft) to 4,000 m (13,123 ft).

The park has 560 km (350 mi) of roads and an impressive 1,300-km (800-mi) network of hiking trails and provides limitless opportunities to strike out into the wilderness to find places where it seems no human foot can ever have fallen before.

*Yosemite Valley*

**DON'T MISS:**
The most famous landmark in the entire Sierra Nevada, Half Dome, is situated where the Yosemite Valley forks. This extraordinary granite pile seems from the valley floor to be just a neatly domed mountain from which one half has mysteriously gone missing – but in fact this is an illusion, as the formation is entirely natural. Note that a permit is required to ascend the Half Dome on certain days (mostly weekends and holidays) using the cable walkway.

**YOU SHOULD KNOW:**
There's no guarantee that the awesome Yosemite Falls will actually be falling – the waterfall is fed mainly by snowmelt and often runs dry in August, remaining so until the winter snowfalls arrive.

# Yellowstone National Park

America's first national park – established in 1872 – is still one of the most impressive. Yellowstone National Park is mainly in Wyoming, with small sections extending into Idaho and Montana. The park covers around 9,000 sq km (3,475 sq mi) and this huge landscape encompasses mountain ranges, canyons, lakes, waterfalls and rivers.

At its heart is the high-altitude Yellowstone Lake, situated over the caldera of America's largest active supervolcano. This is responsible for the lava flows and rocks scattered by ancient eruption that can be seen all over the park, including one of the world's largest petrified forests. Volcanic activity is also responsible for the huge number of geothermal features (half the recorded number in the world) found in Yellowstone. The world-famous Old Faithful geyser is but the highlight of the park's 10,000 dramatic hot springs, geysers and boiling-mud spectacles, many of which can be reached by the paved roads that give access to many of Yellowstone's key sights.

There are eight visitor centres within the park, some of which close in winter, each featuring a selection of interesting ecological and cultural subjects – Yellowstone is rich in flora and fauna and has a large number of archaeological sites. Among other services, they offer advice on where to observe animals such as grizzly bears, wolves, free-ranging bison and elk. A number of official suppliers offer visitor-support activities including transportation, boating, fishing, guided hiking and wildlife viewing, while a wide variety of ranger-guided activities can be booked. But for many the park's the star, and the opportunity to simply drive around, see some of the amazing hydrothermal features, spot wildlife and soak up the stunning scenery is all the stimulus needed to enjoy this extraordinary place, preserved for posterity in the 19th century by forward-thinking conservationists.

**HOW TO GET THERE:**
Fly into a local field like Cody, Jackson, Bozeman, Billings, Idaho Falls or West Yellowstone, many of which have linked bus services to the park. A network of roads surrounds the park (some roads traversing it) with good starting points being Butte (north or west entrance), Bozeman, Livingston and Billings (north entrance), Cody (east entrance), Jackson (south entrance) and Idaho Falls (south or west entrance).

**WHEN TO GO:**
Any time (but winter visits are best conducted as part of a guided tour using snow coaches or snowmobiles, as roads are only open to over-snow vehicles and most entrances are closed in November and March/April to prepare for and clear up after winter).

**DON'T MISS:**
The breathtaking Grand Canyon of the Yellowstone park, carved deep into the rock by the Yellowstone River, downstream of Yellowstone Falls.

**YOU SHOULD KNOW:**
An entrance fee is payable (valid for a week of unlimited re-entry), even by hikers on foot. It is not necessary to book Yellowstone in advance as there is no limit on visitor numbers.

*ABOVE: Colourful terraces atop Mammoth Hot Springs*

*RIGHT: An elk cow and calf standing beside the steaming geyser, Old Faithful*

# Bryce Canyon National Park

Compared to many a vast American national park, Bryce Canyon has modest vital statistics, measuring just 145 sq km (56 sq mi), and its remote location ensures that this dramatic landscape is never overburdened with visitors. Many of those who do venture into the wilds of Utah confine themselves to the scenic drive that offers glorious views over a canyon that isn't really a canyon, but a stunning series of natural amphitheatres populated with huge arches and the extraordinary rock spires known as hoodoos. Indeed, many summer visitors don't even drive themselves, but prefer to park up and take the Bryce Canyon shuttle that tours the most popular viewpoints, thus allowing for uninterrupted sightseeing with no distracting need to watch the road.

Massed ranks of slender hoodoos that can rise to a height of 60 m (200 ft) create a spectacular multi-coloured jumble of red, orange and white rock seen from the canyon rim, which fluctuates between an elevation of 2,400 m (7,875 ft) and 2,700 m (8,860 ft). The 29-km (18-mi) scenic drive ends at the park's high spot, Rainbow Point, but those who prefer to get up close and personal with this unique place have other options.

There are eight waymarked walking trails that can be completed in less than a day, each taking from one to six hours for a round trip from trailheads. Two overnight trails (backcountry permits required) extend the total length of the park's various hiking routes to 80 km (50 mi). Anyone who prefers to let a horse do the hard work can book riding trips between April and October. There are two official campgrounds within the park for those who wish to explore at leisure or indulge in one of the park's most popular activities, landscape photography. Awesome sunrises and sunsets are favourite subjects.

**HOW TO GET THERE:**
The best access route is from US Route 89, then on to Bryce Canyon via Utah Routes 12 and 63.
**WHEN TO GO:**
Any time (many trails are passable on snowshoes in winter, when the park also has a number of marked cross-country ski routes).
**DON'T MISS:**
Seeing stars. Bryce Canyon is one of the darkest sports in the continental USA, offering stargazers the opportunity to see a blazing night sky filled with over 7,500 celestial bodies. There is an astronomy festival in the park every summer.
**YOU SHOULD KNOW:**
The reason so many of the USA's wilderness areas remain empty and unspoilt is that early pioneers found these barren places were incapable of sustaining them without a massive and ultimately unproductive effort. This is illustrated by the determined Mormon settler after whom the canyon is named – the Scot, Ebenezer Bryce – who made a log-cabin home for his family hereabouts during the 1870s but lasted for less than a decade before moving on to Arizona.

*Navajo Loop Trail*

# Zion National Park

Attracting over three million visitors annually, Utah's most popular national park is renowned for breathtaking canyons. People are drawn to this 600-sq-km (230-sq-mi) park near Springfield by extraordinary features such as the enormous Kolob Arch, typical of amazing rock formations that abound. Zion Canyon itself is 24 km (15 mi) long and up to 800 m (2,625 ft) deep, winding between precipitous walls as the north fork of the Virgin River rushes along the canyon floor.

Zion National Park (so named when the original name of Mukuntuweap failed to roll off anyone's tongue) offers incredible views to those who prefer to remain firmly perched on top of four wheels and let the engine do the walking, but this is really a place to hike, climb, camp, bike or explore on horseback. It isn't a vast empty wilderness where no fellow-travellers will seen from one day to the next, but the nature of the landscape is such that there's plenty of opportunity to get away from the crowd and find deserted side canyons or rock scrambles to explore.

There are numerous trails within canyons and along the rims,

rated from easy through moderate to strenuous and technical, so there's something for everyone. But the ultimate Zion experience is the Narrows hike, which follows the Virgin River and involves lots of time in the water – sometimes waist-deep pools. The hike is 26 km (16 mi) long and may be done from top to bottom, with or without camping overnight that allows time to check out tempting features like Kolob Creek and Orderville Gulch. It's possible to tackle the Narrows bottom-up, although only as far as Big Springs. A permit is needed for all but casual hikers at the lower end, to ensure that this wonderful experience is not devalued by processional use.

*Zion National Park*

# Black Canyon

This precipitous gorge at the western edge of the Rocky Mountains is no place for those seeking the solitude of empty wilderness, although that is indeed the status of land surrounding Colorado's Black Canyon. Most people are drawn by one of the most awesome – and unsettling – natural wonders in the USA, and simply seeing it is satisfaction enough. The Black Canyon of the Gunnison National Park may be a bit of a mouthful – and the country's third-smallest national park – but few other experiences match the scary-yet-breathtaking opportunity to perch on the edge and peer down at the jagged rockscape far below.

*The Painted Wall, Black Canyon*

Carved deep into hard rock by the Gunnison River on its way to meet the Colorado River at Grand Junction, this spectacular canyon earned its name because it is so narrow – a mere 460 m (1,500 ft) across in places – and deep – over 610 m (2,000 ft) – that it remains in almost permanent gloom. The sun illuminates the canyon but briefly, and even then falls upon dark walls of volcanic schist. The main focus of visitor interest and most of the park's facilities are to be found on the Black Canyon's South Rim. The main entrance road is 13 km (8 mi) long, and passes the main viewpoints. There are 12 named overlooks, some requiring a short walk from the vehicle, plus opportunities for independent exploration.

The North Rim, accessed by a gravel road, is a better option for those who prefer relative solitude. It has overlooks that equal the spectacle to be seen from the South Rim, a primitive campground and three demanding trails down to the canyon floor – just the job for those who prefer 'I've been there and done it' to a rather less impressive 'I've seen it'.

**HOW TO GET THERE:**
Drive from Montrose, Delta or Gunnison, the nearest towns offering accommodation. There is a campground within the park. Access to the popular South Rim is from County Road 347, a short spur off US Route 50 – a main crossing of the Rockies. Find the North Rim road 18 km (11 mi) south of Crawford.

**WHEN TO GO:**
Any time (but the North Rim road is closed by snow in winter).

**DON'T MISS:**
Colorado's highest sheer cliff, seen from the South Rim. The Painted Wall is 685 m (2,250 ft) tall and shot through with light-coloured granite veins.

**YOU SHOULD KNOW:**
The 80-km (50-mi) Black Canyon has not remained untouched by the hand of man – two thirds of the upstream (eastern) section of the gorge have been flooded as part of a hydro-electric scheme and has become the Curecanti National Recreational Area, offering the usual outdoor activities associated with large artificial lakes.

# Monument Valley

**HOW TO GET THERE:**
Access is from US Route 63, part of
the Trail of the Ancients National
Scenic Byway.
**WHEN TO GO:**
Any time (be aware that the valley
is full of visitors in the summer
vacation period).
**DON'T MISS:**
A thunderstorm rolling across the valley
– a truly awesome sight that explains
why the Navajo place this natural
phenomenon right at the top of their
respect list. As these are rare, an
excellent second prize is seeing the
buttes by night, clearly silhouetted by
the moon's harsh glow and burning
starlight.
**YOU SHOULD KNOW:**
It's best not to plan a visit beginning
or ending with an overnight stay in
any sort of close proximity to
Monument Valley – even the cheapest
of motels (quality and moneywise)
within an easily accessible radius are
ruinously expensive.

'Roll cameras, cue Indians' must have been words frequently uttered in Monument Valley by the great film director John Ford, who shot his first western in this iconic wilderness on the Utah-Arizona border. The movie saw the breakthrough of all-American tough-guy star John Wayne and *Stagecoach* became a classic. Ford returned to use the valley as a location time after time – there could scarcely be a more dramatic backdrop – and many more Hollywood film crews have followed him.

The Colorado Plateau has the greatest concentration of national parks and monuments in the USA, including the Grand Canyon, Canyonlands and the Petrified Forest. Monument Valley isn't among them – it lies within the Navajo Nation Reservation – but has unique scenic qualities that make this atmospheric place as special in its own way as any one of them. The arid floor consists of reddish siltstone and sand deposited by the ancient rivers that eroded the valley, dotted in places with low scrub vegetation. But the main attraction is the magnificent array of red sandstone spires and buttes, sculpted by wind and water over countless millennia into striking masterpieces that rise from the flatlands.

There's a fee for driving through the park on the 27-km (17-mi) dirt road (passenger-car friendly), open roughly from dawn to dusk and starting at the modest visitor centre and shop at Lookout Point, with its great valley views. Guided tours on wheels or foot are available on a choice of routes, including destinations such as Hunts Mesa or Mystery Valley not open to visitors without a Navajo guide. Excursions on horseback are offered at various locations around the park, ranging from an hour or two to a day and more in duration. Camping is available and – for the exotically minded – hot-air balloon rides.

*A Navajo girl poses
for the camera.*

# Chiricahua National Monument

It's billed as 'A Wonderland of Rocks' and the description is more than justified. This may not be America's largest untamed landscape – checking in at just 48 sq km (19 sq mi) – but there's still more than enough rugged terrain to allow an all-day vanishing act by those of solitary bent. Chiricahua National Monument in southern Arizona, some 190 km (120 mi) from Tucson, occupies a remote location. The Chiricahua Mountains are so-called 'sky islands', rising imperiously from a sea of surrounding grassland. The extraordinary rock formations are the main attraction, and these were grotesquely carved by water and ice over millions of years from rhyolite originally formed after the Turkey Creek Volcano erupted, a mere 27 million years ago – a sobering reminder of the human race's fleeting presence in a natural world of infinite age. This thought perhaps explains the awe experienced by those who see this enduring rockscape.

Exploring this special place may be done from the 13-km (8-mi) scenic drive on a paved road, or by using 27 km (17 mi) of hiking trails suitable for anything from short walks to day-long expeditions. There is a comprehensive trail guide available at the visitor centre. One day is the least amount of time anyone should want to spend at Chiricahua, and a select few use the 25-pitch campground to extend their stay (no pre-booking). Quite apart from stunning scenery, there's a fascinating opportunity to visit the Faraway Ranch Historic District, home of the Erickson family of Swedish immigrants who arrived in the late 1880s and subsequently developed a thriving homestead and guest ranch. The grounds may be explored and regular house tours take place. In the wild it's possible to spot black bear, mountain lion, white-tailed deer and assorted smaller creatures, plus a variety of bird life.

**HOW TO GET THERE:**
By car only. From Willcox (close to US Interstate 10) take Arizona State Highway 186 until reaching Arizona State Highway 181, turn left and find the national monument's entrance station. It's a 58-km (36-mi) journey.

**WHEN TO GO:**
Open all year (including visitor centre) although the scenic drive can be closed by adverse weather conditions in winter

**DON'T MISS:**
The one-room log cabin built by the first European settlers, Ja Hu Stafford and his wife Pauline, after they arrived here in 1880.

**YOU SHOULD KNOW:**
Fill the car's tank in Willcox – there are no gas stations on the lonely road between the town and Chiricahua National Monument.

*Hikers on Echo Canyon Trail*

# Grand Canyon

**HOW TO GET THERE:**
The North Rim is served by Arizona State Route 67. State Route 64 runs along the South Rim to Grand Canyon Village.

**WHEN TO GO:**
Not winter, when the canyon may see heavy snowfalls that can prevent access to either rim. The North Rim sees greater precipitation and the single access road can be closed for months. Its facilities are closed from mid October until mid May.

**DON'T MISS:**
The amazing U-shaped Skywalk on Hualapai Indian lands at Grand Canyon West, jutting out above a vertical drop of 240 m (790 ft). This glass-floored engineering wonder has become a huge tourist attraction and is positioned over a side canyon, although it offers stunning views to the main canyon and Colorado River.

**YOU SHOULD KNOW:**
The first Europeans to see the Grand Canyon were a party of Spanish conquistadors in 1540, travelling up from the south under the leadership of Francisco de Coronado. After repeated unsuccessful attempts to descend to the river, they returned from whence they came and no awed European eyes fell on the canyon for another two centuries. The first non-native people – probably the first ever – to run the Colorado River through the entire length of the canyon were members of the waterborne expedition led by John Wesley Powell in 1869. With that track record he went on to head the US Geological Survey from 1881 to 1894.

Thanks to 17 million years of relentless effort by the Colorado River, Arizona has one of the world's great natural wonders. The Grand Canyon lives up to its billing at around 440 km (275 mi) long, ranging between 29 km (18 mi) and 6.5 km (4 mi) wide while plunging to a depth of up to over 1,800 m (5,900 ft). The canyon is a massive rift in the Colorado Plateau, creating a powerful rocky spectacle that may be viewed from either rim.

Most of this awesome gorge lies within Grand Canyon National Park, with headquarters in Grand Canyon Village on the South Rim. This historic settlement dates from the arrival of the Santa Fe railway in 1901 and has many building dating from that era. It is dedicated to servicing the needs of tourists and has numerous museums and information centres that add a dimension to the Grand Canyon experience.

For most, simply seeing this vertiginous canyon is enough, although it's worth noting that Desert View Watchtower at the eastern end of the South Rim, built on a promontory in 1932, is one of the few places from where the canyon floor and Colorado River can actually be observed. Most of the stunning views are of the opposite rim. The less-popular North Rim is considered to have the finest outlooks, yet ironically most visitors stick to the South Rim in order to enjoy the facilities at Grand Canyon Village. It's necessary to make the choice – the drive from one rim to the other is 345 km (215 mi) and takes five hours. For those who want more than scenery, the canyon offers unique hiking opportunities, but only for those prepared to hang tough and carry a lot of water in their backpacks.

*Big sky above the canyons, buttes and plateaux of Grand Canyon National Park*

# Sonoran Desert

North America's largest and hottest place, covering 310,000 sq km (120,000 sq mi), is the Sonoran Desert. It extends all the way from California into Mexico, via Arizona – the latter's name confirming that arid desert terrain covers much of the state. For an apparently unforgiving wilderness, the desert contains a remarkable variety of flora and fauna. Over 2,000 plant types live and thrive in the harsh conditions, while the desert supports over 500 species of animals, birds and reptiles, plus countless insects.

The fact that such vast emptiness exists within the world's most advanced nation is surprising, and provides endless opportunities for those who love to escape from civilization and return to the wild for a few hours or days. Even so, this is America, so the desert must try to pay its way. It is exploited by – among others – animal grazers, so the Sonoran Desert National Monument has been established in Arizona to preserve an unspoilt tract. Find it to the south of Buckeye and Goodyear, east of Gila Bend. It's tiny in the context of the whole desert, but big in itself at 2,000 sq km (770 sq mi).

Perhaps the attraction of a journey of discovery through this extraordinary wilderness is best understood by quoting President Bill Clinton, after the national monument was established: 'The Sonoran Desert National Monument is a magnificent example of untrammelled Sonoran desert landscape. The area encompasses a functioning desert ecosystem with an extraordinary array of biological, scientific, and historic resources. The monument's biological resources include a spectacular diversity of plant and animal species. The monument also contains many significant archaeological and historic sites, including rock-art sites, lithic quarries, and scattered artefacts.' The same things can still be found in much of the Sonoran Desert by those prepared to look.

*Springtime in the Sonoran Desert reveals saguaros, teddy bear cholla, and blooming yellow brittlebushes.*

**HOW TO GET THERE:**
Access is a matter of choice. The two principal cities within the desert area are Phoenix and Tucson, which make good bases for exploration of a vast desert road network.

**WHEN TO GO:**
Any time – although it can be very hot in July and August.

**DON'T MISS:**
The tree-sized saguaro cactus with its distinctive upstretched arms. These grow nowhere else and have served as unpaid extras in countless Westerns.

**YOU SHOULD KNOW:**
California's Colorado Desert is part of the wider Sonoran Desert and home to the Anza-Borrego Desert State Park, which has 12 wilderness areas, numerous dirt roads and an extensive network of hiking trails.

# Bisti Badlands

It's an evocative description, redolent of Wild West bandits and lawlessness, but actually the USA's badlands are just what the name suggests, consisting of arid ground – often with canyons, gullies and tortured rock formations – that early pioneers dismissed as 'bad lands' to settle on or travel through *en route* to more promising territory. The Bisti Badlands in the remote northwestern corner of New Mexico is just such a place – a scenic expanse of weirdly eroded rocks and colourful mounds to delight the modern backcountry explorer, which must have seemed a nightmare place to early 19th-century travellers as it interrupted steady progress across the prairie.

This little-visited 16-sq-km (6-sq-mi) patch of high desert is designated as the Bisti Wilderness Area, but the badlands actually extend much further than official boundaries. In truth, the latter are not much evident on the ground, although occasional fencing and barriers closing off dangerous washes may be seen, but beyond that there is little evidence of human interference – the Bisti Badlands remains an isolated

*Tortured rock formations in Bisti Badlands*

wild place rich in natural drama, much as Nature intended.

To make the most of this unique place a 4x4 vehicle is desirable. Assorted tracks criss-cross sandy hills at the southern boundary of the rocky areas, which are risky options for low-slung cars. The wilderness itself offers a vivid mix of colours – red, orange, brown and grey – and mostly consists of small hills, shallow ravines, dry washes and unusual rock formations, some of which look more like accomplished sculptures than natural artworks. Once away from the approach road, a surreal landscape envelops the bold interloper, going where there are no formal hiking trails and progress is generally made by following ravines with care – the terrain is often unstable and loose petrified wood litters the surface, often mixed with fossils.

**DON'T MISS:**
The Bisti Trading Post – a cluster of abandoned and decaying buildings, including an overgrown children's playground and simple church that is open to visitors. This windswept place is an evocative reminder of the enduring hostility of the adjacent badlands to human endeavour.

**YOU SHOULD KNOW:**
Those with the yen for total isolation should find the 16-km (10-mi) track that leads to the extensive De-na-zin Wilderness. It matches Bisti for colourful rock formations, but some are cloaked with scrub vegetation.

# Sierra Blanca Wilderness

The Lincoln National Forest in New Mexico was established in 1902 and extends to an impressive 4,500 sq km (1,735 sq mi). The high-elevation forest is made up of major portions of four mountain ranges – The Capitans, Guadalupes, Sacramentos and its Sierra Blanca sub range. The latter is named for the extended blanket of snow up to 2 m (6.5 ft) deep that can cover the summits from November until as late as June. It is here that the White Mountain Wilderness Area may be found.

The wilderness soars to a breathtaking (literally) height of around 3,500 m (11,500 ft) and the mountains run in a north-south direction, bordering the Mescalero Apache Reservation at the southern end. The wilderness is about 20 km (12 mi) long and up to the same distance wide, straddling the crest and containing many ridges that branch off. The west side is steep and rugged with numerous rocky outcrops, while the east side is gentler with broad, forested canyons sometimes carrying small streams. The area is heavily wooded, but grassy oak savannahs and meadows are to be found, particularly towards the crest. This is a dramatic landscape of abrupt height changes, varied vegetation, rock promontories, bold escarpments and old avalanche slides.

Any backcountry explorer is sure to spot numerous representatives of the abundant wildlife with (among others) black bears, elk, mule deer, bobcats, coyotes, badgers, foxes, porcupines, skunks and squirrels in residence, along with a thriving bird population headed by wild turkeys. The chance to get among these creatures comes courtesy of a network of lonely wilderness trails, mostly following canyon bottoms and ridges. They range in difficulty from easy to strenuous and the ultimate challenge is the 32-km (20-mi) Crest Trail, offering views to die for in return for the effort required.

**HOW TO GET THERE:**
From the mountain resort town of Ruidoso, New Mexico, reached from US Route 70

**WHEN TO GO:**
Take your pick along with your pack – spring is windy, summer is hot, autumn is wet and winter sees prolonged snow.

**DON'T MISS:**
A visit to the Mescalero Apache's Cultural Museum on Route 70 south of Ruidoso, for fascinating insight into the history and culture of this ancient race.

**YOU SHOULD KNOW:**
Birders will be richly rewarded by a hike in the wilderness, and among many others will hope to spot one or more of the five species for which these mountains provide critical habitat – golden-crowned kinglets, Clarke's nutcrackers, red-breasted nuthatches, northern three-toed woodpeckers and Townsend's solitaires.

# Lostwood National Wildlife Refuge

**HOW TO GET THERE:**
Access to Lostwood is from Highway 8 around 30 km (19 mi) north of Stanley, North Dakota.

**WHEN TO GO:**
Any time, although summer sees the maximum population of breeding birds. Winter weather can be harsh, but cross-country skiing, snowshoeing and hiking take place despite the fact that strong winds can add to the fearsome wind-chill factor.

**DON'T MISS:**
Driving the official auto tour route from Refuge HQ at Thompson Lake, down beside a chain of wetlands and lakes to Upper Lostwood Lake and back, with a dozen key viewing points and overlooks to enjoy during the 22-km (14-mi) return trip, along with any *ad hoc* stops to stretch legs and explore.

**YOU SHOULD KNOW:**
The refuge contains one of the USA's largest populations of sharp-tailed grouse and the males may be seen indulging in their extraordinary mating dance in late April and early May. These prolonged performances take place at established sites known as leks, and carefully sited blinds allow visitors to view the action without disturbing it.

North Dakota contains one of the most important wildfowl breeding sites in the USA, and this area bordering both Montana and Canada is protected by the Lostwood National Wildlife Refuge. It lies in the so-called prairie pothole region – meaning it has a large number of lakes, ponds and boggy patches that provide a perfect habitat for geese, ducks and other aquatic birds. This has earned a designation as a Globally Important Bird Area, and the annual Burke County Birding Festival is held every June.

The 110-sq-km (42-sq-mi) block of old prairie was first settled in the early 1900s, but proved inhospitable to incoming farmers and has been reclaimed and restored since the mid 1930s with wildlife conservation a priority. In 1975, the Lostwood Wilderness Area was established within the refuge. This 23-sq-km (9-sq-mi) enclave provides further protection to the bird life, encompassing vital breeding sites and preventing disruptive activity. However, hiking and photography – plus cross-country trekking on skis or snowshoes in winter – are permitted. In the wider refuge, there are numerous trails providing the opportunity to explore.

Although the principal importance of the refuge lies in its 4,000 wetlands, Lostwood is within the Missouri Coteau region, which consists of prairie and hills. Nearly three quarters of the refuge is virgin prairie, making for a varied habitat that supports all sorts of creatures in addition to the large seasonal and resident bird population. There are around 250 bird species in the refuge, while animals to look out for include white-tailed deer, badger, coyote, fox, rabbit and weasel.

# Badlands

South Dakota's Badlands National Park is the USA's largest mixed-grass prairie, preserved more or less in its original state. It serves as a poignant reminder of vast tracts of similar grassland – where buffalo roamed – that once covered much of America's Middle West, stretching from Saskatchewan down to Texas. The national park covers 990 sq km (380 sq mi), within which 260 sq km (100 sq mi) has been designated as the Badlands Wilderness. The rolling prairie shares this vast wild place with dramatic expanses of rock, eroded into fantastic shapes and patterns.

For centuries these badlands were the hunting ground of the Lakota Sioux tribe, and the last armed clashes between these proud indigenous people and the US Army took place hereabouts at the end of the 19th century. This story – plus a fascinating review of the park's long history from prehistoric times, as evidenced by the wealth of fossils to be found here – is brought to life at the Ben Reifel Visitor Centre, named after the Sioux Nation's first congressman, which has numerous interesting exhibits, some interactive, and a theatre showing the fascinating park movie.

A typical half-day tour consists of a session at the visitor centre during a run around the paved Badlands Loop Road, perhaps with a side trip along the gravelled Sage Creek Road, and pauses at four scenic overlooks. It's easily extended to a full day by using one of five waymarked hiking routes that require from half an hour to three hours for a round trip. There are ranger-guided activity programmes in summer, but those who prefer to stay away from the tourist trail can obtain a topographical map and break out the compass and backpack before heading into the wilderness to do their own thing.

**HOW TO GET THERE:**
The national park is best approached from Interstate 90 – exit 131 at Interior for the Northeast Entrance, exit 110 at Wall for the Pinnacle Entrance. Car rental available at Rapid City Regional Airport for those who fly in.

**WHEN TO GO:**
Spring to autumn is best (winters can be harsh), although the park is open all year.

**DON'T MISS:**
The nearby Minuteman Missile National Historic Site, just off Interstate 90 at exit 131. A reminder of the Cold War, this site preserves a Minuteman II ballistic missile system consisting of a launch control centre and missile-launch silo. Guided tours can be booked at the National Park Service office.

**YOU SHOULD KNOW:**
North America's most endangered land mammal – the black-footed ferret – has been successfully reintroduced to the Badlands Wilderness.

*A fiery sunrise lights up the sky above countless peaks that make up the Badlands.*

# Big Bend National Park

**HOW TO GET THERE:**
Drive to the park from Marathon (to the north, use US Route 385), Alpine (northwest, use Texas Highway 118) or Presidio (west, on super-scenic FM-170, the Texas River Road – if anyone's wondering 'FM' stands for 'Farm to Market').

**WHEN TO GO:**
Any time, although the temperature soars uncomfortably in late spring and early summer and the park is subject to extremes of climate depending on elevation. Peak visitor months are March and April but the park never becomes crowded.

**DON'T MISS:**
Dropping by at least one of the five visitor centres. Three are open year-round – Panther Junction at park headquarters, Chisos Basin and Persimmon Gap. Castolon and Rio Grande Village are seasonal (open November to April). In addition to issuing permits for backcountry camping and river use, these all have informative exhibits illuminating the fascinating geology, natural and cultural histories of the park.

**YOU SHOULD KNOW:**
Plan carefully and go prepared – Big Bend really is remote and it's wise to stock up with gas, water and provisions before driving in. There are four stores serving campers within the park, with basic stock, but the last significant shopping opportunities are in Alpine, Del Rio and Fort Stockton.

This is a truly untouched wild place, much of it appearing today just as it did to the first European pioneers centuries ago. Big Bend National Park in West Texas is three parks in one – big river, desert and mountains. It lies in Brewster County, one of the USA's least-populated areas, and this fabulous park covers 3,250 sq km (1,255 sq mi), protecting much of the Chihuahuan Desert's unique ecology and topography. It also includes nearly 190 km (120 mi) of twisting Rio Grande, the border with Mexico, including a huge V-shaped sweep of river that gives the park its name. And the Chisos Mountains are here, the only range in the USA to be entirely contained within a single national park.

To be appreciated, even for a brief period that barely scratches the surface, this huge wilderness calls for a serious expedition rather than a simple visit. Once there, it is possible to enjoy a wide variety of activities. Simplest of all (and least strenuous) is viewing awesome desert landscape from one of many scenic drives on paved roads. For more adventurous types, the park has numerous unimproved dirt roads suitable only for reliable four-wheel-drive transport, allowing exploration of the remotest places, perhaps combined with backcountry camping (permit required). In either case, it's essential to leave the vehicle from time to time to merge with the landscape. Even from paved roads a few steps lead to timeless desert solitude, while those who want prolonged exposure can use the network of hiking trails.

Beyond that, rafting or kayaking the Rio Grande offers a hugely rewarding experience, through spectacular canyons with near-vertical walls like Santa Elena, Mariscal and Boquillas. It's possible to go solo (permit required) or with the help of many professional guides who organize trips.

*Sunset on the Chisos Mountains*
*in Big Bend National Park*

# Boundary Waters Canoe Area

The Superior National Forest in Minnesota's Arrowhead Region lies between the US-Canadian border and the North Shore of Lake Superior. In this 16,000-sq-km (6,180-sq-mi) tract of woods and water commercial activities like logging take place alongside the type of recreational activities offered by sparsely populated wild places. These include (in season where appropriate) berry picking, mountain-biking, camping, going afloat, hiking, fishing, hunting, cross-country skiing, snowshoeing, snowmobiling, driving scenic byways, off-roading, wildlife viewing and birding.

One of the most interesting and exciting possibilities is exploration within the Boundary Waters Canoe Area Wilderness (BWCAW), which extends along the national forest's northern limit. Renowned for pristine lakes – and the sporting fish that thrive therein – this is the USA's most-visited wilderness. But at 4,400 sq km (1,700 sq mi) there's little chance of this magical place to the east of Lake Superior becoming overcrowded. Actually, much of the BWCAW isn't the least bit canoe-friendly (although going afloat is a great way to explore), because it consists of both boreal forest and deciduous forest, including large tracts of old-growth timber that has never been logged.

For all that, the wilderness contains over 1,000 lakes and motorboats are prohibited on three quarters of them. Plenty of campgrounds that can be reached by vehicle surround the wilderness but, inside, 2,000 backcountry sites can only be reached by boat. With 1,600 km (1,000 mi) of established canoe routes, paddlers are spoiled for choice – although most require frequent portage between lakes. Popular entry points include Trout, Moose, Seagull and Sawbill Lakes, hinting at the abundant fish, animal and bird life to be seen in BWCAW. For those who get seasick on a boating pond, the wilderness has short hiking routes such as Eagle Mountain and Magnetic Rock, plus long-distance trails including the Kekekabic and Border Route trails.

*Canoeing on Crooked Lake*

**HOW TO GET THERE:**
There are many entry points to the wilderness for motorboats, paddlers and hikers – some for day use only, others for overnight trips. The nearest towns are Aurora, Ely, Isabella, Tofte and Grand Marais.

**WHEN TO GO:**
Any time, although winter is not the season to go afloat.

**DON'T MISS:**
Finding incised petroglyphs and painted pictographs on rocky ledges and cliff faces. There are hundreds within BWCAW, created by the Ojibwe people who once travelled these waters using birch-bark canoes and still live locally.

**YOU SHOULD KNOW:**
Overnight camping permits are required for all backcountry expeditions within BWCAW. In addition, advance-reservation permits are required for groups making motorized day or overnight journeys – plus overnight paddle-powered or hiking trips. These are on quota to ensure there's no overcrowding (issued on a first come, first served basis from May to September). At other times no reservation is required, but permits must still be filled out at entry points. The National Forest Service issues a comprehensive trip-planning guide (available online).

# Indiana Dunes National Lakeshore

This protected area on the southern shore of Lake Michigan is long
and narrow –almost 40 km (25 mi) long, with a total area of just
61 sq km (24 sq mi). Gary is at the western end of Indiana Dunes
National Lakeshore with Michigan City to the east. It is not
contiguous, having two roughly equal sections and some privately
owned property within the boundaries. However, it is a magnificent
stretch of impressive lakeside landscape, dominated by sand dunes
that can reach 60 m (200 ft) in height. But dunes, beaches and
crashing waves are not the full story.

Although the long run of beaches along the lake is the principal
recreational resource, the national lakeshore has much more than
that to offer. It is a treasure house of natural delights, including
areas of swamp, bog, marsh, prairie, riverbank, forest and oak
savannah. The biological diversity is staggering, with around 1,100
ferns and flowering plant species to be found. The bird life is
vibrant, with over 350 species recorded, including many migrants
that rest before moving on. Birdwatching is therefore a popular

activity, as is hiking along diverse trails that provide anything from a leisurely stroll to a day-long expedition.

This wonderful expanse of sculpted soft sand may be close to civilization and well used for recreational purposes, but it's still easy to get away from it all. The dunes are extensive, offering every opportunity to find a quiet spot. And by choosing one of the less-popular locations and going during the week it is perfectly possible to imagine that this magnificent lakeshore is the wildest of places scarcely touched by human hand. That's true in summer, so following an inland or dunes trail in the off-season (on skis or snowshoes if necessary!) virtually guarantees solitude.

**YOU SHOULD KNOW:**
Swimming in Lake Michigan is tempting, but there are only a few lifeguards on the most popular beaches (in season) and the lake is notorious for sudden rip currents. If caught, swimmers are advised not to fight the current – which will be too powerful for even strong swimmers – but to go with the flow until able to edge sideways out of the rip.

# Lusk Creek Wilderness

Shawnee National Forest at the southern tip of Illinois is an oasis of natural wonders amid a (relative!) desert of intensively farmed land. Those seeking backcountry experiences are well served, and can concentrate on the wilderness areas within the national forest – Bald Knob, Bay Creek, Burden Falls, Clear Springs, Garden of the Gods, Panther Den and Lusk Creek. All seven are impressive wild places, but if one has to be singled out it is the Lusk Creek Wilderness – if only for the magnificent view that rejoices in the somewhat incongruous name of 'Indian Kitchen'.

This wilderness extends to a mere 28 sq km (11 sq mi), but for once that old saying doesn't stack up – size definitely *isn't* everything, as Lusk Creek is both the second-largest wilderness in the state and a miniature masterpiece to be savoured by lovers of unspoilt wild places. This perfectly formed mini-wilderness consists of rugged terrain and winding canyons – a type of landscape not common in Illinois – where broad ridge tops overlook terraces, narrow ravines and sheer rock walls. Lusk Creek Wilderness is dotted with sinkholes and caves, there is some old-growth timber and wild flowers are abundant in spring.

The wilderness may be accessed from one of two trailheads, at New Liberty Church and Indian Kitchen, and encompasses Lusk Creek itself. This is one of the purest streams in Illinois, attracting fishermen, canoeists and those who simply want to stroll the banks. Horse riding, hiking and camping are other recreational activities that may be practised, but most casual visitors find that simply walking around in tranquil yet dramatic surroundings is satisfaction enough – especially when the highlight is being surprised and delighted by one of the most spectacular overlooks in the state at a precipitous hairpin turn in Lusk Creek Canyon.

**HOW TO GET THERE:**
Lusk Creek has two trailheads. For New Liberty Church Trailhead leave Illinois State Highway 145 on Forest Road 404 then go south on Forest Road 488. For Indian Kitchen Trailhead (and that view) leave State Highway 145 on the Eddyville-Golconda Blacktop and follow the signs. The nearest town is Eddyville.
**WHEN TO GO:**
Any time (May to September for the best weather)
**DON'T MISS:**
The evocative reminders of ultimately fruitless human endeavour in Lusk Creek Wilderness, such as old homesteads, fruit trees, overgrown cemeteries and abandoned dirt roads.
**YOU SHOULD KNOW:**
The 255-km (160-mi) River-to-River Trail passes through Lusk Creek Wilderness shortly after commencing at Battery Rock, overlooking the Ohio River, before continuing westwards to its final destination on the banks of the Mississippi River at Grand Tower, Illinois.

*Tupelo trees in the Cupola Pond Natural Area of Mark Twain National Forest*

**HOW TO GET THERE:**
Main roads through forest areas are Interstate 44 (east-west), US Route 63 (north-south) and US Route 60 (east-west).

**WHEN TO GO:**
Any time, but the show of brilliantly coloured turning Ozarks foliage from mid September into October is world-famous.

**DON'T MISS:**
Driving the 37-km (23-mi) Glade Top National Scenic Byway, a two-lane gravel road near Ava, Missouri, that winds through ridge tops above rolling countryside offering superb far-reaching views to the Springfield Plateau and Boston Mountains down in Arkansas.

**YOU SHOULD KNOW:**
Greer Spring in Oregon County, Missouri, is the largest spring on forest land in the USA. It discharges 840,360,000 l (185,000,000 gal) per day, which is 9,750 l (2,150 gal) per second. This dramatic scenic outflow can be reached and admired after a short hike from Missouri Highway 19.

# Mark Twain National Forest

Missouri native Mark Twain is commemorated by the national forest that bears his name, which consists of around a tenth of his home state's woodland. The Mark Twain National Forest (MTNF) covers some 6,100 sq km (2,350 sq mi) in south and central Missouri, spreading into 29 counties. The native timber had all been logged out when President Franklin D Roosevelt's Depression-era Civilian Conservation Corps – a New Deal work-creation programme – started replanting deforested areas and laid the foundations for what became MTNF, established in 1939 and mostly falling within the Ozark Highlands.

The forest is not in one block, but consists of nine separate tracts with six ranger districts and headquarters at Rolla, Missouri. It offers a variety of recreational opportunities for those who like to hunt, fish, hike, ride on horseback, camp or observe abundant wildlife, which includes over 300 species of birds, 75 types of mammal and 125 different amphibians or reptiles. Mountain-biking and driving are permitted on most forest roads, although not in wilderness areas, and there are also a number of roads where all-terrain vehicles may be used.

There are several prime locations for lovers of wild places. These include the rugged Bell Mountain Wilderness Area with

22 km (14 mi) of wilderness trails, and parts of the St Francois mountain section noted for streams, rivers, lakes, rocky bluffs, woodland trails and fine landscape views. The forest has recreation areas such as Sutton Bluff and Marble Creek with campgrounds and scenic trails. The latter is the trailhead for a section of the long-distance Ozark Trail that leads to Crane Lake. Other popular forest destinations are the Council Bluff Lake Recreation Area, surrounding the forest's largest stretch of open water, and the Silver Mines Recreation Area with its abandoned mine workings.

# Kisatchie Hills Wilderness

Within Louisiana's Kisatchie National Forest may be found 35 sq km (14 sq mi) of the steepest and most interesting terrain in a state not noted for rugged grandeur. Kisatchie is the only national forest in Louisiana. It is located in seven parishes – Vernon, Rapides, Grant, Natchitoches, Webster, Claiborne and Winn – in the northern and central part of the state. The forest protects a wonderful natural world of bayous beneath old-growth pine and bald cypress stands. This magical place may be explored from a comprehensive 4,800-km (3,000-mi) network of forest roads where vehicles (including all-terrain vehicles) are mostly permitted.

One of the no-go motorized zones is the aforementioned Kisatchie Hills Wilderness Area, known locally as 'The Little Grand Canyon'. Relatively small but perfectly unspoilt, the only way of seeing this wilderness is to travel on foot or horseback. There are three established trailheads that provide easy access, although it's possible to enter from any direction. This scenic area features sandstone bluffs and outcrops, flat-topped mesas and varied woodland. There is a designated trail system but no restriction stopping hardy hikers from stepping into the unknown, and camping is permitted.

The four intersecting wilderness trails are for true adventurers. The Backbone Trail speaks for itself, and passes through 11 km (7 mi) of demanding terrain. The others are shorter – High Ridge Trail at 2.5 km (1.5 mi) and the Turpentine Hill Trail, of similar length. The shorter Explorer Trail provides a wonderful taste of wilderness hiking for those unwilling or unable to tackle the more demanding trails, but even there the wilderness is no place for casual strollers. Those who want to spend time in the district will find nine campgrounds in the area, all primitive and some not designed for vehicle use.

**HOW TO GET THERE:**
The wilderness trailheads are on Forest Road 59, the Longleaf Scenic Byway, and Forest Road 339. These may be reached from Interstate 49 using exit 119 and driving for 8 km (5 mi) down Louisiana Highway 119 to find FR 59, where the wilderness is on the right. A right turn onto FR 339 also borders the wilderness back to the point where it meets the forest proper.
**WHEN TO GO:**
Summer (late May to September)
**DON'T MISS:**
The opportunity to drive the Longleaf Scenic Byway from end to end – it's a 27 km (17 mi) paved road connecting Louisiana Highways 119 (east end) and 117 (west end). Better still, find time to add a visit to the Longleaf Vista Day-Use Complex and tramp the interpretive trail – a short loop through the woods with informative signs describing native flora. There are great glimpses of the adjacent wilderness and short spur trails lead to a mesa offering panoramic all-round views over the forest.
**YOU SHOULD KNOW:**
The four wilderness trails are all primitive and very remote and – although it is not compulsory – it is recommended that hikers or horse riders should come prepared to take risks and also leave a check-in form at their chosen trail entrance to inform the Forest Service of their presence and intentions – just to be on the safe side.

# Black Creek Wilderness

**HOW TO GET THERE:**
The wilderness is located in Perry County east of Mississippi State Highway 29, north of Wiggins. The trailhead is at Big Creek Landing.
**WHEN TO GO:**
Any time (although high summer is seriously steamy and the insects can be voracious, so the other three seasons are generally favoured).
**DON'T MISS:**
De Soto National Forest's one other designated wilderness area, also of an aquatic nature – Leaf River Wilderness, between Benndale and McClain off State Highway 57. Although very similar to Black Creek, this is a smaller tract of flood plain, with rising ground at the western edge. It may be appreciated from the short Leaf Trail hiking route.
**YOU SHOULD KNOW:**
Firewood should never be taken into a forest area, even if campfires are permitted. This will help to prevent the spread of three alien wood-boring insects – emerald ash borer, Asian longhorned beetle and Sirex woodwasp – that can be brought in on firewood and, once established, will kill local trees.

On the Lower Coastal Plain of southern Mississippi, Black Creek is the state's largest wilderness at 20 sq km (8 sq mi). This peaceful enclave is located in the broad valley of Black Creek, a tributary of the Pascagoula River so named because the water is stained to a dark caramel colour by tannic acid from decaying vegetation. The creek is Mississippi's only designated Wild and Scenic River and bisects the wilderness. In truth, the emphasis should be on scenic rather than wild, for this is a gentle landscape of oxbow lakes and impressive clumps of old-growth timber that include bald cypress, loblolly pine, sweet gum, red maple, sweet bay and oak. This is not a place of rugged landscapes but rather low, rolling hills and unassuming ridges covered in the pinewoods of De Soto National Forest.

The Black Creek National Recreation Trail runs for 65 km (40 mi) along the Black Creek drainage. To be travelled only on foot, it passes through the length of the wilderness. Nothing motorized – a prohibition that includes bicycles – may enter the wilderness and horses are not permitted on the recreation trail. Hiking, camping, canoeing, kayaking and fishing (bass and panfish a speciality) are the principal activities on, in and around Black Creek. The river has plenty of wide sandbars ideal for pulling up a canoe, pitching camp or having a leisurely picnic in incomparable surroundings.

Black Creek cannot remotely be described as the USA's wildest wilderness, but it remains in pristine condition and on many days visitors will find it hard to believe that canoes have ever navigated the river or another human foot has fallen on this delightful flood plain. True solitude is a precious gift, and Black Creek can give generously.

# Green Mountain National Forest

**HOW TO GET THERE:**
The two blocks of national forest are best explored from Rutland, Vermont, which lies between them. Going north use US Route 7 and Vermont Highway 116 (west) or US Route 4 and Vermont Highway 100 (east). Going south use US Route 7 (west) or Vermont Highways 103 and 100 (east). The state roads are super-scenic.
**WHEN TO GO:**
Any time (although winter conditions can be extreme and the autumn foliage has to be seen to be believed).

There is something for everyone here, for Green Mountain National Forest (GMNF) covers more than 1,600 sq km 620 (sq mi) of protected land in central and southwestern Vermont, forming an impressive north-south spine of public land down the middle of the state. The forest is characterized by great scenic beauty and a wonderful rural atmosphere, with rugged mountain scenery and extensive forests punctuated by charming traditional villages. The extensive forestation is of various age classes, but there are also small treeless upland habitats, wetlands, streams, ponds and lakes.

Three major trails pass through this largely untamed area – the Robert Frost National Recreation Trail, Appalachian National Scenic

Trail and Long National Recreation Trail. Beyond that, there are endless opportunities for wild-place action on the extensive 1,450-km (900-mi) network of local trails. These are used for hiking, primitive camping, cycling, horseback riding, snowshoeing, cross-country skiing and snowmobiling. The forest has three alpine and seven Nordic ski areas for winter sports enthusiasts who come out to play during the long winters that turn the forest into a white wonderland. Hunting (in season) and fishing are also popular pastimes. So, too, is wildlife-watching and photography, with numerous bird species and mammals including black bear, moose, beaver and white-tailed deer to be spotted. Boating opportunities exist, too, along with a number of developed campsites with good facilities.

Around 400 sq km (155 sq mi) are taken up by the eight officially designated wilderness areas within GMNF, a quarter of the total area. These are not for the inexperienced or faint-hearted. Management is minimal, with fallen trees left to rot and helpful aids like rough bridges and marked trails virtually non-existent. But those fit individuals motivated by the spirit of challenge, exploration and self-discovery will find wilderness heaven – total solitude plus awe-inspiring surroundings.

**DON'T MISS:**
A rewarding side trip to East Creek Natural Area near Orwell, Vermont. The creek flows into Lake Champlain and sustains wonderful wetlands that harbour rare flora and wildlife like the American bittern – but one among many bird species to be seen. Other notable inhabitants are painted and snapping turtles, muskrat, white-tailed deer, mink, bobcats and coyotes. Lower East Creek may be explored by rowboat for a special open-air experience.

**YOU SHOULD KNOW:**
The eight wilderness areas in GMNF (in ascending order of size) are Bristol Cliffs, George Aiken, Big Branch, Peru Peak, Joseph Battell, Lye Brook, Glastenbury and Breadloaf. Maps of each are available online at the US Department of Agriculture's Forest Service website.

*A view from Kelly Stand Road, Green Mountain National Forest*

# White Mountain National Forest

It is big, beautiful, wild and spreads into two states – New Hampshire and Maine. It's the 3,175-sq-km (1,225-sq-mi) White Mountain National Forest (WMNF), unsurprisingly contained within the White Mountains. This range offers the most rugged upland terrain in New England and forms part of the mighty Appalachians. It may be big enough to allow wilderness seekers ample scope, but WMNF attracts six million visitors each year. Indeed, the only national site in the USA to draw more is the Great Smoky Mountains National Park, further south on the Tennessee-North Carolina border.

As for wilderness, there are five areas within WMNF, accounting for over 460 sq km (178 sq mi) of forest lands. The Presidential Range/Dry River Wilderness is notable for cloud-shrouded mountains named after prominent US citizens who made their mark on American history, including several presidents, and attracts serious peak-baggers. The Sandwich Range Wilderness consists of rugged terrain that rewards super-fit hikers with outstanding views over mountains, lakes and forest. The Great Gulf Wilderness is a small but spectacular *cirque*, a natural amphitheatre formed by glacial erosion. The largest is Maine's Caribou-Speckled Mountain Wilderness, a place of craggy rockscapes characterized by open ledges, deep notches and wooded ridges. The 'speckled' description comes from vivid splashes of autumn colour created by stands of hardwood trees. Pemigewasset Wilderness encompasses a river watershed surrounded by steep mountain ridges. It is the newest – and most widely used – of the forest's wilderness areas.

There are actually three disconnected areas within WMNF as a whole, together offering 1,900 km (1,180 mi) of hiking trails, numerous official campgrounds and all the usual outdoor recreational opportunities, from autumn foliage photography to zoological observation. As per federal regulations, wilderness areas cannot be commercially exploited and must be used only by non-motorized explorers.

*A swift flowing river runs through White Mountain National Forest.*

# Catskill Forest Preserve

The Catskill Forest Preserve consists of all state-owned land within Catskill Park, encompassing New York State's Catskill Mountains. The preserve amounts to an impressive 1,150 sq km (445 sq mi) that is, as the name suggests, mainly wooded. But it also includes wetlands and meadows, lakes, rivers, waterfalls and cliffs. It is a natural playground affording all sorts of recreational opportunities, not least of which is the ability to get away from civilization and enjoy the solitude of the woods, where the only companions are birds and forest animals, the latter including bear, coyote, bobcat and mink.

The 98 major peaks within Catskill Park form a stirring skyline, and forest preserve land is classified as one of three types – wilderness, wild forest and intensive use. The latter mainly consists of official campgrounds, most of which – while having vehicular access – offer only basic facilities. One exception is the huge North-South Lake campground with many pitches and swimming areas in both lakes.

Wild forest is mostly second- or third-growth woodland that has been disturbed by human activity before being allowed to regenerate. Certain vehicles are permitted on the old logging roads and those leading up to many fire towers that offer superb vantage points with panoramic views over the arboreal sea. These areas are popular with those who prefer driving, with or without accompanying woodland walks.

Wilderness areas must be 'untrammelled by man' and the forest park has four (review pending). These are Slide Mountain and Big-Indian Beaverkill in Ulster County, plus Indian Head and West Kill in Greene County. No mechanical intrusion is permitted – even chainsaws needed to clear fallen trees require a special permit – while trails are narrow woodland paths rather than old roads. It's here that backcountry hikers and birdwatchers can experience true solitude in the great outdoors.

*A view across the beautiful Catskill Mountains*

**HOW TO GET THERE:**
Catskill Park has many routes that offer scenic touring and give good access to forest preserve areas. The park's vast network of minor roads is best reached from Interstate 87 (New York to Albany).

**WHEN TO GO:**
Any time (snow can be deep in winter, but there are still plenty of recreational opportunities like cross-country skiing and there are various winter sports facilities in Catskill Park, such as Belleayre Mountain Ski Centre).

**DON'T MISS:**
The view from the top of Slide Mountain, the highest peak in the Catskills – the main trail to the summit was built in 1892, the first hiking route constructed in the forest preserve at public expense.

**YOU SHOULD KNOW:**
Catskill Park is within a so-called 'Blue Line' encircling 2,800 sq km (1,100 sq mi) in Delaware, Greene, Sullivan and Ulster Counties. Deriving from the blue ink originally used to physically outline Catskill and Adirondack Parks on a map, this became a device ensuring that any land acquired by the state within Blue Lines must legally 'be forever kept as wild forest lands' and incorporated into existing forest preserves.

*Ferns and hardwoods in Allegheny National Forest*

# Hickory Creek Wilderness

**HOW TO GET THERE:**
The Hickory Creek trailhead is close to Hearts Content Recreation Area, 24 km (15 mi) southwest of Warren, Pennsylvania, which is on US Route 6. Follow Scenic Route 3005 (Pleasant Drive) to the junction with Township Road 2002, which leads to Hearts Content with its campground.

**WHEN TO GO:**
Any time – October to enjoy the sensational colours of the autumn trees – although the wilderness trail itself is impassable to all but the most determined survivalists after snowfall.

**DON'T MISS:**
The interpretive Old Growth Trail, a stroll around a loop path from the picnic site at Hearts Content Recreation Area, through a lovely old-growth timber stand that was deliberately preserved by a logging company when all around came down in the mid 1800s. This is the centrepiece of the small but attractive Hearts Content Scenic Area, a National Natural Landmark.

**YOU SHOULD KNOW:**
The Hickory Creek Wilderness is one of only two such areas in the whole of Pennsylvania, the other being the Allegheny Islands Wilderness, consisting of seven islands along a 90-km (56-mi) stretch of the Allegheny River between Buckaloons Recreation Area and the town of Tionesta.

Pennsylvania's mighty Allegheny National Forest has much to offer, but nothing more self-contained and beguiling than the 15-sq-km (6-sq-mi) Hickory Creek Wilderness. This unspoiled gem is located in the forest's Bradford Ranger District in northwestern Pennsylvania and is characterized by beech and black cherry woodland, interspersed with open spaces dotted with stands of oak, maple, birch and hemlock, while at ground level there's a rich variety of mosses, ferns, shrubs and abundant wild flowers. The wilderness encompasses East and Middle Hickory Creeks, where native brook trout can be caught and black bears and deer lurk in the undergrowth along with shy wild turkeys. The trees are populated by the likes of barred owls and woodpeckers.

One of the most rewarding experiences within the national forest – and the only way to fully appreciate the wilderness atmosphere – is following the Hickory Creek Wilderness Trail. This 18 km (11 mi) loop offers a great experience for lovers of wild places, who will understand the lonely challenges faced by the first European pioneers as they explored the forest and empathize with their long-ago experiences.

The round trip is a strenuous day hike or rewarding overnight expedition. This is not one for the unfit or inexperienced walker, with map and compass essential aids. Occasional yellow blazes mark the trail, but these are being allowed to fade naturally and obstructions like fallen trees are mostly left untouched. If this sounds daunting rather than delightful, simply sampling the beginning of the trail gives a flavour of the place. Alternatively, plenty of easier yet worthwhile hiking opportunities are to be found on the 320-km (200-mi) network of well-developed and waymarked trails within the surrounding Allegheny National Forest's 2,075 sq km (800 sq mi) of largely wooded terrain.

# Great Swamp National Wildlife Refuge

New Jersey's Morris and Somerset Counties are the places to find Great Swamp National Wildlife Refuge – an unspoiled corner of this well-developed state within 50 km (30 mi) of Manhattan that's so special it's one of the nation's 500+ wildlife refuges, has been declared a National Natural Landmark and is officially designated as wilderness. So what's so important about this relatively small area – 31 sq km (12 sq mi) – that very nearly became the site of a major international airport in the early 1960s?

The answer is 'birds'. The Great Swamp is within a watershed that provides the source of the Passaic River. Although habitat within the refuge is varied, its predominant character – as the name suggests – is wetland. This environment provides a home and refuge for a huge population of resident and migratory birds. Around 250 species have been recorded and the refuge serves as a vital stopping place on North America's eastern migration corridor. But the 'wildlife' tag applies to numerous four-footed denizens such as deer, coyote, fox, muskrat, raccoon, beaver, red and grey squirrel, plus the occasional bear. There are also turtles, snakes, amphibians, fish and innumerable insects, together enjoying a wonderful natural habitat rich in wild flowers and native vegetation.

There are roads through the Great Swamp at the western end, including Pleasant Plains Road where Refuge Headquarters and the Helen C Fenske Visitor Centre may be found, along with a nature shop. There's a wildlife observation centre on north-south Long Hill Road, which separates off the road-free eastern half of the refuge with its various rewarding hiking trails emanating from convenient trailheads with parking. There are related facilities surrounding the Great Swamp, such as an outdoor education centre in Chatham Township and the Somerset County Environmental Centre.

*A boardwalk stretches across the unspoilt swamplands.*

**HOW TO GET THERE:**
From US Interstate 78 (exit 40) take Hillcrest Road, Mountain Avenue and Meyersville Road. From US Interstate 287 take exit 30A and follow refuge signs.
**WHEN TO GO:**
Refuge grounds are open from sunrise to sunset all year round.
**DON'T MISS:**
The Raptor Trust – based in Millington, New Jersey, and surrounded by the Great Swamp. This is the place to see a huge collection of captive raptors and a large number of assorted wild birds recovering from injury.
**YOU SHOULD KNOW:**
Back in 1968, this was the very first of (currently) nearly 700 locations in the USA to receive official federal wilderness designation under the Wilderness Act of 1964.

# Backbone Mountain

Maryland's Potomac-Garrett State Forest is a 47-sq-km (18-sq-mi) tract of rugged upland forest situated between the towns of Oakland and Westernport. This magical sweep of wild woodland, tumbling streams and deep valleys is a great place to start exploring Backbone Mountain, which straddles the border between Maryland and West Virginia. It is a prominent ridge of the Allegheny Mountains, part of the Appalachians and great Eastern Continental Divide, around 65 km (40 mi) long and runs on a northeast-southwest line from Maryland's Savage River Reservoir to Black Fork on the Cheat River in West Virginia.

Within the State Forest on its Maryland flank may be found Crabtree Woods, a fascinating remnant of the once-vast expanse of old-growth forest that has largely been logged out. It contains mixed hardwoods such as red oak, sugar maple, basswood and cucumber trees, offering a wonderful display of contrasting colours when the foliage starts to turn in late September or October. The forest as a whole offers fishing, trails to suit casual strollers and hardened hikers alike, plus a choice of mountain-bike routes.

Backbone Mountain is a watershed. While the north branch of the Potomac heads off into Maryland, West Virginia gets the white-water Youghiogheny, a tributary of the Monongahela River. The mountain's forested sides are criss-crossed with trails that allow backcountry hikers to enjoy the solitary splendours of nature and abundant wildlife. One feature worth visiting is the Olson Observation Tower at the southern end of the mountain. West Virginia's first fire tower was built there in 1922, although the present structure dates from the 1960s. The tower is not open to the public but, as befits a vital lookout, tree-top views from the last of the 133 steps leading up to it are truly spectacular.

# Cranberry Wilderness

The last North American Ice Age sent its glacial fingers as far south as West Virginia. When they retreated, at their southernmost point they left behind a geological anomaly – a 3-sq-km (1.2-sq-mi) peat bog ecosystem. Maintained by chance microclimate, it's like a piece of Canadian taiga isolated in the dense, temperate woods and rushing mountain rivers of West Virginia's enormous Monongahela National Forest. The bog is called Cranberry Glades Botanical Area. Its spongy soil is so fragile and so full of site-specific flora, including orchids and carnivorous species like the pitcher-plant, that it can be crossed only on protective boardwalk trails.

Cranberry Glades is the jewel in the crown of the 145-sq-km (56-sq-mi) Cranberry Wilderness named after it – and of the additional 105-sq-km (40-sq-mi) 'Cranberry Backcountry' to its west, where wilderness restrictions are fewer). Cranberry Glades has survived untouched; Cranberry Wilderness is in reversion to its primeval state. In the 1970s it almost became West Virginia's biggest strip coal mine and, like most of the eastern United States, it was once clearcut by timber companies. Now, parts of Cranberry Wilderness have already had 100 years to recover. Along the Middle Fork of the Williams River, icy water tumbles across boulders in long cascades or runs through beautiful, tall ferns and broadleaf woods filled with exuberant outbursts of rhododendron. Side trails drop off the high ridges past waterfalls and into mysterious hollows. Others keep the high ground among red spruce and Appalachian hardwoods, with magnificent views across the broad mountains and deep valleys typical of the Allegheny Plateau. As a designated sanctuary for black bears, Cranberry Wilderness has become a haven for all forms of wildlife. It's a privilege to share it briefly with what the 1964 US Wilderness Act describes as 'a community of life . . . where man himself is a visitor who does not remain'.

*A trio of pointed green leaves among a trio of crimson petals identifies this delicate spring wild flower as the Purple Trillium Blossom in the Cranberry Wilderness.*

**DON'T MISS:**
'Hell For Certain' – a particularly lovely, isolated branch stream feeding into Middle Fork Williams River; white-water running in the rushing waters of springtime or lazy river tubing in placid late summer water; the secret hollows along the Big Beechy Trail.

**YOU SHOULD KNOW:**
Some rivers have 'catch-and-return' fishing rules on certain sections. Check licenses and permissions before you go. The Wilderness area is a black bear sanctuary. The backcountry is not. Wear brightly coloured clothing during the hunting season when hiking or camping near the fringes.

# George Washington National Forest

The Appalachians, a glorious range of thickly wooded parallel ridges, deep valleys and shining rivers, sweep southwest, forming the Virginia–West Virginia border. The forests were home to Native Americans, then settlers, who cleared and farmed the fertile land. Logging and mining in the 19th century ravaged and scarred the landscape and almost wiped out the indigenous wildlife. Thanks to the vision and determination of those who recognized the threat to the nation's natural resources, the government intervened to purchase deforested mountains. In 1918, the area which later became the George Washington National Forest was one of the first acquisitions; now it is jointly administered with the Jefferson National Forest further south as a vast area of public land.

The forest is within easy reach for millions of city dwellers, who are drawn by its peace and grandeur and outdoor activities which include hunting, fishing, horse riding, camping and canoeing. Some spots can be quite crowded, but much of the more remote and undeveloped forest has been designated wilderness, and even at busy times walkers can find solitude on the hundreds of miles of hiking trails, which include part of the long-distance Appalachian Trail.

The varied terrain of the forest supports a huge variety of trees and plants and many animals and birds, including white-tailed deer and black bear, wild turkeys and bald eagles. It is splendid walking country and a climb to one of the higher ridges is rewarded with a stunning panorama of rolling, tree-clad ridges, in autumn dazzling with scarlet-and-gold foliage, receding into a softly misty distance. The US Forest Service aims to 'care for the land and serve the people', and here it does both superlatively.

# Red River Gorge

More than 70 million years of weathering have formed the scenery surrounding the central section of Kentucky's Red River Gorge. Wind and water have sculpted sandstone cliffs, hollowing out rock shelters (caves) which slowly erode into arches and bridges and these are the best-known features of the gorge. Unspoilt woods and valleys between the rocky ridges are home to a wealth of plants and wildlife. When the railways opened up this remote countryside in the 19th century, city dwellers flocked here. Entrepreneurs opened hotels and the crowds enjoyed not just the wonders of nature, but restaurants, boating lakes and dance halls. Later, to protect this unique landscape, it was made part of the Daniel Boone National Forest. Red River Gorge is now a designated National Natural Landmark; orchestras no longer play, but there are miles of enjoyable short and long hiking trails.

The river offers excellent canoeing; the tough upper reaches suit experienced canoeists, while the quieter central section is normally safe and easy, with fine views of the rocks around the gorge. 'The Red' is also a world-renowned rock-climbing and abseiling location, with established routes in overhanging sandstone ranging from easy to very difficult.

While several of the spectacular rock arches, such as the famous Sky Bridge, are easily accessible and much visited, many more – there are around 100 – are found on quieter, more demanding trails and can be visited in peaceful solitude. Clifty Wilderness is a spacious, rugged, undeveloped part of the gorge, where a few longer trails wind through towering cliffs and narrow ravines. Traces of its earliest inhabitants, the Native Americans, and of pioneers and settlers can be seen in the area. These are treasured and protected by the Forest Service, which is diligent in its care for all aspects of this extraordinary landscape.

**DON'T MISS:**
The Gladie Cultural-Environmental Learning Center is excellent for background to the geology, wildlife and cultural heritage of the gorge, as well as for information on trails, climbing, camping, etc.
**YOU SHOULD KNOW:**
The cliff edges are often unstable; do not allow children to wander on their own. Canoeists should always check the river level – high water is too fast and low water too shallow for safety. New climbing routes must be approved by the Forest Service.

*Unspoilt woods and valleys lie between the rocky ridges of Red River Gorge.*

# Fall Creek Falls State Park

**HOW TO GET THERE:**
By car, 18 km (11 mi) east of Spencer and 29 km (18 mi) west of Pikeville, Tennessee

**WHEN TO GO:**
Any time for the spectacular waterfalls; summer if you want to jump in the natural plunge pools below the cascades and falls.

**DON'T MISS:**
The Cable Trail, a difficult but rewarding short clamber to the base of Cane Creek Falls; Rumbling Falls Cave, near Dry Fork, the second largest chamber in the USA; watching the brave (or foolhardy) dive from the swing bridge into the swimming hole at Cane Creek, just where it says 'Don't'.

The Cumberland Plateau is famous for its oak and hickory forests stretching from Kentucky down to Alabama. On its western edge in middle Tennessee, between Pikeville and Spencer, the plateau is creased by Cane Creek Gorge, the centrepiece of a geological formation that cuts into the stands of hardwood timber with streams, gorges, cascades and waterfalls. The region is powered by the waters that feed Cane Creek, but it takes its name from the highest of the waterfalls that make it so thrilling to visit: the 84-m (256-ft) Fall Creek Falls. Protected within a 81-sq-km (31-sq-mi) State Park, Falls Creek Falls is a compendium of some of temperate-zone America's most dramatic natural formations – with the added bonus of being highly accessible.

Cane Creek is fuelled by several streams even before it enters Cane Creek Gorge and drops hundreds of feet in less than a mile.

Cane Creek Cascades drop 14 m (46 ft) before falling 26 m (85 ft) at Cane Creek Falls (into the same plunge pool as the 38-m (125-ft) Rockhouse Creek waterfall). Piney Falls tumble 29 m (95 ft) into a minor gorge above its confluence with Cane Creek; and even 76-m (250-ft) Coon Creek Falls seems inconspicuous right next to Fall Creek Falls itself. There are limestone sinks, cave systems, trails and swing bridges (slatted walkways, tethered at each end) high above the gorges. But there are also car parks close to the best overlooks, and facilities that owe nothing to nature.

Fall Creek Falls State Park is a scenic adventure of first magnitude. Away from the obvious choke points, it is still wild and ruggedly beautiful. Woven into its most popular sights are remote trails through mountain laurel, rhododendron and tulip poplar. Invariably, they re-emerge where moving water exercises its universal magic on human imagination – but nobody minds sharing that.

*The scenic wonderland of Fall Creek Falls State Park*

**YOU SHOULD KNOW:**
The multiple waterfalls of Fall Creek Falls State Park served as principal locations for the Disney live-action version of *The Jungle Book*. Not only were the wilderness locations considered perfect – the film crew had the use of the 400-person conference and hotel facilities within the park.

# Congaree National Park

There used to be about 4,850 sq km (1,875 sq mi) of bottomland forest in South Carolina, part of a 210,450-sq-km (81,255-sq-mi) chain of forested swamp that looped from Chesapeake Bay to east Texas. Now just 52 sq km (20 sq mi) survive – 45 sq km (17 sq mi) of them in the protected 90-sq-km (35-sq-mi) wilderness of Congaree National Park. The astonishing old-growth bottomland hardwoods have no equal in the USA. Over 75 species, force-fed by constantly refreshed silts washed down in regular flooding, grow to record dimensions. Loblolly pines, incongruous in any floodplain, reach 52 m (171 ft) alongside giant swamp chestnuts, hickories, sycamores and bald cypresses over 8 m (26 ft) in circumference. Their collective canopy arches high, high above, chased by poison ivy and grapevines. In this silent, warm, watery cathedral, darting bright colours reveal some of the 173 species of birds that fill the forest. Among them are all eight species of southeastern woodpeckers, including the spectacular red-cockaded woodpecker.

In fact the area was only saved because it is a floodplain and not a true swamp. Neither farmers nor logging companies could capitalize on the regular flooding. The trees thrived in the rich wetlands but stayed too green to float down river. Although there are hiking trails, including a 4-km (2.5-mi) boardwalk over water, the best way to see it is by canoe. Cedar Creek meanders lazily through 32 km (20 mi) of oxbows, loops and bends before it joins the Congaree River. Heron, river otters, wild boar, box turtles and innumerable other wildlife in the dappled swamps and pools turn pleasant drifting into an adventure of slightly Jurassic wonder. For hikers, the Oakridge Trail guarantees getting close to the heart of the old-growth trees, especially magnificent old-growth oaks and beeches. There are giants here whose height is only exceeded by California's sequoias – but so many more of them.

**YOU SHOULD KNOW:**
On a floodplain, even giant trees have relatively shallow roots. When Hurricane Hugo smashed many of Congaree's tallest trees in 1989, it was considered a catastrophe – but the damage created dramatic holes in the leaf canopy which have greatly stimulated new growth on the forest floor.

**HOW TO GET THERE:**
Leave your car at the Harry Hampton Visitor Center at the entrance to Congaree National Park, 30 km (19 mi) southeast of Columbia off SC Route 48. Bring your canoe with you.
**WHEN TO GO:**
Any time. It's useful to ring before you go to check the state of flooding.
**DON'T MISS:**
The Low Boardwalk (trail) through bald cypress and water tupelo forest; the mystery of cypress 'knees' – the tangles of roots that grow up to 3 m (10 ft) in the air; wildlife along the King Snake Trail, one of the park's most remote.

*Cypress Swamp,*
*Congaree National Park*

# Cumberland Island National Seashore

**HOW TO GET THERE:**
By ferry from St Mary's, Georgia, or by private boat from Fernandina Beach, Amelia Island, Florida.

**WHEN TO GO:**
Any time. Winter is particularly good for beachcombing.

**DON'T MISS:**
The wild turkey courtship dance of March/April; loggerhead turtles nesting from mid May; the 1898 Georgian-revival Plum Orchard Mansion; the marine wilderness flora and fauna around Lake Whitney on the Roller Coaster Trail.

**YOU SHOULD KNOW:**
In September 1996, the late John F Kennedy Jr and Carolyn Bessette chose to be married in the single-room wooden shack First African Baptist Church, in 'The Settlement' established in the 1890s for African-American workers.

*A wind-bent oak on Cumberland Island*

The largest and southernmost of the Atlantic barrier islands protecting the coast of Georgia, Cumberland Island also includes the biggest island wilderness in the entire USA. It's a vision of an entirely pristine America without noise or light pollution, where native species like wild turkeys, otters, white-tailed deer and armadillos are commonplace among the wild horses, alligators and occasional bobcats that share the fertile island paradise. The island is 28 km (17 mi) long and 5 km (3 mi) wide, big enough to support three distinct ecosystems. Towards the ocean, a perfect sand beach (one of America's top ten) runs up to a kilometre deep the length of the island, backed by dunes which give way to dense palmetto stands, pines and – magically – sun-dappled pastures and woods of ancient oaks festooned with Spanish moss. On the west coast woods and meadows yield to 69 sq km (27 sq mi) of marshes, creeks and tidal mudflats, teeming with 300 species of waders, sea birds and dazzling migrants.

Cumberland Island's haunting beauty is emphasized by the few traces of human occupation that still endure at its north and south ends. Once owned by the Carnegie family, part of the island remains private and closed to visitors; but palatial mansions remain, as ruins or restored luxury hotels, along with the more poignant chattel houses of 'the Settlement' where a small community of fishermen and farmers long ago sweated a living. Hotel guests get a special kind of access to the island's secrets, including wildlife-watching at dawn and dusk when other visitors have mostly gone. Rangers try to keep visitor numbers down to about 300 at any time – and although some arrive by private boat as well as on the daily ferry, Cumberland Island is never crowded. It is one of the Carnegie family's most prescient and valuable gifts to America.

# Florida Bay

Florida Bay is a vast triangle of ultra-shallow sea at the tip of the Florida Peninsular, protected from the Atlantic by the arc of the Florida Keys. To its north the bay's coast is porous. It's where the 80-km (50-mi) wide, slow-moving mass of the Florida Everglades freshwater 'river' merges with the sea in a symbiotic exchange of salt and fresh water critical to the huge variety of subtropical wetland flora and fauna for which the Everglades are so famous. It's not surprising that most of the bay's 2,218 sq km (855 sq mi) are included in the Everglades National Park, because its average depth is under 1 m (3 ft). Here, land and sea are defined by the same topographic and ecological integrity, and mutually dependent. Beneath Florida Bay's shimmering surface lies a marine wilderness as rich in novelty, colour and rarity as any of the Everglades' mainland natural marvels.

*An aerial view of Florida Bay*

The shallow sea only just covers gigantic meadows of seagrass. As a nursery for hundreds of marine species, and food for larger creatures like the manatee and green sea turtle, the grasses ultimately sustain the whole of Florida Bay's ecosystem. Bigger fish lurk round the mangrove islands and in the coastal estuaries and brackish waterways where mangroves form long tunnels and the channels of water run slightly deeper.

Guided boat tours apart, the only way to explore Florida Bay is by canoe or small, powered boat. With Polaroid (non-reflective) glasses you can see deep into the water – as vital for navigating shallow channels as for enjoying the full range of marine wildlife. Canoes are easy (and quiet) to manoeuvre among both mangroves and mudflats, and offer the best opportunities of seeing anything from a saltwater crocodile to some of America's rarest and most beautiful wading birds.

**HOW TO GET THERE:**
By boat from Key Largo or by car from Miami to Flamingo village, where you can rent a boat or canoe, or sign up for a boat tour.
**WHEN TO GO:**
November to April
**DON'T MISS:**
The birdlife around the Eco Pond, close to Flamingo; pottering among the tidal waterways such as Alligator Creek and Terrapin Bay.
**YOU SHOULD KNOW:**
There are marked channels for travelling across Florida Bay: missing them risks a steep fine and almost inevitably running aground. Getting towed off is expensive and extremely damaging to the fragile seagrass prairie – so take the time to study the free navigation charts available at the Flamingo Visitor Center.

# Calakmul Biosphere Reserve

In the language of the ancient Central American Maya culture *Calakmul* means city of twin pyramids. Calakmul was among the Maya civilization's most important sites, second only to Tikal in Guatemala. Its massive pyramids have long been reclaimed by tropical forest and jungle, but the Calakmul Biosphere Reserve, of which the ten square miles of Mayan ruins are only a small part, is intended to protect archaeological history as much as the precarious regional ecosystem. The reserve covers 7,300 sq km (2,820 sq mi) – rather more than the US State of Delaware – bounded by Quintana Roo to the east and Guatemala to the south. It is the biggest tropical forest reserve in Mexico.

The forest would be familiar to a returning Mayan. Five of Mexico's six 'big cats' (jaguar, puma, ocelot, margay and jaguarondi) share the regrown wilderness with 80 other mammals, 358 bird species, reptiles, fish, butterflies, bats and amphibians. Tropical fauna make splashes of colour in the halls of green trees where monkeys swing and parrots chatter. At dusk every day, between two and five million bats wheel into the sky from Calakmul's bat cave to forage for insects. The taxonomy of such rich biodiversity even includes the family of man. The reserve needs to sustain humans, too, and it's in the forefront of the UNESCO 'Man and the Biosphere' (MAB) programme.

It's a balancing act. Calakmul is already expanding both its core wilderness areas and the buffer zones which contain the Mayan ruins and where the *ejidos* (Mexican communities living on communal land) can benefit directly from the forest. The scheme will be successful when the *ejidos* take over the management of the forest, and as guides for ecotourism. The advantage to visitors is beyond price – access to local expertise in one of the world's most stunning tropical ecologies.

# Cumbres de Majalca
# National Park

It is epic terrain. South of the US–Mexican border on the Rio Bravo, the wide-open hill country familiar from Texas becomes even wilder and more rugged. Chihuahua is Mexico's biggest state (half the size of Spain, or the whole of Britain), where the purple mountains of the Sierra Occidental descend to the southeastern plateau of the Chihuahua Desert. The state capital, also called Chihuahua, is one of just two sizeable local cities (the other is Juarez on the US border). The rest is a geological badlands of mountain bluffs and box canyons, where outstanding natural beauty has been baked and then frozen into the land itself. The harsh climate and difficult access have helped preserve its natural secrets. Cumbres de Majalca National Park is one of its best.

It is completely unexpected. The volcanic mountains of the Sierra de Majalca sub-range rise only to 2,600 m (8,530 ft), but from them spring a number of *arroyos* (fast-flowing streams) that cut dozens of valleys into the 1,000-m (3,280-ft) high plateau. Most of it is mantled by thick oak and pine forest; but after rain, every clearing is carpeted with green and dotted with the wild flowers of the high prairie. Everywhere, enormous boulders or chimneys (*cumbres*) of volcanic rock stand isolated – whittled, split and smoothed by water and wind. Like Easter Island statues, the extraordinary volcanic sculptures seem to have individual characters, but share the natural majesty of simply being immense. The dominant forest is typical of its altitude and the extreme hot and cold temperatures. It is a perfect habitat for the black bears who live here, among coyote, eagles, falcons, woodpeckers, and deer.

Visitors come for the hiking, mountain-biking and rock climbing, and become smitten by the Cumbres' sheer beauty. Fortunately, the dramatic geological oddities share their grandeur with more wildlife than people.

**HOW TO GET THERE:**
By car from Chihuahua City – 30 km (19 mi) north on Highway 45, then left on a gravel track for the same distance.
**WHEN TO GO:**
Any time – but in mid winter the high ground is likely to be under snow.
**DON'T MISS:**
The boulders of Salsipuedas (especially if you enjoy rock climbing); the geometry eroded into the Penon de El Cuadrado rock formation; the imaginative formations known as Sleeping Beauty, Soldier's Peak and Eagle's Nest.
**YOU SHOULD KNOW:**
The Mexican phrase to express being dumbstruck with amazement is *Ay Chihuahua!* (Don't ask: just practise). The boundary between the Cumbres de Majalca National Park and the backcountry is not clear. Be prepared to meet police or soldiers looking for the *bandidos* regularly alleged to patrol the area.

# Nevado de Colima

**HOW TO GET THERE:**
By car from Colima or bus from Ciudad Guzman to the edge of the park; or by 4x4 to La Joya. Within the park, apart from that track, only hiking and horse riding are allowed.
**WHEN TO GO:**
November to March, the dry season
**DON'T MISS:**
Carizalillo Lake, where weekenders come to camp, kayak and picnic high on El Nevado; swimming in the stone pool fed by the spring at the bottom of a canyon below the campsite clearing at 3,521 m (11,550 ft); the green water of Laguna Maria, on the trail to El Volcan, a perfect alpine mirror reflecting the smoking crater.
**YOU SHOULD KNOW:**
In the Nahuatl language, *Colima* means God of fire who rules, and refers to Volcan de Fuego's belching eruptions. Yet although both volcanoes have Colima as part of their names, they are both in fact in the State of Jalisco.

From any angle – north to Guadalajara or southwest to Colima on Mexico's Pacific coast – the twin cone peaks of Nevado de Colima (El Nevado) and Volcan de Fuego de Colima (El Volcan) stand out from a distance. El Volcan is active, with a history of major eruptions and semi-permanent fizzing and growling. At any time it can, and does, spill showers of red-hot rocks over its flanks, and as recently as 2005 shot columns of ash 5 km (3 mi) high into the sky. It's a dangerous but fascinating force of nature, still growing in the old caldera formed by the much older and completely dormant El Nevado, a just-comfortable 9 km (5.5 mi) out of range. Between and surrounding the two lie thick forest and scrub, the 204 sq km (79 sq mi) Nevado de Colima National Park. Snowcapped El Nevado looks down from 4,335 m (14,220 ft) on its fiery, 3,900 m (12,795 ft) neighbour. Hiking the first is the best way to see the second.

El Nevado rises out of hot, dusty (and now deforested) plains, through increasingly cooler subtropical and temperate zones of lush coniferous forest near the top. The trees are full of movement, of white-tailed deer, coyote and endemic birds like the highland guan, Aztec thrush and thick-billed parrot as well as woodpeckers, doves and hawks. Reaching El Nevado's summit is a strenuous two-day hike from the edge of the park; but in a 4x4 you can get to La Joya, a solitary cabin at the end of the track from where a short but demanding hike brings you to some of El Nevado's loveliest terrain, and a grandstand view of El Volcan. Stay the night at La Joya and you stand the best chance of seeing the astonishing wildlife dramas that occur during the early hours of daylight.

# Ria Celestun Biosphere Reserve

This is the place where the word 'ecotourism' was invented in 1983. The Ria Celestun Biosphere Reserve protects some of the best-preserved wetlands in the northwestern Yucatan Peninsular, on Mexico's Gulf coast. Its centrepiece is the estuary (*ria*) close to the fishing port and resort of Celestun. The river emerges onto a shelf of shallow sea lined with sand dunes, swamps and mangroves that form domes and tunnels around the coastal lagoons, flooded pastures and lowland jungle on 'shore'. It is bursting with glorious life. Enormous flocks of intensely pink flamingoes (up to 18,000 at a time) strut and flap offshore like a pink Mexican wave. There are storks, egrets, parrots, cardinals, pelicans and hummingbirds among the 320 species here. Crab and shrimp crowd the brackish water where mangroves thrive, and there are turtles, crocodiles, manatee and spider monkeys above and below. Jaguars, tapirs and anteaters are among 75 mammals in the jungle areas. They add up to a dazzling demonstration of species and habitat interdependence, completed by a boat ride at night time. The nocturnal wildlife action in the maze of mangrove waterways gives wings to the imagination.

Ria Celestun Biosphere Reserve is not especially big – 591 sq km (228 sq mi) – but it has added significance in being the source of most of the fresh groundwater in northwestern Yucatan (where all fresh water comes from underground sinkholes). Every development on its increasingly crowded fringes interrupts the free exchange of fresh and saline water, and impacts immediately on the fragile balance of the ecosystem. A new bridge slightly diverted a freshwater channel, causing a reed marsh to stagnate and a large flamingo feeding area to close down. Threats like these to such a beautiful exhibition of natural dynamics can be removed only by inspiring the local economy to put ecotourism first. Which means, go soon and help keep Ria Celestun pristine.

**HOW TO GET THERE:**
Head for Celestun port and rent a boat or bicycle, or take tour boats to different parts of the reserve.
**WHEN TO GO:**
Any time. Flamingoes are most numerous in winter.
**DON'T MISS:**
The 'petrified forest' of hundreds of sun-bleached, long-dead trees – a surreal landscape; swimming 'underground' in a freshwater sinkhole (*ojo de agua*); the reed marsh habitats and fishing grounds.
**YOU SHOULD KNOW:**
Typically, a flamingo hoovers up 2,000 l (440 gal) of water per day, filter-fishing. Celestun has adopted the American Flamingo – the biggest and most deeply coloured of the world's six species – as its 'signature bird'.

*Flamingoes feed in their thousands at the Ria Celestun Biosphere Reserve.*

# Sierra Gorda Biosphere Reserve

**HOW TO GET THERE:**
By car or bus to Jalpan de Serra, at the centre of the reserve in north Queretaro. Transport is fairly easy in the area because Sierra Gorda's small towns are a tourist destination in their own right.

**WHEN TO GO:**
Any time

**DON'T MISS:**
The rare opportunity to sample radically different ecosystems in a short time, and without having to carry lots of supplies. Wilderness areas are seldom as accessible or fringed by such a choice of facilities.

**YOU SHOULD KNOW:**
Sierra Gorda's fame as a tourist hot spot rests chiefly on a group of five villages known as 'the Missions of Sierra Gorda' – five Franciscan convents built in the 18th century and among the best examples of Mexican Baroque architecture and art of the colonial era. They were built for the Pame and Chichimeca indigenous peoples whose fierce resistance to the colonial Spanish lasted until the mid-19th century. Somewhat contrarily, they accepted evangelizing friars and conversion to Christianity centuries earlier. The villages have World Heritage status.

The state of Queretaro in Mexico's central highlands is the meeting point of north and south bio-regions, and it makes Sierra Gorda Biosphere Reserve the most ecologically diverse in the country. The range is vast within a compact area. Mean altitudes go from 300–3,500 m (985–11,500 ft), and local microclimates produce a huge variation in rainfall. The reserve includes deciduous and evergreen tropical forests, cloud forest and dense oak and pine; spiny shrubs and giant barrel cacti in its arid semi-desert areas; and barely penetrable jungle bursting out of its canyons and deep valleys, watered by huge sinkholes and underground river systems. Historically difficult to access, and with a small population bound by poverty, the Biosphere Reserve was established by integrating Sierra Gorda's farms and villages into co-dependency with habitat conservation. There are roads and villages, and some industry – but local people have encouraged the wilderness areas to creep in and around them. Across almost a third of the whole state of Queretaro, their efforts have increased tourism but reduced its environmental impact. It is welcome evidence of an unusual empathy between man and nature.

Sierra Gorda is on the monarch butterfly's flight path. Its mountains and canyons echo with 300 kinds of migrant and native birds, and it's a matter of mood which kind of leafy glade, cooling waterfall or earthy-smelling oak forest to hike in. One of the area's most exciting hikes (or mule rides) is to the Sotano de Barro (Mud Basement) through jungle and across hill country. It's a huge sinkhole 600 m (1,970 ft) across and 450 m (1,475 ft) deep. Every night, it fills with a raucous colony of military macaws roosting; and the sight of them flooding out *en masse* at dawn is as colourful as Queretaro's famous woven shawls.

*A view of the spectacular Sumidero Canyon*

# Sumidero Canyon

Sumidero Canyon, east of Tuxtla Gutierrez in Mexico's extreme southeast, began as a seismic event on the edges of the North American, Cocos and Caribbean plates. It evolved over millions of years from a gash on the edge of the Chiapas High Plains to a majestic chasm carved a kilometre deep out of limestone and basalt by the Grijalva River. The Sumidero Canyon National Park encloses the canyon along 30 km (19 mi) of the river. The topography of its roughly 219 sq km (84 sq mi) varies between 360–1,729 m (1,180–5,670 ft), and a road connects a series of vantage points called *miradores* from which to look down on the canyon's finest features. Hiking the area is tough and uncomfortable. It's better to head straight for the Ecological Reserve established on the river bank. It nestles in a crook of the river before the canyon proper. The lower ground encourages huge ferns and dense jungle foliage around small pools and marshy ground, the habitat of crocodiles and spider monkeys.

Like the Ecological Reserve, the canyon is only accessible by boat. These *lanchas* leave from the town of Chiapa de Corzo (you may have to wait on the jetty for enough people to fill a boat) for the 35 km (22 mi) ride to the lagoon of the Chicoasen Dam. The twisting Grijalva River runs placid and deep, the home of egrets, herons, kingfishers, vultures and cormorants perched on rocky outcrops. Huge crocodiles bask on tiny beaches. The walls of the canyon rise and rise, almost sheer, to 1,000 m (3,280 ft). They are lined with caves, and a magnificent formation called 'the Christmas Tree'. It's a yuletide lookalike made of calcium deposits on trailing mosses, which becomes a waterfall in the rainy season. It fits perfectly into the strange, lost world of Sumidero Canyon.

**HOW TO GET THERE:**
By boat, from Chiapa de Corzo or Cahuare
**WHEN TO GO:**
Any time, in daylight (boats won't operate after dark).
**DON'T MISS:**
*Cueva de Colores* (Cave of Colours); the sunset view from the *mirador* called *La Coyota*; *Cascada Velo de Novia* (Bride's Veil Waterfall); the giant *Crocodylus acutus*, the American crocodiles for which Sumidero is a perfect, and rare, habitat.
**YOU SHOULD KNOW:**
Sumidero Canyon is both exciting and spooky. Its *ambiente* is coloured by its history, of enduring significance to the indigenous Chiapanecas people who still live in the area. Centuries ago, when the Spanish conquistadors over-ran them, the Chiapanecas of Sumidero committed mass suicide in the canyon rather than face slavery.

*The Maya Mountains*

# Bladen Nature Reserve

There are no roads in the Bladen Nature Reserve. Visitors are forbidden. Bladen's 403 sq km (156 sq mi) are set aside as true wilderness where the lavish biological diversity of Belize can 'perpetuate itself' without human intervention. The only way to go there is on a pre-arranged educational research tour or as a volunteer researcher for the scientific teams permitted to do medical or environmental research. Even with a permit, the reserve is difficult to get to. It is entirely surrounded by other protected areas which provide a natural buffer zone against encroachment on its own, pristine rainforest. Bladen is in the Toledo district of southwest Belize. The Maya Mountains and Deep River Forest Reserves lie to the south, the Columbia Forest to the southwest, Chiquibul National Park to the north and the Trio Reserve to the east. Any and all of them are magnificent – but the Bladen Nature Reserve surpasses the best of the rest.

It's breathtakingly lovely – but rugged. The reserve descends the southeast slope of the Maya Mountains and across the Bladen Branch of the Monkey River. The limestone karst under its southern half is full of conical hills and outcrops honeycombed with sinkholes, cave systems and underground streams. The conditions produce towering palms and 70 species of trees; and make giants of the lianas, herbs, ferns, flowers and fruits that crowd round jungle pools and waterfall cascades. In this sanctuary even rare species are commonplace and visible. Peccary, tapir and jaguar are among 300 mammal species; the crested guan and great curassow among the 200 birds; and the reptiles and amphibians are the richest in Belize.

Nobody has lived in the area since the Mayans and, although attempts are made at illegal activities like logging, Bladen has never been much disturbed. It is a verifiable tropical Eden, the adventure of a lifetime, and well worth the effort.

**HOW TO GET THERE:**
By vehicle from Danriga to Mile 59 Southern Highway, then on foot 10 km (6 mi) to the BFREE (Belize Foundation for Research and Environmental Education) field station on the edge of the reserve. Given notice, they might send a 4x4 to collect you.

**WHEN TO GO:**
November to May

**DON'T MISS:**
Hiking in the forest with a local Mayan who teaches ethno-botany and is expert in traditional forest lore; and be sure to swim in one of the rock pools below one of the many falls in the completely pure waters of the Bladen Branch River.

**YOU SHOULD KNOW:**
Visiting the Bladen Nature Reserve is not for everyone. You look creation full in the face – and discover that its exalted beauty lacks even rudimentary comfort for casual visitors. The dedicated can apply for voluntary internships with BFREE; and the Ya'axche Conservation Trust (aka simply 'Ya'axche') rangers sometimes accept volunteers on extended patrol to help observe illegal (usually commercial) forest incursions (Ya'axche recently caught the Belize Hydroelectric Company trying to build a wholly illegal dam in Bladen – without being noticed!).

# Cockscomb Basin Wildlife Sanctuary

Isolated in the far south of Belize between the Maya Mountains and the coast, the Cockscomb Basin Wildlife Sanctuary is the world's only jaguar reserve. It is also one of the few reserves that accept casual visitors on the same basis as serious naturalists. This rudimentary respect stimulates visitors' curiosity and sense of adventure: it's a very effective method of sharpening vision and hearing before hiking into the great unknown.

Learning to 'read' the forest is paramount at Cockscomb. The reserve's 728 sq km (280 sq mi) of jungle are watered by dozens of streams and underground watercourses that emerge in sparkling waterfalls and clear, deep pools ringed by boulders. As in every kind of terrain, but here especially, pug marks and broken vegetation speak for the teeming wildlife – adrenalin-pumping proof of fabled big cats too canny to be easily spotted. There are several trails (graded by difficulty and physical ability) where you can feel completely absorbed into the patterns of nature the sanctuary is at pains to illustrate. The all-day hike to Outlier Mountain covers most important habitats from jungle swamp and tropical rainforest to the rugged tangle of the mountain itself; but shorter trails are intended to be as much about fun as learning something. For the really committed, the four-day hike to 1,120 m (3,675 ft) Victoria Peak is a lifetime opportunity. You need a permit from the Belize Audubon Society and a licensed guide. The area has not yet been fully explored since it was returned to a wilderness decades ago, and you can expect to discover unknown orchids and encounter rare animals.

Cockscomb Basin's willingness to treat serious conservation as potential recreation should be a blueprint for other wildlife sanctuaries of similar stature. Not many of them encourage inner-tubing down their rivers for the thrill of 'looking a crocodile in the eye at its own level'.

**HOW TO GET THERE:**
By car or bus from Danriga to the Maya Center on the Southern Highway (the bus will stop by request). At the Maya Center Women's Group Gift Shop you pay the entrance fee to the reserve; then it's a 10-km (6-mi) hike or local taxi drive on a dirt road to the Cockscomb Basin Visitors' Center.

**WHEN TO GO:**
December to May (the dry season, and the only months Victoria Peak may be visited) – although wildlife generally is much more active from June to July (the start of the rainy season). December is best for migrant birds.

**DON'T MISS:**
Ben's Bluff Trail, a hike through the transition zone of rainforest to mountain pine forest, ending with a swim beneath a 6-m (20-ft) waterfall; inner-tubing on the Stann Creek River; or the antics of Montezuma's oropendola and the white-collared manakin, two of the world's most hyperactive birds.

**YOU SHOULD KNOW:**
The Visitor Center is built on the remnants of what used to be a logging camp, so the reserve is able to offer basic facilities like a small convenience store, bunkhouses and a few guest cottages as well as a campsite. Take advantage of them: they are as much comfort as you'll ever find in the wild.

*A stunning jaguar on the prowl in the Cockscomb Basin Wildlife Sanctuary.*

# Sarstoon/Temash National Park

**HOW TO GET THERE:**
By very small plane to the airstrip close to Barranco; by boat from Punta Gorda; or by local 'bus' from Punta Gorda to Barranco if you are on foot.
**WHEN TO GO:**
Any time
**DON'T MISS:**
Belize's only example of comfrey palm forest, on the banks of the Sarstoon River; the red mangrove forest – the best in Central America; lingering in Barranco for a glimpse of Garifuna (descendants of the original Carib peoples) culture and folklore.
**YOU SHOULD KNOW:**
In the heat and humidity it's easy to drift into somnolence. Stay awake and aware on land and water in Sarstoon/Temash – the crocodiles are not the only creatures who mean business.

The Sarstoon River forms Belize's southern border with Guatemala. The Temash River opens onto the Gulf of Honduras 16 km (10 mi) up the coast in Amatique Bay. Sandwiched between the two deltas are 170 sq km (66 sq mi) of mangrove forests, sandbar and silt-filled creeks, swamps and marshes merging into some of Belize's most pristine jungle forests. It is an ancient place of innumerable shades of green shadow, splashed with flashes of primary brilliance. It is home to species not found elsewhere in Belize, like the scarlet macaw, white-faced capuchin monkey, countless butterflies and Morelet's crocodile. Seldom disturbed by human intrusion, the deeper forests are full of fresh tracks of bigger, rarer mammals like the tapir, jaguar and ocelot – legends of invisibility, but frequently glimpsed.

The crowning glory of the Temash River are the towering red mangroves reaching up on both banks to 31 m (100 ft) or more, and stretching for miles into and along the coast. Orchids and bromeliads decorate the solid 3-m (10-ft) wall of their roots. Between the rivers, the delta of shallow, brackish waters nourishes underwater grass plains where manatee feed and shoals of fish flit away their nursery years. Sea birds wheel in search of the rich pickings of shrimp; and snook and tarpon patrol far upriver.

You need a guide to come here, and a boat to enjoy it. Boats can be rented in Punta Gorda, the biggest community in the Toledo District. More interesting (and easier if you use the little airstrip near the park), is to look for a guide at the thatched Garifuna village of Barraco, known as the 'gateway to the park'. With expert local guidance, you'll be helping to fulfil the park's commitment to sustainable activities – and be certain of getting close to its most extraordinary natural secrets.

# Indio-Maiz Biological Reserve

Nelson did it for glory. Cornelius Vanderbilt did it for gold. Mark Twain called it 'an earthly paradise'. Now, the reason for ascending the San Juan River on Nicaragua's border with Costa Rica is because it is one of only two ways to enter what UCLA (University of Southern California at Los Angeles) biologists called 'the gem of Central American nature reserves'.

The Indio-Maiz Biological Reserve is the biggest area of contiguous rainforest outside the Amazon. Much of it is still not fully explored, but from the Caribbean side it is permitted to use the Indio River (via the San Juan) to get deep inside the 2,590-sq-km (1,000-sq-mi) reserve, most of which is prohibited except to scientists. The only other access point is from the west, via the Bartola River near the historic settlement of El Castillo. This route also connects to the San Juan River, but is used by many more people for frequent, shorter, token visits just inside the reserve.

Visitors must have a guide, and the guide must be a Rama Indian. In a supreme irony of modern 'conservation', the Rama people are no longer allowed to live along the Indio River as they have done for centuries, but visitors can use their former homes to camp within the reserve for a few nights. That aside, their expert knowledge brings the richness of the jungle forest to vivid life. There are deer, sloths, giant anteaters, boars, pacas, pumas, howler and spider monkeys, manatees, freshwater sharks (the world's only species), turtles, crocodiles, caimans, iguanas, yellow-and-black poison dart frogs, reptiles of every hue, toucans, hummingbirds, parrots, and whole rainbows of butterflies, orchids and other tropical flowers – very probably, all of them before lunch. The Indio-Maiz Biological Reserve is where you go to stock the ark; and Mark Twain was right.

**HOW TO GET THERE:**
By road or plane to San Carlos at the foot of Lake Nicaragua on the west side; or by boat or plane (airstrip) to San Juan del Norte on the Caribbean. If necessary, the trip can be organized in advance from Managua.
**WHEN TO GO:**
Any time
**DON'T MISS:**
Staying at least one night within the reserve. It's the only way to get a real impression of the species' diversity and behaviour – even though night-time jungle noises can be spine-chilling. The reward for sleeplessness is the magic of dawn and the reawakening world – and the prospect of seeing twice as many animals and birds as on a short, daytime visit.
**YOU SHOULD KNOW:**
Incredibly, this is not a region for mosquitoes (perhaps because of all the frogs). Be afraid of the caimans and some of the snakes, but not of being bitten by something you can't see.

# La Flor Wildlife Refuge

**HOW TO GET THERE:**
By 'bus' (four-wheel drive) with a guide from San Juan del Sur, 18km (11 mi) away.
**WHEN TO GO:**
The season runs from July to January, peaking in October and November – but there are turtle landings throughout the year.
**DON'T MISS:**
The chance to camp on or near La Flor beach (if possible around the time of a full moon). It takes at least 24 hours to see how the ocean, beach and forest interact on behalf of the turtles, their eggs, and their predators, with some degree of success for them all.
**YOU SHOULD KNOW:**
The hatchlings emerge simultaneously, millions at a time, after about 50 days and there are usually seven or eight major *arribadas* each season. La Flor is open day and night, subject to an entrance fee and camping fees. No facilities are available.

One of Nicaragua's most beautiful beaches lies on the Pacific coast just north of the border with Costa Rica. It looks like a scene from an Elvis movie: the deep crescent of pure white sand is backed by swaying palms, rising cliffs and tropical dry forest, and buffered at each end by thick clumps of mangroves. The rather theatrical perfection is appropriate. This is La Flor, the annual site of a spectacular natural drama. Between July and January, hundreds of thousands of sea turtles haul themselves out of the ocean to nest and lay their eggs here.

How turtles recognize the beach where they were born is as much a mystery as how they synchronize their mass invasions, known as *arribadas* (arrivals). La Flor is one of only two beaches on Nicaragua's Pacific Coast they use; and although all kinds of turtle can be seen there, it is olive Ridley's turtles (known as *paslama* in Nicaragua) which appear night after night, sometimes in groups of 30,000–50,000. They've got to be quick. They have to struggle through the fine, soft sand, competing for the best spaces; laboriously clear a hollow in which to lay around 100 eggs; cover it so that the eggs can develop at the correct temperature; and escape back to sea before they are spotted by hovering predators. Predators are everywhere. La Flor exists primarily to protect the turtles, but its forests are big enough to house monkeys, iguanas and big bird colonies which treat the newly laid eggs – and subsequent hatchlings – as a convenient larder. Their only safety is in their colossal numbers.

Witnessing an *arribada* can be emotional. La Flor is close to Central America's well-trodden surfer and backpacker trails, but inside its boundaries visitors are hushed by its sudden, primal silence; then spellbound by the dawning significance of its almost nightly, natural spectacle.

# Penas Blancas Massif

The Penas Blancas (White Rocks) Massif in north central Nicaragua takes its name from the calcium streaking the rockface. The massif, part of the vast Bosawas Biosphere Reserve, is the highest part of the Isabella Mountains range spanning the Jinotega and Matagalpa districts, the watershed between the Bocay and Coco Rivers on one side, and the Tuma on the other. On a bigger scale, its position between the Pacific and the Caribbean magnifies the significance of its height: it is the key to weather patterns and the life-giving water balance of a much, much larger area. In the recent past, the massif's generous fertility encouraged the development of coffee and other farms on its lower slopes. The realization that stripping the mountains of its rainforest damaged its vital but fragile ecosystem caused a dramatic rethink. Now the lower slopes have been returned to nature, and the Penas Blancas Massif can be appreciated for its unique contribution to the region's biodiversity.

It is unique because the Massif is self-enclosed, and above 1,000 m (3,280 ft) where it has never been developed, its steep valleys and multiple peaks are a mist-filled realm of untouched cloud forest. Evergreen flora grow to giant size with trees reaching 50 m (164 ft). Black oak, granadillo and walnut trees shelter giant ferns, heleconias, orchids and bromeliads. Birds love it. Among the colourful parakeets, warblers, hummingbirds and tanagers the resplendent quetzal is the loveliest, and restricted to its mountain habitat. Waterfalls crash jawdropping distances from the massif's sheer rock walls, and the network of streams and creeks makes hiking wearily wet. There is no prolonged summer interval of hot days. The sun may shine, but the massif's microclimate maintains a year-round temperature 20–24°C (68–75°F) and a steady drip. Damp hikers will appreciate that this is why the scenery and wildlife are so spectacular.

**HOW TO GET THERE:**
By bus or car from Matagalpa to km 195 on the road to El Cua, then on foot or by 4x4 to Penas Blancas community.

**WHEN TO GO:**
Any time. (The prevailing, uniform weather pattern means take warm clothing.)

**DON'T MISS:**
La Pavona, one of the most beautiful waterfalls; *La Media Luna* – a difficult, unmarked hike through utterly compelling cloud forest landscapes; *El Horno* – an adventure hike with an expert guide, high into primary forest to a campsite from where, early in the morning, you can see quetzals flying out to breakfast.

**YOU SHOULD KNOW:**
The Penas Blancas Massif was revered by the Mayans as a sacred sanctuary. Water was the element foremost in their rituals. Each year, during Easter Week, the small population of Mayans still living in the massif cover themselves in white clay and bathe in the streams and rivers. A few people come from several other Central American countries, especially Guatemala, to share the ritual. So can you.

# Braulio Carrillo National Park

**HOW TO GET THERE:**
By car or bus (stops on request) along the Guapiles highway – park up in a hidden spot and hike. It's best to leave the car at a Ranger Station; hikers have been held up, robbed and carjacked on the deserted highway.

**WHEN TO GO:**
Any time. There is less rain in March and April.

**DON'T MISS:**
The Rainforest Aerial Tram through the canopy layers, or the zipline through the canopy itself.

**YOU SHOULD KNOW:**
The 'green miracle' of Braulio Carrillo National Park is that, so far, it has protected central Costa Rica's most important water catchment from the real threats of deforestation and settlement common elsewhere, despite the relatively new road running through it. It's a victory for Costa Rican common sense, only slightly marred by bandits' willingness to point guns at unvigilant visitors.

It takes 30 minutes to go from Costa Rica's capital, San Jose, to Braulio Carrillo National Park, and it's like time-travelling. Although Costa Rica was slow to recognize its own environmental wealth, it responded with enthusiasm to the challenge of preserving it. More of the country is protected as wilderness or an ecological buffer zone than – proportionately – anywhere else in the world. Braulio Carrillo National Park is one of Costa Rica's biggest and best, and it's right on the capital's doorstep.

It covers the western side of the volcanic Cordillera Central, from the edge of the coffee farms and cattle ranches on the highland plateau straight up the mountains to the chilly mists of cloud forest between extinct volcanoes; and then down the Caribbean slope to La Selva's great swathes of humid lowland jungle. Crossing it is a tough four- or five-day adventure with a guide (and permission). It's dangerous, too; from top to bottom 84 per cent of it is primary forest and jungle, and the wildlife includes some of the world's most lethal snakes, touch-poisonous amphibians and other colourful, murderously attractive threats. Fortunately, three Ranger stations on the park's edge provide easier access to short, marked trails. The Barva Station is the start of a climb to the

lake in the crater of the dormant Barva Volcano. The cloud forest here harbours local heroes like the strawberry poison arrow frog, the terrifying *fer-de-lance* snake, and the continent's biggest venomous snake, the bushmaster. Zurqui Station has two major trails taking in the rivers and waterfalls of different forest ecosystems full of howler and spider monkeys, deer, tapir, and the luminous, shimmering glory of quetzals, scarlet-rumpled tanagers, toucans and golden hummingbirds. The old-growth trees, butterflies and burgeoning wildlife have flourished here for thousands of years – untouched and virtually unseen until Braulio Carrillo was declared a national park. There's no easier place to sample such extraordinary diversity.

*Tourists take an aerial tram through rainforest canopy near Braulio Carrillo National Park.*

# Cordillera de Talamanca

Still largely unexplored, the Cordillera de Talamanca is the southern spine of Costa Rica, the continental divide between North and South America and the watershed between the Pacific and the Caribbean. The range soars upwards to Costa Rica's highest peak, Cerro Chirripo – 3,820 m (12,530 ft) – towering over a forbidding wilderness of plunging valleys, glacial lakes and some of the rarest terrain in the whole world: the high-altitude, neotropical ecosystem called *paramo*. It looks like science fiction: peat bogs and swampy grasslands peppered with enormous spiked plants and strange shrubs in profusion. The *paramo* is one of an astonishing number of habitats in the Cordillera, created by differences in altitude, weather patterns, soil and topography. Since every one of them is a mix of flora and fauna from north and south, Talamanca's wildlife is among the world's most abundant and diverse. The isolation of the lush forests of Talamanca's valleys harbours 600 kinds of bird, 500 species of trees and bushes, 150 kinds of orchids and around 265 amphibians and reptiles. Ocelots, tapirs, anteaters, pumas and jaguars are not rare here. People are.

The lower half of the Costa Rican section of the Talamanca range is even better. It's part of a Biosphere Reserve shared with Panama. Known to both as the Amistad National Park, it's the biggest wilderness in either country, and a concentration of colourful and numerous species as rich as anywhere on earth. The terrain is more difficult (even the Conquistadors gave up), but the rewards are phenomenal. Camping and hiking are allowed, but there are no facilities. It's worth the effort to stay a while; of the Cordillera's nine major ecosystems, three are found only on the Pacific side and four on the Caribbean. Between them, the Talamanca range is believed to be home to no less than four per cent of all the species on earth.

*Banana plantations in the Cordillera de Talamanca range*

**HOW TO GET THERE:**
On foot, from the Inter-American Highway. The easiest access is via Las Tablas, near the Las Cruces biological field station at San Vito de Coto Brus.

**WHEN TO GO:**
Any time. Seasons don't really exist in the Cordillera de Talamanca – but the west slope is a little drier from December to March.

**DON'T MISS:**
The surreal rarity of the *paramo* landscape: it's a once-in-a-lifetime chance and worth the necessary altitude acclimatization. Getting there and back provides another chance to spot the red-and-green magnificence of the quetzal among the great virgin forests of moss-covered oak and bromeliad-trailing cypress.

**YOU SHOULD KNOW:**
Among the geomorphic surprises of the Talamanca Range around Chirripo, one of the strangest is the discovery of several perfectly preserved glacial features.

# Rio Bongo Estuary

**HOW TO GET THERE:**
On foot, from Manzanillo in Puntarenas, or from Playa Coyote in Guanacaste; or by boat from the port of Puntarenas around the tip of the peninsular

**WHEN TO GO:**
November to April, for sunshine and the cooling Papagayo offshore breeze; or the beginning of the rainy season in May, for the revival of the lush green flora and the best multi-coloured sunsets. October is a washout.

**DON'T MISS:**
Following the Rio Bongo a little way upstream, past deep pools and small lagoons where countless birds nest in the thickets and somnolent crocodiles swarm on sandbanks.

**YOU SHOULD KNOW:**
The tourist industry has recently become aware of the Rio Bongo's ecological rarity and is proposing wildlife-spotting boat trips. Officially there are no regulations to restrict this because Rio Bongo is not a Reserve. Please remember that visitors enjoy it (and are welcome) by courtesy of its owner, and should respect his ambition to keep it unspoilt by over-intrusion.

The Pacific coast of Costa Rica's Nicoya Peninsular is an endlessly scenic series of curving white beaches punctuated by rocky headlands and mangrove-filled river estuaries. Nicoya's northern section is a mecca for surfing *cognoscenti*, intrepid backpackers and world-weary travellers who recognize that life seldom gets much better than this. The southern section is paradise itself – and the Rio Bongo estuary is its pristine heart. Reaching it involves a 7-km (4-mi) hike north from the village of Manzanillo. It's easy to be entranced by the thick forest crowding the edge of an enormous sweep of fine sand. Be wary. The beach becomes a long spit running parallel to the river. Where it emerges into the sea it's only waist deep, but ford it at your peril. The Rio Bongo is famous for its large colony of crocodiles, once compared in size to African Nile crocs. They flourish for some way up the river, scouting the thick mangroves and sandbanks of its meanders and oxbows; and occasionally startled swimmers find them in the open ocean, miles from the estuary.

Crocs aren't the only giants to survive from the age of dinosaurs. The Rio Bongo beach is one of the most important nesting sites for leatherback sea turtles in the eastern Pacific – and the 1.8–2.4 m (6–8 ft) *colossi* are very picky about their habitat. Happily, the whole beach is protected by a private landowner who refuses to allow any kind of development that might disturb them. His sensible rules include prohibiting camping, but permitting 'night hiking' so visitors can witness the leatherbacks' ancient ritual. Take the opportunity. The sight is as rare as finding a true, tropical beach wilderness – and between the swaying palms, the rhythmic pounding of the ocean, and the river's serene tranquillity, Rio Bongo genuinely reflects nature in harmony.

# Tortuguero National Park

The waterworld of Tortuguero National Park on northeast Costa Rica's Caribbean coast is an ecological adventure playground. It covers a huge region of lowland palm swamps, tropical wet rainforest and mangroves, criss-crossed with natural channels and connected lagoons as well as the freshwater creeks that feed the Tortuguero River itself. Boating on its lazy currents is the only way to get close to its many secrets and electrifying surprises – although the park includes some montane rainforest where volcanic hills climb to 100–300 m (328–985 ft). Hiking among its waterfalls and swimming in rock pools is a beautiful experience, but Tortuguero's magic is in its water margins, where freshwater and saltwater mix and all four elements merge.

With such a wide variety of habitats and the comparative rarity of visitors (in a whole day gliding through the network of canals and rivers, it's possible never to come across another boat), the region is alive with movement. More than half of all Costa Rica's bird and reptile species live here. Monkeys, sloths, anteaters, lizards, caimans and crocodiles exist in the kind of profusion that makes sightings inevitable, even from a boat. Every corner is a nest, breeding ground, or habitat for something in the canopy, mangroves or dense jungle forest islands. Four kinds of marine turtles lay eggs on Tortuguero's sandbanks, including the biggest visiting population of green sea turtles anywhere on the Caribbean coast. Visitors can join 'night walks' to see them crowd ashore (but only the mandatory guide may carry a flashlight, to prevent disorienting the turtles).

The downside of Tortuguero's fertility and abundance is the threat from commercial interests like logging, which can only upset the ecological balance. In practice, that means the more people who come to admire its natural beauty, the more likely Tortuguero can be properly protected.

**HOW TO GET THERE:**
By boat from Moin, north of Limon, or from Puerto Viejo de Sarapiqui
**WHEN TO GO:**
February to April is the nesting season for giant leatherbacks; July to October for green sea turtles.
**DON'T MISS:**
The 2-km (1.2-mi) jungle trail running from the Park Ranger HQ known as *Cuatro Esquinas* near Tortuguero village; and remember the wonderland underwater – with Polaroid lenses it's easy to see the seven kinds of river turtles, manatees, river otters and 50 fish species (including the menacing alligator gar) weaving through the seagrasses below the boat
**YOU SHOULD KNOW:**
The long boat ride to Tortuguero from Puerto Viejo is worth the physical discomfort because it transits the stunningly beautiful Barra del Colorado Wildlife Refuge. It also passes from the Sarapiqui River to the San Juan River, which is technically inside Nicaragua. Be prepared for border checks, in and out.

*Trees overhang the waters in Tortuguero National Park.*

# Chiriqui Highlands

**HOW TO GET THERE:**
By plane to David, then car or bus to Boquete
**WHEN TO GO:**
Any time. Temperatures vary enormously according to altitude rather than season, and the park is a network of microclimates.
**DON'T MISS:**
Central America's finest white-water rafting on the Chiriqui River (the only way to access some of the most spectacular natural features). Listen out for the ethereal call of the black-faced solitaire in the forest canopy, and the ringing croak of the three-wattled bellbird in the shrubs.
**YOU SHOULD KNOW:**
Visitors to Chiriqui may encounter a large community of Ngobe-Bugle (aka Guaymi), Panama's largest indigenous tribe. They come to the highlands for the coffee-picking season, the centre of their social culture. Ngobe-Bugle women wear *naguas*, beautifully crafted dresses in vivid blues, greens and reds, and carry *chacaras*, woven bags decorated the same way. They are accomplished examples of folk art, directly inspired by the colour schemes of Chiriqui's forest birds.

The province of Chiriqui forms Panama's border with Costa Rica on the Pacific slope of the continental divide. Its coastal lowlands are a mix of dense jungles and lively surfing resorts, backed by miles of orderly farmland where the volcanic soil guarantees astonishing fertility. The region is famous for its coffee farms stretching high up into the Chiriqui Highlands, quilting the slopes of Panama's highest peak and only volcano, the dormant 3,478 m (11,410 ft) Baru Volcano. As the farms thin out, montane rainforest takes over, dotted with small villages perched on rocky crags in a landscape of waterfalls and tall trees. It's suspiciously European, and no surprise to discover that most of the villages were built by engineers who came to work on the Panama Canal. Higher still lies a wilderness of primary cloud forest, a cool, misty world filled with the clamour of birds of the brightest colours and fanciest names. Between the mountain villages of Boquete and Cerro Punto, the Quetzal Trail follows a high ridge around the Baru Volcano. Besides the legendary sacred bird of the Aztecs and Mayas, the oak, cedar and laurel trees and the ferns and mosses harbour the spectacled foliage-gleaner, the prong-billed barbet, the buffy tufted-cheek and a jeweller's display of hummingbirds. They share a landscape of rare beauty.

On Baru's Caribbean side the Chiriqui Highlands descend through changing flora and fauna until they merge with the slopes of the Panamanian extension of the Cordillera de Talamanca. This region falls within the Amistad Biosphere Reserve, Central America's biggest reserve, and a pure wilderness. Amistad is shared with Costa Rica, and its Panamanian section forms a biological corridor connected through the Chiriqui Highlands to the lowland jungles and islands of Bocas del Toro. That puts Chiriqui at the heart of one of the planet's boldest ecological endeavours.

*Daybreak over Baru Volcano in Chiriqui province*

# Isla Bastimentos

Of the 68 Bocas del Toro islands spread across 100 km (62 mi) of the Gulf of Chiriqui on Panama's Caribbean coast, only Isla Bastimentos anchors a National Marine Park. Amazingly, it flourishes in the middle of a growing tourist industry centred on the town of Bocas, visible (and sometimes audible) from Bastimentos itself. The 52 sq km (20 sq mi) island is one of Panama's biggest, and although it is a trackless jungle accessible only by boat, it is populated at either end. Only the central section belongs within the park, providing a land bridge between three enormous and mutually dependent marine tracts which are the highlight of any visit to Bocas del Toro. The real wonder is that the indigenous villages and tourist developments on the island see eco-conservation as serving their own interests: Bastimentos is an advanced model of how to combine leisure with ecotourism.

There's plenty to explore. The 16.6 sq km (6.4 sq mi) of interior land corridor is primary rainforest with a full complement of monkeys, sloths, turtles, frogs, lizards, caimans, armadillos, colourful birds, ferns, hardwood trees, bromeliads and orchids. To the south the forest floods to become Panama's largest red and white mangrove swamp, opening onto the shallows of Almirante Lagoon – a sub-marine meadow of waving seagrass dotted with mangrove islands, sandbars and coral reefs.

**HOW TO GET THERE:**
By boat from Bocas town on the tip of Colon Island
**WHEN TO GO:**
Any time, but the turtles come to nest between April and October.
**DON'T MISS:**
Playa Larga (Long Beach), worth braving rough sea and rocks to land on, and Red Frog Beach, named after the numerous bright-red poison dart frogs that swarm there and nowhere else. Red Frog beach is on the edge of the park, and threatened by development.
**YOU SHOULD KNOW:**
Isla Bastimentos, like Bocas del Toro in general, was settled by West Indians centuries ago. The village of Bastimentos used to be called Old Bank and people still speak *Gali-Gali*, a local Creole dialect combining Afro-Antillean English, Spanish and Ngobe-Bugle. At the other end of the island is the purely Ngobe-Bugle village of Quebrada Sal.

*Red Frog Beach*

To the north, the jungle canopy overhangs a coastline of rocky outcrops, sheer cliff faces and freshwater creeks interspersed with long stretches of white beach where four kinds of marine turtle come to nest and lay their eggs. The east end of the marine park takes in the beautiful, uninhabited Zapotilla Cays, part of the barrier reef around Bastimentos, with an underwater landscape of pinnacles, crags, rock chutes and tunnels that make spectacular diving and snorkelling. Afterwards, the cays make a great venue for playing Robinson Crusoe.

*A view looking west along the Rio Dulce from the bridge at the village of the same name.*

# Rio Dulce

**HOW TO GET THERE:**
By bus to the town of Mariscos on the south shore of Lake Izabal; or by boat to Livingston
**WHEN TO GO:**
Any time. The rainy season expands the wetland jungle delta where the Polochic River enters the lake, and the wildlife explodes all along the Rio Dulce.
**DON'T MISS:**
Turning off the outboard and paddling your own *cayuco* among the untouched and seldom-visited pristine jungles and crystal-clear freshwater rivers like Rio Obscuro and Rio Zarquito on the southwest bank of Lake Izabal. Return via the Biotopo de Chacon Machacas – the manatee sanctuary in the seagrass lagoons of the Golfete, a 5-km (3-mi) wide section of the Rio Dulce edged by a lattice of mangrove channels.

The eastern corner of Guatemala between Belize and Honduras is a self-contained watery wonderland called Rio Dulce. The Dulce River itself is short – 42 km (26 mi) – but it is the central feature of a much bigger region of small rivers and jungle islands, of protected swamps, mangroves, and primary tropical rainforest. The river is the outlet for Lake Izabal, Guatemala's biggest, which is fed in turn by the rivers running off the Sierra de las Minas into the Polochic Valley. The glorious logic of this topography and the climate is the ripeness and fertility of all the different kinds of wilderness the region supports. The feeling remains strong despite a thriving tourist industry based on several small towns and villages on its banks, and the major road bridge that crosses it. The human presence actually makes access to Rio Dulce's secrets easier: without it, the jungle would be forbidding and, frankly, scary. But even with its civilization, the giant-size vegetation feels all-consuming.

The Garifuna town of Livingston, on Amatique Bay at the mouth of the Rio Dulce is the only large community at one with its environment – so it's the place to find a guide as well as to have fun.

Since Livingston is accessible only by boat, Rio Dulce's fabulous natural riches are on the doorstep. There are hundreds of connecting channels overhung by trees trailing flowers and filled by chattering monkeys, long-beaked waterbirds and screaming parrots. There are 'hot' waterfalls created by underwater geysers, huge 'meadows' of packed lily pads in bloom, a 10 km (6 mi) white limestone gorge with 120-m (400-ft) high walls festooned with trailing greenery and orchids, and acres of reed beds. A motorized dugout (*cayuco*) opens up the most remote, toucan-friendly creeks and provides a water taxi to some of the amazing jungle trails.

**YOU SHOULD KNOW:**
When pirates roved the Spanish Main, Lake Izabal was a popular pirate haven. The little town of El Estor got its name from English pirates who used to sail up the Rio Dulce to replenish supplies at 'The Store' – *El Estor*. The Castillo, the fort of San Felipe de Lara upstream of the present-day road bridge, was built by the Spanish to repel the Englishmen's regular visits.

# Sierra de las Minas

Undisturbed since the Olmecs and Maya mined jade and obsidian – and gave the mountains their name – the Sierra de las Minas has been protected by the deterrence of its geography. Its shallow soil and steep slopes discouraged farming, and its topography caused local microclimates of opposite and irregular extremes. Scientists love its integrity: six ecosystems and three eco-regions operating in symbiotic harmony, but with different results from anywhere else with a similar range. This is because the Sierra is 3.2 km (2 mi) high, 48 km (30 mi) wide and runs east-west for about 160 km (100 mi) through Guatemala's northeast highlands. Its shape causes 'weather-shadows'. Visitors expect to find the florid glory of tropical exuberance at the lower levels of valleys and ravines, but not dry pine-oak forests below the biggest cloud forest in Central America, and still less the arid rarity of the Motagua valley thorn scrub forest right next to the region's most verdant wetlands around Lake Izabal.

The astonishing variety and quantity of the wildlife can only be appreciated by taking in the Sierra's entire altitudinal range. Between San Agustin Acasaguastlan and Chelasco on the Biosphere Reserve's northern edge there is a 32 km (20 mi) wilderness trail which more than justifies the strenuous effort required. From the bird-filled cloud forests of mossy hardwoods and bamboo stands the trail winds down through evergreen forest so perfect that the Sierra is referred to as 'one of the world's most important tropical gene banks for conifer endoplasm' (it means seed banks are a good thing). It's certainly beautiful, and the descent proves repeatedly that there's more wildlife and more varied fauna even than in the legendary Peten area to the north. It's an extra hike to visit the Motagua Valley – but Motagua has the added attraction of being *chaparral* country, perfect for a cowboy vacation.

**HOW TO GET THERE:**
By bus to Chilasco, Salama or San Agustin Acasaguastlan, in any of which permission and a guide may be sought from Defensores de la Naturaleza (the Guatemalan agency in charge).
**WHEN TO GO:**
Any time. The lowest rainfall is between January and March.
**DON'T MISS:**
Tasting the utter purity of the water – the dense forests of the Biosphere's northern section filter it repeatedly. The montane forest species include very rare survivals of yew and maple stands, where resplendent quetzals are quite usual. The Sierra de las Minas has a big population and it is also an important flyway for North American migrants and overwintering birds.
**YOU SHOULD KNOW:**
Despite considerable efforts since the 1950s to locate them, the Olmecs' sources of jade were considered lost forever – until in 1998 Hurricane Mitch flooded the Motagua River to a height 9.5 m (31 ft) above its flood level, and revealed alluvial deposits which were traced back into the mountains to a jadeite vein 2 m (6.5 ft) wide by 45 m (148 ft), alongside boulders of jade 'as big as a bus'.

# Western Highlands

Guatemala and Central America's highest peak is 4,220 m (13,845 ft) Tajamulco, one of the chain of 37 volcanoes whose steep cones dominate the Sierra Madre highlands of western Guatemala. Parallel to and north of the Sierra Madre is the Sierra de los Cuchumatanes, Central America's highest entirely non-volcanic mountains. Between the two ranges lies an upland plateau of ripe fertility, a temperate network of plunging valleys, waterfalls and craggy granite ridges. In springtime, sheer mountainsides of deep green explode with the colour of wild flowers; but at any time the region is the most spectacularly beautiful in all Guatemala. Its beauty is at odds with its history of violence – yet it remains culturally as well as geographically enclosed. Running down from the spine of the Cuchumatanes is the network of valleys and fast mountain rivers known as the Ixcan, centred on the Ixil Triangle. Conflict as much as location has always isolated the Ixil people, and their language is spoken nowhere else. Their wariness towards strangers originated before the Conquistadors – so it isn't personal – but it adds to visitors' feelings of slight alienation, despite the authentic welcome offered in every Ixil village.

Getting the most from visiting the Western Highlands means revising the usual definitions of nature in the wild. The Sierra Madre's three active volcanoes spit regular fire and fumes, yet their flanks are still terraced for crops wherever possible. In the rain-drenched highlands, forests at every elevation grow giants of their species, with dense under-brush to match. Only the summits are treeless *altiplano*, a mist-wreathed, chilly grassland broken by worn boulders. Yet both landscapes are productive in the hands of the indigenous farmers and shepherds. The Western Highlands and its people have evolved together and belong to each other. It is their symbiosis that makes the region so bewitching.

*Early morning fishing on Lake Atitlan*

# Pico Bonito

The resort beaches lining the Caribbean at La Ceiba are dominated by the looming bulk of Pico Bonito. The highest – 2,436 m (8,000 ft) – peak in the Nombre de Dios range, Pico Bonito rears up from sea level immediately behind the resort. Its jagged silhouette stretches away into the blue yonder, an invitation to an adventure that starts just a few minutes' drive away. The lure is the diversity of wildlife habitats in close proximity; the coastal jungle rises through strata of tropical wet, broadleaf and lowland dry forest, diversifying into cloud forest at around 1,200 m (4,000 ft) – a rare combination guaranteeing the best chance of seeing the widest variety of endemic species. These strata are subdivided by another influence – the mountain's unusually steep valley formations. Tumbling rivers and rushing streams create dozens of cascades and waterfalls on every level. Each harbours its own population of birds, butterflies and bigger animals, from monkeys to river otters. Their abundance is dependent on the harsh topography, which makes Pico Bonito very hard to access, but correspondingly rewarding.

The Biosphere Reserve to which Pico Bonito gives its name remains one of the least explored in Honduras. Some of the most

difficult terrain will stay that way, because access is forbidden to everyone other than professional climbing teams with permission to make ascents. It doesn't matter. Most of the best of the reserve is accessible near its perimeter and at intermediate height. There are eight-cable zipline tours beneath the forest canopy and white-water rafting on the Rio Bonito and the Rio Cangrejal (in the park's buffer zone). Cross the swaying suspension bridge to the visitor centre (one of only two entrances to the park) and a trail system unfolds taking visitors to beautiful waterfalls hung with orchids and guarded by scarlet macaws. The balance between visitor entertainment and nature conservation is sympathetic to both. Bravo.

*Pico Bonito and its surrounding lush coastal jungle*

# Rio Platano Biosphere Reserve

The 'Banana' River used to be the source of 'red gold' – the mahogany that furnished Europe. It is the major river of the Mosquito Coast and is still home to the remnants of three of Honduras' indigenous peoples: the Miskito, Pech and Garifuna. The biosphere reserve was created as much to provide a sanctuary for these cultures as to protect the fabulously complete coastal ecosystems in which, historically, they thrived. It is a humid, haunting wilderness of steaming mangroves, islets of jungle, coastal lagoons and creeks draped in moss-shrouded rainforest. It is the sudden splash and whirling water of the caiman in the shadows, and the squawking crash of flocks of parrots bursting from the canopy. Most of all, it is the silent wariness of the traveller in a dugout, watching, watching.

*Canoeing along the Rio Platano river.*

It is also extraordinarily beautiful and full of surprises. The best are to be found with the guidance of one of the villagers. Each guide is part of the region's living continuity, familiar with its wildlife and weather and alert to the drama hidden in the landscape. Near the Rio Platano's headwaters at Warsaka, and at Lancetillal nearby, there are 1,500-year-old petroglyphs incorporated into major ruins whose occupants used the rainforest as larder and pharmacy just as its current residents do. Descending the river by *cayuco* (motorized dugout) to Las Marias – a Miskito and Pech village on the edge of the vast mangrove forest – provides a glimpse of the subtle complexities controlling every kind of life in these isolated wetlands and shows how Miskito culture is integrated into the fragile eco-chain. There are quicker ways to sample Rio Platano's natural marvels, but the region's rarity is its human connection. Take the time and have the adventure. This is a long, long way from the city.

**HOW TO GET THERE:**
By plane to Palacios, then by boat (five hours) from Raista on the coast upriver to Las Marias. Using a tour company might be less complicated.

**WHEN TO GO:**
Any time

**DON'T MISS:**
Spending as much time as possible in a *pipante* (dugout) or on a raft on the Rio Platano. It's the best vantage point to see every kind of wildlife. The river also passes some of the best archaeological sites, such as the 1,000-year-old village of Los Metates, as well as natural features like El Subterraneo – a white-water gorge lined with flat slabs of rock and full of monkeys, macaws and toucans.

**YOU SHOULD KNOW:**
The Mosquito Coast gets its name from the Meskito people, not because it's a mosquito-infested swamp. Although, in fact, it is.

# Cerro Verde

**HOW TO GET THERE:**
By car or bus to the visitors' car park at the foot of Cerro Verde, where (compulsory) guides will be waiting to do your bidding.

**WHEN TO GO:**
Any time. The rainy season from May to November brings out the best of the flowers and greenery.

**DON'T MISS:**
The dramatic cliffs and lush forest around the blue jewel of Lake Coatepeque, on the flank of Santa Ana. Once the parent volcano, Coatepeque is a huge imploded caldera. Now its shore is peppered with the discreet, luxurious weekend homes of the country's elite – but you can swim there. You can even scuba dive 'in a volcano'.

*Izalco Volcano, Cerro Verde*

Cerro Verde is the centrepiece of three volcanoes set close together on the border between the departments of Sonsonate and Santa Ana. Together they are a powerful reminder of El Salvador's always precarious position along the Pacific Ring of Fire, and although Cerro Verde is extinct and Izalco 'quiescent', the third, Santa Ana, still spurts out sulphurous fumes around its boiling crater lake. All three can be climbed, but Cerro Verde offers a grandstand view of both its neighbours and Izalco, El Salvador's iconic volcano cone (it used to be on the country's banknotes) is in any case most dramatic seen from a distance. Santa Ana's crater is much more interesting. It has four, descending in size from the rim to what was recently a sulphurous lagoon, and is now a reawakened, boiling and bubbling cauldron. There's a wonderful trail from Cerro Verde all the way to the 2,365 m (7,760 ft) rim of Santa Ana, with progressively more staggering views as it rises through the forest and into the volcanic debris.

On Cerro Verde itself, the supernutrients in the volcanic soil

have created a cone wreathed in layers of dense secondary forest that have replaced the coffee farms for which it is still famous at its lower levels. Left to itself, the mountain is ablaze with wild flowers packing the lush vegetation below the towering trees. At about 2,000 m (6,560 ft), the tropical conditions draw the clouds into a misty veil of tepid drizzle, and Cerro Verde's rim and crater are covered in beautiful cloud forest. The Una Ventana a la Naturaleza Trail (a window on nature) leads you into the crater itself. Untouched for 300 years, the trees are giants, and filled with toucans, hummingbirds, parakeets, and rare species like the black chara which feeds other species during their mating season.

**YOU SHOULD KNOW:**
Izalco is the youngest volcano in El Salvador. For 200 years it was in a state of continuous eruption, and its flaring lava streams were visible well out into the Pacific Ocean. Sailors relied on it as 'the lighthouse of the Pacific'. Eventually a hotel was built on Cerro Verde so visitors could enjoy the sight in comfort. A few weeks before the hotel opened in 1967, Izalco's eruptions stopped completely and permanently. Since 2005, when it sprang back into life, Santa Ana (aka Ilamatepec) has been the subject of an 'active' warning.

# El Imposible National Park

Don't be put off by the name. A century ago, coffee was farmed on the steepest mountains. At one point high up, the trail was too narrow for two mules to squeeze past each other: it was 'impossible'. Now the plantations have been returned to secondary forest, in a bid to buffer a precious remnant of El Salvador's once huge primary forests and to form El Imposible National Park on the western edge of the Apaneca-Ilmatepec range. Protection came just in time for many species of bird, mammal, reptile, insect and even amphibians which survive only here. More crucially, by reversing the inroads made by farming and logging, El Imposible has been saved as the source of seven rivers which water a huge part of El Salvador. That's why visitor numbers are controlled and travellers must seek a permit from the government agency, Salvanatura – but the payoff is that the conservation process has restored the mountains to their pristine beauty.

There are only around 36 sq km (14 sq mi) of primary dry forest, but they range in altitude from 274–1,311 m (900–4,300 ft). The mountains and steep gullies are an outstanding sanctuary for over 500 bird species and 1,000 species of trees and plants. One 8-km (5-mi) circuit called Cerro El Leon begins in the florescent humidity of a deep gorge and leads through dense forest of constantly changing fauna and flora to astonishing panoramic views near the summit of Montana de los Aguilares, and returns by way of the Ixcanal and Guayapa river valleys. It's the best trail for birdwatching and for butterflies. Less strenuous is the short – 2.2 km (1.4 mi) – trail from the Mixtepe Visitor Centre at the park entrance, to Mirador El Mulo. It's a perfect introduction to the forest, and leads to a lookout point with dramatic views of the Guayapa valley.

**HOW TO GET THERE:**
By car, or by bus from Cara Sucia or the Ahuachapio River bridge
**WHEN TO GO:**
October to February, when it's dry. The rainy season makes the steep hills too muddy and difficult.
**DON'T MISS:**
The lovely Los Enganches trail to the beautiful forest swimming hole at the junction of the Guayapa and Venado Rivers. It continues upriver to Piedra Sellada (the Stamped Rock), a stone carved with Maya script, and one of several archaeological sites buried in the wilderness. The Hasta La Luna trek follows no trail but leads into El Imposible's heart, and to a stunning series of cascades where you can cool off.
**YOU SHOULD KNOW:**
The main entrance to El Imposible is on the park's southeast edge at San Benito, beyond the tiny village of San Miguelito. It's important to get a visitor's permit in advance either in San Salvador or by calling the park so they can arrange a guide who will collect the permit money on arrival. Guides are usually volunteers who work for a tip in US dollars.

# Los Cobanos

**HOW TO GET THERE:**
By bus, car or boat
**WHEN TO GO:**
The reef population changes with the rainy season between May and October, and the dry season. Avoid Christmas and Easter when Los Cobanos is packed.
**DON'T MISS:**
Taking a boat ride into deep water above the seaward fringes of the reef, where dolphins, sea turtles, rays and the larger game fish come to feed and cavort. Scuba divers can just fall off the boat for a closer inspection, and might see some of the many shipwrecks in the area.
**YOU SHOULD KNOW:**
Los Cobanos is more fragile than most coral reefs because, like many Pacific coast reefs, its growth is limited by blasts of cold, upwelling water which encourage algae. Its coral diversity is low, too, because it is far away from diversity-rich Pacific reefs which might colonize it. It is also threatened by bleaching when El Niño raises the water temperature, and by voracious crown-of-thorns starfish. Despite these drawbacks, it is a living kaleidoscope.

Punta Remedios is a pimple of a headland jutting into the Pacific Ocean from the flattened curve of El Salvador's western coastline. The sandy beaches sweeping for miles to the east break up into a series of volcanic rocky coves around the point itself and along its lee shore. Each cove anchors a spreading web of mangroves – and the combined change of coastal topography is just big enough to deflect the big Pacific currents. The effect is spectacularly dramatic: directly opposite the tip of the point, offshore eddies nourish the only coral reef formations on Central America's Pacific coast between Mexico and Costa Rica. It is a hotspot of marine biodiversity, and has recently come under eco-sensitive scrutiny as El Salvador's first Natural Marine Protected Area, known as Los Cobanos. It includes nearly 40 km (25 mi) of coastline from Playa Barra Salada to just short of the port of Acajutla, all the mangrove forests to their inland limit, and exactly 36 times as much ocean as land mass, with the coral reef at the area's heart.

The wildlife comes in quantity as well as quality. At low tide a thousand rock pools teem with small fish and shell fish, and it's easy to pick a path through the shallow water round mangroves. It's not just a children's paradise. Wading birds pace the flats while ocean predators patrol the skies above the reef looking for the nursery shoals. Big game fish come in raiding packs, a target for fishermen and sometimes each other. Migrating 15 m (50 ft) humpback whales pass close to the shore. In the crystal water, scuba divers and snorkellers get the best view of the reef flora and fauna, and of the giant snapper, barracuda, mahi-mahi, wahoo, yellow-fin tuna, rooster fish and turtles that abound. Los Cobanos has got the lot, and pelicans too.

# Montecristo-el Trifinio National Park

The preservation of the Cerro Montecristo cloud forest is a triumph of political optimism in a region once plagued by sectarian confrontation. The mountain is 'shared' by El Salvador, Guatemala and Honduras. Its 2,418-m (7,935-ft) summit marks the exact spot where the three countries meet, and is proudly known as El Trifinio. Here, visitors are monarchs of all they survey – explorers in a wild and beautiful world that repays the hardships of getting there with a superabundance of plant and animal species born of the region's isolation and blend of exotic microclimates. Montecristo has cloud forest on a gargantuan scale, and the biodiversity to match. Wreathed in mist, oak and laurel trees grow to 30 m (100 ft) with a vault-like canopy shading giant 8 m (26 ft) tree ferns among the mosses, lichens, trailing bromeliads and psychedelic orchids near the forest floor. Even at intermediate altitudes where cypress stands and pine-oak forest dominate (and sometimes alternate – the microclimates produce strange anomalies!) normal expectations are confounded by the richness and rarity of the wildlife – but Montecristo's cloud forest is an ark by comparison.

There are spider monkeys, two-fingered anteaters, pumas, agoutis, wild boar, opossums and coyotes. There are toucans, quetzals, woodpeckers, quail, eagles, nightingales, owls, brilliantly coloured hummingbirds and some 200 other bird species, 53 of which are endangered, and ten of which exist nowhere else. The higher you go, the better the birds.

The isolation which protects Montecristo means that visitors must be self-sufficient and prepared to camp (it's free) for at least one night. Head for Los Planes, a grassy clearing in a bowl at about 1,900 m (6,235 ft) up the mountain. Such trails as exist begin here – but the whole joy of Montecristo is being a tiny speck in a beautiful, mystical giant of a virgin wilderness.

**HOW TO GET THERE:**
By 4x4 taxi (expensive) or by bus from Metapan to the park turn-off and a rough, 11-km (7-mi) hike to Los Planes. Self-drive is an option, but the road is extremely difficult for an inexperienced (4x4) driver.

**WHEN TO GO:**
November to March/April. The summit area above Los Planes is closed at other times for the cloud forest fauna breeding season.

**DON'T MISS:**
The 7 km (4.3 mi) slow hike through the cloud forest from Los Planes to El Trifinio. The trail is whatever you want it to be, and it gets more and more spectacular as the cloud forest's peculiarities invade your senses.

**YOU SHOULD KNOW:**
Besides getting a visitor's permit in advance from the Ministerio de Medio Ambiente, you have to stop at the national park kiosk at La Pluma, a halt half way between Metapan and San Jose, and pay the entrance fee. Day trips to Montecristo are disappointing only because getting in and out leaves no time to do anything else. Take as much food and water as possible, and stay as long as it lasts.

# Sierra del Rosario

Lush tropical forests covered much of pre-Columbian Cuba, but centuries of growing sugar cane and raising cattle reduced them drastically and threatened the incredible biodiversity of the island. Now, as part of a determined reforestation programme, many areas of Cuba are national parks. West of Havana, the Sierra del Rosario is a lovely swathe of rolling, wooded mountains, tobacco plants and orchards to the north of the rocky outcrops of the Cordillera de Guaniguanico. In 1984, a large section of the eastern sierra was declared a UNESCO Biosphere Reserve and now valuable research on the sustainable management of the region's natural resources and the involvement of local people is combined with ecotourism.

It used to be an important coffee-growing area, and small-scale coffee production continues. The village of Las Terrazas, originally built for forestry and conservation workers but now also home to artisans and farmers, has a museum, cinema and research institute. A well-designed hotel complex offers horse riding, mountain-biking, fishing and boating as well as a number of delightful long and short guided walks into the lushly verdant evergreen and semi-deciduous forest. Many of the hundreds of species of plant and wildlife found here are unique to Cuba. South of Las Terrazas is Soroa. Originally a coffee plantation and now part of the Biosphere Reserve, the hotel here also organizes activities and hikes.

Walks in both locations have much to delight botanists and birdwatchers, historians and hedonists. Everywhere, huge bright butterflies and tiny hummingbirds flit around orchids and ferns, while colourful birds flash among exotic trees. Some trails into the forest visit the crumbling, atmospheric remains of 18th- and 19th-century coffee growers' mansions. The area is blessed with many clean, clear streams, and waterfalls and natural swimming pools feature on several of the routes.

*Sierra del Rosario Biosphere Reserve, Pinar del Rio*

# Sierra Maestra

The biggest mountain range in Cuba, the Sierra Maestra rises steeply from the southeast coast. Pico Turquino, at over 1,970 m (6,465 ft) the country's highest mountain, is named for its colour – its slopes are clad in misty, greenish-blue vegetation. Now a national park, the sierra has special historical and emotional significance for the Cubans as a place of refuge. From the Taino Indians' flight from the Spanish in the 16th century to the 20th century when the Castro brothers escaped into the lush greenery and mists to organize the struggle against Batista, these inaccessible wooded valleys and precipitous gorges have sheltered revolutionaries and rebels.

*The lush scenery in the Sierra Maestra Mountains*

The ascent of Pico Turquino is a long, challenging hike best undertaken as a two- or three-day guided trek. Walkers usually start the climb by heading east from Alto del Naranjo, northwest of the peak, and either return there or continue south, descending to the coast at Las Cuevas. This stretch of the southern coastline, with plunging mountains and quiet beaches, is spectacular. The peak can be scaled from here, although this ascent is very steep. Refuges are spaced out along the whole route and guides will organize overnight stops. The walk combines green valleys, open uplands affording panoramas of unfolding mountain ranges and the brilliant-blue Caribbean, and cool forests rich in flora and fauna (pygmy owls and hummingbirds are often spotted).

The Comandancia de La Plata, Castro's revolutionary base, is a shorter hike and can be completed in a day. After the steep road from Santo Domingo to Alto del Naranjo, this trail runs west along sheer ridges to where, in a deep gully, hidden under a canopy of trees, Fidel and Raul built their settlement. Here, visitors can inspect a scatter of huts, including dormitories and stores, Castro's operational headquarters and Che Guevara's hospital. A little museum displays photographs and memorabilia, such as Fidel's fountain pen and the radio equipment used by Che for his Radio Rebelde broadcasts to the nation.

**HOW TO GET THERE:**
Flight or long-distance bus to Bayamo, road to Santo Domingo and jeep taxi to Alto del Naranjo.

**WHEN TO GO:**
December to June

**DON'T MISS:**
Santo Domingo, in its deep, verdant valley, is a delightful village and a good base for visits to the Sierra Maestra, gentler rambles in the foothills and swimming in the river. What is now accommodation for walkers was once another camp for the revolutionaries. The life of the dignified rural community has changed little since then.

**YOU SHOULD KNOW:**
All walks must be guided. The trails are sometimes closed for reasons ranging from bad weather to official visits. Photography is not permitted in La Plata. El Cobre, a copper-mining town west of Santiago de Cuba, is home to the Virgin of Charity, the patron saint of Cuba, whose shrine was visited by Pope John Paul II. Among the many offerings is one from the mother of the Castro brothers and, although it is now locked away, John Steinbeck's 1954 Nobel Prize medal.

# Culebra National Wildlife Refuge

*The Flamenco Peninsula*

Culebra was declared a National Wildlife Refuge in 1909 but was, effectively, a firing range for the US Navy until 1975. Now administered by the US Fish and Wildlife Service, the refuge includes the deeply indented coastline, palm-fringed beaches, parts of the rocky, forested interior and all the satellite islets; all this, and its exceptional wildlife, attracts visitors to this small island with its easy-going brand of ecotourism.

Limited development means wonderfully clean seawater and Culebra's fringe and barrier reefs are some of the most vibrant in the Caribbean. They provide excellent feeding for seabirds and large fish and some very fine snorkelling – anything from angelfish to barracuda may be encountered in the brilliant, glassy waters.

Large coastal mangrove swamps are roosting sites for the endangered brown pelican and nurseries for fish and crustaceans, while the isolated beaches (most are accessible only by tracks) and untouched forest (the Mount Resaca area can be explored by trail) are perfect habitats for a multitude of nesting birds. Terns are particularly numerous on Culebra – a large colony of sooty terns colonizes the Flamenco Peninsula, while roseate, sandwich, bridled and royal terns are widespread. Other birds frequently seen include boobies, tropicbirds and ospreys.

The northern beaches and tiny Isla Culebrita are also nesting sites for endangered sea turtles. Loggerhead, hawksbill, green and leatherback turtles all bury their eggs in the soft sand; the sites are closed during the summer hatching season.

Culebra is only about 11 km (7 mi) long and there is little traffic on the few roads; mountain bikes are a good transport option. By day, the empty beaches of Cayo Luis Pena and Isla Culebrita can be reached by water taxi, although a kayak is a pleasing and ecologically sound way to visit these little desert islands.

**HOW TO GET THERE:**
Flights from San Juan and Fajardo airports; regular ferry service from Fajardo

**WHEN TO GO:**
November to July

**DON'T MISS:**
Summer visitors who volunteer early enough are recruited to assist wildlife refuge rangers count and protect sea turtle nests and hatchlings. Seeing the tiny turtles struggle out of the sand and scuttle to the water's edge is a thrilling and moving experience.

**YOU SHOULD KNOW:**
Keep to the trails as some parts of the island are littered with a legacy of the target practice years – unexploded bombs. The deep, sheltered bay of Ensenada Honda was used by pirates, including Captain Henry Morgan, as refuge from enemies and hurricanes.

# El Yunque

Sometimes the rich Taino, European and African heritage of Puerto Rico seems overshadowed by modern American life, but the island probably owes the survival of its rainforests and rich biodiversity to US colonial rule. Logging and rapid urban expansion resulted in serious deforestation and soil erosion, but in the 1920s extensive areas of conservation forest were set aside and now thousands of tropical plant, bird and animal species flourish in a variety of natural habitats.

Much of eastern Puerto Rico is covered by the forests, hills, streams and waterfalls of El Yunque (previously known as the Caribbean National Forest), the only tropical rainforest under US administration. Now a UNESCO Biosphere Reserve, it is carefully managed and has hiking trails and visitor and research centres. A range of forest types grows here, including most of Puerto Rico's ancient virgin forest – many of the reddish-barked Palo Colorado trees, with their trailing vines, are around 1,000 years old. Sierra palms, ferns and mosses thrive in wetter conditions and, on peaks and ridges, heavy rain and constant winds bend and stunt the cloud, or dwarf, forest. This sumptuously diverse landscape supports a wealth of wildlife. Although the endangered Puerto Rican parrot (which nests in the Palo Colorado trees) is rarely seen, more than 50 bird species, many unique, inhabit the reserve. Resident reptiles include the Puerto Rican boa.

Some of the shorter, paved trails to popular destinations (waterfalls, viewing towers and peaks) can get busy, but longer wilderness trails in the undeveloped south of the forest are often deserted. Serious walkers may leave the crowds behind and relish the cool, pristine beauty of this mountainous subtropical rainforest.

**HOW TO GET THERE:**
There is no public transport to El Yunque, but Highway 191 (off Highway 3 from San Juan) runs right into the forest.

**WHEN TO GO:**
April to June are quiet months in the forest; in the hot summers, islanders flock there to cool down; winter (high season) can be hectic.

**DON'T MISS:**
A night in the rainforest. Camping is permitted off-trail, but it is very basic. Several hotels around the forest perimeter provide an enticing combination of comfort with the unforgettable music of the creatures of dusk and darkness.

**YOU SHOULD KNOW:**
Do not attempt the longer trails without a good map and compass as it is easy to get lost in a rainforest. It rains, so take suitable clothing. The piercing two-note call of the *coqui* frog, the Puerto Rican mascot, is the sound of the forest. This tree frog deposits its eggs in crevices in trees and then guards them. The tadpoles develop inside the eggs and emerge as tiny froglets.

*Palms in the rainforest at El Yunque*

# Armando Bermudez National Park

The Dominican Republic is the eastern two thirds of the island of Hispaniola, with Haiti to its west. It has the second largest economy in the Caribbean, a large portion of which is tourism. Most visitors content themselves with the beautiful beaches and sparkling nightlife, but that means missing the spectacular mountainous interior.

The Armando Bermudez National Park, the first to be established here, is now one of several. Covering the north of the island's highest mountain range – the Cordillera Central -- and bordering another national park, this region boasts the four highest mountains in the Caribbean, with Pico Duarte rising to 3,087 m (10,130 ft).

The scenery is glorious; the forested slopes, including most of the surviving virgin rainforest, encompass the largest areas of the country's originally forested landscape. Rivers allow a lush subtropical mixture of West Indian cedar, orchids, palms, bamboo and tree ferns to thrive; at higher elevations, the trees are mainly Caribbean pines. This is twitcher paradise where Hispaniolan parrots, palmchats – the national bird – Hispaniolan trogons, loggerhead flycatchers and several endangered species such as the La Selle thrush can all be seen. Mammals – wild boar and the endangered Hispaniolan solenodons, a creature like a large shrew – are far less visible.

The park draws those who love the great outdoors. Campsites and trails bring climbers and hikers, but for others the goal is the summit of Pico Duarte. To attempt this, you must take a guide and a mule with you and camp *en route*. The trek is not for the faint-hearted although, after travelling through aromatic pine forests with the occasional meadow affording fabulous views, the tough push to the ancient, barren summit is worthwhile. Once there you feel that you are standing on top of the Caribbean, if not the world.

*Light streams through a cloud forest high in the mountains of Cordillera Central in Armando Bermudez National Park.*

# Eastern National Park

One of the largest marine parks in the Caribbean, the Eastern National Park is situated on the thickly wooded southeastern peninsula of the Dominican Republic, near Bayahibe. To the south is Calderas Bay, opposite which is Saona Island, and to the west the small, uninhabited Catalina Island. Formed in 1975, and a UNESCO World Heritage Site, the park is 808 sq km (312 sq mi), of which 388 sq km (150 sq mi) are marine.

Formed from limestone, the peninsula has shoreline cliffs, white sandy beaches, rocky spurs and mangroves and is riddled with tunnels and caves where pre-Columbian pictographs may be seen. The park is famously hot, with no freshwater streams or lakes; rainwater flows through the porous limestone and collects in sinkholes. The easiest cave to visit is Cueva del Puente, but it's a tough hike nevertheless. Whether approaching from land or sea, take water with you. Around 112 species of birds are to be found here, including the ashy-faced owl and the Hispaniolan lizard cuckoo, both of which are endemic.

However, the shoreline, sea and islands are the greatest attraction in the park. The coastal ecosystem provides habitats for hundreds of species of plants, birds, fish and marine mammals, such as the rhinoceros iguana, bottlenose dolphins, manatees, and several different species of sea turtle. Catalina Island has a wealth of glorious white sandy beaches with crystal-clear waters, so the snorkelling and diving is renowned. Camping permits can be arranged.

Saona Island has two small communities and excellent anchorage. There are no hotels, so visit for the day or anchor offshore and stay longer. It, too, is beautiful with many coconut palm-fringed beaches and fabulous swimming and diving. Many hours can be spent snorkelling over coral reefs and seagrass beds, viewing hundreds of fish, corals, sponges and crustaceans. You may see dolphins and, perhaps, whales in winter.

*A pristine beach on Saona Island*

**HOW TO GET THERE:**
Take your own boat or hire a boat and a guide from Bayahibe harbour and settle the price before you set off. There are entrances near Bayahibe and Boca de Yuma if you go by car. Don't forget to buy entrance tickets from the ranger stations, and hire a guide.

**WHEN TO GO:**
December to February and July to August.

**DON'T MISS:**
The natural swimming pool on Saona Island. Not more than 1 m (3.3 ft) in depth, you can see all kinds of starfish and other marine creatures in this lovely spot.

**YOU SHOULD KNOW:**
Saona Island's original name was Adamanay, but in 1494 Christopher Columbus changed it to Savonesa, which has become Saona over the course of time.

# Jaragua National Park

The largest protected area in the Caribbean, Jaragua National Park lies in the southwest of the Dominican Republic's Barahona Peninsula. Jaragua is unusual in that the third of it on land includes the southern slopes of Bahoruco Mountains, while the remainder consists of protected waters that include Beata and Alto Velo Islands, and a recently formed and still-growing reef platform called Los Frailes.

The park is a fascinating place to explore. The dry, thorny forest hosts a preponderance of cacti alongside endemic shrubs such as the medicinal canelilla, and guanito palms. The land is dotted with caves and many are decorated with petroglyphs and pictographs dating back to 2590 BC; they provide shelter for 11 species of bat. More than 50 endemic species live here: 36 in Hispaniola, 26 in Jaragua itself, four on Beata Island and three on Alto Velo Island. Among these are two iguanas and, at 16 mm (0.6 in) the world's tiniest reptile, the Jaragua Sphaero – a dwarf gecko.

The park is also home to 130 species of birds – some 60 per cent of the country's total – over half of which are seabirds. The country's largest population of pink flamingoes lives at Oviedo lagoon and vast colonies of white-crowned pigeons and the largest known colony of the plain pigeon, a West Indian endangered species, can be found here, too. On the islands and cays the sooty tern has formed its largest Caribbean colony.

Closer to the coast are mangroves. The beaches, many of which are empty and truly idyllic, are nesting sites for leatherback, hawksbill, loggerhead and green turtles which inhabit the extensive coral reefs and seagrass beds – as do queen conch, spiny lobsters and the endangered West Indian manatee. Dolphins are often seen playing in the waters near Alto Velo Island.

*The white sand beaches of Bahia de las Aguilas are fringed by spectacular coral reefs.*

# Lake Enriquillo

The largest lake in the entire Caribbean, Lake Enriquillo is unique. Situated some 44 m (144 ft) below sea level in the southwestern area of the island, it is just 20 km (12 mi) south of the border with Haiti. Part of the ancient sea channel that once divided Hispaniola, its fascinating ecosystem is due to its hypersalinity. Not only twice as salty as the sea, it is also sulphurous. The depth varies considerably as the water evaporates quickly, and storms are required to replenish its volume because the region receives little rainfall.

Lake Enriquillo was declared a National Park in 1995, although in 1974 Cabritos Island – one of three islands in the lake – became a National Park in its own right. The lake is named after Enriquillo, the Taino Indian chief who resisted the Spanish colonizers while hiding in this area; his statue can be seen at a museum in Santo Domingo.

These difficult conditions provide a habitat for a large number of birds and reptiles, including the American crocodile. The largest population in the world may be found here; each day they swim to the mouths of freshwater streams and spend their nights and lay their eggs on Cabritos Island – a flat, arid six-mile-long island where cacti grow in profusion. Two species of iguana – Ricord's and rhinoceros – abound. Some are so tame that they approach visitors in the hope of being fed.

This is also flamingo country and thousands of these lovely birds can be seen. Among the many other species are burrowing owls, West Indian nighthawks, Hispaniolan parrots and several types of heron – altogether some 97 species of land and aquatic birds make their home here. A harshly beautiful area, Lake Enriquillo is well worth a visit.

**HOW TO GET THERE:**
By car from Barahona to La Descubierta – the National Park Station is 2 km (1.2 mi) east of town. Here you can hire a boat and a guide to take you to Cabritos Island. You could also join a tour in Santo Domingo.

**WHEN TO GO:**
December to February and July to August.

**DON'T MISS:**
A strange illusion that can be experienced at Polo Magnetico. As you drive there from Cabral the car will feel heavy although the road is flat. At Polo Magnetico, where the road seems to rise, put the car into neutral and feel it pick up speed as it appears to go uphill.

**YOU SHOULD KNOW:**
On a hill close to the lake is the Las Caritas Indian Cave where you'll find Taino engravings of faces. It is thought that Enriquillo himself hid from the Spanish in this small cave. It has fabulous views of the lake and is extremely hot, so take plenty of water.

*Beyond the cacti – Lago Enriquillo*

*Cockpit Country – home to more than three quarters of Jamaica's birds*

# Cockpit Country

One of the joys of flying from Montego Bay are the views of an extraordinary and beautiful region of Jamaica. From this bird's-eye viewpoint, it looks like a vast inverted egg box: all verdant mounds and hollows, unscarred by roads or settlements. This is Jamaica's unique Cockpit Country. In 1665 the British army took Jamaica from its Spanish colonists, many of whom released their slaves and fled to Cuba. In western Jamaica, the slaves, or Maroons, hid in this wilderness. After many years of guerrilla warfare, they forced the British to cede land, autonomy and freedom to them in the treaty of 1738, and their descendents live there still.

Formed 12 million years ago, subsequent erosion of the limestone plateau produced a large area of regularly spaced, rounded conical hills and flat-bottomed pits, or sinks, probably caused by collapsing cave systems. During storms, soil is brought down from the hills into the valleys, some of which are cultivated and only accessible by trails from surrounding villages. Much of the region remains impenetrable virgin forest.

The region is extremely important for wildlife. More than three quarters of Jamaica's birds are found here, including both the black- and yellow-billed parrot. The island's largest predator, the Jamaican boa, makes its home here, too, as do the endemic blue swallowtail and Jamaican giant swallowtail butterflies and many kinds of bat that roost in the 300 or so caves. At least 101 unique species of plant can be found, some growing on a single hill. These include ferns, bromeliads and six varieties of orchid. You'll need to take a local guide when hiking here – it's easy to get lost and dangerous to go off trail, as you can fall through thin layers of limestone into a deep sinkhole below.

**HOW TO GET THERE:**
The Cockpits are easiest to explore from Accompong, just north of Maggotty. Guided hikes can be taken into the interior, or you can visit with a tour company.
**WHEN TO GO:**
December to March if you are going to camp. For short hikes, early morning is the best time as it is still cool.
**DON'T MISS:**
Wait-a-Bit, the visitor centre at the entrance to Cockpit Country, and the Peace Cave where Cudjoe, the Maroon's Ashanti leader, and the British signed the peace treaty.
**YOU SHOULD KNOW:**
In the 17th century the British chose the name Cockpit Country because the area reminded them of the cock-fighting pits that were prevalent across Jamaica at that time. Cock fighting is now illegal, although it still takes place occasionally.

# Central Rainforest Reserve

St Lucia is one of the Caribbean's Windward Islands and best known for its tourism. It is an extremely beautiful island with superb natural harbours and stunning beaches. Most visitors either visit on cruise ships or remain in their all-inclusive holiday resorts. In recent years, however, the Forestry Department has actively promoted the beauty of the mountainous interior. Clad in tropical rainforest, it contains many rivers that tumble down to the sea.

The Central Rainforest Reserve encompasses 77 sq km (30 sq mi) of the central mountain range. Mount Gimie, the highest peak in the region, rises to 958 m (3145 ft) and is a steep, tough hike of about seven hours. Many shorter hikes are available, however, such as the Enbas Saut Falls trail, which starts 9.6 km (6 mi) east of Soufrière on the island's southwestern coast.

An hour-long trip at the base of Mount Gimie takes you, via many wooden steps, to two waterfalls and natural pools at the head of the Troumassee River. Most hikes require a forestry guide, but this trail can be followed without one. There are splendid mahogany and mahoe trees to be seen and some huge ferns. The trail includes both true rainforest and cloud forest and it's good for spotting birds. The St Lucia black finch, the blue-hooded euphonia, the mountain whistler and even the St Lucian parrot, endemic to the island, may be sighted here.

Hike from coast to coast in a morning, following an old trail used by slaves and their masters during the 17th and 18th centuries. Arrange a birdwatching trip with the Forestry Department and you may see other rare, endemic birds such as the St Lucia peewee and the St Lucia oriole. Along the way you'll spot many beautiful tropical flowers, fruits, orchids and bromeliads.

**HOW TO GET THERE:**
From Soufrière or Vieux Fort
**WHEN TO GO:**
The dry season is from December to June, but don't forget there can be frequent sharp showers in the rainforest.
**DON'T MISS:**
The fabulous World Heritage Site twin peaks of Gros and Petit Piton – ancient forested volcanic cones that rise from the sea on the southwestern coast of the island.
**YOU SHOULD KNOW:**
It is an offence not to have a permit when entering the rainforest. These are available at every trailhead. At about one-and-a-half times the size of the Isle of Wight, St Lucia was named after Saint Lucy of Syracuse by the island's first colonizers, the French.

*Tropical rainforest in the interior of St Lucia*

# Caravelle Peninsula

Martinique, an island lying between Dominica and St Lucia, is an overseas *département* of France and its general standard of living is higher than that of most Caribbean islands. The south, with its fine, white sand beaches, is its most popular region, while the north, dominated by mountains and extinct volcanoes, is carpeted with lush rainforest.

The Caravelle Peninsula is a nature reserve that juts out into the Atlantic on the northeastern side of the island and is an excellent place in which to hike. The peninsula is quite different from the rest of Martinique, being arid with varied landscapes and offering stunning views of the rocky coastline. It is also beautiful.

Start your trip at the 17th-century Château Dubuc, a ruined plantation with wonderful vistas across Treasury Bay. From here hike one of the two paths that lead through the reserve, or go off-piste. The longer trail is 12 km (7.5 mi) and takes some three-and-a-half hours to traverse. It gives the hiker an opportunity to see the different ecosystems of the Caravelle, as well as many types of flora and fauna – some 80 species of sea and land birds, including rare and endangered species, frequent the area.

The trail, shaded by trees such as red gum, passes through

*A view of the Caravelle Peninsula looking towards the mainland.*

mangrove swamps. Wooden boards provide safe passage across the wettest areas, where thousands of small crabs can be seen clinging and scuttling about the aerial roots. Subsequently it becomes a beautiful coastal path, cutting across the tip of the peninsula and affording splendid views of Treasury Bay and out to the open sea, which crashes and foams against the rocky cliffs below. Here the trail has no shade – a hat, sunscreen and plenty of water are essential.

# Morne Trois Pitons National Park

Rugged little Dominica lacks beaches and has avoided mass tourism, but its waters are perfect for diving and whale-watching, its mountainous, forested interior rewarding for birdwatchers and walkers. Much of this 'nature island' is protected and the Morne Trois Pitons National Park is also a UNESCO World Heritage Site because of its rare combination of volcanoes, fumaroles and hot springs with pristine rainforest and a remarkable biodiversity.

Much of the park is accessible via a network of walking trails. Some very popular short walks, such as the Trafalgar Falls and Emerald Pool Trails, pass through luxuriant rainforest where ancient, towering trees with massive, buttressed trunks are festooned in creepers and bright with flowers, to reach cool lakes, plunge pools and waterfalls. Longer trails lead to high, secluded lakes and volcanic peaks – the easiest to climb is the Morne Anglais, in the south of the park. From high ridges where trees are dwarfed by wind and rain, there are views over remote waterfalls and valleys to the circling sea.

The most demanding and exciting hike is to the Boiling Lake and the Valley of Desolation. A three-hour guided climb through rainforest brings the walker to a ridge above the lake, whose water is heated by geothermal activity. It is unwise to linger long here, for the ever-present dense clouds of steam and vapour over the lake are sulphurous. The invisible water can be heard churning as it simmers at just below boiling point. The floor of the Valley of Desolation steams, hisses and belches with numerous scalding geysers, bubbling mud pots, hot springs and steam vents in a blighted expanse of sulphur-stained rocks. On the return path, a dip in Titou Gorge can be very welcome.

*Trafalgar Falls*

**HOW TO GET THERE:**
Buses run from Roseau to most of the trailhead villages.
**WHEN TO GO:**
February to June
**DON'T MISS:**
The aerial tramway near Titou Gorge gives a unique view up to the rainforest canopy and down through clouds of birds and butterflies to the forest floor, where agoutis (rather like long-legged guinea pigs) may be spotted rummaging.
**YOU SHOULD KNOW:**
Guides are essential for longer walks – after rain, the going can be treacherous and mists descend very quickly; when the cruise ships are in, Trafalgar Falls is packed with day-trippers; Dominica is the only island where Caribs (the pre-Columbian residents) still live – their culture and skills survive and they are still expert canoe carvers and navigators.

# Tayrona National Park

Colombia has made huge strides in recent times to clean up its image as a dangerous, crime-infested country where powerful drug barons operated largely unchecked by the forces of law. Now it has become once again a relatively safe and desirable tourism destination. Nowhere is the transformation more dramatically apparent than in the Tayrona National Park in the remote far north of the country. What was until relatively recently a no-go zone for visitors where Marxist guerrillas battled with right-wing paramilitary groups for control of the cocaine business, has now reverted to a secluded paradise containing some of the Caribbean's most stunning unspoilt beaches and most pristine tropical forest.

Tayrona was designated a national park in 1964. Its 150 sq km (58 sq mi) are remarkable for their biological diversity. The park is flanked on its southern edge by the foothills of the world's highest coastal range, the Sierra Nevada de Santa Marta, which includes the country's tallest peak, at 5,775 m (18,950 ft). Tayrona is one of the few places on the planet where you can stand on a tropical beach and see snow-capped mountains. It is home to more than 200 species of bird, including the extraordinary royal flycatcher, and mammals such as howler monkeys, collared peccaries and the elusive jaguar (a nocturnal hunter which you are most unlikely to see).

Tayrona is situated 35 km (22 mi) east of the old coastal city of Santa Marta. There are no roads inside the park so you have to walk or hire a horse for the 45-minute trek through the jungle to the coast at Arrecifes, where a sequence of glorious beaches unfolds to the west.

*Arenilla Beach in Tayrona National Park*

# Canaima National Park

The name of this vast park, encompassing some 30,000 sq km (11,600 sq mi) of remote jungle in the southeast corner of Venezuela, may not be a familiar one but Canaima includes within its borders one of the planet's great natural wonders, the mighty Salto Ángel or Angel Falls. Only discovered by the outside world in 1937 after American bush pilot Jimmie Angel crash-landed his light plane on top of Auyantepui table mountain, Angel is the world's highest waterfall; at 980 m (3,215 ft) it is 16 times the height of Niagara Falls. The phenomenon is caused by the Churún River plunging dramatically off the edge of the Auyantepui plateau into the dense rainforest below. So high is the drop that before the water hits the pool at the base, much of it has turned to mist.

In spite of it being the country's number one tourist destination Angel Falls is not an easy place to reach, although you are unlikely to regret the effort involved. You can arrange to view the waterfall by flying over it in a small plane but it is far better to take your time with an overland trip. This typically takes three days and involves

**HOW TO GET THERE:**
Light plane from Ciudad Bolívar to Canaima, then motorized canoe up two rivers, and a final 1.5-hour trek through the jungle.
**WHEN TO GO:**
The rainy season (June to October) when Angel Falls is at its fullest and most spectacular (although visibility may be affected by cloud and mist cover at the top).
**DON'T MISS:**
The darkly brooding cliffs of Cañón del Diablo (Devil's Canyon) at the base of Angel Falls.
**YOU SHOULD KNOW:**
If you visit Angel Falls in the dry season not only will you see a diminished cascade but you may also have to help carry your boat overland at certain points because of low river levels.

flights, river travel and hiking. The sense of anticipation as you trek the final leg through the rainforest is palpable; you hear the dull roar of the huge cascade long before it comes into view. And spending a night in a simple camp at the base of the east-facing falls means that you see them in the magical light of sunrise.

Canaima offers much more than Angel Falls, though. The beautiful lagoon beside Canaima village, for example, is surrounded by half a dozen smaller waterfalls, including one that you can actually walk behind.

*Mist enshrouds Angel Falls – the world's highest waterfall.*

# Roraima

Until the last 100 years the large plateau forming the summit of Roraima in the southeast corner of Venezuela was largely cut off from the impact of humans. Known as a *tepui* (a local Indian word meaning 'house of the gods'), Roraima is one of over a hundred such plateaus scattered throughout the remote Gran Sabana region. The distinctive 'table-top' profiles of these sandstone mountains, with their flat summits and near-vertical sides rising up out of the surrounding rainforest, are the result of geological processes two billion years ago, making them among the most ancient formations on the planet. Roraima's impenetrable flanks have produced a unique ecosystem on the plateau: endemic species of plants, insects and small creatures found nowhere else on earth. The reports which the first Victorian explorers to reach the summit brought back fired the imagination of Sir Arthur Conan Doyle and inspired his famous adventure story *The Lost World*.

Roraima may not offer the dinosaurs conjured up by Conan Doyle, but the many endemic species of flora and fauna found nowhere else but here make the six-day trek up onto the 2,800-m (9,200-ft) plateau a thoroughly rewarding one for anyone possessing reasonable levels of fitness and stamina. The climb requires no technical skills but it is a long and demanding one. The pay-off is a genuinely other-worldly experience of a kind that is increasingly rare on this crowded planet. The mysterious atmosphere on the barren surface of the summit with its strange rock formations, glinting quartz crystals and bizarre plant life is only enhanced by the frequent mists that cover it. The microclimate on top means that visitors must travel prepared for wet and chilly conditions as well as the heat and humidity of the encircling savannah and rainforest.

*Sunset at Mount Roraima*

# Iwokrama Rainforest

As most of Guyana's population lives on the coastal belt you lose the crowds in no time at all when you head inland. Travelling some 160 km (100 mi) south of Georgetown, the capital, brings you to a very special place. Iwokrama is an area of unsullied tropical rainforest which owes its remarkable survival to a pioneering initiative of the Guyanese government in 1996 to establish an internationally funded project for the conservation and sustainable development of the rainforest. A key feature of the Iwokrama approach is the active involvement of local communities. The Makushi Indian people, whose traditional homeland this is, have been given support and training to develop new and non-destructive ways of earning their living, such as low-impact harvesting of timber and opportunities to work in ecotourism.

*A red and green macaw (Ara chloroptera) flies through the Iwokrama Rainforest.*

The Iwokrama reserve covers an area of 3,710 sq km (1,430 sq mi) and boasts a range of habitats in addition to rainforest, including lakes, river systems, savannah and, at its heart, a 1,000-m (3,280-ft) mountain range from which the area takes its name. Inviting as all this may sound to the intrepid traveller, the strict rules governing the management of the reserve mean that you are not allowed to explore the reserve on your own. Your base is the international field station beside the Essequibo River where you live alongside scientists conducting ongoing conservation and research into Iwokrama's extraordinary profusion of flora and fauna. Nearly 500 species of bird, 130 different mammals and over 400 types of fish (including South America's biggest) are found here and the field station offers lots of nature walks with expert local guides to help you spot the wildlife. With so many creatures hunting at night, nocturnal safaris are also not to be missed.

**HOW TO GET THERE:**
4x4 transport from Georgetown or a flight to Annai and 4x4 transfer to the field station
**WHEN TO GO:**
September to March
**DON'T MISS:**
In the southwest of the reserve there is a 150-m (500-ft) suspended walkway which takes you through the forest canopy, giving a unique view of the treetops and the forest floor 30 m (100 ft) below.
**YOU SHOULD KNOW:**
Although there can be absolutely no guarantees, Iwokrama gives you a better chance than most places of sighting South America's great cat, the shy and elusive jaguar.

*Cotopaxi and Chimborazo volcanoes preside majestically over Ecuador's central highlands.*

# Chimborazo

The snow-capped peak of Chimborazo presides majestically over the central highlands of Ecuador. At 6,310 m (20,700 ft) this extinct volcano is the country's highest mountain and sits at the southern end of what the 19th-century German explorer Alexander von Humboldt dubbed the 'Avenue of the Volcanoes'. The Andes at this point is formed of two parallel mountain chains, with Chimborazo part of the western range. Unlike its famous counterpart Cotopaxi in the eastern range, Chimborazo is no longer an active volcano and its landscape today is one of extinct craters, huge glaciers and ice fields. Cotopaxi may be the world's highest active volcano but Chimborazo has its own claim to fame: lying only a couple of degrees south of the equator, the planet's bulge makes it the world's tallest peak when measured from the earth's core.

Although it is technically not a difficult climb, basic mountaineering experience of snow and ice conditions is required for the ascent of Chimborazo; this normally takes three days with an organized expedition. Because there is a real risk of avalanches during the warm daylight hours, the final eight-hour summit climb is undertaken at night. If you are not in this league, however, it is still possible to appreciate the magnificent landscape with day-treks; for example, by climbing close to the snowline between the two refuges, an ascent of 200 m (655 ft). The highlands surrounding the mountain are protected as a forest reserve and hiking here will familiarize you with the unusual native vegetation and also give you the chance to see llamas and alpacas roaming freely.

**HOW TO GET THERE:**
There is a good road from the town of Riobamba, 30 km (19 mi) to the southeast. A bus will take you to the entrance of the reserve, or a taxi all the way to one of the trailheads.
**WHEN TO GO:**
June and July or December to early January
**DON'T MISS:**
The *quinoa* plant, sacred to the Incas, grows wild in the reserve.
**YOU SHOULD KNOW:**
Bear in mind that serious trekking at Chimborazo is at high altitude – over 3,500 m (11,500 ft) – so you should take care to acclimatize well beforehand.

# Galápagos Islands

So many stories and myths surround the Galápagos Islands that it is sometimes hard to believe that they exist at all but rather inhabit a parallel universe beloved of natural history film makers. Exist they most certainly do, however, in a remote location in the Pacific 1,000 km (620 mi) west of the Ecuador mainland. It was, of course, Charles Darwin who first brought the Galápagos to the world's attention when he visited the archipelago in 1835 and used his observations of the islands' wildlife to formulate his revolutionary theory of evolution. What made such an impression on Darwin was the extraordinarily rich ecosystem which had developed in an isolated location untroubled by man and other major predators.

This ecosystem may be rich but it is also incredibly fragile and struggling nowadays to deal with the pressures of the modern world, not least those resulting from mass tourism. The Galápagos Islands are high on the destination list of most serious nature lovers but be warned that visiting them does not come cheap; indeed the authorities now deliberately hike the prices in an effort to restrict the human flow. Although you can plot your own itinerary once there, you will definitely see more of the remarkable wildlife on an organized boat tour; a typical tour offers onboard accommodation as you cruise among the islands, and numerous onshore excursions. There are opportunities aplenty for observing the astonishing number of species that are unique to the Galápagos, including the world's most northerly penguins, frigate birds, blue-footed boobies, Darwin's celebrated finches, the ubiquitous sea lions, marine iguanas (the world's only seagoing lizards) and, most famously of all, the majestic giant tortoises. Nowhere else on earth can you get up as close and personal to wild creatures which seem so unfazed by your presence.

**HOW TO GET THERE:**
There are flights from the Ecuador mainland to Baltra and San Cristóbal. Public ferries connect the major islands if you are not on an organized boat tour.
**WHEN TO GO:**
Any time of year. You have a choice between warm and wet – and busier (January to June), and cool and dry (July to December).
**DON'T MISS:**
If your visit coincides with the mating season, you should see one of nature's more bizarre spectacles: the courting ritual of the male frigate bird which inflates a flap of scarlet skin on his chest to the size of a balloon.
**YOU SHOULD KNOW:**
UNESCO now has the Galápagos Islands on its Danger List. The pressures on its unique environment have now become so extreme that any responsible traveller should consider seriously the morality of a visit.

*A view of Pinnacle Rock on Bartolome Island*

# Machalilla National Park

On Ecuador's central Pacific coast Machalilla National Park was created in 1979 to preserve its most beautiful stretch of coastline and one of the few remaining expanses of tropical dry forest on the continent. The park covers an area of 600 sq km (230 sq mi), one third of which comprises ocean. Tranquil and isolated beaches are backed by coastal scrub and densely forested hills, while inland the terrain rises and the dry forest gives way to the lush vegetation of a cloud forest. A pass to visit Machalilla can be obtained from the park headquarters in the small coastal town of Puerto López and is valid for five days. There are few maps or waymarkers, however, so you will be dependent on the expertise of local guides. Mighty ceibo trees tower above you on the various hiking trails through the virgin forest as your guide points out exotic orchids and numerous endemic plant species, such as the ivory palm.

You will certainly hear if not see howler monkeys and, if you are lucky, spot anteaters and two rare species of deer, as well as over 350 types of bird. Agua Blanca is a small village in the park with noted archaeological remains from pre-Columbian times. A nearby sulphur pool offers an enticing and refreshing dip, in spite of its pungent odour. For a change of habitat, you can take a boat trip from Puerto López to Isla de la Plata, one of several offshore islands incorporated in the national park. The island provides important breeding grounds for frigate birds and boobies. Pelicans and albatrosses may also be seen and in the winter months the surrounding seas are host to one of nature's great spectacles as humpback whales arrive for the mating season.

# Yasuní National Park

The extensive area of Ecuador east of the Andes range is known, appropriately enough, as the Oriente. And in the far east of this region, brushing up against the border with Peru, lies Yasuní National Park. Covering nearly 10,000 sq km (3,860 sq mi), Yasuní is the largest mainland national park in the country and one of Ecuador's last true wildernesses. Most of the park consists of upland tropical forest, but there is a liberal sprinkling of lakes, rivers and other distinctive wetland environments, too, such as seasonally flooded forest and *igapó*, lowlands that are more or less permanently under water.

What makes Yasuní so special for biologists and nature lovers alike, is the fact that for reasons that are still not clear this area was spared the ravages of the last ice age; as a consequence it has retained a degree of biodiversity found in few other places on earth. Yasuní is home to more than 500 species of bird and nearly two thirds of the mammals found in Ecuador, including three of the continent's 'Big Five' – the tapir, jaguar and giant otter. A recent botanical study discovered 473 different tree species in a single hectare (2.5 acres) – thought to be a world record. The fecundity of this remarkable place has been recognized by UNESCO, which in 1989 declared it an international biosphere reserve.

It comes as no surprise that such a well-preserved natural environment should be a long way from civilization. It is not an easy place to get to and you certainly should not visit the park without a guide (it is a jungle out there, after all). Most people savour the delights of Yasuní on organized tours which are plentiful and relatively cheap; arrange one in advance when you are in Quito.

*A dusky titi monkey at Napo Wildlife Center, Yasuní*

**HOW TO GET THERE:**
The oil town of Coca, eight to 10 hours by bus from the capital, Quito, is the main jumping-off point for Yasuní. To reach the park from here involves a 90-minute drive followed by a two-hour river trip.

**WHEN TO GO:**
Any time of year (but note that May to July are the wettest months).

**DON'T MISS:**
The formidable harpy eagle, one of the world's largest birds of prey.

**YOU SHOULD KNOW:**
Lucrative oil deposits in Yasuní mean an uneasy co-existence prevails at present between the ecology lobby and the oil industry.

# Altiplano

*Altiplano* means 'high plain' in Spanish and the term is now used to denote a vast plateau in the central Andes that spreads into Bolivia, Argentina and northern Chile as well as southern Peru. The wide, empty grasslands of the Altiplano occur at altitudes of 3,500 m (11,480 ft) or more so it is essential to acclimatize yourself properly before visiting the region – a good reason, in addition to the environmental one, for travelling overland to get there rather than flying in. After Tibet, the Andean Altiplano is the most extensive area of high plateau on the planet; it really does feel like being on the roof of the world here. The rarefied air at this altitude is exceptionally clear, affording wonderful views of seemingly limitless horizons beneath stunning cobalt skies.

The most significant feature of the Altiplano is Lake Titicaca, at 3,811 m (12,500 ft) the world's highest navigable lake. Straddling the border with Bolivia the lake is also one of the largest, with a length of 170 km (106 mi) and an average width of 60 km (37 mi). A boat trip on the lake to explore some of the 70 or so islands is an unmissable experience, giving the visitor a chance to witness the fishing communities of the local Quechua Indians as they struggle to retain their distinctive culture against the onslaught of modern commerce and tourism. These communities are also to be found on Titicaca's remarkable floating islands. Resembling enormous rafts, these islands are built from the buoyant *totora* reeds which grow in abundance around the lake and which are also used in the construction of the traditional fishing boats.

**DON'T MISS:**
The *chullpas* at Sillustani and Cutimbo. These extraordinary cylindrical burial towers dominate the landscape in the flat plains to the west of Titicaca and are reminders of an ancient pre-Inca culture that once flourished in the region.

**YOU SHOULD KNOW:**
The Incas believed that Lake Titicaca was the birthplace of the sun and that the first Inca, Manco Capac, rose out of its waters.

*A church and snow-topped mountain on the Altiplano*

# Chachapoyas

If you harbour Indiana Jones-style fantasies of coming across mysterious archaeological remains as you hack your way through dense jungle, then a trip to the Chachapoyas region in Peru's Northern Highlands is a must. There may be established trails now which spare you the hacking but this is still a remote and undeveloped area which does not reveal its surprises easily. The virgin cloud forests surrounding the little market town of Chachapoyas are littered with archaeological sites testifying to an enigmatic ancient culture which at one time rivalled the Incas. Chachapoyas, indeed, was the Incas' name for this culture and may be derived from Quechua words meaning 'people of the clouds'.

The Chachapoyas were a fierce warrior people who liked to show off their trophies of conquest and also practised human sacrifice. Buses and shared taxis run along unsealed roads in some valleys but the only way to reach most of the ruins is on foot or horseback. Many of the remains have been reclaimed by the jungle and are hard to spot so, even if you decide to strike out on your own, you would be well advised to hire a local guide for any serious exploration. The most spectacular ancient site (and a relatively accessible one) is the mighty stone citadel of Kuélap, perched breathtakingly on a mountain-top surrounded by thick forest. Location and vistas rival Machu Picchu, without the crowds.

Only disclosed to the outside world a few years ago, the Gocta Falls deep in the jungle north of Chachapoyas are one of the world's tallest waterfalls, at 771 m (2,530 ft). It's a tough five-hour trek but worth it if you want to see the falls before the inevitable happens and they are opened up to organized tourism.

*Laguna de los Condores in the Chachapoyas region*

**HOW TO GET THERE:**
An 11-hour bus ride from Chiclayo to Chachapoyas. Once there, shared taxis (*colectivos*) are a cheap and efficient way of getting around.
**WHEN TO GO:**
May to September
**DON'T MISS:**
You'll think you've found Shangri La when you first set eyes on the Belén valley west of Chachapoyas, with its river lazily meandering through a fabulously green valley floor and ringed about by mist-covered hills.
**YOU SHOULD KNOW:**
The Gocta Falls remained unknown for so long because the local people feared the curse of a beautiful resident mermaid if they disclosed its whereabouts.

133

# Lomas de Lachay National Reserve

A little over 100 km (62 mi) north of Lima, the bleakness of the Sechura desert which fringes the coast all the way to the border with Ecuador is unexpectedly punctured by the Lomas de Lachay, a spur running down from the Andes. The exposure of these foothills (*lomas* means 'mounds' in Spanish) to the ocean currents created by Pacific trade winds has created a microclimate in sharp contrast to the aridity of the surrounding coastal plain. The rolling mists that blow in off the sea in the winter months produce condensation in the hills which triggers an explosion of growth and life. No fewer than 74 plant species have been recorded in this relatively confined area, one third of which are now on the critically endangered list. Among the 55 types of bird found here are several species of the delicate hummingbird. Mammals to look out for include the *zorro* (red fox), Andean skunk, and grey deer which have been successfully re-introduced in recent years.

The Peruvian government was quick to recognize the significance of this unusual ecosystem and an area of 51 sq km (20 sq mi) is now protected as a *Reserva Nacional*. There may be few other facilities in the reserve but it does offer good waymarked trails and a number of camping areas. Among the profusion of flora and fauna there are also strange rock formations, the result of forces eroding the local granite; some have been given fanciful names, such as *Cerro la Virgen*, said to resemble a praying Virgin Mary. Although these hills are now uninhabited, rock paintings provide evidence that they were once the home of ancient tribes.

# Manu River

Peru takes its responsibility to protect its wilderness areas rather more seriously than its neighbour Brazil, and nowhere is this better demonstrated than in the Manu area deep in the southern Amazon basin. Here the entire watershed of the Manu River is contained within the Manu National Park, the country's largest. Rising on the eastern slopes of the Andes, the river makes its sluggish way south to Boca Manu where it joins the Madre de Dios, which in turn flows eventually (yes, you've guessed) into the mighty Amazon. As with most of the Amazon jungle the river provides the only means of getting around. It takes some six hours to travel upstream by boat from the park entrance to the lake of Cocha Salvador, where one of the park's two lodges is situated.

Manu National Park is half the size of Switzerland but a mere one fifth is open to visitors (the rest is accessible only to indigenous tribes and authorized scientists), so even spending a week here means you are only ever going to scratch its surface. But what a surface! Manu is right up there as one of the most biodiverse spots on the planet; not for nothing did UNESCO declare it a Biosphere Reserve in 1977 (and a World Heritage Site a decade later). The park's boundaries encompass altitudes ranging from 365 m (1,200 ft) to 4,000 m (13,120 ft), and the resulting variety of environments, from lowland jungle to mountain cloud forests, is home to a staggering array of vegetation and wildlife. The numbers are almost unbelievable – there are 13 types of monkey and 1,200 butterfly species alone – but it does mean that, with the help of an experienced guide, you should be richly rewarded with sightings.

*The Manu River*

**HOW TO GET THERE:**
Make this the adventure it deserves to be and travel overland from Cuzco. It's a 24-hour boneshaking drive to Atalaya or Shintuya where you board a boat for the day's river journey to the Manu park entrance.

**WHEN TO GO:**
May to October, when it is hot and humid but the tropical downpours are fewer.

**DON'T MISS:**
The giant catahua tree in the rainforest, used by the native tribes to make their dugout canoes.

**YOU SHOULD KNOW:**
It is illegal to enter the park without a guide. Visitor numbers are carefully controlled by the authorities so it is essential to book your tour well in advance (in Cuzco or Lima).

# Beni Biosphere Reserve

**HOW TO GET THERE:**
It is a 24-hour journey by bus from the capital, La Paz, but as this includes a section through the mountains which has been designated the world's most dangerous road, this may be one occasion when it makes sense to overcome any environmental qualms and take a flight instead to San Borja or Trinidad.
**WHEN TO GO:**
May to October (but note that even though the climate is tropical the area is subject to the occasional *surazo* – a cold wind blowing up from the Argentine pampas – so some warm clothing is advisable).
**DON'T MISS:**
If you are visiting at the end of July the three-day village fiesta at nearby San Ignacio de Moxos is one of the most colourful and exciting in the country.
**YOU SHOULD KNOW:**
In recent years the Chimane homelands and the fringes of the Beni Reserve have come under increasing threat from commercial logging interests.

The enormous Amazon Basin in the northeast of Bolivia still contains great swathes of pristine tropical forest. One of the best is the Biosphere Reserve of Beni which lies in the Llanos de Moxos region west of Trinidad. The reserve protects 1,350 sq km (520 sq mi) of mixed savannah and rainforest and, as its label suggests, is rich in flora and fauna. Around 500 bird species have been recorded here and 100 different types of mammal, including big favourites like the anteater, peccary, jaguar, river otter and spider monkey (although as usual you can count yourself fortunate if you see any of the stars as most are shy and elusive, often hunting or foraging at night). A large adjacent area of forest has been set aside for the exclusive use of the local Chimane people.

The only visitor facilities in the reserve are at El Porvenir on its southern edge, close to the main road between La Paz and Trinidad. This is savannah and the forest proper is some way away but various tours are offered from the visitor centre, a former ranch which offers basic accommodation. You can either take day-long guided hikes out into the jungle or tours on horseback around the more open areas. Viewing towers give you a different perspective on the wildlife. A popular excursion (although that is a relative term in this remote spot) is the river trip by canoe to the Laguna Normandia, a lake filled with rare black caimans. These impressive amphibians may look entirely at home in this lovely setting but in fact they are the descendants of creatures rescued from a failed leather business in the city.

# Laguna Colorada

**HOW TO GET THERE:**
This is a sparsely populated area with few facilities so you should not consider visiting it other than on an organized tour. Three- or four-day tours by 4x4 can be arranged in the nearby towns of Uyuni and Tupiza.
**WHEN TO GO:**
July to October (but remember that the high altitude means that it can be bitterly cold, with temperatures at night falling well below freezing).
**DON'T MISS:**
If you can brave the cold, the night skies of the Altiplano are some of the best you will ever see.
**YOU SHOULD KNOW:**
Flamingoes have a remarkably sophisticated filtering system in their large bills for extracting nutrients from the lake's saline waters.

High up on the *puna* grasslands of Bolivia's southern Altiplano sits a very unusual lake. The name, Laguna Colorada or 'Coloured Lake', provides a clue. Forget the palette of blues, greys and browns you would normally associate with a lake; this one has a striking reddish hue, caused by the algae that flourish in these mineral-rich waters. If you walk around the shores of the lake you can see evidence of the minerals themselves in deposits of white sodium and magnesium. Although the lake covers an area of 60 sq km (23 sq mi), its average depth is a mere 0.8 m (2.6 ft), making it a haven for waders and other waterfowl. Many different species of duck and geese flourish in these brackish waters but the undoubted stars of the Laguna Colorada show, and what most people come here to see, are the flamingoes. All three of the continent's native species are to be seen here, including the world's largest population of the smaller James

flamingo. The stupendous array of colours in this harsh, other-worldly landscape – the lake's waters, the greens of the *puna* scrub, the delicate pinks of the flamingoes, the snow-capped peaks on the horizon, and all beneath a brilliant blue sky – takes your breath away; literally so, since the altitude is well over 4,000 m (13,120 ft).

The Laguna Colorada is in the north of the large Eduardo Avaroa Wildlife Reserve which extends over 100 km (62 mi) down to the borders with Chile and Argentina. Herds of wild llama and vicuña roam the wide open plains and the reserve contains a number of unusual features, including other coloured lakes, a volcano (which can be climbed) and geothermal areas with hot springs, bubbling mud pools and steaming fumaroles.

*A small herd of llamas walks along the shoreline of Laguna Colorado.*

# Salar de Uyuni

You may want to rethink the phrase 'flat as a pancake' once you have gazed on the vast expanse of the Salar de Uyuni in southwestern Bolivia. This extraordinary landscape is like no other; it is a desert, yes, but instead of the more familiar golden hues of sand your eyes are assaulted by a dazzling whiteness. Uyuni is a salt pan, the world's largest, covering more than 12,000 sq km (4,630 sq mi). The Altiplano (high plain) here has no outlet to the sea so mineral-rich waters off the surrounding mountains once collected at the lowest point; high salinity levels left salt deposits which formed a giant saltwater lake. A permanent cover of water has long since evaporated thanks to the fierce Andean sun but beneath the thick surface crust of salt the ground remains largely saturated.

There is an awful lot of salt around and, not surprisingly, there is an industry devoted to its extraction and processing. It is a tough way to earn a living and many locals have realized that a more lucrative avenue is to sell curios and artefacts made from the white stuff to the growing tourist market. Most people visiting the Salar take an organized 4x4 tour which generally involves one night on the salt flats in fairly basic accommodation. Longer tours also take in the Eduardo Avaroa Wildlife Reserve to the south. The desert is entirely flat and featureless apart from a few 'islands', such as Isla Incahuasi with its strange, cactus-covered mounds.

If you are fortunate enough to see the salt flat just after rainfall, you can enjoy the reflections of the sky and clouds in the surface water – an astonishing optical effect where the horizon seems to disappear altogether.

*A fantastic view across the salt lake – Salar de Uyuni*

# Chaco Forest

Paraguay lags behind most other South American countries in the development of tourism, largely because of the long-lasting and repressive Stroessner regime which only came to an end in 1989. What this small, land-locked nation lacks in the way of facilities for the traveller, however, is more than compensated by the integrity and lack of degradation of much of its natural landscapes. Occupying 60 per cent of the country west of the Paraguay River, the Chaco is one of the continent's great remaining wildernesses and its second-largest ecosystem after the Amazon.

*The stunning flower of a midnight queen (*Harrisia bonplandii*)*

With both tropical and subtropical climates, the Chaco encompasses a range of environments; wide plains and seasonally flooded savannahs characterize the lowlands which provide major feeding grounds for waterbirds. The real adventure, however, begins in the High Chaco to the north where the huge dry forest of El Gran Chaco extends over the borders into Bolivia, Brazil and Argentina, covering an area of more than 1,000,000 sq km (386,100 sq mi). It is a harsh, unforgiving landscape of prickly scrub and stunted trees where searing temperatures and fiercely hot winds hold sway. But, unpromising as it sounds, it is also one of the best places to seek out the continent's larger mammals. Both great cats – the puma and the jaguar – live in the Gran Chaco, as well as peccaries, tapirs, anteaters, giant armadillos and the guanaco, a member of the camelid family that includes the llama and alpaca. The best chance of spotting animals is on a night walk. Patience and a torch are the most useful aids, especially at a waterhole or salt lick. Look out, too, for the unique night monkey – the only nocturnal monkey in the Americas.

**HOW TO GET THERE:**
There is only one highway through the Chaco. A bus from Asunción, the Paraguayan capital, takes 16 hours to get into the heart of the Gran Chaco.
**WHEN TO GO:**
May to September
**DON'T MISS:**
You are also likely to spot the rhea, the giant flightless bird that is South America's equivalent of the ostrich and emu.
**YOU SHOULD KNOW:**
If you make your own arrangements to tour the Chaco you will have to hire a 4x4 and travel with plenty of fuel, food and water as there are no supplies available locally.

**139**

*An aerial view of the Anavilhanas Archipelago*

# Anavilhanas Archipelago

The Rio Negro or Black River in western Brazil is one of the major tributaries of the Amazon. Rising in the mountains on the Venezuelan border it joins with the Rio Solimões at Manaus to form the Amazon proper. A day's boat journey upstream from Manaus brings you to the small jungle town of Novo Aírão, gateway to the world's largest group of freshwater islands – the Anavilhanas Archipelago. Over time geological barriers downstream caused the river to flow in narrower channels and the resulting water pressure backed up to create a huge lake-like area up to 20 km (12.5 mi) wide, which is studded by more than 400 densely forested islands – the consequences of sedimentary deposits. Much of the forest here is seasonally flooded, known in Portuguese as *igapó*; during the wet season, indeed, many of the islands in the archipelago are completely submerged.

Riverboat tours introduce you to the delights of the Anavilhanas Archipelago, which has its own ecosystem and an abundance of plant and animal life. Those flamboyant and noisy jungle-dwellers, macaws and parrots, are a common sight, as are toucans and howler monkeys. Among the river creatures you are likely to see are delightful Amazonian dolphins. The dry season exposes some superb beaches on a number of the islands, their fine white sands making a vivid contrast with the unmistakable black waters of the river. It may not be the seaside but you can still enjoy chilling out on these beaches, especially as the Negro's acidic waters mean there are far fewer mosquitoes around than normally in the jungle.

**HOW TO GET THERE:**
Anavilhanas is an eight-hour boat ride from Manaus. (It's a little quicker by bus but it's much more atmospheric to be on the river.)

**WHEN TO GO:**
Any time of year. This region gets a lot of rain; if you really want to avoid the wet stuff, June to October tends to be the driest period.

**DON'T MISS:**
If you get the chance, try your hand at a spot of piranha fishing (don't worry, despite the fish's fearsome reputation you are unlikely to lose a finger let alone your hand!).

**YOU SHOULD KNOW:**
Your odds on spotting wildlife will increase greatly if you can decamp from the main boat and explore the side channels in the peace and quiet of a canoe.

# Aparados da Serra National Park

In the far south of Brazil the dominant landscape feature is an extensive highland plateau, its rock formations the result of layer upon layer of sediment deposited from the nearby Atlantic Ocean. Volcanic and other subterranean activity some 150 million years ago covered the tableland with a thick crust of basalt rock. The forces of wind and water subsequently carved out great cracks in the basalt at the plateau's edges, creating a series of magnificent canyons for the modern visitor to wonder at. The most impressive of these is Itaimbezinho, which forms the centrepiece of the Aparados da Serra National Park. The canyon is nearly 6 km (3.75 mi) long, 720 m (2,360 ft) deep and between 600 m (1,970 ft) and 2 km (1.25 mi) wide. It is a sublime spectacle at any time, but its grandeur is enhanced still further by the regular fogs that roll in off the Atlantic.

The canyon's most striking feature is its sheer rock escarpments; unlike those of the Grand Canyon, though, these surfaces are mostly covered with vegetation. The park lies in a temperate zone, with well-defined seasons, but the special topography of the Itaimbezinho canyon means that it hosts two distinct habitats: the canyon floor is subtropical, while the slopes and higher levels which see relatively little rainfall, display a thick cover of cloud forest. The surrounding tableland is dotted with stands of araucaria pine with their distinctive umbrella shape.

Guided trails, including one that runs around the canyon rim and a more challenging one that descends to its floor, take you into the heart of the park. Aparados da Serra is home to an abundance of bird and animal life. The maned wolf, puma, ocelot and tapir can be found here.

**HOW TO GET THERE:**
The park lies 66 km (41 mi) northeast of São Francisco de Paula. It is a difficult place to get to unless you take a guided tour or have your own transport (4x4 advisable).

**WHEN TO GO:**
Winter (May to August) is the best time to visit; it may be cold but the visibility is clearest and there is less chance of sea fogs spoiling the views. Spring (October and November) can also be chilly but offers a dazzling display of wild flowers.

**DON'T MISS:**
The canyon contains two spectacular waterfalls.

**YOU SHOULD KNOW:**
Visitor numbers to the park are limited to 1,000 per day so if you are not on an organized tour you are advised to book your visit in advance.

*Winter in the Aparados Da Serra National Park*

# Boipeba Island

**HOW TO GET THERE:**
Although you can travel over from Tinharé, the best way to reach Boipeba is direct by boat from the coastal town of Valença (four hours by normal boat or one hour in a speedboat).
**WHEN TO GO:**
Any time of year (although you may want to avoid the rainy season, April to July).

*Boipeba Island is separated from Tinharé by the Rio de Inferno.*

Like most good things the Ilha de Boipeba does not come to you on a plate. It takes some effort to access its various delights but you are unlikely to come away disappointed. Boipeba is one of the three main islands of the Tinharé Archipelago which lies just off the Bahia coast, 100 km (62 mi) south of Salvador. Its larger neighbour, the Ilha de Tinharé, is a famous holiday destination popular with the Brazilian cool set as well as foreign sun-seekers. Boipeba to the south is separated from Tinharé by the vividly named Rio de Inferno (Hell River). The change of atmosphere crossing this narrow and, in spite of its name, relatively placid channel is quite remarkable; the crowds and the buzz that surround the beaches of Morro de São Paulo on Tinharé vanish completely when you step

onto its unassuming neighbour. Yet Boipeba has beaches every bit as sensational but considerably less developed than Tinharé's.

This is a place where you can really slow down and forget the pace of modern life for a while. There are no roads and no cars, just the odd tractor and jeep, so the only ways to get around are on foot or by boat. Besides the palm-fringed beaches the landscape is one of sand dunes, salt marshes, extensive mangrove swamps and, in the interior, dense Atlantic rainforest. The waters around the island are crystal clear most of the year and are superb for snorkelling and diving, especially the coral reefs off the Ponta de Castelhauos at the southern tip of the island. If you are feeling more energetic, surfing, canoeing and horse riding are also available.

**DON'T MISS:**
The amazing array of sea life to be seen in the natural pools that form off the beaches at low tide.
**YOU SHOULD KNOW:**
The island's name is derived from a native Indian word for flat snake, referring to the sea turtles that frequent the local waters.

# Caatinga Wilderness

This vast and sparsely populated region covering 750,000 sq km (290,000 sq mi) of the interior of northeastern Brazil gets its name from the thorny scrub which is its dominant vegetation. Only the hardiest of plants survive in the harsh, semi-desert conditions of these uplands. One of the toughest of all, the cactus, is a common feature of the landscape. Other kinds of tree have adapted to the intense heat and drought-like conditions by remaining leafless for long periods. An integral part of the *sertão*, the Brazilian bush or outback, the Caatinga is a bleak and lonely place where scattered communities eke out a living from subsistence farming. It is little visited by travellers but possesses all the same a raw and unvarnished beauty which feels a world away from the hectic life of the coast.

The towns of Campina Grande and Caruaru are the main gateways for exploring the region if you are heading inland from the coast. The São Francisco River is also an important artery and a vital green lung through what is the largest area of dry forest on the whole continent. With a mere one per cent of it enjoying any form of protection, however, the Caatinga is very much at the mercy of commercial pressures and human activity. The large ranches with their herds of grazing cattle and *vaqueiros* cowboys may look picturesque enough but the introduction of new and intensive agricultural practices is accelerating a process of desertification throughout the region. This is particularly bad news for the bird life, which is surprisingly rich given the unpromising habitat.

**HOW TO GET THERE:**
Distances are huge and public transport erratic so you will need to hire a 4x4 for any serious exploration of the Caatinga.
**WHEN TO GO:**
It is hot and mainly dry all year round, with a rainy season from March to June.
**DON'T MISS:**
If you are here in the wet season you will see much of the landscape transformed by wild flowers and lush new growth.
**YOU SHOULD KNOW:**
In times of severest drought even cactus plants – thorns and all - are used as cattle feed.

*The Chapada dos Guimarães still feels remote and mysterious.*

# Chapada dos Guimarães

The Mato Grosso in western Brazil is a region of flat uplands which extend to the horizon in every direction. At its centre is the Chapada dos Guimarães, a sandstone plateau that rises over 350 m (1,150 ft) from the surrounding plains. As you draw nearer on the road that climbs steadily out of the city of Cuiabá, the precipitous curtain of rock confronting you looks ever more daunting and impenetrable. Do not be intimidated, though, because the national park that covers much of the plateau – 300 sq km (116 sq mi) of it – holds an array of spectacular natural sights you won't want to miss. Although the Chapada is an increasingly popular attraction, it still retains a distinct aura of remoteness and mystery. It can claim, however, to be at the heart of things in one very specific sense, lying as it does at the geodesic centre of the South American continent (it is equidistant between the Pacific and Atlantic oceans).

There are a number of hiking trails around the national park, some of which can only be undertaken with a guide. Natural features include waterfalls, canyons, caves and bizarre rock formations. The Véu de Noiva (Bridal Veil) waterfall drops 86 m (282 ft) down a sheer cliff, while the Cidade de Pedra (City of Stone) is a mesmerizing collection of sandstone shapes around the canyon edges. A flash of blue seen here belongs most probably to macaws which build their nests on the cliff faces. At several sites ancient rock paintings have been preserved. From the highest point of the plateau, São Jeronimo (850 m, 2,790 ft), there are panoramic views of the *cerrado* (high plain) and the Pantanal wetlands to the south.

**HOW TO GET THERE:**
The gateway to the park is the small town of the same name, which is 65 km (40 mi) from Cuiabá. Although you can get there by bus, having your own vehicle is recommended as the distances between the various sights in the park are considerable.
**WHEN TO GO:**
Any time of year
**DON'T MISS:**
The vertical walls of dark-red rock assume a special grandeur at sunset.
**YOU SHOULD KNOW:**
In recent years the Chapada has become popular with New Age followers, attracted by its spiritual qualities and other-worldly atmosphere.

# Itatiaia National Park

Established in 1937, Itatiaia was Brazil's first national park and is still a place where you can escape the crowds and get back to nature with relative ease. It is located in the far west of Rio de Janeiro state, 165 km (103 mi) from the city and close to the state borders with Minas Gerais and São Paulo. The unusual name comes from an indigenous word referring to 'rocks with sharp edges'. The park covers an area of 120 sq km (46 sq mi) on the slopes of the Mantiqueira mountain range; the variation in altitude it encompasses makes for a startling diversity of landscapes, from dense Atlantic forest in the foothills (a type of forest that is now critically endangered in Brazil) through treeless, grassy slopes at higher levels and on up to the mountains themselves. Within the park's borders are two major peaks: Agulhas Negras at 2,787 m (9,145 ft) and Prateleira at 2,540 m (8,335 ft), both of which are popular climbs for those with mountaineering experience.

Because the area escaped use for coffee cultivation or other agricultural purposes its ecology has remained remarkably intact and unchanged. On the various walking trails through the park you will see giant tree ferns, bromeliads, orchids and other characteristic features of subtropical forest. Itatiaia is graced with numerous waterfalls and natural springs which feed the Paraíba River (an important source for Rio's water supply). The water may be bracing, but on a hot day you will probably be very grateful for a refreshing dip in one of the natural pools.

Itatiaia is a paradise for birdwatchers; hummingbirds, owls and toucans are all much in evidence. The park's visitor centre provides a good introduction to the flora and fauna to be seen.

**HOW TO GET THERE:**
By 4x4 or local bus from the town of Itatiaia which lies on the main highway between Rio and São Paulo.
**WHEN TO GO:**
May to August, when it is generally dry but can be chilly at night.
**DON'T MISS:**
Lago Azul (blue lake) with its beautiful setting and clear waters that are ideal for bathing.
**YOU SHOULD KNOW:**
The park is still recovering from a disastrous bushfire in 1988 which swept through one fifth of its area.

*Giant tree ferns can be seen from the walking trails.*

# Lençóis Maranhenses National Park

**HOW TO GET THERE:**
The park is three to four hours by road from the state capital São Luis. Most tours start from the town of Barreirinhas.
**WHEN TO GO:**
June to September, when the lagoons are filled. It is always hot and humid but there is occasional relief from cooling sea breezes.
**DON'T MISS:**
The beaches at Lençóis Maranhenses are exceptional by any standards and you will almost certainly have them to yourself.
**YOU SHOULD KNOW:**
Since access to the national park is carefully controlled you will have to hire an accredited guide if you are planning your own visit.

Brazil is a huge country but it's a fair bet you won't see anything else quite like the Parque Nacional dos Lençóis Maranhenses. Located on the coast of the northeastern state of Maranhão, the park's name translates from Portuguese as 'bedsheets', a suitably graphic description for this unique landscape. When you are only a few hundred kilometres from the Amazon delta you do not expect to find a desert, but that is what you get at Lençóis Maranhenses: an area of over 1,500 sq km (580 sq mi) composed in the main of giant white sand dunes. Their dramatic shapes have been formed over thousands of years from sand deposited by rivers at their mouths, which has then been swept back inland by winds and ocean currents. The dunes now stretch up to 50 km (31 mi) inland and extend 43 km (27 mi) along the coastline.

The play of sunlight and shadow on the dunes is a captivating sight, not least for anyone who fancies themselves behind a lens.

But this is an equatorial climate, with little of the aridity of the Sahara or Arabian deserts. When it rains in the first half of the year it does so with a vengeance and the flat areas between the dunes fill with water, creating hundreds of freshwater lagoons. Some, like Lagoa Bonita and Lagoa da Gaivota, are enormous and provide wonderful swimming opportunities in their crystal-clear waters. Other activities to enjoy in the park include boat trips on the Preguiças river and around the mangrove swamps and riding the dunes in a jeep (authorized drivers only!).

*Sunset over the desert*

# Rio Negro Forest Reserve

There aren't many places on the planet that can still lay claim to being uncharted territory but the upper reaches of the Rio Negro in the far northwest of the Amazon basin come as close as any. The Rio Negro, or Black River, is a major tributary of the Amazon, its characteristic dark waters (more the colour of tea than jet black) joining with those of the Rio Solimões at the Meeting of the Waters below Manaus to form the main Amazon River. The Negro has its source in the Colombian uplands 2,230 km (1,390 mi) away. Close to the source, and hard up against the border with Colombia, lies the Rio Negro Forest Reserve, a protected area covering 38,000 sq km (14,670 sq mi) of virgin tropical forest. Bounded on one side by the Rio Negro and on the other by its tributary the Uaupés, the reserve contains significant swathes of *igapó*, seasonally flooded forest, as well as primary rainforest and *caatinga* scrubland.

There are virtually no facilities in this remote area and the only way to explore the reserve is by hiring a local guide to take you on day treks or camping trips. The town of São Gabriel, a few hours downstream, is the place to arrange this. In terms of wildlife the Rio Negro Forest Reserve is the Amazon at its extravagant best; over half of all the species recorded in the Amazon basin can be found here, although as usual you will need a good deal of patience and luck to spot the rarer and more elusive creatures. Multi-coloured toucans and parrots, pink dolphins frolicking in the river and capuchin monkeys swinging through the canopy should provide ample compensation for any other disappointments.

*Amazon River dolphins (*Inia geoffrensis) *frolic in the Ariaú River, a tributary of the Rio Negro.*

**HOW TO GET THERE:**
A fast boat upstream from Manaus takes five days.
**WHEN TO GO:**
During the dry season, June to November
**DON'T MISS:**
If you're lucky your guide will help you spot the golden-backed uacari, one of South America's most charming but least-known monkeys.
**YOU SHOULD KNOW:**
Unfortunately, the very remoteness of the area has attracted less savoury elements and drug running across the national frontier is a significant problem. You should take official advice before planning a visit to the reserve.

# Serra do Cipó National Park

*A pair of black tufted-ear marmosets*

The Espinhaço Mountains bisect the state of Minas Gerais from north to south, dividing the central Brazilian Highlands from the coastal plain to the east. At the southern end of the range lies the Parque Nacional Serra do Cipó, established to protect a typical *cerrado* landscape of high-altitude grasslands and open savannah of a kind that is increasingly threatened with degradation from human settlement and commercial exploitation. Covering an area of 338 sq km (130 sq mi), the park is criss-crossed by a series of watercourses forming part of the São Francisco basin. Formidable canyons and gorges have been created where the valleys have cut through the mountains; the Cānion dos Confins and the gorge of the Rio do Peixe are two of the best. The park is also blessed with an abundance of beautiful waterfalls, most of which can be reached easily enough on a network of walking trails.

Serra do Cipó is renowned for its biodiversity and boasts a high proportion of endemic species. The conditions in this harsh scrubland hardly seem propitious for growth but a remarkable variety of unusual plants manage to prosper in the sparse and sandy soil, helped by the proximity of fresh water. Among more than 50 species of mammal found here are anteaters, deer, armadillos, monkeys, ocelots and otters. This is also classic habitat for the capybara; you should have no difficulty spotting the world's largest rodent. Besides trekking, Serra do Cipó offers opportunities for horse riding and for kayaking on the Cipó River. As you explore the area keep an eye out for traces in the foothills of the old stone road built by slaves for the prospectors who came looking for gold and precious stones in centuries past.

**HOW TO GET THERE:**
The national park is 100 km (62 mi) northeast of Belo Horizonte, the state capital.

**WHEN TO GO:**
Serra do Cipó has a tropical lowland climate. The best time to visit is between April and October.

**DON'T MISS:**
The clear waters in the pool beneath the Great Waterfall make a marvellous bathing spot.

**YOU SHOULD KNOW:**
North of Serra do Cipó are the towns of Diamantina and Serro, two examples of the *cidades históricas* (historic cities), founded as mining camps in the early 18th century.

# Atacama Desert

If the name Atacama has a familiar ring about it this is probably because in a school geography lesson you will have learned about it as the driest place on earth. In parts of the Atacama, rainfall has never been recorded. The world's highest desert occupies the entire far north of Chile, extending 1,000 km (620 mi) south from the Peruvian border. It is a huge region but its most spectacular sights are to be found in a relatively compact area at the desert's heart, clustered around the town of San Pedro de Atacama. Here you can experience the best of the Atacama in microcosm: a dazzling *altiplano* (high plains) landscape of salt flats, sand dunes, lagoons and hot springs, set against a backdrop of snow-capped volcanoes.

Immediately south of San Pedro the rough white crust of Chile's largest salt flat stretches away as far as the eye can see. The monotone visual palette is dramatically punctured by large flocks of flamingo and other waders attracted to the shallow lakes scattered around the saltpan. On its northern edge the aptly named Valle de la Luna is a world of strange rock formations, the result of millions of years of erosion. The valley is at its most striking at either end of the day when the sun's rays bathe the encircling peaks in hues of pink, gold and purple.

In the other direction El Tatio is the world's highest geothermal field, at 4,320 m (14,170 ft). Early morning is the best time to see the geysers at full strength; the sight of steaming fumaroles against the brilliant azure of the *altiplano* sky is one of many memorable images the Atacama has to offer.

**HOW TO GET THERE:**
The nearest transport hub is the copper-mining city of Calama, 106 km (66 mi) to the west. Regular buses run between Calama and San Pedro.
**WHEN TO GO:**
Any time of year (but remember you are at considerable altitude so nights can get very chilly).
**DON'T MISS:**
A relaxing soak in one of the thermal pools at El Tatio.
**YOU SHOULD KNOW:**
The atmospheric conditions in the Atacama Desert make it a famous location for star-gazing and there are a number of observatories in the area.

*Hikers on the salt flats along the Tuyajito Lagoon in the Atacama Desert*

# Bernardo O'Higgins National Park

Bernardo O'Higgins was the unlikely sounding name of Chile's first head of state after the country had shaken off the Spanish colonial yoke and gained its independence in 1818. A fully paid-up member of the Chilean liberation struggle, O'Higgins was the illegitimate son of an Irishman who is now remembered as one of the nation's founding fathers. His name crops up frequently, but certainly nowhere more substantially than in Chile's largest national park. Straddling the 50° latitude in the deep south of Patagonia, the Bernardo O'Higgins National Park covers a staggering 35,000 sq km (13,510 sq mi). The park has been much less touched by human hands than its more famous neighbour, the Torres del Paine, largely because it is only accessible by boat.

The granite pillars of Torres del Paine may be justly famous among the trekking community but Bernardo O'Higgins is the place to come if you want to hike away from the crowds. Including much of the Southern Patagonian Ice Field within its boundaries, this is a truly elemental world of glaciers, waterfalls, lakes, craggy peaks and untouched fjords. Huge swathes of native forest are interrupted by pampas and the occasional isolated *estancia*. This is the realm of the condor but also of the guanaco, a smaller relative of the llama. It takes several hours to reach the park by boat up the Última Esperanza sound. The name translates as 'Last Hope' but you should certainly not despair as the views on the way are astonishing, as is your eventual arrival at the base of the Serrano glacier, beautiful Mount Balmaceda rising up behind. The only way to do the park full justice, though, is to take one of the longer escorted tours which involves kayaking and camping.

*The west side of Cerro Torre – 3,102 m (10,180 ft) – and neighbouring peaks, from the Southern Patagonian Icefield*

# Pumalín Park

Parque Pumalín (Pumalín Park) is the creation of one man, the American clothing magnate and entrepreneur Doug Tompkins. Tompkins is one of a new breed of environmental philanthropists dedicated to supporting innovative projects in conservation and sustainable living. He purchased his first parcel of land in the area 20 years ago and has added to it steadily since, so that today the park covers an area of nearly 3,000 sq km (1,160 sq mi) in northern Patagonia, running south from outside Hornopirén to just north of Chaitén. This has always been one of Chile's wildest and most rugged regions and Doug Tompkins wants to keep it that way, while at the same time giving visitors an experience of the natural world that is both enriching and humbling.

Pumalín preserves a pristine landscape of temperate forest and pasture criss-crossed by sparkling upland rivers. A jagged coastline with deep inlets carved out by the ocean adds to the drama. By local standards the visitor facilities in the park are exemplary and could serve as a model for the country's national parks. As well as a network of well-marked hiking trails there are sensitively sited lodges and campsites, all designed to have minimum impact on the environment. Tompkins has been careful to involve the local communities; small farms continue to operate privately within the park where the emphasis is on low-impact practices and sustainable agriculture.

There are two points of access to the park. Most people visit from the south where there is a visitors' centre and other facilities at the small cove of Caleta Gonzalo, 60 km (37 mi) north of Chaitén. It is the northern end, however, accessed by boat from Hornopirén, that is wilder and more spectacular and offers the added attraction of hot springs.

**HOW TO GET THERE:**
There is a daily ferry sailing in the summer months between Hornopirén and Caleta Gonzalo.
**WHEN TO GO:**
December to March (in spite of the latitude the sun's rays are still strong so you should always wear sun screen).
**DON'T MISS:**
The giant alerce tree, a member of the cypress family. This hardy evergreen can grow to over 60 m (200 ft), making it the largest tree species on the continent.
**YOU SHOULD KNOW:**
After the eruption of Chaitén volcano in May 2008 many of the facilities in the south of the park were closed. You should check the current status before embarking on a visit.

*A river within Pumalín Park*

*Torres del Paine, Patagonia*

# Torres del Paine

**HOW TO GET THERE:**
By bus from Puerto Natales, 150 km
(93 mi) to the south on a reasonable
gravel road
**WHEN TO GO:**
October to April (although
hardened and experienced trekkers
might choose to go in the quieter
winter months).

Mention the words Torres del Paine to a serious walker and the
chances are you will be met with an expression of awed reverie. This
national park in the far south of Chile has long been a legendary
destination among the trekking community and the eponymous
'Towers' – a cluster of 2,600-m (8,530-ft) granite pillars that make up
the Paine Massif at the heart of the park – have become the defining
image of Patagonia in many people's minds. There are enough
different aspects of elemental nature here to satisfy the most
seasoned of travellers: rugged mountain terrain, thundering rivers in
deep-sided valleys, wide-open steppes and dense green forests. And
being so far south you find a magical extra ingredient in the mix:

huge glaciers and lakes with floating chunks of shimmering blue ice the size of a house. The most accessible is the Grey glacier and its associated lake (which is anything but that colour), although it is still a long day's hike to the base of the glacier.

The breathtaking scenery in this national park fully deserves its reputation but it does mean that it is a popular place and can get very busy with hikers in the summer months. Most walkers come to tackle the 'W', one of the world's classic treks, so called because of the route's shape on the map. The 'W' takes four to five days to complete and there are good campsites and mountain shelters throughout the park. The route includes a number of fantastic viewpoints (*miradores*) and the Valle Francés, a steep-sided valley with spectacular mountain views on both sides. If you have the time and the stamina, the Circuit Trail (seven to ten days) takes you round the back of the peaks and gets you away from the crowds.

**DON'T MISS:**
Being at the Las Torres viewpoint at dawn to watch the peaks suffused by the first rays of the sun.
**YOU SHOULD KNOW:**
In peak season (January and February) it is essential to make advance reservations for your sleeping arrangements while in the park.

# Valdivian Coastal Range

The Valdivian Coastal Range forms part of the Cordillera de la Costa, the western range of the Andes mountains which hugs much of Chile's Pacific coast. Also known as the Cordillera de Mahuidanchi, the range lies towards the southern end of the whole chain. Its ecological significance lies in the fact that it is a rare surviving example of temperate rainforest, a habitat which has been particularly vulnerable throughout the world to intensive logging and other commercial interests. Broadleaf evergreens are the dominant tree type; they flourish in the moist and humid climate created by the prevailing westerly winds blowing off the ocean. The elegant canelo tree is a particularly common sight in the Valdivian forest with its shiny whitish-green leaves. Its durability and adaptation to harsh conditions has given it the nickname of 'winter's bark'.

Although a less-visited part of the country, the Valdivian hills and forests have much to offer the lover of nature. A good place to sample the area's delights is in the Parque Oncol, a 754-hectare (1,860-acre) reserve centred around Cerro Oncol, at 714 m (2,340 ft) the region's highest point. Numerous walking trails and viewing platforms give excellent views of the ocean as well as the area's many volcanoes further inland. The park makes for a good day trip from the city of Valdivia. If you are feeling adventurous there is an extensive canopy tour which provides an excitingly different perspective on the wildlife. Among the animals you might see in the reserve are wild boar and *pudú*, the world's smallest deer.

**HOW TO GET THERE:**
A 4x4 is recommended for the 32-km (20-mi) trip from Valdivia.
**WHEN TO GO:**
Any time of year
**DON'T MISS:**
Chile's national flower, the copihue, grows in these forests. The distinctive shape of its red flowers gives it its common name of Chilean bellflower.
**YOU SHOULD KNOW:**
The canelo tree was considered sacred by the Mapuche Indians who used to inhabit these hills and forests.

# Aconcagua

The Andes mountain chain runs the entire length of the continent
but it is Argentina that can claim the loftiest peak of all within its
borders. At 6,960 m (22,835 ft) Mount Aconcagua is the highest
summit in both the western and southern hemispheres. It is also
one of the most accessible of the world's great peaks, attracting
hundreds of climbers every year to its three routes to the top.
Provided you are fit and have some experience of climbing at
altitude there is no reason why you shouldn't undertake an
organized ascent with professional guides, although you won't be
able to take the family and you will need to allow a good two weeks.

If you hadn't planned on such hardcore activity you can still
enjoy many of the splendours of the Alta Montaña on a tour of the
Andes highlands west of Mendoza. Beyond the city the road soon
starts to climb, leaving behind fertile slopes covered in vineyards
(this is Argentina's premier wine-growing area). The hills become
increasingly barren and denuded of vegetation as the ascent
continues. Pastures and grassland give way to mountain streams,

sudden deep valleys and rocks of strikingly varied hues. Just beyond the winter ski resort of Los Penitentes and at an altitude of 2,700 m (8,860 ft) you encounter one of the region's great sights, the Puente del Inca. This natural stone bridge over the Rio de las Cuevas owes its extraordinary coppery-gold colour to minerals in the water.

A short distance further brings you to the entrance to the Aconcagua Provincial Park. If you have not signed up for the full climbing experience you can still enjoy hugely rewarding day and overnight treks to base camps and mountain shelters beneath the snow line.

*Mount Aconcagua in the Andes Mountain Range*

# Los Glaciares

**HOW TO GET THERE:**
The Perito Moreno glacier is 80 km (50 mi) west of El Calafate, where there is an airport. The main base for the northern section of the park is El Chaltén, reached by a two-and-a-half-hour drive on a paved road from El Calafate.

**WHEN TO GO:**
November to April

**DON'T MISS:**
The opportunity to try your hand (and feet) at a spot of ice trekking on the glacier – equipment and full instruction provided, but not available to children under 12.

**YOU SHOULD KNOW:**
Scientists studying these glaciers to gauge the effects of climate change have reported clear evidence that many are receding at an alarming rate.

The Los Glaciares National Park is formed from the eastern slopes of the Andes in southern Patagonia. Extending for 170 km (106 mi) along the national frontier with Chile, the 6,000-sq-km (2,320-sq-mi) park encompasses a range of habitats as its terrain spreads down from the mountains: to the east lies Patagonian steppe, giving way, as the ground rises, to huge montane beech forests. What most people come to this national park for (and the reason why it is a UNESCO World Heritage Site) is hinted at in its name: *glaciares* is Spanish for glaciers and there are 47 of them in the park, occupying close on half its total surface area. This extraordinary fact becomes more credible when you consider the mind-boggling dimensions of the larger glaciers like Upsala and Viedma; the latter is the biggest in the country at nearly 1,000 sq km (385 sq mi). Together they make up the Southern Patagonian Ice Field, the largest ice mass on the planet after Antarctica and Greenland.

The most celebrated and visited of the park's glaciers is the Glaciar Perito Moreno in its southern section. Although there are fabulous views of the glacier from the well-sited walkways on the Península de Magellanes, the best way to appreciate the splendours of this frozen world is to take a boat tour on Lago Argentino. As well as visiting several smaller glaciers, the boat weaves its way between giant icebergs floating on the lake as it draws close (but not too close!) to Perito Moreno's 60-m (197-ft) high ice wall. If you are very lucky you may experience the phenomenon known as 'calving' in which huge chunks of ice succumb to water pressure and break away from the face of the wall.

*Perito Moreno Glacier and Lago Argentino*

# Lapataia Bay

Were you so inclined you could follow the Route 3 highway out of Buenos Aires all the way south to the very toe of the country where the road finally runs out at Lapataia Bay, a mind-boggling distance of 3,242 km (2,015 mi). A few kilometres west of Ushuaia, the world's southernmost city, Lapataia is a wide south-facing bay overlooking Beagle Channel, which separates the mainland from the islands of Cape Horn. The narrow channel is named in tribute to Darwin's ship which famously cruised these waters. Lapataia Bay lies within the extensive Tierra del Fuego National Park, 630 sq km (243 sq mi) of mountains, forests, lakes, glaciated valleys and unspoilt coastline. Inviting as all this may sound, only a very small proportion of the park (less than five per cent) is open to visitors; this is the section around Lapataia and neighbouring Ensenada Bay. It is more than enough, though, to showcase the very special atmosphere here and to leave you with an indefinable yet potent end-of-the-world feeling.

Extending north across Lago Fagnano, the park encompasses vast swathes of southern beech forest. Walking among the trees as the wind gently rustles the fragrant leaves is a wonderfully refreshing experience. There are half-a-dozen short trails which acquaint you with the park's range of natural features and make for excellent day treks. One trail runs for 8 km (5 mi) along the shoreline while another heads inland along Lago Roca to the national border with Chile. If you are looking for a tougher challenge, the steep climb up Cerro Guanaco – 973 m (3,190 ft) – will reward you with panoramic views from the summit.

**HOW TO GET THERE:**
Lapataia Bay is an easy 12-km (7.5-mi) bus or car ride from Ushuaia. A more atmospheric, if slower, way to reach the park is to take the old narrow-gauge railway which once transported convicts to hard labour in the forests.
**WHEN TO GO:**
November to April
**DON'T MISS:**
If you are here in March or April the trees put on a stunning display of autumn colours.
**YOU SHOULD KNOW:**
It is hard to believe that you would find a species of parrot this far south, but you may be lucky and catch a glimpse of the austral parakeet in the trees.

*Lapataia Bay lies within Tierra del Fuego National Park.*

*A Magellanic penguin with her chicks*

# Cabo dos Bahias

Patagonia's coastal highway runs almost all the way to Tierra del Fuego. The landscape is often hypnotically vast and empty, although in places the road is within sight and sound of the ocean. Here, an extraordinary abundance of wildlife – whales and dolphins, seals and sea lions, penguins and seabirds – nest, breed and feed. The Valdes Peninsula in the north is a prime whale-watching location, while the popular Punto Tombo Reserve is home to South America's largest nesting colony of penguins. Cabo dos Bahias, south of Camarones, is an isolated wilderness of scrub and rugged shore, where land and sea creatures thrive in a peaceful, protected reserve.

Large numbers of Patagonian foxes and the usually timid guanacos (wild llamas) and ostrich-like, flightless rheas, wander fearlessly inland. Seals and big, aggressive sea lions colonize the rocky foreshore and killer whales (orcas), which are actually large dolphins, patrol the waters for sustenance. Numerous resident seabirds include cormorants, skuas and petrels. In spring and summer, beach and hinterland become an enormous nursery where some 25,000 pairs of Magellanic penguins raise their young.

These strikingly marked birds – elegant black-and-white stripes divide dark backs from white fronts – have discordant calls and are also known as jackass penguins. Males come ashore and dig burrows where females lay eggs in October; parents share feeding duties until the chicks learn to swim in February. In March, the young start their migration north, followed by the adults. Watching thousands of penguins seemingly 'planted' in holes and surrounded by grazing guanacos is fascinating – and rather surreal.

**HOW TO GET THERE:**
The reserve is about 30 km (19 mi) south of Camarones by the RP1, a slow, gravel road.
**WHEN TO GO:**
October to March for penguins, although the reserve is a fascinating place all year round.
**DON'T MISS:**
Meeting the penguins. Although the nesting area is fenced off, they potter about and are naturally curious. Visitors who sit and wait will be rewarded, although penguins do nip if anyone gets too close. Land-based residents will also approach, and are not at all camera-shy.
**YOU SHOULD KNOW:**
Gaiman, a small town north of Camarones, which was settled by the Welsh in the 19th century, is famous for afternoon tea. Tearooms and family homes serve strong tea with delicious pies, jams and fruitcake.

# Calchaquí Valleys

The Andean northwest of Argentina is a dry, semi-desert world of striking rockscapes and sparse vegetation that is far removed from the lush pampas to the south. Even so, such an unpromising landscape can yield surprising pockets of fertility, such as the Valles Calchaquíes region. The dramatic contrasts between green valleys, surrounding sun-parched uplands and an ever-present backdrop of snow-capped mountains help to explain the particular appeal of this remote area, lying south and west of the provincial capital Salta. The main artery through the region is the Calchaquí River and most of the valleys link to it. Tumbling mountain torrents have carved a number of remarkable canyons out of the sandstone plateau.

In this thinly populated landscape the few scattered settlements are oases of shade and tranquillity, offering traditional adobe houses, cobblestones, pretty squares and artisan workshops. Cachi is a typical example and boasts an unbeatable setting beneath the towering profile of Mount Nevado del Cachi – 6,380 m (20,930 ft). An area of 650 sq km (250 sq mi) at the heart of the Valles was designated a national park as recently as 1996; the Los Cardones park takes its name from the ubiquitous *cardón* or candelabra cactus, one of the few plants to flourish in these parts. With no other trees growing here, the wood of this giant cactus, which can grow to over 5 m (16 ft), is widely used by local communities as a construction material and for furniture. Its unmistakable profile will certainly be one of your abiding images of a visit to the Valles.

**HOW TO GET THERE:**
The road from Salta to Cachi, which climbs up and over the Cuesta del Obispo, is one of Argentina's most spectacular drives.

**WHEN TO GO:**
Any time of year, although it can get brutally hot in summer (December to February).

**DON'T MISS:**
If you are visiting in the autumn (March to May) you will see lines of red peppers drying in the sun on many of the hillsides.

**YOU SHOULD KNOW:**
The vineyards which proliferate as you approach Cafayate on the southern edge of the Valles Calchaquíes are among the highest in the world.

*The striking rockscape of Calchaquí Valley*

*The Ibera Wetlands – the largest protected area in Argentina*

# Ibera Wetlands

The Esteros del Iberá or Ibera Wetlands are one of Argentina's most important wildlife havens. Situated in the subtropical northeast of the country in the Entre Ríos or Mesopotamia region – so called because it is bounded by the two great rivers of the Paraná and the Uruguay – the Esteros del Iberá were once part of the main course of the Río Paraná. Sluggish currents have combined with silting and sedimentation over time to form the present patchwork of lakes, water channels, swamps, densely wooded marshes and savannah. Floating islands, known as *embalsados*, are a special feature of the waterways, a consequence of aquatic plants and other vegetation accumulating on the water's surface.

This is no ordinary wetland; covering a total area of 13,700 sq km (5,290 sq mi), the Esteros del Iberá is the second-largest wetland in the world after the Pantanal in Brazil. In recent years it has been afforded a measure of protection as a nature reserve but environmentalists, worried about continuing threats to its delicate ecosystem, carry on campaigning for tougher controls and greater regulation. There are no paved roads in the reserve so most visitors don't take their vehicle in. Even though you are largely leaving behind the sounds of human activity it is surprising to discover just how noisy the natural world can be, especially when you are talking about howler monkeys and more than 350 bird species. Waders feature prominently of course, among them the splendid Jabiru stork and the ruddy tiger heron. There can be few more magical experiences than being poled through the marshes in a noiseless flat-bottomed boat as the air around you is filled with the rich and raucous polyphony of the natural world.

**HOW TO GET THERE:**
It's a four-hour bus journey from Mercedes on a dirt road to the centre of the reserve at Laguna Iberá.

**WHEN TO GO:**
Any time of year but you might want to avoid the fierce heat of high summer (June and July).

**DON'T MISS:**
The capybara, the world's largest rodent. Luckily, unlike many of the other South American mammals, the capybara is far from reclusive and can often be seen grazing in large family groups at the water's edge.

**YOU SHOULD KNOW:**
In the language of the pre-Columbian people who once inhabited the area Iberá means 'glittering water'. When the sun is setting or beneath a full moon it is easy to see why.

# Misiones Forest

*The magnificent Iguazú Falls*

The province of Misiones lies in the far northeast of Argentina, in a strip of land that extends like a crooked finger between Paraguay and Brazil. The climate and topography are subtropical and Misiones has some of the largest and least spoilt areas of surviving Atlantic rainforest, a habitat that has been particularly vulnerable to logging and other agricultural activities. In Misiones, where controls on development and commercial exploitation are limited and there are comparatively few areas under government protection, these threats remain acute. As a result it is not as easy as you'd think to find accessible examples of pristine forest for that jungle experience you'd always promised yourself.

Your best bet is to head up to the Brazilian border and avail yourself of the services and infrastructure that have been established around the Iguazú Falls. The magnificent falls are one of the planet's top natural wonders and what of course everyone comes here to see. But set as they are within a sizeable national park which has left the surrounding jungle largely undisturbed, it is surprisingly simple to escape the visitor crowds and head off on a nature trail as it plunges into the depths of the forest. The dense canopy and the luxuriant undergrowth support a staggering array of plants and wildlife. In no time at all the sounds of human activity are behind you and, provided you are patient and tread softly, you should be rewarded with plenty of sightings. While all the stars of the South American animal kingdom can be found here, you can count yourself fortunate indeed if you spot any; what you will see aplenty are multi-coloured butterflies and gorgeous tropical birds like toucans and parrots.

**HOW TO GET THERE:**
The nearest town is Puerto Iguazú, 20 km (12.5 mi) to the northwest, from where regular buses run to the park entrance.
**WHEN TO GO:**
Any time of year
**DON'T MISS:**
An early morning walk in the forest is the best time to see the birdlife.
**YOU SHOULD KNOW:**
If you really want to immerse yourself in the rhythms and moods of the jungle, a stay at a jungle lodge is strongly recommended.

# Valley of the Moon

**HOW TO GET THERE:**
The park is 80 km (50 mi) north of
San Agustin de Valle Fertil, where
some organized tours start.
**WHEN TO GO:**
April to September. Afternoon tours
offer the added bonus of a
wonderful sunset.
**DON'T MISS:**
The museum has displays on
evolution and palaeontology and the
history and work of the park. A must
for anyone with an interest in
dinosaurs, there are fossils,
reconstructions and dioramas of the
palaeoenvironments.
**YOU SHOULD KNOW:**
The rangers usually speak only
Spanish; information in the museum
is also in Spanish, but making sense
of the written word is rather easier.
The roads in the park are gravel and
may become impassable after (rare)
rain. The countryside west of the
park, in the foothills of the Andes, is
delightfully fertile and supports a
thriving wine industry. The San Juan
Wine Route tour is a very refreshing
change from the desert.

Ischigualasto Provincial Park lies high in the semi-arid Sierra de Valle
Fertil amid the lower ranges of the Andes in northwestern Argentina.
This name derives from the Diaguita for 'land without life'. The park
is an extensive area – around 600 sq km, (230 sq mi) – of barren,
eerie emptiness scattered with twisted rock formations. Millions of
years ago its dramatic red-sandstone canyons contained rivers whose
swirling waters eroded the rocks, which were further sculpted by
millennia of weather into strangely shaped red and ash-grey
monoliths. This lifeless landscape is known as the Valley of the Moon.

Much more than a geological curiosity, the valley is a
palaeontological treasure trove. The park is a UNESCO World
Heritage Site, for its fossil-bearing rocks form a unique, undisturbed
sequence of deposits, with perfectly preserved fossils representing

*A typical sight in the Valley of
the Moon in San Juan
province, land of the first
dinosaurs*

the entire Triassic period. Among the important dinosaur fossils are the remains of the carnivorous *Herrerasaurus* and of the small predator *Eoraptor lunensis*, the 'dawn raptor', one of the earliest dinosaurs ever discovered. Fossils of other vertebrates and of ferns, horsetails and giant tree trunks have given palaeontologists a chance to study the evolution of dinosaurs and mammals and to build up a picture of their environment. The lunar landscape was, around 200 million years ago, a flood plain with meandering rivers and dense vegetation.

Rangers lead regular convoys around the park. Tours, which last about three hours and include a visit to the museum, stop at several important and photogenic spots for information and exploration. Special events include magical full moon tours.

# AFRICA

# Farafra Oasis and the White Desert

A huge fertile depression in the Libyan Desert, the Farafra Oasis is the most isolated and least populated of Egypt's oases. No archaeological evidence of occupation in pharaonic times has been found, although it is known that during the reign of Rameses II it was called Ta-iht, the Land of the Cow. It is bordered to the west by the impenetrable Great Sand Sea where, it is said, the army of the Persian king Cambyses disappeared *en route* to Siwa. Repeated searches have revealed no trace of the lost men.

All that remains of an important Roman settlement is a tumbled fort, although a ruined Roman cemetery lies outside the town and evidence of Roman and Byzantine travellers is scattered around springs and pools all over the oasis, particularly at Ain Hadra, an important watering place on the ancient caravan route. Now sleepy Farafra is home to Bedouin who live in traditional mud-brick houses, often painted blue to ward off the evil eye. At nearby Bir Sitta, a sulphurous spring offers a soak after a day in the desert.

The extraordinary White Desert begins about 32 km (20 mi) north of the town; the vast, flat, milky wasteland is broken by hundreds of jagged, blindingly white chalk rocks, shaped by millennia of desert winds into pinnacles, twisted spires, misshapen mushrooms and a bewildering menagerie of mutant creatures. West of the road stand the *inselbergs* – steep, symmetrical rock cones with flattened tops, strangely similar to those seen on Mars. These give some welcome shade for walkers and campers. This surreal landscape is much visited by tour groups, but away from the most popular clusters of photogenic chalk formations, its mystery is compelling.

*White* inselbergs *and yellow sand dunes are characteristic features of the El Qabur area of Egypt's White Desert.*

# Valley of the Whales

Southwest of the Faium Oasis, the Wadi al-Rayan is a protected area of lakes and waterfalls popular with birds and animals and with weekend Cairenes escaping the city's heat. A long unpaved track leads from the wadi out into the desert to a level, pale expanse broken by occasional rocky outcrops. This is the Valley of the Whales which, in 2005, became Egypt's first Natural World Heritage Site. More than 40 million years ago, when oceans covered much of the Sahara, this arid spot was very like the Florida Everglades – a swampy coastal region whose waters teemed with fish and marine life and whose banks swarmed with reptiles, animals and birds.

A remarkable variety of well-preserved fossils, including mangrove roots, sharks and turtles, give palaeontologists a vivid picture of life before the waters ebbed, but it is the fossilized skeletons of whales that give the valley its name and importance. This extinct subspecies of whale, the *archaeoceti*, was carnivorous, streamlined, 18 m (59 ft) long, and land-based. Many of these fossils have not only flippers but also hind legs, feet and toes, and represent a major stage in evolution: the emergence of the whale as an ocean-dwelling mammal.

This incomparable open-air museum is now carefully managed by UNESCO. Marked walking tracks lead around the exhibits, where fossilized whale skeletons (many have been unearthed since the first was found in the 1902–1903 season) lie stretched out on the sand, ringed by stones and low ropes. The site's remoteness and scale are impressive and slightly disorientating. A visitor gazing over the endless surrounding waves of sand which lap around the steep islands of rock, may experience a brief vision of whales slithering between tangled mangrove roots into the ebbing ocean.

**HOW TO GET THERE**:
Organized tour with 4x4s
**WHEN TO GO**:
November to April
**DON'T MISS**:
The visitor centre and information booths around the site. They may seem incongruous, but they are sympathetically built and the maps and information are invaluable.
**YOU SHOULD KNOW**:
The site is so sensitive and important that access is restricted, although pre-arranged tour groups are allowed to camp in the valley. None of the fossils should be touched and there are very heavy penalties for removing anything from the valley.

*Fossilized bones of ancient whales in Egypt's Valley of the Whales*

# Green Mountains

Most of Libya's vast, barren landscape does not receive sufficient rainfall for settled agriculture. Desert lakes are salt and the network of wadis, apart from brief periods after rain, is dry. The Green Mountains (Jebel al-Akhdar) of northern Cyrenaica, where streams and waterfalls flow almost year round, are the exception. The mountains, with their cover of pine, wild olives, cypress and juniper trees, are gloriously verdant. In the south, the desert stretches to the Chad border; to the north, the range drops precipitously to a coastal plain which curves from Benghazi to Derna. Cyrenaica was a province of ancient Greece and several important cities lay on the coast. Then, the lovely Green Mountains were a precious granary; now, this area is little known.

It is possible to explore the Green Mountains from Al-Bayda and Shahat and visit some of Libya's finest classical sites. These include Ptolemaia, Apollonia and magnificent Cyrene, the most complete of the Greek cities. Inland sites like the Temple of Aesculapius at Al-Bayda are less visited. In Qasr Libya a museum displays the remarkable mosaics found in two small Byzantine churches. Laid in AD 539, most depict paradisiacal scenes of flowers and wildlife, although one shows the Pharos Lighthouse at Alexandria. Wadi al-Kuf was the scene of fierce battles in 1927 when, until they were bombed, Libyan resistance fighters halted the advance of the Italian forces. The caves where the guerrillas sheltered can be seen in the steep, rocky walls of the valley.

The fertile rounded hills of the Green Mountains still produce cereals, potatoes and fruit. This is one of the few areas in Libya with a pleasant summer climate, and cliffs, canyons, springs, woodland and deep, shady valleys make for marvellous, relatively cool walking in beautiful, unspoilt countryside.

# Jebel Nafusa

Towns and villages – many deserted and derelict – cling to the rocky hillsides of the Jebel Nafusa. This narrow east-west range rises steeply from the arid coastal lowlands and its southern slopes merge with an immense, empty gravel plain. The landscape appears harsh and inhospitable, yet sheep and goats graze the uplands and, in places, the plateau is golden with grain, shaded by fig and apricot orchards, and scattered with silvery olive groves; regular winter rains support agriculture here.

In the seventh century the Berbers retreated to these mountains. Here they built underground houses, *dammous*, to protect them from the advancing Arabs and the weather. The most impressive of these are dwellings built into the sides of wide, deep pits, reached by tunnels. From a distance, they are invisible. Huge, fortress-like granaries, *qasrs*, some of which are still in use, protected their treasure – the crops. Although now living in modern homes, most of Libya's Berbers still farm the Jebel Nafusa.

Three towns make good bases for exploration. Nalut, near the Algerian border, has an old town built on a rocky bluff and Gharyan, at the eastern end of the range, has some well-preserved underground homes. In the middle, Yefren, built among woods high above the coastal plain, is a lovely old town. A large Jewish community once lived here and a fascinating, ancient synagogue survives.

Steep slopes, deep ravines and high, sunny pastures with breathtaking views north and south make for exhilarating walking. Several villages merit a detour, notably photogenic Tarmesia, whose deserted stone houses blend almost organically into the crags where they perch.

**DON'T MISS:**
The spectacular granary at Qasr al-Haj, an ancient village north of Yefren. This enormous 12th-century 'fortress' stored olive oil in the underground area and grain in the upper three storeys. Some of the rooms, sealed with palm wood doors, are still used; grain stored in these cool, dry spaces stays fresh for years.
**YOU SHOULD KNOW:**
Gharyan is famous for its pottery. Roadside stalls sell wares ranging from intricately decorated bowls and *tagines* to timeless terracotta jars and ewers. The Libyan authorities sometimes restrict access to the more remote parts of the country at short notice.

*Abandoned Berber village in the Jebel Nafusa*

# Ubari Dunes and Lakes

Much of the desert which covers Libya is a flat, gravel wasteland. To experience the thrill and romance of the Sahara dunes, visitors must head for one of the sand seas. The most accessible is the Ubari Sand Sea, which is easily reached from three towns – Tekerkiba, Germa and Ubari. Although much visited, it is not hard to escape the noisy convoys of 4x4s for this is a boundless expanse of reddish sand waves – crescent and ridge dunes which, with their compacted bases, are relatively stable. Early and late, they glow with rosy sunlight and their shadowy valleys make perfect campsites. As the temperature drops and the campfire crackles, the brilliance of the stars in an inky sky and the total silence are awe inspiring. Although 4x4s are a quick and easy option, they do break up the surface of the dunes and a trip into the sand sea by camel is infinitely more satisfactory. As well as being ecologically sound, it allows a glimpse of the true majesty and magic of the desert.

A first sight of the Ubari lakes from the heights of the dunes is unforgettable, for they lie in the tawny sands like gleaming slivers of lapis lazuli set in the deep green of palms and reeds. There are several north of Tekerkiba, and three – Umm al-Maa, Mavo and Gebraoun – are sizeable. A fourth large lake, famous for its changing colour, has almost dried up, as have several of the smaller ones. They are remnants of a wetter past and are now very salt, so that bathing in them – Gebraoun is the easiest to get into – is a float rather than a swim. Lying back in the buoyant, warm water surrounded by towering sand cliffs is a wonderful experience.

*A group of date palms among the sand dunes*

# Bouhedma National Park

Probably Tunisia's most important national park, Bouhedma was created in 1980 and is now a UNESCO Biosphere Reserve. The 165-sq-km (64-sq-mi) park is dominated by a type of gumtree and scrub, the last traces of the savannah that once spread along the northern edges of the Sahara desert.

Lying beneath the Bouhedma Escarpment, but including the rocky slopes, the park is unique in North Africa and looks and feels more like parts of Kenya or Tanzania. This is the place to visit if mammals are of particular interest to you. Dorcas gazelles, scimitar-horned oryx, golden jackals, Cape hares and Ruppell's foxes can be seen, as well as gundis – rodents that live on the rocky foothills of the escarpment. Bouhedma has needed some protection as grazing livestock, land clearance and poaching had begun to degrade the landscape. As part of this effort several animals, such as addax and dama gazelles, have been successfully re-introduced. There are also about 300 plant species and many birds. These include ostriches and several species of raptor, such as golden eagles, Lanner falcons and Pharaoh eagle owls.

The highest peak, which reaches 840 m (2,756 ft), is home to juniper, olive and *Pistacia* – a genus of trees in the cashew family.

Both permanent and seasonal watercourses can be found here, the most important of which is the source of Ain Cherchera. Be alert as you walk, however: there are scorpions all across Tunisia, including some that are potentially deadly.

A small eco-museum and forest station is situated at the entrance to the park, the former offering excellent guidance on its flora and fauna. For those with walking difficulties, there are a few enclosures nearby to ensure that every visitor can see some of the wildlife.

**HOW TO GET THERE**:
By road from Gabès
**WHEN TO GO:**
During the winter months – the summer is far too hot.
**DON'T MISS:**
The remnants of ancient civilizations that occupied this area. There are Neolithic places of worship, Berber tombs, a prehistoric site and old mines to be seen.
**YOU SHOULD KNOW:**
This is one of the few remaining places in the world where the sand or dune cat has been sighted, although no specimens have been collected. Sand cats have very furry feet and can live in extremes of heat and cold, as long as there are enough small rodents for them to eat.

# Ichkeul National Park

Comprising a large lake and wetland area by the side of Ichkeul Mountain, Ichkeul National Park is the only natural area in North Africa to be recognized as a World Heritage Site. Easily reached from the capital, Tunis, this is a wonderful place to visit.

Connected to a large lagoon which is itself connected to the ocean, the 85-sq-km (33-sq-mi) shallow and brackish Lake Ichkeul is an essential refuge for more than 200 species of trans-Saharan migratory birds that gather here each spring and autumn. During the winter season between 200,000 and 300,000 birds can be seen on the lake and its surrounding marshlands. Herons, white storks, spoonbills, flamingoes, ducks, geese, waders and endangered white-headed ducks rest up while, overhead, buzzards, kites, ospreys, falcons and harriers hunt for the perfect meal.

The lake itself is full of life, including otters, frogs, toads, snakes, turtles, crabs and fish such as eels, sole, sea bass and anchovies. Plenty of pondweed provides both food and shelter for many species.

On Mount Ichkeul, jackal, genet, wild cat, porcupine, wild boar and mongoose thrive – there is even a large boa population. During winter, when the area receives the most rainfall, the mountainside is carpeted with flowers and, just at the entrance, a small herd of water buffalo can be seen, often with white egrets on their backs, eating the insects bothering their hosts.

During summer the lake becomes more saline as the rains depart and salt-loving plants begin to colonize the edges. The locals have been known to use lake water for drinking and irrigation and, despite being illegal, cattle, sheep and goats graze in the park, too. Hunting, fishing and quarrying also continues, albeit clandestinely.

# Khroumirie Mountains

The Khroumirie Mountains are situated in the eastern reaches of the Atlas Mountains, which stretch from Morocco through to northern Tunisia. The average height of these peaks is 800 m (2,625 ft) and their 550 km (340 mi) of footpaths and trails provide a wonderful hiking experience. At 1,014 m (3,327 ft), the highest peak is Jebel Biri.

This region enjoys a Mediterranean climate and the town of Ain Draham, deep in the Khroumirie Mountains and developed by the French as a hunting resort, has a European look with its steeply sloped red roofs. It is an excellent base for a visit, surrounded as it is by many paths and tracks leading through this lovely forested region. Trees include mimosa, eucalyptus, pine, juniper and – the dominant species – cork oak. These last are large evergreens with gnarled and twisted branches that live for about 150 years, growing a thick layer of rough bark that can be harvested without damage to the tree about 12 times during their lifespan. The cork layer regenerates, making the trees a renewable resource.

This woodland habitat shelters mammals such as deer, wild boar, jackals, wild cats, porcupines, foxes and mongoose, as well as birds such as partridges, green woodpeckers and cuckoos. Tortoises may be seen trudging about on sunny slopes and rocky verges. Hiking through this shady cork forest, with its springs and waterfalls, valleys and glorious panoramic views is an absolute joy. The region receives more rainfall than most in North Africa, and some snow falls during winter. Much of the wildlife suffered from over hunting by the local population, so steps were taken to protect it. This has been successful in the main but you will probably see more boars' heads mounted on walls than while exploring the forest.

**HOW TO GET THERE:**
By car or public transport from Tabarka or Bizerte on the coast, south to Ain Draham.
**WHEN TO GO:**
It is possible to go at any time of year, but be aware of possible winter snow. Even at the height of summer the Khroumirie Mountains remain reasonably cool.
**DON'T MISS:**
Ain Draham's Women's Weaving Cooperative. Here you can see carpets being woven by hand and buy them from the showroom.
**YOU SHOULD KNOW:**
Tunisia's cork forests are owned by the state and looked after by Forest Administration. The country's main water reservoirs are located here. Locals have the right to graze livestock and gather firewood, some of which is made into charcoal to provide another source of income.

# Erg Chebbi

**HOW TO GET THERE:**
Organized tours can be arranged from most major Moroccan cities, but Merzouga can also be reached by public transport, rental car or 4x4 with a driver.
**WHEN TO GO:**
April, May, June, September and October are the best months to experience the dunes. In July and August many Moroccans visit for sand bathing, a traditional treatment for arthritis and rheumatism.
**DON'T MISS:**
Merzouga and its surrounding area. You may visit Berber villages and an oasis where date palms provide shade and the air is moist and cool. The neat patchwork of fields of vegetables, wheat and alfalfa and the sound of trickling water is a relief after the relentless heat of the desert around you.
**YOU SHOULD KNOW:**
Local folklore has it that Erg Chebbi was formed as a punishment from God. A woman and child were refused shelter by the villagers of Merzouga, which was situated where the dunes are today. As a result, an enormous sandstorm blew up and buried the whole village.

The Erg Chebbi dunes near the village of Merzouga are the most impressive of the two ergs in southeast Morocco. The landscape is flat, desolate, stony desert, but suddenly, and seemingly out of nowhere, these vast Saharan sand dunes rise up to 150 m (490 ft) high, blown there by the wind. They cover an area 22 km (14 mi) long and 5 km (3 mi) wide and are an astonishing sight.

This is the closest to being in the full-on Sahara without first participating in some extremely intrepid travelling, and it is a remarkable experience. It is possible to take a camel ride to the top of the dunes, or hire a quad bike, but the very best way to experience them is on foot. Go to watch the sunset – it will be like no other: an awe-inspiring visual feast of red, pink, orange, yellow and purple – and if luck is on your side, you might even see a green flash.

A walk into the dunes in the dark is also exciting, lit only by the moon and a myriad of sparkling stars in the sky above. Infinitely more stars are visible when there is no ambient light, and the realization of the immensity of the universe is humbling. It is cold at night and, because it is so hot during the day, the body feels the drop in temperature very strongly, so dress accordingly. Sunrise is another good time to be on the dunes.

During the day try dune boarding or have fun just sliding or rolling down the dunes. In the summer months the daytime temperature is often over 45°C (113°F), so remember to take plenty of water, a hat, sunglasses and sunscreen. Visitors may stay in traditional camel-and-goat-hair tents.

*The impressive Erg Chebbi dunes*

# Jbel Tazzeka National Park

Located in the Middle Atlas Mountains some 97 km (60 mi) east of Fez is the old garrison town of Taza, which is the perfect base from which to explore Jbel Tazzeka. This 1,980-m (6,496-ft) peak rises in the centre of the surrounding national park, which is famed for its scenic beauty. There are many routes to take, short or long, but on reaching the summit of Jbel Tazzeka the reward is majestic views of the surrounding forested mountains and snowy peaks in the distance.

The park is a great area for hiking through forests of cedar, cork oak and even olive trees; splashing through clear springs; marvelling at waterfalls and lakes; and exploring canyons and caves. The undergrowth is largely tall ferns and bracken, interspersed with pink cistus – a good habitat for large frogs, brilliantly colourful lizards and birds such as rollers, shrikes, short-toed treecreepers and hoopoes. During spring and summer gorgeous butterflies abound. Don't be surprised to meet goat herders or farmers ploughing small plots with oxen or donkeys. Crops are surrounded by yellow-and-white daisies and blood-red poppies, which add to the pleasure of walking here.

Dayat Chiker is an interesting, large, dry lake with strange rock formations and fault lines. For much of the year crops are grown here and animals are grazed. But the best-known feature in the park is an enormous cave system. Discovered some 80 years ago by Norbert Casteret, a French citizen, the Friouato caves form the largest cave system in North Africa and have yet to be fully explored. They are entered via a 100-m (330-ft) deep shaft, with 580 steep steps down. Then chamber follows chamber, each with spectacular stalactites, stalagmites and even stalactite curtains.

**HOW TO GET THERE:**
By road from Taza
**WHEN TO GO:**
May to November
**DON'T MISS:**
Even if cities aren't your thing, visit Fez. The ancient walled city, Fez el Bali, is a UNESCO World Heritage Site. Utterly fascinating, it is unlike anywhere else in the world.
**YOU SHOULD KNOW:**
If time is short, there is a beautiful 112 km (70 mi) scenic drive through Jbel Tazzeka National Park. It is a good way of seeing a great deal in just one day.

*Sheer rock walls line the dramatic Todra Gorge.*

# The Dades and Todra Gorges

Morocco bursts with dramatic natural beauty and the Dades and Todra Gorges rank high on the list of memorable sights. The pair lie fairly close to each other in the Atlas Mountains, 110 km (70 mi) northeast of Ouarzazate.

At full flow during winter, a river runs through the Dades valley, irrigating wheat, figs, dates, argan and almond trees. In early spring the almond blossom is enchanting, softening the spectacularly vivid red and rocky landscape. Historically, the Berbers fortified this fertile area with hundreds of *kasbahs*: great, castellated buildings made of red mud, straw and lime, their turrets and walls decorated with carvings. Some are inhabited but many stand empty, gradually being reclaimed by the earth.

The entrance to the Dades is by paved track, although it is far more interesting to hike than to attempt to drive. There are fantastic rock formations and a walk through the gorge, with its sheer rock walls, is unforgettable. Both gorges are a big draw for rock climbers, with many different routes to attempt.

The Todra Gorge is the more dramatic of the two. It is 600 m (656 yd) long and cuts through the mountains, the 300-m (985-ft) walls guarding a passage at some points a mere 10 m (33 ft) in width. As sunshine only reaches the bottom of the gorge in the mornings, the stream here is very cold and at night the temperature can drop to freezing. A few families live and farm nearby and can often be seen with sheep, goats or camels, making their way along the dirt track to settlements at the other end.

In the past this area rarely saw tourists and although those days are gone, the sheer drama of the gorges and their surrounding mountains and valleys make them definitely worth visiting.

**HOW TO GET THERE:**
Public transport, shared or privately hired taxi, rental car or organized tours can be arranged from Ouarzazate.

**WHEN TO GO:**
Spring or autumn. The best time for photography in the gorges is between 08.00 and 13.00.

**DON'T MISS:**
El Kelaa M'Gouna, an oasis in the Dades valley that is the centre of Moroccan rose cultivation. It is a great hiking area and every May a traditional Rose Festival is held.

**YOU SHOULD KNOW:**
Berbers lived in North Africa long before the Arabs arrived. Many Moroccans have Berber origins but, as they are often perceived to be 'backward' due largely to their homelands in the most traditional and rural parts of the country, many deny their roots. The Berber language is entirely different from Arabic, and sadly is not recognized as an official language in Morocco, but French is.

# Pico de Fogo

Some 483 km (300 mi) from the coast of Senegal, West Africa, lies the Republic of Cape Verde. An archipelago of ten islands and eight islets, its capital, Praia, is on the largest island, Santiago. Fogo is Cape Verde's fourth largest island and the only one with an active volcano: Pico de Fogo.

Two eruptions shook the island during the last century. In 1951 lava poured down the southern flanks of the volcano and created two new cones. The 1995 eruption was incredibly dramatic. After days of small earthquakes, flaming lava shot 400 m (1,310 ft) into the sky, raining down into the crater and forcing the inhabitants to run for their lives. An ash cloud 5 km (3 mi) high covered Fogo and it was seven weeks before the lava stopped flowing altogether. One village was effectively destroyed.

At 2,892 m (9,488 ft) and dominating every view, Pico de Fogo looms high, and a hike or two around and into the caldera is hard work and exhilarating, providing extraordinary views not only of the volcano itself but also of Santiago. The volcano's eastern slopes are covered with dark lava from eruptions that have occurred over hundreds of thousands of years.

Volcanoes are famously fertile and Pico de Fogo is no exception. The crater is known as Cha das Caldeiras and within it the vast floor is relatively flat, although strewn with lumps of lava. Two small villages exist here, cultivating vegetables and fruit, including grapes that are turned into locally renowned wine. The valleys of the northeastern slopes are also used for agriculture – coffee and vines grow here, amidst eucalyptus trees.

There are many hikes to enjoy: to the summit of Pico, round the crater rim or floor, to the 1995 peak, or the steep descent to the town of Mosteiros, caught between the mountain and the sea.

**HOW TO GET THERE:**
There are daily flights from Praia, and twice-weekly ferries. Those arriving by yacht can anchor at the harbour north of São Felipe, Fogo's capital. An *aluguer* (shared taxi), rental car or a conventional taxi is the best way of getting around once there.
**WHEN TO GO:**
November to July
**DON'T MISS:**
The Cooperativa in the crater, where you can enjoy music and dancing in the evenings; the Bandeira de São Felipe, Fogo's liveliest festival that takes place at the end of April; São Felipe's historic centre.
**YOU SHOULD KNOW:**
The people who live in and around Pico de Fogo are straight haired, sometimes blonde and blue eyed, with light skin. They are believed to be descended from the French Duc de Montrond, who fled here to escape a duel in the 19th century, bringing with him the vines that are now so productive.

*Pico de Fogo dominates the surrounding lanscape.*

*Pelicans inhabit the many sandbanks and small islands.*

**HOW TO GET THERE:**
By public or rented transport from Dakar, then *pirogue* from the park headquarters. It is possible to stay in very basic *campements* on the Langue de Barbarie itself, rather than in Saint-Louis.

**WHEN TO GO:**
November to May is best.

**DON'T MISS:**
The bird-count tours. On the 24th of each month a walking tour takes place and, on the 28th of the month, boats tour the full length of the park. On both occasions visitors may help the professionals spot water birds.

**YOU SHOULD KNOW:**
The name *Langue de Barbarie* was taken from the prickly or Barbary pears that once grew here in profusion. Although the park is just 25 km (15 mi) long, the entire length of the sand stretches from Nouadibou in Mauritania, to Saint-Louis – a matter of some 600 km (375 mi).

# The Langue de Barbarie National Park

The West African city of Saint-Louis is situated on a narrow island some 25 km (15 mi) from the mouth of the Senegal River. A UNESCO World Heritage Site since 2000, this charmingly dilapidated city is in three parts. The historic centre is on the island itself, while Sor, with its tidal marshlands, is on the eastern mainland, separated from the island by the river. To the west the river is separated from the Atlantic by a narrow sand spit, the Langue de Barbarie.

At 30 km (19 mi) long, the sand spit itself has little vegetation – mostly casuarina trees that have been encouraged to grow to help prevent erosion – and can best be explored by *pirogue*. These small, flat-bottomed boats are used by local fishermen and can be easily handled in shallow water – paddled, punted or used with a small sail or outboard motor. The trip alone is interesting as the *pirogue* gently moves through the many sandbanks and small islands. This is an area of great importance to migratory birds, as well as being a haven for marine turtles, many of which nest here.

From early spring until autumn, multitudes of birds breed here, while others overwinter. White and grey pelicans waddle about and pink flamingoes pick their way carefully around the water's edge. Terns and swallows swoop and dive while lapwings and weavers and glamorous sunbirds busy themselves nest building. Herons and ducks are ubiquitous, as are cormorants, which fly steadily over the water, occasionally diving in and capturing an unwary fish. Pata monkeys, lizards and crabs abound, although it is rare to see a turtle – they just come ashore during the summer months to lay their eggs, departing immediately afterwards. The turtles are closely monitored as they are an endangered species, and unfortunately poaching still occurs.

# Kiang West National Park

Kiang West National Park is probably the most important and least visited wildlife park in The Gambia. Located on the south bank of the Gambia River, it is only 145 km (90 mi) from the capital, Banjul. The journey, however, is hard as the road is in poor repair. Established in 1987, the river forms the park's northern boundary.

Kiang West is uninhabited, flat and low. Three *bolongs*, or creeks, run through the interior, which mainly consists of savannah and deciduous woodland, with mangroves and tidal flats. There are many trees: red acacia, kapok, and several species native to the Sahelian biogeographic area that divides the Sahara desert from the southern savannahs.

Most of The Gambia's mammals are found here, including antelopes, warthogs, spotted hyenas, leopards, servals and caracals. This is habitat for marsh mongoose, pythons, cobras and Nile crocodiles. West African manatees and humpback dolphins can sometimes be spotted in the Jarin creek.

The Gambia is famous for its birds and this area is home to half the country's species – more than 300 have been recorded. During the dry season many raptors are found such as eagles – including the bateleur, Kiang West's logo – hawks, harriers, falcons and the ubiquitous vultures. Other birds include hornbills, with their recognizably awkward flight, weavers, parrots, kingfishers, sandgrouse and chats. It is not essential to take a guide, but they are knowledgeable and quick to point out birds that you might otherwise miss.

Make for Tubabkollon Point. Here you are close to the river and antelopes and warthogs can be spotted from the nearby escarpment. A waterhole within walking distance can be observed from a viewing shelter. Here you'll see many animals, including monkeys, coming to drink as the dry season tightens its grip.

**HOW TO GET THERE:**
4x4 on the southern Trans-Gambia highway to Dumbuto, the main base of Kiang West. You can also take tours that go partly by road and the remainder of the way by river boat.
**WHEN TO GO:**
During the dry season, from November to April
**DON'T MISS:**
The Nganingkoi Bolon tidal creek where you will see many wading birds, and possibly marsh mongoose hunting for crabs.
**YOU SHOULD KNOW:**
Kiang West National Park warrants more than a quick look, and it is easy to stay nearby. You can organize this independently or through a tour company.

# Pendjari Biosphere Reserve

**HOW TO GET THERE:**
It is an eight-hour drive from Cotonou, Benin's economic and administrative capital, but only a five- or six-hour drive from Burkina Faso and Niger respectively.
**WHEN TO GO:**
From October to mid February. Pendjari is open year round, but the trip is more difficult during the rainy season.
**DON'T MISS:**
The local tribal villages and the Tata Sombas of the Betamaribe. Benin has several ancient and treasured cultures.
**YOU SHOULD KNOW:**
The dirt roads within are better maintained and easier to drive than the roads accessing the park. A map is available at all the park entrances and you are requested to drive slowly and carefully to minimize disturbance to the wildlife. The best time to see animals is in the early morning or late afternoon, near the river or lakes. Take binoculars, sunscreen and plenty of water.

Situated in the northwest of Benin, Pendjari National Park, some 12,000 sq km (4,635 sq mi) in size, is part of the largest complex of Protected Areas in West Africa, crossing the borders of Benin, Niger and Burkino Faso. During the 1950s Benin, then part of French West Africa, listed Pendjari as a Protected Area and it became a hunting ground for French colonials.

Today, Pendjari still retains three areas for hunters and their professional guides, under the ownership, control and supervision of the local people. A percentage of the fees received for hunting permits is used to improve the lives of those living near the park boundaries; the remainder helps preserve and improve the Biosphere Reserve, which it became in 1986. Much emphasis is placed on the growth of ecotourism and research, and this is a fantastic area through which to hike, go mountain-biking, take canoe trips, join organized safaris or drive independently.

Renowned for its populations of large mammals, the savannah and grassland is home to cheetahs, lions, leopards, hyena, African wild dogs and jackals. Other large mammals include elephants, buffalo and hippos. Pendjari contains several types of antelope and monkeys, but most of all, there are birds.

With a backdrop of the Atakora range and its rocky cliffs, Pendjari park is lush in part, thanks to the eponymous broad river winding through it, bordered by thick, canopied forest. Within its boundaries over 300 species of bird can be found. Birds of prey include kestrels, kites, harriers and eagles such as the booted eagle and the African fish eagle. Smaller species include chats, babblers, waxbills, whydah, white-throated francolin and many more. Purple glossy starlings flash past, their iridescent plumage almost shockingly vivid, disappearing into the shelter of baobabs, palms and other African tree and shrub species.

# Gola Forest

Bordered by the Atlantic Ocean, Guinea and Liberia, Sierra Leone is severely underdeveloped. Its inhabitants still suffer from the after effects of a disastrous civil war, only resolved in 2000. Deforestation has increased since the end of the war, but in 2005 the RSPB and Bird Life International, alongside the Forestry Department and the Conservation Society, joined forces to work on a conservation and sustainable development project in the Gola Forest. It is hoped that by 2012, the forest will achieve national park status.

Gola Forest is the largest area of lowland rainforest in Sierra Leone. It is divided into four distinct areas. Gola North is rugged, fairly high and drained by the Mogbai River, while Gola East and West, separated by the Mano River, are low-lying and swampy. Tiwai Island, situated in the Moa River to the west of Gola West, is a game sanctuary.

The closed canopy forest, which contains 200 species of tree, supports most of West Africa's wildlife. Around 50 species of mammal live in Gola, including ten primates. Several species are vulnerable or endangered, including chimpanzees, elephants and pygmy hippopotami. Other species have only recently been found, such as the leopard, zebra duiker and bongo. There are about 330 different birds. Nine are threatened, six are vulnerable and one, the rufous fishing owl, is endangered. The 770 species of flowering plants in the forest help the very high diversity of butterflies to flourish; over 600 species have been found there, three of which are new discoveries.

It is possible to visit the Gola Forest in a 4x4, with a guide, just for the day. But for a much more interesting visit, full camping kit, complete with porters and a cook can be arranged. If rainforests are of interest, Gola should be visited. This is why the park is known as the country's 'green diamond'.

**HOW TO GET THERE:**
Gola is located in the southeast of Sierra Leone and is accessible by road. The nearest big town, Kenema, is a six-hour drive southwest of Freetown, the capital.

**WHEN TO GO:**
The dry season is between December and May. The average temperature is 26°C (78.8°F) but it can fall to 16°C (60.8°F) at night.

**DON'T MISS:**
The pygmy hippopotamus, the white-necked picathartes which nests in colonies on cliffs in the forest, and the very rare Gola malimbe.

**YOU SHOULD KNOW:**
Despite all efforts, Gola is threatened by logging, hunting and mining, including for diamonds. Famously, blood diamonds were used to finance the civil war. Sierra Leone is rich in diamonds, and corruption is rife. Drug cartels have started to use the country as a place from which to ship drugs to Europe, which may turn it into a narco-state similar to neighbouring Guinea Bissau.

# Comoe National Park

**HOW TO GET THERE:**
Comoe National Park is 410 km (255 mi) by road from Abidjan. A 4x4 is essential.

**WHEN TO GO:**
The park is open to visitors from December to May.

**DON'T MISS:**
Big-game fishing is available on the Comoe River if hiking doesn't appeal.

**YOU SHOULD KNOW:**
The country is edging towards civil war, which has exacerbated the constant problems with poaching, particularly of elephants, overgrazing of cattle and the burning of land for agricultural purposes in Comoe National Park.

Located in northeastern Côte d'Ivoire, south of the country's border with Burkino Faso, is Comoe National Park. West Africa's largest game park was inscribed on the UNESCO World Heritage Site list in 1983, but added to the endangered sites list in 2003. The political turmoil that has overtaken the country during recent years has made 65 per cent of the park 'beyond the control of the staff'.

The Comoe River, which flows south from the northeastern section of the park, is the reason Comoe contains such remarkable plant diversity, including shrub savannahs and dense rainforest normally found much further south. It is best visited when its floodplains seasonally become tall grasslands, tempting many species to leave the forest in search of food.

The park contains a great many birds and mammals. Among these are 17 types of carnivore, including African wild dogs and leopards. Chimpanzees, baboons, colobus monkeys and the endangered Diana monkey can be found here, as can duikers, bongos, hartebeests, kobs and bushbucks. African elephants, buffaloes, warthogs and hippos are also present, but in fairly small numbers.

Comoe is also known for its birds. Some 494 species include five species of vulture, 50 species of other raptors and ten species of heron, including the goliath heron. It is possible to sit by the river's edge with binoculars and observe many of these creatures at close range.

This is a park for adventurous explorers looking for a truly authentic experience. During the dry season, when the park is open to visitors, 500 km (310 mi) of tracks are available. Some of these are rugged and hard to follow, and it is wise to employ a guide. Two tourist zones have been established, but there is an area that is strictly off limits.

*An aerial view of a village in Comoe National Park*

# Tai National Park

Declared a Forest and Wildlife Refuge in 1926, Tai National Park became a UNESCO World Heritage Site in 1982, 46 years later. Situated between the Cavally and Sassandra rivers in the southwest of Côte d'Ivoire, this is the largest area of primary tropical rainforest in the whole of West Africa.

Vast trees soar to heights of 46 m (150 ft), their massive trunks using supporting roots for extra strength. The dense canopy excludes sunlight, making for good hiking as it keeps the undergrowth down. Tai has two recognizable types of forest: the north and southeast supports trees such as palms and ebony on poor, thin soil, while in the southwest the trees are all tropical, rain-loving species, 150 of which are endemic.

There are 47 species of large mammal living in this forest, five of which are endangered. It is not particularly easy to see large mammals – many are elusive – but there are African elephants, leopards, golden cats, various species of duiker, pygmy hippos, Cape buffaloes and colobus monkeys. The chimpanzees of Tai National Park have become famous thanks to years of study carried out by Swiss researchers. The apes live in groups of 70–80, and during the dry season visitors can hear them cracking nuts open with stones. The elephants, which are on the endangered list, aid the region's ecosystem, as secondary forest springs from dung deposited in clearings.

Areas around the rivers are the best places from which to spot both large mammals and birds. There are no fewer than 230 bird species here, eight of which are endangered. Among these is the white-breasted guinea fowl. Tai is protected by a buffer zone some 5 km (3 mi) wide, part of which is farmed, but there are on-going problems with poaching, illegal tree felling and gold mining.

**HOW TO GET THERE:**
Visit the Tai National Park Headquarters in San Pedro for a permit, and take their advice as to which method of visiting the park would suit you best.

**WHEN TO GO:**
The dry season is between December and February.

**DON'T MISS:**
Hiking up Mount Nienokoue, in the south of the park. The effort is more than worth the view of a never-ending sea of green rainforest, and you are likely to see animals and birds *en route*.

**YOU SHOULD KNOW:**
A new strain of Ebola virus has been isolated in Tai National Park. Chimpanzee meat, which has been linked with spreading the virus, is frequently eaten locally. Côte d'Ivoire has been relatively peaceful since 2007, but it is a potentially explosive country. Visit only if you are already familiar with it or if you have family or friends there.

*Walking through the towering trees in Tai National Park.*

# Crystal Mountains National Park

Gabon lies on the equator and contains three well-defined areas: mountains, savannah and the coastal plain. Unusually in sub-Saharan Africa, the economy – boosted by oil revenues – is relatively well distributed and the government has made conservation a high priority. Some 10 per cent of the country is protected in 13 national parks, boosting revenue from tourism as well as protecting Gabon's natural treasures.

The Crystal Mountains National Park is a section of a wide, rocky escarpment situated in the northwest of the country between Equatorial Guinea and the Ogooué River. Mount Iboundji, in the north of the mountain range, reaches just 1,575 m (5,167 ft) and is the highest peak in Gabon.

Stunningly beautiful, the park is the epitome of a tropical African jungle – teeming with life and famed as a biodiversity hotspot. An American research team has been working here since 2004. The flora is exceptional. Trees include hardwoods such as ebony, mahogany and purpleheart, as well as *okoumé* and *ozigo*, all of which produce valuable timber, and there is an extraordinary array of flowers, including endemic orchids and begonias. At higher elevations, clouds envelop the forest, producing a mystical landscape of tangled undergrowth, trees shrouded in lianas, and climbing vines.

This equatorial rainforest provides habitat for a wide variety of wildlife. Elephants, leopards, antelopes, jackals and zebras roam the savannah; crocodiles and hippos haunt the river; lowland gorillas and many other primates swing through branches in chattering groups. Pythons and vipers hunt for small prey at ground level, while toucans and parrots screech in the canopy above.

Take a wildlife safari to the Crystal Mountains and visit the Kinguele Falls in the heart of the region, on the M'Bei River. It is a marvellous opportunity to experience the African rainforest, normally only seen on television screens.

# Loango National Park

In 2002 Gabon's president Omar Bongo Ondimba created 13 national parks. The existing Petit Loango and Iguéla Reserves were joined to form Loango National Park. Its habitat includes forest, savannah and lagoons as well as swamps and untamed coastline, and it quickly became a popular spot for ex-pats living in Libreville. Situated between the Nkomi and Ndogo lagoons, south of the capital, and based on the concept 'tourism pays for conservation', it became the focus of small-scale, low-impact, high-end tourism.

The coastline boasts the largest number and variety of whale and dolphin species, including humpback and killer whales, with the exception of South Africa. The ocean also contains many large fish, and Loango is renowned for its record-sized Atlantic tarpon. Fishing in these waters is an exciting experience.

Four types of sea turtle breed on this coastline, including the Olive Ridley and the leatherback, both of which are endangered. From November to February, visitors may join the data-collection team, going out at night in search of nests or hatchlings. Three species of crocodile may also be seen on such a night-time trek.

Fabulous wildlife abounds in Loango throughout the year and, although the animals are shy, there is a good chance of a sighting from a 4x4, on foot, from a hide or from a boat. Trips around Iguéla lagoon are very rewarding and birdwatching expeditions can be arranged. Expect to see Pel's and vermiculated fishing owls, Forbes's plover, and African river martins among others.

The savannah and forest is home to many mammals, large and small, and although Loango is not like the big game parks in East Africa, on a safari there is a good chance of observing several species such as zebras, herds of buffalo, lowland gorillas and chimpanzees in unusual settings.

*A Western lowland gorilla in Loango National Park*

**WHEN TO GO:**
The best time for little rain and clear skies is December. In the dry season, from June to September, the sky is overcast. Some months are better than others for seeing particular animals, so check before booking if you have a particular interest.

**DON'T MISS:**
Elephants and forest buffaloes walking on the beach at sunset or the whale-watching season from July to September.

**YOU SHOULD KNOW:**
Africa's last Eden, as Loango is often known, is where *National Geographic* photographer Michael Nichols took his photographs of surfing hippos.

*Tourists on the tree-top walkway in Kakum Conservation Area*

# Kakum Conservation Area

Just an hour by road from Cape Coast, the Kakum Conservation Area covers 350 sq km (135 sq mi) of dense tropical rainforest. The area supports a rich diversity of wildlife, including the white-bearded colobus monkey, bush pigs, porcupines and the timid forest elephant. Many species of birds and butterflies also flourish in this lavish land of plenty and the noise of competing wildlife provides a wonderful, if none too peaceful, soundtrack to Kakum.

The conservation area has a number of hiking trails that take ramblers deep into the forest to a land of fast-flowing tropical rivers and spectacular rapids. Park guides are available to explain the area's economic and cultural significance to local people, as well as to lead the way through the dense undergrowth.

It is the 65-m (213-ft) tall giant hardwood trees, however, that are the main attraction in Kakum. Ghana is by no means unique in suffering rapid deforestation and the need for food, timber and even firewood means that what takes hundreds of years to grow can often be destroyed in the blink of an eye. To their credit, the administrators in Kakum have come up with an ingenious way of giving their trees greater economic value by leaving them *in situ* than they would have if they were chopped down. Visitors can now climb high into the canopy by way of a 500-m (547-yd) long tree-top walkway to experience the environment of the high-tree dwellers. A good head for heights is required as the walkway is little more than a narrow width of wood held in a rope cradle. If vertigo can be avoided, it is a magnificent way to view a world that is seen only by canopy dwellers and wildlife cameramen.

**HOW TO GET THERE:**
By bus from Pedu Junction in Cape Coast
**WHEN TO GO:**
All year round, but it's driest from May to August.
**DON'T MISS:**
The area is best seen just after a sharp shower. The mist caused by evaporating rainfall shrouds the dense vegetation in a cloak of tiny water particles.
**YOU SHOULD KNOW:**
Kakum is not the best place to get close to wildlife. Forest dwellers are generally shy and chances are they will hear people before people see them. The best way to view animals in the park is by way of a night-time stakeout, when there is the possibility of sighting the elusive forest elephant.

# Banc d'Arguin National Park

Mauritania is a vast country in West Africa on the western fringes of the Sahara Desert. Its boundaries, save for the Senegal River to the south, are little more than lines in the sand. Its main resource, other than some low-level mining, comes from its Atlantic coastline in the form of fishing. But even here the right to fish very often belongs to others. This makes the National Park of Banc d'Arguin all the more vital for the protection of the ecology of the area.

The park covers the largely desert coastal region of the country between the capital Nouakchott and Nouadhibou. Most of its interior is made up of sand blown by strong Saharan winds but, away from the arid core, Banc d'Arguin contains an astonishing variety of habitats. The area of most significance to the biodiversity of the region is a large expanse of mudflats, particularly those adjacent to the island of Tidra – the largest of 15 significant islands off the coast. Millions of birds head south to escape the European winter and breed in the park, making the mudflats of Banc d'Arguin the largest bird conservation area on Earth. The fish-rich waters are also a magnet for dolphins and sea turtles.

Perhaps the most surprising and remarkable part of the park is its large mangrove swamp. As well as containing the most diverse flora in the park, it offers up clues about the area's very different geological past and about our ever-changing planet. The fact that Banc d'Arguin contains such an assortment of fertile grounds is largely due to its once having been the huge estuary of a river system that flowed from the now-parched Sahara Desert.

**HOW TO GET THERE:**
By road from Nouakchott – a 4x4 vehicle is essential.
**WHEN TO GO:**
All year round – wildlife-watching is best from November to March.
**DON'T MISS:**
Birdwatching – especially from the island of Niroumi – where the colonies of bar-tailed godwit, ringed plover and dunlin represent over half of the total Atlantic population.
**YOU SHOULD KNOW:**
Travel to and within Mauritania is difficult. Advice on safety and security should be taken from the Foreign Office (UK) or State Department (US) before travelling.

*Greater flamingoes are one of many species that breed in the park.*

# Bandiagara Escarpment

When journeying through the flat, unexciting and scorched landscape of Mali, the traveller could be forgiven for recalling the words of Samuel Johnson, who said that there are places 'worth seeing, but not worth going to see'. Such thoughts are quickly dismissed as the road begins a steady incline and one of Africa's greatest natural wonders rises mirage-like out of the desolate landscape. The gigantic Bandiagara Escarpment – a 150-km (94-mi) long towering sandstone cliff of rich ochre colour – runs from Ouo in the west to the Honbori mountains in the southeast and, as well as being a geological phenomenon, is a place of no little human intrigue.

The cliff face itself varies in height from 100 m (328 ft) to 500 m (1,640 ft) and is broken by deep ravines and scree-lined passages. The higher levels of the escarpment have a rich and diverse flora which has all but disappeared at lower levels. Archaeological research has revealed that high up in the cliffs a system of caves and tunnels was created over 2,000 years ago. The caves then lay empty for over a thousand years until the Tellem pygmies arrived and built houses in the crevices. The remains of these elevated structures can still be seen. Today, the cliffs act as protection for a string of over 300 villages belonging to the local Dogon people.

It is hard to leave the area without the feeling that you've visited a place out of time. The flat-topped and cone-roofed clusters of Dogon buildings blend in to seem part of nature and the people themselves have an animist system of beliefs and rituals that is far removed from anything else on Earth.

*The spectacular cliffs of the Bandiagara Escarpment*

# Air and Tenere Natural Reserves

Located in northern Niger towards the border with Algeria, the Air and Tenere Natural Reserves together form the largest protected area in Africa. At 77,000 sq km (29,730 sq mi) they cover an area of arid and semi-arid land on the edge of the Sahara Desert that is roughly the size of Scotland. The combined reserve was created in 1988 and includes the western portion of the Tenere Desert and the eastern peaks of the Air Mountains. Its mission was to provide an environment where wildlife could flourish and it was hoped that sustainable populations of desert fauna could be established in the area. However, years of civil strife have seen wildlife numbers plummet. The addax antelope, ostrich, and dama gazelle have all but disappeared from the region, while the once numerous Barbary sheep and Dorcas gazelle are now seldom seen.

Although denuded of much in the way of wildlife, the reserve is still a place of unusual beauty. The Tenere Desert contains one of the world's largest sand seas and some of the highest barchan dunes in the Sahara. It is a bleak landscape punctuated only by the odd sand-blasted tree whose spiky leaves have evolved to withstand sandstorms and intense heat.

The Air Mountains are positively verdant by comparison. Comprising several massifs above a craggy plateau, they support a wide variety of grasses, shrubs and small trees. The mountains are also a good landmark for migrating birds and their relative greenness provides welcome respite in a land where water is at a premium.

The area was established as a UNESCO World Heritage Site in 1991 and was almost immediately put on its endangered list. Things are now moving in the right direction and one sixth of the reserve is working well as a sanctuary for the addax antelope.

*Sand dunes in the Tenere Desert meet the Air Mountains.*

**HOW TO GET THERE:**
Travel by road from Niger's capital, Niamey, or (more difficult) from Algeria.
**WHEN TO GO:**
During the 'cold' season (October to February) when the heat is less oppressive.
**DON'T MISS:**
The distant view of the Air Mountains that appear to bubble up out of the desert.
**YOU SHOULD KNOW:**
The north of Niger has pretty much been a zone of conflict for the past 30 years. Advice on safety and security should be taken from the Foreign Office (UK) or State Department (US) before travelling.

*Mount Cameroon is the region's highest peak.*

# Mount Cameroon

Dubbed 'the roof of West Africa', Mount Cameroon at 4,095 m (13,435 ft) above sea level is not only the region's highest peak but is also the only active volcano of mainland tropical Africa west of the Rift Valley. It is part of a basalt ridge that rises from the Gulf of Guinea and is a truly awesome sight when viewed from the sea. It is also as wet as it gets. The region surrounding the mountain receives some of the heaviest rainfall on Earth at an incredible average of 10 m (33 ft) per year. This, coupled with the tropical heat of the lower slopes of the mountain, creates a hothouse environment for a diverse and spectacular range of plant life. Some of the insect-attracting plants that thrive there have heads as big as bicycle wheels.

Despite its elevation, the mountain is more of a hike than a climb, but the vertical journey takes the traveller through four distinct habitats. At sea level the area is characterized by dense mangrove forest, which soon gives way to lush evergreen lowland forest. The tall luxuriant growth of the lowlands is then replaced by thinner mountain forest until the land turns to savannah above 2,000 m (6,560 ft). Once at the top the hiker can explore recent volcanic action in the form of craters, lava streams and crater lakes.

The area around the mountain is administered by the youthful and vibrant Mount Cameroon Inter Communal Ecotourism Board which seeks to preserve the area by marrying the mountain's well-deserved popularity with the needs of local people. Portage is compulsory (no bad thing, given the heat and humidity) and there is a series of huts on the mountain for overnight stays.

**HOW TO GET THERE:**
By road from Cape Coast or bus from Limbe

**WHEN TO GO:**
All year round, but the rain is most intense in the months between June and October. The hottest months are between March and May.

**DON'T MISS:**
The view over the Atlantic from the summit. Because the mountain is often shrouded in cloud, it is worth allowing extra time on any climb to have a greater chance of clear weather.

**YOU SHOULD KNOW:**
The climber should arrive prepared for all weathers. The mountain is stiflingly hot at the lower gradients while, at the top, a dusting of snow is not uncommon in the cooler season (September to February).

# Zakouma National Park

The *raison d'etre* of a game reserve is to bring people close to the wild animals they would normally have little access to. This is a happy marriage, as the visitors bring much-needed revenue, which in turn goes towards preserving the animals' habitat. Safety and security in exchange for the disturbance created by a few motor vehicles is no bad deal. For the staff and wildlife at Zakouma National Park this would be a great luxury. Its close proximity to the war in Darfur has had a catastrophic impact on the area and poaching has become endemic. Some wildlife has been killed for food, but one animal has suffered more than most. In a land where *per capita* income is less than $200 a year, the elephant has been targeted by organized criminal gangs for its tusks, which can fetch $100,000 a pair when sold in China or Thailand. In 1970 the elephant population in Chad stood at over 300,000, today it is below 10,000 and falling.

Travel through the park is possible only by journeying with the park rangers who, by necessity, must be as heavily armed as are the poachers. But Zakouma soon reveals itself to be a beautiful place. It is a land of wide open plains broken only by a few clumps of trees, where lions take shelter before heading into the cover of the long parched grass to stalk their prey. This is a magical place, where heat haze distorts distance and clouds of dust rise out of the sun-baked earth, disturbed by the hooves of jinking gazelles. But it is the mighty African elephant that most symbolizes the park. As sensitive as it is strong, its plight is shaming, although it is hoped that, with the help of the Wildlife Conservation Society, it may once again flourish in the region.

**HOW TO GET THERE:**
By plane to N'Djamena, then overland by car
**WHEN TO GO:**
The wet season, from June to September, is less oppressively hot.
**DON'T MISS:**
The sight of a moving elephant which, uniquely among mammals, spreads the burden of its weight evenly between front and rear legs, making it the four-wheel drive of the animal kingdom.
**YOU SHOULD KNOW:**
Currently it is not advisable to travel outside of N'Djamena. Check with the Foreign Office (UK) or State Department (US) before travelling.

*Trou au Natron is a caldera in the Tibesti Mountains where the Toubou people gather rock salt.*

# Tibesti Mountains

The inhospitable plains of the Sahara Desert extend across North Africa from its Atlantic coastline in the west to the Nile Delta in the east. At 9 million sq km (3.5 million sq mi) and growing steadily still, it is the largest arid region on Earth. It is characterized by vast shifting sands that blind and disorientate the traveller. Only the camel has adapted to this extreme environment through its ability to store fat and the development of an extra eyelid that acts as a windshield.

Rising out of this seemingly endless and monotonous landscape are two mountain groups – the Ahaggar in the west and the larger and more imposing Tibesti Mountains in the east. The Tibesti Mountains appear like a mirage from the desert. Composed of black basalt from a now-dormant volcanic chain, they have over the years been sandblasted into a stunning lunar-like landscape. Travel through the range is beset with problems. Sand gets into everything and the area is subject to the largest diurnal temperature range on Earth. Morning temperatures can be below freezing, while by midday they can have soared to half boiling point (in Fahrenheit the range is an astonishing 100 degrees).

Emi Koussi, at 3,415 m (11,204 ft) is the highest and most challenging peak of the area. Surrounded by a corona of dramatic volcanic spires, it provides a test for even the most experienced mountaineer. But, without doubt, the most stunning spectacle the area has to offer is a 5-km (3-mi) wide 750-m (2,460-ft) deep salt-filled crater, Trou au Natron. The contrast between the black mountains and the blinding white of the crater as the sun beats off both provides one of the world's most extraordinary sights.

**HOW TO GET THERE:**
Travel overland from N'Djamena, Chad, or (more difficult) from southern Libya.
**WHEN TO GO:**
The heat is less searing from December to February.
**DON'T MISS:**
The view of Emi Koussi from Tarso Taro
**YOU SHOULD KNOW:**
Travel to and within Chad is difficult. Roads are few and far between and the only public transport is aboard cargo lorries. Advice on safety and security should be taken from the Foreign Office (UK) or State Department (US) before travelling.

# Bale Mountains

There are always wild places to be discovered in this world – often fascinating destinations where sheer remoteness has until recently precluded a visit. One such area is the Bale Mountains in southeastern Ethiopia. This lush landscape of forested mountains and pristine streams offers superb scenic satisfaction, but also introduces visitors to local culture in a manner that provides a blueprint for sustainable ecotourism. As with much of Africa, however, it's a clear case of 'the sooner the better'. There is increasing clearance within forested areas and the level ground at the foot of the mountains is no longer used for pastoral livestock herding. Instead, the land is being cultivated with increasing intensity.

But the locals are friendly and guides may be found to lead visitors into the forest, either on foot or mounted on horseback. Bold trekkers will be rewarded with a wealth of tree and plant life, with distinctly different flora as the elevation increases, right up to heather-covered moors at the highest levels. The hillsides are aflame with torch lilies between June and November, while the bright-yellow flowers of *Hypericum lanceolatum* are everywhere. Honey production is a significant activity and there are far worse tipples than the punchy mead that much of it mysteriously becomes.

The Adaba-Dodola forests harbour a wealth of birdlife, from Abyssinian catbirds to yellow-fronted parrots. These will be more visible than the forest animals – although the likes of Menelik's bushbuck, assorted monkeys, baboons, spotted hyenas, porcupines, warthogs, mongoose, jackals and Ethiopian wolves (among others) are there to be spotted by those with sharp eyes and a light tread. The chances of getting lucky – and enjoying a good all-round experience – are much increased for visitors who book one of the organized mountain expeditions that use primitive but established camps.

**HOW TO GET THERE:**
The gateways to the Bale Mountains are Dodola and Adaba, in the Regional State of Oromia.
**WHEN TO GO:**
Any time. The dry season (November to May) is best, although the mountain climate is generally cool. The rains come in July and August, when damp discomfort is counterbalanced by the intensity and freshness of the vegetation.
**DON'T MISS:**
A daytrip from Dodola town to the Lensho River and spectacular Shebelle Waterfalls
**YOU SHOULD KNOW:**
There is a real threat of terrorist activity in Ethiopia, and not even Addis Ababa is deemed entirely safe for visitors. Extreme vigilance is essential, especially at transport hubs and places regularly frequented by expatriates and foreign travellers.

*The lush landscape of the remote Bale Mountains*

# Omo Valley

**HOW TO GET THERE:**
With difficulty. The area is remote, roads are unpaved and only a few specialist tour companies inside or outside the country organize trips to the area, although there is a guest lodge along the river that has a private airstrip for charter flights from Addis Ababa.
**WHEN TO GO:**
Avoid the rainy season (April and May) when the river floods, Nile-style.
**DON'T MISS:**
A traditional Faro body-painting and dancing event (any time) or a boat trip on the river when the water is high (June to September).
**YOU SHOULD KNOW:**
Photographing the fascinating and diverse local population is irresistible, but it is courteous to ask permission before taking pictures of people or their villages, and a small gratuity will be expected in return. English is Ethiopia's second language and widely understood, at least at a basic level.

The important Omo River falls entirely within southern Ethiopia, rising in the Shewan Highlands and rushing down to Lake Turkana in the Great Rift Valley. Ethiopia's most remote wilderness surrounds the Omo Valley. The valley's natural beauty may be stunning and justify a visit in its own right, but the opportunity to visit colourful local villages adds a fascinating extra dimension. This UNESCO World Heritage Site is a cultural melting pot where the earliest-known fossil remains of *Homo sapiens* were discovered.

The river flows through two national parks – Omo and Mago – but these have few if any facilities and are defined more by lines on maps than much evidence on the ground. With just one significant road providing access – from Konso via Woito to Bako or Omorate – this really is a splendid opportunity for adventurous types to organize the expedition of a lifetime. But however ambitious the journey, there simply won't be time to see and do everything. Photography, birdwatching, wildlife-viewing, fishing, nature hiking and exploring in a 4x4 are just some of the tempting possibilities, but the real joy of this place is people-watching.

There are at least 20 different African tribes within the area – all interesting, all with their own customs, all living a traditional way of life that may be seen today but will inevitably be swept away by 'progress' within a few more generations. Peoples of the lower Omo Valley include the Dizi, Dorze, Hamar, Me'en, Mursi, Nyangatom and Suri. The villages contain mud-and-thatch houses – often of beehive form – and this is the place to see the extraordinary sight of women with mouths stretched to accommodate huge round clay plates. The effort of getting to the Omo Valley may be considerable, but the reward will be a storehouse of memories to treasure.

*Hamar men tending their cattle.*

# Goda Mountains

Located to the northwest of the Gulf of Tadjoura in North Africa's smallest country, the Goda Mountains rise to a height of 1,750 m (5,741 ft) and are Djibouti's largest 'green' enclave – a vegetated oasis amid the country's stony desert landscapes and an area where mist often rises above the lush green slopes and it actually rains sometimes. Small mountain villages like Bankoualé, Dittilou and Randa seem a world apart from the scorching plains at the foot of the mountains and offer the blessed relief of a cooler climate.

It is possible to enjoy a day's hike in the mountains or find accommodation there at a few locally run campsites or in simple huts reserved for tourists in unspoilt areas, either of which can provide a base to explore before it's too late. Much of the forest has been cleared over the past 200 years and only one tenth of its original area remains. Drought, fires, deforestation and overgrazing by ubiquitous livestock are, sadly, continuing the process.

The Day Forest National Park, accessed from the National 9 road, aims to protect much of what is left and contains most of Djibouti's biodiversity. One of three national parks in Djibouti, it is small but has a unique ambiance. It harbours rare plants and birds, some – like the Djibouti francolin – endemic. Birdwatching attracts visitors, while animals such as warthog, monkeys and antelope may also be seen. The forest is located where the plateau of the Goda Mountains is bordered by the Goh and Hamboka cliffs. The Day Massif contains juniper trees and an impressively dense pine forest. However, the attempt to preserve the junipers seems to be a losing battle, as there are now almost too few to ensure survival, let alone mass regeneration.

**HOW TO GET THERE:**
A hired 4x4 vehicle is the transport of choice, with or without the services of a local guide.
**WHEN TO GO:**
Favoured months to visit Djibouti are October to April.
**DON'T MISS:**
A visit to Tadjoura, on the gulf of the Tadjoura Sea and overlooked by the Goda Mountains. Once a slave-trading centre, Djibouti's oldest town is now a busy port notable for white-washed houses and splendid nearby beaches.
**YOU SHOULD KNOW:**
The Djibouti-Eritrea border is disputed and best avoided under all circumstances. There is a general threat of terrorist activity and petty crime such as mugging and bag snatching is not uncommon in Djibouti, which is nonetheless a stable and relatively prosperous country. French is widely spoken in this *petit* former colony, once French Somaliland.

*The green slopes of the Goda Mountains*

# Lake Assal

Anyone who's ever wanted to walk on water must head for Lake Assal, a crater lake 120 km (75 mi) to the west of Djibouti City. There, the impossible almost becomes possible, for this amazing body of water is fed by salt springs that make it more saline than a more publicity-conscious pretender: the Dead Sea. Lake Assal is an impressive 157 m (515 ft) below sea level – making it the lowest point in Africa. The effort required to get there isn't wasted, for remoteness and fierce climate combine to ensure that this eerie landscape remains largely untouched by the heavy hand of tourism.

*Lake Assal – the lowest point in Africa*

The lake is in the Danakil Desert and extends to an area of 54 sq km (21 sq mi). It is surrounded by brooding volcanoes (happily dormant) whose dark presence contrasts dramatically with the lake's brilliant aquamarine colour. A visit to Lake Assal is not for those who like gentle scenery and a temperate climate. It is in an inhospitable area seared by desert winds that is one of the hottest places in Africa, with temperatures capable of reaching nearly 60°C (140°F) and light so bright that a good pair of polarizing sunglasses is an essential travelling companion. But for lovers of wild places and dramatic landscapes its austere charms will be deeply satisfying.

The banks are covered in large salt crystals and saltpans surround the lake. The local Afar people still produce salt to trade into Ethiopia, as they have for centuries, and may be seen coming and going with their camels. The visitor is likely to be offered an unusual souvenir – a large bag of Lake Assal refined salt, costing only a few francs.

# Meru National Park

*Zebra in the Meru
National Park*

International fame came to Meru National Park when Joy Adamson's book *Born Free* chronicled the reintroduction of the lioness Elsa to the Kenyan wilderness back in the late 1950s. This was an important step forward for the conservation movement yet, despite such a positive association, many tourists overlook Meru. This may be a legacy of mismanagement in the 1970s and 1980s, when poaching was endemic and visitors wisely stayed away. Today, that situation has been remedied after an intensive rehabilitation programme conducted by the Kenya Wildlife Service, supported by the International Fund for Animal Welfare. So Meru is once again a haven for wildlife and a stimulating destination but, happily for those who appreciate wilderness exploration, it remains one of Kenya's lesser-known – and visited – parks. That said, there are lodges and self-catering accommodation in Meru along with campsites public and private. Overnight camping is a great experience for those not thrown by the myriad noises of an African night.

The 870-sq-km (335-sq-mi) park consists of riverine palm forests, with wooded grasslands in the west and thorny bush land to the north. The area experiences high rainfall that encourages the growth of tall grass and nourishes extensive swampland, which means that animals are sometimes difficult to spot. But with or without the help of an experienced guide it is possible to see many species, including lion, leopard, cheetah, giraffe (not so hard to detect!), zebra, elephant and hippopotamus, black rhino and rare antelopes. In addition, the bird population is thriving and more than 300 species have been recorded within park boundaries. The park is within sight of Mount Kenya and natural highlights are the Tana River and Adamson's Falls. Game viewing, birdwatching, photography and simply soaking up the scenery of this special place are the principal activities.

**HOW TO GET THERE:**
Meru National Park is around 350 km (220 mi) from Nairobi and most visitors fly in to the Mulika Lodge Airport within the park. Road access is by the main entrance, Murera Gate – 35 km (22 mi) from Maua.

**WHEN TO GO:**
Any time (the hottest months are generally February and March, the coolest July and August).

**DON'T MISS:**
The Meru home of George and Joy Adamson of *Born Free* fame. Elsa herself is buried in the park and some of Joy Adamson's ashes were scattered over the grave of her beloved lioness after the pioneering conservationist was murdered in 1980.

**YOU SHOULD KNOW:**
There is a real terrorist threat in Kenya, which has experienced indiscriminate attacks – notably on places frequented by expatriates and foreign travellers. It is unwise to enter slum and township areas, where crime rates are high. The border area with Somalia is also dangerous and several kidnaps of aid workers and nuns have been recently reported.

**197**

*Clark's anemonefish swimming through magnificent anemone.*

# Watamu Marine National Reserve

**HOW TO GET THERE:**
Watamu is 120 km (75 mi) north of Mombasa and 28 km (17 mi) south of Malindi. The reserve is some 11 km (7 mi) off the main Mombasa-Malindi road – turn towards the Indian Ocean at Gede. It's possible to fly in to Malindi Airport and hire a vehicle or get onward transport from there.

**WHEN TO GO:**
Any time. The coastal lowlands are not as temperate as most of Kenya and have high temperatures and humidity, although these extremes are tempered by sea breezes.

**DON'T MISS:**
Gede ruins – the remains of a 12th-century Swahili village, mysteriously abandoned around 1400 and now an atmospheric place overgrown with baobab and tamarind trees. This National Museum merits exploration and should be followed by a visit to the Kipepeo Butterfly Project – by Gede's entrance – where locals breed forest butterflies for export to live display centres around the world. Another nearby attraction close to the main road is the Malindi Crocodile Farm and Snake Park. Feeding time is 16.00 on Wednesdays and Fridays (volunteers welcome!).

**YOU SHOULD KNOW:**
Neither Malindi nor Watamu is plastic-friendly – both reserves have an entry fee that must be paid in cash, either Kenyan shillings or US dollars are the acceptable currencies.

The jewel in the crown of Kenya's 50-plus national parks, reserves and sanctuaries must surely be the tiny but glittering Watamu Marine National Reserve, itself part of the much larger Malindi Marine National Reserve. Watamu may seem geographically insignificant but that's not the full story. As the name suggests, the glory of this special place lies in its extraordinary marine environment.

This consists of the Mida Creek mangrove forest with its teeming bird-like intertidal rocks, sandy beaches, mud flats, coral cliffs, fringing reefs and a glorious coral garden. The latter lies less than 300 m (328 yd) from shore in the azure Indian Ocean, crying out to be explored by glass-bottomed boat. Snorkelling or diving are even better options for those who want to become part of this unique underwater world, however briefly (snorkels, masks and fins are available for hire). Water temperature ranges from 20°C to 30°C (68°F to 86°F) so immersion is pleasant indeed. Expert guides are on hand to add detailed information to the experience, if required, and there are other splendid snorkelling possibilities outside the main coral garden.

Quite apart from corals – there are around 150 species here, hard and soft, including sponges, brain and fan corals – over 500 types of fish inhabit the waters. The larger denizens include whale shark, barracuda, manta rays and giant octopus, while there are countless brightly coloured reef fish. Another major attraction is the green turtle population, actively encouraged in this haven by a serious conservation programme that involves the active co-operation of local fishermen. Also to be seen is the occasional dugong – the fabled sea cow said to be the inspiration behind mermaid legends. Watamu may not be the wildest place in Kenya, but it's certainly one of the most interesting and colourful.

# Mahale Mountains

In the west of Tanzania, bordering Lake Tanganyika, is a magical wild place. The Mahale Mountains National Park represents the heart of Africa unspoilt, a place with no roads just 100 km (62 mi) from where Stanley found the object of his prolonged search and (allegedly) uttered the immortal words 'Dr Livingstone, I presume'. The park covers 1,600 sq km (620 sq mi) of lakeshore and spectacular upland terrain, with beaches and azure water easily mistaken for those of an Indian Ocean paradise island. The added dimension is mysterious, jungle-clad mountains that tower above the lake, rising to the dramatic heights of 2,460-m (8,070-ft) Nkungwe – the park's loftiest peak.

For those sufficiently determined to reach this remote place, the star attraction may well be chimpanzees, for the park is home to around 800 of the agile tree-dwellers – one of the largest cohesive populations left in Africa. There's every chance of a sighting – about 60 of them belong to the M Group, which has become used to humans as a result of a research programme dating back to the 1960s.

But the park has more to offer than charismatic primates. Some visitors may get no further than the waterside – swimming, snorkelling or fishing in the pristine waters of the world's least-polluted freshwater lake. Others will be seduced by camping safaris to the interior, where forested slopes are home to an amazing array of colourful birds and easily observed red colobus, red-tailed, and blue monkeys. Most will want to do a bit of both, to wring every last drop of rewarding experience from the trip of a lifetime. In season there are three permanent tented camps – with almost every mod con – plus a large general campsite and two small rest houses.

*A chimpanzee in the Mahale Mountains National Park*

**HOW TO GET THERE:**
Take a charter flight to the park from Arusha, Dar es Salaam or Kigoma. Alternatively, go by boat – charter a private or park motorboat from Kigoma (four hours). The weekly steamer from Kigoma takes seven hours, after which a local fishing boat or park boat (by prior arrangement) completes the journey.

**WHEN TO GO:**
The dry season (May to October) is best for forest hiking, although November's light rains are not really problematical.

**DON'T MISS:**
The very special opportunity to see a complete troupe of chimpanzees in the wild (allow two days for the expedition). It's also possible to see chimps acclimatized to human presence in nearby Gombe Stream National Park, a small but beautiful enclave on the lakeshore.

**YOU SHOULD KNOW:**
Be aware of an underlying terrorist threat in Tanzania. However, a more pressing cause of concern should be long-distance buses, which tend to be ill maintained and liable to become involved in accidents, often with fatal consequences. Armed robberies have occurred in the Arusha region and areas bordering Burundi can be hazardous. Once there, however, the Mahale Mountains are quite safe.

# Ruaha National Park

The name of the game is game, and this is the place to see game galore. Ruaha in Central Tanzania is the country's second-largest national park at almost 10,350 sq km (4,000 sq mi), and this vast wilderness consists of semi-arid bush country that is home to a teeming population of animals and birds. The arteries of this rugged landscape are the Great Ruaha River and its tributaries along the park's eastern boundary – raging torrents in the rainy season, dwindling thereafter to a series of still-vital pools amidst a desert of rock and sand.

Africa's most iconic animals are here in numbers. The park has 10,000 elephants, the greatest number in any East African park. There are giraffe, zebras galore, many large lion prides, leopard, cheetah, hippo and crocodile, along with numerous great kudu – characterized by the males' magnificent corkscrew horns, the latter serving as the park's emblem. Among other species to be seen (it's not too hard in dry season, when animals congregate around the remaining waterholes) are lesser kudu, striped and spotted hyena, packs of rare African wild dogs, Grant's gazelle, sable and roan antelope, impala and waterbuck. The bird population is equally impressive, with some 450 different species to 'twitch', including the trilling crested barbet and handsome natives such as the ashy starling and yellow-collared lovebird.

There is a network of tracks designed to facilitate dry-season wildlife-watching along the Great Ruaha River and its seasonal tributaries. These may be driven or hiked, while many visitors with a love of wild places simply can't resist the opportunity to take day walks or a hiking safari through untouched bush land, allowing them to share the wonderment of the first Europeans to explore the African interior's solitary splendour.

*A bull elephant in Ruaha National Park*

# Serengeti

*Migrating wildebeest*

Tanzania's largest, oldest and most popular national park is a world-famous UNESCO World Heritage Site – with good reason. For Serengeti is home to one of the most awesome events in the animal world, when six million hooves pound the plains during an annual migration that sends a million wildebeest, 300,000 Thomson's gazelle and 200,000 zebra in search of fresh grazing to support a population explosion of 8,000 calves every day, before the 1,000-km (620-mi) return journey sorts out the weak from the strong.

The 40-km (25-mi) columns of animals are a moving spectacle as they brave crocodile-infested river crossings to fulfil their annual destiny, but Serengeti has much more to offer. This land of parched savannah, wooded hills, termite mounds and orange dust has different faces, becoming transformed in the rainy season to a green expanse spangled with flowers. The variety of wildlife is extraordinary and this is one of the best places in Africa to watch game doing its own thing in the wild. Apart from the great migration, a highlight of any visit is the sight of one of the great predators pursuing a kill. The park has lion, leopard, cheetah, buffalo, giraffe, elephant, rhino, eland, topi, impala, jackal, hyena and many more, right down to the insect-eating aardwolf. There are also at least 500 bird species.

Serengeti has ample in-park accommodation, from luxury lodges through quality standing tented camps to regular campsites for pitch-it-yourself travellers. Even so, the park is so vast that even a full complement of visitors can quickly vanish into the blue yonder, allowing everyone so minded to enjoy undisturbed solitude in this wonderful wilderness. One exotic activity is a hot-air-balloon safari, while other organized possibilities include guided game-viewing drives, walking safaris, bush picnics or *al fresco* lunch/dinner parties served in Africa's great outdoors.

**HOW TO GET THERE:**
Scheduled or charter flights from Arusha, Lake Manyara and Mwanza. Long-distance road access from the same three starting points, or nearby Ngorongoro Crater.

**WHEN TO GO:**
Depending on the desired spectacle, December to July to follow the wildebeest migration or June to October to best observe predators going about their deadly business.

**DON'T MISS:**
Fascinating rock paintings executed by the indigenous Maasai people – ask in the village of Kolo for a guide to the cave site where they may be viewed.

**YOU SHOULD KNOW:**
Allow at least three days to be sure of seeing wildebeest moving during the great migration – both route and timing can be unpredictable – then add another couple of days if the visit is to include a look at Serengeti's main predators in action.

# The Kitulo Plateau

**HOW TO GET THERE:**
By 4x4 from Cimala – 80 km (50 mi) east of the highland town of Mbeya on the paved Dar es Salaam road – take the spectacular dirt road to park HQ at Matamba and on to the plateau, a further hour's drive away. Basic but erratic public transport (passengers travel at their own risk) to park HQ at Matamba is sometimes available.

**WHEN TO GO:**
December to April for the wild flowers' command performance. The best hiking months for those who are happy with sensational scenery, fewer people and no flower power are September to November.

**DON'T MISS:**
Matema Beach – a fabulous spot on the shore of Lake Nyasa, a half-day hike from the park. It has two affordable church-run hostels.

**YOU SHOULD KNOW:**
Kitulo National Park is being developed apace, with facilities such as campsites within the park for visitors with their own equipment. Mbeya has everything from good hotels to unpretentious guesthouses, while Matamba also has simple guesthouses.

The glittering jewel in the crown of Tanzania's Southern Highlands is the Kitulo Plateau. Locals call Kitulo *Bustani ya Mungu* – the Garden of God – and anyone lucky enough to reach this enchanting place will instantly understand why it has earned that name. For this is where one of the world's most impressive floral displays may be seen during the rainy season. Around 350 types of vascular plant erupt into a botanical spectacle of extraordinary diversity from November onwards, dazzling visitors with sheer variety and scale. Prominent alongside 45 different ground orchids are plants such as aloes, asters, geraniums, giant lobelias, lilies and brilliant red-hot pokers, together creating a riot of competing colour.

The plateau levels out at 2,600 m (8,530 ft) and is protected by Kitulo National Park, which extends to an area of around 415 sq km (160 sq mi). This is an important watershed for the Great Ruaha River, with well-watered volcanic soils supporting the country's most important montane grassland. In addition to this rolling grassland, the area has rounded hills, rivers, waterfalls, crater lakes and forest. Visitors should aim to find the Numbi Valley, a picturesque spot where small streams emerge from grassy hillsides as if by magic.

There are good hiking trails on the plateau, offering easy walking over open grassland and giving access to flowers and a vibrant bird population. The latter is so beguiling that it attracts birdwatchers who see Kitulo's flowers and brilliant butterflies as a great backdrop to the main attraction – rare avian treasures such as Denham's bustard, blue swallow, mountain marsh widow and *Cisticola njombe*. It is also possible to go beyond the plateau to enjoy strenuous hill climbing through sometimes-dense vegetation amidst the rugged surrounding peaks of the Livingstone, Poroto and Kipengere Mountains.

# Kibale Forest

It's a primary primate destination – a beautiful 775-sq-km (300-sq-mi) tract of preserved Ugandan tropical rainforest that supports no fewer than 13 primate species, from chimpanzees to several types of Central African monkey, such as L'Hoest's, Ugandan red colobus and Ugandan mangabey. But for most the main attraction of Kibale National Park will be those appealing chimps. They're sufficiently used to people to go about their lives undeterred by human intrusion – playing, squabbling and grooming in trees bearing the juiciest fruit, demonstrating sublime unconcern for camera-toting visitors with cricked necks.

A network of shaded trails offers almost unlimited hiking possibilities within the forest, also giving opportunities to visitors with a specialist interest. Birdwatchers are drawn by over 300 species, including African grey parrots, noisy hornbills, African pitas, green-breasted pitas and the endemic Prirogrine's ground thrush. Lepidopterists are attracted by shimmering displays of butterflies while botanists (including university researchers) come for the varied flora. In addition to seeing numerous agile primates, animal watchers may be delighted by occasional encounters with buffalo, leopard, bush pig, otter or assorted antelopes. The park's forest elephants (smaller and hairier than plains counterparts) commute to and fro from Kibale to the adjacent Queen Elizabeth National Park, the two protected areas together providing one of the country's most important ecotourism areas. In fact, the latter is Uganda's most-visited game reserve.

Although it looks entirely authentic to the untrained eye, Kibale owes its survival to colonial-era status as a forest reserve that could be (and was) sustainably logged. The national park was created in 1993, alien replanting was removed and the forest has been regenerating ever since. This provides encouraging evidence of the way in which important examples of Africa's rapidly vanishing natural habitats are being preserved thanks to the economic desirability of carefully managed tourism.

*Chimpanzees can often be seen grooming each other.*

**HOW TO GET THERE**:
Access is from Fort Portal in the west of Uganda – Kibale Forest is 35 km (22 mi) away via a dirt road and there is (somewhat erratic) public transport. Fort Portal itself is 320 km (200 mi) from Kampala along a (mostly) paved road.

**WHEN TO GO**:
Any time – the climate is hot but bearable all year. The rainy season is from March to May.

**DON'T MISS**:
The sights and more particularly sounds of the forest on a guided night walk – an unforgettable experience

**YOU SHOULD KNOW**:
It is essential to obtain comprehensive travel and medical insurance before visiting Uganda. Road travel by night outside major towns is not recommended. Kibale itself is safe, with in-park lodges (upmarket and budget) plus a luxury tented camp providing secure accommodation.

203

*A view across the plains of Kidepo Valley*

# Kidepo Valley

**HOW TO GET THERE:**
By air, either using a private charter from Entebbe International Airport or Eagle Air's thrice-weekly scheduled service. The Karamoja region is potentially dangerous and overland travel is not recommended, as violent poachers or cattle rustlers may be encountered. Those who do risk the 700-km (435-mi) road trip from Kampala (a sturdy 4x4 is essential) are officially recommended to hire armed guards for the final leg. This rigmarole may be justified as a 4x4 vehicle is the best way of seeing as much of the park as possible.
**WHEN TO GO:**
Any time (although March and April are prime months for birdwatchers, when all the specials and many transient migrants are present).
**DON'T MISS:**
A visit to the local Karamajong community, which welcomes visitors interested in their timeless way of life. Cultural entertainers will put on a splendid show of traditional dancing for a small fee.
**YOU SHOULD KNOW:**
The Uganda Wildlife Authority's Apoka Rest Camp offers comfortable in-park *bandas* and chalets. Visitors should bring their own food, which can then be cooked for them. For those with bottomless pockets, the exclusive Apoka Lodge in the centre of the park offers every mod con. For visitors on a tight budget, there are two primitive campsites for those with their own equipment.

The Kidepo Valley National Park in the Karamoja region is tucked away in Uganda's northeastern corner, where it meets Sudan. It's the country's most remote national park, boasting rugged landscapes unsurpassed in any other. Kidepo is the ultimate destination for true lovers of unspoilt wild places, for this pristine 1,500-sq-km (580-sq-mi) wilderness of semi-arid valleys is little visited by tourists. Indeed, the word best used to describe those who do make the pilgrimage is 'adventurers'.

Many determined travellers who make the effort needed to visit Kidepo Valley are birdwatchers – often as part of organized ornithological expeditions – attracted by the huge variety of feathered species (around 475) to be found in the varied habitat of semi-desert scrub, open thorn scrub, grassy savannas, assorted woodland and granite outcrops. Among 'specials' not found in any other Ugandan park are some of East Africa's rarest birds, including the Karamoja apalis and black-breasted barbet. But the range is eye watering, from ostrich down to a huge variety of colourful songbirds, with an awesome selection of birds of prey. The animal population suffered during Uganda's catastrophic Idi Amin years, but has recovered. Over 80 mammal species live in Kidepo, including nearly 30 found in no other park. Along with rarities like the bat-eared fox and caracal, visitors can expect to spot the likes of giraffe, elephant, buffalo, lion, leopard, cheetah, reedbuck, waterbuck, kongoni, orobis, kudu, klipspringer, dik dik, zebra, warthog, jackal and mongoose, plus a healthy reptile population.

Guided walks (perhaps augmented by spotlit night drives) offer the ideal opportunity to see the maximum number of animals and birds in the time available. But for those happy to regard the wildlife as part of a rewarding wilderness trek rather than an end in itself, merely being in this magical wilderness is enough.

# Lake Mburo

For a relatively compact national park by African standards, with an area of just 260 sq km (100 sq mi), Lake Mburo offers a very special experience. The name is something of a misnomer, for there are actually five lakes within the park – home to hippos, crocodiles and numerous water birds. The lakes are fringed with swamps that give sanctuary to papyrus specialists like the Sitatunga antelope and the rare Papyrus gonolek, a striking red, black and yellow bird.

This gives a clue to Lake Mburo National Park's key attractions – animal watching and birdwatching. This part of Uganda is covered in acacia woodland, with rich biodiversity supporting its own distinctive fauna. Those intent on seeing a wide variety of game will not be disappointed. There are nearly 70 species of animal to be found within the park, including Uganda's most visible population of giant eland plus impala, topi, the rare roan antelope, zebra and buffalo, with predators like leopard, jackal and hyena waiting to pounce on all but the fittest. Birders have 360 recorded species to pursue, including half a dozen forest rarities and 60 different water birds. The park has strategically placed hides overlooking salt licks where animals may constantly be observed coming and going, while boat trips on Lake Mburo provide an unmissable perspective on the park's flora on fauna, including those wily crocs, hippos and birds such as pelican, fish eagle and the rare shoebill stork.

There is a selection of accommodation (from luxury to budget) in Mbarara, while there is a permanent tented camp at Rwonyo park headquarters. There are three strategically located public campsites within the park and meals may be ordered from the Lake Mburo dining shelter. However, visitors are advised to bring enough food and drink to last for the duration of their stay.

**HOW TO GET THERE:**
By road. The park is about a four-hour drive from Kampala, in the Mbarara District. Turn off the Mbarara to Kampala highway at clearly signed junctions for one of the park's two gates: Sanga or Nshara.

**WHEN TO GO:**
Any time

**DON'T MISS:**
The opportunity to explore swampy Rubanga forest on a ranger-guided trip. It is small but has a closed canopy in places, formed by a rich variety of trees. Look out for fine specimens of Africa's famous flame trees.

**YOU SHOULD KNOW:**
While wandering in the park on foot can be an exciting opportunity to experience nature as nature intended, it is actually mandatory to be accompanied on any such expedition by an armed park official.

*Lake Mburo National Park*

# Semuliki Valley

A remote section of the Semuliki Forest in western Uganda is an extension to the Congo's vast Ituri Forest. This 220-sq-km (85-sq-mi) ecosystem on the Uganda-DRC (Democratic Republic of Congo) border is enclosed by the Semuliki River to the west and north and by the Fort Portal to Bundibugyo road on the other two sides. The land is flat, in marked contrast to the rugged grandeur of the nearby Rwenzori Mountains, and was gazetted in 1993 – thus becoming the only national park in the country to consist primarily of tropical lowland forest.

*Sempaya hot springs are rich in salt and sulphur.*

**HOW TO GET THERE:**
Starting from Fort Portal (reached by two good routes from Kampala), it's 4x4 country. About 50 km (30 mi) along the rough road to Bundibugyo is the park's Sempaya Gate, with park headquarters at Ntandi a bit further along. For true daredevils, regular public transport there and back (until around 16.00) is available from Fort Portal's taxi park. There are also local outfits in Fort Portal that will organize a custom visit.

**WHEN TO GO:**
Any time (but localized flooding occurs during the rainy months – March, April, May, September, October and November).

**DON'T MISS:**
A side trip to Mungilo Waterfall, just outside the park boundary. Another 'must' is the view over the park from the Bundibugyo road as it meanders through the Rwenzori escarpments, with a spectacular panorama visible from Mungu Ni Mukunwa.

**YOU SHOULD KNOW:**
Visitors travelling to Fort Portal from Kampala often choose the longer route via Masaka, Mbarara and Kasese, as this provides the opportunity to visit Lake Mburo National Park, Kyambura Wildlife Reserve, Rwenzori Mountains National Park and Queen Elizabeth National Park along the way.

It provides a wonderful chance to escape Uganda's regular tourist circuit and experience the only real jungle in East Africa. There is accommodation in Fort Portal from which to sally forth, but the very best way of enjoying Semuliki Valley is to camp within the park and spend time exploring on foot. There's much to be seen. A hike along the winding Semuliki River will seem like paradise for birdwatchers, while everyone can enjoy the bright butterflies and perhaps glimpse animals such as pygmy hippo, crocodile, forest elephant, buffalo, leopard and assorted primates (including chimps). For anglers, the river offers great sport fishing. There are campsites within the park (tents supplied or bring your own). An associated canteen offers food and drink with meals prepared to order, but most visitors bring their own provisions. For those with loftier aspirations, the park has a few 'executive *bandas*'.

One unmissable highlight is Semuliki's hot springs, located in a section of mineral-rich swamp land that attracts a fascinating variety of wildlife and is served by a network of trails. The highlights are a jet of super-heated water and pool of boiling water that bubbles up from the depths. The park's party trick is to take some food and boil it on site – eggs a speciality.

# Akagera National Park

The most remote source of the Nile is northeast Rwanda's Akagera River, meandering through a landscape of lakes and swamps on the Tanzanian border. The river is surrounded by typical African savannah that consists of open grassland and acacia woodland – terrain in marked contrast to the country's generally hilly character. In 1936 a 2,500-sq-km (965-sq-mi) area to the west of the river was reserved to form Akagera National Park, one of Africa's finest in terms of flora, fauna and outstanding natural beauty.

All the classic African animals were well represented, including hippo, crocodile, lion, leopard, elephant, giraffe, zebra and many types of antelope, along with a stunning bird population numbering around 500 species. But the preservation of this fabulous place was inevitably set back by the tragic events of the 1990s, when over a million Rwandans died as a result of ethnically motivated genocide. Dedicated conservationists did their best to maintain the park's integrity, but it was an uphill struggle. Refugees returning after the civil war flooded the savannah and this severe human pressure drove much of the wildlife back into the park's more remote areas. The influx resulted in two thirds of the park's original area being degazetted.

However, enough unspoilt terrain remains to ensure a memorable visit, and there is every hope that the lure of hard tourist currency will ensure the park's continuing rehabilitation. This remains big game country with every chance of spotting the big ones – giraffe, elephant, buffalo and zebra herds, plus occasional lions and leopards on the prowl. A dozen species of antelope still inhabits the park, including impala and the statuesque Cape eland. The birdlife is amazing, with some of Africa's greatest concentrations of water birds to be seen along the river, lakeshores and in marshy areas.

**HOW TO GET THERE:**
Akagera is best explored from the town of Kagitumba on the park's northern boundary, reached from Goma by road via Ruhengen and Kabale – a roundabout journey of some 200 km (125 mi).

**WHEN TO GO:**
Avoid the rainy months (December, March and April) when many routes become impassable.

**DON'T MISS:**
The opportunity to camp alongside one of Akagera's lakes, experiencing the true majesty of the African bush as pods of hippos splutter and grunt all day long, large crocodiles sunbathe, and assorted wildlife appears to drink at dawn and dusk – all accompanied by an extraordinary display of colourful birdlife.

**YOU SHOULD KNOW:**
The country is now generally safe but rural areas bordering the Democratic Republic of Congo or Burundi are best avoided. There have been occasional grenade-throwing incidents in Kigali but these seem to be related to local disputes rather than indicate any sort of general terrorist threat.

*Desert-dwelling elephant*

# Nyungwe Forest

**HOW TO GET THERE:**
The forest may easily be visited for a rewarding day hike from the nearby towns of Cyangugu or Butare. The paved road between Huye and Cyangugu runs through the forest.
**WHEN TO GO:**
Prime dry season months for forest hiking are December and January or June to August.
**DON'T MISS:**
An excursion to the forest's fascinating Kamiranzovu Marsh, close to the road between main campsite and rest house, to see habitat quite different from that of the surrounding forest and glimpse localized animals such as the Congo clawless otter.
**YOU SHOULD KNOW:**
This is a true wild place. The forest gets barely 3,000 visitors a year, although numbers are increasing as the country becomes more stable and word of this unspoilt natural treasure spreads. This is underlined by the recent opening of the Nyungwe Forest Lodge, a typically luxurious eco-friendly establishment for visitors with deep pockets. The general area can be hazardous but the national park is regarded as safe.

Southwestern Rwanda's Nyungwe National Park is located on the Burundi border south of Lake Kivu. A long-established forest reserve, it gained national park status in 2004 and covers an area of 970 sq km (375 sq mi). It contains the largest tract of montane forest left in East or Central Africa. Nyungwe Forest with its high canopy is a wonderland of 250 types of tree including ebonies and mahoganies, towering tree ferns, tangled vegetation and orchids galore. Notable among the flora is the spectacular giant lobelia. Nyungwe is home to 275 bird species, countless butterflies, 80 different mammals including 13 primate species, plus assorted amphibians and reptiles. The biodiversity within this area is exceptional by African standards but remains threatened by Rwanda's burgeoning population.

There is an extensive network of well-maintained hiking trails in the national park, designed to show off the huge variety of flora and ensure that all the best scenic valleys, waterfalls and viewing points are accessible. Excellent day walks range in duration from one to seven hours, with guides available to lead the way. For those sufficiently seduced to spend two or more days in Nyungwe National Park, Uwinka Tourism Reception Centre has a good rustic rest house and campsite conveniently located at the edge of the forest, providing an ideal base for extended exploration.

The latter option is definitely worthwhile. Birders will have to look hard to spot feathered gems, with 24 specials endemic to this part of the Rift Valley high on the list. These include giant hornbills, great blue turacos and red-breasted sparrowhawks, so the effort is worthwhile. Looking for primates is hugely satisfying, with chimpanzees ever-popular quarry but plenty of other possibilities to pursue, such as huge troupes of Ruwenzori colobus monkeys, grey-cheeked mangabeys and L'Hoest's monkeys.

*Early morning mists in the Nyungwe Forest National Park*

# Volcanoes National Park

In the far northwest of Rwanda, towering to an impressive 4,500 m (14,760 ft), the Virunga Mountains are home to the oh-so-rare mountain gorilla. The flanks of this rugged range are protected by Volcanoes National Park (officially Parc National des Volcans) – Africa's first national park, gazetted in 1925 to protect those priceless primates. The foothills of the Virungas are cultivated, but as soon as ascending trails enter the park visitors are transported to a different world – a rich cocktail of montane ecosystems consisting of bamboo and evergreen forest, heath and open grassland, lake and swamp.

This elevated rainforest is alive with the sound of birds and a bright array of feathered inhabitants rewards those with the patience to wait and watch. Evidence of the forest's elusive population of buffalo and elephant will be plainly visible, a fleeing bush duiker may be glimpsed and rare golden monkeys chatter in the trees above. Arrow-head mountaintops will be visible through gaps in the canopy, beckoning those with the energy and stamina to tackle some of Africa's highest volcanic peaks, including Bisoke (one day) or Karisimbi (two days).

But the park's main attraction is the gorillas, saved from extinction after eminent American primatologist Dian Fossey brought their plight to international attention. She founded the Karisoke Research Centre in the 1960s and devoted the rest of her life to studying these amazing animals. She was murdered at her home in 1985 – probably by poachers – and is buried in the park among a gorilla population that owes its continued existence to her efforts. Seeing these magnificent but gentle creatures up close in their natural habitat is one of the world's most moving wildlife experiences and a fitting memorial to Dian Fossey, whose story was told in the film *Gorillas in the Mist*.

**HOW TO GET THERE:**
A good starting point is the bustling town of Ruhengeri, in its scenic setting at the foot of the mountains.
**WHEN TO GO:**
Any time (it was famously said of the Virungas by Dian Fossey that 'they're so high up that you shiver more than you sweat').
**DON'T MISS:**
The bridge at Musanze, just outside Ruhengeri. It's an extraordinary natural marvel formed from a solidified lava flow dating from the ancient volcanic eruptions that shaped this dramatic area. A worthwhile side trip is to the remote but beautiful Lakes Burera, Ruhondo and Karago – easily visited and appreciated on a daytrip.
**YOU SHOULD KNOW:**
Permits to visit the mountain gorillas are not cheap, and guided parties are limited to a maximum of eight visitors (and four parties per day), leaving the ORTPN (Rwanda Tourist Board) offices in Musanze after an early morning briefing. Although these magnificent animals may be approached at close quarters – but no nearer than 7 m (23 ft) – gorillas are susceptible to human diseases and anyone with a contagious illness, such as a cold or flu, should not attempt the trip.

*The Virunga Mountains – home to the mountain gorilla*

# Nankhumba Peninsula

**HOW TO GET THERE:**
Visitors to tourist lodges either fly in to the Nankhumba Peninsula on a charter or arrive by private launch. It is possible to drive from Lilongwe to the national park in about three hours, with road improvements promising to speed the journey in future (local roads are generally unmade and potholed and can become impassable in rainy season).

**WHEN TO GO:**
May to October is the prime season for visitors.

**DON'T MISS:**
Chembe village on Cape Maclear – a fishing community at the end of a dirt road from Monkey Bay with a few basic facilities, offering an ideal opportunity to see how the locals live.

**YOU SHOULD KNOW:**
As Africa goes, Malawi is one of the safer destinations. But driving – especially at night – can be hazardous, and the many mini-buses that ply for trade are decidedly accident-prone. Malawi is known as 'The friendly heart of Africa' and Malawians welcome visitors warmly.

Malawi is landlocked, but it certainly isn't short of water – the country is dominated by and shares a name with Africa's third-largest lake, which is surrounded by exceptional landscapes characterized by high mountains, plateaux, rocky outcrops . . . and sensational vistas across the continent's most beautiful lake from the rim of the Great Rift Valley. Combined with a vibrant local economy involving bustling towns, traditional villages, lively markets, endless roadside produce stalls and numerous cottage industries, this creates one of Africa's more tempting destinations – a country that is both relaxed and stimulating.

One of the most attractive sections of Lake Malawi's long shoreline is Nankhumba Peninsula at the picturesque southern end of the lake. The peninsula is a serious tourist destination, capitalizing on the lake's undoubted charms. Lake Malawi National Park encompasses the peninsula's northern tip and is a UNESCO World Heritage Site, the citation referring to its importance in the study of evolution as a result of the incredibly varied endemic fish population. The park is also home to important Neolithic sites. At scenic Cape Maclear within the park, upmarket lodges offer the combination of luxury accommodation and the usual watersports (no jet skis allowed, happily). The main settlement is Monkey Bay.

Those fish are the main attraction, providing an extraordinary display of kaleidoscopic colour and seeming entirely devoid of fear, feeding from the hand and swirling boldly around snorkellers. But the lake is (much!) bigger than the park's relative unobtrusive tourist facilities and the Nankhumba Peninsula as a whole remains an achingly beautiful place, with backcountry that contains wildlife like antelope and baboon and a pristine shoreline. The birdlife is abundant – with squabbling fish eagles ruling the roost – and the adventurous traveller can easily find complete solitude in this truly magical place.

# Nyika National Park

Malawi's largest national park covers an area of 3,200 sq km (1,235 sq mi) and this unique wild place does just what the name suggests. The translation of *Nyika* is 'source of the water' and the national park is indeed one of the country's most important catchments. It extends across a great plateau in northern Malawi and is a vast granite dome hosting an environment like no other in Africa, consisting of rolling grassy hills interspersed with wooded valleys, surrounded by steep escarpments.

The grasslands are richly endowed with wild flowers, including over 200 types of orchid, and the montane vegetation attracts large numbers of antelopes – which in turn serve as a generous larder for one of Central Africa's most concentrated leopard populations. The occasional lion or elephant may be seen, along with zebra and smaller animals like bush pig or warthog. Over 400 species of bird have been recorded in Nyika National Park. Notable among the latter are the endemic red-winged francolin, wattled crane and rare Denham's bustard.

The park attracts specialist visitors like birdwatchers and landscape photographers, but also makes a superb destination for those who simply want to get away from civilization and enjoy this atmospheric wilderness, which is often shrouded in cloud during the rainy season. There are all sorts of attractions to be found, such as a Neolithic shelter, waterfalls, trout pools and the pretty Lake Kaulime. The area may be explored from park headquarters at Chelina Camp, in the centre of the Nyika Plateau, where the log-cabin lodge provides good accommodation that makes a perfect base. Safaris may be undertaken on foot, mountain-bike or horseback, and 4x4 excursions are the easiest way to see as much as possible of this striking country if time is limited.

**HOW TO GET THERE:**
Access is by one dirt road branching off the highway to Katumbi border post, some 60 km (37 mi) north of the town of Rumphi. It continues across the plateau (where it delineates the border with Zambia) before reaching Chisenga border post.

**WHEN TO GO:**
In the rainy season (November to April) to see Nyika's fabulous display of wild flowers.

**DON'T MISS:**
A side trip to Vwaza Marsh Game Reserve – just 50 km (31 mi) south of Nyiki. This remote reserve is not much visited, but its mopane and miombo woodland provides an exceptional opportunity to view a great variety of animals and rich birdlife.

**YOU SHOULD KNOW:**
A small 80-sq-km (31-sq-mi) section of the Nyika Plateau (also called Nyika National Park) falls inside Zambia, but there is no road access so all visitors from that side of the border have to travel via Malawi to see Zambia's own small but perfectly formed wild gem.

*Getting away from it all in Nyika National Park.*

# Zomba Plateau

**HOW TO GET THERE:**
The old 'up' road was a nightmare, but there's now a new paved road to the top of the plateau, well signed from bustling Zomba town, Malawi's former capital (but note that the 'down' road from the plateau is stony and unsurfaced).

**WHEN TO GO:**
Any time. But be aware that the rainy season is from November to April (although rainfall varies and is heavier on the plateau than around Lake Malawi). The driest months are September and October.

**DON'T MISS:**
Emperor's View – with one of the very finest viewpoints on a Zomba Plateau over-endowed with wonderful distant views, this crowning glory was presumably named for Queen-Emperor Victoria by 19th-century British pioneers, who undoubtedly had to work much harder to experience this awesome outlook than today's motorist (although, to be fair, many choose to make the scenic hike to Emperor's View instead of driving).

**YOU SHOULD KNOW:**
Unfortunately, cars left unattended while the occupants explore the plateau are sometimes broken into, so tempting items should be concealed within the locked vehicle.

*Mist hangs over the Zomba Plateau.*

In the south of Malawi is a great massif that rises to 1,800 m (5,900 ft). It supports vast tracts of cypress, cedar and pine woodland, interspersed with a riot of mixed vegetation. Although there are plenty of animals and birds galore, Zomba is not the place to attract dedicated wildlife-watchers – the animals are shy and, although leopards, bushbuck or baboons may occasionally be glimpsed, the cover is so dense that such events are a rarity. However, one type of impressive sighting is guaranteed – brilliantly coloured giant butterflies are everywhere – and more visible birds include the ubiquitous white-necked raven and green louries with their vivid red underwings.

But the main attraction here is stunning scenery. Colonizing Brits in pith helmets once described the sweeping panoramas to be seen from Zomba Plateau as 'The finest views in the British Empire' and it's breathtakingly apparent why they came to that bold conclusion. Far-reaching vistas overlook Lake Chilwa to the north, Shire River to the west and Mount Mulanje to the southeast.

Most of the plateau is managed by Malawi's Department of Forestry, which is doing a fairly sensitive job that respects the original ecosystem. This means that a good network of dirt roads exists, which is ideal for 4x4 sightseeing excursions around this wonderland of tumbling streams, waterfalls and lakes. Other popular recreational activities are trout fishing in season, hiking and horseback riding. For those tempted to spend more than a day enjoying this unique landscape, there is a luxury hotel on the edge of the plateau, along with a large campsite with facilities like hot-water showers and proper sanitation. Another, more primitive campsite is located on the west side of the plateau, an ideal base for those who like getting away from more obvious tourist bases.

# Chimanimani Mountains

This rugged range – part of a chain stretching from Cape Town to the high mountains of East Africa – straddles the frontier between Mozambique and Zimbabwe, mostly falling within the Chimanimani Transfrontier Conservation Area. A national park on the Zimbabwean side is an established destination for organized expeditions, but Mozambique's Reserva Nacional de Chimanimani in Manica Province was only established in 2003 and is as yet undeveloped. It has the country's highest peak – Monte Binga at 2,436 m (7,992 ft) – and offers a number of primitive campsites, staffed by friendly AK-47-toting rangers in smart green uniforms who are happy to offer help and advice. Tourism may be a major contributor to the area's future but for now it is still a truly wild place – with lushly forested slopes that provide the opportunity to explore on foot and highlands that remain a wilderness – that progress (apart from those ubiquitous AK47s) seems to have passed by.

The biodiversity of the Chimanimani Mountains is legendary, but to enjoy their solitude it is first necessary to leave the cultivated areas around villages behind, and avoid many illegal panners working the streams in the hope of finding glinting gold. Local guides are easily found, and essential for everything but the most cursory day hike. For anything longer, it is sensible to hire porters who will act both as guides and carry camping equipment. With their help, it is possible to reach the plateau with its sensational rock formations and far-reaching views, where curious animals such as klipspringers are likely to take a close look at the intruders to their lofty domain. Elephants are quite common lower down, where the forest birdlife is abundant and the butterflies are vivid. Other sights include rock paintings and there are opportunities for canoeing.

**HOW TO GET THERE:**
With considerable patience and much bumping on unmade roads. From the coast, take the EN1 and – after crossing the Buzi River – turn off the paved road and head for Dombe and thereafter find an entrance to the reserve on the Sussundega road.

**WHEN TO GO:**
Tropical cyclone season (November to March) is best avoided, as heavy rain is inevitable and widespread flooding not unusual.

**DON'T MISS:**
The spectacular waterfall of the Muvumodzi River within the reserve (also known as the Martin Falls), plunging dramatically into a deep, rocky bowl.

**YOU SHOULD KNOW:**
Mozambique's Ministry of Tourism is working with the World Bank to develop a programme of ecotourism that will make the Chimanimanias more accessible, rather than calling for the sort of fairly determined individual expedition currently required to explore this unspoilt wild place.

*The Chimanimani Mountains offer some of the most spectacular mountain landscapes in Africa.*

# Maputo Special Reserve

Around 80 km (50 mi) south of Mozambique's capital of Maputo is a world apart from the bustling city with its teeming streets, cultural diversity and fascinating museums. Although sharing its name, the Maputo Special Reserve (formerly Elephant Reserve, a name still widely used) on Santa Maria Peninsula in the country's southern part is an area of outstanding natural beauty forming part of the Lubombo Transfrontier Conservation Area – a grouping of national parks from South Africa, Swaziland and Mozambique itself.

Happily for lovers of wild places, in the aftermath of prolonged civil war Mozambique is some way behind its neighbours in catering for the well-heeled local and international visitors who will eventually transform the national economy. But there's a downside to go with the fact that the reserve therefore remains wild and unspoilt by over-exploitation for tourism (three ecotourist sites planned but as yet unbuilt). That downside is that a 1975 stocking of the reserve from South Africa's Umfolozi Game Reserve introduced a huge population of elephant and rhino that was undone by civil war. Just 200 elephants and no rhinos survived the conflict. However, numbers are now recovering well with a splendid selection of wildlife to be seen – such as expanding elephant herds, hippos, crocodiles, leopards, lions, antelope, zebra, armadillos and red squirrels – within the reserve's sparsely populated 800-sq-km (310-sq-mi) territory. Birds flourish in assorted habitats and there are many rare species, with avian riches attracting birders from all over the world.

Visitors are treated to an extraordinary stretch of pristine coastline on the Indian Ocean with limpid waters offering stimulating diving possibilities. There are also dunes, fabulous beaches and important mango ecosystems. Interior tracts of forest and grassland offer great hiking potential and some splendid wildlife-viewing opportunities.

# Quirimbas Archipelago

*The Quirimbas Archipelago is a chain of mesmerizing islands.*

Northern Mozambique's Quirimbas Archipelago is a mesmerizing chain of 31 islands in the Indian Ocean that contains some of the world's richest coral reefs, supporting a fabulous array of marine life that equals snorkelling and scuba-diving heaven. For non-swimmers, simply seeing the Quirimbas could be the experience of a lifetime. Still, the archipelago's seductive attractions are a relatively well-kept secret and these enchanting tropical islands have never been seriously exploited for tourism and remain a conservation jewel all but untouched by intrusive development – reflected in recently acquired UNESCO World Heritage status and the fact that 11 of the southernmost islands have been integrated into the Quirimbas National Park, established in 2002.

The islands stretch from the coastal town of Pemba up to Cape Delgado and the Tanzanian border, a distance of around 320 km (200 mi). Some are linked to the mainland by coral reefs, sand bars and mangroves. The fortunate few who stray from the beaten track to pay one or more of them a visit are richly rewarded. It won't always be so, for Mozambique's proactive Ministry of Tourism is busy planning a serious campaign to make the most effective economic use of the country's abundant natural wonders, with the buzzword being 'ecotourism'.

It doesn't come much more eco that the Quirimbas. These fine islands – some tiny, some uninhabited, some with lodges built of local materials that hardly seem to intrude on the beauty that surrounds them – are formed of rugged coral punctuated by golden beaches where it is truly possible to feel isolated from the cares of the modern world. Key islands include Ibo, Quisiva and Matemo, which harbour former Portuguese outposts that supplanted pre-colonial settlements – a striking example being Stone Town on Ibo, a monument to Swahili culture over the centuries.

**HOW TO GET THERE:**
By air direct to Pemba from Johannesburg (a five-hour flight thrice weekly) or Dar es Salaam in Tanzania (a 45-minute flight five times a week). Internal flights from Maputo get to Pemba in the end, via a circuitous route. Thereafter it's a matter of making local arrangements for onward travel to the islands (by boat or light aircraft).

**WHEN TO GO:**
It's an any-time adventure.

**DON'T MISS:**
Those who like the Quirimbas Archipelago will also adore the Bazaruto Archipelago, to the south – a national park that has no roads, shops or tourist attractions . . . just breathtaking beaches, pristine waters and stunning coral reefs. Expect to see the fabled dugong, or sea cow, for Africa's largest concentrated population lives here.

**YOU SHOULD KNOW:**
The small island of Medjumbe has a ruined lighthouse plus a hotel that offers chalet accommodation and a pace of life all its own. Medjumbe time (an hour ahead of the mainland) operates and visitors are ceremonially issued with watches set accordingly.

# Kasanka National Park

This is not a national park in the conventional sense, for Kasanka in Zambia's Central Province is operated by a non-profit-making charitable trust that aims to secure the park's biodiversity and make it self-sustaining with the help of carefully managed tourism. The park has assorted habitats – lakes, rivers, swamps, dambos (shallow drainage channels), riverine forest, grassland – and is handsomely endowed with the miombo woodlands characteristic of the area. It is considered to be one of the most picturesque parks in the country.

*Punting in a dug-out canoe on Lake Wasa in Kasanka National Park.*

Despite being relatively small at 450 sq km (175 sq mi), Kasanka is a well-preserved wilderness that serves as a haven for many endangered species – including Sitatunga antelope and blue monkeys from the animal kingdom, plus Ross's lourie and wattled crane from the wonderful world of birds, which here numbers over 400 recorded species. The latter figure underlines the fact that Kasanka has a rich diversity of flora and fauna. There are no vast herds of animals but it's possible to spot a variety of interesting creatures. In addition to the rarities, visitors can look for hartebeest, antelope, bush pig, warthog, duiker, baboon, leopard, waterbuck, reedbuck, hippo, crocodile, otter, elephant, jackal, civet, mongoose and more.

**HOW TO GET THERE:**
By private air charter to a strip in the park. Driving takes around five to six hours from Lusaka or the Copperbelt, using the paved Great North Road to Kapiri town from either direction and turning there towards Mpika and Tanzania.

**WHEN TO GO:**
If a visit can be made at any time, go for November and December when Kasanka sees a spectacular congregation of several million fruit bats. The least favoured months are January to May.

**DON'T MISS:**
The opportunity to visit the Livingstone Memorial, marking the spot where the great explorer died in 1873. It is about 30 km (20 mi) north of Kasanka.

**YOU SHOULD KNOW:**
Petty crime is a problem in Zambia, with bag-snatching, mugging and thefts from parked cars not uncommon. Walking alone after dark is not recommended and there are occasional attacks on tourists in remote areas. However, Kasanka's protected environment is entirely safe.

There are three affordable campsites with basic facilities in the park, requiring visitors to bring their own camping equipment. It is wise to check in advance rather than simply turning up, as conditions may preclude camping, or all three sites may be fully booked. It is also possible to stay at one of Kasanka's two lodges, an option which many combine with a trip to nearby Shebill Island Camp in the vast Bangweulu Wetlands. Wasa Lodge and Luwomba Lodges offer the choice of budget self-catering chalets or a more expensive full-board package that includes some seasonal activities.

# Lower Zambezi National Park

Still relatively undeveloped, Zambia's newest national park is an unspoilt wilderness that extends to an impressive 4,000 sq km (1,545 sq mi). It lies some 450 km (280 mi) downriver from Victoria Falls, where the mighty Zambezi River crosses the fertile floodplains of the Lower Zambezi Valley. Across the river is Zimbabwe's Mana Pools Reserve, and the two parks combine to create a huge wildlife sanctuary. There is a steep escarpment along the northern boundary of the park, confining most animals to the plain. The river's edge is characterized by lush vegetation, the floodplain is fringed with winterthorn trees and mopane forest, while broadleaf woodland cloaks the surrounding hills.

*A canoe safari gets close to a bull elephant.*

There may not be as many different animal species in Lower Zambezi National Park as can be found in some other parks, but they are present in vast quantities and this place offers keen wildlife-watchers a unique experience. This involves taking to the water and observing the likes of abundant hippos, large elephant herds, crocodile, impala, buffalo, zebra, kudu, puku antelope and baboons, all seeming relatively unfussed by waterborne intruders, thus allowing canoeists to get very close. The birdlife is exceptional with a huge variety of species to be spotted, including fish eagles, trumpeter hornbill, Meyer's parrot, Lilian's lovebird, crested guinea fowl, black eagle and vast flocks of quelea.

Day safaris are offered by park lodges – guided or unguided – that allow adventurous visitors to drift downstream at a leisurely pace all day, before being spared the need to paddle back by the arrival of the lodge's motorboat as dusk approaches with the welcome offer of a return tow. Several operators run canoeing trips extending to several days, with nights spent at comfortable bushcamps on the banks. Some established lodges and camps offer vehicular game drives or guided walking safaris.

**HOW TO GET THERE:**
It's possible to drive to the park (using a 4x4) from Chirundu or Luangwa Town. But it's too new to have established vehicle access and most visitors prefer to be picked up from Lusaka or Chirundu after booking in advance with lodge or canoe-safari operators.

**WHEN TO GO:**
Any time, although April to September are the best months, with June to September being the park's high season.

**DON'T MISS:**
If there's one place where the cost of booking a bushcamp or safari lodge is justified by the return, this is it – the park has some of the very best in Africa.

**YOU SHOULD KNOW:**
Fishing (for tiger fish, bream and vundu catfish) is a popular recreational activity in the park and – strangely – the canny locals have discovered that pungent cheap soap is a top bait.

# Sesriem Canyon and Sossusvlei

**HOW TO GET THERE:**
By car to Sesriem and on to Sossusvlei (both are within Namibia's Naukluft National Park) – and by 4x4 for the (otherwise impassable) last 4 km (2.5 mi) to Sossusvlei.
**WHEN TO GO:**
Any time. High season is between June and September.
**DON'T MISS:**
The rock formations and caves within the Sesriem Canyon – a vivid geological record written in sedimentary rock, and the habitat of eagle owls, the lappet-faced vulture and lanner falcon, whose prey lies among the chattering starlings, pied crows and pigeons on the canyon's inner ledges.
**YOU SHOULD KNOW:**
Visitors clever enough to book a camp site at Sesriem during high season (do it *early* – spaces are limited and highly prized) may enter Sossusvlei an hour before sunrise, which means getting a very privileged view of the dunes and their denizens. Sesriem is in any case spectacular – and the National Park campsite has a *swimming pool*, a surreal touch in such extreme wilderness.

The dunes of the Namib Desert are 30 million years old. Whipped by fierce winds into sharp, undulating ridges like colossal red-and-black waves in a granulated ocean, they cover 32,500 sq km (12,550 sq mi), stretching 300 km (186 mi) north up Namibia's coast from Luderitz, and as much as 140 km (87 mi) inland. Nowhere in that vast region are their changing colours and moods more spectacular than in the alien magnificence of Sossusvlei. These are the tallest dunes in the world, over 300 m (1,000 ft). Just to gaze on them is humbling. Between the hours of dawn and dusk they might be coloured blood red, lilac, palest gold, deep yellow or intense orange like rust; and shadowed by a patchwork of soft blue and green, deepening to ultramarine and black.

Incredibly, the bone-dry Sossusvlei dunes mark the estuary of the Tsauchab River, swamped in mid flow by the encroaching desert. The river evaporates into white clay pans like Dead Vlei and Nara Vlei on the edge of Sossusvlei. Sometimes enough water reaches the pans to provide a mirror reflecting some of Africa's most spectacular views, and to bring the desert alive with flowers and birds. But visitors may not stay here: camping is a 63-km (39-mi) drive 'upriver' at Sesriem. A trail from the campsites leads to the 40-m (131-ft) deep and 1 km (0.6 mi) long Sesriem Canyon, carved over a million years by the Tsauchab River. Even from a few metres' distance, the canyon is invisible among the camelthorn trees and scrub. In many places its walls almost meet overhead, and the pools of water it retains are a magnet for all manner of scrambling desert creatures and birds. To get the best of it, start early in the morning and follow the arcing sun from the gorge up onto the dunes.

*Sesriem Canyon*

*The untouched Skeleton Coast*

# Skeleton Coast

The Bushmen called it 'The Land God Made in Anger'. To the Portuguese it was 'The Gates of Hell'. The Skeleton Coast used to mean the whole of Namibia's Atlantic coastline. Now it refers to the 20,000 sq km (7,720 sq mi) National Park that protects the northern one third of Namibia's coast, from the Ugab River to the Angolan border. It is an untouched world shrouded in chilling mists and prolonged fog. The cold Benguela Current sweeps north, pushing Antarctic air into the arid African heat. Although it never freezes, the Skeleton Coast is spitefully inhospitable – but it is a sanctuary to fur seals and marine and wading birds for which the nutrient-rich sea is a perpetually full larder. Inland, huge crescent, hummock and transverse dune systems lie between canyons of rust-coloured rock; and in this rainless transition zone desert scrub is watered by the mist. It's the transition that brings so much wildlife to the area. Rare desert elephants live here, with oryx, springbok, giraffe, ostrich, hyena, black rhino and even lion. Most find refuge in the depths of the canyons and dry river beds where the temperature is higher – pursuers and pursued using the foggy world for hunting cover.

Between the Hoanib and Kunene Rivers the Skeleton Coast may only be visited as part of a 'fly-in safari' that must be organized by a government-licensed concessionary. This northern section is where the coast's hostile reputation is confirmed. The shore is littered with long-ago shipwrecks, surreal sculptures of mechanical bones wedged in the sands. Somehow they are simultaneously pathetic and magnificent: failures in a contest with the raw power of unforgiving nature. Yet for some of Africa's most threatened creatures, the harsh struggle to stay alive here is their shield. The dynamism of that wilderness struggle is what brings visitors, and it's worth seeing.

**HOW TO GET THERE:**
By car to either Ugabmund or Springbokwasser, the only two entrances to the park's southern area; or by pre-arranged 'fly-in safari' to the north.

**WHEN TO GO:**
Any time. From May to September a strong wind blows the fog further inland, bringing moisture and reviving plant and animal life.

**DON'T MISS:**
Giving yourself time. The Kunene River harbours turtles and a big colony of crocodiles. Elephant and lion occasionally scavenge on the beaches, but you are more likely to see them and a huge variety of other creatures further inland. The park has over 250 species of birds and, close inshore, there are dolphins, humpback and killer whales besides the seals. Every habitat on the Skeleton Coast is teeming, if only you have time to explore it.

**YOU SHOULD KNOW:**
The Skeleton Coast is literally a geological jewel. Some of its beaches, especially near Mowe Bay, consist of gemstones polished by wave action. They can include red and maroon garnets, amethysts, quartzes, agate and carnelians. Legend has it that shipwrecked sailors often found alluvial diamonds at their feet – then died of thirst on those interminable beaches, with the wealth of a Croesus in their pockets.

*Spitzkoppe has the silhouette of a sleeping dinosaur.*

# Spitzkoppe

**HOW TO GET THERE:**
By car, on the long gravel turn-off from the road to Henties Bay.
**WHEN TO GO:**
Any time
**DON'T MISS:**
The details – birds in the air, and the flora and fauna of the rock formations and the cracks in the massif. Equally important to Spitzkoppe's compelling sense of identity are the various sites of Bushmen rock paintings. The most complex – and complete – are at 'Bushman's Paradise', where you use a chain handhold to clamber up a smooth slope to see them, on the underside of a long rocky overhang.
**YOU SHOULD KNOW:**
Spitzkoppe is famous among photographers for its fabulous colours and shapes. In Namibia, the massif is considered so beautiful and unusual that images of it inspire a kind of reverence.

On the flat, arid scrub desert of Namibia's coastal plain between Usakos and Swakopmund, Spitzkoppe rears on the horizon as the jagged silhouette of a sleeping dinosaur. Sometimes called the 'Matterhorn of Namibia', the granite massif is the eroded remnant of a volcano that collapsed 100 million years ago. Its twin peaks reach 1,800 m and 1,584 m (5,905 ft and 5,197 ft), but their effect is made much more dramatic by rising, sheer, over 700 m (2,300 ft) above the plain. Wind and rain have sculpted the rocks into weird and wonderful formations, carving out gullies and caves which harbour unusual flora like the yellow butter tree and the poison tree, which oozes a white sap used by Bushmen to poison their hunting arrows. Several sheltered rock faces carry ancient paintings by this indigenous San people.

Spitzkoppe is a magnet for experienced climbers, who over the years have established a system of permanent lines for hikers to pull themselves over rocky obstacles along the various trails. This act of mercy opens up the mountain for less athletic visitors. There are so many trails to so many beautiful, hidden corners, and they cater to every level of fitness. They lead to spectacular views across the plains to the Pondok Mountains (the name comes from the Afrikaans for 'looks like an African hut'), or to vistas along the spine of the Klein Spitzkoppe 10 km (6 mi) to the west. Climbing is much harder than it may look. Even for experts the rock can be too hot to touch, and the round, weathered surfaces defy any sane grip – but outside the summer there are climbing tours to the summit which require spending three nights on the mountain. The less committed will be content with the lower campsites sited in isolated privacy among boulders, with fantastic views and skyscapes.

# Sibebe Rock

Swaziland is landlocked by Mozambique to the east and South Africa everywhere else. It's a topographical jigsaw, with highlands predominant in the west, and hot, dry lowlands to the east, both crammed into an area no bigger than Wales in the UK or New Jersey in the USA. In a single day visitors can easily drive from the cool mountains, forests and waterfalls of the highveld, through hilly central grasslands, to the open savannah of acacia and broadleaf and the baking bushveld of stunted thickets, knobthorn and dry riverine forests. Many drive straight through to South Africa, cheating themselves of some of Africa's loveliest landscapes, and missing world-class geological oddities for which Swaziland is famous.

Outside Mbabane, Swaziland's capital at the northern end of the Ezulwini Valley, a gravel road follows the Mbuluzi River as it winds down the incomparable Pine Valley. The villages and rondavel homesteads seem to grow naturally out of this pastoral beauty: it's made for hiking or horse riding. Then quite suddenly, as river and road loop round a protruding bluff of smooth rock, the trees and shrubs fall away to reveal the bald rock crown of a truly massive granite dome pushing into the blue sky. This is Sibebe, second only to Australia's Uluru as the world's largest single rock. Close-to, it's impossible to guess its real size. The colossal granite monolith is only visible from far away, sheer on all sides, and unbroken anywhere except by gullies formed by erosion. It's even more spectacular from its own summit. It feels like being on top of the world, with views (on a clear day) as far east as the great 'big five' game reserves of Hlane and Mkhaya, and to the south, the twin peaks called Sheba's Breasts, the legendary site of King Solomon's Mines. Informally, Swazis call Sibebe Rock 'the tumescence of Swaziland' – and they might not be joking.

**HOW TO GET THERE:**
By car or bus. There are official 'entrances', but access is permitted across most private land on the perimeter.

**WHEN TO GO:**
June to November, when the western highlands are drier but cooler.

**DON'T MISS:**
The short hiking trails on Sibebe Rock (if the summit proves too ambitious), and guided hikes in the vicinity – like the Mlilwane Hippo Trail or the Lion Cavern, celebrated as the oldest known human mine workings, dating back to 43000 BC.

**YOU SHOULD KNOW:**
Swaziland is sometimes called Africa's last truly traditional kingdom. 'Kingship', personified in the Swazi royal family, is also a mystical notion that informs everyone's daily life and provides the glue securing traditional culture to modern customs. The whole country stops for two major annual rituals – the Incwala, or sacred ceremony of Kingship, and the Umhlanga Reed Dance, in which unmarried girls collect reeds (umhlanga) to make a symbolic windbreak demonstrating their protective loyalty to the Queen Mother, known universally as Indlovukazi, or 'She-Elephant'.

# Kgalagadi Transfrontier Park

Formerly known as Kalahari Gemsbok National Park, Kgalagadi is a joint enterprise by Botswana and South Africa on their Namibian border. With only five park entrances from the three countries, visitors may have to jump through a few bureaucratic hoops to fulfil border as well as park controls. Frankly, it's worth every effort to gain access to one of Africa's and the world's great open wilderness areas. In size alone Kgalagadi represents the rare phenomenon of an entire ecosystem with minimal human interference. The park covers 36,000 sq km (13,900 sq mi) of semi-desert savannah, red dune systems, acacia scrub and woodland, and endless sparse tracts of Kalahari couch grass covered in camelthorn bushes. They are landscapes that belong naturally to huge herds of antelope, and visitors will find migrating oryx, blue wildebeest, grey duiker, red hartebeest, steenbok, impala, gemsbok and the occasional rare eland.

Where they go, the predators follow. No campfire is complete without an evening serenade of the grunts, screams, snarls and coughing roars belonging to some of Africa's most famous carnivores, but a much better time to see them is around midday when leopard, cheetah, spotted hyena and the giant, black-maned Kalahari lion can often be found resting in the shade of camelthorn or acacia trees. Mammals of all sizes concentrate in or near the dry courses of the Auob and Nossob Rivers, including meerkat, pangolin (aka the scaly anteater), honey badger and bat-eared fox. The Nossob is also a byword for spotting an unusual variety of raptors, like the bateleur, snake eagle, lappet-faced vulture, pygmy falcon, kestrel, kite and pale chanting goshawk. With 200 other migratory and resident species, the birds participate in Kgalagadi's magnificent annual cycle of regeneration. The visitor's privilege is to be able to follow its wildlife cast of millions, playing out the game of life in all its glorious, gory detail. Amazing.

*A lion in Kgalagadi Transfrontier Park*

# Tsodilo Hills

*Rock paintings of the San Bushmen in the Tsodilo Hills*

From a distance the desert horizon is a flat line broken by a series of quartzite cliffs rising sheer from the savannah to 410 m (1,345 ft). This is the highest peak in Botswana, and one of four in a line of descending height called the Tsodilo Hills. Standing alone in the western corner of the Kalahari Desert, in Ngamiland near the edge of the Okavango swamps, the hills have a history to match their geological oddity. Alternately baked and scoured by freezing winds, they are the repository of the world's biggest collection of indigenous rock paintings, the summary of 100,000 years of known religious worship and sacred ritual. Throughout that time the Tsodilo Hills have been physical representations of the San Bushmen's spiritual culture. According to height, they are 'the male', 'the female' and 'the child' (with the nameless fourth knoll ascribed to 'the male's first, discarded wife') in the San creation myth, and the resting place of ancestral spirits. Even now, a San guide taking visitors to what is known collectively as the 'Rock that Whispers' will first ask 'permission' from the hill deities to do so.

The 4,500 rock paintings (and thousands of other artefacts) are spread between 400 sites across 10 sq km (3.8 sq mi) of the hills. Most of them, including the best, are on the northern side of 'the female' and, significantly, they are different in style and content from any other known rock art. The feeling of being in a place of mystery and magic can be overwhelming: visitors may come for the archaeology or the cultural aesthetics, but they leave with a profound sense of human indomitability. By investing their enduring faith in these barren, inhospitable and isolated hills, the San Bushmen have created an ark of beauty out of burning hot rock.

**HOW TO GET THERE:**
By small plane to the Tsodilo airstrip; or by 4x4 on a track just south of Sepupa in the Panhandle region
**WHEN TO GO:**
Any time
**DON'T MISS:**
The symbology which challenges presumptions about how long human cultures have been capable of abstract thought. The Tsodilo Hills paintings aren't the only demonstrations of ancient ideas: in one of the rock grottos on 'the female' (from which the gods ruled the world) the stones have been crudely fashioned into a 2-m (7-ft) high, and 6-m (20-ft) long python's head. The python is and has always been central to San culture as the creator of mankind, and the arid stream beds around the hills are held to be the python's tracks, searching for water.
**YOU SHOULD KNOW:**
Some visitors think it is fanciful to ascribe spiritual significance to four outcrops of rock. Some feel their atmosphere so keenly they cannot bear to stay in the area. Many not only feel the strong emotions that the hills engender, but also report feeling an 'unlooked-for empathy' with the San belief that hunting or causing death of any kind in the vicinity will bring misfortune.

# Sehlabathebe National Park

*The Sani Pass, which goes from South Africa to Lesotho, through the Drakensburg Mountains.*

If the 'Kingdom of the Sky' has a garden, it is Sehlabathebe National Park. Like the fabled Shangri-La it is an impossibly remote, sub-alpine paradise protected by its average altitude of 2,450 m (8,038 ft) and its position on Lesotho's eastern border with South Africa, on the lip of the Drakensberg Escarpment. A tectonic quirk raised the Sehlabathebe area higher than its surroundings, pushing a very rare outcrop of Clarens formation (cream-coloured) sandstone clear of the Drakensberg basalt which forms southern Africa's highest mountains immediately to the north. Whittled by the Tsoelikane and other tributaries of the nascent Orange River to the west, the sandstone contributes sensational landscapes like near-vertical cliff faces, river gorges, weird rock formations riddled with caves, waterfalls, magnificent promontories looking over plateaus studded with small lakes – and the sandy sediments which fill its valleys and provide the mineral sustenance for some of the planet's loveliest open grasslands. There are marshes and meadows at every altitude, completing the conditions for an unusual range of biodiversity. Game is restricted to rhebuck, eland, baboons, oribi antelope, mongoose, otters, wild cats and jackals, but the birdlife is magnificent, especially in the highest tarns. With all this, and vast skies and distant views, Sehlabathebe makes gods of hikers and riders. There are no fences.

Sehlabathebe is a designated wilderness that shares a boundary with South Africa's uKhahlamba Drakensberg Park, and a position at the southern end of the 300-km (186-mi) Maloti-Drakensberg Transfrontier Project which rings north and east Lesotho. Although visitors bask in the park's remote perfection, the beautiful surrounding backcountry adds to the quality of the experience by reintroducing the human element. The wilderness survives only if the Basotho people can benefit from it. It's possible to drive to the park – but it's far, far more rewarding to trek in through the surrounding Basotho villages.

# Tsehlanyane National Park

Small by international standards, Tsehlanyane is the jewel in a much larger environmental scheme, and of growing importance to its ultimate success. The park covers 56 sq km (21.5 sq mi) of the highest and most rugged terrain in the Lesotho Highlands. Set deep in the Front Range of the Maloti Mountains, Tsehlanyane's plunging valleys have an altitude range of 1,940–3,112 m (6,365–10,210 ft) and are predominantly sub-alpine. Their beauty is not exclusive – the whole Maloti range is breathtaking – but it is of rare quality. Tsehlanyane includes one of Lesotho's very few remaining old-growth indigenous forests, and preserving it is proving crucial to the Maloti Mountains' role as a source of pure, fresh water, and to a high level of endemism.

The much larger scheme is the development of the Maloti-Drakensberg Transfrontier Project. Tsehlanyane and its environs represent a massive extension of a biological corridor that now runs for hundreds of miles around northern Lesotho along the Drakensberg range that forms its border with South Africa. It is a fragile ecosystem, challenged by human encroachment of every kind – but it's proving to be a model of sustainable development, benefiting the Basotho people as much as the wildlife. Already visitors to Tsehlanyane can see previously non-existent herds of migrating eland, troops of baboons, grey rhebuck and 20 other frequently sighted medium-sized mammals. Even leopard have returned. Yet Tsehlanyane is not a wholly pristine wilderness. There are still villages dotted about. The Maloti Mountains are full of archaeological sites charting Basotho culture over several millennia. Tsehlanyane's forests include che-che woodland and stands of berg bamboo among local flora and fauna that have direct cultural significance for the Basotho. For visitors, trekking on foot or horseback through such natural beauty, it's a joy to participate in a culture so enthusiastic about living in harmony with nature.

**HOW TO GET THERE:**
By car along the Hlotse River valley to the park entrance just past Khabo village. Then by hiking or surefooted Lesotho pony.

**WHEN TO GO:**
Any time – but winter is always cold and snow is not unusual.

**DON'T MISS:**
Riding. It's the ideal travel mode for the steep hillside trails. Tsehlanyane is full of streams, cascades and rock pools for a super-bracing dip, and a really stunning 39-km (24-mi) trail connects the park with Bokong Nature Reserve, perched on a cliff overlooking the Lepagoa Valley and home of the Lepagoa Falls.

**YOU SHOULD KNOW:**
Visitors will find a very friendly welcome in Basotho villages. In typically rural areas like this, Basotho people wear trademark blankets in very bright colours – but only tourists wear the traditional, conical, Basotho headgear. Travellers who enter or leave Tsehlanyane by way of Butha-Buthe should pause to see the fossilized dinosaur footprints on the banks of the nearby Subeng River.

*Maloti Mountains in the Lesotho Highlands*

# Timbavati Game Reserve

*A young lion cub climbing on
its mother.*

South Africa's Kruger National Park is an enormous wilderness showcasing Africa's most spectacular wildlife. Timbavati borders the Kruger's central section, one of a number of private concessions along the Kruger's length which benefit from having no fences to hinder game moving freely between them. Timbavati's 680 sq km (262 sq mi) of low bushveld is the meeting place of the mopane woodlands and the Timbavati floodplain. The combination of savannah grasslands and dense shelter makes the region one of southern Africa's best for viewing all kinds of game. Besides the 'big five' of lion, leopard, buffalo, elephant and rhino, visitors are almost certain to see impala, kudu, giraffe, baboons, zebra, monkeys, cheetah, hippos and crocodiles. Early morning and late afternoon safaris are adventures into the real world of dangerous predators – and even from a vehicle it's not unusual to have to back off quickly if an elephant or buffalo feels threatened.

Of course, getting as close as possible to some of Earth's greatest living creatures is the whole point. Timbavati is organized so that it's never crowded, although it can feel like it during the dry season when three or four land rovers are tracking game to the same waterhole. It takes expert knowledge to get the best from going on safari, which means staying at one of Timbavati's private lodges. Some are bushcamps, others are five-star luxury eco-resorts camouflaged in the vegetation next to waterholes for easy viewing. Each has a speciality, like night tours, or tracking lion on foot, or river trips by dug-out canoe among crocodiles and Africa's most dangerous mammal, the hippo. Some are better placed to see the 500 bird species that regularly visit the Kruger and its environs. The joy of Timbavati is that so much variety is on its doorstep.

# Madikwe

Between the little town of Groot-Marico in South Africa's North West province and the Botswana border lies one of the country's biggest game reserves. Madikwe includes 750 sq km (290 sq mi) of acacia-studded grasslands and bushveld plains that disappear in a blue haze on the horizon, broken only by outcrops of burnished rock and the occasional solitary hill (called an *inselberg*). It is a transition zone between the desperately arid Kalahari thornveld and the dense forests watered by a permanent river and seasonal wetlands in the foothills of the majestic Dwarsberg Mountains. Madikwe is how travellers imagine the African wilderness, with columns of elephant and buffalo shimmering under a heat haze, and the inky blackness of the night canopy. With its varied terrain it supports a phenomenal number and variety of game. The 'big five' are all there, with the biggest elephant herd outside the Kruger, and of buffalo anywhere; white and black rhinos; cheetah, giraffe, hyena, zebra, kudu, springbok and dozens of other species; and a mixture of desert, plains and wetland species among its 300 birds.

Madikwe's success as a reserve has been bolstered by Operation Phoenix, the world's biggest translocation programme. With the enthusiastic support of its residents, in little more than 20 years Madikwe has seen re-introduced species like wild dog and black rhino flourish and spread as former farm and ranching land was returned to a wilderness that would attract the big herds. Local enthusiasm has been crucial, and one of its cornerstones has been the local desire not just to create South Africa's 'best' reserve, but to make it especially attractive to children. Throughout Madikwe, the camps and lodges make a concerted effort to be family-friendly. The facilities for children (and their parents) are unmatched in any other reserve – and best of all, Madikwe is entirely malaria-free.

*White rhinoceros in Madikwe Game Reserve*

**HOW TO GET THERE:**
By 4x4 from Johannesburg – 360 km (224 mi); or Gaborone in Botswana – 28 km (17 mi) to the Abjagterskop reserve gate. This is usually arranged through a lodge concessionary since day visits are not permitted.
**WHEN TO GO:**
July to September, when sparse vegetation makes viewing easier and animals congregate at the remaining waterholes.
**DON'T MISS:**
Bringing the children. The guides at Madikwe love explaining things to kids, and most of the camps have special activities for them, including 'game drives' for under eights! But that doesn't mean they will infantilize the safari for adults – it's a measure of the care that has gone into making Madikwe such a winner. And (say it often) the reserve is *malaria-free.*
**YOU SHOULD KNOW:**
The region of Madikwe is immortalized in the works of Herman Charles Bosman (1905–1951), the South African writer and poet. His most famous story is called *The Mafeking Road*, after the track which runs straight through the reserve. Bosman also wrote – of the contemplative mysticism Madikwe inspires – "It does strange things to you, the Marico moon, and in your heart are wild and fragrant fancies, and your thoughts go very far away." Visitors often feel the same.

*Fish River Canyon is one of Africa's most amazing natural wonders.*

# |Ai-|Ais/Richtersveld Transfrontier Park

**HOW TO GET THERE:**
By four-wheel drive. Visitors from South Africa must go via the Sendelingsdrift border post, and use the recently reactivated pontoon ferry over the Orange River – or face a 485 km (300 mi) detour!

**WHEN TO GO:**
April to October. Depending on good rains, springtime (July to October) brings out the full floral splendour of |Ai-|Ais/Richtersveld.

**DON'T MISS:**
Booking ahead. Numbers are restricted on the Fish River Canyon Trails – Vensterval (four days), Lelieshoek (three days) and Kodaspiek (two days) – to preserve the delicate ecosystem. Ask a local Nama guide to point out the Apollo 11 caves, which contain Namibia's oldest rock paintings, and the 2,000-year-old Khoi rock engravings at sites all over the park.
A guide can also explain the importance of *malmokkies*, the cold fog from the Atlantic Ocean that brings moisture to sustain the birds, reptiles and smaller mammals.

**YOU SHOULD KNOW:**
In the Nama language, |Ai-|Ais means 'burning water', and refers to the thermal springs gushing up into the desert at the place where the Fish River Canyon hike ends.

Nobody does camouflage better than Nature. The unification of Namibia's |Ai-|Ais reserve and South Africa's Richtersveld appears to be the twinning of two equally inhospitable mountainous deserts that face each other across a loop of the mighty Orange River. A closer inspection reveals that the two halves of the Transfrontier Park complete each other to form a single botanical hotspot called the Succulent Karoo biome. The apparently barren landscape of interminable rocky hills scarred by rugged *kloofs* (gullies), dry river beds and valleys filled with immense boulders is a fragile ecosystem adapted to over 1,700 plant species, most of them rare, and over a 100 of which are endemic. As the eye adjusts to the spectacular topography, it begins to take in the enormous variety of life forms it supports. Many are bizarre, like the *halfmens boom* (half-person tree), a 3 m (10 ft) cactus with a crown of leaves like dreadlocks. Wild animals are also numerous, although elusive in Richtersveld's vastness. Even so, hikers will come across klipspringer, springbok and steenbok, baboon, mountain zebra and leopard. The unfamiliar flora attracts 150 specialist bird species, and in the Orange River and some of the larger pools elsewhere, the region has its own endemic fish, like the yellowfish, Orange River mudfish and the sharptooth catfish.

On the Namibian side are two of southern Africa's most amazing natural wonders. One is the hot springs at |Ai-|Ais itself. The other is the second-largest natural canyon in the world. Hiking 90 km (56 mi) of the 166 km (103 mi) Fish River Canyon is one of the great African adventures. There's no marked trail. Hikers take five days to pick their way down the bluffs of the canyon and follow the intermittently flowing Fish River through a chasm with sheer walls 550 m (1,800 ft) high to a world of magnificent, alien beauty.

# Royal Natal National Park

Royal Natal National Park was created long before anyone realized the importance of bio-corridors in conserving flora and wildlife. Now it forms part of the mighty uKhahlamba Drakensberg Park, itself subsumed into the Maloti-Drakensberg Transfrontier Project that rings the border between Lesotho and KwaZulu-Natal. As interest shifts towards the grander plan, it's easy to overlook the jewel in the Drakensberg crown: the original nature reserve, Royal Natal.

It is dominated by the Drakensberg Amphitheatre, a wall of rock 5 km (3 mi) long standing 500 m (1,640 ft) straight up from the surrounding plain. Two 3,000-m (9,840-ft) peaks, the Sentinel and Eastern Buttress, guard each end and several large domes rise from the summit plateau. A French missionary christened the highest of these *Mont-aux-Sources* because seven rivers begin here, including the Orange River. It is a spectacular landscape at any level and from every angle. Experienced hikers get the best of it on the two-day, 45-km (28-mi) *Mont-aux-Sources* Trail; although it's possible to drive to the top as well. A network of shorter trails adapted to every level of competence covers the Amphitheatre. One of the most scenic leads visitors boulder-hopping along the Tugela Gorge, through thick forest with stands of yellowwood trees, over flower-studded grassland and up a chain ladder through a rock tunnel to a cliff with an eye-popping view of Tugela Falls. Tugela is one of the world's highest waterfalls, dropping 948 m (3,110 ft) in five distinct leaps. After heavy rain, the flooding Tugela River can tumble in as many as 18 separate cascades from the lip of the Amphitheatre; and in winter they freeze into enormous sculptured ice pillars. Less crowded now, Royal Natal National Park has never been more beautiful – and it has first-class visitor facilities to match.

**HOW TO GET THERE:**
By car
**WHEN TO GO:**
Any time
**DON'T MISS:**
Swimming in the rock bowls at the top of Gudu Falls, then using chain ladders to climb the cliff chimney called 'The Crack' for the reward of seeing the vast panorama of the rugged Drakensberg; return by clambering down the near-vertical 'Mudslide'.
**YOU SHOULD KNOW:**
Anyone can apply to run the *Mont-aux-Sources* Challenge, an annual 50-km (30-mi) cross-country race usually held in September. Competitors race from the entrance to Royal Natal National Park to the top of the Sentinel peak, and back again. The field is restricted to 250 runners and is popular with 'extreme athletes' – so book early, because there is a waiting list.

*The Drakensberg Amphitheatre, Royal Natal National Park*

# iMfolozi Wilderness

Both iMfolozi and its neighbour Hluhluwe had been game reserves for a century when they were officially amalgamated as the 960-sq-km (370-sq-mi) Hluhluwe-iMfolozi Game Reserve in 1989. Game conservation had not always been completely unselfish: iMfolozi (formerly Umfolozi) was once the private hunting precinct of King Shaka Zulu, and both sections have been threatened by hunting warriors as well as poachers. Hluhluwe in the north is more mountainous, broken by canyons, fast rivers and tropical forests filled with the colours of exotic birds. Its hills and dense shrubbery are the ideal habitat for black rhino, which thrive here. To the south, iMfolozi flattens into a wilderness of acacia-dotted savannah and undulating, thicket-cloaked hills squeezed between two branches of the iMfolozi River.

It is predator and big game country. iMfolozi Wilderness is (relatively) crammed with Africa's biggest and best, and in numbers that make seeing them all but guaranteed. The reserve is famous as a sanctuary for both black and white rhino, and visitors staying at the various park camps and lodges can expect game drives and guided trail safaris to the hides overlooking wilderness pans and waterholes to which all wildlife must come. Elephant, lion, cheetah, leopard, hyena, buffalo, warthog, wildebeest, baboon and jackal pass in a pageant of African splendour. At any time on the savannah they may be joined by zebra, giraffe, waterbuck, nyala, kudu, bushbuck and great herds of impala. The grasslands themselves harbour wild dog, meerkat and dozens of smaller species, and everywhere colourful tropical birds fill the air or patrol the mudflats round the waterholes and river banks. At iMfolozi it really is possible to believe in the notion of an ark of creation. In conjunction with Hluhluwe, the reserve offers the greatest concentration of easily visible big game in Africa.

*Burchell's zebra*

# Kosi Bay

*Fish traps in Kosi Bay*

In the northeastern corner of Maputaland, on the border with Mozambique, Kosi Bay sustains an African microculture that has survived there for over 700 years. Kosi Bay is inhabited exclusively by Maputaland's three oldest existing communities of kwaDapha, eMalangeni and Nkovukeni peoples, members of the Tembe tribal group indigenous to the area. They live in symbiotic harmony with the 12-km (7.5-mi) long system of Kosi Bay's four lakes, which they maintain as the fundamental element of their very existence.

It is a fragile ecosystem. The chain of lakes is connected by a series of channels that lead to the most pristine estuary in South Africa – a sandbar-choked lagoon with just one narrow exit into the Indian Ocean. High tides constantly refresh the system, and the differing salinity of each lake supports a colossal variety of plant life on its banks, including rare forests of raffia palm, five mangrove species, figs, orchids and papyrus. The lakes themselves are strung with a web of fish *kraals*, sited to make the most of every twist in the watercourse and every flood and eddy in the water itself. The fish are so plentiful that Kosi Bay is known as 'the aquarium', and its crystal-clear waters are great for snorkelling and scuba-diving. However, even fishing can be a risky business. Zambesi sharks come up the channels, and hippos and crocodiles live among its marshes, reed beds and overhanging swamp forests. Lots of them. The forests are also home to bushbuck, duiker and several kinds of monkey, and the variety of the terrain brings some of the world's rarest and most beautiful birds in a rainbow of colour to its wetland splendour.

Kosi Bay has the endlessly fascinating charm of undisturbed nature at its most subtle. It is stunning, and deserves to be the destination of choice of every visitor to Africa.

**HOW TO GET THERE:**
By 4x4, slowly and carefully
**WHEN TO GO:**
Any time – but in December and January loggerhead and leatherback turtles come to the beaches to lay their eggs; and humpback whales pass close inshore on their way to calve off Mozambique.
**DON'T MISS:**
Birds to set your imagination ablaze, like the bluemantled flycatcher, pinkthroated longclaw, crab plover, African finfoot, Pel's fishing owl and hundreds more.
**YOU SHOULD KNOW:**
Visitor numbers are restricted, and permits are necessary both to visit and to fish (take-and-return). But with Tembe Elephant Reserve on its doorstep (home to the 'big five' and a lot more), making the effort to see Kosi Bay is doubly worth it. Technically, Kosi Bay is part of the iSimangaliso Wetlands World Heritage Site centred on St Lucia Bay much further south – but that's as much as they have in common. Note that Kosi Bay is a high-risk malaria area.

# Tsitsikamma National Park

**HOW TO GET THERE:**
By car along Route 62, a tiny road passing the edge of the Formosa Nature Reserve, reminiscent of the USA's Route 66 in Arizona and New Mexico. It is lined with a string of small towns preserved since the 1940s and 1950s. Stop and hike into the wilderness.

**WHEN TO GO:**
Any time

**DON'T MISS:**
The Tsitsikamma range rises suddenly east of the Keurbooms River north of Plettenberg Bay, and the area is particularly rich in colourful birds like the giant kingfisher, Knysna lourie, Knysna woodpecker, and sunbirds galore. Head for the mountains' highest peak, 1,675-m (5,495-ft) Formosa, for glorious views over Nature's Valley and the fertile coastal forest.

**YOU SHOULD KNOW:**
*Tsitsikamma* means 'place of many waters', and was named by the Khoi San indigenous people of the region.
The National Park and the Tsitsikamma Mountains are full of ancient Khoi cultural sites, including caves, shell middens and rock art.

*A beautiful bay on the Cape Garden Route*

Most South Africans think of Tsitsikamma as an eco-playground and adventure centre for extreme sports, with Tsitsikamma National Park as its heart. The park includes a marine section extending 5 km (3 mi) into the Indian Ocean, and an 80-km (50-mi) stretch of coast that forms part of the Cape Garden Route, internationally celebrated for its rugged beauty and colourful flora and fauna. Tsitsikamma Forest sits on a 200-m (656-ft) high, thickly forested plateau rising sheer from the waves, bounded by the Bloukrans River to the west and the Eerste River to the east. Its owes its conservation to the development of trails and facilities for mountain-biking, group hiking, bungee-jumping (Bloukrans Bridge over the Storms River gorge is the highest bungee jump in the world), quad bikes, scuba diving, canopy ziplining and trail-driving – yet wildlife flourishes and Tsitsikamma's beauty remains legendary. Visitors love its setting between the ocean and the Tsitsikamma Mountains, assuming both belong to the National Park. They look, but they seldom see.

The Tsitsikamma Mountains are a true wilderness with no formal trails or activities. Their solitude is enhanced by their location within the Formosa Nature Reserve, which itself lies between the remotest part of Tsitsikamma National Park and the Bavvianskloof Wilderness Area inland towards the Great Karoo. The only crowds are of birds which fill the rich afromontane forests, ravines, river banks and towering ferns and shrubs of the wet *fynbos*. Near the pools below mountain cascades there may be bushpig or blue duiker, leopard or elephant; or more likely, butterflies and amphibians and smaller mammals.

The name 'Tsitsikamma' is used to refer to so many other geographical delights that few people realize how incredibly isolated the Tsitsikamma Mountains really are – or how very extraordinary it is that such a pristine region of Africa could still exist untouched, so close to one of the country's major tourist attractions.

# Eastern Cape – The Wild Coast

*The remote Wild Coast*

Not so long ago South Africa's apartheid culture banished 'unwanted blacks' west and north of the Kei River, creating the semi-autonomous Transkei, an unloved territory deprived of economic opportunity and subsidy. For decades Transkei was ignored as a deeply rural backwater, while the rest of South Africa's beautiful Cape coast was heavily developed in the name of local and international tourism. Known as 'The Garden Route', it's still beautiful – but Transkei's pristine coastal dunes, beaches and bays are both beautiful and empty. Rolling hills and grasslands reach back from the rock cliffs and dune systems. Aloe groves fill deep ravines. Dense forests are folded into the land, lining its rivers and dramatic, tidal estuaries. For roughly 250 km (155 mi) from the Great Kei to the Mtanvuna River, the Wild Coast is a gift of nature, unpolluted by light or noise, and accessible only to those willing to hike or ride a horse to get there.

The only communities are the long-established thatched rondavels of fishermen, and the occasional backpacker lodge or small hotel, managed and owned by local people. When democracy turned South Africa on its head, the Xhosa communities of the Wild Coast quickly realized the value of preserving their natural asset intact. Nowhere else in the world is there such an idyllic coastline with a benign, all-year climate, and still virtually undeveloped. The Wild Coast does include several small nature reserves like the tiny Silaka Reserve which protects an enclave of towering forest and lush grasslands; but most are like the Hluleka Reserve south of Port St Johns, useful signposts to areas of unspoilt natural beauty and tranquillity. It's an addictive combination and visitors will discover that the more they entrust themselves to local knowledge about the Wild Coast, the more they will be enriched by its isolated charm.

**HOW TO GET THERE:**
On foot or horseback. Access by 4x4 is strictly limited – and unlike most other places in South Africa, it isn't at all easy just to 'fly in' for the day or weekend.
**WHEN TO GO:**
Any time
**DON'T MISS:**
The coastal hike from Coffee Shack past Baby Hole and Hlungwane Waterfall to the spectacular 'Hole in the Wall' – a pierced rock formation in which crashing waves set up a rhythmic slapping. Closer to Mthatha, the regional capital, Luchaba Nature Reserve is a series of wetlands, grasslands and forest glades that explodes with birds and wildlife. For isolated beaches try Mbotyi in Pondoland.
**YOU SHOULD KNOW:**
Nelson Mandela was born in the Wild Coast region of the Eastern Cape. It is the Xhosa heartland, and Xhosa is the majority first language. The more visitors know of Xhosa traditions and customs, the more they will understand Mandela – and vice-versa.

# Cirque Mafate, Réunion

Conan Doyle would recognize it as his *Lost World*, accessible only by helicopter or long, hard trek. Summit peaks of bald rock lance the tropical sky, almost strangled by a cloak of thick forest and green jungle that plunges down to absurd, handkerchief-sized clearings between the mountains. Separated by huge crags, ravines and waterfalls, the isolated clearings are connected only by difficult trails that wind through tumbled boulders overrun by rainforest vines and giant ferns. The Cirque Mafate is the Indian Ocean volcanic island of Réunion's 'island within an island', one of a 'three-leaf clover' of adjacent calderas (*cirques*) in the north of Reunion (the only active volcano is in the south), each differing radically from the others and from the rest of Reunion. Cirque Cilaos is the most developed. Cirque Salazie is the most exuberantly florescent, and famous for the perfect straw to make straw hats. Mafate is the most remote, protected by inaccessibility. It has always been so: it was untouched until it became the refuge for a few maroons centuries ago. Eventually some stayed, founding the eight *ilets* ('islets', or villages) on the only flat ground they could clear between the almost sheer mountain walls. Each has a different character, although the biggest (La Nouvelle) has only 150 residents. To hike between them, succinctly placed in staggering landscapes of rock and sky and falling water, is to enter enchantment. There is a tamarind forest where the trees grow to 20 m (66 ft), bent by wind and covered in trailing bearded capuchin. Grass-covered ledges skirt precipices, and swaying bridges cross fearsome gorges. Every turn holds a surprise and, with a Mafate guide, every trail becomes a jaw-dropping adventure into raw wilderness.

*The incredible Cirque Mafate*

**HOW TO GET THERE:**
By helicopter or on foot
**WHEN TO GO:**
Any time
**DON'T MISS:**
The Creole culture that persists in Cirque Mafate. It includes a relaxed version of French café culture, and several *ilets* are centred on the *bonhomie* of curiosity and conversation in the communal cafe. Join in to find a congenial guide, willing to take you to places like Ilet Aurere at the foot of Piton Cabris, connected to Ilet a Malheur via a hair-raising bridge over the Bemale gorge.
**YOU SHOULD KNOW:**
The hiking is world-class, with or without a guide. Being French (Réunion is a *Departement d'Outre Mer*, or Overseas Territory) Mafate trails are marked using the *Grande Randonnee* system.

# Ranomafana National Park

When Madagascar split from the African continent it became a living laboratory of evolution and diversity. Isolation prevented almost all forms of species exchange, so that 90 per cent of its flora and fauna is now endemic and exclusive. Yet four fifths of all Madagascar's landmass has been stripped and ransacked for short-term commercial gain. Rainforest once covered the coastal flatlands that now produce just a few corporate export crops like coffee, and more is disappearing as Malagasy farmers are forced to farm on higher ground. Ranomafana National Park protects the best of what's left. About 60 km (40 mi) east of Fianarantsoa, Ranomafama is proof of the richness of the rainforest that once extended along the whole of Madagascar's east coast.

The National Park owes its existence to the golden lemur. Its discovery in 1986 prompted research which revealed 30 species of lemur monkeys, and 60 more in the extended lemur family. Some are really bizarre. The indri has panda markings and somersaults from tree to tree, wailing like a humpback whale. The aye-aye is the stuff of nightmares, with bat's ears, teeth that never stop growing, and a Scrooge-like long skinny finger that enables it to perform the role of a woodpecker where no woodpeckers otherwise exist. Ranomafana's montane rainforest covers 416 sq km (160 sq mi) of teeming wilderness at altitudes between 400–1,200 m (1,310–3,940 ft). Watered by dozens of streams feeding the Namorona River (which crashes out of the eastern escarpment in spectacular falls close to the park entrance), it nourishes more orchid species than in the whole of Africa and flora and fauna like nowhere else on Earth. It is full of colour and beauty, and endlessly exciting encounters with strange life forms: there is no more productive wilderness on the planet.

*A female red-bellied lemur*

# Tsingy de Bemaraha

Just getting in is the hard part, like crossing Manhattan by having to climb up and over each skyscraper in the way. The *tsingys* of western Madagascar are plateaux of karst limestone undercut by groundwater into cavern systems and tunnel fissures, and simultaneously eroded from the top. Collapsed caverns form slot canyons up to 120 m (395 ft) deep with sheer rock walls cracked into a series of razor-sharp pinnacles. Crammed together so tightly they are impassable, *tsingys* (Malagasy for 'where you can not walk barefoot') are labyrinths of jagged rock edges and fluted spikes.

Entering the Tsingy de Bemaraha may be like crossing sky-high fences topped with broken glass, but it's not all bad. The dissected limestone extends over much of the 1,519-sq-km (586-sq-mi) Bemaraha World Heritage Site of untouched forests, lakes, rivers, grasslands and even mangrove swamps. Over half is a 'Strict Nature Reserve', accessible only for research – but the whole region is a biofortress protected by its impenetrable geography. It's full of unknown, unnamed flora and fauna, besides a legion of known species endemic not just to the reserve, but often to specific altitudes on specific pinnacles. The forest crams into the spaces at the foot of each *tsingy*, often creating its own microclimate, and three or four distinct habitats chart its height and exposure to the extreme heat and humidity. These are magic mini-worlds, variants of Bemaraha's greater ecology – but travellers willing to risk its real dangers (just to stumble is to be lacerated) will find lemurs, amphibians, butterflies and birds among wildlife and landscapes that simply don't exist anywhere else. Lemurs at Tsingy de Bemaraha are dominated by the troops of acrobatic sifaka adapted to balancing on razors – and there's a lemur species with long legs and a silly walk named after the British comedian, John Cleese.

*An aerial view of* tsingys

**HOW TO GET THERE:**
By 4x4 from Morondava – 150 km (93 mi) or one day, with luck; by chartered plane from Antananarivo to Antsalova, near the reserve; or by *pirogue* (dugout canoe) with a tour expedition on the Manambolo River.

**WHEN TO GO:**
April to November (closed during the rainy season December to March)

**DON'T MISS:**
The short trail on Great Tsingy, one of the two limestone formations accessible to visitors, goes deep into the 'forest of dagger blades', crossing the pinnacles on hair-raising rope bridges; but a river expedition up the spectacular Manambolo Gorge combines the greatest variety of wildlife-spotting opportunities (like the world's only 'cave crocodiles') with an introduction to indigenous Vazimba culture as well as an easier path into the *tsingy*. Within the park the two- or three-day Anjohimanintsy Trail takes in the highlights of *tsingy* endemism.

**YOU SHOULD KNOW:**
The *tsingys* cannot be underestimated. One hiker who fell described the damage 'like being flensed', and even the stoutest climbing boots get lacerated. On the other hand, Tsingy de Bemaraha is the most fascinating of all Madagascar's marvellously alien wildernesses.

# EUROPE

# Hornstrandir

**HOW TO GET THERE:**
On foot, or more easily by boat from Isafjordur or Holmavik to the west. The boat offers a choice of landings on Hornstrandir.
**WHEN TO GO:**
Mid June to mid August
**DON'T MISS:**
The great cliff of Hornbjarg, 534 m (1,752 ft) at its highest peak. From there, one of the loveliest hikes follows tumbling streams and cascades down into Hornvik cove, towards Hornstrandir's other major cliff, Haelavikurbjarg. Camp below the gorge which opens onto the lagoon-like Hafnaros estuary.
**YOU SHOULD KNOW:**
Take a copy of the *Icelandic Sagas* with you. Hornstrandir features in them, and still evokes their warrior mystique and romance. This may be why the Westfjords Tourist Information Department strongly recommends that travellers to Hornstrandir contact them beforehand for information on 'local weather and other conditions'.

Like a barnacle-encrusted Neptune's triton, the three peninsulars of Iceland's West Fjords region look on the map to be stuck haphazardly to the rest of the country, connected only by a narrow isthmus. The region is as isolated as it looks – and Hornstrandir, at the tip of the most northerly 'prong', is the most remote and solitary of all. It has a coastline out of all proportion to its actual size, made up of deeply incised fjords of widely differing character. The variety – of chilling precipices of black rock, grassy slopes tumbling down to sandy coves, wave-smashed pinnacles and beaches formed from crushed shells – lends itself to constantly evolving marine landscapes that change according to both the weather and the shape-shifting illusions of its spectacular topography. Inland, Hornstrandir's majestic cliff formations are backed by vivid-green grasslands. Everywhere, vistas across lakes and streams to faraway promontories and snow-touched peaks are also reminders of the austerity that living creatures here must endure. It takes a full summer for the ice of the previous winter to melt – so every blade of grass and every field mouse survives on the edge, and visitors need to be hypersensitive to scuffing mosses that may have taken years to root properly. Ungrazed for decades, rare botanicals flourish among Hornstrandir's 260 flowering plants and ferns. Once polar bears roamed here; now it's the domain of arctic foxes and

huge colonies of eider ducks, the sea eagle and the screams of seabirds raging against the wind.

Hornstrandir is about purity. It is free from all man-made pollution. The colours of the sky and land are more vivid and more subtle. It's beauty is a heart-wrenching happiness of living creation going on all around – being. Go there. It's hard work, but you will rejoice.

*Hornstrandir's majestic cliff formations are backed by vivid-green grasslands and wildflowers.*

# Thingvellir

*A view across the stunning rift valley of Thingvellir*

Thingvellir means 'plains of parliament', and it is where Iceland instituted the world's first legislative assembly, the Althing, in the year 980. As a geographic metaphor for democracy, it could hardly be bettered. Thingvellir is a broad, flat plain big enough for any size of public gathering, fringed by a high ridge to the west from which any speaker can be seen and heard. Far beyond the green plain, touched with glistening lakes and rivers, blue mountains blur into the mists. It is a majestic vista with the kind of open natural beauty that inspires visitors to optimism and a sense of reverence – and that's an opinion voiced and written down by visitors to Thingvellir for a thousand years.

Geologically, Thingvellir is just astounding. It is a major rift valley set out like a textbook illustration of plate tectonics. It is where the North American and Eurasian plates drift apart – visibly. A small Natural History Exhibition with an overview of the whole valley explains the significance of the shield volcanoes, glaciers, lava fields and the 114-m (374-ft) deep Lake Thingvallavatn spread below; and visitors can walk down one of the largest faults, Almannagja, to the Oxararfoss waterfalls. Most of the lake's water flows out through Flosagja and its tributary fissures to the east. The greatest adventure at Thingvellir is to go 'fissure diving' in Silfra, one of the world's top-ten dive sites. It is literally the crack in the Earth's crust between the plates, and divers swim 'from Europe to America' between the two faces of rock, wafted effortlessly along on the gentle current. Silfra is 40 m (130 ft) deep in open water, and 60 m (197 ft) in its side caves. Below the surface, the clear water turns a surreal, bright blue. Non-divers may prefer to discuss Viking politics while basking in Thingvellir's hot springs.

**HOW TO GET THERE:**
By car or bus
**WHEN TO GO:**
Any time (note that the weather has no influence on fissure-diving).
**DON'T MISS:**
Exploring the geology of the fissures along Thingvellir's western rim, and along the water margins and meanders of the Oxara River just below it.
**YOU SHOULD KNOW:**
Thingvellir is more than a nature conservation area. Officially it is a 'protected national shrine'. Its unique status derives from the Logberg, or 'Law Rock', from which the 'Law Speaker' proclaimed the laws of the Icelandic Commonwealth. He was supposed to memorize the laws, and was given three years to recite them all; but he had to recite the procedural rules at each summer gathering. The original Logberg was the 'Spongin', the long spit of lava between the branches of the Flosagja fissure.

# Surtsey

Iceland grows about one inch wider each year as Europe and North America continue to pull apart. Tension between the two tectonic plates creates a weak fault line in the earth's crust which cracks under pressure of the welling core magma. Over tens of millions of years the process threw up the submerged mountain chain called the mid-Atlantic Ridge, and pushed Iceland above sea level. Surtsey, newest of the 45 rocky outcrops of the Vestmannaeyjar (Westmann Islands) off Iceland's south coast, is a rare surface demonstration of our planet's dynamic fundamental geology. In June 1963, fishermen saw the sea boil as fiery lava broke the surface, vented from a volcano that rose 130 m (426 ft) from the sea floor in a day, and continued to challenge ice with fire for nearly four more years. By then Surtsey had grown to 2.8 sq km (1.1 sq mi) of still-smoking lava, but although it was already being nibbled by wave and wind, it was untouched by human intervention. In fact, since its birth, only scientists have been permitted to set foot on it, to take advantage of the unrivalled opportunity to chart both its raw geology, and its gradual colonization by coastal flora and fauna. It is an utterly pristine work of nature, in all its forms of development.

Visitors may be forbidden on Surtsey but the other Westmann Islands were formed by the identical process, and Heimeay suffered its own volcanic eruption in 1973. Side by side, visitors can compare the newly created terrain of crusty lava with the beautiful, austere, sub-arctic landscapes into which it might mature. It's already happening on Surtsey. By boat (and the smaller the better), it's quite easy to study the colonizing vegetation and tentative animal life – and to enjoy it at least by analogy on Heimeay, so close by.

**HOW TO GET THERE:**
By air from Reykjavik, or air-taxi from several points along the coast to Heimeay; or by ferry from Thorlakshofn. Small boats for island-hopping can be hired on Heimeay.

**WHEN TO GO:**
June to September

**DON'T MISS:**
Kittiwakes, puffins, razorbills and guillemots wheeling round the caves, cliffs and sea-stacks of volcanic rock between the Westmann skerries and islands. On Heimeay, hike up Eldfell past steaming fissures and vents to the brilliantly coloured mineral deposits at the top.

**YOU SHOULD KNOW:**
Surtsey was named for Sutur, the Norse giant of fire. Its original eruption blasted columns of ash 9,150 m (30,000 ft) into the sky to the accompaniment of non-stop lightning storms. Travellers are asked to applaud this demonstration of Icelandic mythology and not reveal that volcanic ash clouds create electrical charges by friction, just like clouds of vapour.

*A volcanic crater on Surtsey Island*

# Thorsmork National Park

Thorsmork is Iceland's sacred, hidden valley. For at least a thousand years it has been dedicated to Thor, the Norse god of thunder and lightning. Thorsmork means 'Thor's Woods', and in a country that plundered all but one per cent of its trees for firewood, Thorsmork's forested beauty confirms its continuing status. It is approached across 30 km (19 mi) of lichen-covered gravel cut by the myriad shallow channels of the Markarfljot River, braided with its tributary glacial streams. They converge where the mountains rise up on either side into the glaciers of Tindfjallajokull and Eyjafjallajokull. As the river turns north through the hills, it reveals an outlet finger of the Gigjokull spur glacier pushing down a side-gully into a steel-blue lagoon, and magnificent box canyons like Stakkholtsgja gorge, where the towering rock walls narrow to the feathery waterfall at its far end. Another turn in the river and suddenly Thorsmork opens out, an oasis of green vegetation in the rain shadow of the huge glacial and volcanic complexes of Eyjafjallajokull and Myrdalsjokull – both ice caps over major volcanoes. Its microclimate is warmer and less windy than its surroundings. Birds fill the air, attracted by the lichens, mosses, alpine flowers, grassland and birch trees that soften the dynamic geology of volcanic glaciers, moraine and lakes.

Thorsmork is an outstanding destination for hiking and, especially, horse riding. Icelandic horses deal with fording rivers better than any vehicle, besides doing minimal damage to the ultra-fragile ecosystem. The most popular trek is from the lush valley up across the rocky fastness of Fimmvorduhals Pass between the glaciers, to the glorious 60 m (197 ft) waterfall of Skogarfoss near the coast. The descent passes 20 major cascades before the main falls' sheer drop over the escarpment – where a double rainbow forms in the spray every time the sun shines.

**HOW TO GET THERE:**
By 4x4, with a driver experienced in fording rivers, from Reykjavik –160 km (100 mi) away. Horses are available locally.
**WHEN TO GO:**
June to September/October
**DON'T MISS:**
The *Laugavegurinn* or 'Hot Spring Trail' to Thorsmork from the north, including the colourful rhyolite area near Torfajokull and its 11 obsidian lava fields, to Lake Alftavatn (the 'Lake of the Whooper Swans') and the ultimate wilderness beauty of Thorsmork, seen from the multiple-river plain near Fremri-Botnar.
**YOU SHOULD KNOW:**
In March 2010, after 200 dormant years and without any warning at all, two brand-new volcanic fissures several hundred metres long opened on the Fimmvorduhals Pass. The eruption sent molten lava spilling into the Hrunagil and Hvannargil gorges, transforming the Krossa River into a torrent of meltwater, and threatening Thorsmork. Authorities evacuated the entire area. Scientists fear it could trigger a future catastrophic eruption of Katla, the colossus buried under the Myrdalsjokull icecap overlooking the pass – but instability is the chief characteristic of Iceland's vulcanology. Visitors should be aware of the risks and be prepared for the worst.

*Skogarfoss waterfall*

# Lysefjord

The two southernmost of Norway's major fjords meet near the 'oil city' of Stavanger. Lysefjord heads eastwards off Hogsfjord, through a cleft in the rock like the Pillars of Hercules in the Bosphorus. It looks even more like a creation of the gods as it suddenly opens up a dramatic vista along most of its 40 km (25 mi) length, revealing walls of rock facing each other over just 2 km (1.5 mi) of water, and rising to peaks over 1,000 m (3,280 ft) high. The effect of the sheer slabs of light-coloured granite (*Lyse* means 'light') is magnified by the water's other-worldly shade of deep green where it plunges to its maximum depth of 422 m (1,384 ft). Lysefjord was carved by brutal glacial action into the kind of austere landscape that inspired Norse sagas. Its sides are so steep and inhospitable that nobody can live there, and nobody tries. That means one of Norway's most characteristic natural wonders remains a pristine wilderness, easy to access, and highly popular as a destination for both afternoon hikes and serious trekking.

*A walker admires the stunning view from Pulpit Rock 604 m (1,981 ft) above Lysefjord.*

There are two ways to see Lysefjord – from the top or by boat. Boating is glamorous and comfortable. From Lysebotn, the ancient (and only) community at the fjord's innermost end, Lysefjord stretches straight ahead in an overwhelming geometric perspective of sky, rock and water. Almost the same view from the Kjerag Boulder – a giant sphere of rock wedged in a crevice over a sheer, 1,000-m (3,280-ft) drop into the water – feels like looking across the roof of the world, and visitors feel this sense of majesty wherever they look across the fjord to faraway mountain ranges. Fortunately, it's easy to combine a boat trip with a hike to Lysefjord's rim in the same day.

# Utladalen Canyon

Sognefjord, north of Bergen, is Norway's longest. It snakes 205 km (127 mi) inland towards the country's spine, the great mountain wilderness of Jotunheimen National Park. The connecting link is the gigantic glacial canyon of Utladalen, an extension of Sognefjord that remained above sea level when the glaciers melted. Now Utladalen is the southwestern gateway to the biggest concentration of high mountains in Norway. Geologically, it belongs to them, because the whole Jotunheimen is composed of gabbro rock, an ancient and exceptionally hard form of granite that resisted primary glacial erosion. The unusual result is a series of sharp peaks and abrupt rock buttresses, separated by many short, hanging valleys. It took a much bigger secondary glacier to scour out the huge, steep-sided canyon of Utladalen – and the silts it left behind are the reason that Utladalen is so very much more pastoral than the wild, jagged peaks around it (the location, incidentally, of Peer Gynt's frenzied flight on a reindeer's back, in Act One of the opera).

Utladalen is the gentler face of Jotunheimen's dramatic landscapes. Its pine forests are old, and a sheltering cloak to remote hill farms. The rugged terrain is softened by grassy spurs and slopes of scree or shale, and dozens of streams and waterfalls. The occasional farms lend an air of domesticity in tune with, but quite different from the harsh extremities of the alpine Hurrungane mountain region which soars up alongside. The contrast is what attracts both ramblers and the many hikers for whom Utladalen is part of a highway. It has only one obvious attraction – Norway's highest free-falling waterfall, 275 m (902 ft) Vettisfossen – but the valley holds more unregulated major waterfalls than anywhere else anyway. Outstandingly beautiful, geologically fascinating and spiritually fulfilling, Utladalen is a manifestation of the compelling chain that binds human enterprise to nature at its most robust.

**HOW TO GET THERE:**
By car from Ovre Ardal to the Hjellefossen waterfall car park; then on foot
**WHEN TO GO:**
Any time. In winter the waterfalls can become gigantic spears and columns of ice.
**DON'T MISS:**
Exploring the web of trails that criss-crosses the Utla River in search of ever more spectacular mountain panoramas. Short trails like the path from Vetti to the falls make a great day out. Others can be 160 km (100 mi) long and cross from the high tops and glaciers of Jotunheimen, through Utladalen, to the wonders of Sognefjord.
**YOU SHOULD KNOW:**
Jotunheimen is the 'Home of the Giants' of Norwegian folk lore. In fact it has over 50 peaks higher than 2,000 m (6,560 ft), and is the highest section of *Kjolen* (the Keel), the spine of Scandinavia running the whole way north between Norway and Sweden, that looks like the keel of an upturned boat.

# Kullaberg Nature Reserve

**HOW TO GET THERE:**
By car, bus or train to Molle
**WHEN TO GO:**
Any time
**DON'T MISS:**
On the north side, pick your way from the cliff-top forest down to the sea through a ramshackle extravaganza of driftwood towers and tunnels that has grown into a whole maze over 27 years. Called Nimis, the structure is owned by the artist Christo (of Reichstag-wrapping fame), but was created by Lars Vilks, who in 1996 declared the land around it to be an 'independent republic' called Ladonia. Visitors are invited to pay $12 and join the Ladonian nobility. Nimis is still growing, but remains an illegal structure.
**YOU SHOULD KNOW:**
Carl Linnaeus, primogenitor of modern scientific classification and giant of avifauna in particular (as in the Linnaean Society), adored Kullaberg when he came in 1749. You can see why so many birds visit the place – the birch, pine, beech and oak forests with their understorey of juniper, wild honeysuckle and blackthorn, added to the intertidal marine habitats, appeal to an almost unique combination of species.

Part nature reserve and part civic amenity, Kullaberg occupies the very tip of the Kullen peninsula that points a finger of rock northwest into the southern end of the Kattegat. The promontory marks the entrance to the Oresund strait between Sweden and Denmark, a few miles north of its narrowest point, where Helsingborg faces Danish Helsingor (home of Hamlet) across the water. Kullaberg is Sweden's most westerly point – but its fame rests on being the only 'mountain' of any kind at all in Skane, the country's remorselessly flat and featureless southern region.

Kullaberg packs an extraordinary variety of terrain into its 35 sq km (13.5 sq mi). Its highest point is 187-m (613-ft) Hakull, but between this 'peak' and the 40-m (131-ft) cliffs of ancient archean rock that rear above the sea on Kullaberg's north and south sides, there are beech forests, meadows filled with wild flowers, steep gullies and promontories that drop off the central ridge where climbers come to practise. The cliffs themselves are mined by the sea into secret swimming holes, tide pools and prehistoric caves that were inhabited 10,000 years ago. Many of the best are accessible only from the water, but visitors can rent kayaks locally to reach them and some of the 800 climbing routes with intriguing names like Napoleon's Hat or The Kulla Man's Door. The lighthouse at Kullaberg's tip stands only 70 m (230 ft) above the sea, but is visible for 50 km (31 mi); in one form or another it has signalled the murderous dangers of the peninsula for nearly 1,000 years. On misty evenings there is a lovely walk from the lighthouse bluff through woods of gnarled juniper and hawthorn to a place of low stone walls, curled like elfin ramparts in a troll forest. Kullaberg is full of imaginative surprises.

# Sarek National Park

**HOW TO GET THERE:**
By car or bus from Jokkmokk to Ritsem, then by Lapp boat across Lake Akkajaure; or on foot via the Kungsleden or Padjelanta marked trails through adjoining national parks.
**WHEN TO GO:**
Any time. The Northern Lights are usually at their best between November and February.

*Rapa Valley in autumn in Sarek National Park*

The World Heritage Site of Laponia is known more prosaically as Sweden's northernmost province of Norrbotten, and it is the ancestral home of the nomadic Sami reindeer herders. It is a harsh, remote world, far above the Arctic Circle, of glacial lakes and valley wetlands, alpine massifs, ravines, rivers and spectacular mountain peaks rising above glittering icefields and glaciers. Most of it is a trackless wilderness, protected by a series of national parks that border Norway to the west, and stretch almost to Finland in the east. Each park has a signature terrain, but their common heart is Sarek, where Sweden's greatest concentration of high peaks sits in icy majesty. Of some 250 distinct mountains, 87 are over 1,800 m

(5,900 ft) and eight soar over 2,000 m (6,560 ft), packed into a rough circle spanning 50 km (31 mi). Although the park contains nearly 100 glaciers, it suffers a lot of rain which can turn streams into torrents without warning. In fact, crossing rivers is a major hazard in Sarek, where two bridges over key trail junctions are the only facilities available to help hikers. The bridge over the Smaila River at the park's centre is all-important, and visitors use it as both destination and meeting point. From the outside it takes two to three days to reach – from Rinim through the Pastavagge; from Kisuris through the Ruotesvagge; or, most magically of all, from Aktse along Rapadalen.

Rapadalen is Sarek's main artery. Fed by the waters of 30 glaciers, the Rapapaato River flows like threads, braided and spread across the broad valley floor, settling in ponds and small lakes. The water is coloured a bright, ice green against the emerald shrubs on its soggy banks, and fingers of mist shroud nearby mountain tops and hover in side canyons. It's one of Europe's most beautiful places, and worth every effort to see.

**DON'T MISS:**
Laddepakte, Skarjatjakka and Skierfe are easily accessible mountain peaks, with some of the best panoramas over Sarek. Look out for the bizarrely exuberant herbaceous flora of Rapadalen, and dense stands of mountain birch and osier that encourage the presence of bear, arctic fox, lynx, wolverine and the large elk of the region.

**YOU SHOULD KNOW:**
Sarek National Park is not for the inexperienced. Professional polar explorers come here to train, and so do climbers practising for major assaults. Some of the hiking is fairly easy (especially in summer, although the downside is zillions of swarms of mosquitoes), but beginners can be caught out by conditions changing from benign to treacherous in seconds.

*A sailing boat moored amongst the islets in the Stockholm Archipelago.*

# Stockholm Archipelago

Swedes call it the 'garden of skerries' (rocky islets) or *Skargarden*. The archipelago of more than 24,000 islands radiates from Sweden's capital city, Stockholm, in an arc 70 km (44 mi) deep and 150 km (93 mi) from north to south. The largest and most heavily forested islands are closest to the city (and include some fully fledged suburbs). Size and vegetation diminish with distance, so that the smallest outcrops of bare, black rock are closest to the lashing storms of open water. In a continuous geological process, the whole land mass has been rising infinitesimally, exposing new skerries and enlarging the existing islands; and uniquely among the world's major archipelagoes, the islands are extremely close together – many only 100 m (328 ft) apart. Since they are typically formed from the mixture of volcanic ash, sand and clay called greywracke, a bedrock created billions of years ago, Skargarden is simultaneously very old and very young.

It is also very beautiful. The larger, inhabited islands like Fjaderholmarna, 17th-century Vaxholm, or 12th-century Uto, famous as much for its mining heritage as for its nature reserve, combine carefree resorts with idyllic, pastoral interiors of swimming ponds, streams, meadows and forests. Thousands of others show nature at its most deliciously varied and delicate, with sandy beaches, picturesque rock formations, and lush grassy clearings in their thick woods, full of wild flowers and berries. Even where visitors see a summer house discreetly sheltered by the trees, they have *Allemansratten* – every person's legal right to land anywhere (except immediately next to someone's house) and set up camp for as long as they like, anchor their boat, pick berries and mushrooms, and enjoy the fields and woods. The countless seaways are busy in summer with canoes, sailing boats, skiffs and even punts: the Stockholm Archipelago can absorb thousands in their personal quests for solitude within its amphibian magnificence.

**HOW TO GET THERE:**
By ferry along specified routes or by rented craft to wherever you like.
**WHEN TO GO:**
Any time, but note that winter ferry services are greatly curtailed.
**DON'T MISS:**
Vaxholm, which used to defend the all-important sea route to Stockholm, and Grinda, the 'green island' full of tranquil lanes through its pastoral beauty and small enough to enable visitors to connect with nature without abandoning social comfort. Both islands are a reminder of Skargarden's importance in Swedish culture and history.
**YOU SHOULD KNOW:**
The smallest islands are uninhabited and will probably stay that way because of recent legislation prohibiting new building within 300 m (1,000 ft) of the shoreline. Some Swedes call it the 'Robinson Crusoe charter', because it is an encouragement to find your very own piece of pristine solitude.

# Lake Saimaa

The Saimaa lake district of southeast Finland is a shimmering, watery maze of thousands of lakes, 14,000 islands and skerries, green forests, reed beds and narrow strings of grassland dividing one water course from another. Water covers 1,700 sq km (656 sq mi) of the 4,400 sq km (1,692 sq mi) lake district, an area roughly the size of Belgium. Created by uniform glacial upheaval, most of the lakes run roughly parallel to each other, and water flows slowly from north to south through the vast system of connecting channels above and below ground. The twisted, elongated shapes of the lakes and the islands together offer 15,000 km (9,320 mi) of pristine shoreline. In such a huge outdoors, visitors can sail or hike, or both, for days without seeing another person. Even the little summer houses visible on many small islands, or among the forests crowding the shore, are too discreet to disturb the tranquil beauty that characterizes the majority of the region. Visitors can stay in some of them, although facilities are suitably Spartan. Part of Lake Saimaa's ethos is demonstrating rugged individualism, and that includes cooking on an open fire on fish caught locally, as well as hurling yourself into freezing water for fun.

Lake Saimaa itself lies at the heart of the system, and through it run some of the region's 3,000 km (1,865 mi) of canoe or sailing routes, including one running all the way from Helsinki, via the Saimaa Canal and lake, to the resort town of Savonlinna and far beyond. Savonlinna is famous for its opera festival, held at the magnificent medieval castle of Olavinlinna, and from late June to August it's full of vacationers and weekenders. Visitors in search of Saimaa's treasure house of natural wonders will have no difficulty in finding more peaceful domains to call their own.

**HOW TO GET THERE:**
By train to Savonlinna, where boats of every kind can be rented; or by car or bus. Most lakes have a designated slipway to launch boats from car trailers.

**WHEN TO GO:**
Mid June to September – although Saimaa is beautiful in winter, too.

**DON'T MISS:**
Saimaa seals, among the world's rarest creatures and exclusive to Lake Saimaa. They are found only in fresh water, and only 270 remain in the wild. For sheer adventure, sail to Haukivesi, a gigantic lake within the Saimaa system. You can follow the Linnonpoiku Nature Trail in Linnansaari National Park – which is self-contained, with its own, internal lake system, on a 40-km (25-mi) island in the middle of Haukivesi.

**YOU SHOULD KNOW:**
The Saimaa lake district has always been a favourite haunt of visiting Russian elites. Tsar Alexander III came regularly, and visitors can join a luxury cruise that follows the 'Tsar's route' through the Kotka archipelago in the Gulf of Finland to the medieval town of Lappeenranta and Savonlinna. Soviet elites continued the fashion – but now the region's many Russian visitors include the less exalted.

*A low sun over the shimmering Lake Saimaa*

# Lemmenjoki National Park

**HOW TO GET THERE:**
By car to Repojoki or to the
Lemmenjoki Nature Information Hut
at Njurkulahti, from where there is a
motor boat service to the park's
wilderness area.
**WHEN TO GO:**
June to August
**DON'T MISS:**
The introductory 4 km (2.5 mi)
Lemmenjoki Nature Trail; taking a boat
down the Lemmenjoki River valley; or
the 26.5-km (16-mi) circular trail from
Ravadasjarvi Lake to Morgamoja Brook
– the centre of the 1940s to 1950s
Lemmenjoki Gold Rush – and on to
Ravadaskongas waterfall. Visitors may
still encounter the occasional gold
prospector – be advised that they are
characteristically solitary.
**YOU SHOULD KNOW:**
Lemmenjoki is divided into three
areas. All the marked hiking and
canoeing/boating trails are in the
'basic zone', but visitors can go
anywhere within it, although
campsites are designated. In the
'wilderness zone' there are no marked
trails and hikers are trusted to use
their discretion when choosing camp
or fire sites. In the 'restricted' area,
walking is *only* allowed on marked
trails, to prevent erosion and protect
fragile root systems.

*Lemmenjoki National Park*

Nothing else in Europe matches the size of Lemmenjoki National Park as an uninhabited, roadless wilderness. It covers 2,850 sq km (1,100 sq mi) of forests, rivers, low fells and huge mires in the arctic north of Finnish Lapland. At the 'top of Europe', Lemmenjoki shares one boundary with a Norwegian national park (which greatly extends their mutual viability as wilderness); and both Swedish and Russian Lapland are close.

The fragile ecosystem that Lemmenjoki protects has a cultural as well as ecological importance. The park combines natural features which enable the nomadic Lapp people to survive from one year to the next. Along the Repojoki River, the Sallivaara Reindeer Round-up site of round-up fences and cabins is a reminder of the herders' harsh way of life – but Lapps know that Lemmenjoki can also be a garden of opportunity. The slopes of the 70-km (43-mi) long Lemmenjoki River valley and the banks of both Kietsimajoki and Vaskojoki are thick with typically Lappish, short and wide, old-growth pine trees called *aihki*, which are favoured by succulent moose. Above the river valleys pine gives way to birch and the habitat of the rock ptarmigan on the bald hilltops and fells. Where the valleys are broad, *aapa* bogs and deep mires crammed with rarities of arctic flora buzz with a sub-stratum of birds and insect life; and although the spruce forests reach their northern limit in Lemmenjoki's south, the park is permanent home to brown bears, wolverines and golden eagles as well as the foxes, moose and reindeer which thrive here.

Lemmenjoki has unequivocal grandeur, as though its big sky, vast forests and great rivers shake their combined fist at the brutal harshness of the elements; but it also demonstrates how richly varied and fulfilling life – in all its forms – can be on the margins.

# Oulanka National Park

Oulanka National Park sits in the cross-hair of the Arctic Circle and Finland's border with Russia, roughly equidistant from Kuusamo and Salla. It's a Finnish 'National Landscape' which celebrates a uniquely Finnish version of the northern boreal forest zone that encircles the world. The hilly uplands range only from 380 m (1,246 ft) to 150 m (492 ft) in the lowest river valleys, but they are carved by two major rivers and their tributaries into a series of canyons and gorges famous for their white-water rapids, waterfalls, and long, shallow cascades. In the valley bottoms, rich silts deposited by river meanders and oxbows encourage lush meadows full of sub-arctic wild flowers, boreal moths, and butterflies like the copper violet. Big temperature variations between the fells and meadows support even greater species versatility; and the region's calcium-rich bedrock gives a further twist to the selection of rare flora, especially close to Oulanka's chalk springs and ponds. The herb-scented forests higher up shelter mosses where visitors will find plants like the dark-red helleborine, dwarf milkwort, and the calypso orchid (Oulanka Park's symbol). Hiking here is heaven on the senses.

Oulanka's dramas are played out on and by the rivers. The Oulanka River enters the park as rip-roaring rapids plunging down the Oulanka Canyon, and descends a series of stunning ravines to meet the Kitkajoki just before the Russian frontier. Hiking down the Oulanka takes visitors through a selection of the park's finest scenery, across hanging bridges where streams come hurtling in from the side, past Rupakivi Rock and the deafening roar of the Klutakongas waterfalls and rapids, to eventual tranquillity in the water margins of its eastern edge. Not surprisingly, Oulanka's charms make it one of Finland's favourite destinations, for hiking, water-rafting, rapid-running and even swimming, as well as botanizing for idle pleasure. It's a glorious bit of nature.

*A blaze of colour in the forests of Oulanka National Park*

**HOW TO GET THERE:**
By car, to entrances at north and south, or in the middle of the park at the visitor centre close to Oulanka Canyon.

**WHEN TO GO:**
Any time – the new winter Rytisuo Snowshoeing Trail takes in small, open mires, spacious pine forests, and peaceful riverscapes.

**DON'T MISS:**
The breathtaking scenery along the lower course of the Kitkajoki River, from Juuma to the Russian border. Less challenging, and more suitable for families who like canoeing or boating, are the calm waters of the lower Oulanka, from Kiutakongas to Jakalamutka.

**YOU SHOULD KNOW:**
Berry and mushroom picking is (unusually) allowed within the National Park, and there is a profusion of lingonberry, blueberry and crowberry as well as wild strawberry and arctic bramble. Unfortunately, the park's *aapa* bogs and fens produce few cloudberries; and you have to get to any mushrooms before early rising reindeer beat you to it.

# Mols Bjerge National Park

**HOW TO GET THERE:**
On foot or horseback, by bike, or bus or car. The car is important – Danish National Parks are committed to developing car routes for the walking-impaired.

**WHEN TO GO:**
Any time

**DON'T MISS:**
The 49-m (161-ft) cliffs of Jernhatten (the Iron Hat) looking out to Hjelm Island in the Kattegat, and the old beech woods of Troldeskoven (the Troll Forest). The most remote rambles take in the otters of Langeso and Stubbe Lakes and the river valley through the thick broadleaf forests round Ornbjerg Mill. The creaking, ancient structure is Djursland's only preserved, working mill.

**YOU SHOULD KNOW:**
On the western edge of Mols Bjerge the spectacular ruins of Kalo Castle include a 500-m (547-yd) long cobblestone dyke which is Denmark's most important surviving medieval road. A marked trail leads through the mysterious Thyrahytten salt marshes to the epic forests of Hestehave and Ringelmose. You don't need a sixth sense to feel the aura of ancient power in this area.

In a country as flat as Denmark, rolling hills and coastal cliffs have special significance. Mols Bjerge National Park takes its name from the 137-m (450-ft) hill-top of Mols itself – the best-known natural feature of a much bigger, 180-sq-km (69-sq-mi) reserve that includes heath, pastureland, forests, bogs, meadows and a whole range of coastal and marine features. It sits on the twin headlands of southern Djursland, east of Arhus, and extends north as far as Ronde in the west, across to Hyllested on the Kattegat coast. It even includes the open water of Begtrup Bay and much of Ebeltoft Bay, two stretches along the Kattegat, and the offshore island of Hjelm.

Mols Bjerge is a representative catalogue of Denmark's finest landscapes, all of it discreetly signed with trails that make those highlights accessible to hikers and ramblers of every level of experience, and as special as possible for children and the wheelchair-bound. The trail from the Forest and Nature Agency Visitor Centre at Ovre Strandkaer, next to Mols, is typical. It runs through pine and broadleaf woods and across gentle open hills full of grazing longhorn cattle to a spot with far-flung views over

*Wild lupin in Mols Bjerge National Park*

Ebeltoft Bay. Ebeltoft is an historic, 13th-century market town of huge charm and has an ancient harbour flanked by sandy coves. To its south the fascinating salt marsh of Ahl Plantage is crammed with wild flowers, herbs and grasses adapted to its brackish moisture, right next to what was once the mighty Bjornkaer and Egedal forest of oak which fuelled the 17th-century salt-extraction process, and is now recovering its grandeur. A lovely 6-km (4-mi) nature path north to Gravlev passes rich meadows and mixed broadleaf woods. This is nature at its most reticent and domestic – but as dramatic in its detail as anything in the world.

# Rold Skov

One of Denmarks's largest forests, Rold Skov covers about 80 sq km (31 sq mi) in the Himmerland region between Aalborg and Randers on the Jutland peninsular. The forest is an agglomerate of state- and many privately-owned small forests, brought together by common interest not in preservation for its own sake, but in the development of an ecologically integrated plan for a reserve which necessarily spreads in and around villages, farmsteads and small towns. For visitors it helps that Rold Skov is a patchwork of discrete sections. In one, prominence is given to restoring great plantations of North American spruce and fir species, adding to existing forests of dense, old fir which flourish in the moraine soil of sand and gravel. With the considerable rain it gets, Rold Skov is one of the best conifer habitats in Denmark. Elsewhere, in the Rebild Hills and Bjergeskov sections, there are wonderful – and big – growths of natural, old beech forest, where the gnarled and twisted trees have survived long-ago pruning and damage from game. Two sections, Troldeskoven and Urskoven, are set aside to revert eventually to virgin forest. With no human intervention trees will fall, creating their own glades and new flora to fill them; and it is closest to these sections that visitors will see most game and most birds.

Almost equally important as the forest ecology itself are the cultural artefacts and associations scattered throughout Rold Skov, linking the restoration of its forests to those who lived in symbiosis with it. The Northern Well is 600–700 years old, and the Bjergeskoven section alone holds Bronze Age burial mounds, the Stenstuen dolmen, and several ancient, parallel sunken roads. Evidence of various methods of charcoal-burning is everywhere. Hiking through its forest glades, springs and lakes, visitors find that Rold Skov in its entirety forms a really uplifting ecological narrative.

**HOW TO GET THERE:**
By bus or car to Rold or Gravlev; or by train to Skorping
**WHEN TO GO:**
Any time. Each season has distinct flora and fauna.
**DON'T MISS:**
The 'erosion holes' caused by acidified rainwater penetrating cracks and dissolving the lime in the soil, which collapses into serious cavities invisible beneath the forest carpet. In June, you can see Denmark's largest orchid, the Lady's Slipper, in the Bjergeskoven forest – although it's behind railings for its own safety.
**YOU SHOULD KNOW:**
Hikers may like to spice up their journey through Rold Skov with a sudden and unprovoked 'attack' by leering, dirt-smeared, masked bandits of uncivilized mien. This is a service that can be pre-arranged. For a fee, you get three (sort of) medieval 'robbers' (five or six for big occasions) who will ambush you and your party in the forest, at your convenience. With luck, this 'unpleasant half-hour' encounter will end jocularly with a *roverbjaesk*, a drink from a hip-flask. Rold Skov is the only official Danish nature reserve to offer this service.

# Skagen, Grenen and the Raabjerg Mile

If the Jutland peninsula were a silhouette portrait, Skagen would be the cowlick on top of its Pompadour hairstyle. Skagen (pronounced 'skayn') is Denmark's northernmost point, the tip of the spit separating Denmark from Norway across the Skagerrak, and from Sweden across the Kattegat. It is the meeting point of the Baltic and the North Sea, a place of colliding white water and achingly beautiful, blue and gold luminescence, where the elements shimmer in perpetual motion.

History clings like seaweed to the region. Empires have been won and lost on Skagen's whimsical meteorological vagaries: 'the Skaw' (the *Ska* of Skagerrak) is notorious for breaking mariners' hearts. In fact the eccentric resort town of Skagen anchors local geography with its system of stabilized dunes, and the opposing forces of the Skagerrak and Kattegat have gradually moved their principal battleground to Grenen, the curling tongue of sand on Skagen's northern edge which consequently grows by 8 m (26 ft) each year and shifts its shape from day to day. Visitors can ride a blue-and-red tractor-train called the *Sandormen* (Sandworm) from the dunes to the water's edge, and stand with a foot in each sea. Less than a dot in this universe of sky and water, a visitor can almost touch the eternal in Grenen's majestic interplay of light and reflection.

Southwest of Grenen, the 'Raabjerg Mile' demonstrates the colossal natural forces determining the region's character. The Raabjerg Mile is one of Europe's biggest migrating coastal dunes, up to 40 m (131 ft) high and composed of roughly 3.5 million cubic metres of sand, generating a miniature desert of almost a square kilometre (0.3 sq mi). In 300 years it has moved 5 km (3 mi), burying villages and forests which will one day reappear as it continues northeast at an average speed of 18 m (60 ft) a year. It is held in such awe that it is not even desecrated by litter.

*Windswept sand dunes at the Raabjerg Mile, Skagen*

# Llechwedd Slate Caverns

**HOW TO GET THERE:**
Llechwedd Slate Caverns are just to the north of Blaenau Ffestiniog, on the A470 Betws y Coed road.
**WHEN TO GO:**
Any time (temperature below ground is comfortably constant even in winter).
**DON'T MISS:**
Lunch at the traditional Miners' Arms pub overlooking Llechwedd Victorian Village and the stark landscape created by slate mining. A speciality of the house is Lobsgows, a seafaring dish brought back to these parts from the German port of Hamburg by workers who helped re-roof the city with Blaenau Ffestiniog slate after the great fire of 1842. This one-bowl meal consists of blended mashed potato, corned beef and beetroot - and is said to be a great hangover cure!
**YOU SHOULD KNOW:**
The Llechwedd mine owner – one John W Greaves – won an award at the London Exhibition of 1862 for showing a single piece of slate little thicker than paper that measured 3 m (10 ft) long and 0.3 m (1 ft) wide.

Not all the world's wild places remain so because they are unsullied by human hand. Nowhere is this truer than in the confines of the British Isles, where much of the landscape has been shaped by the expansion of agriculture, industry and commerce since time immemorial. But paradoxically, once some enterprises have served their purpose and been abandoned the result can be natural drama of the highest order.

The slate industry is active around Blaenau Ffestiniog in North Wales, where quarries still produce this valuable commodity and spoil tips continue to grow. But Llechwedd Slate Caverns is one example of a not-so-natural wonder once created by industrial activity. This is the place to learn about the Welsh slate industry and the life and times of the hardy miners who made it possible, when huge demand for this quality roofing material arose in the 19th century.

Today, the abandoned caverns offer a unique journey back in time. At the surface is a re-created Victorian Village with pubs, shops, a lock-up, bank and smithy, plus a collection of narrow-gauge wagons once used to haul slate. Below ground it's possible to enjoy two special experiences – riding the Miners' Underground Tramway through a network of tunnels and vast chambers enlivened by tableaux, then exploring the Deep Mine on foot, where dramatic *son et lumière* presentations re-create Victorian mining conditions.

After enjoying the brilliant re-creation of yesteryear above and below ground, the abiding memory of Llechwedd Slate Caverns will surely be the truly awesome grandeur of those magnificent underground cathedrals of commerce, hewn from the living rock with the help of no more than basic tools, gunpowder and muscle power. Long after those tough miners are no more than a memory, their work remains as a dramatic spectacle that Mother Nature herself might envy.

# Clwydian Range

**HOW TO GET THERE:**
Main roads surrounding or going through the Clwydian Range are (from north to south) the A548, A547, A5151, A55, A451, A453, A525, A494 and A5104. Gweryd Lakes are signed from the hamlet of Llanarmon-yn-Ial (on the B5431 road, off the A494 between Mold and Ruthin).

One of only eight protected landscapes in Wales, the wild and wonderful Clwydian Range is a 35-km (22-mi) chain of heather-clad hills stretching from Prestatyn Hillside in the north to the Nany y Garth pass in the south, from the Vale of Clwyd in the west towards the Dee Estuary in the east. Denbigh and Ruthin are in the vale and Mold is on the Dee side.

This is one of the most precious tracts of countryside in North Wales, rising from fertile farmland through coppice woodland and small, hedged fields on the lower slopes to open heather moorland punctuated

*Heather-covered slopes of the Clwydian Range leading up to the summit of Moel Famau*

with limestone outcrops and wooded escarpments on the tops. Deep valleys slash the flanks, notably those carrying the Rivers Alyn and Wheeler. Where the limestone breaks through, there are grasslands rich with orchids and other wild flowers.

The Clwydian Range is best viewed from the Vale of Clwyd, but most folk will want to do more than look. These hills offer the opportunity for every sort of recreational activity, from thrill-seeking challenges like paragliding, abseiling or rock climbing through horse riding, cycling and walking to fishing. Although long popular as a 'green lung' for visitors from Merseyside and Cheshire, these delightful hills have enough roaming room to ensure that anybody who wants to get away from it all need never feel crowded, especially if avoiding summer weekends.

A popular stopping-off point is Gweryd Lakes, towards the south of the range. In enviable surroundings, it offers coarse and trout fishing and is an excellent base for sallying forth into the hills. Afterwards, hikers will find that unspoilt local villages provide a welcome chance to visit traditional pubs such as the Cross Foxes in Nannach, Blue Lion in Cwm, Raven in Llanarmon or Druids in Llanferres.

**WHEN TO GO:**
Any time (although the weather can, to say the least, be unwelcoming to those unprepared for the rigours of winter).
**DON'T MISS:**
One or both of the range's two delightful country parks. Loggerheads has a beautiful wooded valley, dramatic cliffs and limestone outcrops. Moel Famau consists of heather moorland, plus the remains of a tower constructed to celebrate George III's Golden Jubilee – and sensational views.
**YOU SHOULD KNOW:**
The Offa's Dyke National Trail runs for almost the entire length of the Clwydian Range's ridge. Much of the Clwydian Range is open-access land, but there are private areas where walkers are asked to remain on signed public rights of way.

# Nicholaston Burrows

The Gower Peninsula in southwest Wales has plenty of splendid marine scenery along its southern coastline, fronting the Bristol Channel, and back in 1956 the Gower was the first place in the UK to be designated as an Area of Outstanding Natural Beauty. Considering its proximity to bustling Swansea, Nicholaston Burrows can seem incredibly remote, especially out of season. Even in high summer it does not get crowded, because getting there requires a hike through extensive Nicholaston Woods (home to protected ash trees and rare plants such as purple bromwell, butcher's broom and bloody cranesbill), where it's quite possible to spend a rewarding hour before even reaching the Burrows (dunes and beach).

Those in search of sea, sand, scenery and solitude should put Nicholaston Burrows high on their list of must-visit destinations. This unspoilt seaside gem is backed by extensive sand dunes held together by scrub vegetation, themselves well worth exploring on the way to the beach. The western part of Oxwich Bay (where there's car parking) can get crowded in summer, but even then the eastern end next to Nicholaston Burrows never gets too busy, and those with a keen interest in nature may care to explore the Oxwich Burrows reserve, a wonderful expanse of salt- and freshwater marshes.

In the other direction lies Three Cliffs Bay with its impressive jutting rock formations. There's an excellent short walk looping out along the cliff tops looking down, and returning along the beach looking up. When the tide is out beachcombing often produces dividends, especially for lovers of seafood such as cockles and scallops. It's easy to spend a couple of active days exploring the Burrows and environs, but those who simply prefer messing about on a beautiful beach will find ample satisfaction doing just that.

*Oxwich Bay*

# Brecon Beacons

Good enough for the tough-as-nails SAS to use as a training ground, these stern hills to the south of Brecon are neither over-populated nor the easiest of terrain – particularly in winter, when the local mountain rescue team is frequently called into action. That said, at other times of year the Brecon Beacons offer rewarding outdoor opportunities, although they are notorious for sudden weather changes. The range consists of peaks forming a horseshoe around the head of Taf Fechan River, including Pen y Fan, Corn Du, Cribyn and Fan y Big. They're connected by an extended ridge with long parallel spurs.

These are the core of the Brecon Beacons National Park, but there are other sections, giving an overall area of 1,350 sq km (520 sq mi). The Black Mountain is to the west and then comes the sandstone massif of Fforest Fawr. To the east of the beacons lie the Black Mountains on the English border. The park contains some of the most spectacular upland formations in southern Britain and the landscape is mainly high moorland, with forestry plantations and pastureland in the many valleys.

Sightseeing from the comfort of a car is satisfying, with so much rugged scenery to appreciate, but the national park is made for those who enjoy outdoor activities. These include a gamut of leisure possibilities, including hang-gliding, parascending, caving, rock climbing, water sports, canoeing, fishing, horse riding, cycling, mountain-biking, walking and camping. The park's rich past and natural heritage offer another dimension, with numerous archaeological and historical sites to be found. Around 170,000 visitors come each year, which is far too few to deny the secretive SAS their lonely, undisturbed route marches in the park's remote wilderness areas.

**HOW TO GET THERE:**
Working clockwise from the west, the main towns surrounding the Brecon Beacons National Park are Llandeilo, Llandovery, Brecon, Hay-on-Wye, Abergavenny, Pontypool, Blaenavon, Brynmawr, Merthyr Tydfil, Glyn Neath and Ystradgynlais. Several good roads cross the park from north to south and the A40 runs from east to west.

**WHEN TO GO:**
Spring, summer or autumn.

**DON'T MISS:**
Waterfalls. There are dozens in the national park, mainly towards the southern edge, the tallest of which is Sgwd Henrhyd with a drop of 27 m (90 ft), on National Trust land near Coelbren.

**YOU SHOULD KNOW:**
In 2005 the first hiking route to cover the entire length of the Brecon Beacons National Park was inaugurated. The Beacons Way runs from the village of Bethlehem in Carmarthenshire to the foot of Ysgyryd Fawr near Abergavenny, the most easterly of the Black Mountains. The long-distance Taff Trail from Brecon to Cardiff also passes through the national park.

*A view across the Brecon Beacons*

*Porthcurno Beach*

# Porthcurno

**HOW TO GET THERE:**
Porthcurno is after St Levan down a dead-end valley road, off the B3315 some 14 km (9 mi) southwest of Penzance and just 5 km (3 mi) from Land's End. There is a large car park above the beach, which is then reached by a wide footpath.

**WHEN TO GO:**
Forget any thoughts of privacy in the summer months, but midweek forays out of season are another story.

**DON'T MISS:**
A visit to the extraordinary open-air Minack Theatre, on the left up the winding hill to St Levan church from the bottom of Porthcurno Valley. This extraordinary place was the creation of Rowena Cade over half a century, starting in the 1930s and – perched on a Cornish cliff side – must surely be the world's most dramatic stage.

**YOU SHOULD KNOW:**
Porthcurno may seem a scenic Cornish backwater today, but it was once the very hub of world communications. From the late 19th century a network of international submarine telegraph cables came ashore here (there were 14 by the 1930s) and there was a college that trained cable operators. A secure bomb-proof tunnel was bored to house the telegraphy operation in World War II, part of which may be seen during a visit to the award-winning Porthcurno Telegraph Museum.

The Cornish coastline is world famous, and Porthcurno is an ideal place to appreciate its visual grandeur. This little village is almost at the tip of England – an honour reserved for nearby Land's End – but with its triangular beach and flanking cliffs Porthcurno delivers all the rugged splendour anyone could want. The steeply shelving beach has coarse sand and faces to the southeast. It is tucked neatly into the western end of Porthcurno Bay, a sweep of awesome cliffs punctuated by tantalizing coves culminating in rectangular Logan's Rock to the east.

The coastline around Porthcurno is designated as an Area of Outstanding Natural Beauty. The granite cliffs are up to 70 m (230 ft) tall and can be appreciated by exploring the many footpaths, one of which is the long-distance South West Coast Path. Green Bay is a small sandy cove immediately adjacent to Porthcurno Beach that can be reached at low tide. Further towards Logan Rock is Pedn Vounder, another small beach accessed by a steep path from the cliff top. Near the top is a white granite pyramid that serves as a navigational aid. It replaced the building that housed the terminal of an undersea telegraph cable to France, laid in 1880. In the other direction is Porth Chapel Beach, which is named for a ruined medieval chapel.

Lifeguards are on duty at Porthcurno between Whitsun and mid September (there can be dangerous rip-tides off the beach) and a dog ban is in force on the beach from Easter to the end of September. Cornwall cheerfully overdoses on holidaymakers in high season and Porthcurno is a justifiably popular destination, but at other times of year it is possible to find total solitude amid some of the Cornwall's most dramatic coastal scenery.

# Prawle Point

Devon's southern extremity is Prawle Point, a jutting coastal headland. It is to the east of Plymouth in the area known as the South Hams, across the Kingsbridge Estuary from the popular waterside town of Salcombe in the direction of Start Point. The land is mostly owned by the National Trust and the point itself is a ten-minute (uphill) walk from the NT car park. The building on the cliff above the point is a watch station manned by National Coastwatch Institution volunteers (visitors welcome to pop in for a chat and see the display housed there). The volunteers are not alone in observing passing traffic out to sea, as this superb vantage point is a magnet for ship spotters (really!).

Actually, this is not a place to go with the intention of doing particular stuff, because the real joy is being there, surrounded by magnificent coastal scenery in a remote and unspoilt place. That said, ornithologists might beg to differ. The Devon Bird Watching & Preservation Society has a small reserve that features a modest superstar – the sparrow-sized cirl bunting, found only in South Devon. Birdlife is abundant, with major migrations in spring and autumn and a large cast of regulars, including assorted sea birds, ravens and raptors like buzzard, red kite and hobby.

Apart from being a birdwatcher's paradise, Prawle Point will appeal to those who simply want to appreciate the rugged grandeur of this beautiful coastline. The South West Coast Path passes through and it's possible to scramble down to little coves with shingle beaches and explore rocky shelves that run unevenly out to sea from the base of the cliffs. Just to the west is Macely Cove, with its enticing strip of sand enclosed by towering granite walls.

**HOW TO GET THERE:**
From the village of East Prawle (reached via a number of alternative minor roads from Frogmore or Chillington on the A379 from Kingsbridge to Dartmouth), using a single-track road to the National Trust car park.

**WHEN TO GO:**
Any time – even in high summer the place doesn't get overcrowded.

**DON'T MISS:**
Summer nature watch – apart from the birdlife, look out for rare butterflies such as the clouded yellow or green hairstreak on land, while basking sharks and grey seals can be spotted in the water.

**YOU SHOULD KNOW:**
Just after leaving East Prawle, the tall post in a field was erected to play the role of a ship's mast, allowing coastguard crews to practise the use of rocket apparatus – once a crucial aid in shore-to-ship rescues. It was often deployed locally, for many a ship has run aground on Prawle Point over the years. The strange-looking bunker on the left just before the climb to the point is a leftover from one of two radar stations built in World War II.

*Remote Prawle Point*

# Exmoor

The Exmoor National Park is very special and sure to appeal to anyone who loves wild and lonely places. But there's much more than moor to be seen in this 700-sq-km (270-sq-mi) area of outstanding natural beauty that includes the Vale of Porlock and Brendon Hills. It spans the borders of Devon and Somerset, with nearly three quarters located in the latter county. Exmoor has over 200 scheduled ancient monuments and countless historic sights ranging from prehistoric hill forts and mine workings to pretty medieval villages with wonderful old churches. Red deer roam free, as do Exmoor ponies, while sheep graze everywhere and the thriving bird population is represented by species as different as the peregrine falcon and Dartford warbler.

But the landscape's the star and that, too, is hugely varied. The rugged northern boundary is a Heritage Coast 55 km (34 mi) long, a stretch of dramatic coastal scenery that includes Britain's highest cliff – the grimly named Great Hangman near Combe Martin, soaring to an impressive 318 m (1,040 ft) with a sheer face of 250 m (820 ft). The shoreline is often wooded and exploring the coast reveals a wonderland of cliffs, caves and huge waterfalls. There are few settlements on the water – only Lynton-Lynmouth (connected by a cliff railway) and Porlock Weir – so mostly this awesome coast is accessible only to the most determined adventurers.

The park predominately consists of heather-covered moorland, lightly peppered with hamlets and small villages. This hilly former royal hunting ground also has extensive areas of broadleaf and conifer woodlands. There are numerous rivers, notably the River Exe and its tributaries flowing south and several that flow out into the Bristol Channel in the north, and it would be easy to spend a month or more exploring Exmoor's beguiling features.

**HOW TO GET THERE:**
The Exmoor National Park is crossed by two main roads – the A39 from Barnstaple to Minehead and the A396 (from Dunster, off the A39 south of Minehead, to Tiverton). The moor itself has a network of minor roads.

**WHEN TO GO:**
Any time, although extreme care should be exercised if venturing onto the moor proper in winter, when weather conditions can change for the worse with dramatic suddenness and swirling mist can pose a particular threat to walkers. Set against the risk factors, the moor's stern winter face has an austere beauty and when Exmoor is covered in snow it has an ethereal appeal.

**DON'T MISS:**
A stroll across the famous Tarr Steps, an ancient clapper bridge across the River Barle between Withypool and Dulverton.

**YOU SHOULD KNOW:**
Does the Beast of Exmoor really exist? This huge cat is said to stalk the woods and pastures of Exmoor – killing the occasional sheep, leaving the odd large paw print in soft mud and exciting the media every time there's a new sighting. True or false, Exmoor is definitely big and lonely enough to provide sanctuary for shy, night-hunting predators.

*An Exmoor pony grazes on heather-carpeted moorland.*

# Orford Ness

Nearly but not quite as far to the east as it's possible to get in the British Isles lies Orford Ness – a remote natural marvel off the Suffolk coast. The largest shingle spit in Europe is joined to the mainland at Aldeburgh and stretches south past Orford to North Weir Point, opposite the hamlet of Shingle Street. The Ness is separated from the mainland by the River Alde and is an internationally important example of rare and fragile European vegetated shingle habitat. Together with nearby Havergate Island, the spit has been designated as Orford Ness National Nature Reserve.

The Ness is 15 km (9 mi) long – an atmospheric strip of marsh and mudflat, lagoons and tidal river, shingle and sand, grassland and scrub, flowers and shells. This should be a lonely outpost untouched by the hand of man, but instead it has a lighthouse dating from 1792 and an extraordinary collection of abandoned buildings. Damaging one of the world's largest vegetated shingle habitats was of little concern to the British War Office in the first half of the 20th century – had such a thing then been deemed valuable or even defined – and the legacy of the Ness's history as a closed site for weapons testing and other research purposes may be read from a bizarre assortment of structures dating from two hot world wars and one Cold War. Early radar experiments took place in the 1930s and the distinctive 'pagodas' were used for testing nuclear triggers after World War II. The National Trust purchased the site in 1993 and has chosen to preserve the military detritus.

The combination of lonely wild place, wide-open spaces and big skies with a 'mystique of secrecy' generated by the former military establishment makes for weird contrasts and a fascinating visit. The National Trust's self-guiding booklet reveals all.

**HOW TO GET THERE:**
Access is strictly limited to protect the natural habitat, and may be (officially) obtained only by using the National Trust ferry from Orford town quay on a 'first come, first served' basis.

**WHEN TO GO:**
Between April and the end of October, with Saturday sailings only except in July, August and September when open days are Tuesday to Saturday. Crossings to the Ness are between 10.00 and 14.00, with the last boat returning at 17.00.

**DON'T MISS:**
The great Martello Tower built at the top of the Ness, the most northerly of those sturdy round gun platforms built to deter a Napoleonic invasion that never came.

**YOU SHOULD KNOW:**
This is not a wheelchair-friendly place. Access to the ferry launch is via steep and slippery steps, some tracks on the Ness are rough and/or unsurfaced and once there the entire circuit involves traversing shingle areas. Most buildings that may be entered have narrow doorways, thresholds and steps.

*The atmospheric Orford Ness*

# North Norfolk Coast

**HOW TO GET THERE:**
Use the A149 that runs from Hunstanton (north of King's Lynn, passing Sandringham) along the coast to Sheringham and Cromer, due north of Norwich.

**WHEN TO GO:**
Any time – winter to find a tourist-free zone and see the large number of migrating wildfowl on the marshes, notably protected Brent geese that can gather in their thousands.

**DON'T MISS:**
The famous seals off Blakeney Point. Boat trips run from Morston or Blakeney Quay daily in season (April to October), less frequently in the off season. Up to 500 common and grey seals will be seen basking on the sandbanks and some will inquisitively surround the boat. Many trips land on Blakeney Point to allow visitors to study the abundant birdlife, stroll to the Old Lifeboat House, splash about in the water or lie in the sun.

**YOU SHOULD KNOW:**
Lord Nelson spent many boyhood days exploring this coast from his home at Burnham Thorpe, where his father was rector. One of 11 children, young Horatio didn't have that much time to run wild on the salt marshes – he joined the Royal Navy in 1771 aged just 13.

*A summer evening at Holkham Bay on the North Norfolk Coast*

The trendy North Norfolk Coast has become known as 'Chelsea on Sea' after the large number of well-heeled Londoners who have holiday homes in charming small towns and villages that line the water or lie just inland. These include (from west to east) Brancaster, Burnham Deepdale, Burnham Market, Burnham Overy, Holkham, Wells-next-the-Sea, Stiffkey, Morston, Blakeney and Cley Next the Sea. Appealing as these delightful places may be to second-homers, there is another aspect of this fascinating coast that will appeal mightily to everyone who loves wild and lonely places, huge skies, the haunting call of passing curlew and total solitude.

For this Area of Outstanding Natural Beauty (AONB) is a land of extensive marshes and mudflats, creeks and tidal pools, beaches and sand dunes. This is where low tide can see the sea retreating beyond sight from the shoreline, only to rush back when the tide turns, filling the gutters with extraordinary rapidity and threatening to cut off the unwary from dry land with no more warning than the ominous rumble of waves driven by a following wind. Local knowledge is helpful and tide tables are an essential aid for any would-be foreshore explorer.

Wonderful walks may be enjoyed in the Holkham National Nature Reserve. It stretches from Burnham Norton to Blakeney and has every feature that makes this unique coastline so special – foreshore, reclaimed marshland, salt marsh, pinewoods, scrub and dunes. A good spot to start is Holkham Bay, right in the middle of the reserve (a small charge for parking in the convenient access point of Lady Ann's Drive is payable during the summer months). There are some impressive dunes at Holkham, but the very best system of the coast is Winterton Dunes at the eastern end of the Area of Outstanding Natural Beauty.

# Pendle Hill

*Pendle Hill seen from the Ribble Valley.*

The old mill towns of Burnley, Nelson, Clithero and Colne in northeastern Lancashire are grouped around isolated Pendle Hill, rising to a moorland crest 557 m (1,827 ft) above sea level. It is part neither of the Pennines to the east nor of the nearby Forest of Bowland, although included within the latter's designation as an Area of Outstanding National Beauty (AONB). The moist climate that underpinned the area's cotton-producing industry is enshrined in the local saying 'when you can see Pendle Hill it's about to rain, when you can't, it's already started'. Despite that, on a rare clear day it's possible to see the sea from the summit.

This crouching mound has inspired people since prehistoric times – there's a Bronze Age burial site on the summit but Halloween is the time for a completely different historical hike – large numbers gather to climb the supposedly haunted hill each year in memory of the infamous Pendle witch trials of 1612 that accused a dozen locals (including two men) of murdering ten people by witchcraft. One 'witch' died in prison, one was acquitted and ten were found guilty . . . and hanged by the neck until dead. Those who can't (or won't!) make Halloween can follow a signed Witches' Trail on foot at any time to visit key sites.

Pendle Hill is one of those places too wild to be tamed, and has therefore remained much as nature intended. Away from regular paths to the summit it offers compete peace and solitude, while those who like to be organized can follow cycling or walking tours designed to showcase the natural beauty of this great hill and its pastoral surroundings. These include the Pendle Three Peaks Trail, the 70-km (43-mi) circular Pendle Way and Grand Cycle Tour of Pendle.

**HOW TO GET THERE:**
The most popular – and steepest – ascent of Pendle Hill begins in the village of Barley to the east. Other villages around the hill are Newchurch-in-Pendle, Twiston, Downham, Mearley, Pendleton and Sabden. Pendle Hill is north of the M65 at Burnley, with the A59 running to the west and A682 to the east.

**WHEN TO GO:**
Any time (but winter conditions call for hill-walking experience).

**DON'T MISS:**
The British in India Museum in nearby Colne's Hendon Mill, dedicated to telling the story of the British Raj with the help of coins, ivory carvings, commemorative boxes and plates, weapons, photographs, uniforms and model soldiers (open weekdays, find it off Craddock Road in the town centre).

**YOU SHOULD KNOW:**
It was here in 1652 that George Fox, famous founder of the Religious Society of Friends (Quakers), experienced a vision that became enshrined in Quaker consciousness. Those tempted to ascend the hill today should perhaps note his words before starting out on their journey: 'We came near a very great hill called Pendle Hill and I was moved of the Lord to go to the top of it, which I did with difficulty, it was so very steep and high'.

*A view of Ennerdale Water from the northern shore*

# Ennerdale Water

The remote hidden gem in Cumbria's crown is Ennerdale Water. This glacial lake is the most westerly stretch of water in the Lake District National Park and one of the smallest, with a surface area of just 3 sq km (1 sq mi). Although surrounded by famous peaks such as Brandreth, Great Gable, Green Gable, High Crag, Pillar and Steeple, this pristine little lake and its shoreline remain undeveloped and completely unspoilt, helped by the absence of any public road entering its snug Ennerdale Valley location.

Ennerdale Water is fed by the River Liza and various fell streams, before discharging into the River Ehen and thence into the Irish Sea. The water level has been artificially raised to support the lake's role as a reservoir (owned by United Utilities) serving the Whitehaven area. The Forestry Commission manages the environs, ensuring that there is no intrusive tourist-orientated development. Despite proximity to the towns of Egremont and Cleator Moor, the lake is not well known and is little visited in comparison to more popular Lake District destinations, making it all the more special for those who appreciate the solitude of wild places.

Beyond Ennerdale Water's western end the broad vista of the West Cumbrian Plain stretches away to the sea, in marked contrast to the eastern end where awesome crags and fells rise sharply. Along the northern shore of the lake is a favoured path to the summit of the great Pillar – a satisfying climb that will be rewarded with sensational views from on high. Other peaks can be reached from the lake, but the routes are more challenging. The lake itself can be circumnavigated, but those walkers who take it on should be ultra-careful when using the testing path beneath Anglers Crag along the southern shore.

**HOW TO GET THERE:**
The easiest access point for walkers or cyclists is Ennerdale Bridge, a delightful small village reached by minor roads from the B5295/A5086 Egremont to Cockermouth road.

**WHEN TO GO:**
Any time (weather conditions permitting in winter)

**DON'T MISS:**
The magnificent view of Ennerdale Water from the top of Anglers Crag. There may be equally spectacular views in the Lake District National Park, but none can better it.

**YOU SHOULD KNOW:**
The annual Ennerdale Show takes place in the last week of August each year – a typically lively Cumbrian event at Ennerdale Bridge that brings country people together to be entertained by agricultural displays, local arts and crafts, assorted competitions, music and general revelry.

# North York Moors

True Brits (and many others around the globe) who watch the long-running TV series *Heartbeat* will be familiar with regular locations like Aidensfield (actually the village of Goathland) and the stunning scenery of the surrounding North York Moors. The 1,425-sq-km (550-sq-mi) national park is sparsely populated and boasts one of the UK's largest unbroken expanses of heather moorland. This stunning landscape is a place where it's possible to walk for long distances without seeing a soul, listening to the calls of upland birds and enjoying the wide sweep of open moors.

Seductive as wild and lonely places may be, there's much more to the North York Moors National Park than that. Quite apart from the wonderful heather moors, there are ancient woodlands, rivers and a wonderful stretch of Heritage Coast that includes the fascinating old port of Whitby, plus beaches and dramatic cliffs. In addition, there are picturesque sandstone villages, castles, medieval abbeys and churches to be found by those fascinated by built history.

To see how much this special place has to offer, drive – or take the Moorland Explorer bus – to The Moors National Park Centre at Danby and enjoy the interactive exhibition, tearoom, arts and crafts gallery, indoor and outdoor play areas and grounds. The centre also has details of eight specific routes for wheelchairs and pushchairs, encompassing the park's various attractions – high moorland, Heritage Coast, riversides, lakes and an important archaeological site. Superb views are on offer from the network of roads on the moorland plateau without climbing or hiking a single step. It's a place that everyone can enjoy at their own pace, in their own way.

**HOW TO GET THERE:**
The Moorbus Network offers a comprehensive public transport network from April to October in an attempt to reduce the pressure of private cars. Park and Ride (free with a Moorbus ticket) is available at Sutton Bank National Park Centre, The Moors National Park Centre at Danby, Hutton le Hole, Thornton le Dale and Newton under Roseberry. Drive in from any of the surrounding towns – Saltburn, Guisborough, Stokesley, Northallerton, Thirsk, Pickering or Scarborough.

**WHEN TO GO:**
Any time

**DON'T MISS:**
A nostalgic trip on the huffing, puffing NYMR (North Yorkshire Moors Railway). This authentic slice of yesteryear offers steam locos, wood-panelled carriages, old-fashioned conductor service and around 30 km (19 mi) of preserved track through exceptional moorland scenery. Hop on and off at will to explore between late March and the end of October. Grosmont is the terminus for the scenic Esk Valley line that also crosses the park.

**YOU SHOULD KNOW:**
In the 12th century the abbot of Rievaulx Abbey made a timeless comment that happily is as true today as it was then: 'Everywhere peace, everywhere serenity and a marvellous freedom from the tumult of the world.'

*Escape the hustle and bustle of modern life on the North York Moors.*

# North Pennines

The special character of the North Pennines – stretching down from Carlisle to Darlington – is recognized by salutations galore. This low-rise range has been designated as an Area of Outstanding Natural Beauty and at 2,000 sq km (772 sq mi) is the second-largest AONB in England, outranked only by the Cotswolds. As a result of unique geological heritage – unusual flora (including rare alpine plants not found elsewhere in the British Isles) and threatened fauna such as red squirrel – the North Pennines have also achieved UNESCO European and Global Geopark status.

Quite apart from official recognition, everyone who appreciates wide open spaces and the ability to escape into the great outdoors will be instantly captivated by huge expanses of open heather moor, blanket bog, hay meadows bright with wild flowers in season, enticing dales, rushing rivers, waterfalls and wonderful woodland.

Traditional stone-built villages house welcoming traditional communities and the North Pennines has a fascinating industrial past, with evidence of extensive lead mining and quarrying in past centuries still to be found, providing an added dimension to this striking landscape that spans three counties – Cumbria, Durham and Northumberland.

The North Pennines are a magnet to birdwatchers. Thousands of wading birds nest in the area, raptors are easily spotted and so are black grouse, with 80 per cent of England's population here. Horse riding, cycling (on and off road) and hiking are the best ways of appreciating the outstanding qualities of the North Pennines.

For those who prefer organized tramping rather than wandering at will, a major section of the long-distance Pennine Way falls within the Area of Outstanding Natural Beauty. Or try Isaac's Tea Trail – a 58-km (36-mi) loop walk that takes in the villages of Ninebanks, Allendale, Nenthead and Alston. This trail is named after Isaac Holden, a lead miner-turned-tea-seller-cum-Methodist-preacher who roamed these parts in the 19th century.

*High Cup Nick is a spectacular U-shaped glacial valley.*

# Galloway Forest Park

*A view over to Meikle Millyea*

Welcome to the Scottish Borders – one of Britain's most pleasing tracts of unspoilt countryside. Once there, the 775 sq km (300 sq mi) of Galloway Forest Park provides a wonderful opportunity to experience the natural beauty of the Borders at first hand. As the name suggests, this is a woodland park. It is operated by the Forestry Commission, an organization that majors on commercial conifer plantations, and this is indeed the predominant characteristic of Galloway Forest Park. But this is a mixed landscape of forest and moor, lochs and rivers, seashore and mountains – a combination that attracts over a quarter of a million fresh-air enthusiasts who visit every year.

Their motivation is understandable. The park is in Dumfries and Galloway and encompasses much of the Galloway Hills, part of Scotland's Southern Uplands. This is a wild and uninhabited area, allowing enormous scope for independent exploration in the sure and certain knowledge that – despite all those visitors – total solitude is never far away. There is more than enough lonely backcountry to get lost in (hopefully not literally) and there are 27 waymarked trails, covering every type of landscape within the park and catering for every level of ability. Wild camping is a popular summer option, and other recreational opportunities include fishing in stunning surroundings for trout and salmon (in season), canoeing, mountain-biking, horse riding and wildlife-watching (top sightings are red deer, pine marten, otter and red squirrel, golden eagles, black grouse and nightjar).

There are three first-class visitor centres to help point newcomers in their desired direction: Kirroughtree (reached from Newton Stewart or New Galloway), Glentrool (reached from Newton Stewart) and Clatteringshaws (reached from New Galloway). The latter is on the Galloway Red Kite Trail and has a superb interactive wildlife exhibition.

**HOW TO GET THERE:**
Enter the park from any of the surrounding villages – Newton Stewart, New Galloway, Gatehouse of Fleet, Dalmellington or Castle Douglas. The main road to Newton Stewart is the A75. There are three single-track access roads into the Galloway Hills – one from the A712 near the dam at Clatteringshaws reservoir to Craigencallie; one forestry toll road to Loch Doon, Loch Doon Castle and Stinchar Bridge near Dalmellington; and one from Glentrool village to Bruce's Stone.

**WHEN TO GO:**
Any time (even if a winter visit goes no further than Kirroughtree Visitor Centre to introduce the kids to Santa and pick up a sustainably grown Scottish Christmas tree).

**DON'T MISS:**
A visit to Bruce's Stone, high on the northern shore of Loch Trool, which can be reached by car (see above). This memorial commemorates Robert the Bruce's first victory over the English, when he was a fugitive hiding in the Galloway Hills.

**YOU SHOULD KNOW:**
In 2009 Galloway Forest Park was the first place in the United Kingdom to be awarded Dark-Sky Park status by the International Dark-Sky Association, on the grounds of having a UK night sky unusually free of light pollution.

**269**

# Isle of Jura

*The Paps of Jura*

Once the exclusive fiefdom of the powerful Campbell clan, the Isle of Jura in the Inner Hebrides is now split into different estates. There are lots more red deer than people on Jura and deer stalking is a principal contributor to the island's economy. The other is tourism. With an area of around 370 sq km (143 sq mi) and some 200 inhabitants, this starkly beautiful island remains a classic unspoilt Scottish wilderness that draws visitors who love wild and lonely places.

Most people live in the pretty village of Craighouse on the east coast, which has a post-office shop, hotel, tearoom, village hall and church. A narrow road (pretentiously titled the A846) follows the eastern and southern coasts. Jura House in the south has the sheltered Walled Garden, open to the public, featuring many exotic species from the Antipodes. Respecting the awesome power of Atlantic gales, the rugged and unsheltered west coast is uninhabited, but has a number of raised beaches (rocky marine shelves above sea level). The island's western side is dominated by three conical peaks known as the Paps of Jura. These are included in the challenging annual Isle of Jura Fell Race sponsored by the local distillery. Between the northern tip of Jura and neighbouring Scarba is the Gulf of Corryvreckan, complete with notorious whirlpool.

Jura has many historical sites, including Iron Age forts and prehistoric standing stones, but the landscape is the main attraction. The island has assorted habitats – lough, woodland, bog, heather, grassland, mountains, cliffs, bays and beaches – and is a walkers' paradise. Along the way it's impossible not to see red deer, and perfectly possible to spot a wealth of wildlife such as seals, otters, golden eagles, sea eagles, hen harriers, buzzards, assorted songbirds and many species of sea bird.

# Knoydart Peninsula

Travellers tempted to visit Scotland's last great protected wilderness will even enjoy the bit that is sometimes frustrating when it comes to such adventures – getting there. Because, for all but seafarers or those rich enough to hire a helicopter, a visit to the remote Knoydart Peninsula will start with a drive up *Rathad nan Eilan* – the Road to the Isles. This starts at Fort William and goes through breathtaking coastal scenery as it passes through Glenfinnan and Arisaig *en route* to the port of Mallaig. A good alternative is making the same journey by train, using the spectacular West Highland Line.

The peninsula is sandwiched between Lochs Nevis and Hourn. This National Scenic Area, known locally as the 'rough bounds', attracts sailors, hill walkers and mountaineers – the latter including those intent on Munro-bagging, with two of these must-climb mountains on offer. The pretty whitewashed village of Inverie crouches below conifer woodland on the north side of Loch Nevis, beneath the intimidating bulk of Sgurr Coire Choinnichean. The peninsula's one metalled road goes nowhere, making Inverie the largest mainland settlement in Britain not connected to the national road network. Inverie is the ideal base from which to explore Knoydart's dramatic landscape. There are guided ranger walks on Wednesdays that allow day visitors to experience this extraordinary place without staying over, timed to end before the last return ferry to Mallaig.

There are a number of excellent B&B establishments in and around the village of Inverie, and also some self-catering cottages, farmhouses, converted barns and bothies. It's advisable to book early if summer accommodation is required – or take a tent – for some visitors return year after year to recharge their batteries in this tranquil haven far from the hustle and bustle of modern life.

*A house nestled in the tranquil haven of the Knoydart Peninsula.*

**HOW TO GET THERE:**
By boat from Mallaig, or on foot – a modest 30-km (19-mi) hike through rough country. There is also the Arnisdale Ferry Service, from the village of the same name on Loch Hourn – custom trips to the north side of Knoydart Peninsula by small boat a speciality.

**WHEN TO GO:**
Any time, although the peninsula can be bleak in winter.

**DON'T MISS:**
A swift half at the remotest pub in Britain, the Old Forge at Inverie. It has six moorings, offers good food, is open all day for 364 days a year . . . and has that all-important clothes-drying rack by a roaring fire.

**YOU SHOULD KNOW:**
The peninsula is now owned and managed by the Knoydart Foundation, a partnership set up to maintain and manage 70 sq km (27 sq mi) of the wildest county in Britain. This put the peninsula's future back in the hands of the local community, 150 years after most of the inhabitants were evicted and sent to Canada as part of the infamous Highland Clearances.

# Rannoch Moor

**HOW TO GET THERE:**
The A82 crosses Rannoch Moor on its way north from Bridge of Orchy to Gen Coe and Fort William, as does the West Highland Line.

**WHEN TO GO:**
Spring to autumn, unless extreme winter sports are the objective.

**DON'T MISS:**
Breathtaking Loch Ossian, tucked away in the northeastern corner of Rannoch Moor, far from public roads (but just a short hike from remote Corrour rail station on the West Highland Line).

Rannoch Moor can seem like the last place on Earth when the weather closes in, as cloud swirls down from the hills and relentless rain starts falling. This large triangular expanse of boggy Highland moorland stands on its inverted apex to the west of Loch Rannoch and extends to around 130 sq km (50 sq mi). The moor is a level plateau surrounded by mountains and consists of innumerable lochs and lochans, streams and peat bogs, heather and scrub.

The moor is crossed by one road and a railway, but still remains one of Scotland's loneliest enclaves, described thus by Robert Louis Stevenson in his novel *Kidnapped*: 'A wearier-looking desert a man never saw'. He must have seen it on a bad day, for when the sun comes out this dour other-worldly place takes on a sparkle all its own. Weary hikers plodding across the moor on the West Highland Way are re-energized. Others are tempted to park their cars and roam through this extraordinary landscape, while some let the train take the initial strain before doing the same. Achallader is at the moor's southern apex, Rannoch Station is at the northeastern corner, while the northwest is delineated by the mouth of Glen Coe.

The isolated situation of the moor and the fact there is no west-east road crossing is underlined by the realization that anyone who decides to walk the 16-km (10-mi) track between the Youth Hostel near Rannoch Station and the Kings House Hotel on the main A82 road for a refreshing drink is in for a 32-km (20-mi) hike. There's no chance of getting a lift or taking a taxi back to rest weary feet, for the shortest route back to Rannoch Station by road is over 160 km (100 mi) long.

**YOU SHOULD KNOW:**
Those who prefer to look rather than do can get a feel for Rannoch Moor by riding the aforementioned West Highland Line, whose Victorian builders had to support the tracks on a base of imported earth and ashes laced with timber and brushwood to reinforce the boggy ground. It's not a bad option – the 'Iron Road to the Isles' is one of the most scenic railway routes in Britain and is considered to be one of the world's best rail journeys.

*The jagged Cuillin Hills on the Isle of Skye are seen here from Loch Coruisk.*

# Loch Coruisk

**HOW TO GET THERE:**
First get yourself to Skye. Thereafter take a boat from Elgol on the shores of Loch Scavaig at the end of Srathaird Peninsula (easy way) or hike the same trip along the shoreline (hard way, a long walk along a path with difficult sections including the notorious Bad Step above a vertical drop to the sea). An alternative 11-km (7-mi) rough tramp is from Sligachan down Glen Sligachan.

**WHEN TO GO:**
April to October for the boat trip from Elgol

**DON'T MISS:**
A scenic boat trip to Loch Coruisk followed by a couple of hours exploring the environs of this inspiring lake after fellow-passengers have departed, before returning to Elgol on foot along one of the most impressive coastal paths in Scotland.

**YOU SHOULD KNOW:**
Loch Coruisk has inspired many a painter – including the well-travelled J W M Turner – and attracted a number of literary giants such as James Boswell and Samuel Johnson.

'Speed, bonnie boat, like a bird on the wing . . . Over the sea to Skye' is part of a famous Jacobite lament for the lost cause of Bonnie Prince Charlie in the 18th century, commemorating the Young Pretender's flight from Uist to the Isle of Skye with the help of Flora MacDonald, following his defeat at the Battle of Culloden in 1746. In fact, the origins of *The Skye Boat Song* are not traditional – for it is a Victorian invention written after one Annie MacLeod heard and remembered the melody of her oarsmen's Gaelic rowing song in a boat on Loch Coruisk.

Whatever the origins, it's a haunting song, and people are still going over the sea to enjoy the stunning natural beauty of Skye. One of the highlights of any trip to the island must be a visit to that self-same Loch Coruisk, a freshwater lake that takes its name from the Gaelic *Coire Uisg* (Cauldron of Waters). This must surely be one of the most wild and dramatic visions in all the Scottish Highlands. The northern end of the loch is surrounded by the jagged fangs of the Black Cullin range and it is hidden by those inhospitable basalt mountains. A small rill from the southern end discharges into Loch Scavaig, a sea loch.

This fact is a life-saver for those who lack the time, energy or fitness to reach this compelling but isolated natural wonder on foot, for boat trips from various starting points on and off the island deposit people at the iron steps on Lock Scavaig that give access to the short but rocky walk to Scotland's most magnificent freshwater loch. The boat trip alone is worth the entry fee, with Loch Coruisk itself a stunning visual bonus.

# Sandwood Bay

Where's Great Britain's finest beach? You've guessed it – the answer that would be disputed by none who have been there is Sandwood Bay, facing the restless Atlantic Ocean close to the northwestern tip of Scotland. The beach is a 2-km (1-mi) stretch of wide pinkish sand backed by impressive sand dunes and a small loch, which curves between craggy cliffs. An imposing sea stack guards the southern end. For sheer majesty, this place takes some beating, but perhaps its true appeal is that there's every chance of having private use of this beautiful wild place.

Even in high summer it is likely that only a few determined souls will share this special strand, for a real effort is required to get there. Once, it was possible to keep driving after the road started to peter out into a rough track, abandoning the car when further progress was impossible and walking from there. Nowadays, there's a mandatory car park at the dead end of the nearest road, after which a gate and well-defined 6-km (4-mi) path leads across undulating moorland to the beach, passing Sandwood Loch on the way. As the descent to the beach begins, roofless Sandwood Cottage is on the right – providing a good spot to camp for those who think one day in this special place isn't enough.

They're not wrong. Simply sitting on the beach soaking up the stark beauty of this lonely beach is a great beginning, but after that comes the urge to explore – the sand, the dunes, Sandwood Loch, adjoining cliffs. Some imbued with pioneering spirit even set out to follow the shore up to Cape Wrath, a name that says everything about this Atlantic coastline.

**HOW TO GET THERE:**
A minor road leads north from Rhiconich, just past Achlyness on the A838. It winds alongside Loch Inchard to Kinlochbervie and on to Oldshoremore, after which the road expires at Blairmore. Park at the end and walk northwards towards the beach.

**WHEN TO GO:**
Any time – the beach is delightful in summer, but truly magisterial in winter when angry Atlantic waves lash the beach and flying spray clouds the cold air, beneath a dark and steely sky.

**DON'T MISS:**
The honesty box in the car park – Sandwood Bay is owned by the John Muir Trust and contributions help to preserve this priceless beach.

**YOU SHOULD KNOW:**
Not seeing doesn't add up to not believing – powerful local superstition suggests the ghost of a bearded sailor whose Spanish Armada galleon was wrecked on the rocky coast used to knock on the windows of Sandwood Cottage and he still haunts the bay – perhaps intent on pursuing the mermaids said to disport themselves on shore when nobody is around. Approach quietly, just in case.

*The sun sets over Sandwood Bay.*

# Glens of Antrim

*Glanariff – 'Queen of the Glens'*

Known by locals as 'The Glens', this Area of Outstanding Natural Beauty in Northern Ireland is officially designated as the Glens of Antrim. There are nine of these stunning valleys, together offering a concentrated cocktail of awe-inspiring scenery within an area of some 50 sq km (19 sq mi), which includes glacial valleys and tundra plateau, boglands and grazing, rivers and waterfalls, vertical cliffs and sandy beaches.

The Glens radiate from the Antrim Plateau down to the northwest coast and serve as a major tourist attraction. But there's more than enough dramatic scenery to go around so there's no need to feel crowded, especially if avoiding high summer and making an effort to stray from the well-beaten visitors' track. Famed in Irish poetry, song and myth, these lush green valleys seem like secret wonderlands alive with the sound of running water and birdsong.

Each glen has its own character, each merits leisurely exploration. Glenarm – the glen of the army – has a village of the same name. Glencloy is the glen of the hedges. Fertile Glenariff is the so-called Queen of the Glens. Glenballyemon is geographically the middle glen of nine. Rugged Glenaan is the site of legendary Ossian's grave. Glencorp is the glen of the slaughtered, named for a long-forgotten event in Ireland's violent past. Glendun, spanned by a viaduct carrying the main Cushendall-Ballycastle road, is the glen of the brown river. Glenshesk is the sedgey glen and Glentaisie is named for the princess of nearby Rathin Island. It would take a lifetime to explore them all, so it's a case of 'take your pick'. Whichever is chosen there are a few roads, but this is a mission best undertaken on foot armed with no more than a map, stout shoes, a flask of tea and camera with spare memory card.

# Mourne Mountains

The very words have a romantic ring, and the Mourne Mountains in County Down do not disappoint, for this Area of Outstanding Natural Beauty is generally regarded as the most picturesque mountain region in Ireland. Thanks to the words of the popular song penned by Percy French in 1896 ('Where the Mountains of Mourne sweep down to the sea'), they are also Ireland's most famous mountains.

This compact range due south of Belfast overlooks Carlingford Lough close to the Irish Republic. The mountains are contained within a rough triangle just 24 km (15 mi) long by 13 km (8 mi) wide with apex-points formed by Newcastle, Warrenpoint and Kilkeel. Among around 60 high tops in the Mournes are a dozen granite peaks rising to a height of 600 m (2,000 ft) or more, including Northern Ireland's highest – Slieve Donard. Others in this wild landscape have quaint names such as Slieve Muck, Brandy Pad, Butter Mountain, Buzzard's Roost, Cock and Hen Mountains, Devil's Coach Road, Eagle Mountain and Pigeon Rock.

With rugged mountains, grazing pastures, heather moorland, forests, drumlins, lakes, rivers, coastal plains and wonderful sandy beaches, the area is a magnet for get-up-and-go outdoor enthusiasts. Walking is a major activity, with everyone from afternoon strollers to serious hill walkers finding more than enough to satisfy them. Climbers, too, can find pitches to test every level of competence. Seven signed cycle trails offer varying degrees of difficulty and length, while dedicated mountain-bikers with thighs like tree trunks have their own marked course. Fishing and horse riding are also popular options. For those who prefer not to wander yonder on spec, there are wonderful reserves to enjoy (Castlewellan, Tollymore and Kilbroney Forest Parks, Donard Forest, Silent Valley, Cranfield Beach and Murlough Bay).

*Sand dunes at Murlough Nature Reserve with views to Dundrum Bay and the Mourne Mountains*

**HOW TO GET THERE:**
The Mournes can be accessed using a network of minor roads from Castlewellan and Newcastle in the north and Rostrevor in the south, or various turnings off the main A2 coast road from Newcastle to Rostrevor via Kilkeel.

**WHEN TO GO:**
Any time

**DON'T MISS:**
The chance to partake of some *al fresco* dining out in a beautiful spot that has been voted as one of Britain's Top 20 Picnic Sites – Tollymore Forest Park near Newcastle, which offers excellent views of the sea and surrounding Mourne Mountains and is itself handsomely endowed with woodland, green sward and delightful rivers.

**YOU SHOULD KNOW:**
The Great Wall of County Down (actually it's a simple but rather long dry-stone wall more prosaically called the Mourne Wall) runs for 35 km (22 mi) and links 15 mountain summits. It dates from the early years of the 20th century and was built over two decades to define the boundary of an area purchased by Belfast's water authorities to ensure security of supply for Ireland's growing industrial powerhouse. Silent Valley reservoir is a scenic reminder of their efforts.

# Lough Allen

This beautiful lake atop the River Shannon is shared between Counties
Leitrim and Roscommon, with the former having the lion's share and
the latter a mere morsel. This is the uppermost of three loughs on
Ireland's great river and lies beneath the Iron Mountains near the
Shannon's source on Cuilcagh Mountain. Lough Allen is 13 km (8 mi)
long and 5 km (3 mi) wide. The water level is controlled by sluice gates
and can therefore fluctuate by as much as 2.5 m (8 ft), revealing many
ancient crannog dwelling sites when low.

Lough Allen has suffered from insensitive examples of modern
tourist development, but by and large remains an unspoilt gem set in
stunning Leitrim countryside. This is a traditional tract of rural Ireland
that is sparsely populated, with the lough separating the hilly
northwest from a relatively flat southeast. It is a land of extraordinary
pastoral beauty, with soaring mountains and plunging valleys, rolling
pastures and woodland, lakes and rivers – plus a short stretch of
Atlantic coastline.

The lake itself is a wonderful stretch of water, fed by numerous
small streams that descend the slopes of adjacent mountains, which are
steep but not precipitous.

This is wild country – a place of bogs, heather and rocks with some
relatively recent woodland planting. The lake is a noted angling
hotspot, and eco-friendly watersports such as windsurfing and kayaking
are popular. The limit of the Shannon navigation is at the north shore of
the lake, with access from the extensive Shannon waterway system via
scenic Lough Allen Canal at the southern end, originally built to carry
coal from the nearby Aringa mines in the early 1800s. There are many
signed walking routes around the lake and various stables offer the
means to explore the shore and surrounding countryside on horseback.

# The Burren

If there's a more bizarre landscape in all Ireland, it remains a secret – for surely nothing can wrest that quirky crown from The Burren. This karst limestone region – one of Europe's largest – extends to around 300 sq km (115 sq mi) bounded by the Atlantic to the west and Galway Bay to the north. The name comes from the Irish *Boireann*, meaning 'Great Rock', and it's certainly that. These rolling hills are made up of limestone pavements criss-crossed with a distinctive pattern (*karren*) of cracks (*grikes*) and isolated rocks (*clints*).

The Burren seems like a barren wilderness at a first distant glance, but closer inspection reveals rich vegetation growing in the narrow cracks. This habitat is so unusual that Mediterranean, arctic and alpine plants live side by side, with one alpine – the blue spring gentian – serving as The Burren's tourist-board symbol. This wild and empty place will not appeal to people who like their natural wonders to be big and bold, yet more discerning explorers will be captivated by green lanes where it's possible to walk for long distances amidst this unique landscape without seeing a soul. Along the way will be innumerable signs of The Burren's rich heritage – dozens of megalithic tombs, standing stones, Celtic crosses and traces of villages abandoned during the Great Famine.

And those who only do 'big and bold' need not despair, for The Burren's muscular coastline is magnificent – coming to a dramatic high point at the Cliffs of Moher towards the southwestern boundary. These are as big and bold as they come, towering up to 214 m (702 ft) above the Atlantic. There are spectacular coastal views from the top, but these have to be shared. The cliffs attract over one million visitors a year.

**HOW TO GET THERE:**
The Burren is roughly delineated by a circle formed by the villages of Ballyvaughan, Kinvara, Tubber, Corofin, Kilfenora and Lisdoonvarna in northwest County Clare.
**WHEN TO GO:**
Any time (spring for the fabulous wild flowers)
**DON'T MISS:**
The annual Doolin Festival, held over the weekend following the last Friday in February. Dedicated to the world-famous local musician Micho Russell and notable for the West Clare style of lively concertina playing, this is also a wonderful showcase for traditional Irish musicians from all over the country. This small fishing village beneath the Cliffs of Moher describes itself as 'a doorway to The Burren', and visitors who don't make the festival can still enjoy nightly Irish music at any one of three pubs.
**YOU SHOULD KNOW:**
During Oliver Cromwell's brutal mid-17th-century campaign in Ireland his lieutenant general of horse, one Edmund Ludlow, uttered a phrase that has never been forgotten and is enshrined in local history. During the course of operations to suppress resistance in The Burren, he sourly commented 'It is a country where there is not enough water to drown a man, wood enough to hang him nor earth enough to bury him.'

*Limestone criss-crossed with a distinctive pattern of cracks and isolated rocks – a typical Burren landscape*

279

# Beara Peninsula

The Wild West of Ireland isn't what it used to be, with tourist pressures and prosperity brought by Celtic Tiger years inevitably changing this once-remote area. But even though the lower slopes of coastal mountains are now dotted with the white rectangles of new bungalows, one beside each abandoned stone cottage, these are no more than small blemishes on the face of a hauntingly beautiful landscape. One place that – despite some development in its settlements – retains its traditional character is the Beara Peninsula in the far southwest of the country.

*The rural coastal countryside of the Beara Peninsula*

**HOW TO GET THERE:**
Kenmare and Glengarriff are on the N70 coast road.
**WHEN TO GO:**
Any time
**DON'T MISS:**
The wonderful coastal vista to be seen from the top of Healy Pass, which connects north and south coasts of the peninsula south of Lauragh, with a commanding outlook over Beara that stretches away to the neighbouring Iveragh Peninsula.
**YOU SHOULD KNOW:**
Anyone with a day to spare should take the Dursey Island cable car – the only one in Europe specifically used to span a stretch of water, in this case treacherous Dursey Sound with its powerful tidal race. Go in the off season and this wild and lonely isle can be shared with fewer than a dozen inhabitants and their livestock . . . some of which may occasionally be encountered in the cable car as it goes to or comes back from market.

Marooned between the Kenmare River to the north (in true Irish fashion, a bay) and Bantry Bay to the south, the Beara Peninsula was once the stronghold of the O'Sullivan clan and it's easy to understand why it was one of the last strongholds to resist the conquering English in Elizabeth I's reign. Today, the established tourist trail is the Ring of Beara, a 195-km (120-mi) circumnavigation of the untamed peninsula that allows motorists to enjoy some of Ireland's most magical coastline and imagine that – but for their modern chariot and others like it – they have gone back in time.

The ring begins in Kenmare and ends at Glengarriff, passing through Adrigole, Castletown Bere and Allihies along the way. Top attractions include ruined Dunboy Castle, Puxley Mansion, a copper-mining museum and Derreen Gardens. There are also various tourist traps, but for those who like to get away from it all there are countless opportunities to explore the rugged shoreline and/or vanish into one of two mountain ranges that run down the centre, the Caha and Slieve Kish, bisected only by two roads along their entire length. For determined off-road hikers, the breathtaking Beara Way also runs right round the peninsula.

# Marquenterre Dunes

The estuary of the River Somme on the Picardy coast is the largest in northern France at 72 sq km (28 sq mi), but it's shrinking steadily as a result of sedimentation. That means the estuary is a rich vegetated habitat and the prolonged process of silting has created one of Europe's most extensive sand-dune complexes between the Somme and Canche estuaries. Le Marquenterre is an impressive expanse of dunes fronting La Manche (the English Channel) that have been stabilized by pinewood plantations. The place is home to an assortment of interesting wildlife, including a colony of seals, but – apart from satisfying those who can't resist the lure of exploring wild and lonely places – the real attraction is birds, birds, birds.

In addition to a varied resident population, Le Marquenterre provides refuge for an enormous number of migrating birds stopping off to rest and refuel during the long two-way journey from Scandinavia to Africa. This strange land of dunes, pine forests and tamarisk, with salty meres and ponds rich with water plants, provides an ideal habitat and it's possible to wander undisturbed for hours and spot many of the birds that occupy this haunting landscape. But those who need or welcome expert guidance should take their binoculars to the Marquenterre Ornithological Park, one of only two bird reserves in France.

It offers three waymarked walks – a short one taking around 90 minutes and two longer ones needing perhaps three hours. The beauty of these is that they were designed to pass numerous points ideal for observing birds. There are many strategically placed hides along the way, some of which may be manned by knowledgeable guides and have telescopes trained on nesting sites in the breeding season. The park also offers informative ranger-guided walks.

**HOW TO GET THERE:**
The Marquenterre Ornithological Park is situated off the D940 near Rue, an attractive former fishing village marooned inland as the Somme silted up. The extensive dune system is bounded to the east by the D940, which runs north from Le Crotoy on the Somme Estuary via Rue to Conchil-le-Temple, and is roughly parallel to the main A16 road.

**WHEN TO GO:**
Any time (winter visiting to the park between November and March is possible only at weekends, as part of an official guided tour). The northern bird migration takes place in April and May, the return journey from August to October.

**DON'T MISS:**
Ornithologists (and others) will be fascinated by the Maison de l'Oiseau (House of Birds). Find it between Cayeux-sur-Mer and St-Valéry-sur-Somme on the other side of the estuary.

**YOU SHOULD KNOW:**
As one of France's only two bird sanctuaries, Marquenterre is not quite the safe haven the word 'sanctuary' might suggest – as soon as the French waterfowl season opens, the surrounds of the relatively small reserve echo with the sound of gunfire as sporting shooters take full toll of their feathered quarry.

*Le Marquenterre – one of Europe's most extensive sand dune complexes*

# Iles d'Ouessant

In the wild Atlantic Ocean, close to Cape Finistère, lies the one place in Brittany that has a different name in English. Ushant is a corruption of Ouessant, one of only two inhabited islands (the other is Molène, to the southeast) in the rocky Iles d'Ouessant – rocky granite outposts separated from the mainland by treacherous seas. A visit to Ushant involves taking the car ferry – capacity just two cars, so don't bother taking yours as the island's main road extends to just 6 km (4 mi) long and the whole island is only 8 km (5 mi) long and half as wide.

Ushant has one significant settlement. Lampaul has all the necessary facilities, including four hotels, and there is also a campsite for do-it-yourself visitors. Although it is a popular destination, Ushant never gets overrun and this windswept place remains a wild and unspoilt destination even in high summer. The island is surrounded by towering cliffs that plunge into the sea, with nary a guard rail in sight, and intrepid observers can find innumerable spectacular vantage points from which to study this dramatic coastline in all its moods. The interior is a virtually treeless plateau covered in heather and springy turf, with occasional stunted trees and low scrub crouching in hollows. There is gorse and a kaleidoscope of wild flowers in season.

There are few established paths so walkers go where they please, while bicycles may be hired from the ferry terminal by those who prefer pedal-power. Ornithologists love the Iles d'Ouessant, for this craggy archipelago is a welcome stopping-off point for numerous migratory birds such as the wheatear and ring ouzel, with around 350 species recorded. Beyond that, the obvious wildlife seems confined to the large rabbit population and lizards sunning themselves on dry-stone walls.

# Haut Allier

The Auvergne has been described as 'France's best-kept secret' and, if it is, a place that even most French open-air enthusiasts have yet to discover, the unspoilt Haut Allier is even less well known. Located in the western half of the Haute-Loire department in southern Auvergne (although the principal river is actually the Allier, a Loire tributary), this is the driest and sunniest part of the Auvergne, which constantly provides a reminder that the South of France is not far away.

The Haut Allier – unexploited for mass tourism – is emblematic of authentic rural France at its best. The landscape is stunning and includes large tracts of wild country. The River Allier rises in the Cevennes Mountains and features extraordinary riverscapes with awesome rock formations. The river runs through and is surrounded by stunning gorges – usually having no road access – that are often densely wooded. This is France's last great wild river and the area is renowned among those in the know as white-water rafting and canoeing heaven. Primitive camping, backpacking, rambling, day-hiking and mountain-biking are also popular, using an extensive network of paths through this natural playground. Anglers come for the trout and salmon (there is an extensive fry-stocking programme designed to maintain the salmon run).

The Haut-Allier (high valley of the upper Allier) is a place where it's possible to get up close and personal with Mother Nature – either at a leisurely pace or as part of an action-packed adventure, which could be anything from rock climbing through bungee-jumping to dog-sledding in winter. To that may be added the heritage dimension – discovering castles, abbeys, old churches, mills and delightful medieval villages full of vernacular buildings in the mellow local stone, many with traditional weekly markets.

**HOW TO GET THERE:**
The Haut Allier lies to the south of Brioude, a delightful settlement on the banks of the River Allier. Brioude is to the south of Clermont-Ferrand on the N102 road, which strikes off to the east from the A75.
**WHEN TO GO:**
Any time (winter brings enough snow to satisfy any self-respecting cross-country skier).
**DON'T MISS:**
The magnificent Basilica of St Julien in Brioude, constructed between the 11th and 14th centuries – the largest church in the Auvergne, this splendid building has some wonderfully colourful frescoes.
**YOU SHOULD KNOW:**
There is an annual series of summer concerts put on in some of Haut Allier's beautiful medieval churches, running from late June until August and reinforcing the area's status as a *Pays d'art et d'histoire* (Rural place of outstanding artistic and historical merit).

# Millevaches Regional Nature Park

**HOW TO GET THERE:**
The park is criss-crossed by a network of lanes and minor roads. Good starting points for a journey of exploration are the N141-D941 Saint-Léonard-de-Noblat to Aubusson road in the north or the A89 Tulle-Ussel road in the south.

**WHEN TO GO:**
Any time (but note that summer mornings can be very misty and winter days can be very chilly).

**DON'T MISS:**
Millevaches Regional Nature Park at a glance. This unique experience is available at purpose-built Mont Bessou viewing tower at the southeastern edge of the plateau at its high point. Set in an area of woodland just north of Meymac, the tower affords stunning vistas across the park and to the distant Cantal mountains in the south.

**YOU SHOULD KNOW:**
Don't make the assumption that the park is called after the brown Limousin cattle that may be seen everywhere. It is perhaps named for distinctive rock formations that look like cows (*vaches*) – or possibly as a combination of the Celtic *melo* (high) and Latin *vacua* (empty). Take your pick – it has thousands of Limousin cattle, lots of rock formations that look like cows (with a little imagination) and it's definitely both high and mostly empty of human habitation.

Unwilling to do anything by halves, when the authorities created Millevaches Regional Nature Park in 2004 they ensured it fell within all three of Limousin's departments – Corrèze, Creuse and Haute-Vienne. Equivalent to the UK's Areas of Outstanding Natural Beauty, regional nature parks aim to preserve the best of the nation's fine countryside – an asset that France happily still possesses in abundance. Millevaches makes the point in spades.

This marvellous tract of wild landscape is located in the foothills of the awesome Massif Central. It covers an area of 3,150 sq km (1,216 sq mi), thinly populated by around 40,000 people who mainly live in the villages and small towns around the edge of the park that are characterized by wonderful vernacular stone buildings. An extensive granite plateau offers heather moorland and peat bogs, open grasslands and wildflower meadows, deciduous, coniferous and mixed forests, bubbling springs, rushing rivers and lakes. In fact, it is more of a gentle dome than a plateau, ranging in height from 600 m (1,968 ft) to 1,000 m (3,280 ft). The River Varre rises here, flowing north to feed the Loire, and the Vézère originates nearby but flows south into the Dordogne River.

The higher areas are heavily forested with little agricultural activity. Otherwise, a pleasing patchwork of woods and meadows is punctuated by the occasional field of sunflowers or maize. As is to be expected, Limousin cattle are everywhere. This is an area that provides real satisfaction to those who like exploring unspoilt places where they can be alone amid the vastness of nature. But for those who like a little conventional tourist fun, large reservoirs are nearby. These have beaches, campsites and picnic areas, while sailing and boating should appeal to the nautically minded.

# La Coubre Forest

The Avert Peninsula at the mouth of the Gironde Estuary borders the coast and its tip offers the opportunity to go down to the woods – and shore – without feeling in the least bit crowded. With around 500 sq km (193 sq mi) to explore, La Coubre Forest is a real get-away-from-it-all destination. As with so many things in the modern world, La Coubre Forest is not quite so original as it now appears, having been planted in the 19th century to stabilize a large area of sand dunes. Also, this is a commercial woodland and there are tracts of clear felling awaiting replanting – although compared to the vast presence of the whole, these hardly intrude.

It's possible to drive through the forest and see some worthwhile sights – including Bonne Anse Bay, La Coubre lighthouse, La Bouverie forest lodge and Pointe Espagnol, where a path from the car park leads to a particularly fine beach with far-reaching views that was named for a Spanish vessel wrecked in 1823. For those who like being beside the seaside in a natural environment entirely unspoiled by tourist trappings, La Coubre's sandy Côte Sauvage is a terrific find.

That should be part of any itinerary, but in truth La Coubre deserves to be explored at leisure, on foot or two wheels. The considerable expanse of this light-and-airy pine forest is criss-crossed with established trails. Serious hikers will be tempted by the long-distance path from Royan to Ronce-les-Bains and the island of Oléron, although walkers can roam the forest unchecked. For cyclists who prefer established routes to pedalling at will, there is a cycle track from Saint-Palais-sur-Mer to Ronce-les-Bains, a 60-km (37-mi) round trip that takes in both coast and woodland. There are also marked mountain-bike routes in the forest.

**HOW TO GET THERE:**
The D25 road between Ronce-les-Bains and La Palmyre passes through the middle of the forest, a drive of some 20 km (12 mi).

**WHEN TO GO:**
At any time, although July and August do see plenty of visitors, so those who prefer going alone might prefer the off season.

**DON'T MISS:**
The splendid outlook from the base of the Tour de Gardour, a metal communications tower just off the D25. Follow the arrow sign from the road and park, then take the short footpath and enjoy a breathtaking panorama that takes in the forest, Atlantic Ocean and Gironde Estuary.

**YOU SHOULD KNOW:**
Be aware that certain paths and areas within the forest may be restricted on Thursdays, the day reserved for hunting. Guided walks are offered every day in season (barring Sundays and public holidays), starting at 10.00 from La Bouverie on the Côte Sauvage (take signposted road 44 from the D25).

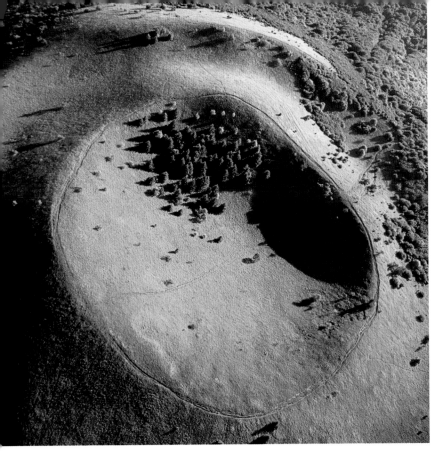

# Chaîne des Puys

A *puy* is a volcanic mountain with a rounded outline. And one of the best places for seeing lots of these shapely domes is the Massif Central's Chaîne des Puys. This run of eight lava domes, 48 cinder cones and 15 maars (volcanic explosion craters) stretches for just 40 km (25 mi) and reaches the high point at the Puy de Dôme towards the middle. This is the highest point in the Auvergne, attracting half a million visitors annually.

There's a regular bus to the summit from Clemont-Ferrand station in summer and there's parking at the lofty visitor centre, but for many the objective is not so much the destination – impressive though that may be – but getting there unaided. This involves ascending an old Roman road, Le sentier des muletiers, or taking the northern path via the Nid de la Poule crater. Cyclists can emulate some famous stage finishes on the Tour de France by using the road during limited periods when it is closed to motor traffic. To be fair, some people aren't that interested in the going up – for numerous paragliders coming down is the high.

If that sounds a bit touristy, the rest of the Chaîne des Puys maintains its unyielding rocky character without any compromise with the modern world. Rocky tops rise above tree-clad flanks, maars have become lonely lakes and occasional isolated farmsteads may be found in the valleys below. Those drawn to wild places can have free rein and it's possible to tramp through this unspoilt mountain landscape for hours without seeing anyone. The Auvergne is an area of great natural beauty where the timeless traditions of rural France are kept alive beneath the watchful gaze of extinct volcanoes, and nowhere is this truer than around the Chaîne des Puys.

*An extinct volcano in the Chaîne des Puys*

**HOW TO GET THERE:**
The Chaîne des Puys is just to the east of Clermont-Ferrand and runs on a north-south axis. Puy de Dôme is just off the A75 road.

**WHEN TO GO:**
Winter to avoid the tourist hordes – and to admire the view of the Chaîne des Puys from the top of Puy de Dôme when there's snow on the ground, which can only be described as breathtaking.

**DON'T MISS:**
It is thought that the summit of the Puy de Dôme has served as a gathering place for special ceremonies since prehistoric times, and the Romans were certainly no exception – be sure to inspect the ruined Gallo-Roman temple built there and dedicated to Mercury.

**YOU SHOULD KNOW:**
When the 6-km (4-mi) road up the Puy de Dôme is too busy in summer motorists are required to park at the foot of the mountain and take a shuttle bus to the summit.

# Massif du Sancy

This ancient stratovolcano in the Auvergne's Puy-de-Dôme department has been inactive for over ten millennia, so it's reasonable to suppose that no eruption is imminent. The Massif du Sancy was created around 250,000 years ago when molten rock exploded through the Earth's crust to spawn a basalt giant. Today, the massif rises majestically from the middle of a plateau and at a soaraway 1,186 m (3,890 ft) takes the crown as the highest mountain in the centre of France – outgunned nationally only by those big guys in the Alps and Pyrenees. Over time it has eroded to a chaotic jumble of steep valleys and spiky needles.

The Massif du Sancy is an imposing sight from afar, a steep-sided monolith crouching along the skyline wearing a white cap of snow long after the surrounding countryside has thawed. Both northern and southern slopes are popular skiing locations, with a number of cable cars and lifts to make the going up easy (although biting winds call for warm clothing, even in summer). Determined mountaineers who prefer doing it the hard way will not be disappointed – some of the routes up the massif's rugged flanks are extremely testing. Despite winter-sports infrastructure, this remains an empty expanse of jumbled rock surrounded by rolling backcountry with fir woods, pastures, rushing streams and waterfalls that echo the mountain's lonely grandeur. The nature of the place may be judged from the evocative names of features such as Hell's Valley and the Devil's Teeth.

The town of Mont-Dore in the valley to the north has a dozen thermal springs known to and enjoyed by the Romans. The restorative waters contain iron, bicarbonate of soda and arsenic, the latter happily in non-lethal concentrations. The park alongside the River Dordogne contains relics of the Roman baths.

**HOW TO GET THERE:**
The nearest big town with an airport is Clermont-Ferrand, from whence a right turn from the southbound A75 onto the D229 at Coudes will morph into the D996 to Mont-Dore. The D203 loops around to the south of the Massif du Sancy.

**WHEN TO GO:**
The climate is severe and the main visitor season for non-winter-sporters is from mid June to mid September, when the autumn foliage is already turning.

**DON'T MISS:**
The truly awesome panoramic view from the Massif du Sancy summit – just reward for those fit enough to beat the meandering yet demanding Puy de Sancy summit trail . . . although lazybones can instead skip up 850 steps to the top from the cable-car station above Le Mont-Dore.

**YOU SHOULD KNOW:**
The valley to the north of the Massif du Sancy contains two streams called the Dore and Dogne that with relentless etymological logic merge to form the River Dordogne.

*The imposing Massif du Sancy*

# Livradois-Forez Regional Nature Park

**HOW TO GET THERE:**
The park is to the east of Clermont-Ferrand and may be reached from the A75 road. The A72 to Thiers crosses the park from west to east and loops down the east side. The park itself has a network of country roads.
**WHEN TO GO:**
Any time
**DON'T MISS:**
An authentic taste of rural France in the welcoming town of Ambert in the centre of the park – the taste in question being that of Fourme d'Ambert, a delicious blue-veined cheese that is the local gastronomic speciality.
**YOU SHOULD KNOW:**
For those debating how to spend their time in the park, an excellent first stop is the visitor centre (Maison du Parc) in Saint-Gervais-sous-Meymont. Those who prefer to view some of the park's scenic charms through eddying steam will leap aboard the heritage steam train complete with observation car that runs (in season) between Courpière in the Puy-de-Dôme department and La Chaise-Dieu in Haute Loire.

They're not big as mountains go, but the Forez Mountains on the borders of Auvergne's Puy-de-Dôme and Haute-Loire departments have pine forests that seem a timeless haven of arboreal tranquillity. Across the Dore river valley is the Livradois, a wooded area of undulating plateau with granite outcrops. Together with gentle hills and slopes around Billom in the west, rolling forested valleys in the southwest and the fringes of the Auvergne's volcanic mountains in the southeast, these contrasting landscapes make up the Livradois-Forez Regional Nature Park, which – in addition to dramatic scenery – is as good a place as any in the land to experience the timeless rhythms of traditional French rural life.

The park has Chateldon and the famous French cutlery capital of Thiers in the north, Ambert and Usson in the middle and Brioude, Lavaudieu and La Chaise-Dieu towards the southern end. But this vast area that stretches from the plains of Limagne to the peaks of the Forez Mountains is essentially a rural backwater dotted with small villages and isolated hamlets. The contrasting terrain gives visitors with limited time available some regional food for thought – there's so much to see that it's hard to decide where to start and what to cram in.

Perhaps the answer is to follow the Route des Métiers – a fascinating circuit that includes castles, ancient monuments, museums and the workshops of craftsmen who still practise country skills passed down over time immemorial in the 21st century. This is not only a great opportunity to appreciate the heritage of this delightful area, but also provides an opportunity to make impulsive diversions into the extensive woodlands, explore river banks, swim in lakes or tramp across unspoilt high moors as the mood dictates. Whatever the choices, this magical nature park rarely disappoints.

# Chartreuse Mountains

**HOW TO GET THERE:**
The mountains fall within a triangle formed by Grenoble, Chambéry and (at a distance) Lyon. The A41 road from Grenoble to Chambéry runs along the eastern flank of the Chartreuses, the A43 Chambéry to Lyon road crosses to the north and the A48 Grenoble to Lyon road provides access to the southwest. There is a network of minor roads within the mountains.

Eastern France's Chartreuse Mountains stretch down from the Lac du Bourget towards Grenoble. They are 45 km (28 mi) long and 25 km (15 mi) wide, forming the most southerly extension of the Jura Mountains and containing many impressive peaks. This limestone range is riddled with underground passages and caves, including the famous *Dent de Crolles* system that extends to an impressive 60 km (37 mi) in length. Above ground, the mountainous terrain makes a great backdrop for a few centres that cater for skiers, although the undeveloped Chartreuse Mountains serve mainly as a magnet for climbers and summer hikers.

They follow in illustrious footsteps. These wild and beautiful uplands were a regular calling point on 18th-century grand tours and subsequently attracted such artistic luminaries as painter J W M Turner and poet William Wordsworth. The mountains remain wild and beautiful, as confirmed by Regional Nature Park status awarded for scenic excellence and interesting cultural heritage. The eastern flanks fall abruptly into the Isère Valley, while the western slopes fall away more gently towards the Rhône Valley. The high ground consists of peaks and valleys. The tallest peak is Chamechaude at 2,082 m (6,831 ft), with other notable summits including Grand Som and Mont Granier.

The internal valleys have small rural communities supported by pastoral farming and sustainable forestry. These little settlements have distinctive vernacular architecture. Square houses sit beneath steeply pitched tile roofs, while shingle-roofed barns with massive cornerstones are constructed with irregular reddish stone. From the inhabited valleys wooded slopes rise to dramatic cliffs, above which the fit and determined hiker will find a magical world of high plateaus and secret valleys covered in grassland and stunted vegetation, beneath those impressive peaks. As wild places go, the Chartreuse Mountains are pretty special.

**WHEN TO GO:**
Summer is best for the backcountry walking, winter for slippery sports centred on Chamechaude.
**DON'T MISS:**
Le Fort du St Eynard, a well-restored 19th-century fortress just south of Le Sappey-en-Chartreuse, perched on a cliff top overlooking Grenoble. The fort is interesting, the views are magnificent and may be enjoyed during some excellent short walks.
**YOU SHOULD KNOW:**
Yes, the famous liqueur is made hereabouts, in the town of Voiron. It consists of distilled alcohol blended with an (inevitably secret) infusion of 130 herbal extracts that improves with age in the bottle. Originally created by monks at the Grand Chartreuse Monastery in the 18th century, revenue generated still helps to support the Carthusian order to this day.

*The superb view from Charmant Som*

# Plateau du Vercors

**HOW TO GET THERE:**
The Plateau du Vercors is east of the
Rhône Valley, standing tall between
the valleys of the Drôme and Isère
Rivers to the southwest of Grenoble.
The Nature Park may be tackled from
any of the surrounding towns –
Grenoble, Romans, Valence and Die.
There is no access from the east
between Grenoble and the
Rousset Pass.

**WHEN TO GO:**
Spring (after the snow melt), summer
and autumn for the hiking and
sightseeing, winter for cross-country
and downhill skiing

**DON'T MISS:**
The extraordinary village of
Pont-en-Royans with its houses
overhanging the River Bourne, and
nearby Saint-Nazaire-en-Royans
beneath a 19th-century aqueduct
that still operates.

The Vercors is a series of plateaux and mountains in the Isère and
Drôme departments, surrounded by vertical limestone cliffs and
divided by deep canyons. This remote and lonely place was the
scene of fierce fighting between German troops and French
Resistance *maquisards* during World War II, as the Maquis de
Vercors group gallantly rose to tie up enemy forces that would
otherwise have been available to counter the D-Day landings in June
1944. The doomed uprising is commemorated by a memorial and
cemetery at the village of Vassieux-en-Vercors in the heart of the
massif, where it all began.

Today's visitor can easily understand why this place was ideal for
resisting the German conquerors (and collaborating French Militia)
during the war. Today, the Vercors massif is a picturesque Regional
Nature Park. But those daunting cliffs and broken terrain remain
the same, explaining why it took 10,000 German soldiers delivered
by glider and parachute to defeat 4,000 guerrilla fighters operating
in territory perfect for ambush and evasion.

The Vercors has distinct sectors. These are the heavily forested Coulmes area in the northwest, the northern plateau nicknamed 'The Four Mountains' for obvious reasons, small western plateaus with their high summer pastures and deep gorges, plus the high plateaus that are the wildest and most remote part of the park. Such contrasting areas give the Plateau du Vercors enormous visual variety, but all of it is impressive. The massif is popular with get-away-from-it-all hikers and there are many signed and well-maintained trails. Many caverns can be explored without special equipment (or undue risk), while paragliding and white-water canoeing are other possibilities. Happily for the action-averse, sightseeing from the relative safety of a car offers breathtaking vistas from some of the most vertiginous roads in France (try the likes of the D76, D518 and D22 through precipitous gorges).

*A lone hiker on the northern ridge of Mount Jocou walks towards the Col de Seysse with views of the Plateau du Vercors beyond.*

# Dourbie Valley

The stunning grandeur of the three Tarn gorges takes the breath away, and of these natural masterpieces the Dourbie Valley is the most picturesque. Its wild slopes are wooded or covered with sparse vegetation at higher levels where the bare rock breaks through, and the stunning array of wild flowers has to be seen to be believed. The smallish but perfectly formed River Dourbie winds down this green valley from its source near Le Vigan in the Cévennes Mountains to join the Tarn at Millau.

The upper valley narrows into two spectacular granite and schist gorges that are 300 m (985 ft) deep. In the Cévennes foothills the river flows through the lush 'Garden of Aveyron', a peaceful green oasis where the charming villages of Nant and Saint Jean de Bruel are located. The Dourbie then begins its home run to the Tarn, snaking between the Causse Noir and Causse du Larzac down an austere yet grandiose valley.

Favoured leisure activities in the Dourbie Valley are rock climbing, white-water canoeing or rafting, birdwatching, horse riding, cycling, strolling beside this lovely river, enjoying some of the best trout fishing in France or hiking up to the limestone plateaus above to find solitude beneath a big sky populated with lazily circling vultures. For some, the scenery ensures that simple sightseeing is enough. In addition to its scenic qualities, the Dourbie Valley has quaint stone-built villages like La Roque-St-Marguerite with its 11th-century church and mill, located near the river below Montpellier-le-Vieux, an impressive labyrinth of rock that simply must be explored. It appears almost man made but was carved by water. The village also has impressive Montcalm Castle. Other medieval villages like Saint Véran and Cantobre cling to the cliffside with stunning views down the valley.

*The Gorges de la Dourbie and the mill (Moulin de Corps) by the river's edge*

**HOW TO GET THERE:**
The Dourbie Valley is accessible from the A75 at Millau, with the D991 actually going up the valley to La Roque-St-Marguerite, Saint Véran, Saint-Sauveur and Nant.

**WHEN TO GO:**
Any time (the winter valley looks great beneath a covering of snow, with not so much as a solitary tourist to be seen).

**DON'T MISS:**
A jar (or two) of the local honey to take home. Made by bees that forage among the Dourbie Valley's pollen-laden expanses of wild flowers, it is said (admittedly by the locals) to be the tastiest in all France.

**YOU SHOULD KNOW:**
Millau's famous Tarn Valley viaduct is the world's highest bridge. Its tallest mast is higher than the Eiffel Tower and falls just short of New York's Empire State Building. This cable-stayed road bridge was designed by Sir Norman Foster.

# Cévennes National Park

Created in 1970, the spectacular Cévennes National Park in the Languedoc-Roussillon region stretches across the departments of Lozère, Gard and Ardèche. Its importance is reflected in a UNESCO World Biosphere Reserve classification. One of the park's objectives is to promote tourism, but happily only the sustainable sort that does not damage this precious landscape of mountains, *causses* (limestone plateaus), deep valleys, forests and alpine meadows. The park has three eco-centres and attracts over 800,000 visitors every year, but this is still a place where it's possible to escape into the vastness of the Cévennes Mountains and enjoy peaceful solitude amid awe-inspiring natural beauty.

Elevations within the park vary from 380 m (1,250 ft) to 1,700 m (5,600 ft) and the climate varies from the continental north to the maritime south. Coupled with differing soil types this ensures an extraordinary variety of flora, with over 2,250 species. Notable among them are huge plantations of chestnut trees and the carnivorous sundew plant, while both alpine and subtropical species may also be found. Animal and bird life is equally diverse, with nearly 2,500 different creatures recorded. Animals such as deer, wild boar, mouflon (wild sheep with large curved horns), beaver and otter roam free, while more visible birds include vultures, woodpeckers and grouse.

There is a network of established trails that extends to 1,800 km (1,120 mi), many designed to be sufficiently user-friendly to encourage visits by families with children. But the park also has more *Grande Routes* (GR long-distance walking paths) than any other French national park, plus bridlepaths, cycleways and winter cross-country skiing routes. There are a large number of *gîtes d'escape* (simple refuges) and rural *gîtes* available in the park for those who want to spend time in this haven of natural tranquillity.

**HOW TO GET THERE:**
The A75 road skirts the park's western side and the N106 runs from Nîmes to Alès, a great starting point from which to start exploring the park.
**WHEN TO GO:**
Any time (take skis or snowshoes in winter).
**DON'T MISS:**
Nobody should visit Cévennes National Park without taking in Aven Armand, north of Meyruis off the D986 road. Discovered at the end of the 19th century on the Méjan Causse by one Louis Armand, this amazing limestone cavern is a fairyland of stalagmites, including the world's largest known example at 30 m (100 ft) tall. Bold visitors can descend a natural shaft on a rope, following the route used by Louis Armand, although most will prefer to use the lift.
**YOU SHOULD KNOW:**
Camping is not allowed in the central area, nor are camper vans or caravans. Visitors' cars, motorbikes or bicycles are not permitted to go off road anywhere in Cévennes National Park, which remains dedicated to preserving the peaceful, unspoilt character of this beautiful area.

*Vultures perch on limestone rocks in the Cévennes National Park.*

# Cirques de Gavarnie and d'Estaubé

**HOW TO GET THERE:**
This is not one for casual sightseers – the natural glories of Cirque de Gavarnie can only be enjoyed after a two-hour uphill tramp from the small mountain village of Gavarnie, close to the Spanish border in the Hautes-Pyrenees. Cirque d'Estaubé calls for a demanding hike via the Gave d'Estaubé (from the D176 south of Luz-Saint-Sauveur).
**WHEN TO GO:**
Summertime, when the going is (relatively) easy and the weather is (usually) in clement mood.

*The stunning Cirque de Gavarnie*

The Pyrenees has rugged mountainscapes aplenty, but two adjoining features that should not be missed are the Cirque de Gavarnie and the Cirque d'Estaubé. In this context a *cirque* (circus) is a valley-head formed like an amphitheatre, open on the downhill side to form a flatter area corresponding to a stage with the valley falling away behind. The upper part of the bowl is a steeper section that might represent the sloping seating area.

The Cirque de Gavarnie is a famous example of the feature. It is around 800 m (2,625 ft) across at the low point and 3,000 m (9,840 ft) wide at the top. It has an impressive natural gap in the surrounding steep cliffs called Le Brèche de Roland. Legend has it that this jagged aperture was cut by Charlemagne's nephew, Count Roland, following his defeat by the Saracens in a nearby battle, as

he unsuccessfully attempted to destroy the legendary sword Durendal to prevent it falling into infidel hands. It's a good story, showing at the very least that memories in these parts are long. The Cirque de Gavarnie also boasts France's highest waterfall, the Grand Cascade de Gavarnie, a tiered falls down a rugged cliff face with a drop of 422 m (1,385 ft). This awesome natural bowl is far from human habitation and ranks as a scenic masterpiece.

The Cirque d'Estaubé is another 4 km (2.5 mi) to the east. It is neither as well known nor quite so spectacular, but this secret grassy enclave amidst encircling mountains is well worth the effort required to get there, although this is really one for serious mountain walkers who are equipped with all-weather clothing and for whom the destination is less important than the journey.

**DON'T MISS:**
A *cirque* hat trick – add the tranquil Cirque de Troumouse to the other pair and admire its amazing curved rock wall that's 10 km (6 mi) long and 1,000 m (3,280 ft) tall. It is not far from the Cirque d'Estaubé and the nearest road is the D922.

**YOU SHOULD KNOW:**
The two *cirques* fall within the Pyrenees National Park on the Franco-Spanish border, an unspoiled mountainous landscape without fences or walls where animals roam free and biodiversity is maintained. The park is home to 70 species of animal and has a wide variety of flora.

# Orlu Nature Reserve

The Ariege Department to the south of Toulouse is little known outside France. The land rises to the high Pyrenees and is steeped in history, as the ruins of numerous romantic Cathar castles atop their rocky outcrops testify. One little gem tucked away in the dramatic mountain landscape of southeastern Ariege is Orlu Nature Reserve. This 40-sq-km (15-sq-mi) chunk of mountain terrain rises from 930 m (3,050 ft) to 2,765 m (9,070 ft) and is sufficiently demanding to ensure that – despite its relatively small size amidst the general grandeur of the surrounding Pyrenees – the determined explorer must still put in a real effort to appreciate everything this special wild place has to offer.

The expedition can start with a quick visit to the museum at the bottom of the reserve, to discover the rationale behind its status as a national hunting reserve – a rarity in a country where anything that moves is likely to end up in the pot. Rangers ensure that the wildlife is protected, scientists study it and intrepid members of the public watch it. Orlu requires the donning of stout shoes and walking. There is an easy hike in the Gaudu Valley and a more demanding three-hour climb to a sanctuary in the middle of the reserve where it's possible to stay overnight.

Orlu Nature Reserve is a place of lush alpine wildflower meadows and forest, tumbled rocks and rushing water. The Oriege cascades down the Orlu Gorge, a splendid mountain torrent that attracts white-water canoeists. There is also an aerial adventure course with zip lines and tree climbing, but this place is really about easily observable wildlife. The stars are chamois and marmots. Birds include vultures, capercaille and ptarmigan.

**HOW TO GET THERE:**
The reserve is near Ax-les-Thermes, on the E09-N20 road between Tarascon-sur-Ariège and Hospitalet près l'Andorre.

**WHEN TO GO:**
Any time (there are four skiing stations for winter-sports enthusiasts).

**DON'T MISS:**
A side trip to Andorra, as one of over ten million annual visitors to this beguiling mountain principality who take full advantage of its duty-free status and enjoy the scenery, usually in that order. Andorra has a joint monarchy, the duties bizarrely being shared by the President of the French Republic and the Bishop of Urgell in Catalonia – not many people know that.

**YOU SHOULD KNOW:**
In the Orlu Valley beneath the Baxouillade peak rumour has it that a Roman gold mine is waiting to be found, although a determined search in the 19th century failed to unearth it. Legend suggests a rich seam is there somewhere, because a long-ago Count of Carcassonne knew the secret and used the bounty to fund the building of his city walls.

# Gorges de Spelunca

**HOW TO GET THERE:**
By road from Porto, or by foot from Evisa or Ota.
**WHEN TO GO:**
Any time of year, but the best time is between April and November.
**DON'T MISS:**
The Forêt d'Aitone National Park, just to the west of Evisa.
**YOU SHOULD KNOW:**
Corsica is renowned for its food and its forests are home to many wild boar. Try the wild boar ham, smoked sausages and stews.

Some 30 km (19 mi) south of Calvi – a popular destination on Corsica's northwest coast – and a short distance inland from the beautiful little resort of Porto, a UNESCO World Heritage Site, is the Gorges de Spelunca.

Set between the mountain villages of Ota and Evisa, this 2-km (1.2-mi) long canyon cuts between the two, its steep, red, granite walls plunging down to the eponymous river below. The gorge is one of Corsica's famous natural sites and it is possible to walk or hike there all year round. Although there are excellent views of much of the gorge from the road, it is more rewarding to make for the mountains, where there is shade and the air is fresh and clean.

Although the gorge is accessible from both villages, most people start from the cemetery just outside Evisa. The descent, at first quite gentle, becomes steeper lower down. The trail leads through shady woods, passing wind-scoured rock pinnacles and bare rock faces to the bottom of the valley and the elegant old Genoese stone bridge, Pont de Zaglia – one of two here. The track through the gorge was once an important communications link, enabling heavily laden mules to be sent from Porto into the mountain villages. Today, the path has been restored using original stones, but it can often feel more like jumping than walking.

Children will also enjoy the gorge, although it will be too strenuous for very little ones. Curiously shaped tiers of boulders, sometimes with one balanced, apparently precariously, on top of another, lead to mini waterfalls and several natural bathing pools. Keep an eye open for the Corsican salamander – this is a great place to see one.

# West Frisian Islands

Germany and the Netherlands share the North Sea's Frisian Islands, with Holland having the best of the deal – it has 14 West Frisians (five inhabited) as opposed to Germany's 12 East Frisians (seven inhabited). In truth, most of the uninhabited Frisians are little more than shifting sandbars that barely stay above water at high tide and even the populated ones are sparsely settled. They are barrier islands, sheltering the shallow Waddenzee from the North Sea proper.

Starting in the west, the largest and best-populated island is Texel. A third of Texel is a nature reserve. The landscape of sand dunes has a network of cycle paths that encourage two-wheeled exploration. Next along is Vlieland, with one major settlement at Oost-Vlieland. Again, dunes are the predominant feature, leavened by meadows and woods. Historic Terschelling is notable for (surprisingly) cranberries. Inhabitants have long used bounty brought by the sea to build eccentric houses and barns, and a barrel of cranberries was washed ashore in 1840. The canny islanders planted them, they thrived and today bakeries and restaurants vie to offer the best cranberry delicacies. Ameland has just four small villages and consists mostly of dunes, but nonetheless has extraordinary biodiversity. Tiny Schiermonnikoog – heavily fortified by the Germans in World War II – hosts Holland's first nature reserve. Small and flat, it nonetheless attracts huge numbers of summer visitors, including many day-trippers.

Island-hopping ferries offer tickets that allow visitors to go at their own pace and check out inhabited islands in turn. This is ideal for hikers and – this is two-wheel-savvy Holland – the many touring cyclists. The West Frisians, particularly outside summer's high season, are wonderfully atmospheric wild places for those who love challenging the elements surrounded by big skies, lonely dunes and restless sea.

**HOW TO GET THERE:**
The islands can easily be reached from Amsterdam by car and ferry from Den Helder. The more easterly islands can be accessed from Harlingen or Holward on the mainland, but Vlieland and Schiermonnikoog do not allow visitors to bring their cars. The latter is served by regular ferries from Lauwersoog.

**WHEN TO GO:**
Any time. Winter can be very bleak, but promises dramatic solitude in return for defying the angry marine elements.

**DON'T MISS:**
The ten-day Oerol Festival on the island of Terschelling. It takes place in mid June and the whole island becomes a stage for the arts, with theatre, music and visual arts put on in the unlikeliest of places - barns, boathouses, meadows, dunes - as well as utilizing the two purpose-built main stages. Tickets are sold as 'passports' allowing people onto the island for all or part of the week and tens of thousands attend this unique event.

**YOU SHOULD KNOW:**
The uninhabited islands of Griend, Rottumerplaat and Rottumeroog are nature reserves that may only be visited if a permit is obtained in advance. However, one 'island' can be visited without going afloat - Wieringen became joined to the mainland after reclamation work in the 1930s.

*A windmill at sunrise on the island of Texel*

# Amrum Island

Amrum is the smallest of the North Frisian group of islands which lie in the North Sea off the west coast of Germany. It is also the least commercialized and offers a very different experience from its lively and sophisticated neighbour Sylt. Amrum is a place to come to unwind and allow your biological clock to slow down to a gentler and simpler rhythm of life. At little more than 20 km (12 mi) long and never wider than a couple of kilometres (just over a mile), the island can be cycled in a few hours and even walked around inside a day. Considering its size Amrum contains a remarkable variety of habitats, including pine forests, heathland and marshes. Its crowning glory, though, and what draws people back to the island year after year, is the Kniepsand, a huge expanse of fine white sand extending for 12 km (7.5 mi) down the entire western side of the island. If you grow tired of the fantastic beaches, the large patchwork of dunes behind await exploration. These cover almost half the area of the island, with some rising to as much as 32 m (105 ft) above sea level.

A single road runs down the spine of the island, linking its five villages. There is a good walk from the lighthouse at Wittdün in the south (the tallest on Germany's coast) through dunes and forests to Norddorf. On the way it is well worth stopping to admire the traditional Frisian houses in the pretty village of Nebel, as well as its well-preserved windmill. A more unusual walk – and one you should only undertake with a local guide – allows you to cross the Wadden Sea at low tide to the island of Föhr.

*An aerial view of
Amrum Island*

# Jasmund National Park

Rügen is a popular holiday island just off Germany's Baltic coast, famous for its fine sandy beaches and rugged coastline. In the 19th century the already fashionable resorts here used to attract the elite of Prussian society during the warm summer months. Writers and artists were also drawn to the island's natural beauty, especially the great German Romantic painter Caspar David Friedrich, who was born in the nearby town of Greifswald. His canvases of Rügen's splendid white chalk cliffs have become not only the island's defining image but also a key icon of European landscape art.

Friedrich was a regular visitor to Rügen and his favourite spot on the island was an area at the end of the Jasmund Peninsula – the Stubbenkammer – from which there are outstanding views of the chalk cliffs stretching south.

This coastline, extending some 10 km (6 mi) to Sassnitz, is now protected as a national park. The cliffs here are the highest sea cliffs in Germany and demonstrate vividly the effects of coastal erosion. The highest of all is the Königsstuhl (king's seat) which plunges 118 m (387 ft) into the emerald-green sea. It is a popular viewpoint, although for a view of the cliff itself you need to head a few hundred metres further along the coast to the Victoriasicht viewpoint. A superb cliff-top walk takes in the entire coastline between the Königsstuhl and Sassnitz, including the craggy Wissower Klinken cliffs.

Although a small park, Jasmund also has fine examples of marsh, wetland and mixed broadleaf woodland; its other claim to fame is the Stubnitz forest of ancient oak and beech trees, some of which are over 700 years old.

*The stunning chalk cliffs of Jasmund National Park*

**HOW TO GET THERE:**
Sassnitz is well connected to the road and rail network. In summer you must leave your car at Hagen and take the shuttle bus or walk the remaining 3 km (2 mi) if you are visiting the Königsstuhl.
**WHEN TO GO:**
April to October
**DON'T MISS:**
A ride on the Rasender Roland narrow-gauge steam train which runs between Putbus and Göhren.
**YOU SHOULD KNOW:**
Jasmund gets very busy in the holiday season.

299

# Harz National Park

Rising above the North German Plain, the Harz Mountains cover an area 100 km (62 mi) by 30 km (19 mi) which straddles the border that once divided the country into East and West Germany. In 2006 the Nationalpark Harz was created out of the amalgamation of two former parks on either side of the old border. The new park protects 158 sq km (61 sq mi) of mountainous granite terrain, much of it covered in dense forests, but there are also areas of high moorland and hidden valleys where birdsong and the babbling of crystal-clear streams are the only sounds you will hear.

At the heart of the national park stands the Brocken, at 1,142 m (3,747 ft) the highest point in the Harz range. You can trek to the top or else take the delightful narrow-gauge steam railway; as it puffs and wheezes its way up the steep gradient you may wonder at times

*Hiking on the Brocken*

whether it is going to make it, but these plucky little engines have been making this journey successfully for well over 100 years. The Brocken itself is steeped in legend and the mists that often shroud the summit serve only to enhance the air of mystery. It is the legendary site of the great witches' gathering on the pagan festival of Walpurgisnacht; lively celebrations in the local towns and villages take place on the night in question (April 30), when lots of locals dress up as – you've guessed – witches and devils.

With some 8,000 km (5,000 mi) of walking trails the Harz National Park is a well-established area for hiking enthusiasts, offering everything from leisurely strolls around beauty spots to long-distance routes such as the Kaiserweg (Imperial Way) and the Hexensteig (Witches' Way) which runs east-west across the entire park.

**DON'T MISS:**
The Grüne Band (Green Line), a 75-km (47-mi) walking trail which follows the line of the old Iron Curtain border.

**YOU SHOULD KNOW:**
Goethe used the Brocken as the setting for the Walpurgisnacht scene in his great drama *Faust*. More prosaically, the Soviet Union used it as an observation post during the Cold War.

# Spreewald

Journey little more than an hour from the centre of Berlin and you could be on a different planet. The Spreewald in the southeast of the state of Brandenburg is one of Germany's most surprising landscapes. This extensive network of rivers, streams and canals was formed when mineral deposits during the Ice Age created natural barriers that forced the River Spree to divert its course and split into a multitude of channels. The resulting marshes and wetlands, with their numerous small lakes and sandy islands, constitute an important ecosystem rare in central Europe; it was duly recognized as such when in 1990 UNESCO declared the region a biosphere reserve.

The Spreewald has over 400 km (250 mi) of idyllic green waterways, many of which are navigable. You can explore them yourself in a canoe or kayak, or else take a trip in a characteristic flat-bottomed boat and enjoy the local knowledge and anecdotes dispensed by your ferryman as he propels you gently along with his pole. These punts are an integral part of a traditional way of life here; in the summer months the post is still delivered by boat to the outlying villages! The wetlands are a haven for water birds and you should have no difficulty spotting many different species, especially at either end of the day.

Another factor which makes the Spreewald such a distinctive place is that it is the historic home of Germany's only indigenous minority, the Sorbs. At festivals and on special days you can still see them in their traditional costumes. The open-air museum at Lehde has fine examples of old Sorbian thatched houses and farm buildings.

**HOW TO GET THERE:**
The twin towns of Lübben and Lübbenau in the heart of the Spreewald are one hour by train from Berlin.

**WHEN TO GO:**
April to October

**DON'T MISS:**
With no hills and a well-developed network of trails running alongside the streams and canals this is a great cycling area for family outings.

**YOU SHOULD KNOW:**
The Spreewald is famous throughout the country for its flavoursome gherkins.

# Lower Oder Valley

The Oder is a name which resonates in postwar European history. The river has formed a significant frontier for hundreds of years and currently marks the border between Germany and Poland. Flowing into the Baltic Sea by Szczecin in Poland, the Oder possesses one of the few delta regions in Europe that have remained largely undisturbed by human interference. A cross-border reserve has been created in its lower reaches to protect and preserve this exceptional environment. The greater part, 105 sq km (40 sq mi), is on the German side where it is known as the Lower Oder Valley National Park. The park covers a 60-km (37-mi) stretch of the River Oder with idyllic riverbank scenery, water meadows, marshes, mixed riparian forests and dry grassland on the surrounding hillsides.

The biodiversity of this relatively compact area is outstanding in Europe. The floodplain is a breeding ground for over 120 kinds of birds, including several endangered species such as the black stork and the sea eagle. Conservation methods have become more radical in recent years and large parts of the park are now completely off-limits to human activity. Even so, the Lower Oder Valley remains a Mecca for serious birdwatchers who are able to get close to the wildlife on foot, on bicycle or by canoe along the riverbank. The visitor centre in the village of Criewen has lots of useful information and is a good starting-point for tours of the park. A recommended day walk is the 14-km (9-mi) circuit of the polder at Schwedt; walking on the raised dyke gives you a good vantage-point for spotting birdlife. Serious cyclists can also do a round trip up and down the two riverbanks (passport needed for the Polish section).

# Saxon Switzerland

Many parts of Europe have had the 'Swiss' epithet applied to them by virtue of their putative resemblance to that country's alpine scenery, although few live up to the grandeur of the real thing. One that does is the region known as Sächsische Schweiz, or Saxon Switzerland, which occupies the land between Dresden and the border with the Czech Republic. It may not boast the snow-covered peaks of its namesake, but Saxon Switzerland possesses drama of a different kind. Soaring sandstone cliffs, canyon-like gorges and flat-topped mountains combine to create a landscape like no other in Germany.

The area, which is also known as the Elbsandsteingebirge (Elbe Sandstone Mountains), owes its existence to the mighty River Elbe which has here carved a tortuous path through the Lusatian Mountains. It is well known for the extraordinary sandstone and basalt rock formations which crop up everywhere, the result of erosion by wind and water. Tall columns with weird shapes and names like Barbarine and the Pillars of Hercules are popular among rock-climbers, but you do not have to go to such lengths yourself to get a buzz from this landscape. It is a paradise for children who love venturing into the myriad gullies and clefts and scrambling up the gentler rock faces. Climb to the top of a sandstone plateau like the Pfaffenstein or the Lilienstein and you are rewarded with magnificent panoramic views of the Elbe valley and the surrounding countryside. The ruins of a medieval fortress are an additional attraction on top of the Bastei rocks which tower 305 m (1,000 ft) above the open fields and rolling hills. An alternative and less strenuous way of appreciating the scenery is on one of the lovely old paddle steamers which ply the Elbe between Dresden and Schmilka.

*Bastei Bridge and the Lilienstein Plateau in Saxon Switzerland*

# Kellerwald-Edersee National Park

**HOW TO GET THERE:**
Kellerwald-Edersee is 30 minutes'
drive southwest of Kassel. The
nearest rail stations are Bad
Wildungen and Frankenberg.
**WHEN TO GO:**
Any time of year
**DON'T MISS:**
Look out for the pretty Cheddar pink
flower, also known as firewitch,
which grows in the cracks of rock
faces around the Edersee.
**YOU SHOULD KNOW:**
The Kellerwald is one of the last
remaining habitats in central Europe
of the wild cat and the eagle owl.

Once upon a time much of central Europe was covered in beech forests but the inevitable pressures of human settlement and exploitation have led to their steady decline, with the result that today they are found only in isolated pockets. The largest such pocket is in the north of the state of Hesse in the so-called 'green heart' of Germany. Such is its importance as a habitat that in 2004 the Kellerwald-Edersee National Park was established to preserve it for future generations. The broad swathe of ancient, gnarled beech trees which makes up the Kellerwald – many several hundred years old – owes its survival to having been a hunting ground for the local nobility in centuries past, which protected it from logging and other forms of exploitation. The majestic red deer is still a common sight in the park but thankfully is no longer hunted.

The beech may be the dominant tree here but it does allow other deciduous species to make an occasional appearance, such as large-leaved limes, ancient oaks and the ash and mountain elms found in the damp gullies which proliferate throughout the park. Numerous nature trails take you along crystal-clear streams, past rock and boulder fields (relics of the last Ice Age) and over meadows covered in wild flowers. The northern boundary of the park is marked by the Edersee, an artificial lake formed by a dam which offers all kinds of water-based activities. A 70-km (43-mi) walking trail takes you right around the lake, while the Kellerwaldsteig is twice as long and links up with the adjacent nature park to the south.

*Kellerwald-Edersee National Park – the 'green heart' of Germany*

# Hainich National Park

Covering an area of 160 sq km (62 sq mi), Hainich Forest is the largest unbroken expanse of mixed deciduous woodland in Germany. In 1997 the southern half of this western Thuringian forest became a national park and a visitor infrastructure was created to promote exploration of the beautiful beech and oak woods. Hainich was formerly part the GDR (East Germany); situated close to the once-sensitive border with West Germany, it was used formerly as a military training area and was off-limits to visitors. There are not many reasons to remember with affection that period of the country's history when Germany was a divided nation, but in this case it meant that Hainich, in common with other rural areas along the heavily fortified border, was for many years spared the pressures of mass tourism. Nowadays it is a delightfully green and peaceful place to visit, with plenty of walking opportunities. One of the more unusual is a high-level walkway near the park's visitor centre at Thiemsburg which takes you through the tree-tops to an observation tower in the heart of the forest, 44 m (144 ft) above the ground. Children will appreciate the different perspective on the forest, as they will the 'Wild Cat Children's Forest', an adventure playground fashioned out of fallen trees and natural materials.

Hainich National Park is in the northwestern corner of the Thüringerwald (the Thuringian Forest), an area of thickly wooded hills and picturesque valleys which was once a favoured haunt of artists of the German Romantic movement. The unhurried lifestyle and relative lack of commercialism which once attracted them still prevail, although the region has sadly suffered significant environmental damage from decades of unchecked industrial pollution during the GDR era.

**HOW TO GET THERE:**
The historic town of Eisenach, on the main east-west A4 motorway to the south, is the best base for visits to the park.
**WHEN TO GO:**
Any time of year. Spring and autumn are particularly good times to visit for, respectively, the wild flowers and the changing tree colours.
**DON'T MISS:**
Eisenach is the birthplace of Bach and the site of Germany's greatest medieval castle, the Wartburg.
**YOU SHOULD KNOW:**
One of the country's best long-distance trails, the Rennsteig, starts outside Eisenach and runs for 168 km (104 mi) through the Thuringian Forest to Blankenstein on the Saale River.

# Wutach Gorge

The 'Grand Canyon of the Black Forest', as it is sometimes billed in the tourist brochures, may be overdoing it a tad, but the Wutach Gorge is an undeniably impressive sight, the more so for being so unexpected in this part of the continent. The River Wutach rises on the Feldberg, the highest point of the Black Forest, and flows east and south before joining the Rhine near Waldshut. This is the far southwest of Germany, close to the Swiss border and to the European Watershed – the line dividing the basins of the country's two great rivers, the Danube and the Rhine. At one time the Wutach was a tributary of the Danube but geologists have yet to solve the puzzle of what caused the river to change its course by 90 degrees in favour of the Rhine.

Outside the small town of Bonndorf the Wutach River has punched its way through the Black Forest rocks to create a spectacular ravine with jagged, near-vertical cliffs which soar skywards and keep the valley in shadow for large parts of the day. The damp, shady conditions have generated a microclimate where unusual plants grow. Well over 1,000 types of wild flower have

*The River Wutach flows through the Black Forest.*

**HOW TO GET THERE:**
There is a good local bus network which offers special passes for exploring the area. The Wutach Gorge is 80 km (50 mi) east of the Rhine motorway linking Basel and Frankfurt. The nearest railway station is Seebrugg, 10 km (6 mi) to the west.

been recorded in this astonishingly fertile environment, which in turn attracts rare birds such as the grey egret and a glorious variety of butterflies and insects. The best way to appreciate this remarkable landscape is to hike the length of the gorge.

The trail runs beside the river between the Schattenmühle and the Wutachmühle. It is 13 km (8 mi) long and takes between four-and-a-half and five hours. It is part of the much longer 118-km (74-mi) path, the Schluchtensteig (Gorge Way), which links the towns of Wehr and Stühlingen.

**WHEN TO GO:**
Any time of year (bring warm clothes as it can be cool in the gorge).
**DON'T MISS:**
If you want somewhere even wilder and more remote, the detour on the gorge trail to the Lotenbach Glen is definitely worth tackling.
**YOU SHOULD KNOW:**
You should take special care on the paths, which are steep in places and tend to be wet and slippery.

# Swabian-Franconian Forest Nature Park

Germany can boast a huge variety of scenery within its borders. While the wooded hills of northeast Baden-Württemberg may not be among the star offerings, they do come as close as any other to presenting what for many is the archetypal German landscape – a mosaic of forests, valleys, fields, gentle uplands, water meadows and pastures where sheep and cattle graze.

Much of this area is now contained within the Naturpark Schwäbisch-Fränkischer Wald. Covering 900 sq km (347 sq mi), the Swabian-Franconian Nature Park gets its name from the fact that it straddles the historical frontier between the medieval duchies of Swabia and Franconia. The border itself ran along the ridge above the valley of the Murr River which more or less cuts the park in two on an east-west course to join the Neckar near Marbach.

The park provides a good example of a reasonably harmonious co-existence between man and nature which has lasted hundreds of years. It is lovely country for walking and cycling excursions and there are any number of marked trails leading you to hidden valleys, viewpoints and peaceful lakes in the woods where a refreshing dip can be very welcome on a hot summer's day. On your wanderings through the spruce and beech forests look out for signs of the *Limes* (pronounced 'lee-mays') – the frontier which for 250 years marked the northern limit of the Roman Empire in central Europe. Unlike Hadrian's Wall, the *Limes* was a timber-and-earthwork fortification and you can still find good traces of the ditch and earth rampart in many places; the foundations of some of the stone watch-towers are also still visible. A walking trail with information panels enables you to follow the course of the *Limes* right across the park.

**HOW TO GET THERE:**
The park headquarters and visitor centre is at Murrhardt, 45 km (28 mi) northeast of Stuttgart.
**WHEN TO GO:**
April to October
**DON'T MISS:**
The archaeological park near Welzheim, which includes a full-scale reconstruction of a twin-towered gateway to a Roman fort.
**YOU SHOULD KNOW:**
In a pioneering venture, the nature park currently offers GPS satellite navigation to its walkers and cyclists.

# Bavarian Forest

Along with the Bohemian Forest across the border in the Czech Republic, the Bavarian Forest (Bayerischer Wald) forms the largest continuous area of woodland in Europe. It covers most of the land between the north bank of the Danube and the Czech border, an area of some 6,000 sq km (2,317 sq mi) on a southeast axis extending from Regensburg to Passau. For a country as heavily populated and highly developed as Germany the Bavarian Forest is a surprisingly wild and unspoilt region and it is certainly a place to come if you want to fill your lungs with green and fresh air. These uplands, which in parts rise to nearly 1,500 m (4,920 ft), are covered almost entirely in dense forest – largely spruce, but beech, oak and pine also feature. Here you can see ancient trees that have grown to gigantic proportions, some as high as 50 m (164 ft) and with girths of 2 m (6.5 ft) and more. Their enormous scale certainly enhances the sense of this being a primeval wilderness.

Although mostly wooded, the Bavarian Forest also has lakes, mountain streams, pastures and areas of high moorland. The landscape is dotted with isolated little villages and farming

*A pair of European lynx*

308

communities. At its southern end is Germany's first national park, also called the Bavarian Forest, which in 2010 celebrated its 40th anniversary. Together with the ?umava National Park in the Czech Republic, it forms the largest area of protected forest in central Europe. With hundreds of kilometres of walking and cycling trails, the park is a nature-lover's paradise and one where you might be lucky enough to spot rare wildlife such as the lynx and the capercaillie (a type of grouse).

**YOU SHOULD KNOW:**
Thanks to the local rock's high quartz component the area has long been famous for its hand-blown glass making. You can visit workshops in Zwiesel and Frauenau to see the ancient craft still being practised.

# Fichtelgebirge

The name of these mountains tells it as it always was and happily still is today – for Fichtelgebirge translates as 'Spruce Mountains' and that pretty much describes this extensive range in northeastern Bavaria. The Fichtelgebirge stretch from the Red Main River Valley to the Czech border and form part of the distinct upland region known as the Thuringian-Franconian Highlands. In truth, these are more like rolling wooded hills than mountains, serving as a reminder that Germany has enough territory to ensure that several large areas of peaceful forest can be allowed to remain relatively undeveloped.

There are numerous towns and pretty villages within the Fichtelgebirge, but this does not detract from the area's natural charms and its unspoilt rural character attracts tourists all year round. For many, simply driving around and seeing the sights is enough, for this is a place of extraordinary granite rock formations and huge tracts of attractive woodland interspersed with moorland, meadows, wetlands and rivers. But Germany wouldn't be Germany without large numbers of enthusiastic visitors bent on embracing bracing open-air activities. These include camping, hiking and mountain-biking in the warmer months, quickly switching to alpine skiing, snowboarding, cross-country skiing and sledding when the snow comes. More pampered incomers head for traditional spas like Fichtelberg, Bad Berneck or Bad Alexandersbad that have morphed into thoroughly modern health resorts offering thermal baths with all the luxury trimmings.

For those who like to get away from the hustle and bustle of modern life, the Fichtelgebirge is an ideal destination. Touring by car offers scenic satisfaction around little-used back roads, plus the opportunity to stop off and picnic or explore tempting corners without seeing another soul. For those on two feet or two wheels, the huge network of forest trails is hiking/biking heaven.

**HOW TO GET THERE:**
The Fichtelgebirge lie between Hof and Weiden, with Bayreuth close to the western fringe. There is good access from *Autobahnen* A 93 and A 9, while Marktredwitz within the Fichtelgebirge has good rail links and is an excellent base for those not equipped with wheels.
**WHEN TO GO:**
Any time
**DON'T MISS:**
The chairlift ride (from either Flecki to the south or Bischofsgruen in the north) to the summit of Ochsenkopf (Ox Head) Mountain, second highest in the Fichtelgebirge range. The views are sensational and it's possible to enjoy them from the Asenturm outlook tower, which conveniently has a restaurant.
**YOU SHOULD KNOW:**
The Fichtelgebirge are the continental divide between the North Sea and the Black Sea and this region is known as 'The Navel of Europe', because four rivers rise in the mountains, each heading off towards a different point of the compass.

# La Pierreuse Nature Reserve

**HOW TO GET THERE:**
La Pierreuse is in the Vaud canton and is easily accessible from the eastern end of Lake Geneva.
**WHEN TO GO:**
May to September
**DON'T MISS:**
The wild flower displays in the high meadows and pastures.
**YOU SHOULD KNOW:**
According to legend the area was once particularly green and lush before being devastated by an avalanche as punishment for the misdemeanour of a local cowherd.

La Pierreuse is the largest nature reserve in Romandie, the historical name for the French-speaking part of Switzerland which makes up the west of the country. It packs a good deal into its 34 sq km (13 sq mi). These foothills to the east of Lake Geneva constitute a prime example of a sub-alpine landscape, with cliffs, meadows, moorland and forests. The reserve is situated south of the town of Château d'Oex on the left bank of the River Sarine. Its core is a broad valley basin which is surrounded by mountains – Le Rocher du Midi to the west, La Videmanette to the east and, to the south, by the sheer limestone wall of the Gummfluh range, which rises to 2,458 m (8,064 ft). There is certainly no escaping the aptness of the name – La Pierreuse translates as 'the stony one' – for the whole area is strewn with large rocks and boulders.

Ibex and chamois are at home here on the screes and rocky slopes, while black grouse live on the moors and birds of prey include falcons and golden eagles. The variety of scenery in a relatively confined area, together with the surprise factor of the scattered rocks, makes La Pierreuse an excellent place for day walks. One of the best begins at the mountain station of the Videmanette cable car and runs through the reserve, crossing over four hills before finishing in L'Etivaz. It is a tough but rewarding six-hour hike with a difference in elevation of 1,000 m (3,280 ft); an easier variation is to walk down from the same starting point to the valley floor at Château d'Oex.

# Lötschental

**HOW TO GET THERE:**
From Goppenstein on the main rail line between Kandersteg and Brig there is a regular bus service, in season, which connects the villages along the valley.
**WHEN TO GO:**
May to September (December to April for winter sports and snow-trekking)
**DON'T MISS:**
The lovely old timber barns and granaries in the village of Kippel, many with richly carved decoration.
**YOU SHOULD KNOW:**
The Lötschental finishes at the base of the Aletsch Glacier, part of the massif containing two of the country's most celebrated peaks, the Eiger and the Jungfrau.

Tucked into the southern fringes of the Bernese Oberland, the high alpine valley of Lötschental can lay claim more justly than most to its promotional tag as the 'hidden valley'. A mere 100 years ago it was still completely cut off from the outside world. It took the arrival of the railway and the engineering feat of a tunnel constructed through the Lötschberg in 1913 to begin the process of opening up the valley. The tunnel links Kandersteg to the north with Goppenstein at the western entrance to Lötschental. Ringed by steep-sided mountains, this is a classic glacial valley through which the River Lonza flows on its journey south to join the Rhône. Although the modern era has caught up with a vengeance and the valley is now a popular winter sports and summer hiking area with the high standard of facilities you expect of the Swiss, its isolation until relatively recently has meant that it has remained largely unspoilt and less developed than many other mountain resorts.

This is wonderful walking terrain during the summer months. From the top of the Wiler cable car the Lötschentaler Höhenweg (high path) takes you high along the northern side of the valley, offering sweeping views before descending to the valley head at Fafleralp. Another classic walk starts from the Lauchernalp ski area and crosses the Lötschen pass into the Gasterntal and Kandersteg.

A further consequence of the valley's isolation has been the survival of old folk customs, including the carnival ritual of Tschäggätta in which local villagers parade through their communities wearing animal skins and fearsome wooden masks. The religious festival of Corpus Christi is marked with a similarly colourful procession.

*The River Lonza runs through the high alpine valley of Lötschental.*

# Murgtal

The Walensee in eastern Switzerland
is one of the country's prettiest lakes.
Lying close to the Liechtenstein
border, this long and slender stretch
of water is framed by dramatic
mountain scenery that invites further
exploration. The village of Murg on
the lake's southern shore marks the
entrance to the Murgtal, a valley
which plunges into the southern
massif. The mountains here may not
be as immediately striking as the
imposing Churfirsten range on the
north shore but they still possess a
wild and untamed air. Their unspoilt
grandeur has been maintained thanks
to a large part of the valley having
been designated a nature reserve.
The reason for the area's protected
status is the mighty stone pine trees
that grow in what are the largest such
forests in the northern Alps. There
are deciduous woods here too and,
close to the lake, the unexpected
sight of large stands of chestnut.

The best way to appreciate the
scenery is to trek through the
chestnut forests and on up the valley
from Murg. Alternatively, you can
make your way to the head of the
valley at Merlen from where a superb
14-km (8.75-mi) circular hike takes
you right round the Hochmättli peak.
Climbing up to 1,800 m (5,900 ft) the
route takes you over moorland
meadows, past bogs and waterfalls
and yields outstanding views in every
direction. It also passes a sequence of
three classic little mountain lakes –
sumptuous watery jewels in this
remote fastness.

*Beautiful Lake Walensee in
Switzerland's 'Heidiland' region*

# Eisenwurzen Nature Park

Tucked away in the far north of Styria, close to the provincial
borders with Salzburg and Upper Austria, the beautiful alpine
landscape that makes up the Eisenwurzen Nature Park looks entirely
natural and unspoilt. Appearances can be deceptive, though; scratch
below the surface and you will find many indicators of man's effect
on the valleys, slopes, pastures and pine forests. Parts of this
landscape would have looked very different 500 years ago when the
mining of iron ore from the surrounding hills was a flourishing
industry. Centred on the town of Eisenerz 25 km (15 mi) to the
south, the mines were a major element in the livelihoods of the
various small communities scattered throughout the Eisenwurzen
region. Whether ferrying logs on wooden rafts down fast-flowing
mountain rivers to feed the furnaces, or working in the area's many
mills, the locals did well out of the industry until mining ceased in
the 19th century. Nowadays virtually all traces of it have disappeared
and it is hard to believe that it was ever here. A few old mills still
stand, including three flour mills close to the village of Gams.

Eisenwurzen is Austria's largest nature park, covering an area of
586 sq km (226 sq mi). As well as its industrial heritage the park has
the lovely valley of the River Enns and boasts many important
geological features in the karst landscape, including caves, gorges
and a lake which has no inlets (it is fed by water entering through
natural springs in the lake bed). There are dramatic walkways along
the narrow Noth and Water-Hole gorges; in the latter the waters
originate from inside a huge limestone cave before dropping 300 m
(984 ft) in a series of five falls into the Salza valley.

# Stubai Alps

The Alps attract visitors at all times of the year, whether for winter
sports or summer walking, and it is not always easy to find that
lonely communion with nature you are seeking. One area where you
stand a better chance than most is the Stubai Alps, a glaciated
mountain chain forming part of the central Alps. Considering their
proximity and ease of access to Innsbruck to the northeast, the
Stubai Alps are a surprisingly quiet and unexplored section of the
mountains; it is not difficult to get away from the crowds, especially
if you are willing to tackle multi-day hikes.

This wild and remote region is made up of a network of steep
escarpments and criss-crossing ridges, with many summits topping
3,000 m (9,840 ft). The principal ridge in the range forms the
border with Italy and includes the highest peak of the Stubai group,

the Zuckerhüttl (literally, 'little sugar loaf') at 3,507 m (11,506 ft). The main access into these mountains is along the Stubaital, a long steep-sided valley which ends at the village of Mutterberg, from where a cable car whisks you up to high-level trekking or, if you are so minded, to skiing on the Stubai glacier. Halfway down the valley the village of Neustift is the starting point for the Stubaier Höhenweg, one of the best long-distance hikes in the whole of the Alps. You need a good week for this challenging route and to ensure enough time to relish the stunning scenery, but it should be manageable by any adult who is reasonably fit. The route crosses several passes at around the 2,700-m (8,860-ft) mark, and paths can be rough and steep, with occasional fixed ropes and ladders to be negotiated in places.

**DON'T MISS:**
If you are a skier, the chance to ski on the Stubai glacier in high summer.
**YOU SHOULD KNOW:**
Austria maintains a well-developed system of mountain huts which provide simple but comfortable accommodation for long-distance hikers.

*A view from Mount Patscherkofel over the Wipptal and Stubai valleys*

# Bohemian Switzerland

**HOW TO GET THERE:**
Bohemian Switzerland is a 90-minute drive from Prague and a two-hour rail journey to the nearest main town, Decín. There are regular buses between Decín and Hrensko and from Hrensko to the heart of the region at Mezná.
**WHEN TO GO:**
April to October

*A peaceful boat trip along the Kamenice Gorge*

It was two Swiss artists of the Romantic movement who first coined the phrase 'Bohemian Switzerland' (*Ceské Švýcarsko* in Czech) in the late 18th century to describe this area of northern Bohemia, although in fact, aside from the occasional meadows and Swiss-style chalets, it is not really alpine in character at all. Striking the landscape undoubtedly is, however, featuring broad expanses of dense woodland covering an elaborate network of bluffs and small canyons where outcrops of sandstone rock have punched their way above the dark-green carpet. Wind and rain have sculpted the soft rock into many strange shapes, creating a paradise for climbers and a gallery of sculptural delights for walkers.

Part of Bohemian Switzerland is now a national park of the same name, but this only accounts for a small proportion of the region which is bounded to the west by the Labe (Elbe) valley and extends eastwards from the German border at Hrensko to Ceská Kamenice. There are many well-marked trails to help you explore the area, of which the most popular is a 17-km (10.5-mi) round route from Hrensko which is manageable in a long day. This trail takes in the region's two most spectacular sights: the Pravcická brána, a huge stone arch that is the largest natural bridge in Europe, and the gorge of the Kamenice River which carves its way through Bohemian Switzerland before joining the Labe at Hrensko. In the east of the region, near Ceská Kamenice, the Panská skála presents another geological curiosity: stacks of basalt columns which, although much smaller in scale, are reminiscent of Northern Ireland's Giant's Causeway.

**DON'T MISS:**
The boat trip along the Kamenice Gorge, a short but dramatic ride in which a ferryman poles you along as you float noiselessly between towering sheer-sided cliffs that rarely see the sun.
**YOU SHOULD KNOW:**
The same geological features spill over the border into Germany where the area is known as Sächsische Schweiz, or Saxon Switzerland.

# Broumov Highlands

A special feature of the central European forests which cover the borderlands of the Czech Republic, Poland and Slovakia are the so-called 'rock towns' (*skalní mesta*). Several are to be found in the Broumov Highlands, an area covering over 400 sq km (154 sq mi) in the far east of the country hard up against the Polish border. Visiting these mysterious landscapes where plateaus, gorges, cliffs and caves are interspersed with strangely anthropomorphic rock formations, it is easy to believe that you are walking through deserted settlements. Two of the best such 'rock towns' are situated next to one another at Adršpach and Teplice in the north of the highlands. Well-signposted trails ensure you don't miss the most interesting rocks and the bizarre shapes which weathering has wrought in the soft sandstone. Grandmother's Armchair, Sugar Cone and the Hand are some of the names that have been applied to nature's work. And at a height of nearly 100 m (328 ft) the Courting Couple at Adršpach is the tallest sandstone pillar in the country.

**HOW TO GET THERE:**
The train journey from Trutnov to Broumov may be slow but it gives you plenty of time to savour the scenery.
**WHEN TO GO:**
April to October
**DON'T MISS:**
The evocatively named Sibir (Siberia) Gorge at the Teplice rock town, which has its own microclimate where cool and damp prevail and towering tree-ferns thrive.
**YOU SHOULD KNOW:**
The great German writer Goethe was one of the first people to put the area on the map when he visited in the 1770s.

Another striking section of the highlands are the Broumov walls, a long thin sandstone ridge which effectively cuts off the town of Broumov to the east from the rest of the country. Approaching from the west in this thickly wooded region you would hardly know the 'walls' were there before coming to the edge of a precipice and being presented all of a sudden with a stupendous panorama of the plain below as it stretches away into Poland. A good vantage point is the little chapel of Panna Maria Snezná, a Baroque jewel built by the great 18th-century architect Dientzenhofer who contributed so much to the cityscape of Prague.

# Šumava National Park

**HOW TO GET THERE:**
Šumava is four hours by bus and five
hours by train from Prague. Local
buses link the main towns and
villages in the region but the more
scenic way to travel is on the two
charming single-track railway lines
that traverse the eastern and central
sectors of the park.
**WHEN TO GO:**
Any time of year
**DON'T MISS:**
The Boubín Virgin Forest, one of the
world's first nature reserves founded
as far back as 1858.
**YOU SHOULD KNOW:**
The Šumava runs along what was
once one of the most heavily fortified
sections of the Iron Curtain, a factor
which ironically has helped spare it
subsequent over-development.

The Šumava is one of very few remaining parts of the crowded continent of Europe that can be legitimately described as a wilderness area. Situated on the southwestern fringe of the Czech Republic, this sparsely populated region forms part of the much larger Bohemian Forest which spills over into neighbouring Germany. It is a land of rolling hills, dark pine forests, meadows, peat bogs and low, humpbacked mountains. With few gradients of serious consequence it is ideal terrain for cycling as well as offering magnificent hiking possibilities. A network of trails gives access to hidden valleys and tiny isolated villages which seem to have grown organically out of their natural surroundings. It may be a deservedly popular destination for lovers of the great outdoors, especially those from Germany and Austria, but the size of the Šumava means there's no problem in getting away from the crowds.

Established only after the collapse of communism in 1991, the Šumava National Park, together with its buffer zone which has the status of a Protected Landscape, covers an area of 1,630 sq km (630 sq mi). The country's most famous river, the mighty Vltava, has its source in the western hills and flows through the length of the park before turning north to Ceský Krumlov. Along the way a dam has created a large artificial lake at Lake Lipno, a popular recreation and watersports area in the summer months. The park becomes ever quieter and more remote and the woods ever thicker the further west you go. The area around Železná Ruda is particularly unspoilt, with two glacial lakes and the lovely Bilá Strž waterfall.

*The confluence of the Cold and Hot Vltava rivers*

# Beskidy Mountains

*It's easy to escape the crowds on the Beskidy Mountains.*

Running for 320 km (200 mi) along the Polish border with the Czech Republic and Slovakia, the Beskidy Mountains form part of the Carpathians, one of Europe's principal mountain chains. With summits rarely topping 1,200 m (3,940 ft) they are not in the same league as the Tatras, their more spectacular neighbours to the west, but these gentle slopes and enticing valleys have an unpretentious and timeless appeal which the discerning visitor can hardly fail to appreciate. The two principal ranges in the central section of these mountains, the Beskid Niski and the Beskid Sàdecki, make for excellent hiking and are well supplied with short day walks and long-distance trails.

Beech and fir are the main trees in these densely forested hills where you will have little difficulty escaping the crowds and communing with nature. You are sharing the woods with bears, wolves, lynx, and wildcats but you need not fret unduly about a close encounter with a predator since these are generally discreet and reclusive hunters who prefer not to be seen. What you will have no difficulty spotting – and one of the special delights of the region – are the wooden churches, some hundreds of years old, which are scattered across the landscape. These extraordinary edifices with their onion domes and richly decorated interiors stand as silent witnesses to a distinctive and almost vanished folk culture which once flourished in these hills. Dedicated to the Orthodox faith, the churches were built by the Lemko people – descendants of nomadic Slavic groups which migrated from the south and east to the Beskidy Mountains in the 13th century; they still speak a dialect that is closer to Ukrainian than Polish.

**HOW TO GET THERE:**
There is a good network of roads along the valleys which penetrate the mountain ranges. Krosno and Gorlice are the best bases from which to explore the Beskid Niski, while Nowy Sàcz and the spa town of Krynica serve the Beskid Sàdecki.
**WHEN TO GO:**
April to October
**DON'T MISS:**
The Poprad River running south from Nowy Sàcz is a particularly beautiful valley in the Beskid Sàdecki hills.
**YOU SHOULD KNOW:**
In the mid-19th century the Beskid Niski area experienced a major economic boom when oil was discovered.

**319**

# Kaszuby Lakes

**HOW TO GET THERE:**
The area's main town, Kartuzy, and the lakeside resort of Chmielno are the best bases for a visit. Public transport is fairly thin so you will need your own means of getting about to get the most out of a visit.

**WHEN TO GO:**
April to October

**DON'T MISS:**
The Kashubians are enthusiasts for snuff. Look out for the hand-carved snuffboxes they carry around.

**YOU SHOULD KNOW:**
The Kashubian is considered a genial and free-spirited character but with a reputation also for obstinacy. There is a phrase in Polish which translates as 'stubborn as a Kaszub'.

*Sunset over the lakes*

The historical region of Pomerania covers the northwest of present-day Poland and has been one of Europe's most bitterly contested territories, changing hands many times over the centuries between Polish, Germanic and Scandinavian overlords. One fascinating legacy of this troubled history is the area of Kashubia (Kazuby), home to one of Poland's most distinctive folk cultures. Kashubia extends for some 100 km (62 mi) southwest of Gdansk and is noted for its tranquil landscapes and serene beauty. This area is not one of nature's scene-stealers but one which wears its modest charms easily and appealingly to anyone seeking a less hurried pace of life and an insight into how the Polish peasantry lived 100 years ago. It is a world of low hills and quiet woodlands dotted with quaint villages containing many examples of the traditional wooden and half-timbered buildings characteristic of Kashubian domestic architecture.

The area's most distinctive features are the many lakes scattered across the countryside – according to legend the footprints of giants

who created the region. A local saying has it that 'wherever you throw a stone in Kashubia, it will land in water'; not surprisingly, the area is a haven for canoeists and kayakers. The Radunia Circle is a particular favourite – a 60-km (37-mi) aquatic loop which takes in ten lakes, all connected by the Radunia River. The loop is in the countryside between Kartuzy and Koscierzyna, a landscape of hills and lakes known popularly as Kashub Switzerland.

You will still hear older Kashubians speaking a dialect of Polish that is thought to derive from an ancient Pomeranian tongue. If you want to learn more about their culture, the outstanding *skansen* (open-air museum) at Wdzydze Kiszewskie in the south of the region is the place to go.

# Stolowe Mountains

Part of the Sudetes Mountains which run for over 250 km (155 mi) along the Polish-Czech border, the Góry Stolowe or Stolowe Mountains have been attracting visitors to this corner of Lower Silesia for more than 200 years. The curious rock formations that are their particular fascination are certainly found nowhere else in Poland. When you look at the characteristic flat-topped profiles of these mountains it is not difficult to see why they are known as the Table Mountains (*stolowe* in Polish). These plateaus were formed as a result of deposits of soft sandstone building up in horizontal strata. Over time the forces of erosion have worn away the softer rock to leave the harder stuff exposed beneath. Inevitably the bizarre shapes thus created have been given names, such as Camel, Elephant, Hen and Pulpit, although it takes quite an effort of the imagination in some cases to appreciate the likeness.

The Góry Stolowe are now a national park. At 63 sq km (24 sq mi) it is relatively small by national park standards, which means you should be able to explore its principal sights in a couple of days. Numerous hiking trails and cycle paths lead through the spruce forests that constitute 90 per cent of the park area, including one that takes you on a large loop from the village of Karlów past various viewpoints and rock formations. After climbing nearly 700 stone steps to the Szczeliniec Wielki, at 919 m (3,015 ft) the highest outcrop in the range, you pass by other striking natural features, including a 20-m (66-ft) deep chasm in the rock appropriately named Little Hell. Elsewhere in the park there is a large group of scattered rocks known as the Petrified Mushrooms and the Bledne Skaly, a huge labyrinth composed of gigantic boulders.

**HOW TO GET THERE:**
The small town of Kudowa-Zdrój on the Czech border to the southwest is the best base for a visit to the Stolowe Mountains. The popular health resort lies on the main Warsaw to Prague highway.

**WHEN TO GO:**
April to October (but be advised that you may still find snow at the bottom of the Little Hell crevice as late as June).

**DON'T MISS:**
If you are in the area you should certainly not miss the Chapel of Skulls in Czermna on the outskirts of Kudowa-Zdrój, a *memento mori* if ever there was one.

**YOU SHOULD KNOW:**
The waters from the area's natural springs have long been known for their curative and restorative properties. There are a number of elegant spa towns close to the Stolowe Mountains.

# Aukštaitija National Park

Lithuania's Lake District has lots of lakes, including 126 in Aukštaitija National Park. None match up sizewise to England's famous equivalents, as the largest is comparatively diminutive Lake Kretuonas with an area of just 8 sq km (3 sq mi). Nor are there dramatic fells, for Lithuania's lakes are scattered among wonderful country consisting of woods, meadows and gentle hills. The park is crossed by the River Žeimena, which is fed by numerous streams and occupies an area of around 400 sq km (154 sq mi) centred on the village of Palūšše, 100 km (62 mi) north of Vilnius beside Lake Lušiai.

Although there are 115 traditional villages within the park, home to over 2,000 people, human presence does not detract from the area's outstanding natural beauty. Three quarters of the terrain is wooded and much of the rest is water, ensuring great biodiversity undamaged by the intrusive scars of modern development. Indeed, some two per cent of Aukštaitija National Park is classified as 'strictly protected' and these sensitive zones may be entered only if accompanied by a member of the park's staff.

The area has a long history – the park has 11 hill forts – and this heritage adds a pleasing dimension to any visit. Stripeikiai is the park's oldest village and hosts the quaintly named Lithuanian Museum of Ancient Beekeeping. Another worthwhile destination is Ginuciai, with its original watermill. But the lakes are magnetic and, since the park was established in 1974, water tourism has become the major leisure activity. Kayaks are easy to hire and a wonderful way of exploring this special landscape, with waterside campsites to encourage extended expeditions. Everyone who takes to the water should be sure to visit Baluošas Lake to explore the seven islands therein, one of which has a mini-lake of its own.

*Aukštaitija National Park –
land of lakes and hills*

# Gauja National Park

Latvia's largest national park is one of four in the country and was established in 1973 in the region of Vidzeme. Running from northeast of Sigulda to southwest of Cesis, Gauja National Park occupies an area of 920 sq km (355 sq mi) along the Gauja River Valley – 60 km (37 mi) long and between 10 km (6 mi) and 30 km (17 mi) wide. Although it follows the river's course, the park also contains lakes – the largest being Lake Ungurs – and around half the terrain consists of dense forest, mainly spruce and pine.

Spectacular sandstone cliffs along the Gauja River soar to 90 m (300 ft) in some places and feature strongly in the park's wilder northern sections around Sigulda, where strict preservation rules apply. There are many amazing rock formations and numerous caves carved from sandstone by wind, weather and water over many millennia. The southwestern parts of the park are more leisure orientated and a natural playground popular with the inhabitants of Riga, who enjoy rafting and canoeing on the river, or hiking, biking and horse riding. The forests provide a home for over 900 plant species, 150 types of bird and nearly 50 different wild animals. There are a number of campsites in the park, including some for river users.

But quite apart from this carefully husbanded nature reserve, those who explore the park will find over 500 monuments testifying to the area's long and colourful history. There are overgrown castle mounds as well as real castles, archaeological sites, old churches, windmills and watermills, fortresses and ancient manors.

The town of Ligatne, which is within the park, has its own fascinating nature park, complete with trails.

**HOW TO GET THERE:**
The historic towns of Sigulda, Ligatne and Cesis are all in the park, while Valmiera is close by and they all provide an ideal jumping-off point for exploration. Sigulda is 50 km (31 mi) east of Riga.

**WHEN TO GO:**
Any time. Winters are short and sharp (generally from January to March). Summers are usually mild but wet.

**DON'T MISS:**
The beautifully reconstructed medieval Turaida Castle, right across the River Gauja from Sigulda. In addition to the original structure begun in 1214, the surrounding museum reserve includes an ancient wooden church and the Dainu Hill sculpture park.

**YOU SHOULD KNOW:**
Gauja National Park and its environs boast the title 'Livonian Switzerland', named for the area's ancient inhabitants and its spectacular scenery. It has been a popular tourist destination since the late 19th century.

*Pine forest in Gauja National Park*

# Matsalu National Park

**HOW TO GET THERE:**
By bus, car, bicycle or train – but only a canoe, skiff or (best of all) a double-prowed fowling punt can take you into the enormous reed beds or across the water. The double-prow means you can go in either direction with minimal fuss or noise.

**WHEN TO GO:**
Any time. Matsalu is always filled with life, but spring and autumn bring the gigantic aerial armadas.

**DON'T MISS:**
The bird colonies on the islands in the bay, equally popular with ringed seals. By the same token, explore the fringe habitats in the woods and bogs around the estuary, home to many of the 275 bird species regularly seen at Matsalu, along with natterjack toads, deer and other mammals.

**YOU SHOULD KNOW:**
Very few nature reserves of Matsalu's size can offer visitors civilized comforts without detracting from their primary purpose as a natural sanctuary. The town of Lihula, on Matsalu's doorstep, holds the Matsalu International Nature Film Festival every autumn.

Every spring and autumn, most of the waterfowl which breed in the arctic tundra migrate along the southern coast of the Baltic Sea. Geese, swans, ducks and waders in their hundreds of thousands stop in western Estonia, on and around the Kasari River delta where it flows into Matsalu Bay and the Vainameri Sea. The entire area falls within 486 sq km (188 sq mi) Matsalu National Park, one of Europe's largest and most important migratory stopovers. It is distinguished both by the extraordinary coincidence of geophysical circumstances that make it so attractive to birds and by the ethereal beauty of its unusual coastal landscapes.

Matsalu belongs to neither land nor sea. Protected by the brackish shallows of the Vainameri Sea from the full onslaught of the open Baltic, Matsalu Bay has no real tides to scour the rich silts that infuse the coastal meadows, reed beds, swamps, bogs, floodplains and slick mudflats that meld into the shoreline. The bay is 18 km (11 mi) long and 6 km (4 mi) long, but barely 1.5 m (5 ft) deep, a sanctuary from everything except the wind and winter ice, which is thicker here, and lasts longer, because of its sheltered position. The 236 sq km (91 sq mi) of open sea within the reserve includes 40 islands which greatly extend the variety of nesting and rest sites available to the two million waterfowl which settle in Matsalu. It's hard to take in their magnificence. On the greyest day, to see 20,000 Bewick's swans materialize from a waterlogged horizon, and listen to the urgent thunder of 100,000 beating wings as greylag and barnacle geese slap down on the water, is to participate in some sort of homage to creation. At dawn in springtime, or in the reddening vastness of a fine-weather dusk, Matsalu is paradise.

# Soomaa National Park

**HOW TO GET THERE:**
By car or bus from Parnu to the park entrance in Joesuu village

**WHEN TO GO:**
Any time. If you can plan a visit to coincide with the spring melt and witness the flooding, so much the better; but the moment varies from year to year.

**DON'T MISS:**
Bog-walking, with an expert guide to prevent disappearance without trace. Look out for rare birds like golden eagles, black storks and various woodpecker species in the swamp forests and flood plains.

Between Viljandi and Parnu in Estonia's southwest, Soomaa National Park protects and celebrates a hydrological anomaly left over from the great Ice Ages. Deep beneath the bogs and forests of the region, the bedrock is inclined at an angle which causes its rivers and streams to drain into a single major river, the Halliste, which then flows into the Navesti River at 160 degrees against its stream. The almost head-on collision of water causes biblical floods every year. In fact, flooding is known locally as 'the fifth season'. Over millennia the same sequence has created five huge bogs separated by thick swamp forests and enormous flood plains; and over centuries, the people who live there have incorporated this bizarre wetland into their own, unique version of rural Estonian culture. For visitors,

Soomaa's international importance as a RAMSAR wetland and World Heritage Site means that every facility now exists to enable them to enjoy both the cultural and ecological highlights of the region.

The best way to get around is by dug-out log canoe, used in Soomaa since the Stone Age, although there are foot and bicycle trails which use traditional trestle bridges erected in times of flood. It's hard to believe the ways water can modify landscapes – especially in the swamp forests (known also as 'carrs') where beaver and otter create river meanders with their building works; the alluvial meadows and river banks coloured blue with wild iris, and harbouring 200 other species including orchids; or the fens and bogs where you might see bear, wolves or lynx. Each of these geographic features is without direct parallel elsewhere in the world. Soomaa is an evolutionary laboratory on a colossal scale, and even its flora and fauna are adaptive. Its peculiar natural history of flooding makes it the most exciting wetland in Europe.

*A view over the swamp forests of Soomaa National Park in early spring*

**YOU SHOULD KNOW**:
Soomaa is full of so many anomalous natural forces that some visitors can start to feel light-headed. The more effort visitors make to see and understand how local communities have adapted, the easier it is to give free rein to enthusiasm, without losing the sense of wonder that makes Soomaa so special.

# Teberdinsky Nature Reserve

The Caucasus mountain range on Russia's southeastern border has exercised a potent hold on the European imagination ever since Alexander Pushkin, Russia's national bard, celebrated the region's elemental grandeur and exotic atmosphere in richly romantic verse after being exiled there in the 1820s. In spite of these magnificent mountains being involuntary witnesses to many of the fiercest territorial disputes which have flared up in the aftermath of the break-up of the former Soviet Union (Chechnya is the most notorious), their mystique and rugged beauty have been preserved remarkably intact. The Communist regime was taking no chances, though, and in 1936 designated the lands surrounding the upper reaches of the Teberda River as a nature reserve.

The Teberdinsky Nature Reserve encompasses an area of 851 sq km (328 sq mi) on the northern spurs of the western Caucasus. With a vertical elevation of nearly 3,000 m (9,840 ft) within its boundaries the reserve displays an astonishing range of environments, from temperate mixed woodlands through dense conifer forests to high alpine meadows above the tree-line. Teberdinsky protects one of the most unspoilt and biodiverse ecosystems in Europe, a fact recognized internationally in 1997 when it was awarded biosphere reserve status by UNESCO.

The reserve offers splendid hiking opportunities but you should take a local guide with you, especially in the southern reaches which abut a sensitive national frontier (Abkhazia, a small breakaway republic from neighbouring Georgia, is on the other side). The forests are home to brown bears, bison, lynx and wild boars while on the rocky higher slopes you should have no difficulty spotting chamois and *tur*, the wild goats which with their large curved horns are found only in the Caucasus.

**HOW TO GET THERE:**
The nearest railhead is at Cherkessk, from where it is a three-hour bus journey south to the village of Dombay, a winter sports resort and the best place from which to organize your visit to the reserve.
**WHEN TO GO:**
May to September
**DON'T MISS:**
The gorgeous displays of wild flowers in the high meadows during the summer months
**YOU SHOULD KNOW:**
The Caucasian bison is Europe's largest native mammal. By the 1920s it had been hunted to extinction in the region but has been re-introduced to the Teberdinsky reserve.

*The Teberda River, near Dombay*

# Kaluzhskie Zaseki Nature Reserve

In times past the vast forests of the central Russian uplands formed a natural defensive barrier protecting the fledgling principalities of northern Russia from marauding tribes and horsemen invading off the great southern steppes. City-states such as Novgorod and Muscovy (modern-day Moscow) relied on the impenetrability of these forests, although local rulers strengthened them still further with fortifications of their own. The use of felled trees stacked one on top of another was one such defensive measure; referred to normally by the French term *abatis*, its Russian name, *zaseki*, has been given to one of Russia's newest nature reserves, created since the end of the Soviet Union.

The Kaluzhskie Zaseki Nature Reserve is situated in the Kaluga region southwest of Moscow. Large parts of this region were formerly covered by mixed deciduous woodlands but, once the military threats from the south had diminished, the forests fell prey to logging and other forms of human exploitation and dwindled fast. Although a country as big as Russia can still hold plenty of secrets, scientists were surprised when as recently as the early 1990s they came across an undisturbed tract of old-growth broadleaf forest. Considering the political turmoil of the times it was quite an achievement that they were able to safeguard this precious survival by establishing an area of 185 sq km (71 sq mi) as a nature reserve.

The reserve is criss-crossed by streams and wetlands but the vast majority of it is woodland and home to a remarkable proliferation of wildlife. Moose, deer, wild boar and wolves are the larger mammals that inhabit the forest; it is also home to over 160 different birds, including golden eagles, hawks and other birds of prey. No fewer than 189 species of mushroom have been recorded.

# Kostomukshsky Forest

The province of Karelia in Russia's far northwest has always been a land alive with legend and shrouded in romance. Inside the huge dark forest an air of mystery mingles with an almost oppressive stillness and, as you contemplate the serried rows of pines receding into the far distance, it becomes easy to imagine the spirits of the woodland that populate the rich folklore of the region. Indeed, it was on the banks of Lake Kamennoye that the poems and songs of the *Kalevala* had their probable origin (the great national epic of Finland which has proved such a fertile source of inspiration for the country's artists, most notably the composer Jean Sibelius).

The 10,500-ha (25,946-ac) Lake Kamennoye is the largest of some 250 lakes found in the Kostomukshsky Nature Reserve in northern Karelia. The reserve was established in 1983 to protect 476 sq km (184 sq mi) of virgin coniferous forest along Russia's border with Finland. This is a classic landscape of the boreal or northern taiga: dense pine and spruce forests interspersed with waterways, swamps and peat bogs. It is home to large animals like the reindeer and brown bear, and to predators like the wolf and the lynx. Sadly, reindeer numbers in the reserve have halved over the past two decades, partly because of poaching but also because the barbed-wire border fence has impeded the creatures' natural east-west migrations. Among the birds to be found in Kostomukshsky are the capercaillie and black grouse, and birds of prey such as the golden eagle, osprey and great grey owl.

**HOW TO GET THERE:**
The nearest town, Kostomuksha, is located 200 km (124 mi) west of the main St Petersburg to Murmansk railway line.

**WHEN TO GO:**
June to August

**DON'T MISS:**
They may be an endangered species but you should be lucky enough to spot white-tailed sea eagles, either in their lofty bankside perches or circling and swooping over the rivers and lakes.

**YOU SHOULD KNOW:**
Thanks to a special joint agreement, Kostomukshsky is now part of a much larger green belt which incorporates other reserves across the border in Finland.

# Yugyd Va National Park

**HOW TO GET THERE:**
The northern part of the park is reached from the towns of Pechora and Inta, both on the Moscow to Vorkuta railway line. The southern part is best reached via Vuktyl, 230 km (143 mi) east of Ukhta rail station. Vuktyl is also home to the park headquarters.
**WHEN TO GO:**
May to September (the spring snow melts offer the best rafting conditions).
**DON'T MISS:**
The neighbouring Pechoro-Ilych Nature Reserve which, together with Yugyd Va, comprises the UNESCO World Heritage Site known as the Virgin Komi Forests.
**YOU SHOULD KNOW:**
Yugyd Va is situated within the Komi Republic, one of 21 autonomous republics that make up the Russian Federation.

It is only fitting that a national park within the largest country on Earth should be on a similarly epic scale and Yugyd Va certainly does not disappoint. At almost 19,000 sq km (7,336 sq mi) it is practically the size of Wales and covers a 400-km (248-mi) length of the northern Urals. This mountain range forms the continental border with Asia, although Yugyd Va is firmly on the western, European side of the mountains. The park includes prime examples of taiga and Europe's largest remaining expanses of virgin spruce forest. As you move east into the foothills, the landscape changes to predominantly tundra. The Urals are not a high range – the highest peak, Mount Narodnaya, which is located within Yugyd Va, is less than 2,000 m (6,562 ft) – but the park lies just outside the Arctic Circle so it comes as no surprise to find glaciers and frozen lakes.

If the Siberian spruce dominates the landscape of the lower slopes, the monotony of dark green is relieved occasionally by broad stands of that most evocative of Russian trees – the birch. There are established populations of elk, reindeer, sable and brown bears in the park, and you are likely to hear wolves even if you don't see them. Yugyd Va covers much of the basin of the River Pechora, one of Europe's longest, which flows north into the Barents Sea. Adventure rafting on its feeder rivers as they tumble down from the mountains is an increasingly popular activity but Yugyd Va is still seriously off the beaten track; with relatively few visitor facilities in the park the only practicable way to experience its many delights is to sign up for a guided tour with camping under canvas or in primitive shelters.

# Tsentralno Chernozyomny Nature Reserve

The city of Kursk lies 500 km (310 mi) south of Moscow on the northern fringes of Russia's fabled Chernozyom, or Black Earth belt. This region, much of it now in present-day Ukraine, was once known as the breadbasket of the Russian Empire, thanks to its deep, nutrient-rich soil. A well-drained humus layer, as much as 1 m (3 ft) deep, has provided one of the most fertile and productive agricultural landscapes anywhere on Earth. One 19th-century writer, indeed, called the Chernozyom 'the Tsar of soils, more valuable than oil, more precious than gold'. Unsurprisingly, it has been intensively farmed over the centuries, which makes the 130 sq km (50 sq mi, including buffer zone) of the Tsentralno Chernozyomny Nature Reserve outside Kursk all the more astonishing a survival.

The reserve is important because it protects a small but precious area of pristine steppe habitat that has never fallen under the plough. It marks the point where the wide open plains meet the belt of temperate forest to the north; roughly half its area consists of broadleaf woodlands. Fringed by the basins of two of Russia's mightiest rivers, the Don and the Dnieper, Tsentralno Chernozyomny also has its fair share of swamps and marshland. The forests are home to elk, roe deer and wild boar while smaller mammals include the Siberian polecat and the stone marten. Black kites are a common sight hovering overhead and the exotic hoopoe with its striking feathered crest and pinkish colouring can also be found here. The grasslands in the reserve put on a fine display of wild flowers in the spring.

**HOW TO GET THERE:**
Kursk is connected to Moscow by bus and rail services. The journey by train takes eight hours.
**WHEN TO GO:**
April to October
**DON'T MISS:**
The beautiful flute-like song of the golden oriole, a summer visitor to the reserve which you are unlikely to see, however, as the bird tends to stay in the tree-tops.
**YOU SHOULD KNOW:**
Because the reserve is divided into six separate tracts it is more vulnerable to pressures from surrounding settlements. Conservationists are trying to establish a system of linking corridors.

# Mount Elbrus

**HOW TO GET THERE:**
The city of Nalchik in the foothills to
the north is the base for visits to the
Elbrus region. Connected by rail (38
hours) and by air to Moscow, Nalchik
is a three-hour bus journey from the
head of the Baksan valley.

**WHEN TO GO:**
June to September (but note that
there is also a skiing and winter
sports season from December to
May).

**DON'T MISS:**
The park's many beautiful waterfalls
and the natural mineral springs near
Baydaevo.

**YOU SHOULD KNOW:**
The walking routes that go up the
southern slopes of the valley
towards the border with Georgia
require you to have a border permit.
This is a free document but can
involve you in a lot of bureaucracy
so you might prefer to join a tour
which will take care of the
formalities for you.

If you accept that the Caucasus Mountains are part of Europe
(some people consider them to be in Asia), then Mount Elbrus is
the highest peak in Europe at 5,642 m (18,510 ft) – significantly
superior to Mont Blanc in France. Its distinctive twin peaks, under a
permanent cover of snow, are an impressive sight at any time of
year but, unless you are an experienced climber or a winter sports
fanatic, you will need to come in the summer months if you want to
see them. Elbrus is situated at the head of the Baksan River valley,
on a spur projecting north from the central Caucasus range. The
mountain forms the heart of the Prielbrusye National Park, a vast
wilderness area comprising 1,000 sq km (386 sq mi) of alpine
meadows and pine and birch forests in addition to the mountains
themselves. Jagged ridges and lofty peaks flank the valley on both
sides, offering spectacular panoramas in every direction.

Various trails lead off from the valley floor along smaller side
valleys, presenting options for easy day-treks or longer, more
strenuous hikes involving overnight stays in campsites or shelters.
You cannot see the summit of Mount Elbrus itself from the Baksan
valley, but a three-hour walk up the Terskol valley brings you to a
dramatic hanging glacier (one of several in the park) where great
shards of ice 'drip' over the cliff edge; from here there is a fine view
of the twin peaks. The more popular and less effortful way of seeing
the summit, though, is to take the cable car at the end of the valley
to the Mir Bar station at 3,500 m (11,483 ft).

*Mount Elbrus, Europe's
tallest peak*

# Shulgan-Tash

*Some of Europe's most ancient rock paintings can be found in the Kapov Caves within the Shulgan-Tash Nature Reserve.*

There are many reasons for protecting our precious natural environment but few can be stranger than the one which has given birth to Shulgan-Tash Nature Reserve in the rolling hills of the southern Urals. The reserve was established in 1990 in order to protect the natural habitat of the humble Burzyan honeybee. Renowned for the quality of sweet golden honey they produce, these wild bees are able to survive very cold weather and Shulgan-Tash is the only place in the world where they are still found in the wild. The bees colonize hollows in trees and feed on nectar from linden trees and the fireweed plant (more popularly known in Britain as rosebay willowherb). The hives are now tended by rangers on the reserve, many of whom have inherited beekeeping skills passed down through generations of Bashkir families.

Bounded on its northern edge by the Nugush River and by the Belaya River to the south, Shulgan-Tash reserve is located in the autonomous republic of Bashkortostan, some 200 km (124 mi) south of the capital Ufa. The landscape is predominantly one of old-growth deciduous forests which cover the hills and low mountains and are occasionally punctuated by clearings of meadow and grassland. Mountain tributaries of the main rivers wind their way through the terrain, creating dramatic canyons through the limestone ridges. Besides the bees, Shulgan-Tash's other claim to fame is the Kapov Caves, a huge underground complex of grottos and passages carved out of the karst by the Shulgan river. The caves, which can be visited on guided tours, contain some of Europe's most ancient rock paintings, estimated to be at least 15,000 years old.

**HOW TO GET THERE:**
The nearest point of access on the railway network is the industrial centre of Magnitogorsk, 100 km (62 mi) to the east.
**WHEN TO GO:**
May to September
**DON'T MISS:**
The chance to sample the product of those busy bees. The amber nectar may not come cheap but is rightly prized by the local population.
**YOU SHOULD KNOW:**
Conservationists are currently campaigning against a proposed hydro-electric dam on the Belaya River which they fear would flood important habitats in Shulgan-Tash.

# Dilijan National Park

**HOW TO GET THERE:**
By minibus van from Yerevan to the upper Avtokayaran, then another to Ijevan that will stop at Dilijan. That said, a taxi from Yerevan is not expensive, even for budget travellers. Car hire offers freedom to see more of the park and its environs.

**WHEN TO GO:**
The Armenian climate varies considerably according to specific location, but the preferred time to explore Dilijan National Park is during the cool and moist summer. Autumn visitors will be delighted by the turning foliage, however.

**DON'T MISS:**
The fabulous Haghartsin Monastery, in a beautiful wooded hillside setting near Dilijan. Constructed between the 10th and 14th centuries, it has many impressive buildings (some ruined) and the centrepiece is St Astvatsatsin Church with a wonderful dome that has no fewer than 16 facets.

**YOU SHOULD KNOW:**
The resort of Dilijan is actually a modest spa town, renowned for its energizing mineral waters – although definitely not quite so grand as Bath or Buxton.

It initially seems somewhat chaotic. Dilijan National Park in northeastern Armenia's Tavush Province – one of two national parks in the country – was created in 2002 to succeed a state nature reserve, itself the scene of forestry enterprises until the late 1950s. Although it spreads across slopes of the Pembak, Areguni, Miapor, Ijevan and Halab mountains, all the high pastures are actually excluded from the park. There are numerous cultural monuments and settlements located within the park – including eponymous Dilijan town – and a railway line passes right through the middle. Tension between well-meaning nature conservation and commercial activity is endemic.

Sounds . . . unpromising? Actually, the largely forested Dilijan National Park is rather good, with plenty of unspoilt, wild terrain awaiting the adventurous traveller looking for an unusual destination. Dilijan itself is a charming old town nestling in the picturesque hills, and provides an ideal base for sallies into the surrounding countryside. This may remind visitors of Switzerland, as it has forests and alpine meadows very reminiscent of the land of alpenhorns and tinkling cowbells. Happily, this remote corner of Europe is gnome-free and anything but a tourist hotspot – seeming all the better for that.

The park cries out to be explored and is rich in flora and fauna. There are over a thousand plant species and a wide variety of trees, including oak, beech, hornbeam, lime, maple, ash, pine, juniper and many wild fruit trees. Around 150 species of bird have been recorded, including real corkers like golden eagle, goshawk, black kite, honey buzzard, black grouse, Caspian snowcock and eagle owl. The animal population is scarcely less impressive, numbering the likes of brown bear, wolf, lynx, wild boar, wildcat and red deer among its 50 or so members.

# Chornohora Mountain Ridge

The mighty Carpathian Mountains frown down on Ukraine, and remain one of Europe's great unspoilt wilderness areas. The Chornohora Mountain Ridge is the highest section, and gives access to the country's tallest peak – Hoverla mountain in western Ukraine at 2,061 m (6,762 ft). Chornohora's main range extends for some 40 km (25 mi) from the Chorna Tysa River in the west to the Chornyi River in the east. The ridge forms the watershed between the rivers Prut and Tysa and is divided by a deep pass. The western end is jagged and the monolithic eastern massif contains the highest peaks, including Hoverla, Pip Ivan, Shpytsi and Tomnatyk. The geology has been shaped by glacial action in the last Ice Age, as evidenced by many lateral and terminal moraines.

Postglacial depressions bottom out in lakes or peat bogs and narrow valleys slash the slopes of Chornohora. The lower elevations are heavily forested with beech and spruce trees, then there's a belt of alder and juniper brush before the alpine meadows and barren rock fields that make up the ridge. The local Hutsul people are mainly occupied with traditional animal herding on high pastures during a five-month season, although tourism is starting to play an increasingly important role in the regional economy.

That said, the mountains are still isolated, lonely and potentially hazardous. So this is really one for an organized hiking tour led by a guide who knows the rugged terrain intimately. A number of treks are offered, lasting from one day to a week. Go-it-alone types should not be tempted to tackle the Chornohora Mountain Ridge unless their self-sufficiency skills and backcountry experience are well honed, although modest day hikes are comfortably within the reach of anyone who is reasonably fit and active.

**HOW TO GET THERE:**
Tourism in the Ukrainian Carpathians centres on the towns of Bystrets, Rakhiv, Verkhovyna and Vorokhta. The best starting points for Chornohora are Bohdan in the Bila Tysa River Valley and Yasinia in the Chorna Tysa River Valley. The nearest rail station to the latter is at Ivano-Frankifsk.

**WHEN TO GO:**
For something very different, be around on August 24, Ukraine's Independence Day, when thousands of Ukrainians make a pilgrimage to the summit of Hoverla. If that's not on, any time in summer is good and any time in the long winter is bad.

**DON'T MISS:**
Anyone tackling the all-day ascent of Hoverla Mountain should be sure to take the short diversion south of the main trail to view the impressive waterfall on the Prut River, a tributary of the Danube. Alternatively, this is a worthwhile hike in its own right if the summit climb is too demanding.

**YOU SHOULD KNOW:**
Continuing tension between Ukraine and Russia was reflected in 2007 when vandals suspected of being Russian activists defaced official Ukrainian national symbols at the summit of Hoverla.

# Synevyr Lake

Ukraine's largest mountain lake is in the picturesque heart of the Synevyr National Nature Park, the country's third such protected area. This impressive tract of mountainous landscape extends to 400 sq km (154 sq mi) in the southern part of the Gorgany Mountains, themselves the centre of the Ukrainian section of the mighty Carpathians. Wooded slopes and mixed habitats provide refuge for a variety of wildlife, including brown bear, wolf, lynx, deer, ermine, badger and marten. Among protected bird species, the rare horned owl stands out.

Synevyr Lake itself is at an elevation of nearly 1,000 m (3,280 ft). It has an outflow into the Tereblya River and was formed when a landslide dammed the steep valley it occupies. It rejoices in the title 'Blue Eye of the Carpathians', encouraged by the presence of a tiny island in the centre that represents the pupil. This small but deep lake has recently been classified as a wetland of international importance. Although the surrounding mountains are wild and lonely – an ideal challenge for the hardy hiker who loves self-sufficient wilderness exploration – the lake is a popular destination.

The drive to the lake is an experience in itself, as the road winds up the steep Synevyrskiy Pass, far above the white dwellings of Svnevry village which are scattered around the silver thread of the Tereblya River. To see the lake in its marvellous setting from afar before actually going there, continue to the summit of nearby Ozirna Mountain before returning to the lake (road open in summer only). A word to the wise – Synevyr Lake's crystal-clear waters may look tempting, and often attract hardy swimmers, but think carefully before joining them. The water temperature rarely rises above 5°C (41°F), which makes the average cold shower seem, well, warm.

# Grand Canyon

Forget travelling all the way to the USA – Europe has its very own Grand Canyon, tucked away in southern Ukraine. The Grand Canyon of Crimea may be found on the peninsula of the same name, which juts into the Black Sea and is an autonomous republic within Ukraine. This geological marvel is situated on the northern slopes of Ai-Petri Mountain, behind Yalta, and in no way measures up to its cousin in Arizona when it comes to the awesome natural wonder stakes – although it is still a sublimely beautiful wild place.

The canyon walls tower up to an impressive height of 320 m

(1,050 ft) and – amazingly – it is a mere 3 m (10ft) wide at the narrowest point. The fast-flowing Kuru-Uzen races along the canyon's rocky floor, creating dynamic small waterfalls, pools and white-water rapids before joining the Auzun-Uzen River towards the canyon exit. Despite those dizzying rock faces, much of the canyon has shallower sides. They – along with the canyon surrounds and floor – are densely wooded.

There are two routes for hikers who want to travel along the Grand Canyon and enjoy its astonishing rock formations close up. One route follows the canyon floor beside the water, another passes along the right flank of the canyon. The former is impassable in winter and spring, when a raging torrent invariably overwhelms the path, but the latter may be used all year round. The favoured direction for hiking is from the upper to the lower end. This through-trek can be done in a day but is anything but a casual stroll. A good level of fitness is essential, for either route is demanding physically. In addition, there are side paths that lead nowhere and anyone tempted to follow one can end up hopelessly lost amidst tangled vegetation.

*The walls of the Grand Canyon of Crimea tower up to a height of 320 m (1,050 ft).*

**DON'T MISS:**
A short day-hike along the canyon floor from the car park, to find the popular Blue Pond and Bath of Youth pools – anyone tempted by the promise implicit in the latter should be aware that the water temperature never rises above 11°C (51.8°F) and is often colder.

**YOU SHOULD KNOW:**
Those exploring the canyon floor should have small-denomination used notes handy – rangers usually expect a non-voluntary 'contribution'.

# Malá Fatra National Park

**HOW TO GET THERE:**
There is a regular bus service from Žilina, 25 km (15.5 mi) to the west of Malá Fatra.
**WHEN TO GO:**
Any time of year. May and September are particularly good months if you want to escape the crowds and the snows.
**DON'T MISS:**
Golden eagles nest in these mountains; you may be lucky to see these majestic birds circling high overhead on the thermals.
**YOU SHOULD KNOW:**
Terchová is famous in Slovakia as the birthplace of a Robin Hood-like folk hero called Juraj Jánošík.

The Malá Fatra is a mountain range in central Slovakia, 226 km (140 mi) of which is protected as a national park. The focus of the park is the beautiful valley formed by the Vrátna River as it carves its way deep into the mountains. The village of Terchová stands at the entrance to the valley but the real gateway comes a short distance south as you enter the dramatic rockscape of the Tiesňavy gorge, with sheer cliffs and towering limestone pinnacles on every side. Further up the valley, exciting vistas open up of mountain-tops rising above slopes which are covered in pine and beech forests. The valley is completely encircled by brooding peaks which leave you in no doubt that raw nature holds sway here. From Chatna Vrátna at the head of the valley, 7 km (4.3 mi) south of Terchová, you can take a cable car 750 m (2,460 ft) up the mountain to the Snilovské saddle from where it is a 40-minute hike to the summit of Velký Kriváň, at 1,709 m (5,607 ft) the highest peak in the park. If the weather holds you will be rewarded with panoramic views not only of the Vrátna valley but also over the Veľká Fatra range to the south.

There are some terrific hikes through the Malá Fatra; some include steep sections featuring ladders and chains which are not for the faint-hearted. The trek to the Rozsutec massif in the east of the park is a particularly satisfying one, giving you access to a cave below Mount Malý Rozsutec as well as a number of hidden valleys and the narrow Dolné Diery gorge.

*Limestone cliffs in Malá Fatra National Park*

# Pieniny Mountains

*Tri Koruny peak in the mighty Pieniny Mountains*

The Pieniny Mountains form part of the border between Slovakia and Poland. A northern spur of the Carpathians, this small range lies in the shadow of the High Tatras to the west, and while it may lack the grandeur of its mighty neighbour, its unspoilt landscapes possess an undeniable appeal. This is in no small part due to a small national park which, together with a sister park on the north bank in Poland, exists primarily to protect the lovely valley of the Dunajec River which forms the actual frontier. Jagged limestone peaks rise above the thick forests which cover nearly half of the park's 21 sq km (8 sq mi). Much of the rest is given over to small fields and richly grassed meadows, testimony to a traditional way of farming largely untouched by the modern age.

The best way to appreciate the mountains is from the river. Although it is what everyone comes to the Pieniny for, you should definitely not miss the trip downriver on one of the large wooden rafts. Starting at the 14th-century Red Monastery, the 90-minute journey takes you down a jaw-dropping 8.5-km (5.3-mi) gorge past cliffs which rise sheer from the water and tower over you. This is no white-water trip so you have plenty of time to admire the dramatic scenery as you are poled along by rafters in their traditional embroidered waistcoats. The views change constantly as the river winds its way through the limestone hills. Your guide will point out the main features, such as the three rocks known as the Stone Monks and the Tri Koruny (Three Crowns); at 982 m (3,222 ft) these are the highest peaks in the range, but Poland claims them as they are on the north bank.

**HOW TO GET THERE:**
The Pieniny Mountains are 120 km (75 mi) from Košice, the main city in East Slovakia. Buses are infrequent so it is best if you have your own transport.
**WHEN TO GO:**
May to October
**DON'T MISS:**
Look out for otters in the water or on the riverbanks.
**YOU SHOULD KNOW:**
At the end of the raft ride at Lesnica you can return to your starting-point on a riverside trail, either on foot or by hiring a bicycle.

# Vihorlat Highlands

**HOW TO GET THERE:**
There are railway stations at Humenné and Michalovce, from where local buses reach the heart of Vihorlat at Remetské Hámre, a village 7 km (4.3 mi) south of the lake.
**WHEN TO GO:**
April to October
**DON'T MISS:**
The traditional wooden churches of the area, a curious blend of western Catholicism and eastern Orthodoxy and the most visible reminder of the local Rusyn culture.
**YOU SHOULD KNOW:**
Late September/early October is a particularly rewarding time to visit the Vihorlat Highlands when the beech woods are a blaze of autumn colours.

In the easternmost part of Slovakia the Vihorlat Highlands are a range of tree-covered volcanic hills which provide some of the country's best walking. With the highest points barely scraping 1,000 m (3,300 ft) there are no flamboyant peaks here but the nature-lover will find more than enough compensation in the varied vistas and the peace and serenity of an area that has been designated a Protected Landscape. The woodlands of the Vihorlat are composed mainly of mixed deciduous trees, with beech being the predominant species. In 2007 parts of these woods, along with counterparts in Ukraine, were inscribed on UNESCO's World Heritage List as Primeval Beech Forests of the Carpathians.

A hidden gem in the Vihorlat Highlands is the Morské oko lake, perhaps the most beautiful and unspoilt in the whole of Slovakia. This glacial lake owes its unusual name (*morské oko* means 'sea eye') to its distinctive blue-green colour. If you sit quietly on the shore you may see the black storks which nest in these parts and honey buzzards and eagles as they circle high overhead. From the northern lake shore it is a two-hour hike to another natural marvel of the region, the Snina stone, a great slab of rock which rises precipitously above the tree line. The strenuous climb to the top is up steep iron ladders attached to the cliff face but the outstanding views from the table-top summit, 1,005 m (3,297 ft) high, make the effort eminently worthwhile. On a clear day you can see all the way over the eastern border into Ukraine.

# Hortobágy National Park

Rather like the Prairie in North America, the Steppes in Russia or the Veldt in South Africa, the Puszta not only indicates a vast flat grassy area, but also carries with it a meaning that portrays a way of life. The great Hungarian Plain is not only the largest natural grassland in Europe but is also a place of special harmony between humans and nature. On the Puszta herdsmen on horseback tend their grey cattle and Racka sheep, while oxen haul trailers brim full with bales of hay. It is a traditional place little changed since before the birth of Christ.

Within this great plain lies Hortobágy National Park. Created in 1973, it was the first to acquire national park status in Hungary and its unique ecosystem was further recognized and protected when it was afforded World Heritage status in 1999. The park covers 800 sq km (309 sq mi) of meadows, low-lying scrub, bogs and lakes which provide a diverse range of habitats for a wide array of flora and fauna. Over 300 bird species have been identified in the park. One in particular provides one of the most spectacular avian displays in the world when, in the late autumn (October) evenings, cranes gather in numbers as great as 80,000 to rest on the park's lakes – in flight they almost block out the sky.

The neoclassical white Nine Span Bridge, completed in 1833, is the most famous man-made landmark in the Hortobágy and at 170 m (558 ft) is the longest stone bridge in Europe.

The Hungarian Puszta is an exceptional example of a cultural landscape shaped by the pastoral activities of mankind. In a world of ever more intensive agriculture and increasing carbon footprints, it is a special place worthy of preservation.

**HOW TO GET THERE:**
By train from Budapest to Debrecen (Hungary has an excellent railway system).
**WHEN TO GO:**
It's best from April to October.
**DON'T MISS:**
The Tisza Lake Water Trail – a 1.6-km (1-mi) boardwalk into the lake's wetlands, complete with watch towers and hides
**YOU SHOULD KNOW:**
The Hortobágy once filled Hungarian dissidents with terror. The former communist rulers built labour camps there in an effort to quell rebellion after World War II.

*Cranes fly over the great Hungarian Plain at Hortobágy National Park.*

# Bicaz Canyon and Red Lake

**HOW TO GET THERE:**
Red Lake can be reached from Ghoergheni by taking the national road 12/C and then following the road through to the canyon.
**WHEN TO GO:**
It's beautiful all year round but clear of snow from April to October. The area is most beautiful in autumn (September and October) when the trees change colour.
**DON'T MISS:**
The view of Red Lake from the slopes of Killer Mountain
**YOU SHOULD KNOW:**
It is said that when the mountainside came down to form Red Lake, shepherds and their sheep were buried beneath the rubble. Legend has it that their cries can still be heard over the lake.

Located in the northeast of Romania, Bicaz Canyon (Cheile Bicazulu) is a deep gorge burrowed out by the fast-flowing Bicaz River. The canyon is not only a destination in itself but also acts as a corridor linking the regions of Transylvania and Moldavia via a precipitous snaking road – which is definitely not for the faint-hearted – for 8 km (5 mi). Within the limestone walls of this most imposing canyon are hidden two remarkable caverns: the Black Cave and Waterfall Cave. As well as offering ample opportunity for a spot of spelunking (cave exploration), the canyon is a favourite among rock climbers. Huge walls up to 300 m (984 ft) high rise to fantastic hanging ceilings, with deep scars in the rocks and huge clear spaces providing an adrenalin-filled climb for those skilled enough to take up the challenge.

Upstream from the canyon lies a spectacular lake, which in geological terms is barely out of the maternity ward. Sometime in the summer of 1837, after a huge storm system hit the area, an enormous chunk of Killer Mountain became dislodged and blocked three creeks, producing a natural dam which flooded the valley. The result was Red Lake (Lacu Rosu) – made red by alluvial deposits and the reflection from the purple flanks of Suhardu Mic Mountain in the water. The lake has an eerie appearance as stumps of pine trees poke out from beneath its surface. In winter it freezes and the gorge is covered by a blanket of snow, while in summer the lake is the perfect place for a leisurely row.

*Bicaz Canyon – a favoured spot for adrenaline-seeking rock climbers.*

# Piatra Craiului

Piatra Craiului (pronounced Cry-ooh-loo-e) is a 150 sq km (58 sq mi) national park in the Carpathian Mountains of Romania dominated by a mountainous ridge from which it takes its name. The north of the park, near the Barsa River, is made up of sloping intense-green pastureland which in spring and summer is dappled with wild blue orchids and yellow buttercups. But it is the spectacularly stark 25-km (15.5-mi) long black ridge, marbled with snow, that is the main attraction in the park. Hiking along the sharp-crested serrated ridge takes two to three days and, as well as offering spectacular panoramic views, takes the walker into the domain of *Ursus arctos* – the northern brown bear. Unlike the Alps or the Pyrenees, where bears have been hunted to virtual extinction, Piatra Craiului has a healthy population with estimates put at around 5,000.

Chamois (a goat-like antelope) forage along the precipitous mountain slopes, nimble and fleet of foot so as to elude the wolves and lynx that prowl the area. Falcons soar on the thermals thrown up by the sun-warmed scree, scouring the ground for the slightest movement that might indicate a meal. An area's environmental wellbeing can be measured by the number and diversity of its bird and butterfly populations, and Piatra Craiului triumphs on both counts as 120 species of birds have been identified in the park and more than twice as many species of butterflies. Of the thousand species of plants to be found, one-fifth are unique to the area.

The highest peak of the ridge – Vârful La Om at 2,238 m (7,342 ft) – may be only half the height of Mont Blanc, but the climb is so arduous that it has the feel of a much greater mountain.

*Storm clouds gather over Mount Piatra Craiului.*

**HOW TO GET THERE:**
By bus from Brasov to Zarnesti, which acts as a gateway to the park.
**WHEN TO GO:**
From May to September is best for hiking on the ridge.
**DON'T MISS:**
The views of the Barsa Valley from the Crapaturii Saddle (a relatively easy hike)
**YOU SHOULD KNOW:**
In geological terms the ridge is an *arête*, formed at the head of two opposing glaciers. Post-glaciation, the slopes have been further steepened by the action of frost and winter ice breaking rocks into scree.

*Autumn in the Zsil Valley in the Retezat Mountains*

# Retezat Mountains

Sometimes called the Transylvanian Alps, Retezat is the highest section of the Southern Carpathian range in Romania and covers around 500 sq km (193 sq mi). The range has a distinct 'H' shape with two parallel rims (Retezat and Little Retezat) connected by a short ridge. The spectacular scenery of the area was carved out by glaciers of the Pleistocene epoch and the range, which has an average elevation of more than 1,500 m (4,920 ft), comprises spectacular granite and limestone massifs speckled with numerous turquoise tarns.

Although starkly beautiful when covered by snow in winter, the mountains gradually come to life after the spring melt. Alpine meadows blossom on the middle elevations in an area that boasts over 1,000 different plant species, with around 100 being unique to the region. The melting ice gives added force to the many waterfalls that cascade down the mountainsides, as bears and marmots slowly shake off their winter sleep. Lynx, otters, chamois and wolves all add to the remarkable diversity of life, while salamanders and vipers seek out sun-warmed rocks to raise their body temperatures.

The most spectacular scenery is to be found on the route between Mount Peleaga and Mount Judele, where a series of stunning lakes on the southern slope of Judele culminates in Lake Bucura, Romania's largest glacial lake. The area is ideal for hiking and in late summer the smaller mountain lakes warm up enough to provide pleasant conditions for swimming. However, frost-cracking means that the higher elevations are formed of unstable scree which can make progress difficult. Serious climbing can be had on the twin peaks of Bucura mountain in the northern ridge of the range, where the northeast ascent of Bucura II is via a sheer rock face.

**HOW TO GET THERE:**
By train from Deva or Petrosani to Ohaba de Sub Piatra, then by bus to Cabana Cârnic.
**WHEN TO GO:**
All year round – it's warmest from May to October but wettest in June.
**DON'T MISS:**
The view of the chain of mountain lakes from the higher elevations of Mount Peleaga.
**YOU SHOULD KNOW:**
Any exploration of the higher elevations of the range should be approached with caution. The area is notorious for its hostile weather, winds of over 80 kph (50 mph) are not uncommon, and when it rains, it pours.

# Cape Kaliakra

Located on Bulgaria's Black Sea coast near the border with Romania, Cape Kaliakra is a formidable place – so formidable that even the colour of its rocks is said to come from the blood of those who have defended it (although iron oxide in the soil provides a more prosaic explanation). It is where East meets West and where history and legend meld into one story. Dragons have been slain, great treasure lost in its caves and maidens have leapt to their deaths to avoid religious conversion.

The word *kaliakra* is of Medieval Greek origin and can be translated as 'Beautiful Fortress' – a fitting description of the cape on both counts. Formed of limestone created beneath the prehistoric Sarmat Sea, it stretches 2 km (1.25 mi) into the sea and is protected by 70-m (230-ft) high sheer cliffs. The inaccessibility of the place made it ideal for the construction of a citadel – named Tirisis – which was successively used by Thracians, Romans and Byzantines. A small yet informative museum houses relics left behind by the ancient settlers.

In 1941 Kaliakra was declared a nature reserve which encompasses not only the land of the cape but also the waters around it. It has healthy populations of bird species all year round. Grebes and cormorants flourish in winter while eagle owls, alpine swifts and black-headed bunting breed here. Dolphins are a common sight out to sea, but the plight of the monk seal has brought into sharp focus the fragility of the cape's ecosystem. Once a common sight, they are now rarely seen.

Hiking along the top of the cape is popular, but great care should be taken as its rocks are subject to constant erosion. The Black Sea can be accessed via steep steps.

**HOW TO GET THERE:**
Take the coast road north from Varna (Bulgaria) or south from Constanta (Romania).
**WHEN TO GO:**
All year round, but it's very warm in July and August.
**DON'T MISS:**
The museum, which as well as being a treasure trove, has the bonus of being housed inside a cave.
**YOU SHOULD KNOW:**
Of all the legends associated with Kaliakra, perhaps the most poignant is that of the 40 maidens. It is said the young women wove their hair together and jumped *en masse* into the sea to avoid capture by the Turks, and hence conversion to Islam. An obelisk called 'The Gate of the 40 Virgins' stands on the spot in their honour.

*Cape Kaliakra, where East meets West.*

# Central Balkan National Park

The Central Balkan National Park is one of the largest and most important protected areas in Eastern Europe. Established in 1991, the park covers 720 sq km (278 sq mi) and encompasses nine distinct nature reserves. The park's topography includes alpine meadows, sheer rock faces, deep gorges, waterfalls and rapids, as well as 20 peaks above 2,000 m (6,562 ft). Old-growth forest of beech, spruce, fir, hornbeam and sessile oak cover over half of the park.

The area is home to bears, wolves and otters as well as around 120 species of birds, including the eagle owl and golden eagle. Of equal importance are the hundreds of species of fungi, moss and algae, and over 100 medicinal plants, that grow there. The park is popular with those seeking outdoor thrills and has ample opportunity for rock climbing, mountain-biking, mountaineering and caving. Exploration of the park can be undertaken on horseback or by hiking.

The reserves contain many astounding geological features. The granite and sandstone bedrock has been sculpted by erosion into weirdly wonderful shapes, most notably the fragile vertical stone pillars of Kalchovi Kamani and the rock bridge, Skalniya Most. Another breathtaking formation is a chain of ravines in the valleys of the Stara Reka and Cherni Osam Rivers. Underwater springs feed fast-flowing rivers and at many points their passage is interrupted by impermeable bedrock, thus creating many impressive cascades and waterfalls.

The park is of global significance and its management board seeks not only to preserve its unique natural scenery, but also the heritage and livelihood of the 31 communities contained within its boundaries. An increased demand for ecotourism is making their task easier.

*Snow-covered Central Balkan National Park*

# Rhodope Mountains

The Rhodope Mountains start south of the Bulgarian capital, Sofia, and run for around 240 km (150 mi) across the border into Greece. They have throughout the ages been the home of Thracians, Ancient Greeks, Romans and Slavs and each has left its mark not only on the architecture of the area but also on the myths and legends associated with this enigmatically beautiful landscape. The area was reputedly the home of Orpheus, who is said to have visited the underworld and returned; perhaps the region's many caves and gorges acted as portals in his journey.

The range is split geologically between east and west. The western section is classic karst terrain – limestone bedrock cut by deep gorges and pitted with caves. To the east, the younger igneous rocks have been eroded to leave rock mushrooms and sharp peaks. The western section has the more spectacular scenery, most notably at Trigrad Gorge – a deep canyon bounded by sheer marble rocks. It is here that the Trigradska River is diverted underground into the Dyavolskoto Garlo (Devil's Throat) Cave, one of the highest underground waterfalls in Europe.

About 8 km (5 mi) from Trigrad is one of the most impressive caves in Europe. The Yagodina cave is on five levels and is around 10 km (6 mi) long. Tours take the visitor into a subterranean wonderland of illuminated stalactites and stalagmites which was home to a troglodyte clan in prehistoric times. Other natural wonders are to be found near the Aidarsko Dere River, in the shadow of the Chernatitsa Ridge. The Chudnite Mostove (Wondrous Bridges) Arches are possibly the remnants of a collapsed cave system where, over time, the elements have sculpted two natural marble bridges.

*A summer landscape in the Rhodope Mountains*

**HOW TO GET THERE:**
A bus links the gateway villages of Kesten, Trigrad and Devin.
**WHEN TO GO:**
From May to October is best
**DON'T MISS:**
Orlovi Skali (Eagle's Rocks) – a relic of ancient Thracian culture
**YOU SHOULD KNOW:**
The Rhodope Mountains is a huge range covering 14,750 sq km (5,700 sq mi) which would take months to explore fully. The village of Trigrad is a useful base, being close to several places of interest and easy to get to.

# Dadia Forest

**HOW TO GET THERE:**
Buses run daily to Dadia from Alexandroupoli, which has good bus, train and air links with the rest of Greece.
**WHEN TO GO:**
The reserve is open year-round. Raptors may be spotted all day from October to March, and young vultures leave the nest in autumn. In May, many migratory birds are preparing to fly.
**DON'T MISS:**
The Evros Delta, south of Dadia, is an atmospheric landscape of wetlands and dunes, and an interesting ornithological contrast. The visitor centre offers minibus and boat trips to see migrating waterfowl such as purple herons, little egrets and pelicans.
**YOU SHOULD KNOW:**
The only other nesting colony of black vultures in Europe is in Spain. The Dadia Forest Reserve does valuable work with local communities, encouraging the understanding of and participation in conservation. The municipality of Dadia runs the Ecotourist Centre and Hostel, and shares profits with the reserve.

Towards the end of the 20th century, the black vulture faced extinction in Europe. The Dadia Forest in northeastern Greece was still home to a few pairs and, with active support from the World Wildlife Fund, an inner zone was set up – a protected reserve where black vultures and griffon vultures (also very rare in Europe) are now well established. The forest reserve covers a succession of volcanic ridges and its diverse habitats are home to a huge variety of flora and fauna, but it is most famous for birds. Its position on major migration routes attracts countless visiting species, but its prime importance is as a refuge for birds of prey. Of Europe's 38 diurnal raptors, 36 are seen here, including imperial and golden eagles, falcons and hawks.

A visit to Dadia Forest begins at the Ecotourist Centre, with informative displays and videos on the birds and on the work of the reserve. This includes augmenting the vultures' food as the greatest threat to their health comes from eating carrion picked up outside the reserve, which may be poisoned. A van takes visitors up to the well-designed observation area where binoculars, telescopes and knowledgeable staff help birdwatchers identify species. There is a very good chance of seeing vultures feeding in the canyon below the hide. Marked trails through the sunlit clearings and the shady, hushed depths of the forest allow silent walkers the sight of rare birds among the trees, or silhouetted high above. Birds of prey can be seen at closer quarters as they take to the air, and a night in the Ecotourist Hostel gives a marvellous early-morning opportunity to watch them soar and take advantage of the first thermals.

# Pindos Mountains

**HOW TO GET THERE:**
A limited bus service runs to some of the villages from Ioannina, which also has good bus links to Konitsa, for the northern areas.
**WHEN TO GO:**
May, June, September, October. Accommodation in the *Zagorohoria* can be hard to find at weekends.
**DON'T MISS:**
The Vikos Gorge is a truly great walk. In one of the world's deepest ravines the foaming river twists and tumbles through narrow defiles and shaded valleys. From Monodendri to Papingo, the hike is 14 km (9 mi); the going is only difficult after rain.

The magnificent Pindos Mountains stretch south of Metsovo and Ioannina from the Albanian border. Logging, road building and ski slopes have partly denuded the range but two national parks safeguard large areas of diverse, unspoilt landscapes and endangered wildlife. With deep river valleys, thick conifer and broadleaf forests and sweeping alpine pastures, both are superb trekking country.

The remote, northern Pindos National Park is home to some of Greece's rarest large animals. Lynx, jackals, wolves and brown bears are not often seen, but at dawn and dusk deserted hillsides echo with the howling of wolves. Zagori, south of the Aoos River, is more accessible but no less wildly beautiful. The Vikos-Aoos National Park covers part of a region which is remarkable not only for its dramatic, rugged landscape but also for the *Zagorohoria* – its numerous, traditional villages. Built on mountain ledges – level ground is used for cultivation – these were winter settlements for the shepherds, who traditionally spent summers on the mountains with their flocks. Greek-speaking Sarakatsani, and Vlachs who speak an ancient Romance language, still make up most of the settled population, although many abandoned the harsh seasonal life. The almost deserted villages are now being restored and some of the traditional stone houses and the surprisingly grand 18th- and 19th-century mansions are guesthouses.

The towering peaks of the Pindos, including Smolikas, the highest in the range at 2,640 m (8,660 ft), and Gamila, whose sheer face drops hundreds of metres to the river below, are long and challenging ascents even for experienced climbers. But the whole area is crossed by tracks – many used by shepherds for centuries – through ravines and forests, over uplands and ridges, to isolated villages and high lakes.

**YOU SHOULD KNOW:**
Even experienced climbers must have specialist guides and equipment and should never climb alone. There is no formal mountain rescue service in the Pindos and the weather changes rapidly – check conditions with the Ioannina Tourist Office. All walkers need sticks, not just for the terrain, but for fending off the all-too-common semi-wild dogs. The steeply arched, slender packhorse bridges which span rivers and link the stony mountain trails were, until the mid 20th century, the only routes between villages and were built, mainly in the 19th century, by groups of itinerant workers who practised their skilled craft around the Balkans.

*Rousanou Monastery in the magnificent Pindos Mountains*

*Detail of a fossilized tree in the Petrified Forest*

# Petrified Forest, Lesvos

Lesvos is a large island and most of its hilly terrain is very fertile, with fields of grain, orchards and olive groves interspersed by dense forests of oak and pine. For the Romans, this was a holiday island and for the Ottoman Turks, a productive larder. But the landscape of the far west is, in surprising contrast, almost desert, with spectacularly bare hills and stony, barren plains. A massive prehistoric eruption buried and transformed – completely and forever – the forested countryside around the volcano. A thick layer of volcanic ash and the action of heavily mineralized water turned all living things to stone, making this strange part of Lesvos a treasury of fossils.

Sigri, the little west-coast harbour town, has an excellent museum with permanent exhibitions on the primeval landscape and

**HOW TO GET THERE:**
Regular charter and internal flights and ferries to Lesvos. Infrequent buses between the capital, Mytilini, and Sigri pass not too far from the forest.
**WHEN TO GO:**
Although the forest is open all year, it is very bleak in winter and shadeless and parched in summer.

the geology and evolution of the Aegean which will enhance a later visit to the Petrified Forest with vivid images of this ancient world. On display are the fossilized trunks, twigs and leaves of the trees and plants which grew here between 15 and 20 million years ago, and a few fossils of creatures that inhabited the forests. Although sequoia and palm have disappeared from Lesvos, a surprisingly large number of the fossilized trees – which include beech, oak, cypress, walnut and plane – still grow here and examples are planted around the museum alongside the standing stumps of petrified trees. To the east of Sigri, the Petrified Forest covers the sun-baked eastern face of the extinct volcano, Ordhymnos. About 3 km (2 mi) of walks are laid out for visitors around the strange, scattered logs and stumps. There is an evocative ancient and lonely atmosphere in this place of eerie, almost lunar, beauty.

**DON'T MISS:**
The Byzantine monastery of Ipsilou, close to the Petrified Forest, is dedicated to St John the Theologian. It is surrounded by a fittingly apocalyptic wasteland, scattered with a few fossilized tree trunks. In contrast, the courtyard is filled with flowers, the interior sumptuous and the small museum excellent.

**YOU SHOULD KNOW:**
Lesvos produces half the world's supply of ouzo. Some of the island's small distillers use secret recipes and produce outstanding spirits. Pre-ouzo rituals among the island's many imbibers include rapping the bottle three times to prevent the contents harming the drinker.

# Island of Evia

Although in some places less than 50 m (165 ft) from the mainland, Evia, which is more than 150 km (93 mi) long, is Greece's second largest island. Very easily reached by road-bridge or one of several short ferry hops, it has long been a favourite with Greek holidaymakers, although relatively few foreign tourists visit. The ancient name, Euboea, means 'rich in cattle' and, although now better known for lamb and kid, Evia remains famously fertile. Particularly popular with Athenians are the picturesque fishing villages and beaches and the world-famous spa, Loutro Edipsou (visited by celebrities from Aristotle to Greta Garbo), on the accessible and sheltered west and north coasts.

Most of inland and eastern Evia is remote, with forested mountains, shady hillside villages and unspoilt beaches. In spring, the countryside becomes a flower garden and, in autumn, open slopes are bright with cyclamen and autumn crocuses. On hills and cliffs, resident and migratory birds of prey include falcons, eagles and buzzards, while coastal wetlands and the reed beds of Lake Dystos are home to large numbers of waders and waterfowl.

Evia has two wonderfully untouched mountain ranges. From the delightful village of Steni there are good treks around the forested foothills of Mount Dirfys and to some lovely, deserted beaches on the central east coast; but the peak itself is a very difficult climb. Mount Ohi is also demanding, although the walk up limestone slopes above the village of Myli is an easier approach. This route passes ancient quarries scattered with chunks of marble and unfinished columns. The southern port and resort, Karystos, is a good base for exploration.

**HOW TO GET THERE:**
Rail and bus from Athens to the capital, Halkida; ferries to points north and south. Buses from Halkida run to some of the larger villages.

**WHEN TO GO:**
May and June or September and October. At weekends, accommodation can be scarce.

**DON'T MISS:**
A cluster of massive stone arches, like Stonehenge's trilithons, stands north of the village of Syra and a single, even larger, one near the summit of Mount Ohi. They are known as *dhrakospita*, dragon houses, because whoever shifted the blocks had to be superhuman. They may be 6th-century BC temples.

**YOU SHOULD KNOW:**
Neither of the peaks should be attempted without the right equipment. The Halkida Alpine Club can provide maps, trail guides and advice. Every few hours, the current in the narrow Evripos Straits changes direction – it can be watched from the old drawbridge at Halkida. Aristotle was reputedly so enraged by his failure to explain the phenomenon that he threw himself into the water; scientists remain baffled.

# Lousios Gorge

Central Arcadia, with its green hillsides, beautiful old villages, fertile valleys, olive groves, orchards and flowery meadows sweet with herbs and tinkling with sheep bells, seems touched by ancient, idyllic magic. The narrow, serpentine road between Dimitsana and Stemnitsa allows glimpses of the Lousios Gorge, one of Greece's loveliest and most interesting hikes.

The trail from Dimitsana – a fascinating little town with fine 18th-century mansions and glorious views into the valley – descends through garden plots to the deep, wooded valley whose flanks narrow into sheer rock faces which, in places, reach almost 300 m (985 ft). Marked hiking trails cross the river at several points and, hidden among the trees, a clutch of monasteries cling to the crags. On the west side of the narrows, Nea Filosofou monastery has some fascinating 17th-century frescoes and the remains of the 10th-century Palea Filosofou monastery seem to merge into the surrounding stone. The remarkable Prodromou monastery clasps the eastern face of the gorge; it is built into the rocks, tucked away like a martin's nest, and occupied by about a dozen young monks. A long track zigzags to the road above.

The path up to the charming village of Stemnitsa, once an important metalworking town and now home to a school for gold and silversmiths, branches off a little further downstream. It is also worth walking along the valley to the Kokkoras Bridge – a high, elegantly arched medieval structure, once a major road link for Arcadia. This spot, with dappled shade and the cold, clean, fast-flowing river, is popular with trout fishermen and with walkers. Although the actual gorge is only about 5 km (3 mi) long, time becomes mysteriously elastic in this entrancing Arcadian landscape.

# Taygetos Mountains and the Mani

From the olive groves of Kalamata to the very south of mainland Greece, the middle 'finger' of the Peloponnese is dominated by the Taygetos Mountains, which divide the Mani east-west into 'Sunward' and 'Shadowed' coasts. North of Areopolis, Outer Mani's landscape is one of dramatic peaks, snow covered until May, steep slopes whose thick forests were, sadly, devastated by recent summer fires, and a narrow coastal plain, watered by mountain streams. South, the mountains taper to craggy bare hills in the remote, sparsely populated Inner Mani, which is generally visited only as part of a daytrip. Fishing villages are scattered along the rocky and rather inaccessible east coast, while in the west, stony tracks over the austerely beautiful ochre and tan landscapes lead to villages of towers, sprouting from the hillsides, and tiny, richly frescoed and isolated Byzantine churches.

Further north is Gytheio. This attractive, friendly port provides a comfortable base on the east coast; on the west coast there are two popular resorts – Stoupa with its fine sand beaches and Kardamyli, where the highest point in the Taygetos, 2404-m (7887-ft) Mount Profitis Ilias, soars above the coast. The peak can be attempted by experienced climbers from the Vyros or Rindoma Gorges, along steep, rocky escarpments and knife-edged ridges, or by hikers via the saddle between the sharp, pyramidal summit and a summer settlement reached by a dirt road.

Around Kardamyli, *kalderimi* (cobbled mule tracks) fan out into the foothills and offer a number of excellent hikes, including a short walk to a pair of burial chambers known as the tombs of the Dioskouri – the Gemini twins. One of the tracks from Exohorio, a hamlet high above the Vyros Gorge, descends into the ravine where two monasteries shelter beneath towering rock faces.

The rocky shoreline of the
Mani Peninsula

**WHEN TO GO:**
Late April (late May for climbers) to June and from September to early October

**DON'T MISS:**
The spectacular road from Sparta to Kalamata crosses the high mountains, climbing through plane-shaded river valleys and ridge after ridge of jagged peaks. In the starkly dramatic Langada Gorge is a rock where the ancient Spartans abandoned infants considered too weak to become soldiers, and the Langada Pass – highest point 1,524 m (5,000 ft) – is reached by a dizzying series of hairpin bends.

**YOU SHOULD KNOW:**
The Taygetos is one of the most beautiful ranges in Greece but is also very hazardous. All climbers, even experienced ones, should seek information and advice on routes.

# Imbros Gorge

Although Crete's White Mountains – the Lefka Ori – are capped in snow for half the year, they are named for their sun-bleached limestone. The journey south from Hania passes isolated villages, high plains and pockets of fertility among the barren, tumultuous peaks. Hora Sfakion, squeezed between steep mountains and the sea, is the chief town of Sfakia, Crete's stoniest and most independent region. The little port is regularly packed with crowds making their way to and from the Samaria Gorge, but the White Mountains are carved by a dozen or so other deep canyons and 'local' gorge hikes include the very challenging Aradhena to the west and the delightful Imbros to the east.

The distance from Imbros to Komitades is about 10 km (6 mi); before the road was built, the ravine was the main route towards the coast and it is generally well cobbled and undemanding – an excellent walk for anyone not seeking an endurance test. For years, Imbros was something of a secret, but it is now on the coach-tour itinerary. The first bus up from Hora Sfakion, or a tranquil night staying in Imbros village, ensures a head start and a peaceful and lovely walk down a path following the stream through steep green valleys, under a rock bridge and into narrow, sheer canyons. In this gaunt landscape, only plants inaccessible to hungry goats thrive, and in spring these steep cliffs are a flower-decked, vertical rock garden and the air is sweet with oregano, thyme and dittany, a favourite Cretan hangover cure. Green and golden lizards scuttle, butterflies dance and songbirds and cicadas chirp in the thick vegetation which shades much of the gorge. High overhead, huge birds of prey hang motionless in the bright day.

# Gavdos

In recent years, the island of Gavdos has changed. There is a big new concrete dock, some newly asphalted roads, new wells and – although the rumble of beachside diesel generators still augments the evening chorus of cicadas – an electricity station. In summer Cretans and mainland Greeks occupy ramshackle beach houses at Sarakiniko and Korfos, or join campers and nudists for a bohemian interlude. But, off-season, the little island retains its magic.

The appeal is not the landscape, as scrub covers much of the low-lying interior, or the architecture – the few 'villages' and even the 'capital', Kastri, are no more than clusters of simple cottages, mostly deserted. Its archaeological remains are fragments of Neolithic and Minoan pottery and its history, apart from a Byzantine period when the population of 8,000 included a bishop, is unremarkable. By the 20th century, when it was used as a place of exile for political prisoners, many of Gavdos's inhabitants had chosen an easier life in Crete.

A visit, though, can be potently nostalgic. The island is about 10 km (6 mi) long and there are good tracks over the undemanding terrain. The longest hike is to rocky Tripiti, the southernmost point of Europe, where swimmers in the crystal-clear waters find themselves surrounded by small fish. The many beaches – sand or pebble, rocky or dune-backed and tamarisk-shaded – are often deserted. Tents can be pitched anywhere and driftwood fires, the slap of wavelets, and a star-jewelled inky sky, are alluring options. But it is the small permanent population (about 50 residents from six families) that makes a long stay feasible and enjoyable. With friendly tavernas, barbecued fish, boat trips, even beer *en route* to Tripiti, Gavdos is a desert island without tears and offers a delightful, illusory isolation.

**YOU SHOULD KNOW:**
In autumn, the 50 km (31 mi) of deep water between Gavdos and Crete is often rough and ferries may be delayed or cancelled. Although Gavdos has plenty of fish, lamb, kid and some locally grown vegetables, most supplies are shipped from Crete. The local thyme honey is delicious, but long-staying vegetarians may go hungry. Gavdos is one of several suggested locations for Calypso's enchanted island, where Odysseus stayed longer than he intended on his way home, but it is better documented as a pirate's lair.

*Agios Ioannis beach*

# Lura National Park

**HOW TO GET THERE:**
The closest town is Peshkopi, 25 km (15 mi) to the east. The easiest route from Tirana is north through Miloti, then west via Rreshen.
**WHEN TO GO:**
April to October, although in winter the snowy forest and the frozen lakes are lovely.
**DON'T MISS:**
One of the southern lakes is named the Lake of Flowers because it is covered with water lilies. When they bloom, the water is invisible beneath the overlapping leaves and the galaxies of starry white flowers.
**YOU SHOULD KNOW:**
Although this park was established in 1966, it has been little developed. A new ecotourism initiative aims to establish 'adventure activities', guides and facilities, and to encourage the involvement of the local community. It is to be hoped that the untouched peace of the Lura Lakes can survive.

Until 1990 Albania was a closed communist country and it remains somewhat mysterious. Despite a sorry legacy of ecological vandalism, much of its rural interior is unspoilt and now industrial activity is monitored and national parks preserve landscape and wildlife. The Lura Mountains, northeast of Tirana, are part of Albania's mountainous spine. On the eastern slopes of the mountain massif known as Lura's Crown, Lura National Park protects a wide belt of forest and a glacial landscape of ridges, ravines and high lakes.

The beautiful, cool forest consists chiefly of beech, fir and pine, and is home to many animals and birds. Pine marten, roe deer and capercaillie may be spotted, while the remote and inaccessible parts of the forest are said to shelter rare and elusive animals, such as brown bears, lynxes and wolves. Amphibians, including newts, live in the chilly waters. The Lura Lakes are well known to Albanians, but little visited by tourists. Numbering about a dozen, they lie like jewels among the trees; some are inky dark, reflecting the conifers, others bright with the blue of the open sky. From the upland village of Fushe Lura several circular walks begin, looping round the upper or lower group of lakes, or climbing the heights of Lura's Crown before descending through the forest. A large swathe of alpine pasture in the south of the park, the 'Field of Mares' is a popular place to relax. In spring and summer it is absolutely radiant, a glorious tapestry of wild flowers.

# Djavolja Varos

Devil's Town (Djavolja Varos) occupies the watershed of two steep ravines – Devil's Valley and Infernal Valley – on the slopes of Mount Radan in southern Serbia. About 200 elongated cones, many over 15 m (49 ft) high, topped by flat, dark stone caps stand crowded together like a multitude of tall, silent, sinister giants. Thousands of years of water erosion carved them from the soft red stone and their evolution continues – old towers change shape and crumble away, others grow slowly from the ground. When the wind blows, they seem to shriek, sigh, groan and wail. Close by, traces of habitation can be seen, as well as the ruins of a church, still visited despite the oak tree which has grown up through the altar. Those who once lived here invented stories about the place and named it – and the two highly mineralized springs – the Devil's Water and the Devil's Well.

Similar geological oddities exist worldwide, but these 'devils' are unusually tall and closely packed – it is almost impossible to squeeze between them – and Devil's Town was recently nominated for the new 'Seven Natural Wonders' list. Although it was not placed, visitor numbers have increased and current development projects will provide amenities and floodlighting for night tours. Independent travellers who want the place to themselves can walk there from Prolom Spa. The enjoyable 9 km (5.5 mi) hike, the Path of Health, crosses fertile farmland and climbs past isolated hamlets before descending through thick woods to the site. There is a strange, unsettling beauty to the twisted towers in a desert of reddish scree, surrounded by the watchful green forest.

**HOW TO GET THERE:**
Regular buses run from Nis and Kursumlija to Prolom Spa. The tourist office in Kursumlija can arrange visits.

**WHEN TO GO:**
May to September

**DON'T MISS:**
A detour from the Path of Health. After the last hamlet, the main path turns downhill, but an uphill track between two ancient oaks (one is roughly carved with *Dj. Varos*) leads to the edge of a precipitous gorge, high above the 'devils'. Looking down on the bristling throng as the light changes with the scudding clouds, the colours shift and seem to flicker, like infernal firelight.

**YOU SHOULD KNOW:**
The most colourful of the folk tales about the Devil's Town concerns a wedding party making its way to church. God, wishing to prevent extreme wickedness of some sort – the precise details vary from jealous rivalry and violence to incest – turned them all to stone.

# Krka National Park

**HOW TO GET THERE:**
Several buses run daily from Sibenik
to both entrances.
**WHEN TO GO:**
April to October
**DON'T MISS:**
A boat trip. Walkers and
birdwatchers may relish the peace of
the land, but the voyage between the
towering cliffs of the narrow gorge is
thrilling, and the view of the
monastery on its tiny island in the
tranquil lake is quite magical.
**YOU SHOULD KNOW:**
Its position near one of the few
passes through the high Alps has
always given Knin strategic
importance. When Croatia became
independent in 1990, Serbs from the
region made the town capital of an
independent state. It was re-taken in
1995; the Serbs left and now the
Croatian flag flies over what is
almost a ghost town.

The Dinaric Alps extend down the Adriatic coast from Slovenia to Albania. Rugged parallel ranges of porous karstic limestone, broken and riddled by ravines, underground rivers and caverns, form most of mainland Croatia, while its myriad islands are the summits of a long-submerged western chain. The mountains are scattered with ruined fortresses – the daunting peaks have been a stronghold against invaders from early times – but the landscape is sparsely populated. The geology and wildlife of several areas are now protected as national parks.

The Krka River rises in the mountains near Knin and Mount Dinara and descends, through a typical karstic landscape of gorges, lakes and cascades of 'steps' built up from tufa to the fine old city of Sibenik, and the sea. The riverside scenery of the Krka National Park is diverse and dramatic – cliffs and caves, woods and marshes – with a remarkable range of plants and wildlife and some interesting architectural features. Entry to the park is from either side of the river, at Skradin or Lozovac. It can be explored on foot by paths and walkways, or by boat. Deserted watermills stand by the waterfalls, the Orthodox Krka Monastery at the head of the valley and the Franciscan Samostan Visovac is picturesquely sited on an island. This wonderful patchwork of natural habitats is particularly important for birds. Resident and migratory species range from raptors, including osprey and eagle owls, to tiny, brilliant bee-eaters. The river flows swiftly all year and there are two very dramatic cascades – Roski Slap, at the end of a deep canyon and Skradinski Buk, a flight of 17 ever-widening steps, with fierce torrents gushing around rocks and surging down into the large lower lake.

*The picturesque cascades of the Krka waterfalls*

*Hills reflected in Cerknica Lake*

# Cerknica Lake

In the beautiful, unspoilt countryside south of Ljubljana, wooded hills, upland and valley farms, streams and isolated villages seem scarcely touched by the modern world. Between the Bloke Plateau and the Rakov Škocjan Regional Park lies an area which on some maps appears as an expanse of water, on others as wetland. This is Lake Cerknica, famous from ancient times for its mystifying periodic disappearances. Full, it measures about 10 x 5 km (6 x 3 mi) and is Slovenia's largest lake; empty, it is a low-lying area of lush hayfields. In 1689, the Slovenian scholar Valvasor proposed an explanation which so impressed the Royal Society that he was made an honorary member. The limestone of this region is perforated by caves and channels and when autumn rains swell streams above and below ground, water bubbles up into a depression which rapidly – often in a few days – becomes a lake. When the subterranean waters eventually recede, the lake empties through karstic sinkholes over a period of several weeks. This intermittent lake has always been a valuable natural resource for farmers and fishermen and, although misguided 19th-century attempts to regulate the flow endangered its ecological balance, the area is now fully protected.

Activities on the lake include boating, windsurfing and skating as well as fishing. Its reed beds, an important habitat for huge numbers of nesting and migrating birds, including storks, reed warblers, corncrakes and lapwings, are a great draw for birdwatchers. The area's other attractions are grouped around the lake. There are good hikes into the hills (the views from the top of Velika Slivnica are superb); picturesque villages, including Otok which is, seasonally, Slovenia's only inhabited island; and, to the east, the little visited Krizna Water Cave, a remarkable network of tunnels and caverns, rivers and lakes.

**HOW TO GET THERE:**
Regular buses run from Ljubljana to Cerknica; local buses are sporadic. Bicycles can be hired.
**WHEN TO GO:**
The lake usually fills in October and starts to empty in late May.
**DON'T MISS:**
The Museum of Lake Cerknica, in a café-bar in Dolenje Jezero, is a family museum. Its displays include objects connected with life by the lake and a slide show, but the star attraction is the owner's working scale model of the area, which demonstrates how the lake fills and empties, with background sounds of locally recorded bird song.
**YOU SHOULD KNOW:**
The museum only opens on Saturday afternoons, although group visits can be arranged. At Sneznik Castle, south of the lake, there is a Dormouse Hunting Museum. Dormice are considered a great delicacy here and the castle hosts an annual Dormouse Hunting Night to celebrate the start of the season.

*A view of Logarska Dolina and the Kamnik-Savinja Alps*

# Kamnik-Savinja Alps

**HOW TO GET THERE:**
Regular train and bus service from Ljubljana to Kamnik and buses north from Kamnik. In summer, one bus a day runs from Kamnik to the Logar Valley.

**WHEN TO GO:**
May to September for walking and climbing, December to March for winter sports.

**DON'T MISS:**
The Logar Valley is accessible to vehicles and can be overrun by organized tours, but for visitors with plenty of time it is a real joy. There are caves and waterfalls, quiet walks through lovely beech woods, a

The Kamnik-Savinja Alps are part of the long chain of the Southern Alps. Although relatively low by alpine standards, they are dramatically steep and rugged and their sheer north faces are very challenging – mountaineering skills are essential. The gentler southern slopes, though, can be climbed by energetic hikers with good boots, maps and common sense. One group of peaks, which includes 2,558-m (8,392-ft) Grintovec, the highest in the range, can be reached from Jezersko, an alpine resort near the Austrian border. Winter activities – cross-country skiing and waterfall ice climbing – also take place in this area.

Pretty Kamniska Bistrika, deep in a wooded river valley north of the pleasant old town of Kamnik, is the starting place for several walks – long tough hikes up into the mountains and more leisurely rambles around forest, ravines and waterfalls. About 10 km (6 mi) from Kamnik, a combination of cable car and chairlift runs to the top of the high limestone plateau, Velika Planina. In winter, this is a popular skiing and snowboarding area, while in summer its rolling pastures are home to herdsmen and their cattle, and walkers. Hikes up to the plateau and around its scattered settlements, over a gloriously open landscape with views north to the jagged peaks, make a wonderfully gentle introduction to alpine walking.

At the eastern end of the range, the Logar Valley is a favourite with visitors. Here, at the famous Rinka Falls, the river plunges (except in high summer) 80 m (262 ft) from the craggy heights to a beautiful green valley.

profusion of flora and fauna – from rare orchids to golden eagles – and longer hikes into the *cirque* of high mountains around the Rinka Falls or to peaceful, road-less alpine valleys.

**YOU SHOULD KNOW:**
Some of the narrower, circular trails from Kamniska Bistrika are one way. Sleepy Kamnik was once an important town and has some fine monastic buildings and two ruined castles. One of these was home to the legendary Countess Veronika (half woman, half snake) and her jealously guarded hoard of treasure.

# Pohorje

Lying west of Slovenia's second city, Maribor, the Pohorje massif is geologically part of the Central Eastern Alps. There are no towering peaks, but this is Slovenia's favourite winter sports location and home to the annual Golden Fox World Cup women's skiing competition. From the outskirts of the town, a cable car whizzes skiers and snowboarders up to Maribor Pohorje for miles of uncrowded cross-country ski tracks and *pistes* (mostly easy or moderate) and an exhilarating downhill night run. At the western end of the massif, built around the highest peak, Rogla is another popular ski centre.

Pohorje is a year-round destination and when the snow melts, ski tracks become routes for hikers and cyclists. This is a lovely 'big sky' area of rolling, undemanding terrain – thickly forested hills, high moorland and marsh, lakes and waterfalls. It is dotted with isolated farms and tiny churches and criss-crossed by long and short walks over unmade roads and forest tracks from both resorts. A particularly enjoyable hike from Rogla meanders through ancient forest to the Lovrenc Marsh Lakes, where walkers should be careful not to disturb the pools – the resident goblin brings bad weather if angered.

Trails from Maribor start at the Bolfenk cable car terminus. Several of the longer routes pass through Areh; a popular walk continues along a high path with stunning views to the Sunik waterfalls, deep in one of Europe's few tracts of virgin forest.

Maribor is a relaxed and interesting old town and a very good base. South of Rogla are the spa town, Zrece, and the delightful 'City of Flowers and Wine', Slovenske Konjice.

**HOW TO GET THERE:**
There are good bus and rail links to Maribor.

**WHEN TO GO:**
May to October for walking, December to March for skiing.

**DON'T MISS:**
The pretty little church of St Areh stands high in a clearing; inside, a stone monument to St Henry (whose name became Areh) was brought here from the Carthusian monastery in Zice. Outside, the spring is thought to have healing properties and the nearby lodge provides welcome sustenance for walkers.

**YOU SHOULD KNOW:**
Maribor is a wine-producing region and the vine which grows on one of the medieval houses is, at 400, the world's oldest. It still produces a few bottles of wine from grapes picked, with great ceremony, every October.

# Val Grande National Park

At 120 sq km (46 sq mi), Val Grande National Park is the largest wild area in Italy and lies 100 km (62 mi) north of Milan, in the Italian Alps. The heart-shaped park, which is surrounded by mountains, is centred on two valleys: Val Pogallo and Val Grande. Until the mid 20th century it contained a number of alpine villages, but war and poverty drove the inhabitants out, leaving nature to take its course. Val Grande was made a National Park in 1992, when it was realized that it had become a wilderness.

Trekking here is exacting and hikers are advised to take extreme care as there are many precipitous ravines. The best plan is to use an official guide because while the major routes through the park have been kept up, there are many others that can be attempted. For those with limited time, Monte Faié is accessible all year round. With an altitude of 1,352 m (4,436 ft), the spectacular view from the top includes the Pedum peaks, Lake Mergozzo and the valley itself.

The valley floor and lower slopes are largely pasture and stands of birch, linden, willow and, most importantly, chestnut. Higher up are ancient beech woods as well as firs that segue into green alder, ferns and moss, then rhododendron and bilberry and, finally, alpine meadows and wild flowers such as gentian, columbine and arnica. The ravines are full of maple, lime, yew and alder.

Many small mammals live here as well as chamois, roe deer, foxes, stone martens and badgers. Bullhead and brown trout thrive in the many streams and rivers, and birds include black grouse, woodpeckers, owls, hawks and eagles.

This is a remarkable place, its remote, silent grandeur the more extraordinary given its proximity to one of Italy's most visited areas: Lake Maggiore.

*A view of the lush Val Grande National Park*

# Maremma Regional Park

Located in the southwestern corner of Tuscany, Maremma Regional Park extends from the mouth of the Ombrone River to Talamone, a 25-km (15-mi) stretch bordered inland by the Aurelia highway. Founded in 1975, the park has a typically southern Tuscan landscape and is dominated by the Uccellina Hills. Softly rounded and covered by dense, shrubby Mediterranean vegetation, the lower slopes consist mainly of pasture and olive groves.

The woods within Maremma are dominated by huge holm oaks, maples and myrtle, and both aromatic and flowering plants such as lavender, rosemary, juniper, clematis and broom bring bright splashes of colour. In spring, several species of orchid can be found. It is this mixture of habitats that prompted the protection of the area.

The park descends gently from the hills across the marshes and dunes close to the estuary, through farmland and pasture to the coastline. To the south, steep cliffs are evidence of coastal erosion. Sandy beaches, protected by indigenous Italian pine forests, are perfect for looking for shells and swimming.

The Ombrone estuary offers splendid birdwatching opportunities; waders, ducks and herons are common. Inland, woodpeckers, finches, bunting, owls, buzzards and kestrels may be seen. Mammals include wild boar, skunks, stone martens, foxes, deer, and many smaller species such as rabbits and hedgehogs. The luxuriant pastures support both horses and the renowned, long-horned Maremma cattle, watched over by *butteri* – Italian cowboys. They not only work with the animals, but also present shows from time to time.

The park offers several trails to follow and organized cycling or horse-riding tours are available. Hire a canoe and follow the Ombrone down to its estuary, it's a bewitching journey.

*The coastal landscape of the Maremma Regional Park*

**HOW TO GET THERE:**
By car, train to Grosseto and Alberese stations, or bus to Grosseto on weekdays only

**WHEN TO GO:**
All year round. From March 23 to September 30 Maremma is open from 08.00 until 17.00. The rest of the year the park is open from 08.30 to 13.30.

**DON'T MISS:**
The scuba diving at Argentario and the islands of Giglio and Giannutri.

**YOU SHOULD KNOW:**
There are important Etruscan sites at Roselle, Saturnia, and Pitigliano and modern thermal spas at the base of Monte Amiata. In Talamone, the remains of a Roman villa may be seen.

# Gran Sasso e Monti della Laga National Park

Encompassing three mountain groups, the Gran Sasso and Monti della Laga National Park is one of the largest protected areas in Europe. Formed in 1991 and part of the Appenines, the park includes both their highest peak, Corno Grande, at 2,912 m (9,554 ft), as well their only glacier, the Calderone. Within its territory are hundreds of villages and 44 towns.

The protected area is so vast and covers such diverse landscape and habitat that it is rich with rare flora and fauna, some of which is unique. Over 2,000 different species of plant is found here and mammals include the Abruzzo chamois, red and roe deer, wild cats, wild boar, foxes, polecats, martens, porcupines, small packs of Appenine wolves and many smaller species.

Birdwatchers often make for the Forca di Penne and Campotosto Lake where thousands of migrating birds rest by the shore, although birds can be seen throughout the area. At lower levels, where there are fields and pasture, Ortolan buntings, crested larks and red-backed shrikes may be found. At higher altitudes there are snowfinches, pipits, alpine accentors and choughs. This is also great country for raptors; golden eagles, lanners, goshawks and peregrine falcons are all at home here.

There are many activities to enjoy in the park and wonderful opportunities exist for exploring on foot, horseback, mountain-bike or by canoe. Rivers and streams rush down into the valleys and there are some spectacular waterfalls which, in winter, form an extraordinary sight when they sometimes freeze. Campo Imperatore, a high plateau, is one of Italy's oldest and most popular ski resorts. With guaranteed snow during winter, the park is a magnet for advanced skiers, with off-piste descents attracting free-riders from across Europe. Cross-country skiing is also popular, as is mountaineering and ice-cascade climbing.

# Ausoni and Aurunci Mountains

The Ausoni and Aurunci Mountains, located in central Italy, run from the Appenines to the promontory of Gaeta on the Mediterranean coast. Part of the Antiappenini, and also sometimes known as the Volsci, derived from their Roman name, there is no official dividing line between them. The highest peak in the range, Monte Petrella, stands at 1,533 m (5,030 ft).

In 1997, the Monti Aurunci Natural Park was created. If time is limited, this offers an excellent overview of these mountain ranges, from the plain to the top of Monte Petrella with its glorious vistas across the mountains to the sea. Magnificent beech trees cloak the northern slopes, and there are oaks, maples, hornbeams and chestnuts, too. In spring wild flowers such as hellebores, snowdrops, cyclamen, violets, anemones and saffron are abundant. Meadows cover the valley, where brooms, Judas trees and 50 species of orchid thrive. The southern sector is on the route of many migratory birds, but there are also owls, nightjars and nightingales to be seen. Raptors are found at higher levels, where mammals such as wild boar, wildcats, foxes, martens and hares make their homes in the dense woodland.

The rainfall in the mountains, which have typical karst topography, sinks through the limestone to reappear as springs and vernal pools on the lower slopes. This is good habitat for amphibians, and four types of salamander as well as four types of frog can be seen here.

A network of trails for both hikers and mountain-bikes runs throughout the park, and both inside and outside its boundaries the mountains are criss-crossed with small roads linking little medieval villages. Many of the inhabitants still raise cattle and work on the land and in the forests. The villages, with their ancient squares, cobbled streets, archways and churches, are well worth visiting.

**HOW TO GET THERE:**
By car or train
**WHEN TO GO:**
Any time of year, but the spring and early summer are best for wild flowers.
**DON'T MISS:**
The historic town of Fondi with its castle, palazzo, cathedral and medieval churches
**YOU SHOULD KNOW:**
The Abbey of Montecassino, located just the other side of the Rome to Naples motorway, was founded by St Benedict in AD 529. In February 1944 it was destroyed during fighting between the Allied and German forces. Paid for by the Italian government, reconstruction took ten years. The Polish War Cemetery can be seen from the Abbey.

*The Aurunci Mountains*

# Pollino National Park

One of the largest national parks in Italy, Pollino National Park straddles the boundary of Basilicata and Calabria in southern Italy. Its highest peak, Monte Pollino, rises to 2,267 m (7,438 ft). Founded in 1992 to protect the palebark pine, the park's symbol, this is one of the last remaining areas in Italy where it is found.

This vast area of 1,820 sq km (703 sq mi) is fascinating, including as it does many interesting towns as well as archaeological sites and glorious wilderness. It is a region best savoured at length, thus a walking holiday is ideal. Serra Dolcedorme is a major attraction, but there are other lovely ranges, too, including Serra di Crispo where the palebark pine grows right to the peaks – all twisted trunks and branches shaped by the wind. From higher altitudes a view of both coasts may be enjoyed and, with luck, a golden eagle might be soaring through the blue sky above.

As well as mountains there are never-ending upland plains dotted with peacefully grazing sheep, rolling hills and lush valleys, and a profusion of flowering plants and bushes, particularly during spring. Many protected creatures inhabit the region, from wolves, roe deer, hares and black squirrels, to snakes, otters, salamanders and the yellow-bellied toad. Birds include peregrine falcons, red kites, lanners and buzzards as well as numerous smaller species, such as woodpecker and chough.

*The primeval Calabrian, or palebark pine, in Pollino National Park*

Rivers and streams are plentiful, plunging through gorges that have been gouged from the rock over millennia. Cave systems, too, are numerous and rich in both prehistoric sites, such as the Romito Caves, and archaeological sites. Castles and monasteries, ancient villages where the older inhabitants still wear traditional dress, ethnic Albanians who maintain their traditional culture and speak their own dialect – all this can be discovered in Pollino National Park.

# Gargano National Park

The Gargano Peninsula sticks out into the Adriatic Sea like a spur above the heel of the Italian boot. This mountainous massif, comprising several peaks, is situated in the province of Foggia. Almost all of it is part of the Gargano National Park, formed in 1995, which also has lower-lying wetlands and flatlands.

The heart of the park is the wonderful Umbra Forest. Once covering the entire peninsula, the 15 per cent that remains is glorious – broad-leafed trees such as beech, maple, hornbeam, oak and chestnut grow to enormous heights and, beneath them, anemones, violets and cyclamen grow in profusion. Some 35 per cent of all species of flora found in Italy are here, including an extraordinary number of orchids: 61 varieties and still counting.

Mammals include about 100 rare roe deer, martens, badgers, wildcats and numerous smaller species, while forest birds include raptors and four types of woodpecker – again, very rare in Italy. Another reason the area is protected is because of its wetlands. There are lagoons, marshes, lakes, vernal pools and springs, as well as the sea. These provide habitat for numerous amphibians and water birds, some of which arrive during their migration to and from Africa and central and eastern Europe.

Between the forest and the sea are large stands of Aleppo pines, olive trees, and typical Mediterranean shrubland. On the coast itself the sea and wind have sculpted wonderful shapes into the limestone cliffs, creating a jagged coastline with many small beaches of sand or stones, often only accessible by boat. There are 128 known caves on the peninsula, 52 of which were used by prehistoric man. Several of the caves can be visited by boat, including the spectacular 47-m (154-ft) high, bell-shaped Grotta Campana.

*A natural limestone arch in Gargano National Park*

**HOW TO GET THERE:**
The best way to explore Gargano is by car, although there are local buses from Foggia.

**WHEN TO GO:**
Best between April and September.

**DON'T MISS:**
The Sanctuary of Monte Sat'Angelo sul Gargano. Dedicated to Archangel Michael, this is the oldest shrine in Europe and has been a place of pilgrimage since the 6th century.

**YOU SHOULD KNOW:**
12 km (7 mi) off the coast are the Tremiti Islands, also part of Gargano National Park. Take a boat trip around the islands to enjoy the beaches and ancient ruins, or scuba dive in the clean, clear waters.

# Supramonte Plateau

**HOW TO GET THERE:**
From Nuoro or Oliena by car
**WHEN TO GO:**
April to June, September and October
**DON'T MISS:**
The prehistoric village of Tiscali,
which is built inside a huge cave in
Monte Corrasi.
**YOU SHOULD KNOW:**
The village of Orgosolo lies at the
bottom of the mountains and has
become famous for its political and
social wall murals, depicting the
struggle between the traditional life
and culture of the local inhabitants
and the views of the State.

Found inland from the Gulf of Orosei, eastern Sardinia, close to Orgosolo, is the high plateau of Supramonte in a mountain range of the same name. Reminiscent of the Dolomites, this limestone massif is covered with forest and is a wonderful region for walking and trekking.

The plateau itself ends abruptly with drops of 1,000 m (3,280 ft) down to the Oliena Plain and its north faces are well known for their difficult and lengthy climbing routes. There are, however, two short routes to the plateau for straightforward hikers. The plateau is weird and wonderful, its typical karst formation laced with drainage gullies and virtually no trails other than the route up Monte Corrasi. This is the highest peak in the area at 1,391 m (4,564 ft). The terrain is bleak, stony and harshly beautiful, with long views across the plateau to the Barumini Mountains. Isolated groups of red peonies appear to live in stone. Beneath the barren summit, gullies shelter many wild plants such as rosemary, cyclamen and lilies.

Visit the region of the Flumineddu River, which is surrounded by a thick forest of holm oak, yew, juniper, holly and oleander. Here the Flumineddu has cut the mountain in two and formed the Gorropu Gorge – one of Sardinia's most impressive natural sites. It is possible for experienced canyoneers to negotiate it with the correct equipment, but part of it is accessible anyway via a pretty path from the valley. There's even the opportunity to enjoy a quick dip along the way.

The mountains are home to mouflon sheep, notable for their curved horns, as well as wild boar, wildcats and pine marten and several smaller species. The great slabs of rock walls provide perfect nesting spots for several raptors, including golden eagles, goshawks and sparrow hawks.

# Cies Islands

The Cies is a group of three granite islands off the northwest coast of Galicia, northern Spain. They have been a nature reserve since 1980 and, with six other islands and archipelagos, in the year 2000 they were declared part of the National Land-Marine Park of the Atlantic Islands of Galicia. Once mountains, their cliffs on the Atlantic Ocean side rear sharply from the water and are riddled with caves formed by the action of wind and waves. The eastern aspect is far less severe; here trees and shrubs abound and rare plants grow in the sand dunes.

Although inhabited for centuries, the Cies suffered so many invasions that by 1700 they were deserted and re-populated only when a lighthouse was built on the island in the 19th century. Today, Las Islas Cies are best known for Playa de Rodas, a superb beach of fine, white sand that links Isla de Monte Agudo to Isla do Faro. At high tide the sea covers the area nearest the rocky shoreline, forming a lagoon but leaving a curved sand 'road' linking the two islands.

Many visitors head for the beach, but exploring further is worthwhile. There are marked trails, the toughest of which makes for the lighthouse at the highest point of Monte Agudo, where the views are superb. For those who prefer a gentler climb there is a delightful short hike through woods. Damaged by climate and human activity, one quarter of the woodland has had to be reforested with pine and eucalyptus.

Birdwatching is another delight. There are important colonies of seabirds here, the largest being some 22,000 breeding pairs of yellowfoot gull. Green cormorants and Caspian gulls also breed here and the noise can sometimes be deafening. The Cies Islands are a resting point during the migration of many other birds.

**HOW TO GET THERE:**
From June to September, travel by boat from Vigo, Baiona or Cangas to Monte Agudo, or join a tourist cruise.
**WHEN TO GO:**
Between June and September, unless you have your own boat
**DON'T MISS:**
The three lighthouses on the islands and the two observatories
**YOU SHOULD KNOW:**
It is possible to camp in the Cies, but permits have to be obtained from the port at Vigo. There is a supermarket and a restaurant but visitors have to take their rubbish away with them as there are no litter bins.

*San Martino Island as seen from Monte Agudo*

# Picos de Europa

**HOW TO GET THERE:**
The easiest way to see the Picos de Europa is by car, from Oviedo or Santander.
**WHEN TO GO:**
All year round, but spring, summer or autumn are probably best.
**DON'T MISS:**
The village of Bulnes. Until 2000 it was only accessible by mule track, but the building of a funicular railway has made it easier to visit and encounter its hardy, independent inhabitants, whose way of life is so completely different from most Europeans.
**YOU SHOULD KNOW:**
Since 1983 the Vuelta a España, one of Europe's elite road bicycle races, has often used the road from Covadonga up to the lakes. The toughest section is the final 7 km (4 mi), which includes an average 15 per cent gradient for 800 m (2,625 ft).

Extending across three regions and part of the Cantabrian Mountains, Picos de Europa is situated some 20 km (12 mi) from Spain's northern coast, halfway between Oviedo and Santander. Formed of limestone, the impressive karst landscape consists of the Western, Central and Eastern massifs, the first two divided by the spectacular 1.5-km (1-mi) deep Cares Gorge. Spain's first national park was formed here in 1918 and in 1995 the designated area was almost quadrupled. In 2003, it became a UNESCO Biosphere Reserve.

Climbers and hikers are drawn to these mountains and the refuge huts are well used. The highest peak, Torre de Cerredo, reaches 2,648 m (8,688 ft) and many more are almost as high. It is also popular with cavers, as some of the country's deepest caves are found here. Its proximity to the sea means there is often snow, regardless of the season.

Each massif has different characteristics. The western massif boasts the Lakes of Covadonga – two perfect glacial lakes.

Covadonga is accessible by car and there is an easy and beautiful hike round the shores of both lakes, winding through beech woods and across swathes of green pasture where shepherds guard flocks of sheep and goats, and delicious cheeses are produced.

The flora and fauna of the Picos de Europa is exciting: Cantabrian brown bears, Iberian lynx, wolves, wild boar, wild horses, roe deer, chamois and ibex are all found here, and birds include buzzards, vultures, golden and short-toed eagles, capercailles and hundreds of smaller species.

It is possible to ride, fish and white-water raft, but simply hiking through the spectacular scenery of mixed forests of oak, beech, walnut, chestnut and maple, and lush valleys filled with wild flowers and butterflies cut with sparkling crystal-clear streams, is both peaceful and healing.

*Hikers walk along a trail in Cares Gorge.*

# Cap de Creus

Situated at the northern end of the Costa Brava, close to the border with France, the Cap de Creus juts out into the Mediterranean. A nature reserve since 1998, protecting both land and sea, the peninsula is the largest uninhabited area of the Spanish Mediterranean. Although the region's holm oak and cork forests were badly damaged from frequent forest fires and over-grazing, thousands of cork oaks have been re-planted.

*The rugged coastline of Cap de Creus*

The coastline rises stark and rugged from the deep-blue sea, indented with tiny bays and rocky islets, many of which are only accessible by boat. The rocks, scoured by centuries of high winds and waves, are notable for their bizarre shapes, some of which resemble birds and animals – for example, the eagle of Tudela.

This is prime birdwatching territory, partly because, as the easternmost point of the Iberian peninsula, it is a magnet for migratory birds. From the highest point at Sant Salvador, several types of swift, black-eared wheatear, rock thrush and crag martins can been seen during summer. Thekla lark, blue rock thrush and black wheatear are permanent inhabitants. Peregrine falcons breed here and Bonelli's eagles hover overhead.

Different species, such as Dartford and Sardinian warblers, inhabit the shrub land that forms most of the landscape – mainly cistus, broom, lavender, gorse and several Mediterranean herbs. Lupins and orchids also thrive, but the most interesting flora, including several endemic species, cling to the narrow coastal strip.

In spring and autumn both Cory's and Mediterranean shearwater fly past, and kittiwakes, skuas, razorbills and gulls arrive for the winter. The clear, unpolluted sea contains a mass of fauna, including precious red coral, as well as spiny lobsters, scorpion fish and sunfish, among others. Certain areas are out of bounds for fishing and scuba diving, but a fascinating underwater world waits for divers.

**HOW TO GET THERE:**
By car from Roses, or take an excursion by boat from Roses to Cadaqués.
**WHEN TO GO:**
April to October unless you are a particularly keen ornithologist. Strong northerly winds are a feature of Cap de Creus during winter.
**DON'T MISS:**
The lighthouse, with its remarkable views over the Mediterranean. Its old administrative building is now a pleasant bar/restaurant.
**YOU SHOULD KNOW:**
Salvador Dali, the artist, visited Cadaqués many times from childhood onward and in later life had a house nearby. The extraordinary rock formations along the coast greatly influenced his art. The mayor of Cadaqués donated a rock from the area that will form part of the new headquarters of the Dali Museum in Florida.

*The Sierra de Gredos near the village of Puerte de Piornal*

# Sierra de Gredos

The Sierra de Gredos, part of Spain's central mountain range, is within reach of Toledo, Ávila, Cáceres and Madrid. Popular with climbers, it also offers great opportunities for hiking, walking, horse riding, mountain-biking and paragliding. A Special Bird Protection Zone, this regional park is home to a wealth of flora and fauna, including over 20 species of raptor.

The highest peak in the largely snow-capped Sierra de Gredos is Pico Almanzor. At 2,592 m (8,504 ft), it is also the highest peak in central Spain. Below the mountain's north face is the Laguna de Gredos, a glacial lake with paths to five other lakes. The scenery is glorious, changing from Mediterranean to alpine – depending on elevation. At lower levels, on the southern side, walk beside clear, sparkling rivers and along old Roman roads or stop to relish a picnic in valleys full of wild flowers, lemon and almond trees, and olive groves. Oak, pine, mountain ash, poplar and birch trees grow in quantity and, in autumn, a great variety of fungi can be found. Thyme, rosemary and oregano scent the air. Experts should look

**HOW TO GET THERE:**
By bus from Madrid to Arenas de San Pedro, or by car from the north or south. There are guided hikes and birdwatching excursions available from Madrid.
**WHEN TO GO:**
Spring, summer or autumn
**DON'T MISS:**
The traditional villages, monasteries, and fortresses that can be found within the mountains or the Neolithic cave paintings called El Collado Braguillas, close to El Raso.
**YOU SHOULD KNOW:**
The Sierra is snow-covered during winter, and cross-country skiing, mountain skiing (including extreme descents) and snowshoeing are all possible activities.

out for endemic species of sedum, saxifrage and antirrhinum.

Higher up, the landscape changes to alpine meadows with swathes of yellow broom and, finally, bare rock face decorated with lichen. Mammals in these mountains include elusive wild cats and beech martens, but Gredos ibex may be seen and otters slip and slide in the many rivers; there are also several endemic amphibians to be spotted. Raptors include golden eagles and several other eagle species, as well as kites, hobbies sparrowhawks and vultures. Altogether, including migratory visitors, over 120 types of bird may be seen in these mountains.

# Sierra de Guadarrama

Within easy striking distance of Madrid and Segovia, the Sierra de Guadarrama offers a great escape from the stress of city living. A continuation of the central mountain chain that runs from Spain to Portugal, this range is somewhat lower and gentler than the Sierra de Gredos, its principal peak, Peñalara, reaching 2,428 m (7,966 ft). Running from southwest to northeast, Guadarrama contains many interesting features, including the Peñalara Natural Park and the unusual granite range of La Pedriza.

Many rivers have their source in this region, noted for its high annual rainfall, and there are many small dams in the mountains. The natural park, on the southern slope of Peñalara mountain, contains many small glacial lakes which, during spring, produce small waterfalls and streams from meltwater. At the highest elevations, rock roses, lavender, juniper and ferns abound. Below 2,000 m (6,562 ft) are, firstly, pine forests – in autumn bursting with delicious fungi such as morels and chanterelles; and, secondly, Pyrenean oak – a protected species. A certain amount of logging is permitted here each year to provide the mountain villages with supplies of firewood.

La Pedriza, on the southern slopes of the Sierra de Guadarrama, is one of the largest granite ranges in Europe. Its peaks and cliffs are intersected with valleys and rivers as well as great boulders – some smoothly rounded, others weirdly eroded – which look as though giants have been playing bowls. There must be a thousand different routes for rock climbers, some easy enough for children – although not tots – to manage. Much of the rock is bare, but there are areas of scrub. Raptors are numerous, including over 100 pairs of griffon vultures. The river flows through the valley, cascading into several delightful pools in which to cool off after hiking in the heat.

**HOW TO GET THERE:**
By train, bus or car from Madrid
**WHEN TO GO:**
All year round, if you don't mind the snow and ice between December and February
**DON'T MISS:**
The Royal Monastery of San Lorenzo de El Escorial. Full of world-class art and ancient manuscripts, it is a UNESCO World Heritage Site.
**YOU SHOULD KNOW:**
Because of its proximity to Madrid, the Sierra de Guadarrama is criss-crossed by road passes and railway routes and caters well for tourists. It can get busy during the summer months but, even so, it is relatively easy to find a peaceful and beautiful spot in which to relax.

373

# Sierra de Espuna National Park

**HOW TO GET THERE:**
Sierra de Espuna is about 90 minutes' drive from Alicante airport and is easily reached by road from Alhama de Murcia, Totana and Lorca; but try to start from the visitor centre.
**WHEN TO GO:**
All year round, but May to October or November is probably best.
**DON'T MISS:**
The 'badlands', known as Los Barrancos de Gebas, in the eastern part of the Sierra de Espuna, and the Walls of Layva – an area of limestone walls that attracts climbers.
**YOU SHOULD KNOW:**
On December 8, 9 and 10 each year, a barefooted pilgrimage takes place. Starting from Totana, the statue of Saint Eulalia is carried from the ornate Sanctuary of Santa Eulalia to San Roque, where she remains until January 7.

Situated about 40 km (25 mi) from the coast, between Mucia and Lorca, is the National Park of Sierra de Espuna. A forested area rising to 1,585 m (5,200 ft), the park is a pleasant retreat in which to enjoy both hiking and numerous other outdoor activities. In summer it is cooler and offers more shade than the rest of this flat, dry region.

While there are no rivers in the park, there are many springs and streams, enabling it to remain verdant throughout the year. The highest peak, El Morron de Espuna, reaches 1,583 m (5,194 ft) and is often snow-covered during the winter. Pines are plentiful, although oak, cottonwood, elm, poplar and maple also grow on these hills. Forest footpaths and well-maintained tracks make for pleasant walking, horse riding and mountain-biking. On the slopes, hawthorn, juniper and shrubs such as thyme, rock rose and honeysuckle thrive.

Towards the summit of El Morron is a group of 26 curious, circular domed wells called the Las Pozos de Nieve. The remains of snow pits, they were used from the 16th century until the 1920s when new refrigeration techniques took over. During winter, snow was collected and packed into these wells, to be cut into ice blocks and sold to businesses and individuals in nearby towns during the rest of the year.

Wild boar, Barbary sheep, genet, wild cats, foxes, red squirrels, rabbits and hares enjoy this habitat, along with many species of birds – including raptors such as golden eagles, goshawks, sparrowhawks and owls. It is worth spending a night or two camping or staying in a rural refuge to get the most from a visit. For the more adventurous, hang-gliding and paragliding are both available and one of the longest caves in Murcia – which can be found in Pliego village – is waiting to be explored.

# Cabo de Gata-Nijar Natural Park

The first terrestrial and maritime Protected Area in Andalusia is located east of Almeria, in southeastern Spain. A UNESCO Biosphere Reserve since 1997, the park is Europe's driest area and contains a wide variety of habitats, including semi-desert steppe, saltmarsh, beaches, dunes, cliffs and a large marine area. Volcanic by origin, ancient calderas, volcanic domes and lava flows are centred around the headland of Cabo de Gata.

This is a wild and rugged landscape. The mountains are craggy and ochre coloured, white sand beaches and secret coves are backed by steep, 100 m (328 ft) cliffs, and lookout towers along the coast are testament to a history of incursions by Berber pirates seeking safety in this inaccessible corner of Spain. The terrestrial area of the natural park is home to low-growing vegetation that has adapted to drought conditions, such as cacti, dwarf fan palms and jujube, or red date. There are several endemic species, including the pink snapdragon. Scrub land consists of wild herbs, Kermes oaks and olives.

Most of the 1,100 species of fauna here are birds, although genets, wild boar and weasels can be seen. The Salinas de Cabo de Gata, a saltwater lagoon separated from the beach by a wide sandbar, is home to many resident birds such as flamingoes, herons, cranes and storks as well as thousands of migratory birds that rest here during their lengthy, biannual journeys. Seabirds include terns, shearwaters, shags and gulls, and the quantity of prey attracts raptors such as ospreys and peregrine falcons.

The pristine waters of the marine reserve cover vast swathes of Posidonia, a seagrass endemic to the Mediterranean. This provides shelter for a mass of marine life such as sponges, corals, sea urchins, anemones, sea stars and diverse fish such as halibut, cardinal fish and sea bream – they all make diving and snorkelling a delight.

**HOW TO GET THERE:**
By car. The visitor centre is between Retamar and San Miguel de Cabo de Gata.

**WHEN TO GO:**
Any time of year, but it is probably best between May and October.

**DON'T MISS:**
The local handicrafts – particularly the rugs and blankets of Nijar.

**YOU SHOULD KNOW:**
Spanish dramatist Frederico Lorca set his famous tragedy *Blood Wedding*, in the harsh, arid, sparsely inhabited inland area here and Monsul Beach, one of the most stunning coves in Gata-Nijar Natural Park, was where Steven Spielberg filmed the scene in *Indiana Jones and the Last Crusade* when Sean Connery, playing Indiana's father, brings down a German plane by scaring a flock of birds into the propellers.

# Sierra de Grazalema Natural Park

A UNESCO Biosphere Reserve since 1977, the Sierra de Grazalema is a magnificent area of karst landscape in which cliffs, gorges, caverns and valleys spread across the province of Cadiz and part of the province of Malaga, in southern Spain.

Its 517 sq km (200 sq mi) is scenically spectacular, bursting with flora and fauna, and encompasses 13 pretty white towns and villages, or *pueblos blancos*, within its boundaries. Grazalema itself is one of the most attractive villages and lies between two mountain peaks. Notoriously, the region receives the most rain in Spain, but the upside of this is that 1,300-plus species of plant, including endemics, thrive here. Part of the park is a special reserve area within which grows the best-preserved forests of Spanish fir in the country. Native to southern Spain, this species is very rare, despite having been in existence since the Tertiary Era (1.6–65 million years BC). Other species that grow well are juniper, maple, Portuguese oak and ash, while willows and poplars flourish alongside the streams and rivers.

Fauna include mountain goats, deer, genets, foxes and mongoose, and naturally there is a wealth of birds – including many raptors. The most renowned bird in the Sierra de Grazalema is the griffon vulture. The cliffs in the special reserve host Europe's largest colony.

The Sierra is a superb place to hike through, with many routes of varying degrees of difficulty to be explored. Other activities include exploring the Hundidero-Gato – Andalucia's largest cave system – which can be tackled by experienced cavers with a permit from the local tourist office, plus mountain-biking, horse riding, climbing and canoeing. And for those who love adventure, there are also some excellent spots within the park for hang-gliding.

*Sierra de Grazalema*

# Sierra de Tramuntana

The island of Mallorca, off Spain's eastern coast, is usually thought of as a holiday destination catering for mass tourism. While this is partially true, life inland is calmer and the scenery a delight. The Sierra de Tramuntana is a mountain range in the northwest, stretching from Andratx to the Formentor Peninsula.

Many ancient trails and cobbled pilgrims' routes weave through the mountains, connecting the little medieval villages of the interior. Here, too, are Mallorca's highest peaks: Puig Major, at 1,445 m (4,741 ft) and Massanella, at 1,352 m (4,436 ft). The former is decorated with military installations, but Massanella is a beautiful hike of some three hours, ending with a superb view over the entire island, with Menorca in the distance on a good day.

Walk through the almond groves and gnarled olive trees of this timeless landscape; wild rosemary and other herbs scent the air and the hillsides glow with clumps of yellow broom – during January, February and March, almond and citrus blossom is an added bonus. Higher up, the vegetation changes to Spanish oak forest, carob and pine. Goats and sheep graze the hillsides, while black vultures hang in the sky above, keeping watch for a potential meal. Along the coastal trails, the visitor is blessed with wide, dramatic vistas from high cliffs, interrupted by small, secluded bays. Ospreys and sea eagles can be seen lazily skimming the water in search of food.

The more adventurous may visit the Torrent de Pareis, a gorge that is accessible only to walkers. One of the most spectacular walks on the island, it begins at Sa Calobra, and offers about five hours of scrambling over rocks through fabulous limestone scenery, along a dry river bed.

*A flower meadow adds vibrant colour to the Sierra de Tramuntana.*

**HOW TO GET THERE:**
Hire a car or book a taxi to drop you off and pick you up later at a designated meeting place. You can also travel by bus from Palma.
**WHEN TO GO:**
To avoid crowds, go during the winter months. During summer the region is busier, but the area is cooler and fresher than staying by the coast.
**DON'T MISS:**
Sa Seu, Palma's 14th-century cathedral, or Bellver Castle, located above the city.
**YOU SHOULD KNOW:**
The writer, Robert Graves and the artist Joan Miró both lived in Deia, a charming village in the Sierra de Tramuntana.

# Garajonay National Park

**HOW TO GET THERE:**
By air or sea from Tenerife or Gran Canaria
**WHEN TO GO:**
Any time of year
**DON'T MISS:**
The Juego de Bolas Information Centre, at the park boundary or the old centre of La Calera – a lovely white town perched precariously on a mountainside, its steep steps and narrow lanes clear of cars.
**YOU SHOULD KNOW:**
The park and its peak are named after Gara and Jonay, a local myth of two unfortunate lovers who were forced to kill themselves rather than face separation. Wooden statues of them can be seen at Garajonay.

The Canary Islands, part of Spain but situated close to Morocco, is a group of seven islands, five of which are popular holiday destinations. Enjoying constant sunshine and very little rain, they are all that remain of a volcanic mountain range. La Gomera, the least heavily populated island, is relatively untouched by tourism; it is also blessed with a unique UNESCO World Heritage Site: the Garajonay National Park.

During the Tertiary period, humid, subtropical forests covered much of the Mediterranean region, but most of them disappeared during the Ice Age. Located in the centre of the island, the 40 sq km (15 sq mi) of Garajonay is one of the best-preserved laurel forests still in existence. Made up of several species of non-deciduous hardwood laurels and laurel-type species, the largest variety reaches up to 40 m (130 ft).

The park is usually wreathed in cloud and mist and the many small

streams and springs ensure extraordinarily lush vegetation, in complete contrast to the aridity of La Gomera's coastal area and that of the other Canary Islands. The place has a magical air about it, as though it has stepped from the pages of Tolkein's fantasy, *The Lord of the Rings*. Huge rocks lie scattered about and trees grow in bizarre, twisted shapes. Large ferns form dripping clumps, and the forest floor is rich with undergrowth providing cover for birds, invertebrates and bats. Two endemic pigeons can be found here, as well as the Gomeran lizard and the Gomeran skink.

The Garajonay National Park comprises mountains and valleys, cliffs and ravines, and there are several routes through and across this unusual landscape. Make for the highest point on the island – 1,487 m (4,880 ft) – which is the summit of the eponymous peak, and enjoy the panoramic view.

*Looking over the forests of Garajonay National Park*

# Alvão Natural Park

**HOW TO GET THERE:**
It takes about an hour by car from Porto.
**WHEN TO GO:**
Spring, summer or autumn is when it is at its best.
**DON'T MISS:**
The traditional villages, such as Lamas d'Ôlo.
**YOU SHOULD KNOW:**
BTCV, the international volunteering organization, began its International Working Holidays in Alvão Natural Park in 1994. Since then, volunteers have helped with clearing new invasive species, re-creating traditional meadow management, dry-stone walling and enhancing the health of the various ecosystems.

Located northeast of Porto, Alvão Natural Park spreads across 70 sq km (27 sq mi) of the ridge and western slopes of the Alvão mountains. Formed in 1983, Portugal's smallest Natural Park reaches the height of 1,330 m (4,364 ft) and the Nature Conservation Institute works hard to promote conservation of species as well as the traditional culture of the small villages within its boundaries.

The park bestrides the transition area between the humid coast and the arid interior, and thus falls naturally into two separate components. At its highest altitude, in a rugged, rock-strewn region, the source of the River Ôlo springs from a large granite basin; at its lowest, the river runs through narrow valleys. The geology here – granite and schist – has produced great drops, and probably the most sought-after 'sight' in Alvão is the Fisgas de Ermelo waterfall. This waterfall cascades down a 300 m (935 ft) slope above the picturesque village of Ermelo.

Much of the park consists of green, leafy, mixed species forest that includes black and English oak, silver birch, hazel, holly, bay, chestnut and wild pear. The heathland is mainly covered in heather, gorse, broom and bilberry. Some of the valleys are terraced and planted with rye or with vines, and fruit and olive trees are also grown. There are still wild-flower-rich meadows in which cattle and goats graze. This mixed environment is home to diverse species of fauna; amphibians and reptiles thrive here, and it is a perfect habitat for bats.

Mammals are mainly small – field mice, rabbits, wild goats, wildcats and, very occasionally, wolves. Several types of raptor can be seen, including round-winged eagles and peregrine falcons, as well as many smaller species such as choughs, bullfinches, flycatchers and water pipits.

# Cape St Vincent National Park

Cape St Vincent National Park runs for 150 km (93 mi) down the Atlantic coast to the southwestern tip of Portugal, from Porto Covo in Alentejo to Burgau in the Algarve. Truly a national treasure, the park has been protected since 1995 and could not be more different from the popular tourist destinations of the Algarve, being possibly the last genuinely wild coastal area in Europe.

Varying in width from 2–20 km (1.2–12.4 mi), the park is sparsely populated, but rich in flora and fauna – including rare and endangered species. Because of its location and long months of sunshine and very little rain, the flora is mostly formed of thorny shrubs and bushes, bulbs and annuals. Including seaweeds, there are at least 750 species here, 12 of which are unique to the area. *Silene rothmaleri*, a charming little white flower that was believed extinct since 1984, was re-discovered at Cape St Vincent in 2000.

The Cape itself is the most southwesterly point of Europe. The cliffs here rise almost vertically from the ocean, on the edge of which stands a lighthouse, built in the 1840s on the ruins of a 16th-century Franciscan monastery. A myriad of birds nest along this coast, many building precariously perched nests on the rocky cliffs. There are kites, peregrine falcons and Bonelli's eagles, as well as rock thrushes and pigeons. This is the only place in the world where white storks nest on rocks. Another unlikely creature to be found is the otter – rarely found in a marine habitat.

This is a coastline of towering – often ochre – cliffs, small, rocky coves and pristine beaches, backed by rolling hills, pine forests and almond groves. The best way to see it is slowly: walk, cycle or travel on horseback to truly appreciate the area.

**HOW TO GET THERE:**
Rent a car from Faro or Lisbon.
**WHEN TO GO:**
Any time of year, but in spring or autumn you will catch the annual migratory birds.
**DON'T MISS:**
The utterly delicious fish and seafood that can be sampled up and down the coast, or the excellent surfing.
**YOU SHOULD KNOW:**
Cape St Vincent, sacred since Neolithic times, is where Henry the Navigator built the first great research and training school for navigators, sailors and astronomers. After the famous sea battle of the same name in 1797, when the British defeated the much larger Portuguese fleet, Nelson was knighted and made Rear-Admiral for his efforts.

*Cliffs, rocky coves and pristine beaches near Cape St Vincent*

*The Montesinho Mountains cloaked in heather.*

# Montesinho Mountains Natural Park

One of the least visited and wildest regions in Portugal, Montesinho Mountains Natural Park was formed not only to protect the rare fauna that survives there, but also the unusually traditional way of life still led by its approximately 9,000 inhabitants. Found in the far northeast of Portugal, its north and eastern edges form the border with Spain.

The villages, such as Montesinho and Franca, have cobbled streets and stone houses that are traditional to the region. Scattered across the slopes are *pombal* – round, medieval dovecotes with horseshoe-shaped roofs. These were built for rearing doves to be eaten, their droppings used as fertilizer.

This is a region of curved mountains separated by valleys, some of which are very steep, others gently sloped. The altitude ranges from 438 m (1,437 ft) at the Mente River to 1,481 m (4,859 ft) at the peak of Montesinho. The eastern section is the most easily accessible, but paths run throughout the park, enabling the visitor to explore the more remote and lush western section.

Along the edges of the streams and rivers running through the park are ash, alder, black poplar, wild cherry trees, willow and hazel, mixed with herbs such as apple mint, and honeysuckle, jasmine and peonies. Meadows are bursting with scented herbs and wild flowers, including orchids and several endemic species. Chestnuts are an important source of local income and in agricultural areas great stands of sweet chestnut trees can be found.

Higher regions are cloaked in oaks, then heathers and, finally, outcrops of granite. The varied habitat is home to wolves, wild boar, foxes, wild cats and deer, as well as 150 species of bird, including three types of eagle and other raptors. The rivers teem with fish and are a playground for otters.

# Serra da Malcata Nature Reserve

The Serra da Malcata lies on the Spanish border at the eastern edge of central Portugal and was created in 1981 in order to preserve the critically endangered Iberian lynx. Their preferred habitat consists of Mediterranean scrub with open forest that includes old trees and dense thickets, as well as meadows in which to hunt.

The nature reserve is perfect country for wildlife of all sorts. Rising to just 1,078 m (3,537 ft), the rolling hills are covered with heather and there is plenty of old oak forest with chestnut and wild cherry trees. At higher levels rare strawberry trees can be seen and, during spring, white and yellow broom provides brilliant splashes of colour. Some of the land just within the reserve's boundaries is used for agriculture, including fruit orchards that look beautiful when in full blossom. Rivers and streams run through the area, beside which grow stands of willow, ash and alder. Small, riverside beaches provide opportunities for paddling, swimming or canoeing.

The Serra da Malcata Nature Reserve is an important region for breeding pairs of various birds of prey, including short-toed and booted eagles and Montagu's harrier. Black vultures also nest here. Mammals include foxes, wildcats, wild boars, badgers, genets, as well as smaller creatures such as hares and rabbits. Otters hunt and play in the rivers, which are full of fish, and every species of amphibian in mainland Portugal has a presence here. It is thought that the Iberian lynx may have become extinct in the reserve, but as they are extremely hard to see, and hunt at night, this is a matter of debate. To be on the safe side, a captive breeding programme is being run across the border in Spain and in due course some of these animals will be introduced to Serra da Malcata.

**HOW TO GET THERE:**
By road from Castello Branco. The main information office is in Penemacor.
**WHEN TO GO:**
Between April and October
**DON'T MISS:**
If you are in central Portugal, don't miss the opportunity of visiting the historic city of Coimbra.
**YOU SHOULD KNOW:**
The Iberian lynx is about twice the size of a domestic cat, but it has longer legs, a bobtail and pointed ears topped with black tufts. The main reason for its drastic decline is because of a shortage of rabbits – its favourite food.

**383**

# EASTERN MEDITERRANEAN & MIDDLE EAST

# Akamas Peninsula

**HOW TO GET THERE:**
By 4x4, or take a bus from Paphos to Polis.
**WHEN TO GO:**
From February to November, but between early March and the end of April for the marvellous show of wild flowers, including orchids. Take plenty of water with you if you are there during the height of summer.
**DON'T MISS:**
Kykkos monastery, a Byzantine marvel founded in 1100; Kourion, a superb archaeological site and the painted churches in the Troodos Mountains.
**YOU SHOULD KNOW:**
There is an on-going battle over the future of the Akamas Peninsula between the forces of conservation, such as Greenpeace and the European Environment Agency, and the government and developers. Some illegal hotels have already been built, including one overlooking turtle nesting sites.

Jutting into the sea at the northwestern tip of Cyprus is the Akamas Peninsula, named after one of the sons of Theseus and his second wife, Phaedra. The third largest island in the Mediterranean, Cyprus has Turkey lying just 75 km (47 mi) to the north and Syria and Lebanon roughly 106 km (66 mi) to the east.

Covering about 230 sq km (90 sq mi), the Akamas Peninsula is the island's most wildly beautiful area. During the 1980s and 1990s, the British used Akamas for military exercises which, ironically, kept it free of the kind of development that was occurring elsewhere on Cyprus. Thus it remains a superb place in which to walk, mountain-bike, or even explore in a 4x4.

On this mountainous peninsula discover perfect, sandy bays, deep gorges, and forested heights. Thanks to its physical location between Europe, Asia and Africa, an unusually high number of plant species thrive here – 530, of which 33 are endemic – as well as 168 bird, 20 reptile, 16 butterfly and 12 mammal species. The headland is forested with pine, juniper, oak, laurel and myrtle and there are large areas of Mediterranean scrubland, gorges, cliffs and dunes, thus providing several diverse habitats. The most important natural site on Akamas is Lara Bay, where both endangered green and vulnerable loggerhead turtles come to lay their eggs in peace.

Trails snake around the peninsula – one of the loveliest is named after the goddess Aphrodite, who emerged from the sea just off the Cyprus coast and is the island's patron. Starting from the Baths of Aphrodite, it ascends to her sanctuary, noted for a resplendent oak tree that is over 800 years old. Climb higher still to reach a flat, rocky area from which the view is magnificent.

*The Akamas Peninsula*

# Karpas Peninsula

The Karpas Peninsula, otherwise known as 'the Panhandle', lies in the northeast of Cyprus, stretching from close to Famagusta to the far northeastern tip of the country. It is an area of small villages, where the inhabitants either farm in the traditional style, or fish for their living, and the countryside is unpolluted by towns or industry.

The hills, which reach 1,000 m (3,280 ft), are blanketed with pine, cypress and the trees of the Mediterranean scrubland. The beaches, some sandy, some rocky, are not only glorious but also remarkably empty and include Golden Sands Beach. This 6 km (4 mi) stretch of sand and dunes is thought to be the best beach on the entire island, and is a nesting site for rare green and loggerhead sea turtles. Offshore, Mediterranean dolphins are frequently seen dashing and leaping through the sea.

The rare Andouin's gull can be spotted here, too. These fish eaters nest on the Klidhes Isles, just off the tip of the peninsula. Cyprus is good for birdwatching. It lies on the north/south migratory route, which is used by some 300 species of bird. Griffon vultures with their great 2.4 m (8 ft) wingspan overwinter and breed here, and one can also see the endemic Cyprus pied wheatear, the golden oriole, the Cyprus warbler, bee-eaters and rollers.

The Karpas Peninsula is also rich in wildflowers and from February until June the region is bursting with hundreds of brightly coloured species, including yellow crowfoot, purple iris and exquisite pink rock roses. While there are no rivers running through the peninsula, there are 15 springs and many underground reservoirs that enable fruit trees, olives and tobacco to be farmed. Hundreds of wild donkeys roam the peninsula – set adrift after the Turkish invasion of 1974, they have lived and bred here quite happily.

**HOW TO GET THERE:**
Access is by car only, via Famagusta.
**WHEN TO GO:**
Arrive in spring for wild flowers and migratory birds, autumn also for the latter, and summer for making the most of the beaches.
**DON'T MISS:**
The Apostolos Andreas Monastery, a major place of pilgrimage for the Orthodox Church of Cyprus, or the ancient ruins of Salamis.
**YOU SHOULD KNOW:**
Reptiles wake from their hibernation in May and, although most of them are harmless, the blunt-nosed viper can be deadly.

*Golden Sands Beach on the Karpas peninsula*

*Gobekli Lake in the Salacur Valley*

# Kackar Mountains

**HOW TO GET THERE:**
Occasional *dolmuses* (shared taxis) climb the rough road to Barhal from Yusufeli, which is well connected with Erzurum. A summer service runs between Trabzon and Ayder, and from Ayder to Camlihemsin, which has a regular,
year-round service to Pazar on the coast.
**WHEN TO GO:**
Late May to late September for walking, July and August for climbing the peaks. By September, the longer nights are cold. In summer, it is almost impossible to find accommodation in Ayder at weekends.

The Kackar range, whose densely clustered peaks soar dramatically above the Black Sea coast, is increasingly popular with walkers. It lies outside the troubled Kurdish regions, is relatively straightforward to reach and is remarkable for its beauty and for the Hemsin people – summer inhabitants of the high pastures.

On the southern foothills, villages amid cherry orchards cling to a deeply fissured, wildly rocky landscape, famous for white-water rafting. The walking here is tough, but the weather is excellent. The northern slopes are extravagantly lush. Above the Black Sea tea plantations, where rivers rush and cascade through dense forests, the beautiful, remote Hemsin Valleys are home, in winter, to the pastoralists. This is the wettest place in Turkey.

Experienced climbers head for the Kackar's precipitous alpine peaks but the network of fine walking tracks attracts most visitors. From villages in the lower highlands, long and short treks – with or without guides – make use of the paths which link the *yaylas*, the stone-and-wood summer settlements. Each belongs to a valley village and several can provide meals, even rooms, for hikers. The walking is glorious: the views are breathtaking, the steep meadows are brilliant with flowers and butterflies, the hundreds of glacial lakes reflect the immense, blue, light-filled sky. Grazing cattle, often pompom-bedecked, may be accompanied by Hemsin women, splendid in traditional black-and-orange headdresses. Trekking across the range is very rewarding. From Barhal in the south, the route climbs over the scree slopes of Mount Kackar, Turkey's fourth highest mountain – 3,932 m (12,900 ft) – and down to the alpine village, Ayder. Here, hot springs ease the strains of two or three days' walking before the descent to the coast.

**DON'T MISS:**
The Hemsins. At the end of May, after days of celebration, all the families take their livestock up to the *yaylas* where the women make butter, yoghurt and cheese. At weekends, Hemsins from cities and overseas rejoin their families for the festivities. Organized treks introduce visitors to the work, culture and merry-making of these remarkable people, thus sharing with them Turkey's tourist income and helping to safeguard their ancient way of life.
**YOU SHOULD KNOW:**
Weather is unpredictable in the Kackars – even in summer, Ayder can be completely fogged in for days – and hikers should never set out without a guide, local information, or a good map. Kate Clow has produced an excellent walking guide to the mountains.

# Kaz Daglari

Kaz Daglari (Goose Mountain), or Mount Ida of Greek classical antiquity, is a conglomeration of peaks above the northern shore of the Gulf of Edremit, southeast of Troy. Its modern name refers to a Turkish folk tale. The summits are windswept and bare. The highest, Kirklar – 1,774 m (5,820 ft) – is a fairly easy climb and the views in all directions are superb. The thickly forested slopes are home to a remarkable abundance of indigenous flora and a recent study of the biodiversity included interviews with plant gatherers and recorded the local names and traditional uses of the herbs and medicinal plants for which Mount Ida is famous.

A number of pleasant villages in the fertile northern foothills are linked by narrow roads and tracks. Attractions for visitors include treks, rides, plane-shaded riverside restaurants and some excellent local produce, including herbal teas, cheeses and tobacco. Higher slopes are thickly clad with pine and beech, threaded by streams, dotted with lakes and waterfalls and criss-crossed by paths.

Above the coast, precipitous southern hillsides are fractured by cliffs and canyons. These are challenging hikes and experience and specialized equipment are essential. Walks from Gure and Zeytinli, pretty little towns at the eastern end of the gulf, are delightful. Good tracks lead through the woods to an impressive waterfall, to some hot springs and up into the hills. In spring, streams race and flowers cover the meadows; in autumn the mountains are clothed in gold and scarlet and visitors gather chestnuts alongside the locals. To walk along quiet trails, away from popular villages and picnic areas, is to experience a landscape rich in ancient legend and traditional rural life.

**HOW TO GET THERE:**
The north of the range can be approached from Bayramic or Kalkym, the south of the range from the Assos to Edremit coast road. Buses or *dolmuses* (shared taxis) run to all these places.
**WHEN TO GO:**
May, June, September, or October. Avoid weekends, when Turkish town-dwellers visit and accommodation can be scarce.
**DON'T MISS:**
In the delightfully named Village of the Wooden Birds (Tahtakuslar Koyu), near Akcay, is Turkey's first private ethnographical museum. As well as a fascinating collection of objects from the nomadic Turkic people – carpets, tents, bridal costumes and so on – it displays contemporary arts and crafts and information on the many legends of Mount Ida and its medicinal plants.
**YOU SHOULD KNOW:**
The most famous story set on Mount Ida is the *Judgement of Paris*. Paris of Troy was asked to decide who was the fairest goddess: Aphrodite, Hera or Artemis. He chose Aphrodite because she promised him the most beautiful woman in the world – Helen. He sailed for Sparta, abducted Helen, and the Trojan War began. An annual beauty contest now commemorates his fateful decision.

# Koprulu Canyon

The sandy coast east of Antalya is strung with beach resorts, but much of the mountainous hinterland is wild and empty, sliced by rivers which race to the Mediterranean. The Koprulu National Park covers a large area of rugged, forested mountains through which the Kupru Irmagi (Bridge River) flows between the towering cliffs of the Koprulu Canyon, below the remains of the ancient city of Selge.

The journey from the coast is lovely; the road meanders through wooded hills and past isolated settlements, becoming increasingly steep and serpentine, with views of distant misty peaks and the silvery river. After Beskonak, a track leads to a narrow Roman bridge, still used to cross the river to an area offering refreshment at waterside restaurants, plus activities on land and water and tracks to the park's other attractions. Near a second bridge (an elegant Ottoman structure) the river forms still, blue pools; upstream, for about 14 km (8.5 mi), it flows deep and calm between tree-clad cliffs, or white and turbulent through narrow, towering ravines. The forest around the gorge comprises huge swathes of dark cypress and mixed woodlands and is home to wild animals which include deer, wolves and wild boar.

The beautiful 12 km (7.5 mi) trail to Selge climbs through thickets of olive, maple and carob trees, past eroded rock formations and the precipitous gullies which once provided an impregnable defence for the Roman city, reputedly home to 20,000 people. The ruins are scattered in tumbled heaps among the stone cottages of present-day residents. The remoteness of this site has hindered archaeological work, but its situation – on a high plateau surrounded by the fields and orchards of Altinkaya and backed by the jagged Kuyucuk mountains – is wonderfully picturesque.

**HOW TO GET THERE:**
Tours from Antalya, Side and other resorts visit the canyon. The track from Beskonak can be driven with care almost as far as Selge. A daily minibus runs from Antalya to Altinkaya and back.

**WHEN TO GO:**
Late April to June, September or October

**DON'T MISS:**
Ancient Aspendos is very close to the route to Koprulu. Extensive remains lie on the hill behind what is, although extensively restored (notably by Ataturk), one of the world's finest Roman theatres. The acoustics are still perfect.

**YOU SHOULD KNOW:**
Activities in the canyon include rafting, kayaking and hikes into the mountains. Selge, at 900 m (2,950 ft) is noticeably cooler than the lower areas. A bright-green shrub seen growing among the dark trees is *Styrax officinalis*, whose aromatic gum was highly prized for medicinal use and is still used in perfumery. The people of Selge valued the plant so greatly it appeared on their coins.

*Rafting in Koprulu Canyon*

# Mount Latmos

Mount Latmos is actually a ridge of many spurs and its modern Turkish name, Besparmak, means five-fingered. It looms above the northern shore of Lake Bafa, once the Latmian Gulf. The serrated crest reaches 1,500 m (4,921 ft); it is wild and formidable, littered with huge boulders and strange rock formations, pierced by caves, and eroded by streams into steep ridges. Guides are recommended for longer climbs – even the redoubtable Freya Stark found herself 'curiously uncertain as to where the confines of reality end or begin' on Latmos.

The ancient Carian town of Latmus was a sizeable port before the gulf silted. The Romans built Herakleia ad Latmus along the western ridge of the mountain, and modern Kapikiri lies among its remains. This traditional Turkish village is a delightful community of small farmers and fishermen, a refuge from mass tourism and the starting point for some excellent walks. The Roman ruins, surrounded by a remarkably well-preserved wall, cover a large area along the lake and up into the foothills. Long hikes (which can be arranged in the village) involve climbing up the stony slopes and through hushed, ancient forests, ascending to the caves which from the 8th century sheltered Christian hermits, and to their monasteries, higher in the peaks. These long walks usually include a night under the stars.

The lake has several small beaches with clean, safe swimming, and some excellent birdwatching opportunities. Flamingoes and storks are among the hundreds of visitors to this huge expanse of water, which can be explored by kayak. The view from the lake – the village and the mountain, mirrored in the still, blue water – is ravishingly romantic.

**HOW TO GET THERE:**
The main road from Soke to Milas runs along the south of Lake Bafa. Minibuses run to Bafa from Soke, Milas and Bodrum. Only taxis continue to Kapikiri.

**WHEN TO GO:**
May, June, September, October

**DON'T MISS:**
Several of the caves on Mount Latmos were occupied 8,000 to 9,000 years ago by people who decorated their walls, as the monks did later. The remarkable artwork is being studied and documented and some of these caves can be visited. Linear figures, all executed in red, are clearly seen engaged in social and religious scenes.

**YOU SHOULD KNOW:**
Another cave dweller was the legendary Endymion, locked into eternal sleep by jealous Zeus and visited nightly by the infatuated moon goddess, Selene. The Christian monks adopted him as a saintly mortal who resisted temptation and studied the moon. Pilgrims to his shrine opened the tomb annually, hoping to learn the true name of God from the mysterious humming emanating from the bones.

*The ancient ruins of Herakleia lie beneath Mount Latmos on the shores of Lake Bafa.*

# Saklikent Gorge

**HOW TO GET THERE:**
Day trips run from all the Lycian resorts. There is a frequent minibus service from Fethiye.

**WHEN TO GO:**
The gorge is open from April until late September. In early spring the water may be excessively fierce and cold; later, although the walking is easier, the water is less exciting.

**DON'T MISS:**
The archaeological site Tlos is close to Saklikent. It was inhabited, on and off, from the Bronze Age until the 19th century. There are remains of the important Lycian city and of Roman, Byzantine and Ottoman buildings. The site is delightfully rural, high above the lovely Xanthos valley.

**YOU SHOULD KNOW:**
Suitable shoes are essential – they should be non-slip and waterproof; rubber sandals are available for hire, but are not very comfortable.
A change of clothes is useful.
Saklikent was only discovered late in the 20th century, during a survey of locations for trout farms. The name means 'Hidden City'. The caves in the gorge's cliffs were occupied by prehistoric people, and by the Romans.

Inland Lycia, despite coastal development, retains a wild, remote beauty. This is a region of barren mountains, dark forests, rushing streams and precipitous valleys and intensively cultivated fertile areas. The route to Saklikent Gorge is along narrow country roads, through fields of cotton, tobacco, wheat and vegetables; women in traditional dress walk their goats and old men play backgammon in shaded village cafés. For holidaymakers in Lycia's beach resorts, a day trip to Saklikent is a 'must' and in summer long queues wait in an entrance area jammed with stalls and makeshift restaurants, before they can escape the intense heat and enjoy the cool, watery depths of the gorge.

With a total length of about 18 km (11 mi) and cliffs soaring to 300 m (985 ft), this is Turkey's longest and deepest gorge and it is truly spectacular. Independent travellers are fortunate – they can visit out of season and, by staying in the nearby campsite, choose a time to walk before or after the coach parties. The gorge proper begins after a long wooden walkway. About 4 km (2.5 mi) can be walked – the steep upper reaches are accessible only to fully equipped climbers and cavers. Water gushes and bubbles from the rocks and cascades in waterfalls; in some places the terrain is muddy or slippery over pebbles and rocks, while in others walkers must paddle or wade through fast-flowing water. The massive rock walls are awe-inspiring, closing in until the roof of the gorge is no more than a crack through which little sun and no warmth penetrate. Far below in the dim chill, with icy water surging between stupendous cliffs, the landscape is thrillingly Gothic.

*Saklikent Gorge*

# Yedigoller National Park

The region of Bolu, about halfway between Ankara and Istanbul, is one of Turkey's greenest with about 60 per cent of the countryside forested. Although rarely visited by foreign tourists, this is a favourite mountain recreational area for Turks, particularly residents of Ankara. Its many attractions include a small winter sports resort, a large lake and a famous hot-springs spa and hotel. The area is also very popular with hunters – some of the local wild boar are as big as small cows. One of Bolu's most tranquil and beautiful spots, the Yedigoller National Park, is reached by a drive through a wonderful, unspoilt, almost alpine landscape.

The Seven Lakes of the park's name were formed when mudslides blocked the small, steep valleys; they lie on an upper and lower plateau and are fed by mountain streams. Around them grows some of Turkey's loveliest forest, much of it dense, native mixed woodland, with fir and pine, towering beeches and monumental, ancient oaks. Birds and animals live safely here and bears and wolves are among the many creatures found deep in the forest. A section has been designated a deer park – set up to protect the endangered Caspian red deer, a large animal which, like other red deer, roars and has huge antlers.

In spring the lakes brim with cold, clear water from the melting snow and wild flowers bloom among the brilliant rhododendrons and uncurling, bright-green ferns. In summer the cool shade is a welcome respite from the heat of the sun. In autumn, as deciduous trees change colour, the mountains blaze with yellow, flame and red, and in winter, frost and snow lend the whole area a still, ethereal magic.

**HOW TO GET THERE:**
The park is reached by forest roads, either heading north from the Ankara-to-Istanbul highway at Bolu town, or west from Mengen, which lies on the road from Yenicaga to the Black Sea coast.
**WHEN TO GO:**
The park is open all year. The road from Bolu is closed in winter and three of the lakes dry up in summer.
**DON'T MISS:**
There are a few bungalows that can be booked through the Forest Service. The accommodation is simple, but each has a fireplace, with a table and barbecue outside – visitors can grill fish from the local trout farm and enjoy the velvet darkness of the forest before a night of deep sleep.
**YOU SHOULD KNOW:**
The little town of Mengen is famous for producing the best cooks in Turkey. It has a cookery school whose graduates are chefs for some of Turkey's best hotels and for the President in Ankara. There is a food festival and cookery competition every August.

*The Al-Shouf Cedar Nature
Reserve in winter*

# Al-Shouf Cedar Nature Reserve

Lying between Dahr al-Baidar to the north and Jezzine in the south, the Al-Shouf Cedar Nature Reserve lies draped across the ridge of Mount Lebanon's western chain, with views to the Shouf area to the west and the beautiful Bekaa valley to the east. The largest of Lebanon's nature reserves, covering perhaps five per cent of the country, it was declared a UNESCO Biosphere Reserve in 2005.

Oak forests carpet Al-Shouf's northeastern slopes, and mixed oak and juniper cloak its southeastern slopes. But the jewels in the reserve's crown are the three superb cedar forests preserved within its boundaries – Al Barouk, Ma'aser Al-Shouf and Ain Zhalta/Bmohray. Some of these cedars are believed to be 2,000 years old, and this is the southernmost area in the world in which they can be found.

The altitude varies from about 1,000 m (3,280 ft) to 2,000 m (6,560 ft) and thus far 500 species of flora have been identified here, including 48 that are endemic to Lebanon, Syria and Turkey, as well as 24 species of tree, although the main work is to re-forest areas that were previously logged. Al-Shouf is known for its regenerative powers – trees here spread naturally and provide habitat for 32 mammals, including grey wolves, golden jackals, striped hyenas, wild cats, mountain gazelles and Cape hares.

Birds are also plentiful, with some 200 species to be spotted – although many are migratory. Birds of prey, in particular, do well and the pheasants and partridges that were introduced to Al-Shouf for hunting have successfully colonized the area.

The Al-Shouf reserve is a wonderful place in which to hike, and trails for different levels of difficulty are available. It is also good for mountain-biking and, in winter, snowshoeing. Visit the Barouk information centre for details of cultural sites in the reserve, as well as hiking routes and other activities.

**HOW TO GET THERE**:
By car from Beirut or the Bekaa Valley.
**WHEN TO GO:**
Spring, summer or autumn, unless you want to enjoy the winter snowfall.
**DON'T MISS:**
The cave castle Qalaat Niha, the last remains of a stronghold once used by Arabs, Crusaders and princes of Mount Lebanon, including Prince Fakhr-al-Din.
**YOU SHOULD KNOW:**
The Lebanese cedar forests were documented by the Sumerians over 3,000 years before the birth of Christ. They feature in *The Epic of Gilgamesh*, one of the world's earliest pieces of literature.

# Jeita Grotto

Located some 18 km (11 mi) north of Beirut, close to Jeita in the Nahr al-Kalb Valley, lies the longest cave ever found in the Middle East. Tucked away beneath the lower slopes of Mount Lebanon, this startling cave complex is a wonder of the natural world.

Inhabited by prehistoric man, the lower cave was 'rediscovered' in 1836 by the Reverend William Thompson, an American missionary who halted at the underground river. It was not explored further until the early 1870s, when engineers from the Beirut Water Company made their way deep inside, to a distance of 1,060 m (3,480 ft). The caves were known as the Grottoes of Nahr al-Kalb, after the underground river whose source the engineers found here and which supplies much of Beirut with fresh water. Subsequent exploration continues to this day, but 9 km (5.6 mi) has been revealed thus far, as has an interconnected upper gallery.

Take a tour of the lower galleries, which involves an electric boat trip along a black, underground lake. At first the dank, chilly atmosphere resounds with the sound of falling water but, as the boat slips further into the cave, other than your own breathing, total silence reigns. Modern lighting spotlights incredible shapes, columns

and stone draperies carved by water across millennia, all within vast, vaulted caverns. The upper galleries, opened in 1969, can be visited on foot. The Red Chamber, so called because of its colour, towers to 106 m (348 ft), although the third chamber is even higher. But the White Chamber has the best of the formations, including the longest stalactite in the world at 8.2 m (27 ft).

*Stalagmites and stalactites at Jeita Grotto*

**HOW TO GET THERE:**
By car from Beirut
**WHEN TO GO:**
The caves are open all year, with the exception of January, but during the winter the lower galleries are closed if the water level becomes too high.
**DON'T MISS:**
Deep within the lower chamber named The Pantheon, past the magnificent Maxwell's Column, the engineer explorers of the 1870s wrote down their names and sealed them in a bottle that they left on top of a stalagmite. During the past 150 years limestone has completely covered the bottle and joined it to its base.
**YOU SHOULD KNOW:**
Beirut itself is fascinating. This ancient place has been continuously inhabited for some 5,000 years and contains wonderful archaeological remains, some of which have been discovered as a result of bombing attacks on the city in the recent past which pulverized existing buildings but enabled the legacy of history to come to light.

# Ajloun Forest Reserve

Some 200 years ago, most of northern Jordan was covered with Mediterranean-type open forest, dominated by Palestine oak (*Quercus calliprinos*). Today only one per cent of Jordan is forested, of which the Ajloun Forest Reserve is a significant part. Established in 1988 by Jordan's Royal Society for the Conservation of Nature, the 13 sq km (5 sq mi) area, located north of Amman in the Ajloun highlands, shelters many rare animals and plants.

The reserve is in a lovely region of small hills and winding valleys, with wild pistachio, wild strawberry and carob trees as well as oaks. In spring, the forest floor is carpeted with great drifts of wild flowers: anemones, rock roses, several species of orchid and wild tulips. The black iris, Jordan's national flower, also thrives here.

This is perfect habitat for forest animals such as wild boar, red fox, striped hyena, stone marten, golden jackal, wolves, Indian crested porcupine and Persian squirrel. Once home to roe deer, the RSCN has introduced a captive breeding programme here, bringing the animals from Turkey, and have now added a similar programme for Persian fallow deer. In 2000, the reserve was recognized as an important area by BirdLife International.

Five trails run through it, designed not only to show the visitor different environments but also to intersect with local communities with whom the reserve authorities have established some co-operative initiatives through raising public awareness. A successful educational programme has been introduced for local young people to learn about biodiversity. The Rockrose Trail, which takes four or five hours to complete, takes hikers through villages and olive groves, for which the area is famous, across forested ridges and valleys, with occasional fantastic views to Lebanon's snow-capped Jebel Sheik, Syria and the West Bank.

# Dana Nature Reserve

From the heights of Jordan's Rift Valley to the low-lying desert area of Wadi Araba, Dana Nature Reserve extends across a long chain of mountains and valleys that are remote, stunningly beautiful and packed with both natural and archaeological treasures. Dana village, overlooking the astonishing gorge of Wadi Dana, boasts a visitors' centre, where information on hiking trails, guides and accommodation is available.

The landscape of Dana, which covers 308 sq km (1,209 sq mi), varies from wooded mountains and red rock slopes to stony plains, majestic sandstone cliffs and classic sand dune desert, and therefore supports a variety of flora and fauna. This is home to Phoenician juniper, pine, evergreen oak and the world's southernmost areas of Mediterranean cypress, as well as acacia and desert shrubs. Mammals include wolves, sand cats, red foxes, hyenas, jackals, porcupines, hares and rabbits. Captive breeding programmes have saved the Nubian ibex and three species of gazelle that were almost extinct here. Birds to be found include Palestinian sunbirds, Sardinian and spectacled warblers, black-eared wheatears, white-throated kingfishers and Syrian serins – their largest breeding colony is in the reserve. Many raptors make their homes here, including houbara bustards, saker falcons and migratory species such as steppe and honey buzzards and steppe eagles.

Wadi Rum, in the southwestern corner of the country, is a renowned protected area of extraordinary sandstone and granite mountains and sandy valleys. Etched by the wind into fantastic shapes, narrow canyons protect ancient rock drawings, and there are 19 special sites of natural and archaeological significance to be visited, on foot, by 4x4 or truck, or riding camels or horses. Camp under sublime starry skies on trips organized by local Bedouin tribes, centred on the Rum village tourism co-operative, and experience the depth of peace and silence that reigns in this remarkable area.

**HOW TO GET THERE:**
To reach Dana, drive or take a minibus from Tafila to Qadsiyya. Minibus passengers then face a walk. For Wadi Rum, drive or take a tour from Aqaba, Petra or Amman.
**WHEN TO GO:**
From March until the end of November
**DON'T MISS:**
The sublime, ancient rose-red city of Petra, a UNESCO World Heritage Site
**YOU SHOULD KNOW:**
The remains of King Solomon's mines can be seen at Khirbet Feinan. T E Lawrence based himself at Wadi Rum before attacking Aquaba in 1917, and David Lean filmed much of *Lawrence of Arabia* here. Several other movies, such as *Red Planet* and *Transformers – Revenge of the Fallen* have also been filmed in Wadi Rum.

*Sunrise in Wadi Rum National Park*

# Wadi Mujib

**HOW TO GET THERE:**
By car or taxi from Madaba or Sweymeh

**WHEN TO GO:**
The reserve and chalets are open year round, but check on your preferred hike in advance – some are only possible between November and March.

**DON'T MISS:**
The rock formation believed to be the 'statue' of Lot's wife, who famously turned her head to look back at Sodom and Gomorrah against advice and was turned into a pillar of salt. Also worth a visit are the hot springs and waterfall of Hammamat Ma'in.

**YOU SHOULD KNOW:**
The reserve has a successful captive-breeding centre for threatened Nubian ibex, which may be visited.

A genuinely remote and wild place, Wadi Mujib, part of the Mujib Nature Reserve, is a gorge that extends to the eastern shore of the Dead Sea some 90 km (56 mi) south of Amman. Established in 1987, the reserve protects 220 sq km (85 sq mi) of the mountainous hinterland and, at 410 m (1,345 ft) below sea level, is the lowest nature reserve on earth.

The mountains in the reserve reach to 900 m (2,953 ft) above sea level, and the large variation in elevation, combined with constantly flowing water from seven tributaries, ensure unusual biodiversity of flora, fauna and, especially, birds. The landscape of harsh sandstone mountains, desert and plateaus, is intersected by steep cliffs and gorges, with a lake at the bottom of the wadi where a dam has been built.

It is not possible to camp independently here, but there is an excellent visitor centre and facilities to stay right beside the Dead Sea. There are several terrific hikes to undertake, all but one of which must be guided. In part this is because of the sensitive nature of the reserve, but it is also because this is dangerous terrain. Highly experienced hikers can easily become lost and, as with all wadis, flash floods can suddenly appear. The Siq trail is straightforward but the rest are tough, requiring a good degree of fitness, the ability to swim and no fear of heights.

Scientists continue to explore and document Mujib and thus far ten species of carnivore have been found, including Arabian leopards, caracals, wolves, jackals and hyenas. Mujib is a haven for birds, and not simply because it is a resting place for migratory species. Raptors include griffon vultures, Bonelli's eagle, lammergeiers and Levant sparrowhawks, and there are many smaller species to be spotted.

*Wadi Mujib is Jordan's Grand Canyon*

# Dasht-e Lut

*Dasht-e Lut contains the tallest and largest sand dune fields in Iran.*

Iran is a large country – the 16th largest in the world – and it shares its borders with seven other countries. Iran's mountains provide a protective barrier that virtually encircles the whole country, within which is a large central plateau, divided into drainage basins. At 480 km (300 mi) long and 320 km (200 mi) wide, Dasht-e Lut is one of the largest of these basins and is a bleak and alien place.

The eastern region of the Central Plateau is formed of two deserts: Dasht-e Kavir, the Great Salt Desert and Dasht-e Lut, the Desert of Emptiness, which extends southwards. The former, which is even larger, is named after its many salt marshes. Travel is fraught with danger. Virtually uninhabited and never fully explored, the marshes, apparently covered by a solid crust of salt, behave like quicksand – drive onto it and sink. Few oases exist in Dasht-e Kavir, where people eke a living from breeding camels, sheep, and a little agriculture, using a clever system of irrigation wells.

Much of Dasht-e Lut is a desert of sand and stone, although it too contains a large salt marsh. It is a place utterly hostile to man. Totally covered with black volcanic lava, it absorbs the extreme heat of the sun, becoming a wind tunnel due to the difference of temperature between it and its surroundings, which are at a higher elevation and a lower temperature.

Dasht-e Lut is the hottest, driest region of the world and absolutely nothing lives there. In 2004 and 2005, a NASA satellite recorded surface temperatures of almost 71°C (160°F). In the central area of the desert, the wind has carved ridges and troughs that look like a choppy sea of sand. Known as yardangs, the ridges reach 75 km (47 mi) high.

**HOW TO GET THERE:**
By car from Bandar Abbas, Zahedan or Bam
**WHEN TO GO:**
Spring or autumn
**DON'T MISS:**
The UNESCO World Heritage Site of Persepolis
**YOU SHOULD KNOW:**
Iran is a troubled country and there are areas where it is unwise to visit. Check current Foreign Office advice before travelling. Do not attempt to drive across Dasht-e Lut.

# Golestan National Park

Golestan National Park is situated in the north of Iran, stretching across a thickly forested area of the Caspian highlands and the steppes of Khorasan province. The very varied terrain includes temperate rainforest, high cliffs, rivers, springs, marshes and grassland plains. Protected since 1957, this lovely area is the oldest national park in the country.

The variety of habitats in Golestan has made it an important sanctuary for wildlife, and mammals include the Persian leopard, brown bear, wild cat, wild boar, Persian ibex and mountain goat, all of which survive happily in the hot summers and snowy winters of the park. Over 150 species of bird also live here, including lammergeiers, three other types of vulture and golden eagles. The lammergeier, unlike other vultures, does not have a bald head and is sometimes mistaken for an eagle. It is a symbol of luck and happiness in Iran. Golestan is also on the route of many migratory birds. As well as the forested hills and rocky crags, the park is home to many wild fruit trees and bushes, such as mulberry, wild pear, fig, barberry and raspberry, and many of the smaller plants are used as traditional remedies.

Sadly, Golestan is under threat for a variety of different reasons. One of these is hunting, but worse still is the construction of a road right through the forest, allegedly with the welfare of local inhabitants in mind. Despite numerous pleas to put the road around the area instead, the authorities have so far refused to budge. Just an hour's drive from the Caspian Sea, Golestan is very popular with Iranian tourists during the summer months.

*Golestan is the oldest national park in Iran.*

**HOW TO GET THERE:**
By car from Gorgan, Golestan's provincial capital

**WHEN TO GO:**
May to October

**DON'T MISS:**
The town and beautiful beach of Bandar Gaz; and don't forget that the Caspian Sea is the main source of Beluga caviar.

**YOU SHOULD KNOW:**
Lammergeier vultures feed mainly on other vultures' leftovers. They drop bones and tortoises from great heights onto rocks, breaking them into edible pieces. Aechylus, the ancient Greek playwright, was killed when a tortoise landed on his head.

# Mount Damavand

Situated in the midst of the Alborz Mountains and within easy striking distance of Teheran, Mount Damavand is not only Iran's highest peak at 5,671 m (18,606 ft) but also the highest peak in the Middle East. Long dormant, this classically shaped volcano produced a large new vent in its crater in 2007 that continues to belch sulphuric gases, smoke and steam. The crater itself has a huge diameter surrounded by yellow, sulphuric rocks, and is about 30 m (100 ft) deep. The summit lake is usually frozen, although at the height of summer it may disappear completely. There are permanent glaciers on Mount Damavand, the largest of which is on the east face.

Although there are 16 known ascent routes on the volcano, most are for experienced climbers only and it is the south-face route that is normally used. This is often compared to the route up Mount Kilimanjaro, in Tanzania, because although it is not technically difficult, it is a long, hard slog. Climbers not only have to be fit and strong, but they must also acclimatize themselves. The volcano's flanks are particularly beautiful in spring, when vast poppy fields come into flower, along with wild tulips, iris and other species of flora. The best climbing time, however, is during summer when much of the snow has melted.

It is advisable to set aside four days for an ascent of Mount Damavand, allowing enough time to acclimatize and for the possibility of sudden bad weather. Refuges and camps exist on every face, although it is wise to book in advance as the volcano is popular with Iranians as well as foreigners. Don't forget that climbing to the summit is not essential – hiking the slopes is less strenuous and equally worthwhile.

**HOW TO GET THERE:**
By car or public transport from Teheran. It is probably sensible to join a guided tour if you intend to climb to the summit.

**WHEN TO GO:**
May and June for hiking and flowers; June, July and August for climbing; January, February and March for skiing

**DON'T MISS:**
The thermal springs at Abe Garm Larijan at the base of the volcano – just what is needed after a tough climb.

**YOU SHOULD KNOW:**
Mount Damavand is important in ancient Persian literature and poetry, standing as a symbol of resistance against foreign rule. It features in both Zoroastrian mythology and *Shahnameh*, the Persian poet Ferdowsi's epic masterpiece.

*Looking through a gap in the rocks towards snow-capped Mount Damavand.*

# Socotra

**HOW TO GET THERE:**
By plane from Sanaa and Aden
**WHEN TO GO:**
From January to May – unless you want to wind surf, in which case go in July.
**DON'T MISS:**
Taking a boat safari – not only will you see whales, but you may also be able to swim with dolphins.
**YOU SHOULD KNOW:**
Socotra became a UNESCO World Natural Heritage site in 2008. The word *socotra* derives from Sanscrit and means 'island of bliss'.

*The Zaheg Dunes near the southern shores of Socotra Island. The Shaab Escarpment is visible in the distance.*

Socotra, a small archipelago lying 380 km (240 mi) southeast of the Arabian Peninsula, is part of the Republic of Yemen. Its extreme isolation, together with the fact that the archipelago was originally part of a continental landmass, and not volcanic, makes Socotra unique – one third of its flora is endemic – and it is often described as being the most alien looking place on earth.

The archipelago consists of four islands and a few tiny, rocky outcrops. Most of the inhabitants live on Socotra Island, with a few hundred living on two others, leaving the remainder uninhabited. Until recently, Socotrans have survived by fishing, rearing animals and cultivating dates. Now, however, ecotourism is becoming an important new source of revenue.

There are only two species of mammal – bats and civet cats – native to the islands, but there are plenty of camels, donkeys and goats to be seen. The great strength of Socotra is its insects, reptiles, marine biodiversity and birds. The most extraordinary tree on Socotra is the Dragon's Blood tree. Looking like an umbrella, its name comes from the red resin exuded from the bark. *Dorstenia gigas*, a giant succulent tree of the fig family with a bulbous trunk, the Socotran cucumber tree and Socotran pomegranate are all highly visible, strange looking, endemics.

Birds are numerous, too: there are 180 species of land bird alone, six of which are endemic; and 45 species of migratory birds also breed here. The uninhabited islands are important for sea birds and the marine life is spectacular, with fish species to rival those of the Red Sea, endemic corals and crustaceans, and numerous whales and dolphins in the surrounding sea. Socotra Island itself is stunning, and offers landscapes that vary from lagoons and white dunes to the misty heights of the Haggier Mountains.

# Bu Tinah

Bu Tinah is a tiny horseshoe-shaped group of islands and shoals some 25 km (15 mi) from Zirku Island, the oil-exporting terminal for Abu Dhabi's vast Zakum oil fields. Part of the UNESCO designated Marawah Marine Biosphere Reserve, the largest protected area of the UAE, Bu Tinah is so low lying – its highest point is perhaps 3 m (10 ft) above sea level – that at low tide the islands and shoals are more or less joined.

The main island has a sheltered, mangrove-lined lagoon to the south and the shoals are surrounded by seagrass beds and coral reefs. These reefs fascinate marine scientists because the conditions in which they thrive are very hard. The Persian Gulf is both extremely salty and very warm. In the height of summer the water temperature can reach up to 35°C (95°F), which would kill most corals in the world. Here, at least 16 species survive happily and are rich with marine life.

The Persian Gulf is home to the world's second-largest population of dugong, 60 per cent of which – some 600 individuals – live in the waters around Bu Tinah. Dugong is the only sea mammal that is entirely herbivorous, hence its common name: sea cow. It is a critically endangered species, still illegally hunted by man, and the seagrass which is its main diet is under threat from oil and chemical pollution. Other marine creatures, including three species of dolphin, abound. The rare hawksbill sea turtle nests on the sandy banks of the shoals and three other species of sea turtle can be found here.

Large numbers of birds live here, too. The island is an important nesting site for ospreys and the shallow waters are perfect for flamingoes. Several species of migratory bird visit Bu Tinah, including the rare Socotra cormorant, and white egrets and herons lurk among the mangroves.

**HOW TO GET THERE:**
The Marawah Biosphere Reserve, including Bu Tinah, is privately owned, but as there are plans to permit limited, supervised visiting, intrepid travellers may yet experience this magical spot.
**WHEN TO GO:**
Between November and April
**DON'T MISS:**
The archaeological sites – Stone Age, Bronze Age, Iron Age, pre-Islamic and Islamic – on Marawah
**YOU SHOULD KNOW:**
Bu Tinah has reached the final 28 candidates for the New7Wonders of Nature campaign. The winning seven places will be announced in 2011.

# Musandam Peninsula

**HOW TO GET THERE:**
Drive from Dubai to Khasab –
ensuring you have all the correct visa
entries; fly from Muscat or take the
world's fastest diesel-driven
catamaran.
**WHEN TO GO:**
November to March
**DON'T MISS:**
Khasab Fort, Kumzar village – only
accessible by boat, Tawi with its
prehistoric rock drawings, or Khor
As-Sham – the largest fjord in
Musandam
**YOU SHOULD KNOW:**
Khasab has long been a port through
which Iranians bring livestock for
sale in the UAE and Saudi Arabia,
sailing back loaded with goods that
are illegal in the Islamic Republic.
This is a dangerous journey as the
Strait of Hormuz is a busy oil tanker
lane and full of other vessels,
including those of the Islamic
Republic's coastguard.

An enclave of Oman, the Musandam Peninsula is separated from the rest of the country by the United Arab Emirates and protrudes into the narrow Strait of Hormuz. At just 55 km (34 mi) from Iran, the local capital, Khasab, has much to offer.

Often referred to as the 'Norway of Arabia', the Musandam Peninsula has an extraordinary coastline of rugged mountains cut with *fjords* or channels, hidden bays and villages that cling like limpets to towering walls of rock that reach to more than 2,000 m (6,560 ft) and where traditional customs of *dhow* building and fishing remain unchanged. This is the Ru'us al Jabal, the dramatic finish of the Hajar Mountains and an important eco-region. A road runs through the interior and a highway has been built that hugs the coastline, offering superb views and access to the mountains, Khasab, and to the only fjord accessible by road – the Khor A'Najd.

There is so much to see and do here. Explore remote villages by 4x4; hike in the mountains among wild olive, fig and juniper; or wander the valleys lush with pomegranates and apricots. Vultures, mountain gazelles and Arabian tahrs, an endemic, goat-like animal, thrive here. Paragliding or paramotoring offer spectacular views of this fantastic coast, or simply stick to the sea. The warm waters contain one of the richest marine environments in the world, with coral gardens and an immense variety of marine life. Rent a boat, cruise on a *dhow*, or join a dive boat and swim, snorkel or scuba dive to your heart's content. Fishing trips are also popular – there are more than 900 species of fish in these waters – or rent a kayak, relax and take it easy.

*Khor A'Najd – the only fjord accessible by road*

# Rub' al Khali

*The vast sand dunes of Rub' al Khali*

The notion of a vast expanse of sand desert is, for some reason, wildly romantic. The Rub' al Khali covers most of the southern third of the Arabian Peninsula, including parts of Yemen, Oman, UAE and all of southern Saudi Arabia, and is some 1,000 km (620 mi) long and 500 km (310 mi) wide. Far from being romantic, this desert is a harsh, unforgiving environment.

Rub' al Khali was inhabited by prehistoric man before the region was desertified and there is much evidence of the presence of both man and animals, especially around what were once lakes. Stone tools, fossilized clam shells and the fossilized bones of various mammals, including water buffalo, goats and hippopotami, have been found. There are also traces of camel caravans that carried frankincense across areas now almost impassable and home to no one.

A recent expedition to Rub' al Khali, led by the Saudi Geological Survey, discovered 31 new plant species and varieties, as well as 24 species of bird. The scientists will examine the adaptations made by the flora and fauna that have enabled them to survive such severe conditions. The dunes can reach over 300 m (985 ft) and, in summer, temperatures may soar to 55°C (131°F) in the middle of the day and sink to below 0°C (32°F) at night. Rub' al Khali slopes from 1,006 m (3,300 ft) in the north, where a long, narrow corridor joins it to the Nafud desert, down to almost sea level in the east. Salt marshes exist in the southeast and, around the edges of this inhospitable region, a few Bedouin feed their camels on the sparse vegetation living in the sand.

**HOW TO GET THERE:**
It is possible to join organized trips from Saudi Arabia, Oman, Yemen and the UAE.
**WHEN TO GO:**
October to January
**DON'T MISS:**
The horse and camel racing that takes place in various different towns around the country between September and June.
**YOU SHOULD KNOW:**
Most of Rub' al Khali belongs to Saudi Arabia, and it is here that vast oil reserves have been found, including the largest oil field in the world, Ghawwar Field, some of which lies under the northern desert.

ASIA

# The Pillars of Lena

*The pillars of Lena are best
viewed by boat.*

From a distance they could be the soaring towers of medieval castles, or the massive ramparts and arched colonnades of some ancient Troy. Massed together on a bend in the river in the sharp shadows of sunlight, the biggest formations look like ominous visions of skyscraper cities, inexplicably ruined and stranded in the endless forests of the Siberian taiga. The extraordinary Pillars of the Lena River are a geological freak – a serrated edge of limestone and dolomite rock spikes carved along an 80-km (50-mi) section of the edge of the Prilenskoye plateau by the mighty Lena River, halfway along its epic 4,472-km (2,780-mi) course from Lake Baikal to the Arctic Ocean.

Formed from an 80-million-year-old Cambrian-era sea-basin, the pillars owe their vertical stability, their 150–300 m (490–985 ft) height and their bizarre shapes to specifically Cambrian-era geological conditions. The Lena Pillars, and the 485-sq-km (187-sq-mi) Nature Park that contains them, are a geological capsule of a vital stage in the development of life on Earth. The area is rich in all kinds of fossils of the Cambrian biodiversity boom, and of later fossils including mammoth, fleecy rhinoceros and Lena horse. The land itself is stamped with frozen ground reliefs like frozen karsts, silt pinnacles and geographical oddities like the 'fluttering sands' called *tukulans* – miniature desert dune systems punctuating the forests on the river bank opposite the pillars, and unique to the region.

The pillars are best seen by boat, or even raft, with a tour company – arranging the correct permits to go it alone on the weekly ferry from Ust'-Kut to Yakutsk is a nightmare. The whole park is glorious with adventure, but it is a vast, lonely wilderness too: visitors on an agency tour may be glad of the company.

# Lake Baikal

Fabulous science and outrageous statistics only enhance the enduring mystique of Lake Baikal. It is a mighty, 11-million-year-old gash in the earth's fabric, a V-shaped rift nearly 11 km (7 mi) deep stopped up by roughly 9 km (5.6 mi) of silts from the 336 rivers that feed it, and still deep enough to hold 20 per cent of all the fresh water on the planet. Buoyed up 456 m (1,500 ft) above sea level by surrounding mountain ranges, the 31,500-sq-km (12,160-sq-mi) crescent-shaped lake supports major and minor ecosystems with so many endemic species of flora and fauna that it has been called the 'Siberian Galapagos'. It's not an idle boast. Lake Baikal is 636 km (400 mi) long and as much as 79 km (49 mi) wide, a jewel of aquatic purity with 1,000 species of specialized flora, 29 endemic variations of a single kind of fish, and the nerpa (endemic Baikal) seal. The same level of biodiversity is apparent across the wildly different topography of a dozen different microclimates on Baikal's shores. There are warm, shallow coastal lakes, boggy river deltas, alpine meadows, boreal forests carpeted with moss, huge mountains cut with ravines and river valleys, and windswept taiga forests.

Zabaikalsky National Park on the eastern shore is typical of Baikal wilderness, a boreal Eden of squirrels, ermine, otters, brown bears, leaping fish, berry-filled shrubs and towering mountain forests. It's one of a chain of parks and reserves surrounding Baikal, and travellers seeking more than the summertime beach life on Olkhon Island offered by many tour agencies might head instead to Baikalo-Lensky Zapovednik on the lake's northwestern rim. It sings with 240 species of birds, and in spring numerous brown bears come to the shore to feed on the caddis flies swarming on the rocks where Baikal seals haul out. That's Baikal magic.

*Sunset over Olkhon Island on Lake Baikal in Siberia*

**HOW TO GET THERE:**
By bus, car or tour bus from Irkutsk to Listvyanka at the southern tip of Baikal (all year); or by hydrofoil (summer only) down the Angara River. Independent local travel around the lake is difficult – but tour agencies in Irkutsk arrange small expeditions to each of the national parks for hikers.
**WHEN TO GO:**
May to October
**DON'T MISS:**
The spectacularly intimidating 10 km (6 mi) long Rytoye Gorge in Baikalo-Lensky Park; the vintage engineering of the 84-km (52-mi) long Circum-Baikal Railway's 200 bridges and 33 tunnels, at Baikal's southern tip; the Kyltygey Islands, Lake Arangatui and the hot swamp springs of Zmeiny, Nechaevsky and Kulinye; and rafting on Baikal's white-water feeder rivers. At Listvyanka, the Institute of the Russian Academy of Sciences sponsors a small but brilliant museum of Baikal's flora and fauna.
**YOU SHOULD KNOW:**
Lake Baikal is full of landmark natural formations which are both spectacular and sacred to the shamanist beliefs and practices of the region. Olkhon Island is one of the most important shamanist centres, and local residents proudly display ceremonial artefacts relating to their beliefs to interested visitors.

# Kronotsky Biosphere Reserve

Sited on the transition zone between tundra and boreal ecosystems, the Kronotsky Reserve on the Pacific coast of Russia's Kamchatka Peninsular turns nature on its head. Geothermal heat meets glaciers; active volcanoes and

*Fumaroles in the Valley of Geysers*

**HOW TO GET THERE:**
By helicopter (or occasionally, boat) from Petropavlovsk-Kamchatsky to a campsite within the Kronotsky Reserve; then on foot
**WHEN TO GO:**
July to August is best for trekking – but the drama of volcanic activity is sensational against the white-out of winter.
**DON'T MISS:**
Bathing in hot springs near the 'Steaming Valley', the fizzing mud crater lake of Burlyaschy Volcano that contains demonstrations of every type of volcano, in miniature; the red, yellow, green and bright blue of the Uzon caldera, a landscape of mineral-rich rock and forest so beautiful that it is a sanctuary for animist worship among indigenous Italmen peoples; or inshore whale-watching for seven species of whale, sea otters, and the amazing bird colonies along the high Pacific cliffs of the reserve.
**YOU SHOULD KNOW:**
Visitors are virtually compelled to travel with a tour agency, which will arrange all necessary permits except individual Russian entry visas. Visitors are advised to consult their doctor before coming to Kamchatka, about precautions against encephalitis from tick bites; and to bring strong mosquito repellents. Walking poles are useful for river crossings and boulder fields.

Pacific storms constantly remodel a multicoloured universe of mineral-rich bogs and swamps, silicon-blue lakes and huge, dark-green valleys. Nights flicker with the hellish red glow of major and minor volcanic eruptions; and morning can reveal whole mountain-sides flensed of forest and vegetation by the steaming coils of fresh lava flows. The dynamic geology of the 11,421-sq-km (4,410-sq-mi) reserve transforms the sullen pallor of the glacial north into a primary-coloured catalogue of the world's most magnificent landscapes. Eleven active volcanoes and the hydrothermal anomalies of as many extinct cones double the mountain and maritime ecosystems represented within it, concentrating the highest biodiversity in Kamchatka into a relatively small area. Visitors can only gaze in wonder at brown bear – by the dozen – grazing in berry-filled valleys or fishing the waterfalls for Pacific salmon against a background of sea eagles and 260 other bird species wheeling over a panorama of distant snow-capped mountains, glaciers and the red and yellow autumn lightshow of larch forests. It's pure Hollywood, but real.

Nowhere in Kronotsky is the thrill of engaging with nature at its most unpredictable greater than in the Valley of Geysers. Hidden by ancient rockfalls on a tributary of the Shumnaya River, it is a giant ravine of bubbling mud pools and 20 major geysers jetting boiling water and steam high into the air. Minerals make a painter's palette of the boulder-strewn mountainsides, and cascades of warm water encourage grasses and trees to grow with tropical exuberance. The valley bewitches all the senses, but beware! – the seductively lush grass meadows can dump unwary visitors head-high in burning mud. Kronotsky's wilderness is as beautiful and dangerous as a tiger.

# Kedrovaya Pad Biosphere Reserve

A mere 20 km (12 mi) across Amur Bay from the ceaseless turmoil of the great port of Vladivostok on the Sea of Japan lies a sanctuary for one of the world's rarest creatures. Dependent on ecologically pure wilderness for its very survival, the Amur ('Far Eastern') leopard steadfastly resists the relentless encroachment of toxic urbanization on its shrinking habitat. Some 30 of these magnificent predators are regularly seen in Kedrovaya Pad, including two families known to breed and live permanently within the reserve. If a similar population exists elsewhere in the world, nobody knows of it.

In fact Kedrovaya Pad is crammed with as many rare birds, trees, flowers and vegetation as mammals. Although small – 179 sq km (69 sq mi) – it benefits from the collision of northern boreal forests with the dense deciduous jungles of subtropical forest ecology. Watered by dozens of streams spilling down the low ridges of the Manchurian (Black) Mountains' coastal spurs where they push into Russia from China and North Korea, the reserve is warmed by ocean currents and southern air coming up from the Phillipines. 'Islands' of pristine forest reflect its dual character. Manchurian oak, Siberian fir and yeddo spruce represent the Korean taiga; but elsewhere Mongolian maple, elm, birch and ash predominate. The warm summer monsoon encourages exuberant vines of trailing clematis and thick ropes of lianas in the canopy, and the dense undergrowth that provides habitats for deer, wild boar, raccoon, badger, black bear, flying squirrels and innumerable other marvellous creatures.

A breathtaking trail along the Kedrovaya River valley demonstrates the reserve's wilderness riches. Crystal-clear mountain water tumbles down a narrow canyon terraced by a series of waterfalls and boulder fields. The bright flashes in the forest green are the luminous colours of flowers, butterflies and hundreds of birds, singing sweetly. Nature's north meets nature's south in transformative joy – and leopards rule, if you see one.

**HOW TO GET THERE:**
By bus, car or train from Vladivostok (three hours), or by ferry across Amur Bay

**WHEN TO GO:**
Any time – but with flora and fauna from north to south, spring is an explosion of blooms and birds; and the red and golden glories of autumn are without parallel.

**DON'T MISS:**
The exotic warblers, nuthatches, flycatchers, buntings, buzzard-eagles, grey goshawks, scops owls and 150 other species that nest in Kedrovaya; the otters proliferating on the reserve's lakes; the lady's slipper, peonies, Dahurian lily and 54 other colourful floral rarities; and the arcaded groves of 55-m (180-ft), ramrod-straight Manchurian firs

**YOU SHOULD KNOW:**
Kedrovaya Pad is the oldest reserve in Russia's far east, but is under threat from poaching, illegal harvesting of valuable plants like ginsengs, nuts and ferns (a delicacy in Chinese and Korean cuisine), and ruthless arson – people hoping to squeeze extra farmland out of the reserve's margins regularly set fires that raze the forest and wildlife together. Its future depends on the sustainable economics of ecotourism.

# Mount Belukha

As the highest peak in the Katunsky range of the World Heritage 'Golden Mountains' of Altai, and the highest in all Siberia, 4,506-m (14,783-ft) Mount Belukha is a trophy summit. Reaching the top needs at least the technical know-how of experienced trekkers, but fixed-rope climbing and glacier traverses (and even the exciting, technically challenging sideshow climbs) are the least of its attractions. For any reasonably fit person, the adventure of a lifetime is just getting there. Mount Belukha presides over the 'bandit country' of Russia's border with Kazakhstan and the ancient mountain passes to both China and Mongolia. Trekkers must travel 750 km (466 mi) by bus from the nearest big town, Barnaul, to the trailhead in the village of Tyungur. Decanted into an ecologically pure mountain wilderness, most people feel profound shock, intensified by realizing that this is 'old' Russia, populated (thinly) by *Staroveri* (Old Believers) faithful to shamanistic traditions abandoned by the industrial world. The perception invests the already stupendous scenery with a deeper beauty – and it is energizing. The foothills of Mount Belukha conceal a cross-section of all the natural treasures of the Altai Mountains: steppes, dense taiga, alpine meadows filled with flowers, chains of glacial lakes, mountain tundra, boggy river valleys, craggy ravines resounding to rushing streams, broad valleys of emerald grassland, glacier moraines and the sky-borne ridge where clouds merge into the highest snow caps. The evolving panoramas make light work of serious trekking; and on foot – or horseback – they are shared by all manner of wildlife from bear and ibex to eagles and sprinting, bobbing hares.

Too remote and too wild ever to have been tamed, Mount Belukha emanates the kind of grandeur that makes travellers feel they have walked with gods. And they probably have.

*Mist rising over Yazevoye Lake with Mount Belukha behind*

**HOW TO GET THERE:**
By bus from Barnaul to Tyungur; then on foot or horseback
**WHEN TO GO:**
July to September, when the region is at its most varied and colourful best.
**DON'T MISS:**
The birds in the wetland flood plains around Ak-kem Lake; the Katun Gorge, and rafting on the wild Katun River; the dramatic landscapes of the Chuysky Trakt; the seven lakes of seven colours in Ak-Ojouk Valley; ice-training on the Arbuz Glacier; and the cedar forest below Karatiurek Pass.
**YOU SHOULD KNOW:**
Independent travellers need a special permit to be in Russia's border area, in addition to other major bureaucratic hurdles they have to jump, like hiring guides, packhorses or whatever. Agency-organized groups are small, largely bureaucracy-free, and provide mutual support against very real climactic dangers and the threat of hostile encounters with, literally, bandits. The proximity of Kazakhstan's border (on Mount Belukha's southern slopes) suggests that travellers consult the Foreign Office on the local situation before they go.

# Dalnevostochny Morskoy

**HOW TO GET THERE:**
By public ferry or private boat from
Vladivostok
**WHEN TO GO:**
Any time. July to September is
considered the prime season.
**DON'T MISS:**
The cranes, storks and many other
species for which the wetlands are a
crucial stop on the migratory
flyways; diving the vertical rock walls
and underwater sea stacks of
Bolshoi Pelis and Furugelm Islands;
and the haunting beauties of an
evening sail through the wild
archipelago to Telyakovskogo Bay.
**YOU SHOULD KNOW:**
Some eastern sections of
Dalnevostochny Morskoy are closed
to any kind of human intervention;
and the reserve's western and
southern seas, including their islands,
are considered to be restricted
primarily to scientific research.
Special permissions may be needed
to land on certain islands or rock
outcrops, or for diving in their
vicinity. It's best to be sure in
advance, because the reserve is also
a Russian Border Area, where
(especially independent) travellers
should do everything by the book.

A thin sliver of territory extends Russia's far eastern coast a little way south of Vladivostok to the Khasan region bordered by North Korea. Much of Khasan's coast falls within Dalnevostochny Morskoy (Far East Marine) Nature Reserve, which protects 643 sq km (248 sq mi) of rocky coast, wetlands, islands, outcrops and open water in the Sea of Japan. All together the reserve's four sections cover a tenth of the waters of Peter the Great Gulf, centred on the Rimsky-Korsakov Archipelago, the north part of Posyet Bay, Furugelm Island and Popov Island, which is closest to Vladivostok and the regional centre for marine tourism. Popov Island's environmental centre and short, ecological trails provide visitors with an explanation of the importance of Peter the Great Gulf among marine ecosystems. For many visitors it is the only chance to admire the reserve's spectacular biodiversity – and it should be the first stop for intrepid travellers hoping to get much closer to its submarine wealth.

Peter the Great Gulf is the biologically richest part of the Sea of Japan. The convergence of warm and cold ocean currents and colliding air masses attracts plants, trees, fish, marine mammals and hundreds of species of marine, coastal and forest birds at their northern and southern limits. Even the topography helps: rocky islets support big colonies of egrets, cormorants, loons, puffins and murrelet; while shallow coves are ideal for breeding fish which serve a local food chain extending to whales, sea lions, dolphins and the seal rookeries on the islands. Underwater reefs, caves and shallow ravines harbour giant octopus, Kamchatka king crab, sea urchins, starfish and a living carpet of warm- and cold-water species. Although only two per cent of the reserve is terrestrial, it includes meadows, marshes, brackish wetlands and sculpted cliffs, enhanced by the anomaly of both temperate and subtropical forest cover. With so much to marvel at, it's too easy to take this beauty for granted.

# Sikhote-Alin Mountains

**HOW TO GET THERE:**
By car or tour agency bus to Lazo,
Arkhipovka or another village in
Chuguevsky district
**WHEN TO GO:**
May to October. (Note that the unique
combination and rarity of tree and
shrub species makes autumn a visual
extravaganza.)

The Primorye region is the southernmost part of Russia's far east, between China and the Sea of Japan. The Sikhote-Alin mountain range is its 900-km (560-mi) long coastal spine, an ocean of highland forests and plunging valleys that is the last redoubt of the world's biggest feline, the Amur (or Siberian) tiger. The magnificent creature may be more symbol than fact (although some 30 tigers still survive in the wild here), but its rarity and beauty are more than matched by its exotic habitat. The south-central Sikhote-Alin is a glorious demonstration of what happens when the northern temperate zone merges with the subtropical ecology borne from the south on warm winds and ocean currents. Coupled with altitudinal hallmarks of the 1,500-m (4,920-ft) ascent from the valley floor, the Amur tigers' hunting grounds include mossy jungles of ferns, broadleaf woodlands, small lakes, waterfalls and bubbling rivers. A little higher, Manchurian walnut, Mongolian oak and cedar stand next to pine and evergreen forests, giving way to spruce and fir, with stone birch and upland shrubs nearest the alpine tundra of the highest peaks. Trekking here is a jaw-dropping botanical adventure of colourful lilies, orchids, irises, rhododendrons and hundreds of lichens, mosses and ferns. Highland meadows and the Mutta tract, an alpine marsh in the middle of a larch forest, are further anomalies of biodiversity in a wilderness where Himalayan and brown bear, wild boar, racoon, wolf, lynx and many deer are commonplace, and every small change in forest ecology has its own population of fabulous birds.

The heart of Sikhote-Alin is almost uninhabited and barely explored. It is a labyrinth of forested beauty, radiant with colour and the music of living nature – and the glow it engenders in every visitor is intensified by the knowledge that somewhere, an Amur tiger is enjoying the view, too; and the view could be you.

**DON'T MISS:**
Bears catching salmon on the Perekatnaya River; the source of the giant Ussuri River on Snezhnaya Mountain and the panorama of the Sikhote-Alin ridge from its summit; rafting on the Ussuri headwaters; hiking from Elamovskie springs to the canyon rapids and cascades of the Beneskie waterfalls; and the Museum of Nature at the Lazovsky Nature Reserve

**YOU SHOULD KNOW:**
There are reserves all round and within the Sikhote-Alin Biosphere (Ussuriysky, Khanka, Lazovsky and Zov Tigra among others), which help focus conservation efforts and limited access to visitors. The whole of south-central Sikhote-Alin is equally stunning and crammed with marvels of geography and nature. All you need is a (mandatory) ranger to guide you to favourite places.

*The forested Sikhote-Alin Mountains*

# Bayanzag Flaming Cliffs

A romantic mystique clings to the Gobi Desert. It is a desert with many faces – Mongolians can distinguish 33 separate kinds of 'Gobi' to describe a vast territory of high mountains, springs, forests and rolling steppe grasslands as well as the arid semi-deserts and wind-whipped dune systems of popular imagination – and every one more than matches its mythology. Partly it's a matter of scale. Where there are sand dunes, for example, they are the highest, longest, and most bizarre. The dunes of Khongoryn Els rise in a sand massif 20 km (12 mi) wide, 100 km (62 mi) long and some 800 m (2,625 ft) high, with individual dune peaks over 30 m (100 ft). Travellers can hear the dunes 'sing' from miles away, a musical drone similar to a light aircraft caused by the grating of billions of grains of sand in the sighing wind.

The dunes are in Gobi Gurvansaikhan in Mongolia's south, a national park that protects some of the Gobi's most spectacular features. There is an escarpment that rises out of a forest of desert-hardy saxaul trees, a ragged wall of reddish, sedimentary rock eroded over millions of years that blocks the horizon. At sunrise and sunset the cliffs of Bayanzag radiate orange, scarlet and crimson against an arc of cerulean sky. Seen from a short distance, it's as though the horizon itself is exploding in flames. Close-to, visitors bathed in the fiery reflections feel a primal rush, as though nature itself claimed sacrifices for its spectacular furnace.

That's not all. The Flaming Cliffs were named by explorer Roy Chapman Andrews, who excavated the first dinosaur eggs on this very spot. The terrain has yielded whole skeletons of various dinosaur species and many mammals; and Andrews himself found the skeletal remains of a hornless rhinoceros, the largest mammal known in the world.

*The Flaming Cliffs are where the first dinosaur eggs were found.*

# Khangai Mountains

*Gers along Orkhon River*

These are the sacred hills of Chinggis Khaan, the epic highlands he chose as the centre of his Mongol Empire and the site of his capital, KaraKorum. The Khangai Mountains stretch northwest from central Mongolia to the Russian border, parallel with the longer Altai range to the south, and reach their highest peak on 3,905 m (12,812 ft) Mount Otgontenger, east of Uliastai where Zavkhan meets the Aimags of Arkhangai and Bayankhongor. Otgontenger is popular with serious mountaineers but, for ancient religious reasons, women are not allowed to climb it. In any case, this central section of the Khangai Mountains is a famously beautiful configuration of thick forests dotted with snow-capped peaks, lakes, white-water mountain rivers, hot and cold springs, and alpine meadows full of musk deer, antelope, lynx, bear, curly-horned wild sheep, ibex, bustards, golden eagles, black vultures, storks and Dalmatian pelicans. The spectacular landscapes spread a huge distance to the southwest, where the Khangai Nuruu National Park also includes the eight descending freshwater lakes of Khuisyn Naiman in Ovorkhangai Aimag. Connected by an underground system of channels, they are one of Mongolia's most intriguing geological sites, and one of the loveliest panoramas in the country.

To the east the Khangai range gradually merges into the steppe grasslands. The broad, sweeping river valleys were the Great Khan's private hunting ground, across the Orkhon River from KaraKorum itself. For travellers, it's a chance to trek by horse to Takhiin Zal in the foothills, where wild Przewalski horse herds have been successfully reintroduced, and the rolling steppe where Mongolian nomads live by horse-wrangling. The mountains in the far distance include the extinct Khorgo volcano and Terkhiin Tsagaan Lake – a fantastic landscape of craggy bluffs, the Chuluut River canyon, and pastures where wild, long-haired yak and horses graze. Visitors can bathe in hot springs and dream an ancient dream.

**HOW TO GET THERE:**
By 4x4 from Ulaanbaatar to regional centres like Tsetserleg, Bayankhongor and Uliastai. Horses and camels are available locally.

**WHEN TO GO:**
May to October

**DON'T MISS:**
The eight stone stele dating back to the 7th–9th century BC with intricate carvings of deer in the wilderness of Shiluustei soum (sub-province) near Khukh Nuur, the mountain lake on the south flank of the Khangai famous for its rich wildlife and lack of visitors; and KaraKorum itself – the 108 towering *stupas* of the Erdene Zuu Buddhist monastery, which replaced the 1220 Imperial Capital in 1586, stand on a ridge above the Orkhon River, and give a terrific suggestion of the palace's vanished magnificence.

**YOU SHOULD KNOW:**
More than anywhere, the Khangai Mountains and foothills represent ancient Mongolian culture and its incorporation of both animist and Buddhist belief systems. It is a huge wilderness – yet everywhere in its most remote fastnesses you find unadorned shrines connecting millennia of nomadic traditions to the fullness of nature. The wildlife confirms it.

*A glaciated valley in the Kharkhiraa Mountains*

# Uvs Aimag

Mongolia's Uvs Aimag (province) occupies the great lakes depression of the country's northwest, between the high mountain extension of the Khangai range to the east, and the 4,000-m (13,120-ft) peaks of the northern Altai Mountains to the west. Even disregarding Uvs Nuur, the province's biggest lake and a World Heritage Site, Uvs Aimag is a remote wonderland of mountains, dune deserts, steppe scrublands, salt and freshwater lakes, tearing rivers and swampy meadows. The least-visited and least-populated of Mongolia's regions, it is crammed with exotic wildlife and a thousand habitats – and several national parks help to ensure that travellers get to see them.

Tsagaan Shuvuut is a Strictly Protected Area in Uvs' extreme north, by the Russian border. Steep elevations up to 3,000 m (9,840 ft) guarantee an amazing variety of mammals and birds in their different ranges, and political hesitancy guarantees that they flourish. It's the same at Turgen Uul, where the 4,000 m (13,120 ft) Kharkhiraa and Khankhukhii peaks dominate one of Mongolia's most beautiful regions, a meld of glaciers, stark cliffs, white-water rivers in forested canyons, waterfalls and flower-carpeted forest glades. Rare animals include the legendary snow leopard.

Khyargas Nuur National Park includes Kyargas Lake – twice as salty as the sea, difficult to reach through its surrounding reed beds, and a paradise for migratory birds – and its freshwater neighbour, Airag Lake, famous for its (alas, dwindling) Dalmatian pelicans. By far the loveliest of the province's lakes is Achit, equidistant from Ulaangom and Olgiy. Besides its scintillating sunrises and sunsets, its fresh water attracts huge flocks of geese and wetland birds, and even fishing eagles – too bad about the mosquitoes.

Uvs Aimag covers 69,600 sq km (26,870 sq mi), but has a population of only around 86,000. Its terrain and wildlife represent a cross-section of Central Asia's magnificent wilderness heart.

**HOW TO GET THERE:**
By plane, car or bus to Ulaangom, capital of Uvs Aimag; then by local arrangement
**WHEN TO GO:**
Any time for birdwatching or climbing; June to October for a modicum of warmth and comfort.
**DON'T MISS:**
The Buurug Dune, covering 4,000 sq km (1,545 sq mi) and the biggest single dune in Mongolia; rafting on the Tes or one of the many brilliant rivers; the stones, temples and other indicators of Uvs Aimag's diverse ethnic mix of Khoton, Dorvod, Bayad, Khalkh, Torguud, Zakhchin and Uriankhai peoples.
**YOU SHOULD KNOW:**
Although 'strict protection orders' cover many of Mongolia's nature highlights, travel permits to these areas are available to independent travellers as well as organized groups. Guides are not always mandatory, but only a brave heart would consider entering the back country without one. Wild life is real, and not always friendly.

# Uvs Nuur Basin

The World Heritage Site and Biosphere Reserve of Uvs Nuur Basin covers 10,689 sq km (4,125 sq mi) of northwestern Mongolia. The lake itself is 3,423 sq km (1,320 sq mi) and roughly 80 km (50 mi) long and wide. Set at just 759 m (2,490 ft) above sea level it is Mongolia's lowest point, but its waters are five times saltier than the ocean and it has no edible fish. It has no outlet either. The 38 rivers that flow into it evaporate in the enormous wetlands on its shores – the feeding, nesting and breeding grounds of some 362 bird species including cranes, spoonbills, geese, swans, snow herons, egrets, steppe hazel grouse and gull species which fly thousands of miles from the South China Sea for a brief northern summer. Their habitats are the salt marshes, reed beds, feather grass, swamp, sedge, willows and aspen that fringe different parts of the lake, and they share it with over 70 kinds of mammal.

The 'closed' system of Uvs Nuur Basin makes it as fascinating to scientists as it is to travellers. In fact it is usually uncomfortable for both. It is one of the hottest places, and always the coldest, in Mongolia, with temperatures ranging from over 40 to –57°C (104 to –70.6°F), and these extremes make it an ideal subject for studying climate change. The basin's extraordinary hydrology (the system including the surrounding mountains and feeder rivers) makes it possible for scientists to determine the rate at which the lake became saline and eutrophic during millennia of unchanged use by pastoral nomadic peoples. Perhaps more important to travellers is that the basin is made up of 12 protected areas that represent the major biomes of eastern Eurasia – like very few places on this Earth, Uvs Nuur can be all things to all kinds of visitor. Your choice.

**HOW TO GET THERE:**
By bus, car or plane to Ulaangom from Ulaanbaatar – 1,425 km (885 mi)
**WHEN TO GO:**
May to October
**DON'T MISS:**
Altan Els, the world's northernmost dune desert ecosystem, and the Bayan Nuur oasis close by – where horses and camels can be hired to ride the dunes; the scenic river valley of the Kharkhiraa Gol (river) which flows into Uvs Nuur, and the hiking trails into the restricted area leading off it.
**YOU SHOULD KNOW:**
Many of Mongolia's national parks and nature reserves charge some kind of entrance fee, but don't be surprised (or offended) if you can't find anyone to pay. Worry instead that you have the right permits before you enter a park, or 'strictly protected area' or 'border area', or occasionally all three, as you might in certain parts of the Uvs Nuur Basin.

*The Uvs Nuur Basin photographed from space.*

# Yolyn Am

The three ridges of the Gurvan Saikhan Mountains run from west to southeast across the northern edge of the Great Mongolian Gobi in Mongolia's southern Omnogovi province. The Zuun Saikhanii Nuruu (the Eastern Beauty) sub-range has peaks over 2,600 m (8,530 ft), shrouding whole valleys in more or less perpetual gloom and creating microclimates that seem to confound natural laws. The most extraordinary is Yolyn Am – 'Eagle Valley' or 'Vulture's Mouth' depending on your opinion of the lammergeier that wheel above it.

Yolyn Am is a long, deep and narrow gash set high in the mountains. The jagged gorge winds for miles, almost concealed by the overhang of sheer rock walls that block out the sunlight, deflect the winds and trap winter in the canyon's depths. Where sunlight falls, the rock is burning hot, and the combination of extremes produces a unique desert ecosystem. There is a small spring in the valley's depths. Even in the 45°C (113°F) air temperatures of high summer it barely flows, because the valley floor hardly ever warms sufficiently to melt the constricting ice that builds for nine months of the year, every year, over millions of years. Summer releases pockets of ice in the canyon walls, but the hundreds of dripping waterfalls only feed the ice field, which becomes several metres thick by the end of winter and several kilometres long. Sunlight reflects from on high onto the cracked slabs of ice, flashing prisms of colour across the defile and a spectacular abstract of blues and greens deep into the hollows. The 'Gobi Glacier' feels like a dream world, a Gobi myth that evaporates where the gorge opens out into a wide mountain valley.

Travellers to this special and beautiful place are urged to arrive by Bactrian (two-humped) camel or at least horseback, and transform an exotic adventure into an indelible memory.

# Fan Mountains

The western border of Kyrgyzstan is shaped like giant pincers, squeezing the meeting point of Uzbekistan, Kazakhstan and Tajikistan. Politically and geographically, it's a confused area. The pincer's upper joint follows the most northerly spur of the Tien Shan Mountains to its western end. Across the intervening lowland slices of Uzbekistan and Tajikistan, the southern arm runs back eastwards on a parallel ridge, gaining serious altitude between the Turkestanskiy sub-range and Pamir-Alai Mountains, which form the northern limit of the famous 'Pamir Knot' and the mountain corridor linking it to the Tien Shan. These southerly hills are an integral part of the giant mountain system of Pamir and Tien Shan, but distinctive enough to retain their own name – the Fan Mountains.

Within Kyrgyzstan, the Fan Mountains are seventh heaven for trekking on foot and on horseback. Most of the 11 summits over 5,000 m (16,400 ft) and 30 above 4,000 m (13,120 ft), including 5,489-m (18,008-ft) Chimtarga, the highest, lie over or on the border with Tajikistan; and the very highest 7,000-m (22,966-ft) peaks, like Pik Lenin (now officially called Koh-i-Garmo) far to the east, are in or shared with Gorno-Badakhshan. Apart from the staggering experience of driving the Pamir Highway from Khorog to Osh – clean across the region – only serious mountaineers want to risk the encounters with armed personnel that are a feature of trekking the trophy peaks. The high peaks are impressive, but the Kyrgyz Fan Mountains are beautiful. They are heavily forested, with sapphires for lakes, alpine meadows, canyons terraced with rocky bluffs, wild orchards in pretty river valleys and, above the tree line, glacial moonscapes and just enough snow-capped bare rock for cheerful self-congratulation. Blessedly empty of 'altitude tourists', the Fan Mountains in Kyrgyzstan are a revelation awaiting the kind of experienced trekkers who see and understand the magnificence in the smallest as well as the greatest manifestations of nature.

**HOW TO GET THERE:**
By helicopter or 4x4 to the high peaks; on foot or horseback anywhere else, from the towns and villages on the valley floor
**WHEN TO GO:**
July to September is the most comfortable trekking season, but it depends on altitude. The glacier line in the east is around 2,800 m (9,200 ft), but 5,000 m (16,400 ft) on the western Murghab plateau, where alpine meadows are full of flowers and butterflies late in the season. Low-altitude trekking in autumn is sublime.
**DON'T MISS:**
The weekly farmers' markets in Daroot-Korgon, Kashka-Suu and Sary Moghul for the food you need to take with you and the craic; the Achik Tash meadows with the Big Peaks in the distance; any of dozens of local festivals featuring Kyrgyz bareback horse racing and oiled wrestling; drinking fermented mare's milk in a felt yurt with Kyrgyz mountain shepherds.
**YOU SHOULD KNOW:**
Requirements for visas and permits change constantly. Travellers are recommended to make their arrangements through a tour agency even if they plan to travel independently, and to travel with a guide. The Fan Mountains are considered to be 'safely accessible' but it is dangerous to make any assumptions, so consult your own government for an update on civil or international strife in the region.

*Lake Iskanderkul and the Fan Mountains*

*Lake Song-Kul*

# Lake Song-Kul

**HOW TO GET THERE:**
By four-wheel drive from Bishkek –
300 km (186 mi)
or Naryn – 150 km (93 mi)

**WHEN TO GO:**
June to September

**DON'T MISS:**
The ride over 32 Parrots Pass to
where the Song-Kul River meets the
lake and where herds of semi-wild
horses come to bathe; the Tyulek
River ride to a village where women
weave traditional carpets invested
with coded folklore; the water birds
in the marshes of the lake's nature
reserve; any chance to eat and drink
with nomadic shepherds and lake
fishermen.

**YOU SHOULD KNOW:**
Lake Song-Kul is the place to go
native. This means not only camping
in yurts, but helping to pitch and
repair them as part of the trek. Most
of all it means responding to
extremely friendly – and wholly
genuine – overtures of hospitality
with the same warmth, even if it
feels a little uncomfortable for
urbanized city folk on an exotic
break. Song-Kul is all beauty and no
artifice – natural or human – at all.

The nomadic culture of Kyrgyzstan is written into the spectacular landscapes of Song-Kul, an alpine lake shimmering in a 3,000-m (9,840-ft) high plateau of steppe grassland. Every year, herders bring their livestock up from the Kochkor Valley to graze on the lush pastures stretching out from the lake to the surrounding ring of mountains, yet centuries of repetitious custom have left no blemish on its tranquil serenity. Instead, travellers are greeted by a creation scene of almost biblical drama. Untethered horses graze freely among yak and sheep all along the lake shore, watched over by enthusiastic children chasing each other on scraggy ponies at breakneck speed to the apparent disinterest of the adults doing chores by the felt yurts erected for the duration. This timeless scene of human domesticity – in unselfconscious harmony with the natural order – has the power to move even stony hearts, and it sets the tone for travelling in the region.

Nearly 30 km (19 mi) long and 18 km (11 mi) wide, the lake is small enough to feel like a self-contained world, and big enough to change colour from blue to pink to violet with the time of day and the weather. It is alive with movement and sound – songs and shouting and laughter as well as the cackle of thousands of wild geese, ducks and waterfowl. Only at night does the clamour fade to the rise and fall of conversations round crackling open fires, and an occasional solitary hooting over the lapping water.

Some travellers can spend weeks drinking in the fragile simplicity of the idyll – but all around the lake there are fantastic trails to ride or trek, like the descent to the Tyulek River over the Aktash Pass, or the Moldaashu ravine. Many visitors swear that however many times they come, Lake Song-Kul is where Kyrgyzstan makes them feel at one with nature's family.

# Saryarka

Saryarka – Steppe and Lakes of Northern Kazakhstan is a UNESCO World Heritage Site. Inscribed in 2008, it is made up of two protected areas: Korgalzhyn Nature Reserve and Naurzum Nature Reserve, with a combined area of over 4,500 sq km (1,737 sq mi). The reserves are situated in a wide band of steppe grassland which extends from Ukraine in the west to China in the east. Bounded by evergreen forest to the north and an arid area to the south, they are a fertile oasis of wetlands, lakes and open grassland. More than 15 million migratory birds, many rare and endangered, use the area's precious saturated lowlands as a hub on their journeys from Europe, Africa and East Asia to breeding grounds in Siberia. Birdwatchers from around the world flock to the reserves at news of sightings, including the imperilled Siberian white crane as well as the more common Dalmatian pelican and pink flamingo.

The reserves are also crucial to the survival of *Saiga tatarica*, an antelope which once roamed the plains in vast herds but is now on the verge of extinction through hunting and illegal poaching. Travel within these golden grasslands is easy and the recent growth in ecotourism has rewarded the efforts of the reserves' authorities, even though tourism was only a secondary consideration when they sought to preserve this area of immense ecological importance.

In this land of big skies there are numerous hilltop mausoleums, built by nomadic peoples to honour their ancestors and to mark out grazing rights. These round-roofed structures, although now in a state of disrepair, are a reminder that the area has long been a place where humans have lived in harmony with nature.

**HOW TO GET THERE:**
By air to Sary-Arka Airport (Karaganda) from Almaty, Moscow or St Petersburg
**WHEN TO GO:**
It's wettest in June and July and very cold from October to March.
**DON'T MISS:**
Lake Balkhash, now the largest lake of Central Asia since the dramatic shrinkage of the Aral Sea.
**YOU SHOULD KNOW:**
When travelling in Kazakhstan care should be taken to stick to authorized routes. There are several 'closed areas' which require advance permission to enter. Also, there are numerous military no-go areas that are often not signposted – if in any doubt, check with the local police first.

# Sayram-Ugam National Park

**HOW TO GET THERE:**
By overnight train from Almaty
**WHEN TO GO:**
July to September are the warmest
and driest months.
**DON'T MISS:**
The crystal-clear waters of the River
Sairamsu – located in a glorious
ravine of the same name.
**YOU SHOULD KNOW:**
When travelling by air to and within
Kazakhstan it should be noted that
very few of the country's carriers are
allowed into EU airspace due to their
poor safety records. It is advisable to
look at the Foreign Office (UK) or
State Department (US) website
before travelling.

Located in the Kaskasu River valley in the Tole Bi District of southern Kazakhstan, Sayram-Ugam National Park is a wildlife sanctuary. Perfect terrain for trekking on foot or on horseback, the park is an area of beautiful valleys framed by the imposing peaks of the Ugam Mountains at the western edge of the Tien Shan range. It is a land that is the kingdom of the snow leopard, lynx, mountain goat and white-pawed Tyanshan bear, while its skies are ruled by golden eagles, peregrine falcons and bearded vultures which ride the thermals thrown up by the steep mountainsides.

The Ugam Mountains offer unspoilt beauty, characterized by huge glacial valleys, turquoise morainal lakes and steep-sided ravines covered in birch and juniper forest. A road takes the traveller into the heart of the mountains, but stops abruptly near the lower slopes. It is then time for a change of pace as the impressive sight of Sayram Peak, at 4,238 m (13,904 ft) the park's highest point, dominates the skyline. The area has a rich history and was once a strategically important section of the Great Silk Road route that carried goods from east to west. There are also numerous ancient monuments, mausoleums and burial mounds scattered across the park which bear witness to its ancient cultural history.

The area is popular with mountaineers and the best climbing is to be found on Kizil-bush and Druzhba which are both over 4,000 m (13,120 ft). Less demanding but still challenging, the most scenic hiking trail is along the slopes of the scree-lined Kaskasu ravine. Sayram-Ugam is a place of rare and exceptional splendour, a tranquil place far removed from the hustle and bustle of modern life.

# Pamiro-Alai Mountains

Pamiro-Alai is a mountain system of central Asia stretching 800 km (500 mi) from the region of Pamir towards the Sino-Tajikistan border. It is made up of five mountain ranges – Alaiskiy, Zeravshanskiy Turkestanskiy, Karateginskiy and Gissarskiy. In Persian, *Pamiro-Alai* translates as 'paradise at the roof of the world'. While its exceptionally harsh environment and extreme remoteness may not be everyone's idea of paradise, it fits well with the local Sunni Muslim belief that paradise should be hard to reach.

The ranges are composed of a succession of huge sheer rock faces with over 30 peaks above 5,000 m (16,400 ft). Roads are few and far between, particularly in the west of the area where access is only really possible by helicopter. Where roads do exist, such as the one near Chimtarga Peak, they are often so narrow and steep that traffic has to be tightly controlled and it is customary to drive up in the morning and down in the afternoon. The area was often chosen to host the all-Russian climbing championships during the Soviet era and it presents some of the most challenging rock climbing anywhere in the world. The season is short, with only August being dry and warm enough to allow full access. Progress on the precipitous rocks can be slow, with advances of only a few hundred metres per day possible on the toughest stretches. This, combined with the need to carry at least a week's provisions, means that only the most experienced climbers can attempt the harder climbs.

The most accessible and perhaps the most beautiful climb in Pamiro-Alai is a route that links Lake Alaudinskie with Lake Kulikalon. A full day's hike along the scree-lined Shogun-Aga pass takes the walker into an area surrounded by towering peaks, while the descent offers incredible views over Lake Kulikalon and across the lavishly green Laudan river valley.

**HOW TO GET THERE**:
By helicopter from Samarkand or Dushanbe. It is possible to reach the area by road, but this involves an arduous journey and it is very easy to get lost.

**WHEN TO GO**:
August is the only time when the weather is likely to be benign.

**DON'T MISS**:
The view of the northwestern face of Mount Chapdara from the Shogun-Aga pass.

**YOU SHOULD KNOW**:
The mountains were a favoured hideout of the ruthless ruler Genghis Khan, from where he led his hordes in a bloody expansion of empire across Asia and into Europe. There is an outside chance that he is buried along with great treasures somewhere in the area, but since he ordered the killing of everyone present at his funeral (some 2,500 men) the mystery of his tomb's location will probably never be solved.

*The remote Pamiro-Alai Mountains*

# Chitral Gol

**HOW TO GET THERE:**
By air to Chitral, then 4x4 to Chitral National Park – about 90 minutes' drive
**WHEN TO GO:**
The beginning of May to the end of September
**DON'T MISS:**
The historic city of Peshawar, the centre of Pashtun culture and arts
**YOU SHOULD KNOW:**
This area of Pakistan is dangerous to visit at this time, due to fighting between the Taliban and Pakistan's army. Members of Al Queda, including Osama bin Laden, are thought to be hiding in these mountains that separate Pakistan and Afghanistan.

Situated in the Hindu Kush, a sub-range of the Himalayas in Pakistan's North-West Frontier province, Chitral Gol is a remote region of valleys and rushing streams encircled by snow-covered peaks. Chitral's highest mountain is Tirich Mir at 7,708 m (25,289 ft). The Chitral Valley was once part of the Silk Road, when caravans from China and central Asia crossed the high passes bound for India. Today, the region remains isolated, cut off from the rest of the world from December to April when the routes in and out are impassable.

Within this area, the Chitral Gol National Park may be found alongside the Chitral River. It used to be the private game reserve of His Highness Sir Shuja ul Mulk, and is still owned by the family, although the Wildlife Department is now responsible for the wildlife. This is a stunning area of ancient deodar cedar trees, pine oaks, junipers and birch stands. In late spring and summer wonderful carpets of wild flowers – blue geraniums, anemones, delphiniums, buttercups, alpine primroses as well as many herbs and medicinal plants – cover the high pastures.

The park is renowned for its markhor goats. The national animal of Pakistan, the markhor is a large and endangered type of wild goat with superb, spiral horns. Siberian ibex and Ladakh urial can also be found here in small numbers, along with carnivores such as the yellow-throated marten, red foxes, jackals, wolves and visiting snow leopards. The birds that may be seen include golden eagles, Lammergeier's and peregrine falcons, snowcocks, Monal pheasants, and many ducks and other waterfowl which pass through *en route* to India. Hunting is a popular pastime here and unfortunately ducks, in particular, make an easy target.

*Chitral Gol remains remote
and isolated*

# Khunjerab National Park

*Herders with grazing cattle on Khunjerab Pass*

One of the highest national parks in the world – more than 50 per cent is over 4,000 m (13,120 ft) – Khunjerab is situated in the Karakoram mountain range and was set up in 1975 to protect the magnificent display of alpine flora and increase the population of snow leopards and Marco Polo sheep – the latter only found in this region of Pakistan.

Starting 30 km (19 mi) from Sost, the valley is at first narrow, with mountains forming high walls to either side, but soon it widens out into broad and beautiful alpine meadows where 66 species of bird live, including kestrels, falcons, sparrow hawks, marsh harriers, Himalayan griffon vultures, golden eagles and Lammergeiers. But Marco Polo sheep and snow leopards are the stars of the area. Marco Polo rams have the longest horns of any sheep, averaging about 140 cm (55 in) and spiral in shape, with the tips pointing out, away from the head. They have been under threat from illegal hunting, but the World Wildlife Fund has created a local organization to help with their protection.

It is thought that the highest density of snow leopards in the Himalayan ecosystem live in this region. These beautiful solitary and secretive cats, active at dawn and dusk and very well camouflaged, are difficult to count but the Snow Leopard Trust is conducting studies at several sites in the North-West Frontier province.

Within the boundaries of the park are the Ghuzerav mountains, at the heart of which rises the perfect pyramid of Sonia Peak. Technically simple, with two routes to choose from, this is a wonderful mountain to climb.

**HOW TO GET THERE:**
The Northern Areas Transport Corporation offers transport from Islamabad to Sost. From here transport is available to Khunjerab. It is also possible to join an adventure tour.
**WHEN TO GO:**
March to September
**DON'T MISS:**
The Hunza Valley, one of the most scenically spectacular places in the world. The valley is supposed to be the inspiration for Shangri-la in James Hilton's book, *Lost Horizon*.
**YOU SHOULD KNOW:**
If you wish to climb Sonia Peak, check in advance whether a permit is necessary, and try to be there in August when river levels are at their lowest.

*A Rhino with her calf in Royal Bardia National Park*

# Royal Bardia National Park

Previously a royal hunting reserve, Royal Bardia National Park became a wildlife reserve in 1976, and in 1988, after being extended to encompass the Babai River Valley, it was established as a national park. Remote and undisturbed, the wilderness covers an area of almost 1,000 sq km (386 sq mi).

Located in Western Terai, much of Bardia lies on the slopes of the Shiwalik hills that form its northern border. The land slopes gently down to rivers in the south and west, while in the east a section of highway bisects the park. More than 70 per cent of the park is covered with forest, mostly sal trees, but the grassland, savannah and riverine forests forming the remainder provides wonderful habitat in which many endangered animals live and breed.

Bardia is bursting with wildlife. Greater one-horned rhinos were successfully relocated here from Chitwan National Park, and now there are 100 of these rare animals. One of the last known herds of wild elephants often pass through as they tramp these remote western Nepalese jungles and six species of deer, gaur, nilgai, Himalayan tahr, serow, and jackal can be seen. In pride of place are Royal Bengal tigers, of which there are thought to be over 50 individuals. Around the rivers, gharial and marsh mugger crocodiles snooze, otters and water birds splash and play, and Ganges river dolphins leap through the blue waters.

Take a guided tour by foot, 4x4, or elephant. These magnificent animals carry their passengers deep into the park through tall, whispering grasses and past vast termite mounds, picking their way delicately through streams *en route*. With luck, many birds and animals will be seen, and even a glimpse of a tiger is a possibility.

**HOW TO GET THERE:**
Fly to Napalgunj, rent a 4x4 and drive to Thakurdwara, the park office and lodges.
**WHEN TO GO:**
From October to early April
**DON'T MISS:**
What may be the largest Asian elephant in the world, named Rajah Gaj, lives in Bardia. He stands 3.4 m (11 ft) at the shoulder. Also look out for the rare and threatened bustard called the Bengal florican.
**YOU SHOULD KNOW:**
An unusual and exciting way to reach the park is by an organized rafting trip down the Karnali River.

# Pindari Glacier

The Pindari glacier, in the Kumaon Himalayas, is situated between Nanda Kot, 6,861 m (22,510 ft) and Nanda Devi, 7,817 m (25,646 ft). A steep, imposing glacier, Pindari measures 3 km (1.9 mi) in length and 250 m (820 ft) in width. A trek here is an adventure for anyone who is fit and the reward is well worth the climb.

Starting at Song, on the banks of the Revati Ganga River, the route is via Loharkhet, where the forest begins. This dense forest is at a relatively low altitude and is bursting with ferns, rhododendrons, wild flowers, berries and moss. Troops of langurs, India's sacred monkey, bound around the forest floor and swing through the trees above.

At Dhakuri Khal pass, a small detour brings the valiant trekker to a small, beautifully situated temple. This is the hardest day, but as the misty dawn reveals the first snow-clad mountains, anticipation grows for what is yet to come. The path runs beside the pristine Pindari River, the source of which rises at the glacier, before reaching Dwali and the treeline.

The climb from here to Phurkiya is tough: the air is thin and cold, with frozen streams to cross, even in midsummer. The river, too, is frozen, but water can still be seen, flowing beneath a thick slab of ice. Skirting the edge of a deep valley, the views are stunning and there is even a slender waterfall to admire. Phurkiya is the last stop before the final ascent to Zero Point.

Pure white, with touches of blue and brown, Pindari glacier gleams in the sunshine and is an exhilarating sight. Although this is an arbitrary place to stop, only serious mountaineers continue – ordinary mortals can only sit and stare at what must be one of the grandest views in the world.

**HOW TO GET THERE:**
By train from Delhi to Kathgodam, then by road to Song
**WHEN TO GO:**
From May 1 to June 30, or September 1 to October 15
**DON'T MISS:**
Views of Nanda Devi
**YOU SHOULD KNOW:**
The trek to Pindari Glacier can be done through a trekking company or individually. It is roughly 90 km (56 mi) to Zero Point and back, a trip of at least five days.

*The imposing Pindari Glacier*

# Pin Valley National Park

Located in the north of Himal Pradesh, right up by the Tibetan border, Pin Valley National Park, in the valley of the Pin River, is cold, high and remote. Its elevation varies from between 3,500 m (11,500 ft) to something over 6,000 m (20,000 ft). Declared a National Park in 1987, it covers 650 sq km (250 sq mi) and has a buffer zone of 1,150 km (715 mi).

The Pin Valley is an astonishing place. Austere, beautiful and other-worldly, it has a distinctly Buddhist atmosphere, due in part to the monasteries and culture of Tibet which is all-encompassing here. Because of the altitude, vegetation is sparse, dominated by alpine trees, stands of Himalayan cedar and rare medicinal plants. By mid June the snow has melted and the vegetation begins to grow. Rapidly, the lunar landscape is transformed by a carpet of wild flowers, and some of the park's rare animals descend to lower levels to feed.

The park was largely formed to protect the endangered snow leopard, the grey ghost of the Himalayas, but these animals are notoriously hard to spot. However, it is home to many other animals including ibex, Tibetan gazelle, blue sheep, woolly hare, fox, wolf and bear. As vegetation is thin, it is easy to view wildlife here and it's wonderful for twitchers, who may spot Himalayan snowcock, chukor, snow partridge, several species of finch and wagtail, pigeon, red-billed chough, golden eagle and Himalayan griffon.

There are several paths to trek, of varying difficulty and all over 3,000 m (9,840 ft), and huts in which to stay overnight. Porters and local guides are available to help, and there are even Chhumurthi horses for hire. It is impossible to drive in the park, so for those who are not so fit, trekking on horseback is a good option.

*Striking patterns of stria in the rocks above Mud, the Pin Valley's uppermost village*

# Gangotri National Park

*Bhojbasa in Gangotri National Park*

Northwest of Nanda Devi, in Uttarakhand and on the border with China, is the enormous Gangotri National Park. An enormous expanse of 2,390 sq km (920 sq mi), the park is characterized by high ridges, mountains, glaciers, gorges, narrow valleys and alpine meadows, all of which contribute to the wide range of ecosystems within its boundaries.

Gangotri's forested areas are made up of Himalayan cedar, fir, spruce and, at lower elevations, oaks and wonderful stretches of colourful rhododendrons. But major landslides have caused areas of irreversible isolation between some of the forested areas. This may prove hazardous in the long run for the welfare of some of the wildlife, which thus far includes 15 species of mammal and 150 species of bird. Mammals such as black and brown bears, musk deer, tahr, blue sheep, Nepalese Bengal tigers and the mysterious snow leopard live in the forests and high crags.

This is a park for those seeking adventure, not simply for nature lovers. Here visitors can raft on the rivers, paraglide, hang glide and ski as well as climb, trek or take a Jeep safari. The mountains themselves are a magnet for climbers and form a magnificent, snow-clad background, with their gleaming, pure-white glaciers.

However, Gangotri is probably best known as a sacred place of pilgrimage. The Gangotri glacier, which flows from Chaukhamba – at 7,138 m (23,419 ft) the highest peak of the Gangotri group – is the source of the River Ganges and is one of the holy Hindu shrines. Pilgrims travel here to bathe in the icy waters of the river, before visiting the three other sites of the Himalayan Chhota Char Dham, representing all three major Hindu denominations.

**HOW TO GET THERE:**
The nearest airport and railway station are at Dehradun, about 220 km (137 mi) from Gangotri town. From there, travel by road.
**WHEN TO GO:**
From May to October
**DON'T MISS:**
Rishikesh, another sacred site about one day away from Gangotri. Nicknamed the 'world capital of yoga' for its many yoga centres, there are also many *ashrams* here, including the now-closed *ashram* of Maharishi Mahesh Yogi, where the Beatles wrote much of the *White Album*.
**YOU SHOULD KNOW:**
In the Hindu religion, the Goddess Ganga took the form of a river to cleanse the sins of King Bagirath's ancestors. Lord Shiva captured her in his matted hair to prevent her from flooding the Earth.

# Chopta Valley

**HOW TO GET THERE:**
Fly to Bagdogra airport in West Bengal, then by helicopter to Gangtok. From there go by road to Chopta Valley via Mangan and Thangu.
**WHEN TO GO:**
May to September, but July and August for the best of the wild flowers.
**DON'T MISS:**
The trek from Chopta Valley to Muguthang Valley. At 4,572 m (15,000 ft), this magnificent valley has awe-inspiring vistas to enjoy.
**YOU SHOULD KNOW:**
It is essential to obtain a permit to enter Sikkim. The political sensitivity of the area has led to a significant military presence here, and visitors should be careful about what they photograph.

The Chopta Valley is located in north Sikkim, at an elevation of 4,023 m (13,200 ft). India's second-smallest and least-populated state, Sikkim is bordered by Nepal, Tibet and West Bengal, and has long attracted tourists to its biodiversity, culture and outstanding natural beauty. Set in the Himalayas, Sikkim boasts the world's third-highest mountain, Kangchenjunga, which can be found on its border with Nepal.

Chopta Valley is pristine and magnificent, surrounded by snowy mountains, whose peaks are always frozen, and deep, green forest. The valley floor is crossed by lovely meandering rivers and in June and July, when the snow has melted, the streams and rivulets run free. But for much of the year they are frozen, enabling visitors to walk over or along them. This is an uninhabited area but, during the summer months, nomadic Tibetans bring their yaks up to graze on the lush alpine pasture. At this time of year, Chopta Valley is like the Garden of Eden, smothered with glorious wild flowers of many species and hues, including gentians, saxifrage, violas, busy lizzies, primulas and anemones. On the higher slopes, low grasses and cushion plants succeed in growing among the scree and boulders.

Large mammals live in the mountains – snow leopards, Tibetan wolves, Himalayan musk deer, blue sheep, takins and serows – but the casual visitor is more likely to be impressed by the birds. Sikkim has over 550 species of bird, some endangered, and it is possible to see golden eagle, snow partridge, snowcock, lammergeier and griffon vultures as well as smaller birds such as babblers and robins.

This serene valley – the peace only broken by birdsong – is both a salutary reminder of the insignificance of humanity in the face of nature and of the damage man has inflicted on so much of the natural world.

# Ranthambore National Park

**HOW TO GET THERE:**
The Delhi to Kota train stops at Sawai Madhopur, the closest town to Ranthambore. Buses run from here to other towns in Rajasthan. Taxis and autorickshaws, or organized tours, continue to the park itself.
**WHEN TO GO:**
October to April. The park is closed between July and September.
**DON'T MISS:**
The walk up to the fort is excellent for nature spotting and for atmospheric architecture. Originally built in AD 944, this area was the scene of endless battles until it became part of the kingdom of Jaipur in 1569.

Ranthambore is an expanse of stony jungle scrub, grassland and dense, dry forest, hemmed in by rocky ridges. Hilly southeastern Rajasthan is relatively green and the reserve, bounded to the north and south by rivers, is well watered and dotted with small lakes. It is named after a ruined fort which stands on an isolated rock towering 210 m (690 ft) above an area which was a hunting reserve for the maharaja of Jaipur until 1970, even though it had been declared a national park in 1955.

Famous as a tiger reserve, Ranthambore is one of the best places in this part of India to see these magnificent creatures in the wild; and tiger numbers have become quite healthy after a recent, distressing decline. Although the reserve is part of India's Project

Tiger, it was government officials who were, eventually, implicated in poaching tigers. At the time of their disappearance, the decrease in population was blamed on villagers and farmers. Tiger-spotting trips around the park are in six-seater 'Gypsies' – open-topped jeeps – or in 'Canters', trucks with seating for 20 people.

There is of course plenty of other wildlife in Ranthambore and good walks to various observation points – the lakes, near one of which stands an enormous banyan tree, are particularly rewarding for birdwatchers. Over 250 resident and migrating bird species have been recorded here and, in addition to delightful flocks of colourful birds flying in the open spaces of the park, waders and waterfowl throng the lakes. Frequently seen species include pelican, bittern, flamingo, ibis and kingfisher. Also resident in the lakes is a large population of marsh crocodile.

**YOU SHOULD KNOW:**
In 2008 one male and one female tiger were sent from Ranthambore to the Sariska Tiger Reserve, north of Jaipur. Sariska, one of India's most important tiger reserves, revealed in 2005 that its tiger population had been eliminated. It is clear that poaching for the Chinese 'medicine' trade was responsible. It is to be hoped that tigers are successfully re-established here.

*A wild Bengal tiger in Ranthambore national park*

# Kanha National Park

*An Indian elephant enjoying a
dust bath.*

Covering 1,945 sq km (750 sq mi) of southeastern Madhya Pradesh, Kanha is one of India's largest national parks and has, since 1955, dedicated itself to preserving a variety of animal species. Today, it is one of the most beautiful reserves in Asia. The Surpan River meanders through a central area of undulating grasslands, jewelled in the dry season with flowering trees such as laburnum with its scented yellow cascades, and brilliant flame trees. To the east and west grow thickets of bamboo and ancient forests of deciduous and evergreen trees, while rocky escarpments north and south provide panoramic views.

The forests are home to troops of monkeys and numerous shy, nocturnal animals; the grasslands are grazed by herds, ranging from tiny mouse deer to enormous gaur. Kanha is particularly proud of its large population of barasingha, a rare swamp deer saved from extinction by excellent conservation work. The herbivores provide prey for the 80 or so tigers (and the smaller carnivores) in Kanha. Jeep safaris tour the whole park, and some parts can also be visited on foot. Well-established nature trails lead from the visitor centres at Khatiya, Kisli and Mukki gates. The varied habitats are a joy for birdwatchers; birds of woodland, plain and the numerous small lakes include hoopoe, bee-eater, parakeet, pond heron and stork.

Kanha is one of several places claiming to be the setting for Kipling's *The Jungle Book* and there is indeed a real magic here in a vast, ancient landscape that is still home to two tribal groups. The Gonds are farmers and herders and the Baiga live by cutting firewood and gathering wild honey in the depths of the forest.

# Chilika Lake

*Fishing on Chilika Lake*

The world's second-largest lagoon, Chilika Lake is separated from the Bay of Bengal by a long sandbar with a mouth that allows saltwater into the lagoon. It then mingles with the outflow of several rivers and this brackish habitat and its unique marine ecosystem is the largest wintering ground for migrating birds in the whole of India. Late in the dry season the lake measures about 600 sq km (230 sq mi); with the monsoon, it almost doubles. Recent silting resulted in decreased salinity, the invasion of freshwater species such as water hyacinth and a reduction of fish stocks, on which villagers from around the lagoon depend. The Chilika Development Authority cut a new mouth in the sandbar, and the delicate balance was restored. The CDA has received awards for its conservation work.

On one of many tiny islands in the lagoon stands Kalijai temple, where Hindu pilgrims flock every January to worship the sun god, Suraya, at the *Makar Mela*. Another island, Nalabana, is central to the bird sanctuary. After the monsoon, as the mudflats re-emerge from nutrient-rich waters, over a million birds fly in from as far away as Siberia. The whole lake, its wetlands and marshes, shallows and sandbars, is alive with birds. Among the hundreds of species are heron, flamingo, stork, spoonbill, kingfisher and osprey.

On the mainland shore some villages have accommodation, often with lake views, and regular ferries run to Nalabana and to Satapada, a headland settlement with an excellent visitor centre complete with upstairs observatory and bird-identification charts. From here, boat trips tour the lake and sandbar.

**HOW TO GET THERE:**
The railway from Kolkata (Calcutta) follows the western shore, with several stops. Frequent buses ply the parallel road between Berhampur and Bhubanesar.
**WHEN TO GO:**
November to January for the greatest concentration of birds.
**DON'T MISS:**
A boat trip. Regular trips are run by a co-operative and tour the whole lake area for birdwatching. They also visit the temple, the sandbar and its pristine beach, and head out to sea to look for Irawaddy dolphins – the only known population of the critically endangered species in India.
**YOU SHOULD KNOW:**
Fishing by traditional, sustainable methods has provided a living for the villagers of Chilika for centuries. Now prawn fishing has become increasingly remunerative and has attracted the interest of outside enterprises. If the government of Orissa auctions fishing rights to the highest bidder, the lives of the fishermen and of the lake itself could be drastically changed.

# Bhagwan Mahavir Wildlife Sanctuary

Even those tourists for whom Goa is synonymous with beaches and bars will notice the exotic butterflies and birds in their hotel gardens. This tiny state has a lush interior of rivers and wetlands and forested mountains and a wealth of wildlife. The Bhagwan Mahavir Sanctuary was founded in 1969; it now includes Mollem National Park and is the largest of Goa's protected areas, and one of the most tranquil. The Western Ghats, in whose foothills it lies, are a formidable barrier for man – very few roads cross the mountains – and a route for animals to travel unmolested. Herds of elephant regularly make their way through the park and tigers are occasional visitors.

Macaque and langur monkeys, sloth bears and porcupines, leopards and wild dogs (considered by the locals more dangerous than tigers) are among the inhabitants of the well-watered, moist deciduous forest and evergreen canopy trees. Venomous snakes include Russell's viper, the deadly 'speckled band' of the Sherlock Holmes story. A rainbow of small birds with names as pretty as their plumage – golden oriole, emerald dove, fairy bluebird, paradise flycatcher – are just a few of hundreds of species found here, and many more, unseen in the depths of the forest, can by identified by their calls. Many of Goa's glorious resident butterflies are also seen here, including the large, slow-flying malabar tree nymph and, during and after the monsoon, India's largest butterfly, the southern birdwing, whose wingspan reaches 250 mm (10 in).

Most animals in the sanctuary are nocturnal and avoid people; even birds are more visible at dawn and dusk. Visitors who spend a night in Mollem's pleasant forest accommodation have a better chance of seeing them and will enjoy not only the glorious scenery but also the enchanting atmosphere and evocative sounds of nightfall and sunrise.

**HOW TO GET THERE:**
Buses travelling east from Ponda and the coast stop at Mollem, close to the forest checkpoint. There is a railway station at Colem, near the south entrance to the park.

**WHEN TO GO:**
November to March

**DON'T MISS:**
Dudhsagar Falls – the name means 'Ocean of Milk' – is south of Colem and can be reached by a dirt road and a rocky scramble. It is a tiered waterfall, one of India's highest and absolutely spectacular after the monsoon. The railway runs very close to it, over a viaduct; some local trains slow to allow passengers a good view.

**YOU SHOULD KNOW:**
Goa is intensively mined for manganese and iron and road journeys east are memorable for the endless jams of trucks carrying iron ore on steep roads and fearsome, stunted landscapes and villages covered in thick, red dust. Despite conservation laws, the sanctuary is threatened by pollution and the illegal dumping of truckloads of waste.

*Dudhsagar Falls*

437

# Biligirirangan Hills

**HOW TO GET THERE:**
Trains run from Bangalore via Mysore to Chamrajanagar. Regular buses run from Mysore and Chamrajanagar to the sanctuary.
**WHEN TO GO:**
The sanctuary is open all year and serious naturalists may choose to visit during the monsoon, when animals flock to newly filled waterholes. October to April is more comfortable.
**DON'T MISS:**
The temple can be reached by road, tracks and steps and makes a fine walk. There are picnic areas on the open hilltop and views over the whole area are terrific. The deity in the temple is an unusual standing form of Ranganatha, an avatar of Vishnu. Crowds of pilgrims worship him at an annual car festival.
**YOU SHOULD KNOW:**
Visitors not staying in the sanctuary need a permit, obtainable in Chamrajanagar. The Biligiriranga (white cliffs) Hills are probably named for the pale, towering rock face where the temple stands, although the name could also refer to the almost constant silvery white mists and clouds that hover around the peaks.

The Biligirirangan Hills in southeastern Karnataka are part of an extensive protected area, the Biligiri Rangaswamy Temple Wildlife Sanctuary, more conveniently known as the BRT Sanctuary. The hills form a biological bridge between the Western and Eastern Ghats, allowing animal migration throughout the Deccan plateau. Since early studies by a British coffee planter, the region has been of great interest to naturalists. Temperature and rainfall differ markedly between lower and higher altitudes in the sanctuary, resulting in a fine mosaic of habitats from grassland, scrub and thick deciduous forest to stunted trees and montane grassland.

Most visible of the animals are wild elephant wandering round the mountains. The grasslands are home to herbivores, including the rare four-horned antelope and the gaur. This massive wild ox, commonly and incorrectly called the Indian bison, can stand almost 2 m (6.5 ft) at the shoulder; tigers are its only predator and their absence has allowed the magnificent gaur to thrive.

The average height of the hills is around 1,500 m (5,000 ft); one of the rocky peaks is the site of the temple to Lord Rangaswamy around which the sanctuary was originally created in 1974. Jeep safaris and elephant rides can be arranged from the Wilderness Camp, where most visitors stay, and there is a good network of hiking tracks. Walkers will spot some of the smaller animals and large numbers of birds. Among hundreds of species seen here are the crested eagle, the racquet-tailed drongo, with its trailing feathers, and the tiny, multi-coloured purple-rumped sunbird, which flits between flowers, sipping nectar.

# Anamudi Peak

**HOW TO GET THERE:**
Road surfaces around Munnar are bad, but it is on the main road from Kochi (Cochin) to Madurai. There are frequent buses to Kochi and a few to other towns. The park and peak can be reached by autorickshaw from Munnar.
**WHEN TO GO:**
November to March
**DON'T MISS:**
Munnar, once called the High Range of Travancore, is the commercial centre for the surrounding tea estates – some of the world's highest. It is busy and not very pretty but its fresh air and the glorious surrounding countryside make it a good base for hill walking. There is a museum on the practicalities and history of tea.

The Western Ghats range extends from Mumbai (Bombay) almost to the southern tip of India. These mountains are exceptionally verdant – forests cover the rugged heights, while foothills, cloaked in tea or coffee bushes, billow like emerald eiderdowns. The British-built hill stations high in the ridges are escapes from the searing heat of summer, where the air is cool and unpolluted and the mountains and woods are home to a multitudinous flora and fauna. Just north of Munnar in Kerala, Anamudi Peak – 2,695 m (8,842 ft) – is the highest in the range, and in the whole of southern India. It is surrounded by Eravikulam National Park, once a hunting ground for the British.

Nowadays, with its rivers and streams, rolling hills and lush forest, the park is a beautiful place and very good trekking country. A wealth of plants and flowers grow here, from rare mountain orchids to blankets of rhododendron. One shrub, the *kurinji*, grows only in the Western Ghats and blooms only once every 12 years – the last time was in 2006 – covering the hillsides with a mist of purplish-blue. Pine, bamboo and teak forests shelter innumerable reclusive animals and the grasslands are home to several species including the Nilgiri tahr, one of the world's rarest mountain goats.

*Anamudi* means 'elephant's forehead' and the peak is a blunt, hunched mass. Walkers can climb to the summit up technically easy slopes to the north and south, starting from a base elevation of about 2,000 m (6,560 ft). To the west and east it is much steeper, with challenging rock faces and deep gorges. The views over the dark forests and rolling tea estates, bright green, trim and tidy, are superb.

**YOU SHOULD KNOW:**
Independent trekkers must obtain permits from the Divisional Forest Office. Restrictions for walkers are to safeguard the Nilgiri tahr (a breed of goat), whose trusting nature makes it an easy target for hunters – it almost became extinct. Groups of the sociable animals gather at the park gates, waiting hopefully for savoury treats – they are addicted to salt and the posters prohibiting feeding them are often ignored by visitors.

*Rolling grasslands and Anamudi Peak*

# Periyar Wildlife Sanctuary

**HOW TO GET THERE:**
Periyar is 100 km (62 mi) east of
Kottayam. The bus from Kottayam
takes four hours, from Madurai in
Tamil Nadu five-and-a-half hours.
**WHEN TO GO:**
December to April is best, during the
dry season when the skies are clear
and the humidity is less draining.
**DON'T MISS:**
The blue-winged parakeet and the
great pied hornbill are two of the
spectacular birds you should look out
for in the forest.
**YOU SHOULD KNOW:**
Longer, overnight treks in the jungle
are also available to anyone who is
medically fit and over 14.

The casual visitor to India has about the same chances of seeing a tiger in the wild as of winning the lottery, but that doesn't stop thousands of people making the journey each year to the Periyar Wildlife Sanctuary in the hope of catching a glimpse of this most formidable of predators. One of Kerala's principal animal reserves, Periyar lies in hill country in the south of the state close to the border with Tamil Nadu. An extensive plateau forms the west of the reserve, while undulating peaks rising to over 1,700 m (5,600 ft) predominate to north and east. Within its 777 sq km (300 sq mi), two-thirds of which is covered by evergreen and semi-evergreen forest, the wildlife sanctuary contains the watershed of two of the region's major rivers, the Periyar and the Pamba.

A small portion only of the reserve (seven per cent) is accessible to visitors; this is centred around the large artificial lake in the western section, which was created by the British when they dammed the Periyar River in 1895 to improve the water supply to Tamil Nadu. Boat trips on the lake are a popular activity here; you will boost your chances of seeing wildlife greatly if you take one early in the morning when animals such as elephants and sambar deer come down to drink at the lakeside in the relative cool of dawn. Better still is to take a three-hour guided trek through the jungle; leading groups no larger than five, a local guide (who may once have been a poacher) will use his trained eyes to introduce visitors to the rich activity of the forest. With more than 260 recorded bird species, you should not come away disappointed.

*Elephants at the Periyar
Wildlife Sanctuary*

# Royal Manas National Park

The Royal Manas is the crown jewel among Bhutan's national parks. The first area of the country to be given protected status – in 1966 – as a wildlife sanctuary, the Royal Manas was declared a national park in 1993. Today it encompasses an area of 1,023 sq km (395 sq mi) in the south of the ancient mountain kingdom. Along with the Black Mountains National Park to the north and India's Manas National Park over the border to the south, it forms a 5,000-sq-km (1,930-sq-mi) highland fastness covering a huge diversity of habitats, from tropical grasslands and temperate moist forests to alpine meadows and scrublands. Over 90 per cent of the park itself is still forested, making it one of the best examples of an undisturbed ecosystem in the eastern Himalayas.

The border here used to be a dangerous one and for many years the region was off-limits to travellers because of the activities of separatist groups in India. The absence of visitor numbers in recent times has contributed to the pristine, unspoilt nature of the Royal Manas and for the past 15 years the World Wildlife Fund has been working with the local authorities to keep it that way. A comprehensive conservation management plan has recently been agreed, designed to enable the park to meet future challenges, especially those associated with tourism development and climate change.

All the big players on the wildlife scene of the Indian sub-continent can be found in the Royal Manas National Park: rhino, elephant, buffalo, bear, the ox-like gaur and several species of deer. Tigers and leopards also make their home here, although they are rarely seen.

**HOW TO GET THERE:**
Travelling independently in Bhutan is still difficult. The easiest way to visit the Royal Manas sanctuary is on an organized tour from the capital, Thimphu.
**WHEN TO GO:**
November to February (the dry season)
**DON'T MISS:**
There are no fewer than four types of hornbill among more than 350 species of bird that have been recorded in the park.
**YOU SHOULD KNOW:**
Although the Royal Manas is once again on the itinerary for tour groups you are advised to obtain official travel advice if you are contemplating a visit to this still-volatile region.

*A rhino in Royal Manas National Park*

# Bokor National Park

**HOW TO GET THERE:**
The nearest town to Bokor is Kampot, 148 km (92 mi) from Phnom Penh. It takes about two hours to negotiate the steep and twisting gravel road to the park entrance, 30 km (19 mi) northwest of Kampot.
**WHEN TO GO:**
December to April
**DON'T MISS:**
The walk from the hill station through the jungle to the Popokvil Falls.
**YOU SHOULD KNOW:**
Although the area is now officially safe, the danger of land mines still exists, as everywhere in Cambodia, so you should be careful to keep to the marked trails.

On Cambodia's coastline southwest of the capital, Phnom Penh, Bokor National Park is one of the country's most important protected areas. Lying at the southern end of the Chuor Phnom Damrei, or Elephant Mountains, a wild region of impenetrable forests and sheer rock outcrops, Bokor encompasses 1,581 sq km (610 sq mi) of primary rainforest. Moist evergreens predominate on the lower slopes while mixed deciduous trees occupy the higher levels. The forest is home to populations of Asian elephant, Asiatic black bear, pangolin and pileated gibbon, but you shouldn't get too excited about seeing wildlife because many of these creatures are active mainly at night and tend to keep well away from the tourist trails.

This area was formerly a stronghold of the Khmer Rouge and witnessed some of the fiercest fighting between their forces and the Vietnamese army. What sets Bokor apart from other wildlife reserves in the tropics is the presence within its boundaries of an abandoned hill station. Built by the French in the early 1920s as a refuge from the oppressive heat of the coastal plain, the station sits at an altitude of 1,080 m (3,543 ft). Having fallen into disuse after the war, the once grand colonial edifices are now in ruins; they include the Black Palace which was once Prince Sihanouk's summer retreat, a Catholic church and a huge hotel and casino complex. Wandering around these deserted buildings is an atmospheric but decidedly eerie experience, especially when the frequent mists close in over the hills. The cooler temperatures are definitely a boon, though, and once the mists clear there are spectacular views over the coast and ocean.

# Cardamom Mountains

**HOW TO GET THERE:**
Bus or shared taxi from Phnom Penh or Sihanoukville. There is virtually no public transport around the region so river travel where available is your best bet, unless you are prepared for the rigours of a seat on the back of a motorbike.
**WHEN TO GO:**
November to March
**DON'T MISS:**
A good base from which to get a feel for this exceptional area is the village of Chi Phat, 40 minutes upriver by fast boat from Andoung Tuek, which is being carefully developed as an ecotourism centre.

The Cardamom Mountains in Cambodia's remote southwest are one of the last true wildernesses in South East Asia. That this vast area of some 10,000 sq km (3,860 sq mi) has so far survived the depredations of land speculators and developers, as well as the commercial threats posed by loggers and farmers, is thanks largely to an unlikely saviour; following the Vietnamese victory in 1979 the defeated rump of the Khmer Rouge regime retreated to these mountains where they continued a sporadic guerrilla campaign for the next 20 years. The presence of these forces and the constant threat of landmines ensured that locals and visitors alike stayed well away.

Now that peace and relative stability have returned to Cambodia, the Cardamom Mountains are set fair to capitalize on their undisturbed state. In this poor and under-developed nation commercial pressures, however, remain as intense as ever and it is only with significant help from a number of international conservation charities that the Cambodian government is able to move slowly forward to a more sustainable future for the region and its native population. With few roads and little in the way of infrastructure, visiting the Cardamoms is really only for the intrepid traveller who reckons with a degree of inconvenience and discomfort in order to experience nature at its most rawly beautiful. The dense virgin rainforest which covers the mountains is home to an astonishing profusion of wildlife, including elephants, bears and the rare Siamese crocodile – not a man-eater but probably best avoided as a swimming companion. The most accessible part of the Cardamoms is the Koh Kong Conservation Corridor which skirts the NH 48 road between Sihanoukville and the border town of Krong Koh Kong.

**YOU SHOULD KNOW:**
One of the animal world's most mysterious creatures lives only in the Cardamom forests. The kouprey, also known as the Cambodian forest ox, was unknown to western science before 1937; there are now thought to be only a few hundred still in the wild.

*Dense virgin rainforest covers the mountains.*

# Sihanoukville Coastal Islands

If you want to see what Thailand's Ko Samui looked like 30 years ago, then the islands off Cambodia's coast are the place to go. Although development is slowly getting under way, many islands remain gloriously unspoilt and largely untouched by the tourist dollar. White sand beaches fringed by palm trees present a picture of a tropical paradise that really is as perfect as it looks. Apart from a few picturesque fishing villages, the islands are for the most part uninhabited, offering the ideal refuge from the rat race. They lie mostly off the coast surrounding the once fashionable seaside resort of Sihanoukville. Situated on a peninsula at the mouth of Kompong Som Bay, Sihanoukville has lots of operators offering day and overnight boat trips to the islands.

The islands form three distinct groups: the Kompong Som Islands are due west of Sihanoukville and, being the easiest to reach, are popular for day trips, while the Ream Islands are scattered offshore to the east. The Koh Tang Islands, meanwhile, are further out to sea and best visited with an overnight stay in mind. All the islands provide good swimming, snorkelling and diving opportunities, although Koh Rong Samloem in the Kompong Som group and the more isolated Koh Tang Islands are particularly favoured. The seas here are rich in marine life, with large fish, excellent visibility and sunken wrecks that can be explored with local guides. If you like to catch your own food, there are plenty of game fishing opportunities here, too, including the chance to bag the prized barracuda.

# Khammouane Province

One of 18 provinces that make up the country, Khammouane is situated at the narrowest point of Laos where its long heel begins. Sandwiched between Thailand and Vietnam, the province is predominantly rural, the majority of the population living in the riverside settlements along the Mekong which marks the Thai border. Khammouane owes its relatively undisturbed state to a remarkably enlightened programme of the Laos government which in the early 1990s established a network of National Protected Areas (NPAs). A total of 20 NPAs are scattered throughout the country and Khammouane is fortunate to have three of them. Nakai Nam Theun and Hin Nam No lie adjacent to one another along the Vietnamese border and are part of the Annam Highlands, while Phou Hin Boun is in the north and centre of the province.

Covering some 6,300 sq km (2,430 sq mi) in all, the three protected areas are typical examples of a karst landscape: limestone plateaus, cliffs, bluffs and steep escarpments, dissected by flat-bottomed valleys. Many of the rivers flow underground and, this being limestone country, there are numerous caves, the most spectacular of which is the Kong Lor cavern, a 7.5-km (4.7-mi) long underground tunnel which you can travel through by boat. The semi-evergreen and mixed deciduous forests which cover much of the land are home to elephants, bears and several types of monkey, including gibbons and macaques. Thakhek is the starting point for guided treks into the Phou Hin Boun area; these treks visit caves, waterfalls, ethnic villages and the serene Kuhn Kong Leng Lake. A justly popular tour option in Khammouane is the so-called 'Loop', a three-day trip involving a combination of motorbike and boat which takes in various natural features and good swimming spots.

*Hin Nam No is a National Protected Area.*

**HOW TO GET THERE:**
The river port of Thakhek, six to seven hours by bus from the capital, Vientiane, is the main base for tours exploring Khammouane province. If you have time, a passenger ferry along the Mekong is a much more atmospheric way to do the journey.

**WHEN TO GO:**
October to February (although if you are prepared to brave the heat and wet of April you will be able to catch the spectacular New Year festivities).

**DON'T MISS:**
The famous Buddhist cave at Tham Pa Fa which contains 229 bronze images of the Buddha, many of which are over 300 years old.

**YOU SHOULD KNOW:**
One of the world's rarest mammals, the saola, lives in the forests of Nakai Nam Theun. Looking like a cross between an ox and an antelope.

# Luang Nam Tha

The northwestern province of Luang Nam Tha has been an important crossroads on human migration routes for hundreds of years. This is amply reflected in the rich ethnic mix of the province's inhabitants, with more than 20 distinct ethnic groups making up the population. A common border with Myanmar (Burma) and China adds to the diversity; the Tai, who are the cultural and ethnic ancestors of the Lao people, originated over the border in China's Yunnan province. Tai Dam, Tai Yuan and Tai Lue are among the groups who live in the region today. Ethnic minorities, indeed, outnumber the Lao population of the province by two to one.

Most of the province comprises mountainous terrain covered in evergreen and deciduous forests interspersed with lush valleys. The omnipresent rice fields are the clearest indicators of human activity, although a less happy reminder are the areas which have suffered heavy deforestation as a result of commercial logging and the slash-and-burn agricultural practices of local farmers. For all the wear and tear the scenery is still captivating, nowhere more so than in the Nam Ha National Protected Area which accounts for roughly a third of the province. Ecotourism is the name of the game here and the Laos government, with support from various international agencies, are committed to developing tourism along environmentally responsible lines. A wide range of trekking tours is available taking you into the hills and forests, often involving overnight stays in remote ethnic villages. It is illegal to trek in Nam Ha without a licensed guide; tours have to follow strict guidelines on frequency and group size as a means of regulating the impact of tourism.

# Plain of Jars

Everyone likes a mystery and the Plain of Jars in central Laos harbours one of archaeology's great unsolved riddles. The name is an apt one to describe this large area to the west of Phonsavan, the provincial capital, although the terrain is more one of rolling grasslands than flat plains. It is part of the Xieng Khuang plateau, an extensive highland area which is bordered to the south by the country's highest mountains. The plateau is an agriculturally fertile region, although farming remains a somewhat precarious activity as a result of the indiscriminate bombing during the Vietnam War period. From 1964 to 1973 the USA conducted one of the most sustained aerial bombardments in history, dropping two million tonnes of bombs, one third of which failed to detonate. The result is a country scarred by unexploded ordnance which it is estimated will take another 100 years to clear.

Thousands of huge jar-shaped vessels fashioned out of the local sandstone lie scattered across the grasslands and hillsides around Phonsavan. The jars have an average diameter and height of 1.5 m (5 ft), although some are up to 3 m (10 ft) tall and weigh around 15 tonnes. No one knows for certain who built them, their date of construction, nor what they were used for. The most comprehensive investigation to date was conducted by a French archaeologist in the 1930s who concluded that the jars were funerary monuments of a Bronze Age culture which flourished some 2,000 years ago. More recent research has cast doubt on this theory, suggesting instead that the jars may have had a more prosaic function as storage vessels for rice and wine. Whatever the explanation, they present a singularly bizarre and impressive sight.

**YOU SHOULD KNOW**:
Even though the main visitor sites have been declared safe, you should still stick to the paths and follow any instructions given by the guides.

*The mysterious Plain of Jars*

*Taat Fan waterfall is one of the tallest in the area.*

# Waterfalls of Bolaven Plateau

With an average elevation of 1,200 m (3,940 ft) the Bolaven Plateau in the far south of Laos boasts a surprisingly temperate climate. Rising high above the Mekong Valley to the west, Bolaven is 10,000 sq km (3,860 sq mi) of fertile uplands spread over four different provinces. The lion's share belongs to Champasak Province and most visits to the Bolaven Plateau start from the provincial capital, Pakse. The plateau is a lovely patchwork of rivers, forests, grasslands and fields where the crop is grown for which the area is famed. It was the French who introduced coffee plantations; after a considerable hiatus caused by the Vietnam War, coffee production has been revived by local farmers and is flourishing once more. Sadly, but inevitably perhaps, the success of the business has generated intense pressures to clear land for further cultivation; this has now become the single greatest threat to the local environment.

The Bolaven Plateau is also noted for its many waterfalls. These are no show-stealers but, with temperatures rarely rising above the high 20s °C and plenty of shade afforded by the lush surrounding vegetation, they provide wonderful places for relaxation and tuning in to the sounds of nature. At Taat Lo on the Seset River northeast of Pakse you can swim beneath the broad, 10-m (33-ft) high falls, while Taat Fan and Katamtok demand a more respectful distance as their waters crash down more than 100 m (330 ft). A particular delight of exploring this area is to trek to remote waterfalls and believe that you really could be the first people to have discovered them. One of the best places to go trekking is in Dong Hua Sao, a national protected area of dense forests which rise up the steep western slopes of the plateau.

**HOW TO GET THERE:**
Buses from Vientiane take nine hours to reach Pakse, from where it is a further two hours to reach the heart of the Bolaven Plateau.
**WHEN TO GO:**
Any time of year (although if you visit between November and February you should be prepared for temperatures to drop significantly at night).
**DON'T MISS:**
The bustling market at Paksong, where the region's farmers gather to sell their coffee crop and tribespeople come down from the mountain villages to sell their wares.
**YOU SHOULD KNOW:**
On the far bank of the Mekong west of the Bolaven Plateau stands the UNESCO World Heritage Site of Wat Phu, a Hindu and Buddhist temple complex which predates the temples of Angkor.

# Dong Phayayen Mountains

Dong Phayayen is a mountain range in central Thailand which is a continuation of the Phetchabun Mountains to the north. Dong Phayayen extends on a north-south axis for 230 km (145 mi). Once entirely covered in forest, the range has been largely stripped bare as a consequence of intensive agriculture and logging. The few stands of virgin tropical forest that remain owe their survival to the establishment of a number of national parks and wildlife sanctuaries in the mountains. The most well-known of these is Khao Yai at the southern end of the range. Thailand's oldest national park now protects an area covering 2,168 sq km (840 sq mi), one of the largest undamaged monsoon forests on the Asian continent. Much of Khao Yai lies on a rolling plateau of sandstone; its highest peak, at 1,351 m (4,432 ft), is Khao Rom.

Most of the park is covered by dense, primary evergreen forest, with small areas of secondary-growth scrub and savannah, the result of cultivation by villagers and poachers who have long since been evicted from the park. While development within the park is now strictly controlled, these man-made open grasslands provide important grazing areas for many large mammals and thus offer some of the best wildlife-viewing opportunities. The evening is the prime time for observing sambar deer, gaurs, wild pigs and bears. Khao Yai is the best place in Thailand for seeing elephants in the wild; there is a population of around 200 in the park. On jungle treks you should see gibbons swinging through the canopy and are unlikely to miss the distinctive profile of the hornbill; keep your eyes peeled around fig trees as this is their favourite fruit.

**HOW TO GET THERE:**
The town of Pak Chong, 200 km (125 mi) northeast of Bangkok, is the main base for visits to Khao Yai. It is a three- to four-hour journey by road from the Thai capital.
**WHEN TO GO:**
November to February is the cool and dry season, but you have a better chance of seeing wildlife during the rainy season from June to October.
**DON'T MISS:**
The wreathed hornbill, one of four types of hornbill found in the national park. Outside the breeding season wreathed hornbills often congregate in large flocks of up to a thousand birds.
**YOU SHOULD KNOW:**
As always, if you are walking in tropical forest you should use mosquito repellent and wear good boots as a defence against leeches.

*Khao Yai - Thailand's oldest national park*

# Khao Luang National Park

The mountain of Khao Luang is the highest point on the Thai peninsula. Rising to 1,835 m (6,020 ft) it stands at the heart of the national park to which the peak gives its name. The park encompasses 570 sq km (220 sq mi) of mountains, valleys and tropical forests. The variation in elevation creates a range of habitats, from moist evergreen forest in the lowlands to cloud and montane forest at the higher levels. Khao Luang is particularly noted for a number of beautiful waterfalls located throughout the park which are at their most impressive at the end of the rainy season in December and January. Nature trails lead to two of the best falls, at Karom and at Krung Ching, both of which are good half-day walks.

For a more challenging trek the summit of Khao Luang itself beckons. The ascent is best undertaken as a three-day trek starting in Khiriwong village, where you can arrange the services of a local guide. The ascent takes you up through dense rainforest and some of the world's largest tree ferns. Over 300 types of orchid thrive in the humid environment of the lower levels; your guide will enlighten you on the varieties. Although tigers, clouded leopards, elephants and macaques are all found in Khao Luang you are unlikely to see them. What you will undoubtedly see, however, are some of the dazzling birds that are resident here, including sunbirds, eagles and three species of hornbill. You will also come across evidence of an unusual form of agriculture practised by local farmers: fruit orchards which grow using the shade from indigenous trees.

# Pha Daeng National Park

In the far north of Thailand the small town of Chiang Dao is the gateway to the Pha Daeng National Park which covers an area of 1,155 sq km (446 sq mi), extending north and west to the border with Myanmar (Burma). The park comprises two mountain ranges divided by a central lowland area which includes two villages displaying the distinctive cultures of local hill tribes. The western ranges are covered by lush tropical forest while the more exposed limestone mountains to the east include peaks with dramatic profiles such as Doi Pha Tang and Doi Pha Daeng itself. Both summits offer superb views of the surrounding landscape. The park is studded with secluded valleys and waterfalls; the sparkling streams that originate in these mountains feed into one of northern Thailand's principal rivers, the Ping. The hot springs at Pong Ang are an unusual feature which are well worth visiting for the variety of birdlife they attract throughout the year.

*An elephant trek through Pha Daeng National Park*

Limestone means caves and underground rivers, and there is no shortage of either in Pha Daeng. While none are as grand and extensive as the famous complex outside Chiang Dao, caves such as Chaeng-Pa Hok and Rom in the north of the park offer spectacular stalactites and stalagmites and an absence of the crowds you find at Chiang Dao. In the cave at Krab ancient human remains have been found deposited in coffin-like niches.

Pha Daeng National Park is contiguous with the Chiang Dao Wildlife Reserve which has been a sanctuary for the region's animals and birds since 1978. Sadly the biodiversity has been significantly impoverished by years of intensive hunting, but there have been encouraging signs of recovery in more recent times.

**YOU SHOULD KNOW:**
The Thai government runs an aid programme to the highlands around Chiang Dao aimed at assisting the hill tribes to develop viable and sustainable agricultural alternatives to opium cultivation.

# Phang Nga Bay

The same geological process which threw up the Himalayas was responsible for producing the unforgettable seascape of Phang Nga Bay in southern Thailand. Long-buried layers of limestone were exposed and fractured, then subjected to steady erosion by monsoon rains. Plant roots split open the rocks and water seeped into the cracks, eventually creating underground streams and enormous cave systems. All along this western coastline fluctuating sea levels and the movements of the tides have sculpted the limestone into a stupefying array of formations. Drowned karstland is the term geologists use to describe this extraordinary environment of towering limestone crags and pinnacles which plunge dramatically into an azure sea.

Much of the bay now enjoys protected status in the Ao Phang-nga Marine National Park. Vegetation clings precariously to the sheer cliffs of the 40 or so islands lying within the park. A wide range of boat tours operates from the park headquarters south of Phang Nga town; they take visitors on cruises around the bay and include landings at some of the larger islands for a closer look at their natural highlights, including some striking caves. A more ecologically friendly way to explore the bay and its islands is to rent a canoe. Provided you heed local guidance, these smaller, lighter vessels should enable you to penetrate to the mysterious *hongs* within several of the more isolated islands – secret sea chambers that are completely enclosed by cliffs.

In spite of the growth of tourism, fishing remains the principal livelihood of the local population. You will find little fishing villages, some built on stilts over the water, scattered throughout the bay area, as well as evidence in the form of mussel farms and floating fish traps among the tidal channels and huge mangrove swamps.

*One of the many karst (limestone) islands in Phang Nga Bay*

**HOW TO GET THERE:**
Phang Nga town is 95 km (59 mi) northeast of Phuket. If you do not have your own transport you will need to take a taxi or a *sawngthaew* (truck-bus) from there to the marine park headquarters where the boat tours depart.

**WHEN TO GO:**
November to May, especially if you want to dive or snorkel as the seas are clearest at this time of year.

**DON'T MISS:**
If you see what look like crocodiles swimming around the mangrove swamps, fear not, they are most likely to be water monitors. The world's second-largest lizard can grow to more than 2 m (6.5 ft) in length.

**YOU SHOULD KNOW:**
The sheltered location of Phang Nga Bay meant that it was spared the worst ravages of the 2004 tsunami. Unfortunately, the more exposed parts of the country's Andaman coastline were not so lucky.

# Phu Kradung

The imposing sandstone plateau of Phu Kradung in northeastern Thailand is visible from a huge distance. Covering an area of 348 sq km (134 sq mi) – the plateau itself comprises 60 sq km (23 sq mi) – it has been a national park for nearly 50 years. The classic table-top mountain looms more than 1,200 m (4,000 ft) above the surrounding forests, which once covered the summit as well; regular fires and the thin soils have turned the plateau into rolling grassland, dotted with pines. Small patches of the original evergreen forest do still survive on the plateau; because of the cooler temperatures, these so-called 'relic' forests abound with tree species more usually associated with temperate zones, such as oak, chestnut, hornbeam and birch. Indeed, the park generally is a haven for plant species that prefer a cooler climate.

With no road access to the summit of Phu Kradung, the only way up is on foot. It is a tough 9-km (6-mi) trek to the edge of the plateau, including some very steep sections; from there it is a further 4 km (2.5 mi) to the upper park headquarters. The relative isolation of the plateau gives it a 'lost world' atmosphere which amply repays the effort involved. Once on top you have a choice of over 50 km (31 mi) of marked trails which lead to waterfalls, flower meadows and cliffs with stunning viewpoints. There may be no dinosaurs up here but the park is noted for the diversity of its plant life, including many rare and unusual orchids and several carnivorous plants, such as pitchers and sundews, which compensate for the poor soil on the plateau by absorbing the nutrients they need from the insects which they trap and digest.

**HOW TO GET THERE:**
Phu Kradung is 70 km (44 mi) south of the provincial capital Loei. The journey takes 90 minutes by bus.
**WHEN TO GO:**
During the cooler months of October to February (but note that temperatures on the plateau can fall close to zero).
**DON'T MISS:**
The crimson leaves of the maple tree which add a splash of brilliant colour to the forest floor when they fall in the dry season.
**YOU SHOULD KNOW:**
Legend has it that lovers who help each other to reach the top of Phu Kradung will stay together forever, but if they quarrel along the way they are fated to separate.

*Sunset at Mak Duk Cliff, Phu Kradung National Park*

# Thung Salaeng Luang National Park

**HOW TO GET THERE:**
Via highway 12 from Phitsanulok or Lomsak

**WHEN TO GO:**
The temperature rises to above 30°C (86°F) between June and September. The cool season is between November and February. Most of the wild flowers bloom in November.

**DON'T MISS:**
Sitting on one of the ledges of Poi Waterfall and feeling the invigorating spray.

**YOU SHOULD KNOW:**
The Siamese fireback pheasant is considered to be so special that, in 1862, a pair was presented to Emperor Napoleon III to encourage trade with France.

Established in 1972, Thung Salaeng Luang National Park is an area of vast open fields surrounded by statuesque pines and dry oak forest. Within it are limestone caves, thundering waterfalls, cascading rapids, salt deposits and beautiful wildflower meadows. Situated in the Phitsanulok and Phetchabun Provinces of Thailand, near the Laotian border, the park covers 1,262 sq km (490 sq mi). It is home to elephants, civets, wild pigs and the occasional visiting tiger. Birds flourish in the area with around 200 species being identified, including herons, eagles, woodpeckers and the majestic Siamese fireback pheasant.

The park was originally earmarked to be a reserve as long ago as 1960, but the activity of communist guerrillas and encroachment by hill tribes, who sought to farm the untouched land, delayed the process. That the park now has only rudimentary facilities adds to its charm. With room for only around 100 overnight guests, it is the perfect place for undisturbed wildlife-watching. The best places to start for those inexperienced in tracking are any of the park's many salt licks. These natural deposits of sodium, calcium and zinc attract animals from miles around and the minerals are a vital part of their diet, facilitating the development of bone and muscle.

The area is blessed with three spectacular waterfalls, with Namtok Kaeng Sopha being the most impressive. Dubbed 'Thailand's Niagara Falls', it is a many-layered staircase cascade and, in the rainy season (July to October), it throws up such a volume of spray that the valley is shrouded in a cloak of mist. The area is also popular with cavers and two classic karst caves can be found there in the shape of Wang Daeng and Dao Duan, while the Kaeng Wang Nam Yen Rapids (scene of an annual inter-village boat race) is great for white-water rafting.

# Ba Vi National Park

An isolated triple-peaked limestone mountain, Ba Vi is some 50 km (30 mi) west of the Vietnamese capital Hanoi and forms the centrepiece of the national park to which it gives its name. The mountain rises suddenly out of a flat, densely forested plain and at the higher elevations the gradients reach one in three. The highest of the three peaks is Dinh Vua at 1,296 m (4,252 ft), followed by Tan Vien at 1,226 m (4,022 ft) and Ngoc Hoa at 1,120 m (3,675 ft). With the notable exception of the Da River in the western section of the park, Ba Vi has no permanent bodies of water of any great size. However, during the rainy season (May to October) many steep-sided, fast-flowing streams emerge to carry the run-off from the mountain and they are often of such magnitude that landslides are frequent.

Although the national park is relatively small at a little over 74 sq km (29 sq mi), it is considered by locals to be the 'lungs of Hanoi' and its lush greenness is certainly striking. The unique ecosystem is home to over 1,000 rare plant species (many with medicinal properties), 45 species of mammal, 25 kinds of reptiles and amphibians and over 100 species of bird. The mountain is more often than not shrouded in mist, offering only tantalizing glimpses of its peaks. Access to the peaks is straightforward as, during the colonial period, the French built a hill station at Ba Vi which included a road that takes the traveller to an altitude of 1,100 m (3,610 ft). Once at the top, if the weather is kind, the views of the forest below are stunning. If it is not, then an 11th century shrine to Saint Tan Vien, one of the four immortal founders of Vietnam, makes the climb worthwhile.

**HOW TO GET THERE:**
By bus from Hanoi or drive via National Highway 32 to the town of Son Tay.

**WHEN TO GO:**
It's cooler and much drier from November to April.

**DON'T MISS:**
Ao Vua Waterfall: a three-tiered cascade that flows into an emerald-green lake that is best viewed from above.

**YOU SHOULD KNOW:**
The park is home to the indigenous Dao ethnic group who have maintained their traditional forest-dwelling life by adapting to change and now are active in the harvesting of the area's many medicinal plants.

# Halong Bay

**HOW TO GET THERE:**
It is a three- to four-hour bus journey
from Hanoi to Halong City.
**WHEN TO GO:**
It is cooler and drier in spring (March
and April) and autumn (October and
November).
**DON'T MISS:**
Bo Nau (pelican) Cave – a
wide-mouthed classic limestone cave
bristling with stalactites and
stalagmites. It is so called because
pelicans often take shelter there.

Legend has it that, soon after the Viet people founded their country, invaders came from the sea. As the raiders approached the shore the Jade Emperor sent Mother Dragon and her children down to Earth to aid the people in their resistance. The dragons opened their mouths and spat out a shower of pearls which turned into thousands of islands. Unable to stop, the attackers crashed into the rocks and the boats were smashed to smithereens. After the battle the dragons stayed on Earth in the place that is now known as Halong Bay, with their tails forming a long sandy beach called Long Vi.

Whatever its true origin, Halong Bay, located in Vietnam's Quang Ninh Province near the border with China, is a place of remarkable beauty. Travel around the bay is best undertaken aboard a junk, the iconic Indo-Chinese mode of transport. The boats cut their way through crystal-clear water, weaving in and out of the numerous limestone pillars that fill the bay. The islands and islets are sprinkled with countless beaches and grottoes created by the combined power

*Islands in Halong Bay*

of wind and waves. The shallow waters are home to over 600 species of fish and mollusc, but it is the islands that steal the show. This surreal seascape has been moulded by 500 million years of erosive forces into astonishing shapes. Ga Choi islet looks like a pair of fighting cocks (a popular sport in Vietnam), while Voi islet resembles an elephant. Another looks like a sail and one is even perceived to take the shape of an incense burner.

Aside from its outstanding natural beauty, the bay has a wide diversity of ecosystems. These include sandy beaches, swamp and mangrove forest, coral reefs and small rainwater lakes. These eerily beautiful habitats are home to numerous mammals, birds and reptiles – including monkeys and iguanas.

**YOU SHOULD KNOW:**
The junks that transport visitors around the bay may look basic, but many are quite luxurious inside. If travelling in the hot and rainy season (May to September) it is advisable to book one with air conditioning throughout.

# Mount Fansipan

Although Vietnam's recent swift increase in food production has been of great benefit to its economy, unsustainable farming methods have seen a rise in habitat destruction, pollution, soil leeching and water degradation. The effect on the country's biodiversity has been startling. However, there is a growing number of fledgling projects that seek to marry the changing needs of local people with preservation of the area's pristine rainforest environment. One such community-based project is centred on the Hoang Lien Mountains, a 100-million-year-old range in Northern Vietnam. The wordily named, but undoubtedly worthy, Community-based Conservation of the Hoang Lien Mountain Ecosystem Project is seeking to arrest the fragmentation of the rainforest and so protect the area's threatened flora and fauna. Ecotourism is an integral part of the project.

The range's biggest draw is its tallest peak. At 3,143 m (10,312 ft), Mount Fansipan is also the highest point on the South East Asian Mainland. The most popular route up the mountain starts in Sapa, which is reachable by road and is just over halfway up the mountain. The beginning of the hike takes the traveller through terraced paddy fields and hill-tribe villages, before crossing the Muong Hoa River near the village of Cat Cat, which gives the route its name. Above 2,000 m (6,600 ft) the vegetation changes to arrowroot plantations and then to thick bamboo, which has been used to construct a basecamp at 2,300 m (7,550 ft). The last stretch of the climb is the most challenging as the trail passes through primary forest of giant pine trees as well as dense bamboo. At the summit of Fansipan, the 'roof of Indochina', the air is wonderfully pure and the panoramic views are stunning.

**HOW TO GET THERE:**
By train from Hanoi to Lao Cai, then by bus to Sapa
**WHEN TO GO:**
Either side of the rainy season, which lasts from May to September
**DON'T MISS:**
Thac Bac (Silver Waterfall), just outside Sapa – a steep-sided cascade traversed by a wooden bridge
**YOU SHOULD KNOW:**
Other than the Cat Cat route up the mountain there are two other main paths. One goes through Sin Chai hamlet and the other starts from O Quy Ho Hilltop.

# Pu Mat National Park

**HOW TO GET THERE:**
By road from Vinh City
**WHEN TO GO:**
It is cooler and drier from November to April.
**DON'T MISS:**
Ma Nhai Stele – an historical site commemorating the Tran Dynasty army's victory over Mongol invaders from China's Yuan Dynasty around 700 years ago.
**YOU SHOULD KNOW:**
Do not film in the villages of the park's indigenous people as they consider it overly intrusive.

Pu Mat National Park is situated in Vietnam's Nghe An province, around 140 km (90 mi) from Vinh. The park covers three districts – Tuong Duong, Anh Son and Con Cuong – with an area of 910 sq km (350 sq mi). It takes its name from the Thai *Pù Mát*, which translates as 'high slope' and this is an accurate description of this densely forested section of the Annamite Mountains.

The true value of Pu Mat, however, is as a sanctuary for the region's unique and increasingly endangered plants and animals. The park is home to around 900 flora species, 240 different types of mammal, 140 bird species, 25 types of reptile and 15 kinds of amphibian. Many of the animals, most notably the saola antelope, are on the World Conservation Union's red list of endangered species.

Aside from the unique array of wildlife, this ancient forested landscape has many beautiful geological features. Among the attractions are the 150-m (500-ft) high Kem Waterfall which verges on the torrential during the rainy season and the wide Giang River, perfect for exploration in a traditional wooden boat. The park is also home to several ethnic minority communities and visits to their villages are a must for those interested in traditional arts and crafts, such as *tho cam*, a colourful highly prized woven fabric.

Pu Mat is a unique and important place of mutual education and benefit for both its inhabitants and the outside world. Botanists, backed by advanced DNA techniques, have used their skills to identify several new and endangered species, while the indigenous people of the area can teach the outside world about living in harmony with the forest, as they have done for hundreds of years.

# Java's Beaches

Java is the world's most populous island and this is in greatest evidence in its often stiflingly hot gridlocked cities. Thankfully, Java is also blessed with many fine beaches where the waters of the Indian Ocean and the Java Sea take the edge off the humid heat. The island's finest beaches are to the south of Indonesia's ancient capital, Yogyakarta, where an abundance of strands stretch for hundreds of miles along the Indian Ocean coastline.

The most popular beach, Parangtritis, is only 30 minutes by car from 'Yogya'. This long, snaking piece of shoreline is famous for the variety of its scenery. The beach is framed by mountains on its eastern side and the dark, volcanic sand contrasts wonderfully with the crests of the giant rollers that pound the shore. A graceful way to explore the area is aboard a *bendi* – a local horse-drawn carriage. The beach does, however, have it drawbacks as the ocean at this point on the coast is turbulent and unpredictable and swimming is banned. Also, especially during weekends and public holidays, it can feel as though the entire population of Yogyakarta has descended on the area.

Thankfully the Javanese 'Riviera' offers a wide variety of beaches for all tastes: divers should head for Drini and Kukup beaches for their beautiful coral reefs, lying just offshore; at Baron beach there is an underground river perfect for bathing in the shade; Wediombo beach is ideal for swimming as it has a shallow bay flanked by gleaming white sands; at Ngrenehan beach traditional fishing methods are fascinating to watch and provide some of the island's freshest and finest seafood, while Sundak beach is a place favoured by the young.

**HOW TO GET THERE:**
By coach from Yogyakarta
**WHEN TO GO:**
It is hot and humid all year round, but driest from May to September.
**DON'T MISS:**
Langse cave (east of Parangtritis beach). Situated 400 m (1,310 ft) up a cliff, it contains a sulphur spring said to cure skin ailments – but anyway certain to relax aching limbs after the arduous climb.
**YOU SHOULD KNOW:**
Wearing green on Parangtritis beach is said to bring bad luck. Local legend has it that the beach is home to Nyai Loro Kidul, the Goddess of the South Sea. Those wearing green may be swept away to an undersea world to work as her slaves. The myth reinforces the idea that it is a good idea to stay away from the water, as swimming in the fierce Indian Ocean is hazardous.

*Exploring Parangtritis beach aboard a local horse-drawn carriage.*

*The idyllic island of Karimun*

# Karimunjawa Islands

Karimunjawa is a 27-island archipelago that runs in a northwesterly direction in the Java Sea 80 km (50 mi) from Jepara. The islands are characterized by rainforest plain, fringed by seagrass and mangrove swamps. Each island is edged with long golden strands, ideal for those who like to walk with sand between their toes or simply lie down and soak up the sun in this tropical utopia. But the real treasure of Karimunjawa is to be found just out to sea in the form of coral reefs whose importance to the world's biodiversity has earned them the tag of the 'rainforests of the sea'.

The main island is Karimun and a further six are inhabited. Others are in private hands, are nature reserves or are used by the Indonesian Navy. The islands and the seas immediately around them are highly protected and the island chain is divided into four distinct zones. Zone 1 is totally protected and is out of bounds, Zone 2 has limited access while Zone 3 is open to all. Zone 4 acts as a buffer zone whose status can be changed if the needs of conservation demand it. It is a system that works well to preserve these island and underwater gems.

The coral reefs are the islands' main draw. Many of the reefs have grown up around shipwrecks and could not have been better designed for diving. The waters off the archipelago support 90 types of hard, soft and red corals as well as sponges and sea fans. Over 240 species of brightly coloured fish live in the reefs, including the rare crocodile fish and leafy scorpion fish. Larger creatures patrol the waters near the islands and the majestic whale shark is a year-round resident.

**HOW TO GET THERE:**
By ferry from Jepara or by air from Semarang (a shuttle service operates from Jakarta to Semarang).
**WHEN TO GO:**
It's hot all year round but drier from April to September.
**DON'T MISS:**
Karang Kapal – a huge submerged reef, home to large bumphead parrotfish and the whitetip reef shark.
**YOU SHOULD KNOW:**
Carrying a first-aid kit is essential when visiting a reef as many of the corals and the creatures that live within them are poisonous. Other than damaging the coral, injury is the best reason for not treading on them.

# Mount Merapi and the Dieng Plateau

Located in central Java, Mount Merapi is a very active stratavolcano 25 km (15.5 mi) north of Yogyakarta. Its steep ash-covered slopes rise to a height of 2,970 m (9,740 ft). Dense vegetation clothes its flanks as the volcanic ash nourishes the soil, making the area attractive to both wildlife and local farmers. But living in the shadow of such a raging monster can be a perilous existence. Merapi erupts on a regular basis with small eruptions every couple of years, larger ones every decade or so and devastating eruption at roughly half-century intervals. Known as the Sacred Mountain of Fire, Merapi provides a breathtaking spectacle when viewed from afar, as constant plumes of white smoke can be seen emerging from its many craters. When docile, it is safe to climb and this can be done in about five hours.

Travelling northwest from Merapi a less volatile but equally striking landscape can be found in the form of the Dieng Plateau. The Dieng, which translates as 'Home of the Gods', is an ancient volcanic caldera plateau 2,000 m (6,560 ft) above sea level. It is an astonishing landscape and, although the volcano is now dormant, there is still a great deal of thermal activity. Steam vents send clouds of gas high into the sky, turquoise lakes fizz with sulphurous fumes and craters filled with boiling mud gurgle. All this is taken for granted as a backdrop to the everyday lives of farmers who tend their potato fields – an unusual crop for the region made possible by the combination of volcanic-ash-enriched soil and the plateau's altitude. In the heart of the Dieng lies the Candi Arjuna complex, a collection of ancient Hindu temples now in a state of semi-ruin. These relics are among the most important remnants of the island's religious past.

**HOW TO GET THERE:**
North by road from Yogyakarta or south by road from Semarang
**WHEN TO GO:**
The region is hot all year round but is driest from June to September.
**DON'T MISS:**
The view of Merapi at sunrise – best seen from the resort of Plawangan.
**YOU SHOULD KNOW:**
The eruption of Mount Merapi in 1006 was so large that it covered most of the island in ash. The ensuing destruction and failure of the harvest led most of the islanders to abandon their Hindu faith and convert to Islam.

*The Dieng Plateau in Central Java with Mount Merapi in the distance and Gunung Sundoro in the foreground*

# Gunung Murud

Located in the northeast of Malaysia's Sarawak state on the island of Borneo, sandstone Gunung Murud is in the isolated Kelabit Highlands. There, a traditional way of life is still the norm in settlements reached with difficulty by taking a ride on one of the MasWings Twin Otters that fly in to all sorts of simple airstrips, weather permitting. Failing that, it's a matter of travelling rough tracks in a 4x4 (although not in rainy season), hitching a ride on a logging truck or slogging into the backcountry on foot. Worth it? You bet!

The Kelabit Highlands is an extensive upland plateau with scattered villages in the valleys. There are few roads and rivers have rapids that make boat travel impossible, so the only way to explore one of the world's last great wilderness areas is to go afoot, ideally with the help of a local guide (the indigenous Kelabits were once fierce warriors but are now entirely welcoming). This is not the place for a casual visit, although it is possible to take a return flight for a quick look. Instead, a well-planned expedition is called for.

Gunung Murud is an excellent objective, starting from the regional centre of Bario (basic airfield, no mains electricity, a few shops including one solar-powered internet facility open for a few hours most days, three public satellite phones, most cooking on firewood stoves). The trail goes through Pa Ukat, Pa Lungan, Long Repung, Pa Remusu and on to the summit of Sarawak's highest mountain, first ascended by a European as recently as 1922. Along the way will be a fascinating glimpse of life in local longhouses, lush tropical foliage, leeches galore, lots of uphill slogging – and breathtaking scenery (if anyone has any breath left, that is) reaching a dramatic climax at the summit of Gunung Murud.

# Kinabatangan River

*Mangroves along Kinabatangan River in Borneo*

For zoologists, botanists and casual observers of wildlife, the Kinabatangan River is a very special place. Situated in the Sabah region of the Malaysian section of Borneo, it is the country's second-longest river. From its source in Banjaran Crocker, it travels 560 km (350 mi) down to a wide saltwater mangrove swamp estuary and finally into the Sula Sea. The river creates an extraordinary diversity of ecosystems that contain a concentration of wildlife found nowhere else on Earth. It is one of only two places in the world where ten species of primate live, including the solitary Bornean orang-utan, the more social proboscis monkey, the maroon leaf monkey and the Bornean gibbon.

The river cuts right through otherwise impenetrable rainforest, where Bornean pygmy elephants can be seen emerging from the dense growth to feed on its banks, always wary of the saltwater crocodiles that patrol the water's edge. It is easily navigable upstream for about half its length and, together with its larger tributaries, the Lokan and Kuamat Rivers, provides the only thoroughfare between the interior and the coast.

The area is best explored by a combined boating and hiking trip. There are a small number of chalets dotted along the river and there is much to see in its basin, most notably at the Gomantong Caves. These limestone wonders are home to several species of swiftlets – small birds that nest in their millions inside the caves. The birds' nests are highly prized for food and medicine in China and at various times throughout the year a perilous harvest takes place. Using rattan ladders and bamboo sticks collectors climb the 60-m (200-ft) high walls of the caves to scrape the tiny nests from the roofs using a tool called a *jalok*.

**HOW TO GET THERE:**
There are direct flights to Sabah from China, the Philippines, Indonesia and Japan and then by road to Sandakan or Lahad Datu.

**WHEN TO GO:**
The northeast monsoon occurs from November until January; outside of these months expect high daytime temperatures and exceptionally high overnight temperatures.

**DON'T MISS:**
The Sepilok Orang-Utan Rehabilitation Centre, a special sanctuary dedicated to the preservation of this most special of animals.

**YOU SHOULD KNOW:**
Such is their docile nature, it was wrongly believed that Bornean pygmy elephants were descended from a domesticated herd abandoned some 500 years ago, but recent World Wildlife Fund research has shown that they are indeed a subspecies, worthy of preservation.

# Semenggoh Nature Reserve

**HOW TO GET THERE:**
The reserve is 20 km (12 mi) south of Kuching, the capital of Sarawak, and may easily be reached by road (car, taxi or local bus – the latter requiring a 30-minute walk to the reserve).

**WHEN TO GO:**
Any time

**DON'T MISS:**
Orang-utan feeding time at Semenggoh's rehab centre – this happens twice daily, between 09.00 and 10.00, then 15.00 and 15.30. But be aware that sightings are not guaranteed as the adult animals are encouraged to forage in the forest as part of their rewilding programme, and sometimes only show up later to collect the free bounty. The young orang-utans are caged but released for part of the day, usually being called back in the early afternoon.

*An adult orang-utan at the wildlife rehabilitation centre in Semenggoh Nature Reserve*

For those seeking to cram in as many of Borneo's natural wonders as possible into a relatively short time, a trip to Sarawak's Semenggoh Nature Reserve should be high on the must-visit list. At just 650 ha (1,600 ac) it's not vast, but still offers a great variety of rewarding things to see and do in a single day. This former forest reserve is now an important facility for conservation and a showcase for Borneo's incredible biodiversity. The Sarawak Forestry Department has an experimental station at Semenggoh that houses a botanical research centre, wildlife centre and arboretum. These provide a fascinating start to the visit, before getting out into the reserve.

The wildlife rehabilitation centre is the place to see strictly protected orang-utans, for here animals that have been incapacitated or confiscated from poachers are readied for release to boost Borneo's shrinking wild population of these endearing primates. The centre has a number of large mammal and bird enclosures, plus animal and bird captive-breeding programmes. The botanical research centre has an orchid nursery, orchard and dedicated gardens for the likes of ferns and bamboo.

Interesting though these attractions may be, Semenggoh is a place to wander at will through mixed lowland dipterocarp forest consisting of primary jungle, well-established second-growth trees and patches of

kerangas forest. The primary jungle contains incredibly rich flora – watch out for the world's largest flower, the 1-m (3-ft) spotted red bloom of the parasitic *Rafflesia arnoldii*, but enjoy this phenomenon from afar. It's also the world's worst-smelling plant, emitting a truly noxious odour that smells like rotting meat, to attract pollinating insects. There are waymarked trails complete with informative notices explaining the flora, but it's quite possible to step off the paths and imagine that this beautiful place is the remotest of rainforest, populated with a bright assortment of birds, gibbons and giant squirrels.

**YOU SHOULD KNOW:**
There is a small fee payable for a permit to enter the reserve. Visitors are reminded not to approach the orang-utans, as they are susceptible to certain human diseases and are being prepared for the wild. Animals must never be fed by visitors and the picking of plants is also forbidden.

# Tabin Wildlife Reserve

At Borneo's northern tip, Malaysia's Sabah state offers more wild places than the average occasional adventurer could explore in a lifetime. But nowhere is safe from inexorable exploitation of tropical rainforests and that spells trouble for the creatures that live in them. Tabin Wildlife Reserve on Dent Peninsula in eastern Sabah was therefore created in 1984 to protect some of the island's endangered species. It consists of 1,225 sq km (475 sq mi) of lowland dipterocarp forest and swamp that provides refuge for three of Sabah's largest residents – the Borneo pygmy elephant, Sumatran rhinoceros and tembadau (wild cattle) – along with nine species of primate, three types of cat and many other animals, birds, reptiles and insects.

Ironically, much of the reserve is second-growth forest after the original was logged out, although some untouched jungle remains. Sterile palm-oil plantations surround Tabin, except to the north, so the reserve is a haven for displaced wildlife. Ecotourism is big business in the Third World and the Tabin Wildlife Resort located within the reserve is designed to cater for those who prefer their backcountry forays to be well organized and fairly comfortable. This commercial resort offers guided activities from bird- and animal-watching to jungle trekking with transport, accommodation and food included.

There are 'mud volcanoes' that provide exceptional wildlife-viewing opportunities as animals and birds arrive to take advantage of rich mineral content, while the mud also provides a free face pack with legendary properties for those into serious skincare. Other possibilities include jungle trekking, fascinating night walks with the help of a torch-bearing guide, night or dawn safaris in open-topped vehicles and plunging into cooling water at scenic spots like Lipad waterfall. But those who prefer to go it alone will find a wealth of unique experiences to enjoy in the lonely solitude of this unspoilt corner of Planet Earth.

**HOW TO GET THERE:**
The starting point is Lahad Datu, from whence it's a 75-minute drive to the reserve. Get to Lahad Datu by air (MasWings from Kota Kinabalu). Make the same journey on the road and it's seven hours. It can also be reached by road from popular destinations such as Sandakan, Tawau and Semporna (all taking about four hours of driving).
**WHEN TO GO:**
Any time, but be prepared for high humidity.
**DON'T MISS:**
On the way to, or coming back from, Tabin Wildlife Reserve it's possible to go via Sandakan to see the extraordinary Sepilok Orang-utan Rehabilitation Centre, which does precisely what the name suggests and provides a unique opportunity to study these magnificent primates at close quarters. After that, a visit to nearby Selingan Turtle Island adds another fascinating wildlife dimension to the Borneo experience.
**YOU SHOULD KNOW:**
Attempts to track the rare Sumatran rhinoceros within the reserve are being hampered by elephants. Researchers use cameras triggered by motion sensors to try and capture images of the iconic rhinos, but when elephants set off a camera they are alarmed by the flash and tend to retaliate by destroying the offending intruder. The best methods are therefore traditional – following spoor, finding dung and analysing damage caused by rhinos when feeding. So much for 21st-century technology!

# Cordillera Central

**HOW TO GET THERE:**
Fly in to Loakan Airport in the bustling city of Baguio, a tourist centre and communications hub that serves as a natural base for forays into the surrounding mountains or expeditions to more distant parts of the Cordilleras.

**WHEN TO GO:**
Any time – the Cordillera Central are cooler than the rest of the Philippines, and Baguio became the country's summer capital after being established by the Americans in the early 1900s. Dry season is November to April.

**DON'T MISS:**
The Banaue Rice Terraces in Ifugao Province. These are a prime example of amazing man-made rocky terraces in the Cordilleras that date back two millennia and are collectively designated as a UNESCO World Heritage Site. At Banaue, it is said that the huge number of steps within the terrace complex would go halfway around the globe if laid on the flat. Locals welcome visitors who come to see their extraordinary mountainscape, bringing much-needed revenue.

**YOU SHOULD KNOW:**
The Cordillera Central terminate abruptly at Pasaleng Bay in Ilocos Norte Province, where the only way for traffic to bypass the massive obstacle of these unyielding mountains is a dramatic viaduct lapped by the sea.

*Early morning view across the mountains of the Cordillera*

Bordered by the Philippine and South China Seas, Luzon features the massive Cordillera Central, a mountain range that dominates the northwestern part of the island. This is the only extensive highland area in the Philippines, mainly lying between 1,000 m (3,300 ft) and 2,400 m (7,900 ft) above sea level, rising to the high point of Mount Pulog at 2,922 m (9,587 ft) and extending to 18,300 sq km (7,065 sq mi). This vast wilderness is no place for the casual visitor, but offers virtually limitless possibilities for the adventurous traveller or backcountry explorer.

The mountains have both tropical sub-montane and montane zones. Apart from agricultural crops, the main types of vegetation are broadleaf evergreen forest and dominant pine growth, leading to the 'Pine Region' tag used by botanists. The catch-all Cordillera Administrative Region (CAR) encompasses seven landlocked provinces – Abra, Apayao, Benguet, Ifugao, Kalinga, Mountain Province and the regional centre of Baguio City (in Benguet). The mountains are occupied by different hill tribes collectively known as the Igorot – nomenclature indiscriminately imposed by occupying Americans a century ago – and experiencing the variety of local culture is a main attraction for intrepid visitors to the Cordilleras.

Natural resources – both timber and minerals – have long been exploited to the detriment of a once-pristine environment. The CAR is a major contributor to the national economy with extensive production of rice, vegetables, fruit and livestock. But these impressive uplands still contain more than enough wild places to challenge the determined visitor. The terrain can be extremely rugged, with steep slopes and deep river valleys, plateaus and isolated flatlands, dense forests and open grassland. It's possible to get around and see as much of the Cordilleras as possible using (somewhat erratic) public transport, but trekking and rough camping tempt backpackers with the self-sufficiency skills necessary to be at one with the natural splendour of these magnificent mountains.

*A spectacular river journey through the winding cave system of Puerto Princesa*

# Puerto Princesa National Park

From the mountains to the sea, this UNESCO World Heritage Site on the island of Palawan covers a complete ecosystem, including some of Asia's most important old-growth forests. Puerto Princesa National Park also features a spectacular limestone karst landscape that has an underground river. What makes this magnificent example different from others is that it discharges into the sea, with the lower section subjected to tidal flows. So great is this attraction that the park's title is sometimes extended to Puerto Princesa Subterranean River National Park, or PPSRNP as it's snappily known by the acronymically inclined.

The river is magical and should not be missed. Local boatmen paddling small craft propel visitors from the South China Sea into a winding cave system that extends to more than 8 km (5 mi). This world of stalactites and stalagmites features huge caverns and is said to be the world's longest navigable underground river. It becomes a weird and wonderful shadowland in the light of torches or oil lamps carried by the boats.

The river journey may be special, but there's a steady procession of boats and those who like a slice of solitude may resist temptation and leave the sandy beaches to head into the remote interior. There are no fewer than eight forest types to be explored – ultramafic, limestone, montane, freshwater swamp, tropical lowland evergreen, riverine, beach and mangrove. If some of those sound obscure, they add up to impressive biodiversity with a variety of trees and rich plant life. The forests are alive with birds. Over 150 species have been recorded, including sea eagle, Palawan hornbill, hill myna and blue-naped parrot. There are animals, too, such as the bearcat, bearded pig and monitor lizard (but beware of the Palawan stink badger and the spiny Palawan porcupine).

**HOW TO GET THERE:**
The park is in the undeveloped Saint Paul Mountains, on the north coast of Palawan about 50 km (32 mi) from the city of Puerto Princesa. The entrance to the subterranean river is a short hike along the coast from Sabang, with boats trips to the cave (20 minutes along the coast) bookable at the Visitors Assistance Centre there. El Nido to the north of Sabang has a ferry service from Busuanga on nearby Coron Island, and thence to Luzon Island.

**WHEN TO GO:**
Any time

**DON'T MISS:**
The park's only primate, the long-tailed macaque. Spot these acrobatic animals in the forest canopy or boldly foraging along the shoreline at low tide. Another thrill is seeing monitor lizards that are sufficiently tame to feed from the hand.

**YOU SHOULD KNOW:**
Palawan is a great destination for lovers of wild places. It has over 2,000 km (1,200 mi) of irregular coastline offering many pristine white sand beaches, countless islets, numerous small islands and hundreds of rocky coves. The interior is largely undeveloped and contains huge stretches of old-growth forest that cover the island's mountainous central spine.

# Lake Karakul

**HOW TO GET THERE:**
By car or bus from Kashgar or Tashkurgan
**WHEN TO GO:**
May to late September
**DON'T MISS:**
Exploring on horseback or camel. Hiring the animals also provides an opportunity to meet the Uygur and Kyrgyz herders who live in the yurts along the lakeshore. Travellers who take the chance to eat or stay the night with them learn something of Kyrgyz culture as well as the folk mythology attached to Karakul itself.

*Kongur Tagh and Lake Karakul*

The Karakoram Highway is one of the world's most spectacular drives. The road links Kashgar, the great cultural melting pot on China's extreme western border with Tajikistan and Kyrgyzstan, and Kashmir across the Khunjerab Pass. It rises relentlessly, and contorts itself through barren dune systems and river gorges that cleave through some of the world's highest mountains, on the eastern edge of the 'Pamir Knot' where the Pamirs divide into the Kunlun and Karakoram ranges. Every switchback reveals a new panoramic drama, yet even so Karakul, the 'Black Lake' of Kyrgyz legend, comes as a magnificent surprise. About 200 km (125 mi) from Kashgar, the terrain opens out suddenly onto a plateau filled by the surreal double-image of the east Pamir ridge mirrored in the lake's glassy surface. It stops travellers in their tracks. The clarity of the air at 3,600 m (11,810 ft) intensifies colour and perspective, but Karakul

doesn't need sunshine. Weather changes foster the illusion of the lake as a living creature of infinite moods. It is equally beautiful in summer sun, covered in roiling black clouds or cloaked by mists into a washed abstract of vastness.

Karakul is dwarfed by 7,546-m (24,757-ft) Muztagh Ata, closest to it, and by the even higher peaks of Kongur Tagh and Kongur Tiube in their distant splendour. Their contribution is strictly scenic. Several trails explore the grass and scrub pastures between the lakeshore and the shale foothills – worthwhile if only to avoid being near the road at lunchtime. Improvements to the Karakoram Highway have increased traffic, and now it is usual to share Karakul's harsh alpine beauty with tour buses stopping for a brief, midday photocall and yak-milk tea. Karakul is one of the great natural sights of Western China and it's a lot more rewarding than that.

**YOU SHOULD KNOW:**
Learn to enjoy yak-milk tea. It starts as basic green tea and yak's milk is a taste you can (eventually) acquire. The problem is the huge percentage of salt added to the tea. However, you may not be offered any alternative in the backcountry, and the tea may provide your only chance to dunk rock-hard Uygur bread (delicious in all other respects) until it's soft enough to eat. It's especially important to be comfortable with local food because Karakul lies in a sensitive border area where permit and visa checks cause frequent delays.

# Taklamakan Desert

One of the world's biggest sandy deserts, the Taklamakan has been horrifying and fascinating travellers for centuries. Over 1,000 km (620 mi) long and 400 km (250 mi) wide, it straddles central Asia between the Tien Shan and Kunlun mountain ranges in China's far west Xinjiang Province, splitting the ancient Silk Road by forcing travellers to detour north or south. The centre is a waterless death trap that a recent traveller described as 'like walking into a hairdryer', and where Marco Polo warned that travellers went mad, hearing voices and seeing spirits beckoning them to leave the road in pursuit of mirages. But for those who dare, the Taklamakan Desert is a rare and beautiful wilderness, dotted with the ruins and remnants of vanished cultures and their bold attempts to challenge nature.

Taklamakan is a 'moving' desert. Its shifting sands have buried Turkic, Mongol and Uygur fiefdoms as well as Chinese; and even obliterated some of the handful of oases which make crossing the desert possible. The latest Chinese attempt to halt its remorseless advance is the oasis of Korla on its northern edge. In the hope of exploiting Taklamakan's vast subterranean reserves of oil and gas, Korla has been remodelled as a desert metropolis of steel and glass surrounded by millions of newly planted trees and 'farmland' irrigated at crippling expense. The project's futility has only emphasized the desert's real treasures, like the enormous alluvial fan of the Molcha River spreading meltwater from the Kunlun glaciers into springtime wetlands full of rare birds, the moonlit 'waves' of the dunes in the Tarim Basin sand ocean, and the simple magic of finding living creatures and plants in that beautiful, arid emptiness. So close to the freezer of Siberia, Taklamakan's flora and fauna are uniquely adapted to its special demands. See it before corporate exploration turns it into a giant dustbowl.

*The shifting sand dunes of Taklamakan Desert*

# Kunlun Mountains

Where the 'Pamir Knot' of central Asia's highest mountains unravels to the southeast, the Karakoram range leads towards the Himalayas, and the Kunlun connects Kashmir with China's Sichuan Province. Between the two lies the Tibetan Plateau, and the Kunlun Mountains form its 2,500 km (1,550 mi) northern rim. Imagination recoils at the thought of anywhere more remote, difficult to reach, or apparently hostile – and the Kunlun are all these things. The hundreds of miles of dun-coloured mountain steppe and interminable rolling hills of sun- and frost-shattered rock shale may conjure a certain poetic beauty, but little in the way of comfort. Indeed, the extreme western end of the Kunlun/Tibet Plateau is the Aksai Chin area disputed between Pakistan, India and China, so even the meagre attractions of the Karakash (Black Jade) River don't justify the inherent political risks to travellers.

There are, though, potentially life-changing compensations. The mountains' historic isolation, and changes in political and environmental thinking, have between them rejuvenated endemic wildlife in several gigantic reserves in the central and eastern Kunlun, and on the north Tibetan Plateau and the north slopes facing the Tarim Basin. It's the only place in the world travellers can expect to see large herds of big, hoofed animals in the wild. It is heart-stopping. The Arjin Shan Reserve may be vast, but there's no hiding 10,000 wild yak, 30,000 wild asses (*kiang*), 75,000 Tibetan antelope (*chiru*), gazelle, Argali sheep, blue sheep, lynx, wolves, leopards and steppe cats; nor even family groups of up to 50 wild Bactrian camels or the originals of the endemic wild horses later named by the explorer Przewalski. The Kunlun Mountains are their Great Plains, and they are multiplying where the terrain includes grasslands and even forests, and the glaciers produce enough meltwater for them to flourish. Go east for a revelation about the meaning of natural abundance.

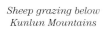

*Sheep grazing below
Kunlun Mountains*

**HOW TO GET THERE:**
By 4x4 cross-country, then extended treks on (domestic) camel with yak porterage, and on foot. Distances are huge and planning is necessary.

**WHEN TO GO:**
April to October, depending on altitude

**DON'T MISS:**
The unspoilt wilderness of 330,000 sq km (127,500 sq mi) Chang Tang Reserve, adjoining Arjin Shan. The whole ecosystem is intact, and shared only with a handful of nomads.

**YOU SHOULD KNOW:**
In Chinese mythology, the Kunlun Mountains feature as the Taoist Paradise, and the place where King Mu (976–922 BC) of the Zhou Dynasty discovered the Jade Palace of the mythical Yellow Emperor Huang-Di and met his beloved Hsi Wang Mu, known as 'Queen Mother of the West' and the object of a major religious cult. Intriguingly, some scholars believe Hsi Wang Mu is another name for the Queen of Sheba, described in the biblical *Book of Deuteronomy* as vanishing after securing the future of her son Solomon. She is thought to have come here and found spiritual enlightenment – hence 'Queen of the West'. The dates match.

471

# Lake Xingkai/Khanka International Nature Reserve

Although it lays claim to just 1,160 sq km (450 sq mi) of a 4,190 sq km (1,620 sq mi) total water plane, China is the senior partner in the Lake Xingkai/Khanka International Nature Reserve. The border between China's Heilongjiang Province and Russia's Primorsky Krai is the border between an attitude as well as two countries. The whole lake is a World Biosphere Reserve and Ramsar-cited wetland, but only China protects the whole of its territory, including the buffer zones of the lake's drainage basin to east and west. In fact, China's section also includes a secondary, much smaller lake, separated from Xingkai by a narrow, sandy causeway which transforms one of the world's most important sanctuaries for migratory birds into a unique ecosystem of unparalleled rarity.

Xingkai's complex wetlands include marshes, grasslands, swampy meadows, some forest, beach and even cliffs on the northwest shore, as well as the water itself. For centuries it has been famous for its luscious fish, the fare of Chinese emperors in the Middle Ages. The 74 species include black carp, black Amur bream, Soldatov catfish, Chinese soft-shelled turtles and enormous 600 kg (1,320 lb) Kaluga fish. The area is also a biogeographic crossroad attracting both Indian and Chinese species – and more than three quarters of all the bird species protected as migratory or endangered pass through, overwinter, or breed within it. They also attract predators to the margins of the shallow waters. The spit between the two lakes provides just enough cover for Amur wildcats, raccoon dogs, Siberian weasels, and even bears, wild boars, wolves and (regularly seen) Amur tigers to stalk unwary prey. In a relatively small area, the biodiversity is astonishing and extremely exciting. Xingkai is certainly difficult to reach, and travellers need to remain conscious of being in a sensitive border area – but the rewards are astronomical, and completely justify the effort.

# Lake Manasarovar

In Tibet, like most of China and India, natural – geographical – beauty is inextricably linked to the spiritual life of the human community. Lake Manasarovar, Mapam Yumco in Tibetan, is the 'eternal and invincible jade lake' that honours the triumph of 11th-century Buddhism over contemporary Bon beliefs, but for at least 1,000 years before that it was already the most sacred lake in Tibet for both Buddhists and Hindus. Small wonder, since it lies just to the south of

Mount Kailash, the 6,714 m (22,027 ft) diamond-shaped peak of black rock that is both the source of the Indus, Sutlej and Brahmaputra Rivers, and the sacred centre of the spiritual world of the Buddhist, Jain, Bon and Hindu faiths. It is a sacrilege to set foot on it. Instead, pilgrims come in their thousands to make the Kailash kora – a 53-km (33-mi) circumambulation from the little town of Darchen. The act cancels a pilgrim's bad *karma* (evil deeds). And if the pilgrim continues, and walks around Manasarovar, the further benefit of salvation is guaranteed. The lake is the second half of the pilgrimage.

It's quite beautiful. In the clarity of the air at 4,556 m (15,000 ft), it often glows the intense, deep blue of outer space, or mirrors the surrounding Olympian drama of mountain wilderness and vast bowl of sky. It can change colour to emerald green in the centre, and in moonlight it is magical. Manasarovar is the highest freshwater lake in the world, and important monasteries line its 88 km (55 mi) shore. The monks officiate at the many rituals specifically associated with the lake pilgrimage, like the annual Manasarovar Yatra ceremonial bathing. Travellers are welcome but need to be self-sufficient in the holy wilderness. Respect for the gods includes leaving no trace behind – other than prayer flags and a profound wonder at the mystique of faith and nature.

**DON'T MISS:**
The nine monasteries around the lake. Each plays a different role in the complex rituals that re-enact key stories from Buddhist scriptures, Hindu mythologies and Jain and Bon legends. Gyiwu and Curgu monasteries are especially well known: the shore next to Curgu is the holiest and purest bathing place of all.

**YOU SHOULD KNOW:**
Travellers need a military permit to reach Lake Manasarovar. Tour companies in Llasa or Kathmandu can arrange it, but guides, pack-yaks, drivers and vehicles can be hired independently in Darchen. In any case, foreigners must register their presence in Darchen, and pay an admission fee covering the Manasarovar area. It's worth paying to salute what Buddhist scriptures call 'the mother of the rivers in the world'.

*Pristine Lake Manasarovar is a sacred pilgrimage site.*

# Yarlung Zangbo Canyon

**HOW TO GET THERE:**
By car or bus to Pai, the community at the upstream entrance to the canyon, then on foot. The new airport at Nyingchi is making access much easier for many more people to make brief visits.
**WHEN TO GO:**
May to October
**DON'T MISS:**
Getting a guide who can show you a fraction of the wondrous natural sights and also explain how they are integrated into local belief systems and culture. The 33 m (108 ft) Hidden Falls are the biggest of dozens of cascades along the gorge, and so sacred that Monba shamans concealed their existence for years. Rafting offers the most awe-inspiring way to see at least some of the canyon – but some sections are dangerous even for professionals.
**YOU SHOULD KNOW:**
It takes about a month to trek the whole canyon, and just trekking from rim to river needs real stamina. But Yarlung Zangbo delivers colossal rewards even to visitors flying in for a quick look, and much more in proportion to the effort invested in seeking out its delights. It's one of the richest adventures on the planet. When you go, try to live it slowly, and with relish.

The Yarlung Zangbo is a sacred river, running 2,057 km (1,280 mi) along the northern slope of the Tibetan Himalayas from its glacial source on Mount Kailash before flowing south to India, where it is called the Brahmaputra. At the great bend the river hard-turns 130 degrees to squeeze between the two 7,500-m (24,606-ft) peaks of Namchak Bawa and Jialabailei, cutting the Himalayas in two and carving a gorge with an *average* depth of 5,000 m (16,500 ft) throughout its 496 km (310 mi) length. Incredibly, it was only in 1994 that Chinese scientists discovered – by accident – that it was longer and deeper than Colorado's Grand Canyon.

Its revelation to the world is almost a pity. The superlatives of its size, splendour and dramatic features pale beside those of its biodiversity. It is not the bleak and stony Tibet that the world knows, but an ocean of forest green nourished by warm monsoon winds sucked through the gap in the Himalayas and constricted by the steep canyon walls. Even so, that altitude means that every ecological zone from polar to tropical rainforest is represented distinctly within the canyon itself. And it is pure, primeval, untouched. Only a handful of indigenous Monba and Lhoba have ever shared the lush forests and rushing rivers, the waterfalls literally pushing through fairytale trains of hanging orchids, or the stands of giant dragon spruce higher up, teeming with golden monkeys and birds more radiant with colour than an Audubon first edition. To science, the canyon is a universal medicine cabinet, a seed bank, a menagerie for the world, a living laboratory of climate change and a hotspot of thermal tectonics. For travellers willing to get stuck in, it distils the beauty, drama and abundance of nature in all its moods and guises – elements many people spend lifetimes trying to assemble from different journeys. Yarlung Zangbo Canyon has the lot on its doorstep.

# Jiuzhaigou

**HOW TO GET THERE:**
By car or bus from Chengdu (ten hours), or by air to Huanglong (be prepared: the airfield is 3,445 m (11,300 ft) up a mountainside!) and a one-and-a-half-hour bus ride.
**WHEN TO GO:**
Any time

The Valley of Nine Villages, Jiuzhaigou lies at the southern end of the Minshan Mountains that dominate northwest Sichuan, some 340 km (206 mi) north of Chengdu. It is a giant picture-book fairytale fantasy of nature, with added giant panda appeal, quality-stamped by UNESCO as a World Heritage Protected Landscape and a Biosphere Reserve.

Jiuzhaigou got its name from the nine ancient Tibetan villages along its Y-shaped valley floor, seven of which are still populated by a former farming community which now caters to tourism within the

*Arrow Bamboo Lake*

protected area. There's a lot to protect. The word 'picturesque' was created to deal with the achingly pretty waterfalls, the rainbow of jewelled lakes, the bird-filled forests, flower-choked glades, rocky bluffs and distant, snow-capped peaks that smite the traveller's eye at every turn. No picture or even series of pictures or film can do justice to the magnificent profligacy of nature in carelessly cramming together so much pristine beauty into a mere 1,320 sq km (510 sq mi) of reserve and buffer zone. Each feature also tells a story drawn from the massive body of Chinese folklore and faith-based legend and mythology. Within a few minutes of arriving, visitors find themselves intoning the fairytales associated with or incorporated into the names of the woods, lakes and mountains around them, drawing them together into a kind of mantra which brings the wonderland to a whirlwind life of princesses in gold chariots plunging from the skies and 108 dropped pearls that became Jiuzhaigou's 108 lakes. The cumulative 'naming' helps distract from the walkways, roads, bridges and other artificial aids to reach the best viewing points. Without them, the ubiquitous natural opulence would soon be trampled indiscriminately. Jiuzhaigou doesn't need to sell itself with pandas, although there are a few. The whole fantastic valley is a coded cultural history written in the four elements, to breathtaking effect.

**DON'T MISS:**
The 'story' of the scenery. The Shuzheng Lakes are just one of several series, each comprising at least 18 ribbon lakes, stepped down a side valley, all different but with connecting folklore. A line of willows across the 100-m (328-ft) wide top of Nuorilang Falls is said to be the tines of a princess's comb untangling the water.

**YOU SHOULD KNOW:**
Jiuzhaigou is a vast reserve, but shuttle buses make it easy to travel between major highlights. They are much less intrusive than you might imagine. The remote Zharu Valley is not on the obvious tour trail, and it's open to those wanting to trek for days or weeks where no facilities exist. It's the best place to see wildlife – even a panda – but it would be a mistake to visit Zharu at the expense of more popular sites, because they completely justify their sky-high reputation and you'll want to linger.

*A captive panda eating bamboo in Wolong Nature Reserve.*

# Wolong Nature Reserve

At the pinnacle of China's environmental protection initiatives, the giant panda sanctuaries of northwestern Sichuan are the Last Chance Saloon for the world's favourite species of bear. Perhaps the pandas know it too – they occupy the nation's heart and the nation's heartland in the Minshan Mountains, which form a natural barrier between the densely populated lowlands of the Yellow and Yangtze River basins and the eastern edge of the Tibetan wilderness plateau. The territory is an ideal combination of high mountains, thick forests and deep, lush valleys, but the seven nature reserves and nine scenic parks protecting Sichuan's pandas are not (yet!) contiguous. Until they are linked to form an effective bio-corridor with the potential for pandas to increase their gene pool in the wild, Wolong Nature Reserve is their showpiece.

Wolong is the centre of China's giant panda research and breeding programme. It protects over 150 giant pandas (roughly half of them in captivity) on the maxim of what's good for pandas is good for lots of other species of fauna and flora. The vertical spectrum of broadleaf, mixed and coniferous woods, with alpine marsh and grassland, bare rock and the snow line above them, guarantees that visitors enjoy Wolong's floral fairyland of diverse habitats as much as the aesthetics of rare creatures like red panda, golden monkey, white-lipped deer, gnu and hundreds of birds. Yingxiong and Yinchang Valleys offer especially lovely views, but visitors come to see Hetao Village, where they are encouraged to coo over baby pandas and get close to their mournful-eyed parents. Pandas can be 'adopted', and bulletins on their progress sent all over the world; and because so many of Wolong's pandas are tagged, visitors with a guide and a GPS can be certain of finding them even in the depths of the vast bamboo stands on which the gorgeous creatures rely to live.

**HOW TO GET THERE:**
Travel by bus or car from Chengdu (three hours) to the reserve entrance at Yingxiu on the Min River.

**WHEN TO GO:**
Any time – although with so many rare trees in its varied forests, autumn turns Wolong into a burnished technicolor treat.

**DON'T MISS:**
The Hero Valley, Mount Siguniang – 6,250 m (20,505 ft) – Reserve in the Qionglai Mountain range, and trekking the wildlife watchtowers up the Zheng He River to Zheng He Lake.

**YOU SHOULD KNOW:**
Just as pandas carry the flag for the World Wildlife Fund and 'the environment' in general, Wolong is a symbol of China's determination to improve its environmental image.
Badly damaged by the 2008 earthquake, the reserve is still catching up on repairs – to animals, access and facilities – by increasing its programme of dedicating individual pandas as 'goodwill ambassadors' overseas, and by giving them to other countries as 'national treasures'.
As impressive as the panda conservation programme itself, is the deft way eco-politics has learned to exploit the shameless emotional appeal of 'Brand Panda'.

# Qinling Mountains

Giant pandas used to be found in the high mountains all over south and western China. Now they are found in just 20 or so isolated habitats in the margins of Gansu, Sichuan and Shaanxi provinces, in the Minshan and Qinling, two mountain ranges at roughly right angles to each other in the very centre of the country. With peaks over 3,700 m (12,140 ft) the Qinling mountains are the watershed between the Yellow River and the Yangtze. They form a natural barrier between north and south China, blocking cold northern winds and soaking up the warm southern rains which make it rival Minshan as a biodiversity hotspot. Inevitably, Qinling's rich forests are threatened by legal and illegal logging, but thousands of years of encroachment in the region have left intact a core area full of endemic flora and fauna. Hillsides flaunt dozens of brightly coloured rhododendron species beneath Chinese yew and Qinling fir trees, and the gingkos and forest understorey of dwarf bamboo varieties support rare species like golden monkey, crested ibis, takin, and surprising numbers of wild giant panda.

Protecting the Qinling wild pandas means protecting their habitats rather than introducing breeding programmes. The success of the four panda reserves at Foping, Changqing, Taibai and Zhouzhi led in late 2009 to the opening of two more at Sangyuan and Qingmuchuan, both almost completely forested and rich in arrow bamboo, giant pandas' favourite food. Foping is the best-established, and it has a higher density of wild giant pandas than anywhere else on Earth. The first sighting in the wild makes your pulse race – but gradually you realize that Qinling pandas have smaller skeletal frames, bigger side teeth, and traces of brown in the familiar black-and-white fur livery. Only very recently scientists discovered that they are indeed a distinct subspecies of China's other giant pandas – and Foping has between 110 and 130 of them.

**HOW TO GET THERE:**
By car or tour bus from Xi'an – 200 km (125 mi) to the end of the road at Lianfengya, then on foot into Foping. Changqing Reserve is adjacent, and the others are all fairly close.

**WHEN TO GO:**
April to October. (Note that wild giant pandas descend to lower elevations seasonally, when they are easier to track: check with the reserve in advance on their movements.)

**DON'T MISS:**
Practise tracking pandas from their droppings, broken bamboo shoots, fur caught on plants and paw prints – most likely they will be feeding in the swathes of Farges cane and umbrella bamboo at Sanguanmiao or Xihe in the heart of Foping Reserve, or near the waterfall at Niangniangtan pool.

**YOU SHOULD KNOW:**
Foping's pre-eminence among the Qinling reserves means it is equipped with good facilities for visitors. Independent travellers must arrange their own permits to enter each reserve, and separate fees for sightseeing, environment protection and guide. While you wonder where it all goes, reflect that a giant panda can grasp bamboo with its enlarged wrist bone, which works like an opposable thumb. Humans have much greater dexterity, yet on the steep, often slippery hillsides, are no match for surprisingly nimble bears.

*A giant panda cub standing up looking for food.*

# Yunnan Stone Forest

Southeast of Kunming, capital of China's Yunnan Province on the border with Laos, the Shilin (Stone Forest) National Park proclaims a 350 sq km (135 sq mi) area of ancient karst, the spectacular remnants of a 270-million-year-old seabed of limestone sediment. Concertinaed by tectonics into a ridged plateau, then whittled by 200 million years of water and weather into other-worldly rock formations, Shilin's sculpted contortions are like a giant's fantasy playground petrified into shards of jagged rock; and like everywhere else in China, each major formation, and the individual rocks, pillars, air bridges, streams, waterfalls, caves, stalagmites, stalactites, cliffs and ravines that contribute to them, are integrated into the sacred mythologies of local culture.

The park consists of seven distinct Scenic Areas. Zhiyun Cave is 400 m (1,310 ft) long, and has caves within caves big enough to hold 1,000 people. The cave walls are hollow where stalactites once hung, and ring musically when struck. Small formations resemble pagodas, old men with walking sticks, beds and other things deemed to have been abandoned by 'celestial beings'. It's typical of Shilin that Zhiyun's highlights should have names like Jade Elephant Propping Up Sky, Hanging Golden Chickens Upside Down or White Dragon Sacrificing. The process is very effective at making the shock of each natural spectacle manageable. The Stone Forest itself is so far beyond usual human experience it needs mythologizing. Thousands of razor-sharp pinnacles rear up like a skyscraper megalopolis, emanating danger but inviting close examination. When it was a wilderness, it must have been terrifying to enter, but now manicured grass walks make visiting an exotic promenade, a curiosity instead of an adventure. It's unmissable, but imaginative travellers will understand more about Shilin's revered place in ethnic culture from the less-visited but equally amazing scenic outposts like the Dadieshui Waterfall, Moon Lake, Bushaoshan and Liziyuanqing.

*The Stone Forest resembles a giant's fantasy playground.*

# Shangri-La, Zhongdian

Ever since James Hilton wrote his 1933 novel *Lost Horizon*, the county of Zhongdian in northwest Yunnan has basked in visitors' compliments. Hilton imagined a perfect community concealed by impassable mountains in an idyllic valley called Shangri-La. In a masterful demonstration of quality environmental self-marketing, Zhongdian lapped up the suggestion that Shangri-La had been modelled on its own stunning landscapes, and in 2002 officially changed its name. Now you can get a ticket   to Shangri-La.

You won't be short-changed. Shangri-La/Zhongdian is every bit as beautiful as Hilton's original, and its local culture, an unusual ethnic mix of Tibetan, Lisu, Naxi and Yi, is hallmarked by traditions of ancient harmony, tranquillity and faith in living nature. The whole region falls within the Three Parallel Rivers World Biosphere, where the upper reaches of the Yangtze, Mekong and Salween Rivers roar south down vast gorges a few kilometres apart from each other; but Shangri-La county is itself made up of a series of smaller reserves protecting the snowbound ridges and high peaks, sweeping alpine prairie meadows, gorges deep enough to harbour subtropical forests, limpid blue lakes and crystal mountain torrents. Every feature is named, illuminating every landscape with the extra dimension of its religious significance. The aeons of calcium deposits that transformed the Baishui Terraces below the Haba Snow Mountains southeast of Zhongdian town into a sculpted masterpiece of descending, overlapping pools represent much more than mere mineral science. To the Naxi, whose Dongba culture was born on the magnificent Bashui Tableland, the terracing is like a huge, white jade representation of the most holy spirits of nature, set off by the surrounding mantle of green; and every year they assemble to sing and dance in celebration of them. This is the true spirit of Shangri-La, echoed in a hundred places within the county – the joy of its people, and a siren call to every traveller.

*The calcium deposits of the spectacular Baishui Terraces*

**HOW TO GET THERE:**
By air from Kunming to Zhongdian (town); then by car or bus around Shangri-La (county)

**WHEN TO GO:**
April to October – but Shangri-La's high altitude means it is often chilly during summer, too.

**DON'T MISS:**
The magnificent sprawl of 1679 Songzanling Monastery – like all Shangri-La's lamaseries, an integral part of the landscape and not just a building; Tiger Leaping Gorge; Bitahai Lake Nature Reserve in the subtropical zone on the edge of Shangri-La, full of bears, parrots, monkeys and cranes. It's only one feature of Pudacuo National Park, notable for its miles of walkways protecting rare plant species.

**YOU SHOULD KNOW:**
Judging by the warmth, generosity, and general benevolence of its ethnically mixed inhabitants, Shangri-La has a strong claim to be an authentic utopia. Hopefully, the high mountains that have made access historically difficult will continue to provide a safe – and stunningly lovely – haven against the growing crowds who come hoping to take away a piece of paradise, instead of just admiring it.

*Amazing rock formations in Zhangjiajie National Forest*

# Zhangjiajie National Forest

Zhangjiajie National Forest in northwest Hunan Province is fundamental to the central strand of Chinese history, aesthetics and mythology. It is also as geologically weird as anything on Earth, and as beautiful – for real – as any dream you can remember enjoying. Its most memorable landscapes are the sandstone and limestone karst formations that make it a convoluted rocky labyrinth of sky-high pillars, needle-sharp mesas, Rubik's Cubes of four-level cave systems, towering, multi-peaked mountains and plunging valleys that seem to twist impossibly on their axes between high and low. With morning mists wisping through its serried peaks, or veiled by imperceptible drizzle, it is the reality of what the western world regards as 'classic' Chinese art. But you can walk into it and belong to it – and that is a rare and exclusive feeling.

Zhangjiajie forest is considered foremost of the four major scenic areas of Wulingyuan World Heritage Site and Geopark, and the two names are often used interchangeably. Its relatively sudden rise to international prominence has brought a colossal influx of Chinese and foreign visitors, and it's not yet clear if the numbers can be controlled without damaging the extraordinary features that make it so special. The Bailong Elevator catapults people 326 m (1,070 ft) vertically up a mountain for the panorama over some of the forest's 3,000 200–300-m (650–1,000-ft) rock columns and sky bridges; and there is a cable car to Huangshizhai for perhaps the best overview of all. With fast-food stands lining the major boardwalk trails on the valley floors, Zhangjiajie might seem on its way to becoming a geological and historico-cultural theme park instead of representing something of the national soul. It isn't, but travellers have to work harder to find its wild heart. Ask a guide for help with Zhangjiajie's cultural significance – the aesthetics and geology speak for themselves.

# Sanqingshan National Park

Not so much a mountain as a map of Taoist principles and metaphors, Sanqin Mountain is also a geological marvel of extremely rare granite landforms, and of exquisitely subtle beauty. The geology obviously came first, but it is no longer possible to treat Sanqingshan's breathtaking sightlines and individual natural oddities separately from its spiritual implications. Every tree, column, rock formation, hillside, spring and peak is incorporated into a schemata of essential Taoist philosophy first noticed and ordered over 1,600 years ago by the great Taoist Master Ge Hong (284–364), who spent years on the holy mountain trying to devise an elixir for immortality and determine a working relationship between Taoism and Confucianism. Although nothing has been physically altered – other than by wind and rain – in the landscape, the infrastructure available to visitors makes it impossible to view the mountain in any other way.

Sanqingshan has triple peaks, equated with the three divine spirits. It is also exceptionally steep, and its position high above the coastal plain of the China Sea means it attracts heavy mists for 200 days of each year. With thick fog or wispy tendrils spiralling through the crags and parting suddenly so that sunshine seems to focus on one or another feature, it's easy to appreciate how the faithful might interpret this randomness as divine. Modern visitors have the advantage of the 'east' and 'west' 'plank roads', each over 3 km (2 mi) long and rising to 1,600 m (5,250 ft) on either side of the peaks, with a forested mountain on one side and a deep canyon on the other, with views to what feels like infinity. From them it's possible to see most of the 48 granite peaks and 89 granite pillars worked into a grand design that includes 230 cultural relics – pagodas, temples, pavilions, pools and bridges – still acknowledged as the ideal blueprint for a Taoist layout. Sanqingshan is unique, and its beauty is genuinely harmonious and inspirational.

# Cape Ashizuri

HOW TO GET THERE:
The best bases for exploring
Ashizuri-Uwakai National Park are
the towns of Tosa-Shimizu and
Uwajima, while Cape Ashizuri is a
comfortable seaside walk from the
small town of Ashizuri, just north of
the cape.

**WHEN TO GO:**
Any time. The subtropical climate is
humid with heavy summer rains.

**DON'T MISS:**
A trip in a glass-bottomed boat to
inspect the colourful marine life
surrounding the long coral reefs in
Ashizuri Marine Park.

**YOU SHOULD KNOW:**
The first Japanese person ever to
visit America, when Japan was a
closed society and leaving (or rather
returning after leaving) was
punishable by death, was a
fisherman shipwrecked off Cape
Ashizuri in 1841 and rescued by an
American ship. Nakahama 'John'
Manjiro learned English and returned
not to sudden death, but a valued
role as an interpreter after Japan was
forcibly opened up to outside
influences.

The southernmost point of Japan's Shikoku Island is Cape Ashizuri, which is part of Ashizuri-Uwakai National Park. Shikoku is often described as Japan's 'Forgotten Island'. It lies to the south of Honshu and lovers of wild places will not be disappointed by the fact that many Japanese regard the place as something of a rural backwater. There are few headline attractions, but the mountainous interior offers great hiking possibilities. The national park encompasses some of Japan's finest coastal scenery and includes offshore islands in an area of sleepy fishing villages that provide an opportunity to experience traditional culture along with tropical plants, an unspoilt environment, crystal-clear sea and pristine white sand beaches.

Cape Ashizuri itself is a famous beauty spot, much appreciated by the landscape-conscious Japanese as a place where the exquisite harmony of the azure Pacific Ocean crashing against towering 80-m (265-ft) granite cliffs is complemented by the clean white pencil of Japan's tallest lighthouse, built in 1914 and visible 40 km (25 mi) out to sea. There are two observation decks that offer stupendous maritime views and a 2-km (1-mi) nature trail takes visitors through a spectacular tunnel of camellia plants to the gaping mouth of Hakusan sea cave and various other points of interest. A star attraction is Kameyobiba ('Place to summon turtles') where there's every chance of spotting these magnificent sea creatures. The park's main attractions are concentrated at the end of the cape and can easily be covered on foot.

Two nearby vantage points offer good views of the cape itself and make interesting stop-offs. The Ashizuri Observatory and the Tengu-Nose Observatory stand high above the waters of the powerful north-flowing Japan Current where it makes its nearest approach to land, carving out dramatic features like the Hakusan Do-mon, a wonderfully dramatic rock arch.

*Camellias at Cape Ashizuri*

# Kamikochi

The Nagano Prefecture on the island of Honshu is blessed with some of the most beautiful scenery in Japan, much of it contained within the Chubu Sangaku National Park. This takes in the northern and central regions of the mountains known as the Japanese Alps. And like the European Alps, the Japanese version sees heavy snow in winter, attracting skiers, while summer visitors hike, climb or simply enjoy the stunning landscape.

An accessible starting point for those interested in seeing these splendid uplands is Kamikochi in the Hida Mountains. This is a popular destination that shuts down in winter, with some limited development to service the many visitors drawn by Kamikochi's stunning setting. Facilities include hotels, shops, restaurants, a campground, waymarked trails and mountain refuges for climbers. This suggests that Kamikochi isn't the wildest of places and it's certainly true that plenty of people arrive in high summer. But this 15-km (10-mi) river valley has plenty of room for everyone and those seeking solitude can quickly find it in the surrounding mountains, with Mount Hotaka at the northern end and the active volcano Mount Yake to the south.

There's excellent day-hiking along the Azusa River, starting with a crossing of the Kappa-bashi suspension bridge near the bus terminal. Trails lead up and down the valley. Highlights include the attractive Takezawa Marsh, tranquil Myojin Pond with nearby Hotaka Shrine, Tashiro Pond and the extraordinary Lake Taisho, formed by a volcanic eruption that dammed the river in 1915, which still has skeletal dead trees standing in the water. Preserved in its natural state, Kamikochi has been designated as one of Japan's National Cultural Assets. Those lucky enough to see this special place will understand why, for this is mountain scenery at its very best.

*The Azusa River runs through beautiful mountain scenery.*

**HOW TO GET THERE:**
Private cars are banned from Kamikochi so access is by bus or taxi. Some buses start from Matsumoto but the best way is to take the Matsumoto Electric Railway to Shin-Shimashima and take the bus from there. Buses also run to Kamikochi from Takayama. Cars must be parked at the entrance gate and the journey completed by bus or taxi – Kamikochi is on National Route 158 between Matsumoto and Takayama.

**WHEN TO GO:**
Kamikochi is open from mid April to mid November. Serious forays into the mountains are best undertaken between June and September. Alpine wild flowers put on a great show from mid May to July, while autumn foliage is at its best in mid October.

**DON'T MISS:**
Kamikochi Visitor Centre for lots of information on the flora, fauna, geology and folklore of the area, plus help for those who intend to hike into the surrounding mountains.

**YOU SHOULD KNOW:**
The Japanese Alps were so christened by Walter Weston, a 19th-century British missionary who introduced recreational mountain climbing to Japan. There is a memorial to him at Kamikochi.

# Lake Biwa

Japan's largest freshwater lake is in Honshu's Shinga Prefecture, close to the former Japanese capital of Kyoto. Lake Biwa extends to 670 sq km (260 sq mi) and is filled by rivers that drain the surrounding mountains, causing the water level to rise dramatically after both the spring snow melt and autumn typhoon season. Regular replenishment is important as the lake serves as a reservoir providing drinking water to the cities of Kyoto and Otsu, which is on the lake. The impressively engineered Lake Biwa Canal connects the two. Other communities around the lake include Hikone, Nagahama and Sakamoto.

*Lake Biwa*

The characteristic lakeshore consists of extensive reed beds, but despite protective ordnances and designation as a UNESCO RAMSAR Wetland, development has inexorably encroached. However, this beautiful expanse of water is large enough to ensure that considerable unspoilt stretches – especially on the northern and western shores – remain to satisfy those who like to appreciate Mother Nature's spectacular creativity, untrammelled by the intrusive contributions of humankind. The sunsets over the mountains to the west of the lake, viewed from the opposite shore, are as good as they get.

Lake Biwa is a popular tourist destination. The sternwheeler *Michigan* plies the lake, lake cruises are available and workaday ferries operate, connecting Chickuba, Hikone, Okishima and Otsu. The islands of Chikubu and Okishima are popular destinations for visitors and pilgrims. Boats and bicycles can be rented in many places and there is an excellent network of cycle paths around the lake. Cyclists who want to see it all can undertake the full 220-km (140-mi) circumnavigation, finding accommodation along the way. Fishing is a popular pastime, along with birdwatching and the usual watersports. Others simply enjoy the beaches. For those hankering after lonely places, there are some splendid hikes in the Hira-san Mountains on the western side of the lake.

**HOW TO GET THERE:**
There are excellent rail services with several lines serving the eastern and southern coasts of the lake, while the J R Kosei Line is ideal for exploring the quieter northern and western shores.

**WHEN TO GO:**
Any time. Note that the temperate climate is subject to sudden weather changes and the more accessible areas of the lake and its shore get crowded during the summer holidays.

**DON'T MISS:**
The Biwako Incline on Lake Biwa Canal, ideally in spring to see the cherry blossom. The incline is no longer used for its original purpose of moving barges between the canal's two levels – they were lifted from the water and transported up and downhill on flat cars.

**YOU SHOULD KNOW:**
There is architectural heritage aplenty around the lake. Japan's oldest remaining train station is in Nagahama, which also has other pleasing historical buildings, interesting temples and shrines, plus a reconstructed castle. One of only a dozen remaining original Japanese castles is at Hikone. The UNESCO World Heritage Site of Enryaku-ji Tendai monastery on Mount Hiei is near Sakamoto.

# Towada-Hachimantai National Park

At the northern tip of Honshu are the unspoilt natural wonders of a national park largely unsullied by the insensitive hand of man. The northern section of Towada-Hachimantai National Park surrounds Lake Towada, while the southern section encompasses the Hachimantai Plateau and the surrounding peaks of Iwate, Koma and Nyuto. The area is one of Japan's most precious scenic gems with a wealth of sylvan vistas, waterfalls, rushing rivers, crystal-clear lakes, marshland, swamps, primeval forests and alpine plants set within rugged landscape dominated by volcanic cones.

Lake Towada is a large crater lake with a surface area of 60 sq km (23 sq mi). The shores are crowded by trees and the road around the lake skirts two promontories at the southern end that reach out and enclose three delightful bays, imaginatively named West, Middle and East Lakes. These may be viewed from the water by taking a trip on one of the pleasure boats that ply the lake between Yasumiya and Nenokuchi (April to October only). The whole emphasis is on allowing visitors to get close to nature and sensitively developed areas like Yasumiya at the base of the Nakayama Peninsula offer facilities like campgrounds, lodgings and nature trails with free guided walks. There is a lakeside promontory and a nearby observatory with wonderful lake views.

To the south is the Hachimantai Plateau, a dramatic upland shaped by volcanic activity that hasn't ceased, as boiling mud pools and assorted vents emitting steam or smoke soon testify. This is great hiking country with stunning views from summits such as that of Mount Hachimantai in the centre of the plateau. This is high moorland at its scenic best, with wetland ponds like Hachiman-numa providing aquatic punctuation. There are various nature trails – Goshogake and Onuma being good examples – while notable peaks include Yake with the impressive Onigaja lava dome and Mount Nyuto with its sweeping distant views.

**HOW TO GET THERE:**
A road follows the shores of Lake Towada, with Yasumiya being the area's largest settlement and a good base for exploration. The Towada Science Museum is located there. The Hachimantai Plateau is crossed by a road from Hachimantai to Koma. A (somewhat erratic) bus network covers the area from the principal towns of Aomori, Towada-Minami and Morioka. These have good rail links and there are regular commercial flights into Aomori from Tokyo.
**WHEN TO GO:**
Any time, although winters can be very cold, especially in the mountains, and adverse weather conditions between November and March can disrupt public transport.
**DON'T MISS:**
The Hakkoda Mountains, south of the coastal town of Aomori. A good base for hiking among these extinct volcanoes and dense forests that clothe their flanks is Sukayuonsen. The autumn foliage is amazing and those reaching the highest summit – Mount Odake – are rewarded with a spectacular panorama stretching away over the rugged landscape to the Sea of Japan to the west and Pacific Ocean to the east.
**YOU SHOULD KNOW:**
The prevalence of volcanic hot springs in the area has led to the establishment of numerous health spas such as Fukenoyu, Goshogake, Tamagawa and Toshichi, which are clustered at the foot of Mount Yakeyama. Many of the developed springs are unsophisticated facilities that offer visitors a great opportunity to get off the usual tourist track and meet the local people who use them.

*Mount Iwate in Towada-Hachimantai National Park*

# Seorak-san National Park

Not far from the DMZ (Demilitarized Zone) that separates South Korea from its insular twin lies Seorak-san National Park, close to the Sea of Japan. This encompasses a considerable section of the Taebaek Mountains and consists of rugged forested landscape with many rushing streams, spread across four counties – Sokcho, Inje, Goseong and Yangyank. It has three sections – Outer Seorak, Inner Seorak and South Seorak.

A huge number of South Korean and international visitors are attracted by the park's scenic splendour, which rivals any mountain scenery in the world and outscores most. For many, the first valley they see upon arrival is quite enough to satisfy their love of wild places, offering almost too much to see and do in a day. This valley houses the main entrance and contains several natural wonders and man-made ones in the form of historic Buddhist temples. Two waterfalls – Biryong (Flying Dragon) and Yukdam – may be seen on the left side of the valley, less than an hour's walk from the car park. The Biseondae is a rock platform above a stream, from whence a cave with stunning views may be reached by those of athletic bent. Further from the entrance lies the Valley of a Thousand Buddhas, so named because the rock formations look like a legion of timeless statues representing the deity.

Beyond immediately accessible areas with friendly nature trails that anyone can tackle lies a wonderland of mountains, rivers and valleys just waiting to be discovered by keen explorers who are prepared to do some serious hiking. They will be rewarded with bizarre rock formations, waterfalls and fascinating flora and fauna. The ultimate challenge is the park's highest peak, Daecheong-bong, which has a refuge close to the summit (advance booking required). The view from the top is awesome, and sunsets there have to be seen to be believed.

**HOW TO GET THERE:**
The main entrance to Seorak-san National Park is close to the city of Sokcho, and regular buses run to the park village of Seorak-Dong and on to the park's entrance, which is a 15-minute drive from town for those with their own transport.

**WHEN TO GO:**
Autumn is prime time, when the stunning reds and yellows of foliage against the rocky landscape are mightily impressive. But be warned – so many people turn up at autumn weekends that local roads can become gridlocked. Go midweek.

**DON'T MISS:**
Rocking the rock – that's the famous Heundeulbawi, a spherical rock encountered on the 900-step climb to the park's notable Ulsanbawi rock formation, an ascent that also passes two temples. The deceptive Heundeulbawi can be rocked quite easily but, despite countless efforts, has never been toppled from its perch. Those who can't face the climb can content themselves with the stunning reflection of Ulsanbawi in Yeongrangho Lake, or take the cable-car ride to Gwongeumseong, an ancient ruined fortress site atop Dol Mountain.

**YOU SHOULD KNOW:**
The park is close to the ocean, but unfortunately access to the sea is denied by tall fences as a reminder of an incursion from North Korea that took place in the late 1990s.

*You can get close to the top of Ulsan Rock – if you climb more than 800 steps!*

487

# Taroko Gorge

One of Taiwan's Eight Scenic Wonders, Taroko Gorge is a marble-and-granite canyon with 3,800 m (12,467 ft) Mount Nanhu at one end and the Pacific Ocean a mere 20 km (12 mi) away at the other. Walking, rafting, biking or driving it is a national sport and entertainment, and one of the first-choice weekend recreations of the millions of Taiwanese living in and around the capital, Taipei. Drivers benefit from the Cross Central Highway, which runs from coast to coast but is specifically designed to give them stunning views of the dramatic scenery in Taroko Gorge. Hikers can choose from several trails either alongside the milky green, swirling water of the Liwu River which carved out the whole unlikely creation, or tributaries like the Shakadang, a secondary chasm marked by gleaming scars where fresh slabs of marble have splintered from the rockface. The most sensational section of any of the trails is Jiucyudong (Tunnel of Nine Turns), where several sheer 900 m (3,000 ft) cliffs angle into each other in a sequence that resembles a coiled dragon. It's like walking inside Taroko's geology, under and through its joints and folds, and the overhang narrows the gorge to just 10 m (33 ft), but with a terrifying drop to the Kelan tributary below.

Taroko Gorge is a national park as well as a world-class geological masterpiece. Away from the waterside trail (in fact, the original single-track road of tunnels and ledges) the occasionally maddening crowds melt away. Hikers starting above Tienhsiang, the ethnic village at the upper end of Taroko Gorge itself, can head through a 380-m (415-yd), pitch-black, marble tunnel, high up a dizzying ledge to the Baiyang Waterfall and a whole series of curtain waterfalls beyond. Serious trekkers will prefer the solitude of the high peaks and alpine grasslands of Hehuanshan on the park's western edge.

*The road through Taroko Gorge which runs alongside the Liwu River.*

# AUSTRALASIA & OCEANIA

# Cape Arid

At the far western end of the Great Australian Bight – the vast bay which does indeed look as though a gigantic bite has been taken out of the country's southern coastline – stands Cape Arid, a wilderness that has an isolated beauty all of its own. The area is now a national park, its 2,800 sq km (1,080 sq mi) covering an extensive stretch of shoreline as well as a large rugged interior. The coast here is one of rocky promontories and sweeping beaches with excellent swimming, especially at Mount Tagon bay, around the mouth of the Thomas River and at Yokinup Bay (also a good location for windsurfing). Further back, young sand dune systems support coastal heathlands with patches of banksia and paperbark stands. From the top of Mount Arid on the cape itself there are fine views of the varied coastal scenery and the many little offshore islands which make up the eastern end of the Recherche Archipelago. As you move inland sandy plains give way to low granite hills and more arid vegetation. The terrain is dominated by mallee scrub and small eucalypt woodlands. The main feature of the north of the park are the hills of the Russell Range which include the highest point in the park, the aptly named Mount Ragged – 594 m (1,949 ft).

While it is home to animals such as wallabies and possums, the park's chief glory is its birdlife. More than 160 species have been recorded, including several that are rare and threatened. Oystercatchers and terns are among the waterfowl and waders to be seen in the Thomas estuary, while Cape Arid is one of the few remaining habitats of the Cape Barren goose and the western ground parrot.

# Peron Peninsula

The Peron Peninsula forms the middle prong of the W-shaped landmass enfolding Shark Bay, the westernmost point of the Australian mainland. It is a wild realm of sandy plains covered with mulga scrub and acacias which have adapted to the mercilessly dry conditions. The dramatic red cliffs of the bluffs and headlands around the coast present a vivid contrast with the blue waters and white beaches below. The far north end of the peninsula is now the Francois Peron National Park, named after a pioneering French zoologist. The area now covered by the park, 525 sq km (203 sq mi), was formerly a sheep station; you can still see the old homestead to get an idea of what life must have been like in such a remote location. One unusual feature of the landscape are the gypsum claypans that were once saline lakes; in some places, such as at Big Lagoon, the sea has broken through into the claypans to form a shallow inland bay.

Shark Bay itself is a protected marine park and its shallow, clear waters are rich in marine life. The cliff tops of the Peron Peninsula provide good viewpoints for spotting dolphins, turtles and manta rays; even the threatened dugong, a gentle giant of a sea creature, can sometimes be seen grazing in these waters. With fabulous coral reefs to entice divers the bay also boasts the largest number of seagrass species ever recorded in one place anywhere in the world (12, since you're wondering). But the most remarkable feature of all is what thrives in the shallow waters of Hamelin Pool on the eastern side of the peninsula: colonies of sediment-trapping algae, known as stromatolites, which are direct descendants of the earth's earliest life forms, dating back over three billion years.

**YOU SHOULD KNOW:**
The national park is part of Project Eden, a state government initiative to re-establish native wildlife species by eradicating feral and imported animals such as cats and foxes.

*Tyre tracks in the red sand of a road which cuts through the flat scrubland of the Peron Peninsula.*

# Kalbarri National Park

Rock formations and colours are the main attractions of Kalbarri National Park which lies on Australia's west coast some 600 km (375 mi) north of Perth. The striking landscapes are the result of geological processes over millions of years, during which the terrain has been shaped by deposits of deep, horizontal bands of multi-coloured sands. The centrepiece of the park is the Murchison River which flows out into the Indian Ocean where the small coastal resort of Kalbarri is now located. The spectacular red-and-white banded gorges which the river has carved out of the rock as it winds its serpentine way to the sea are definitely not to be missed. They are best seen from two sites on the upper Murchison, reached by a turning off the Ajana road east of Kalbarri. The cliff top of Z Bend offers the most dramatic viewpoint where you can gaze down to the river far below; you can also walk around the Loop, a wide horseshoe bend in the river, in two to three hours, depending on how many times you are tempted by swimming spots (best to do the walk in the early morning). On the way you will come across a natural rock arch known as Nature's Window.

Still within the park, there are similarly spectacular cliffs along the coast south of Kalbarri town. Tidal inlets and creeks have created a series of coastal gorges which you can enjoy at sites with evocative names like Rainbow Valley, Mushroom Rock and Red Bluff. The view out to the ocean from the cliffs above the Natural Bridge will make you feel very small. A demanding but rewarding coastal trail connects Natural Bridge with Eagle Gorge, 8 km (5 mi) away.

*Rugged cliffs along the Indian Ocean south of Kalbarri.*

# Ningaloo Reef

*Spangled emperor fish*

For those in the know, Ningaloo Reef on Australia's northwestern coast surpasses the Great Barrier Reef itself. It cannot, of course, compete in terms of sheer scale and variety but Ningaloo has so far managed to escape the worst effects of mass tourism and the other commercial pressures which bedevil its renowned eastern counterpart. The country's largest fringing coral reef, Ningaloo harbours a marine environment of global importance; its entire 300-km (186-mi) length is now protected as a marine park. Proximity to the continental shelf is what gives the reef its stunning diversity of marine life. With some 250 different types of coral and over 500 species of fish recorded, the reef is a diver's paradise, although it also provides exceptional scope for ordinary snorkellers owing to the fact that, in contrast to the Barrier Reef, it lies so close to the coast. Indeed, Ningaloo is the world's only large reef found so close to a continental land mass. Never more than 7 km (4 mi) from the coastline, in some places it is barely 100 m (330 ft) offshore; from the beach at Coral Bay, for example, you can clearly see the white swell breaking over the reef.

If you can tear yourself away from the enchanting world beneath the waves, the North West Cape headland affords a suitably stark contrast. An elevated range with weathered limestone plateaus forms the spine of the peninsula, extending all the way to North West Cape from where there are fine views of the Muiron Islands. The Cape Range National Park covers 506 sq km (195 sq mi) in the northwest of the peninsula. Its arid, exposed terrain is criss-crossed by deep rocky gorges, such as those at Mandu Mandu and Yardie Creek, where you should look out for rock wallabies.

**HOW TO GET THERE:**
Coral Bay is 227 km (140 mi) north of Carnarvon by road. Exmouth, the main town on the peninsula and the principal base for boat tours to the reef, is a further 129 km (80 mi).
**WHEN TO GO:**
April to September
**DON'T MISS:**
In April and May many people come to Ningaloo for the awesome experience of swimming with the world's largest fish, the whale shark. It is a justly popular activity and you should be prepared to pay for the privilege.
**YOU SHOULD KNOW:**
If you have a 4x4 and the tides are in your favour it is possible to drive the entire way south along the beach from Cape Range National Park to Coral Bay.

*A rock formation at sunrise in
Purnululu National Park*

# Purnululu National Park

One of the most extraordinary natural sights in a region full of scenic wonders, Purnululu National Park is much better known as the Bungle Bungles. This mighty sandstone massif (*purnululu* means sandstone in the local tribal language) burst on to the world stage as recently as the early 1980s; until then, its remote location had ensured it was known only to the nomadic Aboriginal peoples whose ancestral land this was and to the odd cattle drover and pilots of the outback. Nowadays this landscape of hundreds of weather-beaten rock domes is a standard feature of Australian tourist brochures, as iconic an image of the country as Uluru.

The terrain is the result of millions of years of erosion and uplift, in the course of which the soft sandstone has worn away to form these curious beehive shapes. But it is not only the shapes that are unusual; the colouring of the rocks is equally remarkable. It is now thought that sediments from two different sources were deposited in alternating strata to create the orange-and-black banding which is such a distinctive feature of the domes. The colouration is caused by the different minerals present: iron and manganese in the case of the orange, while the darker bands are composed of more permeable material where water has supported algal growth.

Spectacular as the stripes appear, they are in fact a fragile crust over a soft and powdery interior that is all too easily eroded. The best way to appreciate the contours of this exceptional landscape is from the air. If you want to reduce your carbon footprint (although probably not by much), the alternative is to take a 4x4 into the park to explore stunning features like Echidna Chasm and Cathedral Gorge.

**HOW TO GET THERE:**
The ranger station at Three Ways is 53 km (33 mi) east of the Great Northern Highway on a dirt road (4x4s only). The driving time is four hours from Halls Creek to the south and five hours from Kununurra to the north.
**WHEN TO GO:**
April to December (but note that it is always hot here).
**DON'T MISS:**
The awe-inspiring walk along Cathedral Gorge with its ever-narrowing ravine and sheer, towering cliffs.
**YOU SHOULD KNOW:**
There is some dispute over the origin of the name Bungle Bungles; it derives either from the corruption of an Aboriginal name for the area or from a misspelling of one of the grasses commonly found here, bundle bundle grass.

# Watarrka National Park

Deep in the Red Centre of Australia the Watarrka National Park is as rugged and isolated a location as you could wish for from the Outback. It comes as a surprise, then, to discover just what a range of environments the park encompasses; as well as the expected desert plains and rocky spurs, you also find plateaus, gorges, red sandhills covered with desert oaks and spinifex, and hidden springs with delicate ferns and cycads growing in profusion around them. It is a surprise, too, to learn that the park is home to more than 600 different types of plant; its name, indeed, refers to the unmistakable umbrella bush which is a common feature of the area.

Watarrka National Park includes the western end of the George Gill Range, itself an extension of the MacDonnell Ranges that frame Alice Springs. At its heart lies Kings Canyon, the natural feature that most people come to Watarrka to see. The sight of the canyon's sheer sandstone walls, rising to 100 m (330 ft) in places, is breathtaking, especially in the early morning sunlight. This is definitely the best time to undertake the 6-km (3.75-mi) walk around the canyon rim, before the day's temperatures become too punishing. The route takes you through a curious maze of little sandstone domes – miniature Bungles – and past a lookout offering a fine view of the imposing southern wall. At the head of the canyon, and roughly halfway along the walk, a surprise awaits you: a sheltered chasm filled with palms and ferns. This haven of greenery is known as the Garden of Eden and it comes complete with a shady pool where you can take a refreshing dip.

**HOW TO GET THERE:**
Watarrka is 450 km (280 mi) southwest of Alice Springs on sealed roads, so it is accessible in a conventional vehicle.
**WHEN TO GO:**
April to September
**DON'T MISS:**
The play of early morning sunlight on the red rocks and cliff faces.
**YOU SHOULD KNOW:**
Bernadette achieved her ambition of standing on the rim of Kings Canyon in all her finery for the closing scene of the cult film *The Adventures of Priscilla, Queen of the Desert.*

*The magnificent Kings Canyon*

# Cobourg Peninsula

Places don't come much more remote than the Cobourg Peninsula on Australia's northern coast, which juts out into the Arafura Sea northeast of Darwin. Although it is possible to fly in or to reach it by boat (two days sailing from Darwin), the biggest adventure is certainly the overland one which involves an epic 4x4 journey across Kakadu and Arnhem Land. Arnhem Land is a huge wilderness that has remained in Aboriginal hands; access by non-indigenous visitors is carefully managed. A limited number of vehicles is permitted to cross Aboriginal land and no overnight stops are allowed. Camping is possible, however, within the bounds of the Garig Gunak Barlu National Park which covers the entire peninsula. The land area of 2,200 sq km (850 sq mi) is more than doubled by the surrounding waters of Van Diemen Gulf and the Arafura Sea, along with neighbouring islands, which form a marine reserve; extensive coral reefs and seagrass meadows support a rich array of marine life.

The Cobourg Peninsula is a wild and beautiful mosaic of coastal grasslands, dunes, beaches, mangrove swamps, lagoons and patches of rainforest. The ranger station on Smith Point is the base for a visit to the park, although since there aren't any tracks other than the main access route you might as well relax and make the most of the magnificent white sand beaches. There are good birdwatching opportunities, too, as this is an important habitat for waterfowl and migratory birds. If you absolutely have to go on an expedition, then the ruins of Victoria Settlement, a failed attempt in the 1840s to establish a British colony and trading post, await exploration; as they lie on the other side of the Port Essington inlet, however, you need a boat to reach them.

*Surf washes onto a rocky beach along the Cobourg Peninsula.*

# Elsey National Park

The Roper River is one of the principal rivers of the area around Darwin, popularly known as the Top End. Flowing into the Gulf of Carpentaria to the east, the river is a green lung in the arid plains and grasslands south of Katherine. Its upper reaches are protected within the Elsey National Park, which also includes a number of springs that feed the river. During the dry season the Roper presents a picture of calm serenity as it courses its gentle way through large waterholes and over rocks and tufa dams. In the wet season, however, it is an entirely different proposition and you would be hard pushed to believe the raging torrent before you was the same river.

*The Roper River - a picture of serenity during the dry season*

This is a world which encourages a slower, simpler way of life. Fishing and canoeing are popular activities here, as is swimming, although as with anywhere in the Top End you should heed local advice about where it is safe to enter the water. Cruises along the Roper River are the best way of appreciating the scenery, taking you into an extensive area of freshwater wetlands like the beautiful Red Lily Lagoon. If you prefer to stay on dry land, however, there are numerous trails – including an 8-km (5-mi) return walk beside the river to the Mataranka Falls where you can cool off in the gentle rapids.

A different bathing experience is offered by the thermal pool at the western end of the park. The natural springs at Rainbow Spring pump crystal-clear water into a large pool at a constant 34°C (93.2°F). Fringed by shady palms and set within a patch of rainforest, it is a great place to unwind after a day on the road.

**HOW TO GET THERE:**
The turn-off to Elsey National Park is a short distance south of Mataranka on the Stuart Highway. Mataranka is 103 km (64 mi) south of Katherine.
**WHEN TO GO:**
April to October (during the dry season)
**DON'T MISS:**
An old wartime Aboriginal army camp is an intriguing historical relic within the park.
**YOU SHOULD KNOW:**
This area was the setting for a famous Australian book, *We of the Never Never*, Jeanie Gunn's classic 1908 tale of the spirit of the pioneering outback.

*Kakadu is Australia's greatest national park.*

# Kakadu

**HOW TO GET THERE:**
The western boundary of Kakadu National Park is 150 km (93 mi) east of Darwin. From there it is a further 100 km (62 mi) to the park headquarters at Jabiru. You can also enter Kakadu from the south by turning off the Stuart Highway at Pine Creek.

**WHEN TO GO:**
Any time of year. Most visitors arrive during the dry season months of May to August when the temperatures are at their most tolerable; but connoisseurs reckon the true spirit of the place is revealed only in the wet season, when nature bursts forth in all its verdant profusion.

**DON'T MISS:**
A boat trip on the Yellow Water billabong, preferably in the early morning or late afternoon. These wetlands provide exceptional opportunities for spotting wildlife.

**YOU SHOULD KNOW:**
After a period when they were abolished to counteract a decline in visitor numbers, entrance fees for the park have now been re-introduced. A pass gives you access for 14 days.

Everything about Kakadu draws you to superlatives. The facts about Australia's greatest national park are staggering for a start: an area the size of Wales – nearly 20,000 sq km (7,720 sq mi); more different reptile species than are found in the whole of Europe; five out of the world's seven types of turtle; one third of the entire bird species of Australia; over 5,000 rock-art sites. It can all seem rather overwhelming on a first visit, and you wonder whether it is possible ever to get the full measure of the park. The truth is, the most you can hope for is a flavour of this extraordinary place, but what a flavour it is! A huge variety of land forms and habitats are featured in Kakadu, an area large enough to encompass the entire catchment area of a river. As the South Alligator River flows north into Van Diemen Gulf, the landscape changes from sandstone plateaus and heathlands in the south through savannah woodlands and paperbark swamps to the coastal belt, which is made up of tidal wetlands and mangrove forests. Presiding over all is the imposing Arnhem escarpment running down the eastern side of the park.

Kakadu is jointly managed by the Australian government and the local Aboriginal groups who still live in the park and are the traditional owners of the land, much of which remains sacred to them and is consequently inaccessible to the casual visitor. Other sites are only for serious off-road types; at certain times of the year they are not even reached by 4x4s. Places which everyone can get to on sealed roads include the incredible sites at Ubirr and Nourlangie, outdoor galleries of rock art depicting animals, birds, humans and ancestral spirits in paintings, some of which are 20,000 years old.

# Kata Tjuta

The stunning assemblage of giant sandstone rocks known as Kata Tjuta in central Australia would be a major destination in its own right were it not for the fact of its world-famous neighbour down the road, mighty Uluru. As it is, the Olgas, as they were formerly known by early European explorers, seem happy enough to cede star billing to the monolith that has become for many people the defining image of the country. But it would be a pity if, having made it all this way to visit 'the Rock', you didn't also allow yourself the time to explore the Olgas as well.

The two natural wonders are just 50 km (31 mi) apart and are both contained within the same national park, which is managed jointly by the local Aboriginal community, who own the land, and the federal government. *Kata tjuta* means 'many heads' in the Aboriginal language, an entirely apt description for this cluster of 36 domed rocks divided by narrow chasms and broader valleys. Whether or not you climb Uluru is a controversial subject these days, but there is no such dilemma here as you are not allowed to climb on the Kata Tjuta rocks. Their smooth, rounded tops may look inviting but the sheer sides of many of the rocks make it an unfeasible prospect. The eastern part of the complex is completely off-limits to visitors since this is a sacred site to the Anangu Aborigines under their men's law. You can still get an outstanding impression of the site, though, by doing the Valley of the Winds walk, a 7-km (4.4-mi) loop trail through a desert landscape of sand hills covered in spinifex and small stands of desert oak.

**HOW TO GET THERE:**
Uluru-Kata Tjuta National Park is 440 km (275 mi) southwest of Alice Springs.
**WHEN TO GO:**
May to September (but as this includes the winter months, note that temperatures in the desert can drop significantly at night).
**DON'T MISS:**
The viewing area on the road to Kata Tjuta from Uluru. The profile of the rocks several kilometres to the north looks stunning, especially at sunrise.
**YOU SHOULD KNOW:**
Many people are surprised to learn that the largest of the Kata Tjuta rocks, Mount Olga, is actually 200 m (656 ft) higher than Uluru.

*The giant sandstone rocks of Kata Tjuta*

# Litchfield National Park

A couple of hours' drive south from Darwin brings you to the boundary of Litchfield National Park. Less well known – and at 1,500 sq km (580 sq mi) a lot smaller than its neighbour Kakadu – Litchfield is nevertheless many people's preferred option for a taste of a subtropical wilderness. Its scale is more manageable, and the principal sights are more readily accessible than is the case with Kakadu.

The park encloses much of the Tabletop Range, a rugged sandstone plateau with eroded cliffs which drop away to black-soil plains covered in spear grass. The dominant trees of the forest here are the Darwin woollybutt and the stringybark, while sand palms, acacias and banksias proliferate closer to the ground. Litchfield's most famous features are the waterfalls which tumble off the plateau at various points throughout the park. Often set in pockets of dense rainforest, they come with deep plunge pools at their bases, perfect for a refreshing dip following a walk. Wangi Falls are easily the most popular and can get very crowded. Tjaynera Falls are just as attractive and much quieter, as befits their more isolated location. Tolmer Falls are the most impressive, although you can only view them from the cliffs opposite.

The so-called Lost City is a jumble of sandstone pillars and blocks which in places resemble ruined buildings. Genuine man-made ruins are to be found elsewhere in the park in the form of the remains of an old homestead and of a tin mine which operated here in the 1870s. Billabong cruises on the Reynolds River are a good way of seeing Litchfield's abundant and colourful birdlife.

*Wangi Falls*

# Nitmiluk National Park

*The Katherine Gorge*

The Jawoyn Aboriginal people own Nitmiluk National Park, which is situated near Katherine in the Northern Territory. The visitor centre features informative displays about the park, presented from their perspective. If their many stories and myths can seem a bit bewildering, you should take comfort from the fact that most 'whitefellas' are granted access to only a small part of their Dreamtime cosmology.

The big attraction at Nitmiluk is the Katherine Gorge, where the Katherine River has carved a spectacular 12-km (7.5-mi) course through the Arnhem Land plateau. Although described as 13 separate gorges, which are separated from each other by rapids of varying length (many of which are just rock bars during the dry season), this is really one continuous canyon which turns first this way then that, depending on the prevailing fault lines. The sheer gorge walls may not be especially tall, but when bathed in sunlight their orange hues present a gorgeous spectacle.

The best way to appreciate the gorge is from the water. If you are an intrepid spirit and possess the requisite energy you can explore the gorge under your own power in a canoe. But most visitors take one of the cruises on offer which travel upstream as far as the second, third or sixth gorge, depending on the length of the trip. It's not all plain sailing, though; there are places where you have to disembark for a scramble over rocks in order to board another boat further upriver. Although this sounds like hard work, it actually adds to the sense of adventure and you are given several opportunities to relax with a swim in the mercifully crocodile-free water.

**HOW TO GET THERE:**
The entrance to Nitmiluk is 30 km (19 mi) northeast of Katherine along a sealed road. There is a shuttle bus from the town to the visitor centre.
**WHEN TO GO:**
May to September
**DON'T MISS:**
The cliff-top lookout over the river near the visitor centre. It's a stiff climb but the views are superb.
**YOU SHOULD KNOW:**
In contrast to its neighbour Kakadu, Nitmiluk National Park actively encourages bushwalkers to tackle its range of marked trails.

# Ormiston Gorge

*Early morning in impressive Ormiston Gorge*

The West MacDonnell Ranges in the heart of Australia boast a number of striking gorges and chasms. The deep shadows cast by their towering walls have made them important refuges for a rich variety of flora and fauna, including several relict plant species surviving from an ancient tropical past. Ormiston Gorge is perhaps the most impressive of all. The presence here of a permanent waterhole, up to 14 m (46 ft) deep, has generated a surprising range of habitats in a relatively confined area: slopes covered in spinifex, mulga woodland, rocky plains and stands of lofty red river gums.

If you come here on a tour from Alice you will probably walk up to the Gum Tree lookout which gives a fantastic view of the 250-m (820-ft) high gorge walls soaring over the pools below. But if this is all you do you will miss much of the magic of this spot; far better to come independently and prepared for a longer trek. The Ormiston Pound circular walk is particularly worthwhile. Starting at the information centre the route traverses rocky slopes before crossing the flat expanse of remote Ormiston Pound and returning down the gorge itself and past the waterhole – perfectly placed for a refreshing dip. The best time to do the walk is in the early morning when the sun lights up the mighty cliffs ahead.

The small campground at Ormiston Gorge is a good base for a longer exploration of the western half of the West MacDonnells. From here it is a good day's walk to Bowmans Gap, or two days to Mount Giles. Spending a night on the mountain is recommended for the stunning view at sunrise over Ormiston Pound to Mount Sonder and its surroundings.

**HOW TO GET THERE:**
Ormiston Gorge is 135 km (84 mi) west of Alice Springs.
**WHEN TO GO:**
April to October
**DON'T MISS:**
The unusual plants you can see here, many with exotic names like Maiden Hair Fern and Glory of the Centre Wedding Bush.
**YOU SHOULD KNOW:**
Not far from Ormiston is the bed of the Finke River. Dry for most of the year, the Finke is one of the world's most ancient rivers and is thought to have followed much the same course for the past 100 million years.

# Simpson Desert

It doesn't come much bleaker than the Simpson Desert, 150,000 sq km (58,000 sq mi) of emptiness straddling the borders of the Northern Territory, South Australia and Queensland. Largely devoid of human activity and as inhospitable as it seems, anyone who has spent serious time in a desert will know that appearances are deceptive and that these environments possess a raw beauty all their own. Habitats you might expect to find, such as gibber plains and mulga scrub, are joined by more surprising ones like gidgee woodland and coolabah plains; these support a fragile but profuse ecosystem of some 800 plant species, 180 types of bird and over 90 different reptiles. If you are fortunate enough to visit immediately after a rare rainstorm you will find the Simpson transformed by carpets of wild flowers which emerge for a brief moment in the sun.

The reason most people come to the Simpson Desert, however, is the sand dunes; rows upon rows of them stretching to the horizon. The Simpson is one of the world's outstanding sand-ridge deserts; the dunes run parallel to one another in a direction dictated by prevailing winds. Crossing the Simpson Desert is one of the outback's great adventures but it is strictly for the experienced and well-equipped 4x4 traveller. The most direct route, the so-called French Line, is also the toughest since it strikes straight across the dunes in a punishing succession of climbs and descents, some as high as 40 m (130 ft).

You do not have to be an adrenalin junkie, though, to get a taste of the Simpson's endless expanses. There are 4x4 day tours from Alice Springs that follow the line of the original Ghan railway, taking you deep into the desert to sights like Rainbow Valley and the mighty sandstone column of Chambers Pillar.

**HOW TO GET THERE:**
Chambers Pillar, the furthest point of most day tours to the Simpson Desert, is 165 km (103 mi) south of Alice Springs.
**WHEN TO GO:**
April to September
**DON'T MISS:**
Don't be too surprised to see camels in the desert. They are the wild descendants of the original beasts brought here by Afghan cameleers before the Ghan railway reached Alice in 1928.
**YOU SHOULD KNOW:**
Most people crossing the Simpson on one of the long-distance tracks do so from west to east because the dunes' eastern slopes are steeper and therefore a tougher climb.

*Sand dunes in Simpson Desert*

# Mount Remarkable National Park

**HOW TO GET THERE:**
Drive 45 km (28 mi) north of Port Pirie on Highway 1, then on to park headquarters at Mambray Creek – which is another 5 km (3 mi). The picturesque 13-km (8-mi) drive to Alligator Gorge is from Main Road North, just south of Wilmington. Hiking access to the park is from these two locations and also Melrose at the foot of Mount Remarkable itself.

**WHEN TO GO:**
Autumn to spring is the preferred time, when vegetation thrives, wildlife is active and the weather is mild. Reflecting this fact, bush camping is permitted from May to October only. Summer visits require serious preparation as the heat can be searing.

**DON'T MISS:**
The park's beautifully marked yellow-footed wallabies. After being hunted to near extinction for its fur, this delightful rock-hopper is still around – although in nothing like former numbers. They may be seen here because the park runs a conservation programme.

**YOU SHOULD KNOW:**
There is vehicle-based camping at Mambray Creek with facilities such as a water supply, flushing toilets, solar-heated showers and communal fireplaces (firewood supplied). Bush camping is restricted to 11 designated sites within the park. The Mambray Creek Cabin and lodge at Alligator Gorge must be booked in advance.

In the Southern Flinders Ranges, not far from Adelaide and South Australia's better-populated areas, the opportunity to explore a true wilderness awaits. Mount Remarkable National Park – named after the 960-m (3,150-ft) summit of the same name – offers splendid scenery in diverse terrain that stretches up from coastal plains west of the Flinders Ranges to foothills above the town of Wilmington.

The park is at the intersection of South Australia's two ecosystems – arid north and wetter south – making for interesting combinations of flora and fauna. Native vegetation includes assorted woodland containing trees such as eucalyptus, northern cypress pine, acacia, peppermint box, sugar gum and blue gum. Imposing river red gums line watercourses and there's a brilliant display of wildflowers in springtime. A diversity of wildlife ranges from kangaroos through over 100 bird species to numerous amphibians and reptiles such as the rare carpet python.

The variety of animals and plants adds interest to a rugged landscape that's a star in its own right. The eroded sandstone Mount Remarkable range dominates the park's eastern side. This massive hogsback has impressive outcrops, like Cathedral Rock, with vertical rock faces. To the west, the Alligator Syncline features Mount Cavern and Alligator Gorge. The latter is the top natural attraction in the South Flinders Ranges – a spectacular gorge between ragged quartzite walls, cut over countless millennia by Alligator Creek. The gorge floor is reached by steps and it's possible to go north to the rippled terraces of a fossilized lakeshore or south between red walls along creek banks green with moss gardens.

Mount Remarkable National Park has numerous hiking trails. These escalate from good short walks at Alligator Gorge and Melrose to the challenging long-distance Heysen Trail. Car parks at Mambray Creek and Blue Gum Flat near Alligator Gorge have excellent facilities, including trailheads.

# Black Mountain (Kalkajaka) National Park

The name of this interesting national park on Cape York Peninsula in the remote far north of Queensland includes the bracketed Aboriginal name because the area is an important part of the indigenous Kuku Nyungkal people's culture – *kalkajaka* translating

*Granite boulders covered in moss, algae and lichen*

**HOW TO GET THERE:**
Start from Cooktown, serviced by two daily flights from Cairns. For old-fashioned outbackers, the park's entrance is 25 km (15 mi) to the south of Cooktown along the primitive but ambitiously named Cooktown Developmental Road. In fact, since 2006, a genuine modern development – the paved Mulligan Highway from Mareeba to Cooktown – has provided easier access.

**WHEN TO GO:**
Any time. The tropical climate can be hot, wet and humid but the coolest, driest months are June to September.

**DON'T MISS:**
The James Cook Museum in eponymous Cooktown, where the great explorer arrived as a lieutenant in command of *His Majesty's Bark the Endeavour* in 1770, steering his crippled ship into what became Cooktown Harbour at the mouth of the Endeavour River, to effect repairs after striking a reef. Housed in a grand former convent, it's rated as Australia's finest provincial museum. It has the anchor and cannon of *Endeavour* along with wide-ranging indigenous, pastoral and mining displays – plus a tribute to the Chinese immigrants who played an important role in the development of Cooktown back in Victorian gold-rush days.

**YOU SHOULD KNOW:**
Serious hikers take note – Cooktown is the northern trailhead for the Bicentennial Heritage Trail. It's as well to make an early start, because the southern terminus is 5,330 km (3,310 mi) away in Healesville, not far from Melbourne. This is the world's longest such trail, running the length of the Great Dividing Range and following old stock routes, wagon roads, river banks and fire trails through Queensland, New South Wales and Victoria. Originally intended for horse riders, it is now tempting hardy walkers and mountain-bikers in whole or part (mostly part!).

as 'spear place'. The prosaic English description is more explicit as the park features an imposing mountain range that appears to be, well, black. In fact, that should read blue-green, because the jumbled pile of massive granite blocks is covered with a film of algae that absorbs light and looks darker than it is from afar. That said, contrasting white patches stand out vividly from their surroundings where boulders have fractured (sometimes explosively) as a result of erosion exacerbated by extreme heat. A few patches of stubborn greenery also intrude on the rocky slopes.

The park is at the top of the UNESCO Wet Tropics of Queensland World Heritage Site in northeastern Queensland's section of the Great Dividing Range, where it meets drier savannah woodlands. The resulting 'Black Mountain' environment has a unique combination of flora and fauna, supporting at least three species – the rock-haunting frog, Black-Mountain gecko and Black-Mountain skink – found nowhere else in Australia. Other interesting creatures include ghost bats and Godman's rock wallabies.

There are excellent observation points for those who simply want to stroll and look (binoculars essential), but anyone getting in among the park's intriguing landscape of monolithic boulders – many the size of houses and stacked in a way that apparently defies gravity – should take sensible backcountry precautions. There are age-old Aboriginal legends and a number of sacred sites, but white incomers soon added their own tales of horses, cattle and even prospectors who entered the Black Mountains in the 19th century . . . never to be seen again.

# Carnarvon Gorge

**HOW TO GET THERE:**
Drive from Brisbane to Roma – 400 km (250 mi). Proceed via Injune in the direction of Emerald until reaching the signed Carnarvon Gorge turn-off – another 200 km (125 mi). Then it's another 20 km (12 mi) along an unpaved road to the gorge itself, which may become impassable after heavy rain. Nobody said it was easy!

**WHEN TO GO:**
Whenever. The coolest months are April to October. The driest months are July, August and September. February is the wettest month but the climate can be unpredictable at any time of year.

**DON'T MISS:**
The Amphitheatre, behind the ancient rock wall of Carnarvon Gorge. Entered through a narrow vertical crack, this incredible crevice can only be described as awe-inspiring – and anyone who raises their voice will find that it has the most amazing acoustics, too.

**YOU SHOULD KNOW:**
Visitors are forbidden to feed the birds, although many ignore this regulation. As a result, bold and opportunistic species such as the laughing kookaburra and pied currawong have become proficient scroungers and developed unnaturally large populations at the expense of less brazen birds, also consuming more than their fair share of natural food resources. Resist their determined advances!

*Carnarvon Gorge*

In southern-central Queensland, Carnarvon Gorge is the centrepiece of the national park that bears its name. Hidden in rugged uplands of the Great Dividing Range, this 2,900-sq-km (1,120-sq-mi) preserve not only encompasses the mountains but also the inaccessible and heavily vegetated Consuelo Tableland. This is a place where truly awesome landscape vistas roll away in every direction, although most visitors hurry to the enclosed world of Carnarvon Gorge – and what a wonderful world it is for those sufficiently determined to get there. This requires effort (see left) but around 65,000 people make the pilgrimage every year and are well rewarded.

The gorge is 30 km (19 mi) long and 600 m (2,000 ft) deep at the mouth, carved into sandstone by the passage of water and time. Most visitors get no further than the first 10 km (6 mi), as this stretch offers a wonderful variety of natural and cultural features that would require weeks of extended travel and exploration to experience anywhere else in the state, if they could be found at all. The main trail follows the limpid creek where platypus may be seen diving into pools, while an extensive network of graded side trails perambulates through tall eucalyptus trees and lush greenery that includes palms and giant ferns. Side gorges and waterfalls abound, offering exciting voyages of discovery. More remote tracks, including Devil's Signpost and Battleship Spur, are for experienced hikers only.

Carnarvon Gorge is alive with birds – 180 species from the tiny weebill to the mighty wedge-tailed eagle – and home to a fascinating range of animals. To the natural sights and sounds may be added appreciation of the spiritual ambiance of the gorge, as expressed in sacred places such as Cathedral Cave and Art Gallery, where Aboriginal rock art may be seen.

# Great Barrier Reef

*Great Barrier Reef, Queensland*

It's a UNESCO World Heritage Site and has been voted one of the seven natural wonders of the world. Queensland's Great Barrier Reef in the appropriately named Coral Sea is in fact a conglomeration of nearly 3,000 individual reefs and 900 islands stretching for more than 2,600 km (1,600 mi), covering an area of around 345,000 sq km (133,200 sq mi). Bramble Cay, at the top end of the reef in the Torres Straits, is the northernmost point of land in Australia. The reef's southern extremity is Lady Elliot Island, off the city of Bundaberg, around halfway down Australia's east coast.

This vast natural treasure house supports a huge variety of life, too numerous to list in detail but including headliners like whales, dolphins, porpoises, dugongs, sea turtles, sharks, stingrays, seahorses and over 1,500 fish species, plus 200 types of bird that visit or breed on the reef's islands. The majority of the reef is protected by the Great Barrier Reef Marine Park, which seeks to ensure that human intrusion becomes neither excessive nor damaging. Even so, tourism is of major importance to the local economy, with a large number of visitors drawn to the Queensland coast by the opportunity to experience a little piece of this magical marine masterpiece.

Many of them holiday at eco-resorts on reef islands – around 30 cays now have such facilities – while others come simply to look and marvel. The ways of so doing are many and varied, ranging from boat trips in regular or glass-bottomed boats to helicopter overflights, day trips or longer cruises. There are even underwater observatories. But the most popular activity by far is getting up close and personal by snorkelling or scuba diving, often from live-aboard dive boats. Although tourism is economically vital, it is carefully policed to protect the reef for posterity.

**HOW TO GET THERE:**
Bundaberg rejoices in the title 'Gateway to the Great Barrier Reef' and is an excellent base for offshore exploration. The Whitsunday Islands are another major tourist centre, as is Cairns in Far North Queensland.

**WHEN TO GO:**
The reef is an all-season destination, with winter seeing the most visitors. June to September are the driest months, October to March the hottest.

**DON'T MISS:**
The Mon Repos Conservation Park on the mainland near Bundaberg, which has the largest concentration of nesting marine turtles in eastern Australia, including the most important nesting population of loggerheads. Laying season is November to March, but the best period to observe nesting turtles on the beach is from mid November to February. Hatchlings emerge and head for the sea between mid January and late March.

**YOU SHOULD KNOW:**
It's not only man-made climate change and pollution that is threatening the Great Barrier Reef – nature poses a threat too, as periodic upsurges in the population of crown-of-thorns starfish pose a constant threat to the reef's wellbeing. These spiny sea stars prey on the coral polyps that form the living reef and a single starfish can destroy 6 sq m (65 sq ft) of coral in a year.

# Kanangra-Boyd National Park

The extensive Blue Mountains Wilderness is west of Sydney. Some
of the most inaccessible terrain in this wilderness – and New South
Wales – can be found in Kanangra-Boyd National Park. The scenic
park provides almost limitless potential for those self-reliant souls
who love solitude to indulge their passion for lonesome wild places.

It has two sections. The gently undulating Boyd Plateau is
relatively accessible, has stunning views and offers everything from
gentle strolls to stimulating day hikes. An unmade road leads to a
campsite at Boyd River and on to the Kanangra Walls area. These
are ideal bases for bushwalking or simply enjoying stunning distant
views from the rim of the plateau. Some of those views roll away
across the labyrinthine Kanangra wilderness area, a broken jumble
of thickly vegetated valleys, overgrown streams and sandstone cliffs
that stretches for 60 km (37 mi). This empty backcountry should be
tackled only by the most experienced and self-reliant of
bushwalkers – ideally those also possessing climbing skills.

The park's best-known features are Kanangra Walls –
spectacular orange-and-grey sandstone cliffs that tower above the
shadowed Kanangra Creek Gorge below – and the 225-m (740-ft)
Kanangra Falls, a scenic cascade that spills down an angled rock
face. The car park at Kanangra Walls is the starting point for most
of the park's established walks, including the wheelchair-friendly
path to the first lookout or a stroll down to the nearby falls. The
established Plateau Walk is longer, delivering awesome views of
Kanangra Walls, Falls and surrounding cliffs. Longer hikes lead out
along the Gangerang Range to Mount Cloudmaker and on as far as
Kaloomba, or south to the Gingra Range and thence to the
Kowmung River. It's all wild and wonderful, and the views alone are
worth the effort needed to reach this remote place.

**YOU SHOULD KNOW:**
The Kanangra wilderness area
should not be tackled lightly. In 2000
two experienced leaders of a
university mountaineering club on a
canyoning expedition died of
hypothermia, and it took the seven
survivors three days to walk and
climb out of the wilderness.

*A lookout point offers
spectacular views over
Kanangra-Boyd National Park.*

*Washpool's rainforest is both varied and original.*

# Washpool National Park

This is the destination *par excellence* for wilderness walkers who like hugging trees, serving as a happy reminder that the interior of Australia may be relatively empty but it's definitely not all arid desert. Washpool National Park in Australia's New England protects some of the most varied and original rainforest in New South Wales, including now-rare Australian red cedars and (wait for it!) the world's largest stand of coachwood trees.

The park was established in 1983 and is an important part of the UNESCO Gondwana Rainforests of Australia World Heritage Site, which underlines the ecological importance of this unique area with its lush flora and interesting fauna. A dramatic landscape of steep gorges, broad ridges, pristine waters and forested escarpments is a haven for threatened animals like the koala, parma wallaby and spotted-tailed quoll, a beautiful cat-like marsupial. It is also a rich habitat for birds, with nearly 150 different species recorded in this unspoilt 650-sq-km (250-sq-mi) reserve.

Washpool National Park offers walking trails to suit every level of fitness and ability, including some limited wheelchair access on short sections of surfaced tracks from the car parks. But the park's true beauty can only be appreciated fully by those willing to venture away from the immediate environs of the highway. The four-hour Washpool Walk regularly features towards the top of lists nominating this wild-at-heart continent's best short wilderness hikes. This inspiring trek takes visitors along twisting paths beside

**HOW TO GET THERE:**
Washpool is 75 km (47 mi) northeast of Glen Innes and 90 km (56 mi) west of Grafton. It is 500 km (310 mi) north of Sydney. Access is from the Gwydir Highway, taking Coachwood Drive via Gibraltar Range National Park, itself a distracting alternative.

**WHEN TO GO:**
Whenever – there is no worst time.

**DON'T MISS:**
The Coombadjha Nature Stroll, linking the picnic areas and campsite of the same name (see below). The track along Coombadjha Creek has signs that provide an informative introduction to the park's features – and there's a delightful shallow pool where swimming is allowed.

rushing boulder-filled streams and through awesome rainforest beneath canopies of tree ferns, accompanied by the distinctive call of bellbirds. For the serious backpacker, the Gibraltar-Washpool World Heritage Walk encompasses an 80-km (50-mi) network of hiking tracks that can occupy up to five days of rewarding exploration in rugged mountain country above the Clarence River Valley on the edge of the Northern Tablelands. Despite difficult terrain – ridges, tors, dry and wet forest, streams and wild rivers, waterfalls and swamps – this walk can be tackled by anyone who is reasonably fit.

**YOU SHOULD KNOW:**
Two campgrounds serve as basecamps for those undertaking extensive exploration. They are at Coombadjha and Bellbird. The former is at the end of the aforementioned Coachwood Drive and features the beautiful Washpool Walk, a signed 8-km (5-mi) round trip through rainforest. Bellbird is on Coombadjha Road off the Gwydir Highway. Both have basic facilities, including bring-your-own-firewood barbecues.

# Yengo Wilderness

As part of the Greater Blue Mountains World Heritage Site, the newly established Yengo National Park stretches for over 70 km (45 mi) from Wisemans Ferry to the Hunter Valley, much of it remote wilderness characterized by predominantly sandstone gorges and rocky ridges. The park is rich in cultural heritage and Mount Yengo, in particular, is sacred to local Aboriginal communities who co-manage the park. The area is still criss-crossed with their traditional routes, established over thousands of years. The Finchley Cultural Walk from Finchley campgrounds leads to an Aboriginal engraving site and has explanatory signs.

The habitat is mainly eucalypt forest – dry on ridge tops and northern slopes, wet in gullies and on southern slopes. There are smaller areas of wet and dry rainforest and some open woodland. Wildlife to watch out for includes koalas, wombats, gliding possums, geckoes and endangered brush-tailed rock-wallabies. A disparate assortment of over 150 bird species has been recorded, including wedge-tailed eagles, masked owls, rare regent honeyeaters, lyre birds and black cockatoos.

Numerous opportunities for short walks exist and there are overnight hiking routes for experienced walkers. Scenic car tours for those disinclined to go afoot, such as the Finchley-Yango-Boree loop that starts near Laguna and gives an excellent overview of the dry sandstone terrain, are well worthwhile. Another scenic drive goes from St Albans via Mogo Creek Road to Bucketty, taking in extensive wetlands and historic Deans Quarry, plus the pleasant must-stop-for-lunch Mogo Creek Picnic Area. Tough types can do the 4x4/trailbike/mountain-bike Big Yango Loop Trail that circles Mount Yengo, with great views over the wilderness area, or tackle the Howes-Yango Trail across the northern section of the park – a five-hour return trip driving a sturdy 4x4. A number of the park's unmade roads are open to vehicle traffic.

**HOW TO GET THERE:**
From Sydney drive via Wisemans Ferry and the historic township of St Albans to Mogo Campground and Bucketty. For the Big Yango/Finchley area use the F3, take the Peats Ridge exit and go through Central Mangrove and Bucketty to find Yango Creek Road. From Newcastle drive via Cessnock to Bucketty and Mogo Campground, or for the Big Yango/Finchley area take the Wollombi Road from Cessnock.

**WHEN TO GO:**
Take your pick – summers are very hot, winters are cooler. The heaviest rainfall occurs between December and January.

**DON'T MISS:**
The awesome vista to Mount Yengo across an expanse of eucalypt dry forest from Finchley Lookout, which has information boards explaining surrounding landforms and much more besides. The lookout is reached from Yango Creek Road, off George Downs Drive near Laguna township.

**YOU SHOULD KNOW:**
The historic Old Great North Road is a hugely impressive example of 19th-century convict road building that follows the park's southeastern boundary. Note, especially, the sturdy stone remains of the historic Circuit Flat Bridge dating from 1831, which remained in use until the 1930s but has now lost its timber roadway. Ironically, conservation work was done on the bridge in the 1990s by a prison crew from St Heliers Correctional Centre in the Hunter Valley.

# Murray-Sunset National Park

**HOW TO GET THERE:**
Those starting from Melbourne or Adelaide are in for a long drive. Once in northwest Victoria the park can be approached from Red Cliffs, Mildura and Renmark in the north or Murrayville and Ouyen in the south. The Sturt Highway passes through the park's northern section but the remainder is remote wilderness bounded to the south by the Mallee Highway and to the west by the Calder Highway.

**WHEN TO GO:**
Summer temperatures are very high and anyone bold enough to think of going during the scorching months may find the park has been closed for safety reasons, should a Code Red (Catastrophic) Fire Danger Rating be in force.

Close to South Australia and New South Wales in northwestern Victoria is the state's second-largest national park. This protects one of the last semi-arid regions in Australia that has almost (but not entirely) escaped human interference – there was once a salt production industry and residual evidence of gypsum mining remains. But that's a pinprick set against Murray-Sunset National Park's impressive 6,300-sq-km (2,430-sq-mi) expanse of untouched wilderness. The flattish landscape is filled with grasslands, mallee eucalypts, porcupine grass, saltbush and buloke, broken by stands of native cypress-pine and belah woodlands. River red gums line creeks and black boxwoods surround flood plains. The park has four salt lakes – the Pink Lakes, so called because of their colour in late summer when they've dried out to leave a crust of carotene-tinted salt.

*The Pink Lakes - so named due to their colour in late summer when they dry out to leave a crust of carotene-tinted salt.*

There are first-class walking trails in the Pink Lakes area, but Murray-Sunset National Park deserves a longer stay. The campground on the shore of Lake Crosbie has good facilities, including a supply of scarce-in-the-park clean drinking water. There are alternative campgrounds at Rocket Lake, Lake Becking, Mount Crozier and Mopoke Hut. Accommodation can also be booked at an old shearer's hut. There are remote campsites with primitive facilities in the wilderness. Those are the very best places to truly appreciate the park's vast isolation and enjoy its wide-open landscapes, incredible sunsets and brilliantly lit starry night skies.

Although vehicles are prohibited in the park's remoter areas and wilderness zones, a number of unmade roads are suitable for road cars – notably the Pink Lakes Track from Linga, Settlement Track along the northern boundary and access roads to Lindsay Island or the Murray River. Beyond that there are numerous routes suitable for exploration with the help of a 4x4. But all tracks are liable to become impassable during or after adverse weather conditions.

**DON'T MISS:**
Red kangaroos. The park is one of the few areas in Victoria where these iconic creatures can be seen in anything like their original numbers.

**YOU SHOULD KNOW:**
Campers should not pitch tents or rest up beneath or near river red gum trees, tempting though the cooling shade they cast along creek banks may be. These mighty trees grow to 45 m (150 ft) in height but they can and do quite often drop heavy branches without warning.

# Wilsons Promontory

*The beautiful coastal wilderness of Wilsons Promontory*

Perhaps appropriately for such a vast and relatively empty continent, the southernmost point on the Australian mainland is the largest remaining coastal wilderness in the state of Victoria. Colloquially known as 'The Prom' by Victorians, Wilsons Promontory is an unspoiled peninsula jutting into the Bass Strait that boasts a stunning 130-km (80-mi) girdle of inspiring coastline consisting of bold granite headlands, tumbled boulders, sheltered coves, intertidal mudflats, dunes, swamps . . . and beautiful beaches. It has been protected since the late 19th century and is now a national park.

One Tidal River is just what the name suggests, swelling with each tide as it discharges into Norman Bay. The river water has a strange purple-yellow colour as a result of tannin emanating from the large number of tea trees in the area. The other Tidal River is the immediately adjacent settlement that serves as a focal point for visitors, not least because it has one of the park's finest sandy beaches. Also, the drive from Yanakie to Tidal River is super-scenic (don't hurry, abundant local wildlife that includes assorted marsupials, kangaroos, wallabies, koalas and emus is liable to stray onto the road).

The park's information centre at Tidal River has a wealth of information on the park's history – from Aboriginal occupation going back at least 6,500 years to the activities of rough-and-ready sealers in the early 19th century – plus general displays on the park's geology, flora and fauna. This is also the place to learn about disabled access to nearby sites such as Squeaky Beach (named for the sound made when tramping the fine white quartz sand) and the Lilly Pilly nature walk. For those adventurers who wish to look beyond Tidal Bay's siren attractions, there are stimulating wilderness hiking trails that require overnight camping.

# Bay of Fires

The wild and wonderful coastline known as the Bay of Fires offers fascinating opportunities to explore an unspoilt wilderness coastline and experience the rich diversity of backing woodlands. The bay is on Tasmania's northeastern coast, extending from Eddystone Point to Binalong Bay. Some falls within Mount William National Park while the rest is a conservation area. This is a place of white beaches that shimmer in the sun, intense blue water and orange-splashed granite (the colour coming from lichen).

The northern section is from Eddystone Point to the Ansons Bay outlet, which cannot be crossed. This is in the national park and can be accessed from Eddystone Road, just before the lighthouse. There's a brisk walk across dunes to the shore and visitors should take all necessary supplies, especially drinking water. This is for day use only but Deep Creek campground is close to Eddystone Point.

The middle section encompasses Ansons Bay and is the destination of choice for those who want to spend time communing with nature. The primitive Policemans Points campground offers numerous sites scattered among the trees, many with direct beach access, but happy campers will become unhappy unless they bring everything necessary for their stay, including a portable loo – there are no on-site toilets, no water nor firewood, no rubbish collection. The southern section stretches from The Gardens to Binalong Bay and has several campsites, but again they offer no facilities other than pitches.

This is an outdoor paradise with activities to match – messing about on beaches, swimming, snorkelling, surfing, fishing, boating, camping, birdwatching and walking. These pleasurable pastimes may be possible in many places, but in the case of the breathtaking Bay of Fires it is not what but where – it's the environment that counts and, for those who crave it, the blessing of solitude is guaranteed.

*Orange lichen gives the rocks their striking colour along the coastline of the Bay of Fires.*

**HOW TO GET THERE:**
Travel north on minor roads (some paved, some not) from St Helens, which is on the A3 Tasman Way between Scottsdale and St Marys.

**WHEN TO GO:**
Tasmania's weather is unpredictable and the climate not only varies in different parts of the island but also from day to day. Winters (May to August) can be quite cool and summers are pleasantly warm with long twilit evenings.

**DON'T MISS:**
The opportunity while on this light-pollution-free island to observe the magnificent *Aurora Australis*, the Southern Lights. It's one of the wonders of the cosmos and, short of travelling to Antarctica, Tasmania is one of the best places in the world from which to view this extraordinary light show. Prime months are April and October but the lights can switch on at any time.

**YOU SHOULD KNOW:**
The Bay of Fires was so named in 1773 by one Tobias Furneaux, a Royal Navy officer who was part of Captain Cook's second expedition and became the first man to circumnavigate the world in both directions. He was also first to chart much of Tasmania and decided to pen 'Bay of Fires' onto his embryonic chart upon observing a large number of Aboriginal fires burning along the shoreline. Aboriginal middens (shell and bone deposits) are found in the dunes and should not be disturbed.

# Ninety Mile Beach

Forget the perennial problem of finding somewhere to lay down that fleecy towel without treading on another sunbather – as the name suggests, Ninety Mile Beach has room for just about everyone in New Zealand, then some. This extraordinary beach is located on the west coast of the North Island's far north Northland, which still makes it quite far south by international standards. A stunning expanse of white sand arches along Aupori Peninsula from just west of Kaitaia, terminating at the rocky headland of Scott Point near Cape Reinga at the northernmost tip of New Zealand.

Ninety Mile Beach faces the Tasman Sea and is backed by dunes up to 6.5 km (4 mi) wide and up to 140 m (460 ft) tall. They are higher at the northern end, where they resemble nothing so much as the Sahara Desert when approached from the landward side. The dunes steadily decrease in height towards the south where they are stabilized by marram grass and lupins, but elsewhere they are bare but for occasional patches of scrub and constantly being reshaped by the wind. This austere 260-sq-km (100-mi-sq) sea of sand is a lonely wilderness that may soon become pine forests.

There are beachside campgrounds and motels at the southern end, but as a whole Ninety Mile Beach is a wild and lonely natural wonder. Getting onto the beach isn't actually that easy, with few access roads. The best way to see it is to drive. Warning signs suggest that Ninety Mile Beach is a potentially hazardous place for anything with four wheels, particularly for a couple of hours either side of high tide, but it was used as a runway for early airmail flights in the 1930s and with reasonable care provides a perfectly usable scenic highway and a wonderful outdoor adventure.

*Ninety Mile Beach*

# Bay of Islands

Close to the northern tip of New Zealand's North Island, in the appropriately named Northland Region, lies the beautiful natural feature that seduced the first European settlers to arrive in the country. Captain Cook named the Bay of Islands after coming upon this natural harbour in 1769. Whalers soon followed, whose profane ways attracted missionaries. The first European child to be born in New Zealand was delivered there in 1815 and the towns around the bay are rich in national heritage sites.

The bay area is as attractive to people today as it was then. This irregular inlet on the northeastern coast is 16 km (10 mi) wide with several arms that extend inland. It is a special destination and its pristine environment attracts plenty of visitors all year round, drawn by wonderful coastal scenery and the opportunity to enjoy a variety of activities from simply romping on white sand beaches to cruising, boating, sailing, sea kayaking, swimming with dolphins and whale-watching. Other popular possibilities are paragliding, jet boating, big-game fishing, scuba diving, snorkelling, cycling, bushwalking, horseback trekking and camping.

But despite the plethora of recreational temptations, the Bay of Islands Marine Park has 144 islands that remain a natural wonderland of native forests, secluded bays and subtropical beaches. This ensures that there are always lonely corners to be found, where those who value solitude can escape the tourist zone. This is particularly true for anyone who goes afloat, exploring the islands until finding a suitably remote spot to land, like an early pioneer stepping ashore for the first time.

In addition to abundant natural charms, the bay is something of a cultural centre, with pleasant towns like Paihia, Russell, Opua, Kerikeri and Waitangi offering craft galleries, museums and heritage trails. There are numerous opportunities to explore Maori culture, too.

**HOW TO GET THERE:**
The bay is around 60 km (37 mi) northwest of Whangarei. Take State Highway 1 to Kawakawa and turn right for Russell. There are daily flights into Bay of Islands Airport at Kerikeri from all major centres in New Zealand.

**WHEN TO GO:**
The bay area often experiences fairly heavy summer rainfall in December. It's best to avoid mid December to early February anyway, as school holidays see a serious influx of camper vans, tourists and noisy children. The winter months (June, July and August) are much quieter and a good bet for those who don't like sharing wild places with too many others.

**DON'T MISS:**
The Mission House (also known as Kemp House) in Kerikeri. This weather-boarded structure with a wraparound veranda is New Zealand's oldest standing building, dating back to 1822.

**YOU SHOULD KNOW:**
The Bay of Islands has the second-bluest sky in the world, second only to the intense dome above the Brazil's Rio de Janeiro, and that's official. This ensures that the bay's waters, too, are a brilliant blue.

*Moturua Island, Bay of Islands*

# Waipoua Forest

Early navigators soon discovered that New Zealand had one priceless asset – kauri trees. These magnificent straight-growing conifers were ideal for the replacement of masts and spars and also – having great rot-resistant properties – hulls and decking. It didn't take long for emergency ship repairs to be replaced by small-scale commercial logging, which became large-scale commercial logging as the new British colony developed during the 19th century. If the forests weren't logged, they were burned by Maoris and settlers to clear land for farming. Serious logging continued right up to the scandalous decision to clear-fell Warawara state forest in the 1960s. Result? Almost all native kauri forests have been lost to the saw or fire, with only around four per cent of the original stock of these noble trees remaining, mostly in small pockets.

Kauri trees are not necessarily the most abundant species in the forests that bear their name but that merely encourages the huge variety of flora that flourishes beneath spreading crowns. The best opportunity to roam original kauri woodlands with their lush undergrowth – and appreciate what so much of New Zealand was once like – is at Waipoua Forest, although happily around three quarters of Warawara to the north survived after logging was stopped in 1972 following a huge public outcry. Together with neighbouring Waima and Mataraua Forests, Waipoua is the largest remaining tract of native forest in the Northland and home to a large population of nocturnal brown kiwi.

A road through the forest passes impressive kauri stands and provides a wonderful feel for the place. Beyond that, there are plenty of established walks and tramping tracks, ranging from short scenic strolls to long hikes that require overnight bush camping. Full details of these may be obtained at the information centre in Dargaville, where the Waipoua Forest Visitor Centre is also located. The Hokianga Visitor Centre in Omapere is also worth a visit.

*Tree ferns grow among the largest remaining stand of mature Kauri forest.*

**HOW TO GET THERE:**
State Highway 12 passes through the middle of Waipoua Forest. It lies to the north of Dargaville and south of Omapere.

**WHEN TO GO:**
This is a relaxing all-season destination.

**DON'T MISS:**
The super bonus of the Kauri Coast. The forest touches the sea but its trees give their name to a much longer stretch of headlands, wild beaches with pounding surf, sculpted sand dunes and imposing stands of kauri trees. It should be explored!

**YOU SHOULD KNOW:**
The country's most famous kauri trees are a major attraction in Waipoua Forest and easily reached from the main road. Tane Mahuta, named after a Maori forest god, is the biggest living kauri. This magnificent tree soars to over 50 m (165 ft) and has a massive girth of nearly 14 m (46 ft). Te Matua Ngahere (Father of the forest) is shorter but fatter, with a girth of 16.5 m (54 ft). A kauri with a circumference of 22 m (72 ft) was felled at Mercury Bay in 1870, ending around 1,500 years of life.

# Coromandel Peninsula

Not far from New Zealand's largest city in distance – but a world apart in terms of both ambiance and population – the happy-go-lucky Coromandel Peninsula is separated from the bustling North-Island metropolis of Auckland by Hauraki Gulf. This sparsely populated spur offers awesome scenery, extending for more than 80 km (50 mi) from its starting point at the Karangahake Gorge, a deep fissure at the southern end of the peninsula's mountainous spine, the Coromandel range.

A world apart, when just 55 km (35 mi) of water separates the two? You bet. Coromandel's inhabitants are concentrated in relatively small settlements, with only Thames having a population of more than 5,000. What's more, these historic communities are clustered along the southwestern and southeastern coasts, with population density decreasing rapidly towards the northern tip of the peninsula. The hilly interior is almost completely undeveloped, with steep slopes largely covered in rainforest. Much of the Coromandel range is protected as a lush forest park, providing a challenging opportunity for adventurous bushwalking. But those who prefer to be beside the sea will be gratified to discover long stretches of dramatic coastline where rocky headlands punctuate deserted beaches, with the added bonus of many scenic offshore islands. One highlight should be digging (and relaxing in) a natural spa bath on aptly named Hot Water Beach.

Either way, ecotourism is the local buzz phrase, and many former residents of Auckland have relocated to the southern end of the Coromandel Peninsula in search of the good life and now commute. Residents and visitors alike revel in open-air activities such as surfing, swimming, diving, fishing, kayaking, boating, windsurfing and horse riding – not to mention enjoying the laid-back café society for which towns like Coromandel have become famous.

**HOW TO GET THERE:**
A good starting point for exploring the peninsula is Thames, which has good road links with Auckland to the north and Tauranga to the south. Thereafter the only roads on offer are State Highways 25 and 25A that loop around the peninsula's shoreline, plus a few minor dead ends and a network of lanes (many unsealed) in the far north. The roads can get busy in summer.

**WHEN TO GO:**
An all-season destination, but lovers of wild places should note that the Coromandel Peninsula gets very busy during long Christmas holidays (to the end of January) when many active Aucklanders take summer vacations in small towns like Whangamata, Whitianga, Pauanui and Matarangi. But even in high season it's not hard to chase solitude on the peninsula.

**DON'T MISS:**
The Cathedral Cove recreational reserve with its famous rock arch (now closed – health and safety rules even in New Zealand). Never mind, this loop walk from the end of Grange Road in Hahei still gives access to Gemstone Bay, Stingray Bay and Cathedral Cove's beautiful sand beach. Here is some of the most spectacular coastal scenery on the North Island.

**YOU SHOULD KNOW:**
The quirky Driving Creek Railway near Coromandel Town in the northwest offers an amazing one-hour return journey through kauri forest via two spirals, three short tunnels and five reversing points up to a mountain-top terminus called – with typical New Zealand humour – the Eyefull Tower. The panoramic view of forested valleys and mountains, coupled with a great outlook over island-studded Hauraki Gulf is pretty special.

*Beautiful Cathedral Cove on the Coromandel Peninsula*

# Waimangu Volcanic Valley

Stand by to be wowed by another world superlative – the globe's youngest geothermal system, the Waimangu Volcanic Valley to the south of Rotorua. As a bonus, the world's largest hot-water spring also awaits (the sizzling Frying Pan) beside the ominously titled Inferno Crater. This protected scenic reserve and wildlife refuge is set in pristine bush country. An extraordinary new landscape was shaped by the eruption of Mount Tarawera in 1886 and the valley now consists of seven craters. Tarawera split in half, opening up a 16-km (10-mi) rift valley and reshaping the landscape into a weird and colourful volcanic wonderland soon to be colonized by verdant vegetation and wildlife, notably wallabies and black swans normally found only in Australia, introduced with help from 19th-century governor and premier of New Zealand, Sir George Grey.

This geothermal masterpiece was named for the Waimangu Geyser, first seen in 1900. It was another top dog, namely the world's most powerful geyser. But four years later it stopped as suddenly as it had started, although not before claiming the lives of two over-curious couples who wanted a closer look and thought they knew better than their guide. It's perfectly possible to make unassisted visits to Waimangu, but local companies offer assorted guided tours for those who prefer not to go it alone.

A paid-for outing usually includes a fascinating cruise on Lake Rotomahana, notable for exotic birdlife and smoking geothermal features of its own. The lake consists of 15 interlinked craters and is the deepest on the North Island. Serious hikers should take the Mount Hazard Trail from the Inferno Crater. This elevated route offers fabulous views down onto the valley floor and across a wider landscape that includes Rainbow Mountain, Mount Tarawera and Lake Rotomahana.

*The steaming Waimangu Volcanic Valley*

# Kahurangi National Park

*Beach at Kohaihai River Mouth*

It's wild, it's new, it's big, it's exciting – it's New Zealand's latest national park, occupying most of the northwestern corner of the South Island. Kahurangi National Park extends to 4,500 sq km (1,740 sq mi) – a vast wilderness area offering a huge variety of landscapes from rocky coastline to wild rivers, glaciated mountains to deep valley floors, plateaus to alpine meadows. Many spectacular landforms include areas of marble and granite sculpted into tortured shapes, arches and caves by the relentless action of water.

Wonderfully diverse terrain provides an ideal habitat for more than half of New Zealand's 2,400 native plant species. Palms on the coast impart a tropical look, while the vegetation changes from podocarp forest with lush undergrowth in the west to beech forest in the east. There's a thriving bird population that includes iconic species such as the great-spotted kiwi and blue duck. Among the less appealing wildlife are giant cave spiders and carnivorous giant snails that luckily prefer worms to people. A number of programmes will initially protect and hopefully enhance threatened flora and fauna in various areas of the park.

Kahurangi National Park is definitely a destination for two types of visitor, who may actually be one and the same. For this is a place where those who revel in outdoor recreational activities will be well served, as will self-sufficiency types who have the opportunity to heft a backpack into the Tasman Wilderness Area and get away from the stresses and strains of modern life. Demanding caving, kayaking and rafting are popular, while the Karamea River is renowned for trout fishing. A network of walking and hiking trails begins with short strolls from roadends through half- and full-day walks to week-long expeditions. The park has many backcountry huts and several campsites.

**HOW TO GET THERE:**
State Route 6 runs along the south of the park, while the coastal State Route 60 runs up beside the park to its northern extremity (both from Nelson). A road up the water from Westport (indeed to the west of the park) goes to Karamea and on to a dead end at Oparara. There are no roads but some unsealed vehicle tracks in the park itself. The gateway towns are Motueka, Takaka, Karamea, Tapawera and Murchison.

**WHEN TO GO:**
Any time. The weather is very changeable. Heavy snowfalls occur in winter and after heavy rain many rivers become impassable.

**DON'T MISS:**
A guided tour of the splendid limestone Honeycomb Hill Caves at Karamea, world famous for their collection of bones from moa and other extinct bird species. It's also worth doing the kayak trip to the impressive Honeycomb Hill Arch.

**YOU SHOULD KNOW:**
The long-established 80-km (50-mi) Heaphy Track crosses the park from west to east, taking in stunning coastline, lush forests and extensive downs. It offers ever-changing views. There are huts and campsites along the track (advance booking required), but even on this established trail hikers should have proper clothing, food and backcountry experience. Those making any trip into the interior of Kahurangi National Park should be sure to notify someone of their plans as a sensible precaution (or take a satellite phone!).

*Maud Island in the beautiful Marlborough Sounds*

# Marlborough Sounds

Although the Marlborough Sounds occupy no more than the northeastern tip of the South Island, this jumbled assembly of sea-drowned valleys between Tasman and Cloudy Bays accounts for one fifth of New Zealand's entire coastline. The DOC (Department of Conservation) manages over 50 reserves in the area, indicating how important this marine marvel is in ecological terms. That awareness notwithstanding, there have been spirited battles between conservationists and commercial interests like ferry companies and scallop dredgers.

The port of Picton at the head of Queen Charlotte Sound is the busy terminus for South Island's road and rail networks – and ferry traffic to and from the North Island – but the hauntingly beautiful Marlborough Sounds remain a sparsely populated jigsaw of winding sounds, craggy islands, peninsulas, quiet bays and steep wooded hills where many small and isolated communities or individual homesteads can only be reached by boat. This makes exploration difficult, but transport may be hired in the form of launches, yachts, motor boats and sea kayaks. Although some visitors go afloat simply to explore, sailing and sea kayaking are popular pastimes in their own right. There are, of course, numerous passenger boats offering cruises for those who like their scenery to come with minimal effort and all the trimmings, while water taxis ply from Picton and Havelock at the head of Pelorus Sound to D'Urville Island.

Serious hikers should essay the Queen Charlotte Track (at least in part). This super-scenic route follows paths established by the original Maori inhabitants of the area or early settlers who mined and farmed hereabouts. The 71-km (44-mi) ridge tramp offers fantastic views over Queen Charlotte Sound, with numerous intriguing side paths down to the water. Those in a hurry can mountain-bike the whole thing in a strenuous day.

# Paparoa National Park

Just over 300 sq km (115 sq mi) of prime South Island coastal real estate was lost to developers when Paparoa National Park was established. As it happens, they probably wouldn't want it, for this is wild land described thus in the proposal that led to the park's classification in 1987: 'It contains scenery of distinctive quality, ecosystems of outstanding scientific interest and beautiful and unique natural features. These result from an unusual combination of natural history, geological history and climate which has created an area which has no parallel in New Zealand and perhaps worldwide.' Motion carried, obviously!

Today's visitors may not have a dedicated interest in every then-lauded aspect of Paparoa, but simply enjoying its contrasting landscapes is enough for most. The park covers an area on or near the coast of the northern Westland and rises up to the top of the Paparoa Ranges. A separate section to the north surrounds Ananui Creek. There are many geological variations in the park but the most important is karst landscape – the only lowland karst in New Zealand with undisturbed forest cover, featuring gorges, caves and streams that mysteriously vanish or reappear.

Much of the park is covered in contiguous lowland and montane forest with diversity unmatched anywhere else in the country – wonderful habitat that supports an abundant bird population. It is a vital refuge for the endangered great-spotted kiwi and supports the only known breeding colony of black Westland petrel. The park is also perfect for dedicated backcountry trampers. There are pleasing possibilities for anything from short strolls to day walks and one longer route – the Inland Pack Track cut through the forest in the 1860s to bypass coastal cliffs – but beyond that it's a lonely wilderness crying out to be explored. Other outdoor activities include caving and kayaking.

**HOW TO GET THERE:**
With great satisfaction, after driving one of the most spectacular coastal roads in New Zealand – State Highway 6 between Westport and Greymouth. The gateway to Paparoa National Park is the township of Punakaiki, which offers shops, accommodation, camping and various organized activities such as canoeing, horse riding, guided caving and scenic tours.

**WHEN TO GO:**
Winter temperatures average a cool 9°C (48°F) so most visitors prefer the other three seasons – especially summer, with its acceptable average of 17°C (63°F). Take waterproof clothing as the area has a high average rainfall and a reputation for unleashing torrential rain.

**DON'T MISS:**
The famous Pancake Rocks near Punakaiki. This awesome maze of blow holes and eroded rock formations named for their layered appearance may be viewed from a high-grade walkway that circles the sea cliffs on a promontory south of the Pororari River.

**YOU SHOULD KNOW:**
The park was the site of the infamous Cave Creek disaster in 1995 when the collapse of a badly constructed scenic overlook resulted in the deaths of 14 people – and the resignation of New Zealand's Minister of Conservation.

*Pancake Rocks in Paparoa National Park*

# Arthur's Pass National Park

**HOW TO GET THERE:**
State Highway 73 (unless blocked by snow, rock falls or landslips, in which case reschedule).

**WHEN TO GO:**
Those not interested in snow should make it anything but winter (when there's lots of it).

**DON'T MISS:**
The splendid viaduct built over the Otira Gorge in the late 1990s to make travel over the pass's rugged terrain less hazardous – it's one of New Zealand's engineering marvels.

**YOU SHOULD KNOW:**
Gold was discovered on the West Coast in the 1860s and a route connecting the new bonanza with Christchurch became an urgent necessity. Incredibly, a road was driven across inhospitable Arthur's Pass in less than a year after it was surveyed in 1864 by (you guessed it) an Arthur – Arthur Dudley Dobson.

In the heart of Ka Tiritiri o te Moana – or the Southern Alps as non-Maori speakers sometimes guiltily call them – lies Arthur's Pass National Park. It consists of high country that features tall mountains, extensive scree slopes, plunging gorges and wide rivers. A historic railway and road 'pass' through the middle *en route* from Canterbury to the West Coast. The small community of Arthur's Pass offers a welcoming base from which to explore the park and has a good visitor centre offering general park information and interpretative displays. There are basic campsites at most of the park's entry points and many backcountry huts connected by a considerable network of walking tracks and tramping trails.

The pass sits on the South Island's backbone and there is a marked difference between western and eastern slopes. To the west, luxuriant podocarp rainforest and red-flowering *rata* boasts a lush understorey of shrubs, ferns and mosses. To the east is dry beech and tawhai forest. Snow tussock and alpine meadows may be seen (and visited) from the summit of Arthur's Pass itself. Birdwatching is a popular pastime, with many species to be found in and around Arthur's Pass village. Good 'twitches' include kea, blue duck, rock wren, South Island robin, bellbird and fantail. The endangered great-spotted kiwi may be heard whistling away at night, but will rarely be seen.

*Waimakariri River Flats, Arthur's Pass National Park*

More demanding activities include mountaineering (Mount Rollaston is a popular target), mountain-biking (formed tracks only) and 4x4 driving (approved roads only). But this is really a place in which to walk, walk, walk. Gentle strolls from the road allow sedentary types to enjoy champagne mountain air with great views. For more serious hikers there are numerous established half- and all-day hikes, plus more than a dozen overnight routes, including the demanding two-day Mingha/Deception Track over Goat Pass – a classic east-west traverse.

# Rangitata River

A liquid rollercoaster drains the eastern side of the Southern Alps between the Lyell and Godley Glaciers and rushes 120 km (75 mi) to the sea near Temuka. The Rangitata River is formed by the confluence of two major tributaries and its most spectacular stretch is in the mountains. Once on the fertile Canterbury Plains it becomes a typical-for-these-parts braided river – a network of small, shifting channels divided by sand bars – before splitting and forming a large island delta, then discharging into the Pacific.

But the gentle pastoral beauty of the Canterbury Plains is not what attracts adventurous types to the swift Rangitata River. Jet boats whizz hither and thither, fishermen exercise their skills (it has some of the best salmon fishing in New Zealand), kayakers test their abilities. If that isn't enough, white-water rafting on the upper river is surely the most exciting way to view the stunning mountain scenery, with various companies offering three-hour white-water, white-knuckle rides that are nonetheless suitable for beginners, with a period of relative calm for safety instruction and familiarization before finally hitting fearsome Grade 5 rapids swirling between monster boulders – the infamous 'Pinch' in the rocky Rangitata Gorge that conducts the racing river out of the mountains.

Those interested in savouring the stunning scenery of the Upper Rangitata Valley as opposed to running the river can drive up either side of the gorge from Arundel, past Mount Peel and on to Erewhon sheep station (right bank) where the Clyde and Havelock rivers merge to form the Rangitata. This was named by Samuel Butler, the first white settler to own nearby Mesopotamia station and author of a famous satire on Victorian life also called *Erewhon*, which almost but not quite spells 'nowhere' backwards. That's how Butler intended it to be read and the name seems entirely appropriate in these back-of-beyond mountains.

**HOW TO GET THERE:**
Arundel is just past Coopers Creek, off State Highway 79 north of Geraldine. Rafting trips often include transport from Christchurch.

**WHEN TO GO:**
Any time, although winter with its Antarctic blasts is not for everyone. The weather in the Southern Alps is bracing from June to August, but at least the snow line remains at around 900 m (3,000 ft) and that white mountain topping makes for even more spectacular sightseeing. The Rangitata rafting season runs from September to the end of May.

**DON'T MISS:**
Rafters can enjoy the sheer thrill of white-water swimming and a daring leap into the river from the famous Jump Rock halfway down Rangitata Gorge. It's the four-metre rock for wimps and the ten-metre rock for anyone more afraid of looking like a wimp than of taking the fearful plunge.

**YOU SHOULD KNOW:**
The Rangitata Valley in the centre of the Southern Alps was the setting for filming important sequences in *The Lord of the Rings: The Two Towers* and *The Return of the King*. The landscape around Mount Sunday became J R R Tolkein's Kingdom of Rohan in Middle-earth and the Edoras hill-fort set was built there.

527

*A hiker on Cascade Saddle Route in Mount Aspiring National Park*

# Mount Aspiring National Park

## HOW TO GET THERE:
State Highway 6 – the South Island's wonderfully scenic road down the West Coast – cuts through the eastern end of the park from Haast Beach through Haast Pass to Lakes Wanaka and Hawea. The nearest town to Mount Aspiring itself is Wanaka. The park's access points are at the townships of Makarora, Haast and Glenorchy.

## WHEN TO GO:
The perfect time to explore the park is summer and early autumn (November to March), especially if the intention is to cross scenic passes between valleys. Off-season is best left to experienced wilderness trekkers and snow-sports enthusiasts who can't resist the heli-skiing. That said, the Matukituki Valley can be walked safely at any time of year.

## DON'T MISS:
The Upper Wilkin Valley – one of the most picturesque in the whole of New Zealand, which is saying something. It's a long-weekend trek starting from Makarora and going via the Kerin Forks Hut on the Gillespie Pass Circuit.

## YOU SHOULD KNOW:
The Red Hills mineral belt in the southwest of the park is a visual surprise. The high concentration of minerals in the soil accounts for the rusty-red colour and ensures that only the hardiest of plants can survive there.

Nothing beckons lovers of remote places more seductively than Mount Aspiring National Park. A huge wilderness in the South Island's wild west guarantees a soaring sense of freedom, for this vast area is an unspoilt land of stunning views, mountains, glaciers, alpine lakes, valleys and white-water rivers. Beech forests predominate below the bush line, while higher up the vegetation consists of snow-tussock grassland and herb fields bright with wild flowers in spring and early summer.

It's easy to get lost – the park extends to an impressive 3,500 sq km (1,350 sq mi), straddling the end of the Southern Alps and stretching from the Haast River in the north to the Humboldt Mountains in the south. But the awesome spike of Mount Aspiring is a great reference point, proving an irresistible challenge to experienced alpinists. However, the main activity in the park is walking. As ever, there are countless short walks – mostly from the main highway, access roads or local towns – for those content to soak up the awesome scenery without straying too far from folding chairs and picnic lunch.

But serious visitors head for one of the long-distance hiking routes that lead into the interior and often link to adjacent areas. These include the Greenstone and Caples tracks (two fabulous valleys, moderate five-day round trip), Rees-Dart Track (a four-day circuit taking in two rivers and some of the park's best scenery) and the ever-popular three-day Routeburn Track (linking Mount Aspiring and Fiordland National Parks). There are campgrounds and numerous huts within the park (pre-booking advisable in summer), plus plenty of primitive campsites along the various tracks. Peace and quiet are not absolutely guaranteed. This being New Zealand, the sound of jet boats may be heard in the vicinity of the park's larger rivers.

# Haleakala National Park

In the southeast of Maui, Haleakala National Park is a wilderness of two halves stretching from brooding volcanic heights at Mount Haleakala down through the clouds (often literally) to verdant coastline at Kipahulu. The island's highest peak often delivers dramatic views across a sea of clouds and this island in the sky is a starkly sculpted landscape of contrasting colours unlike any other.

Haleakala's slopes and the surrounding wilderness offer backcountry hiking against a magnificent backdrop, with access to rare endemic plants and birdlife. It's one of the few accessible places in Hawaii where native species thrive in abundance. This dramatic area on top of the world offers many contrasts, from the dry, cold air of the mountain with its towering cindercones to moist cloud forest rich in ferns at lower altitudes. The wilderness can be accessed from two trailheads near the summit, Halemauu at 2,440 m (8,000 ft) and Keoneheehee (Sliding Sands) at 2,970 m (9,750 ft). The trails eventually merge and lead down to the park's coastal zone. Along the way there are primitive campgrounds and historic cabins that can be booked in advance by overnighters, although the wilderness is also suitable for anything from short strolls to day hikes.

The coastal part of the park is reached by road from Hanu along Maui's spectacular northeastern coast. There is a campground but this area is remote and there is no piped water supply. Ocean swimming can be dangerous but there are plunge pools on the stream that runs down the Oheo Gulch, where the short Pipiwai Trail is popular with day hikers enjoying verdant tropical greenery. Whales, dolphins and turtles can sometimes be spotted offshore.

*Cinder cones in Haleakala Crater*

**HOW TO GET THERE:**
There is no public transport to the park. Road access from Kahului to park headquarters and Haleakala's summit is from Routes 37, 377 and 378 (90 minutes). The coastal section may be reached from Kahului in three hours via Routes 36, 360 and 31.

**WHEN TO GO:**
All year round (but park authorities warn that sensible precautions are needed in this remote area where the weather may be 'hot, dry, wet or cold in any part of the park at any time'). Temperatures range from a high of 27°C (80.6°F) on the coast to a low of –1°C (30°F) atop the mountain.

**DON'T MISS:**
Seeing stars from the summit of Mount Haleakala on a clear night. Hawaii is one of the best places on earth for astral viewing and Mount Haleakala is one of the best places in Hawaii. The intensity of the Milky Way has to be seen to be believed.

**YOU SHOULD KNOW:**
There is a park visitor centre at Kipahulu on the coast, one at park headquarters and another near the summit of Haleakala Naturalists are on hand to answer questions and the centres all have cultural and natural history displays.

# Kealakekua Bay

The Kona (leeward) Coast of the Big Island of Hawaii is an area of historic settlement with many heritage sites and stern natural beauty. One of the highlights is Kealakekua Bay, 19 km (12 mi) south of Kailu-Kona, the main town in West Hawaii. Horseshoe-shaped Kealakekua is the largest sheltered bay on the island, measuring 2.5 km (1.5 mi) in length and 1.5 km (1 mi) in width. Access is to the south end, where a road winds down to a wharf and Napoopoo Beach.

This is no remote wilderness – just a beautifully unspoilt stretch of rugged coastline with volcanic cliffs rising above an inviting expanse of blue water. The bay offers some of the best snorkelling and scuba diving in the Hawaiian Islands. It's a Marine Life Conservation District and an extensive coral reef protects the bay, creating a calm haven where visibility can be as much as 30 m (100 ft) in water that is invitingly warm. The corals are stunning and host colourful arrays of tropical fish. A pod of Hawaiian spinner dolphins frequents the bay and turtles are frequently sighted. Those who wish to explore the shore must be prepared to do some serious scrambling down steep terrain and brave dense vegetation that crowds the water on gentler slopes.

Kealakekua Bay is famous as the spot where Captain James Cook was killed by indigenous Hawaiians in 1779, having estimated upon arrival that there were two thousand people living in two villages on the bay. A sheer cliff face was the burial site for Hawaiian kings and there were royal residences nearby, but by the early 20th century the once-thriving community had declined to the point where the bay was returned to nature's tender embrace, with abandoned village sites quickly invaded by kiawe trees.

*Spinner dolphins frequent Kealakekua Bay.*

# Molokai

In the geographical centre of the Hawaiian Islands is Molokai, one of the least developed and most interesting parts of the USA's 50th state. The island lies on a west-east axis between Oahu and Maui, measuring 60 km (37 mi) by 16 km (10 mi). The few thousand inhabitants have fiercely resisted efforts to turn Molokai into a non-floating tourist barge. That said, the locals – with a higher percentage of native Hawaiians than any other island – are extremely friendly and their principled stand has preserved much of Molokai's natural beauty for the benefit of visitors more interested in wild places than lying on white sand beaches (although there are plenty of those, including Papohaku, Hawaii's longest and widest).

The arid western end of the island with its scrubby grazing land and pineapple plantations is less interesting than the eastern half, although both northern and southern shores have some of the most remote and beautiful beaches in all Hawaii. Molokai was formed from two volcanoes. East Molokai's volcano split in half 1.5 million years ago, collapsing into the Pacific Ocean and leaving the world's highest sea cliffs behind (as featured in the movie *Jurassic Park III*). This is an area of breathtaking tropical landscape – a high plateau rising to 1,500 m (4,920 ft) at Kamakou's impressive peak with lush forests that form an extremely diverse ecosystem.

In addition to those awesome cliffs, there are numerous waterfalls – including the pounding 530-m (1,740-ft) Kahiwa Falls – deep gorges and rugged coastline. This is not tourist central – much of this marvellous terrain can only be reached by hard hiking, after access roads suitable only for 4x4 vehicles run out well short of the best sights, including those famous sea cliffs. In fact, the best way to appreciate their soaring grandeur is to take a sight-seeing helicopter ride from Maui.

*Towering cliffs on the north shore of Molokai*

**HOW TO GET THERE:**
Fly to Molokai airport, which is served by Hawaii's network of internal flights. Vehicles can be rented at the airport.

**WHEN TO GO:**
Any time (but the weather in February can be volatile and unpredictable).

**DON'T MISS:**
The coastal dunes at Mo'omomi, in northwestern Molokai. The western end of the island has been degraded owing to poor land management and over-grazing by goats. Mo'omomi is a Nature Conservancy preserve that protects a lonely area of sand dunes that contain some of the last intact coastal shrublands in Hawaii.

**YOU SHOULD KNOW:**
Molokai is famous for the work of the now-canonized Father Damien de Veuster, a Catholic priest who cared for leprosy sufferers at a colony on the island in the 19th century before himself dying of the disease aged 49. Ironically, that once-forbidden enclave on the Kalaupapa Peninsula is now one of the easier places to reach on Molokai's rugged north coast, by air or down a tortuous mule path. It is populated by (leprosy-free!) descendents of the original sufferers.

*Palmyra Atoll is a tiny National Wildlife Refuge.*

# Palmyra Atoll

Halfway between Hawaii and American Samoa the true adventurer will (with a little help) find Palmyra Atoll, a tiny speck in the vast North Pacific administered by the USA that extends to 12 sq km (4.5 sq mi). The 14 km (9 mi) of coastline has just one safe anchorage, West Lagoon. An extensive reef system protects two shallow lagoons and 54 sandbars and reef-rock islets that are almost all connected. The largest of these – and the site of Palmyra's airstrip – is Cooper Island. Palmyra's islets are heavily vegetated, with species like stands of rare pisonia beach forest, coconut palms, ferns and shrubs that thrive as a result of heavy equatorial rainfall.

The atoll is a tiny National Wildlife Refuge, protecting both land and marine environments. Palmyra provides the only nesting site for seabirds in a huge expanse of ocean and attracts over one million birds in the breeding season. Resident species include red-footed boobies, brown boobies, masked boobies, white and sooty terns. The atoll is a haven for the endangered green turtle, while the surrounding reef and lagoons are populated by an extraordinary diversity of hard corals – 125 different types, which is three times more than Hawaii or the whole Caribbean can boast. The reef fish are as brightly coloured as the corals they patrol and include various sharks. Whales are frequent visitors.

Palmyra is a stunning marine wilderness and has no indigenous population, although scientists have a base on Cooper Island from which to study the corals. The previous residents were US Navy flyers, for Palmyra was a naval air station in World War II. The crumbling and overgrown remains of this era are still visible, serving as a reminder that everything in paradise is not always idyllic.

**HOW TO GET THERE:**
With great difficulty. It's possible to fly in to the airstrip maintained by the Nature Conservancy for visiting scientists, but the cost of a private charter is prohibitive. The few visitors privileged to see this magical atoll (and dive on its stunning reef) tend to arrive in cruising yachts.

**WHEN TO GO:**
Any time – the temperature is a more-than-balmy 29°C (84°F) all year round.

**DON'T MISS:**
The world's largest land invertebrate, the rare coconut crab. Watch one husk and crack a fallen nut and be mightily impressed.

**YOU SHOULD KNOW:**
Palmyra Atoll was specifically excluded when Hawaii became the 50th state in 1959, thus becoming the only privately owned overseas territory administered by the USA. Everything but two islets was sold by the then owners to America's Nature Conservancy in 2000, an organization that will preserve Palmyra's unique attributes for future generations.

# Western Highlands

The outside world didn't know about the place until 1933, when an aerial survey of the highlands in Papua New Guinea (PNG) found the large, well-populated Wahgi Valley in the Western Highlands. That discovery of a thriving but hitherto unknown culture provides a sobering comment on how far the world has shrunk in 80 years, leaving no stone unturned nor corner unphotographed (if only from space). That initial discovery was followed by a traditional footslogging expedition that built an airstrip close to the Mount Hagen volcano and a virgin site now occupied by the town of Mount Hagen, Papua New Guinea's third largest.

Even so, the vast majority of PNG's population still practises a traditional rural way of life and Papua New Guinea – occupying the eastern half of the island of New Guinea – remains one of the world's least-developed nations. It is also one of the most fascinating destinations for lovers of faraway places, as it is one of the globe's least explored places. That's culturally – with over 800 indigenous languages and tribes – and geographically – with many undiscovered plants and animals said to lurk in the undocumented interior. Only recently has access become possible for tourists, as opposed to the most determined of serious travellers.

The Western Highlands are typical of PNG. This is a dramatic landscape of rainforested mountains, fertile valleys, rushing streams, rivers and swamps in the Lower Jimi Valley. Mount Hagen is an excellent base for exploration of habitats that range from lowland forest to alpine grasslands, dotted with coffee plantations that produce the local cash crop. There are a few hotels and tourist lodges, but this remains a primitive destination not for the faint-hearted. The Wahgi Valley remains a lush green oasis that is intensely cultivated, but Mount Hagen is the gateway to the wild and undeveloped areas further west.

**HOW TO GET THERE:**
Mount Hagan Airport at Kagamuga is served by private flights for mine personnel and an irregular public service from Cairns in Queensland and local centres including Moro and Port Moresby. Road access is via the Highland Highway from the coastal cities of Madang.

**WHEN TO GO:**
Any time. The climate is tropical but the uplands are cooler than the coast. Rainwear is essential in the monsoon season from December to March.

**DON'T MISS:**
The annual Mount Hagen Cultural Show in August, when national, regional and local tribal groups get together at Kagamuga to celebrate their heritage. This vibrant sing-sing sees representatives of the various tribes don wildly differing traditional costumes, paint themselves up and peacefully share common ethnicity through dance and music. Up to 50 tribal ensembles perform enthusiastically before up to 50,000 spectators.

**YOU SHOULD KNOW:**
Travellers on the Highland Highway face more than the landslips and potholes that bedevil this largely single-track road. The stretch in the Hagan Highlands is notorious for hold-ups and robberies committed by armed bandits rather underwhelmingly known as 'rascals'.

*The Baiyer River Sanctuary*

# Ofu Island

It doesn't represent much of a Pacific empire, but since quitting the Philippines American Samoa is as good as it gets for the USA – and very good indeed for get-away-from-it-allers. This alluring tropical destination is not as high on the must-visit-islands list as it deserves to be. First impressions are not favourable – the capital of Pago Pago on the main island of Tutuila is tattily commercialized – but that's just a visual glitch. The rest of the island is a natural paradise. Towering peaks surround the town's harbour, lonely roads crowded by dense forest switchback over isolated mountain passes and stunning palm-fringed beaches more than match up to the picture-postcard Pacific white-sand/turquoise-sea standard.

The most discerning travellers head for American Samoa's Manu'a Island group in general and Ofu Island in particular. This volcanic isle is completely uncommercial and unspoilt, while Ofu beach on the west coast must be one of the world's finest. This 3 km (2 mi) stretch of pink coral sand is stunningly beautiful, with a backdrop of swaying palm trees, jagged volcanic peaks and lush greenery. This is a place to swim and walk, often in complete solitude – enjoying the sun, sea and scenery of this dreamy hideaway. Snorkelling off the beach is first-rate, offering wonderful coral formations and vivid underwater life, but it's essential to take the necessary kit. Ofu is not a place where equipment can be rented.

The National Park of American Samoa encompasses 42 sq km (16 sq mi) of land and water on Manu'a islands of Tutuila, Ofu, its twin Olosega and Ta'u, protecting their wild locations from unseemly development. This hopefully precludes the sort of tourist pressure that often overwhelms unspoilt beauty that attracted visitors in the first place. American Samoa remains a dream destination for those willing to make the effort needed to plan a visit.

*A beautiful deserted beach*

# Namenalala Island

Sometimes, getting away from it all requires a fat wallet and a little help from those who cater for those who can afford to get away from it all in singular style. A visit to the privately owned Fijian island of Namenalala offers just such an experience and the ultimate escape. Until the 1980s this 45-ha (110-ac) islet 25 km (15 mi) off the coast of Vanua Levu was uninhabited. From the air the island has an uncanny resemblance to an elongated dragon rising from the azure Koro Sea and might still be uninhabited, but in fact dense vegetation conceals a very exclusive eco-resort.

Just six hexagonal *bures* (Polynesian-style houses on stilts made from timber and woven bamboo) have been built among tall native trees on the dragon's tail, accommodating no more than a dozen guests at any one time, who are treated to the ultimate in desert-island living. Each *bure* overlooks beaches, reefs and a great sweep of sea from a vantage point on the cliff top, while the food is based around fresh produce grown on the island or caught from the surrounding ocean. This is not the sort of resort where pampering is the norm – there is no electricity in the widely spaced *bures* so this is one for those who hanker for a return to nature.

The rest of the island is completely undeveloped and provides the opportunity to explore a manageable stretch of original tropical rainforest. But for most visitors the main attraction will be snorkelling or scuba diving along the 30 km (18.5 mi) of Namenalala's pristine barrier reef, with its brilliant assortment of corals and tropical fish. Other possibilities include sport fishing outside the reef, canoeing, windsurfing, birdwatching . . . or simply relaxing in this secluded paradise.

**HOW TO GET THERE:**
By boat or seaplane from Vanua Levu

**WHEN TO GO:**
Any time, although the dry season from May to October is cool, with lower humidity than at other times.

**DON'T MISS:**
The evidence of Namenalala's mysterious past – the intriguing remains of an ancient ring fortification at the island's highest point, dating back for at least two millennia.

**YOU SHOULD KNOW:**
There is a generator that runs periodically to recharge batteries for guests' equipment. It is wise to take a selection of basic medications and toiletries as stocks on the island are extremely limited. Stout walking shoes are adequate for the forest trails and an old pair of trainers is useful for exploring tidal pools in rocky sections of the shoreline.

*Namenalala Island – the perfect escape*

# Taveuni

Cigar-shaped Taveuni is Fiji's third-largest island after Vanua Levu and Viti Levu, extending to 435 sq km (170 sq mi). Taveuni is the tip of a massive shield volcano that rises from the floor of the Pacific. The island is dotted with volcanic cones and has suffered less from land clearance than Fiji's other islands. Consequently, it has an abundance of lush foliage and is known as 'The Garden Island of Fiji'. With a number of small resorts, it is becoming a popular tourist destination but remains a largely unspoilt destination. Many visitors ignore the interior in favour of diving on the island's famed coral reefs but those who prefer to remain ashore will find plenty of wild country to explore, featuring mountains, lakes, rainforests, breathtaking ocean views, mangroves and beaches.

One of Taveuni's most spectacular natural attractions is Lake Tagimaucia, a crater lake at a height of 800 m (2,625 ft), nestling beneath the impressive Des Voeux peak. This is the place to see Fiji's national flower, the red-and-white Tagimaucia that grows nowhere else. See this woody vine high in the forest canopy on the approaches to the lake, which is covered with floating vegetation. It's a healthy all-day hike to Lake Tagimaucia, but non-trampers can get most of the way there using a 4x4 vehicle and view this scenic gem from afar.

Other major attractions on the island are the plunging Bouma Falls and the picturesque Lavena Village with its pristine beach and nature walk. The international dateline used to bisect Taveuni, until some spoilsport rerouted it to stop people hopping from yesterday to tomorrow and back. There is a marker indicating a spot where this once happened, but that's as near to time travel as it's now possible to get.

**HOW TO GET THERE:**
Fly in to Matei Airport from Nadi via Savusavu, or direct from Suva. The ferry from Savusavu takes around seven hours, or there is a small passenger ferry from Buca Bay on the east coast of Vanua Levu.

**WHEN TO GO:**
Any time – but it has to be October to December to see the fabulous Tagimaucia flowers at their very best.

**DON'T MISS:**
The extraordinary orange dove, a superstar of Taveuni's vibrant bird population. The male has green-speckled plumage that turns to fluorescent orange in the breeding season.

**YOU SHOULD KNOW:**
The island's most imposing edifice is the Wairiki Mission, a fine example of colonial Romanesque architecture, noted for the superb singing at Sunday morning mass (visitors welcome). It overlooks the site where local warriors defeated a large number of Tongan invaders in a canoe battle fought just off the beach. The victors celebrated by cooking and eating the vanquished.

*The beach at Lavena Point on Taveuni*

# Barrier Reef

The French overseas collectivity of New Caledonia in the southwest Pacific Ocean has one indisputable claim to fame, which also happens to be a natural wonder that will appeal mightily to lovers of unspoilt places. New Caledonia's Barrier Reef is the world's second longest at 1,500 km (930 mi), surrounding the main island of Grand Terre and various smaller isles. The coral reef encloses an amazing lagoon that extends to 24,000 sq km (9,300 sq mi), recently listed as a UNESCO World Heritage Site.

Despite damage to the reef's eastern section as a result of nickel mining effluent, this unique eco-region remains in rude good health and provides safe haven for a great variety of life, including endangered dugongs (sea cows) and green turtles. Such is the diversity of species that new fish and invertebrates are regularly discovered. So far, 1,000 types of fish, 5,000 different crustaceans, 5,500 molluscs, 600 sponges and 23 species of breeding bird, including the charming red-footed booby, have been recorded.

Coral formations are outstanding and can provide the experience of a lifetime for scuba divers and snorkellers who boat out to the reef, although non-water-babes can get a feel for the place by taking to glass-bottomed craft or indulging in numerous water sports, from kayaking to windsurfing. The lagoon is large enough to ensure that a wonderful sense of lonely adventure is possible, and sub-aqua sights have to be seen to be believed. Grand Terre itself has much to offer. Most tourists focus on New Caledonia's capital of Noumea, a sophisticated colonial town known as 'The Paris of the East'. But the rugged interior and verdant northeastern coast where torturous rivers and jagged peaks tumble into the lagoon are wild places, while trips to the outlying islands reveal a local culture hardly touched by 150 years of colonial influence.

**HOW TO GET THERE:**
On a cruising yacht (Noumea is the only official point of entry) or by air using long-haul flights to regional centres like Fiji and onward flights using Aircalin. Be aware that visitors without return air tickets are always refused entry. Local Air Calédonie flights serve the outlying Loyalty Islands and the Isle of Pines, as does the fast catamaran *Betico* (at half the price).

**WHEN TO GO:**
Any time. Bastille Day (July 14) is the excuse for an uninhibited celebration that includes an impressive military parade and fly past. Other notable events are Noumea's August jazz festival and agricultural fairs featuring rodeo and the like in Koné (April) and Bourail (mid August).

**DON'T MISS:**
The Isle of Pines, where the Kuto/Kanuméra area is a picture-perfect tropical paradise with pristine Pacific beaches backed by stands of towering pine trees.

**YOU SHOULD KNOW:**
The striking Jean-Marie Tjibaou Cultural Centre in Noumea was designed by the famous Italian architect Renzo Piano and completed in 1998 at a cost of $50 million. This extraordinary collection of ten 'unfinished' hut-like structures was created in celebration of vernacular Canaque buildings and named for an assassinated Canaque leader.

# Antarctic Peninsula

It's the end of the book, and the end of the world. Antarctica underlies the South Pole and is the sixth continent. Technically a desert with virtually no rainfall, the coldest place on earth is experiencing rapid global warming that threatens to alter its icy face for ever. The planet's last great uninhabited wilderness is covered by ice that averages 1.5 km (1 mi) in thickness and, if it all melted, sea levels around the world would rise by nearly 20 m (66 ft). No need to panic just yet . . . but it is happening. During the summer's 24 hours of daylight constant solar radiation punctures holes in a protective ozone layer weakened by greenhouse gases.

Nowhere is the big thaw more obvious than in one of the most accessible (a relative term!) areas. The Antarctic Peninsula is the northernmost part of the mainland. Its coasts have the mildest (another relative term!) climate in the continent and are snow-free in summer months. The peninsula is characterized by offshore

islands connected to the mainland by ice and stand-alone ice shelves – many of the latter retreating or disintegrating at an alarming rate. Even so, the wildlife (penguins, seabirds, seals and whales), seascapes and mountainous interior remain spectacular. It's one of the most awe-inspiring places on earth.

Antarctic cruises cater for various tastes. Ships are small, rarely carrying more than 150 passengers and often fewer. Expedition ships offer varying levels of luxury, while some with ice-strengthened hulls go where intrepid passengers can enjoy activities like sea kayaking and mainland camping. At the sharp end (literally) are icebreakers that go where no other ship can venture. Zodiac transfers for scenic shore outings are commonplace, helicopter shuttles and overflights less so. Cruises invariably employ experts who lecture on subjects such as wildlife, geology, oceanography, glaciology and the history of Antarctic exploration.

**WHEN TO GO:**
The polar summer (a couple of months either side of Christmas).
**DON'T MISS:**
One or more of Antarctica's unique climatic spectacles – the glowing *Aurora Australis* (southern lights) in the night sky, diamond dust (a low-level cloud made up of tiny ice crystals) or the sun dog (a spot of bright light beside the real thing).
**YOU SHOULD KNOW:**
Further south, huts on Ross Island in Erebus Bay (named for the island's active volcano) were used as home bases by polar heroes Captain Robert Falcon Scott and Ernest Shackleton. They have been preserved as historic monuments just as they were left by the departing expeditions.

*Adelie penguins resting on a piece of glacial ice in the Antarctic Peninsula.*

## COUNTRIES AND REGIONS